The WILEY advantage

Dear Valued Customer,

We realize you're a busy professional with deadlines to hit. Whether your goal is to learn a new technology or solve a critical problem, we want to be there to lend you a hand. Our primary objective is to provide you with the insight and knowledge you need to stay atop the highly competitive and ever-changing technology industry.

Wiley Publishing, Inc., offers books on a wide variety of technical categories, including security, data warehousing, software development tools, and networking — everything you need to reach your peak. Regardless of your level of expertise, the Wiley family of books has you covered.

- For Dummies® – The *fun* and *easy* way™ to learn
- The Weekend Crash Course® – The *fastest* way to learn a new tool or technology
- Visual – For those who prefer to learn a new topic *visually*
- The Bible – The *100% comprehensive* tutorial and reference
- The Wiley Professional list – *Practical* and *reliable* resources for IT professionals

The book you now hold is part of our new *60 Minutes a Day* series which delivers what we think is the closest experience to an actual hands-on seminar that is possible with a book. Our author is a veteran of hundreds of hours of classroom teaching and he uses that background to guide you past the hurdles and pitfalls to confidence and mastery of ASP.NET in manageable units that can be read and put to use in just an hour. If you have a broadband connection to the Web, you can see Glenn introduce each topic — but this book will still be your best learning resource if you download only the audio files or use it strictly as a printed resource. From fundamentals to security and Web Services, you'll find this self-paced training to be your best learning aid.

Our commitment to you does not end at the last page of this book. We'd want to open a dialog with you to see what other solutions we can provide. Please be sure to visit us at www.wiley.com/compbooks to review our complete title list and explore the other resources we offer. If you have a comment, suggestion, or any other inquiry, please locate the "contact us" link at www.wiley.com.

Finally, we encourage you to review the following page for a list of Wiley titles on related topics. Thank you for your support and we look forward to hearing from you and serving your needs again in the future.

Sincerely,

Richard K Swadley

Richard K. Swadley
Vice President & Executive Group Publisher
Wiley Technology Publishing

Bible

DUMMIES

Wiley Publishing, Inc.

more information on related titles

Wiley Going to the Next Level
— Available from Wiley Publishing —

60 Minutes a Day Books...
- Self-paced instructional text packed with real-world tips and examples from real-world training instructors
- Skill-building exercises, lab sessions, and assessments
- Author-hosted streaming video presentations for each chapter will pinpoint key concepts and reinforce lessons

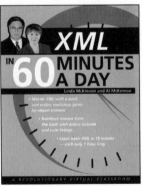

WILEY

Wiley Publishing, Inc.

Available at your favorite bookseller or visit
www.wiley.com/compbooks

ASP.NET in
60 Minutes a Day

ASP.NET in
60 Minutes a Day

Glenn Johnson

WILEY

Wiley Publishing, Inc.

Executive Publisher: Robert Ipsen
V.P. and Publisher: Joseph B. Wikert
Senior Editor: Ben Ryan
Editorial Manager: Kathryn A. Malm
Development Editor: Jerry Olson
Production Editor: Vincent Kunkemueller
Media Development Specialist: Angela Denny
Text Design & Composition: Wiley Composition Services

Published by Wiley Publishing, Inc., Indianapolis, Indiana
Published simultaneously in Canada

For general information on our other products and services please contact our Customer Care Department within the United States at (800) 762-2974, outside the United States at (317) 572-3993 or fax (317) 572-4002.

Wiley also publishes its books in a variety of electronic formats. Some content that appears in print may not be available in electronic books.

Library of Congress Cataloging-in-Publication Data is available from the publisher.

ISBN: 0-471-43023-4

Printed in the United States of America

10 9 8 7 6 5 4 3 2 1

A Note from the Consulting Editor

Instructor-led training has proven to be an effective and popular tool for training engineers and developers. For conveying technical ideas and concepts, the classroom experience has been shown to be superior when compared to other delivery methods. As a technical trainer for more than 20 years, I have seen the effectiveness of instructor-led training firsthand. *60 Minutes a Day* combines the best of the instructor-led training and book experience. Technical training is typically divided into short and discrete modules, where each module encapsulates a specific topic. Each module is then followed by "questions and answers" and a review. *60 Minutes a Day* titles follow the same model: each chapter is short, discrete, and can be completed in 60 minutes a day. For these books, I have enlisted premier technical trainers as authors. They provide the voice of the trainer and demonstrate the classroom experience in each book of the series. You even get an opportunity to meet the actual trainer: As part of this innovative approach, each chapter of a *60 Minutes a Day* book is presented online by the author. Readers are encouraged to view the online presentation before reading the relevant chapter. Therefore, *60 Minutes a Day* delivers the complete classroom experience—even the trainer.

As an imprint of Wiley Publishing, Inc., Gearhead Press continues to bring you, the reader, the level of quality that Wiley has delivered consistently for nearly 200 years.

Thank you.

Donis Marshall
Founder, Gearhead Press
Consulting Editor, Wiley Technology Publishing Group

This book is dedicated to my parents, Theodore and Ruth Kosiavelon, who may not be computer gurus, but still managed to give me exactly what I needed to get where I am today. I love you, Mom and Dad.

Contents

Acknowledgments

I would like to thank Donis Marshall of Gearhead Press for giving me the opportunity to write this book. I would also like to thank Jerry Olsen for his patience during the writing and editing of this book.

Thanks to everyone at Wiley Publishing, Inc. for their help in getting this book to the market, especially to Ben Ryan, Kathryn Malm, and Vincent Kunkemueller, for their support and patience. This book is substantially better due to all of your input.

Most importantly, thanks and love to my wife, Susan, and my sons, Gary and Randy. Your patience and understanding has been greatly appreciated. The only promise that I can make is that the next book will be just as stressful, but since we are now veterans at this, it won't feel as bad.

About the Author

Glenn Johnson is a Microsoft Certified Trainer, Microsoft Certified Solution Developer, Microsoft Certified Systems Engineer, and Microsoft Certified Database Administrator. Glenn has an electronics background and has worked with computers since his first Radio Shack Color Computer (circa 1984). He was the Director of Information Technology and Technical Support for a Tyco International company in Westlake, Ohio, and the Advanced Education Group Training Manager for Xerox Connect in Cleveland, Ohio. Although Glenn has held many management positions, his true love is teaching.

Glenn is currently the owner of Glenn Johnson Technical Training (http://GJTT.com) in Avon Lake, Ohio, and provides contract training, consulting, and programming, primarily in .NET technologies. He also provides Web hosting and may be reached at GlennJohnson@GJTT.com.

Introduction

Active Server Pages (ASP) technology has grown in popularity since the technology was introduced, primarily due to its ease of development. Users have flocked to get onto the ASP bandwagon and have been using it to write code for Web sites of all different sizes. With such a success, why is there a need to change? How can a change make ASP better?

ASP.NET is the latest version of Active Server Pages technology. ASP.NET provides a platform that allows developers to continue writing code in a text editor program, if the developer chooses. In addition, code can be written in Visual Studio .NET, which provides many more options.

This book provides you with an approach to the latest version of Active Server Page technology.

How This Book Is Organized

This book is organized into 17 chapters with a bonus chapter found on the Web site, each of which contains a brief chapter opener followed by several questions that are commonly asked by students when they are being taught in a real-world classroom environment. Next, the chapter goes into its subject's details, presenting many examples along the way. Thereafter, a lab exercise builds on the reading. The chapter ends with a brief summary of several of the key points that were made in the chapter. The chapters are briefly summarized here.

Chapter 1: Introducing ASP.NET

This chapter examines the problems associated with Active Server Pages, followed by a look at the benefits of ASP.NET and programming language choices. Then, this chapter covers the setting up of the development environment, which is used extensively in this book.

Chapter 2: Solutions, Projects, and the Visual Studio. NET IDE

This chapter starts by covering the creation of a folder structure, creation of projects in the folder structure, and storage of these projects in Visual Source-Safe. The last part of this chapter covers the Visual Studio integrated development environment (IDE), its customization, and methods of getting Visual Studio .NET help.

Chapter 3: Exploring ASP.NET and Web Forms

This chapter explores Web Forms. Web Forms bring the structure and fun back to Web development! The chapter starts by looking at the two programming models for ASP.NET, then at how ASP.NET uses server controls, and then at the HTML and Web Controls. It finishes by looking at the view state and post back procedures.

Chapter 4: The .NET Framework and Visual Basic .NET Object Programming

This chapter covers the .NET Framework as well as many aspects of object programming, such as inheritance with Visual Basic .NET. This chapter can be especially useful for traditional Visual Basic programmers, who may be accustomed to using objects, but may not have experience creating objects.

Chapter 5: Working with Web Server Controls

This chapter identifies many of the common properties that are available through inheritance. After that, many of the server controls that are available in Visual Studio .NET are looked at in detail.

Chapter 6: Using Data-Bound Web Controls

This chapter looks at methods of binding data for the purpose of presenting the data to the user. Since database access hasn't been covered yet, the source of the data in this chapter will primarily come from an ArrayList. It's important to understand the data binding basics, which will be somewhat consistent regardless of whether the data source is an ArrayList, an Extensible Markup Language (XML) file, or a database.

Chapter 7: Building User Controls and Custom Web Controls

This chapter covers user controls. After that, the chapter looks at creating custom Web controls from scratch, and it finishes by exploring the ability to inherit from existing Web server controls.

Chapter 8: Data Access with ADO.NET

This chapter starts by comparing connected and disconnected data and then covers the primary ADO.NET objects, looking at details and examples. After covering the objects, this chapter covers different methods of performing data manipulation, sorting, and filtering using the DataGrid control.

Chapter 9: Working with XML Data

This chapter looks at Microsoft's approach to XML in the .NET Framework. The chapter examines the XML classes and then presents various ways of implementing these classes.

Chapter 10: Streams, File Access, and Serialization

This chapter explores streams in detail. After that, it covers file and folder classes. Finally, this chapter covers serialization.

Chapter 11: Working with GDI+ and Images

This chapter starts by looking at the image and bitmap classes. These classes can be used to work with images by using most of the techniques that have been defined in previous chapters. The latter part of the chapter looks closely at GDI+ and the ability to create images on the fly.

Chapter 12: ASP.NET Applications

This chapter explores several aspects of ASP.NET application programming. The first section covers the global.asax file and the HttpApplication class. Next, the chapter explores HTTP handlers and modules. After that, state management in an ASP.NET application is explored in detail. This chapter also covers several other items that come in handy when connecting pages together.

Chapter 13: Site Security

This chapter covers many of the aspects that ensure that only authorized people have access to private data.

Chapter 14: Performance Tuning and Application Instrumentation

The topics covered in this chapter are not meant to replace formal load testing. Instead, they are intended to help the developer to think about performance before formal load testing. This chapter focuses on a developer's ability to optimize the software, although the developer's ability to identify potential hardware bottlenecks can also play a key role in determining the hardware that should be provided in a production system.

Chapter 15: Building and Versioning .NET Components

This chapter covers the methods of creating components, or reusable assemblies, by first creating a component and then using it. After that, the versioning of assemblies is discussed. This chapter also explores the differences between private and shared assemblies. Much of the discussion is spent on exploring strong names and binding policies. This chapter finishes by looking at cross-language inheritance.

Chapter 16: Creating Web Services

One of the best features of Visual Studio .NET is its ability to work with Web services seamlessly. This chapter explores Web services from the Visual Studio .NET perspective by looking at some of the Web service basics and then consuming an existing Web service. The balance of the chapter focuses on creating a Web service.

Chapter 17: Deployment and Migration

This first part of this chapter explores some of the methods of migrating from ASP code to ASP.NET. The chapter then examines methods of using COM components based on both early and late binding techniques. The last part of this chapter covers some of the methods of deploying ASP.NET Web applications.

Bonus Chapter: Mobile Computing

This chapter, which is available on the Web site for this book, covers the Mobile Internet Toolkit, which can be used to solve many of the problems that are associated with the diverse selection of mobile devices that are on the market today.

Who Should Read This Book?

This book is intended to be read in a linear fashion by a person who has had some Visual Basic programming and HTML experience, and who is now trying to expand into ASP.NET. This book does not cover basic programming constructs such as if-then statements and syntactical constructs. This book is intended to fill in the gaps that a Visual Basic developer may have by covering object-oriented programming in detail, and examining inheritance, encapsulation, and polymorphism as it relates to ASP.NET and Visual Basic .NET. Readers who are already familiar with the .NET Framework and Visual Basic .NET may choose to skim the some of the chapter.

Evaluators of this book for use in a school curriculum should consider placing this course directly after a Visual Basic .NET prerequisite course.

Tools You Will Need

The following is a list of software that is required to successfully complete all of the book's labs. Most labs can be done without Visual SourceSafe, but this a good time to bite the bullet and get onto a version control system. Chapter 1 covers installation of this software, while Chapter 2 covers the setting up of Visual SourceSafe and project configuration.

- Windows (2000 or .NET) Professional or Server
- Internet Information Server 5.0+ (included in Windows Professional and Server)
- Visual Studio .NET Enterprise Architect Edition 2002+
- Mobile Internet Toolkit (included with Visual Studio .NET 2003+)
- SQL Server 2000+ Developer Edition
- Visual SourceSafe 6c+

What's on the Web Site?

The Web site contains copies of the sample code that is used throughout this book. Be sure to check the Web site for updates to the code, as well as tips and tricks that may be added to the materials. The URL to access the book's Web site is www.wiley.com/compbooks/60minutesaday.

Introducing ASP.NET

Around 1996 and 1997, a new platform called Active Server Pages (ASP) was introduced to the world. ASP allowed users to execute code written in a scripting language, such as VBScript or JScript, on the server, which could access databases and programmatically create Web pages that could be delivered to the Web browser.

Active Server Pages version 1.0 was first introduced with Internet Information Server (IIS) 3.0 as part of Windows NT Service Pack 3. Version 2.0 was released in December 1997 as part of Windows NT Service Pack 4. The Windows NT 4.0 Option Pack included ASP 2.0 with IIS 4.0 and Personal Web Server (PWS) for NT 4.0 Workstation and Windows 9x. ASP Version 3.0 was released with IIS 5.0 in Windows 2000. Finally, we have ASP.NET, which is packaged with the .NET Framework Software Development Kit (SDK) 2, which is a free download from Microsoft. The .NET Framework SDK is also installed when Visual Studio .NET is installed.

ASP is not a language; it's a platform that can host scripting languages like VBScript and JScript. This platform runs on a Web server, typically IIS, but ASP is also available from third-party vendors for use on other Web servers.

This chapter will look at some of the problems associated with Active Server Pages, followed by a look at the benefits of ASP.NET and programming language choices. Then, this chapter will cover the setting up of the development environment, which will be used extensively in this book.

Problems with Older Versions of Active Server Pages

One of the problems with programming traditional Active Server Pages is that the server-side code is mixed in with the HTML and client-side code. We have somehow managed to migrate back to unmanageable spaghetti coding. It's hard to believe that this has become an acceptable method of programming large-scale enterprise applications.

Due to the nature of HTML behavior, many of the ASP development environments required the creation of tables, and nested tables, in order to obtain the desired position of controls such as text boxes and buttons.

Another problem with traditional ASP programming is that the code is interpreted rather than compiled, resulting in slower performance.

ASP exposed an object called the session object. This object was very easy to use, but programmers often ran into problems when an additional Web server was added, thereby creating a Web farm. The problem is that session state is not shareable within a Web farm environment.

ASP also uses late binding when making calls to compiled COM components, resulting in slower performance.

The Benefits of ASP.NET

To say that ASP.NET is just the latest version of ASP is an understatement. ASP.NET represents an exciting new platform for creating Web sites with the .NET Framework, using any .NET language. Some of the benefits of ASP.NET are:

Structure.   ASP.NET brings structure back into programming by offering a *code-behind* page, which separates the client-side script and HTML from the server-side code.

Layout control.   Using Web Forms in ASP.NET and positioning controls such as text boxes and buttons is easy, and Visual Studio .NET will create the appropriate HTML code for the target browser that is selected. For instance, to be compatible with most browsers, Visual Studio .NET will create tables, and nested tables to obtain the desired positioning of the controls. If the application only needs to be compatible with the latest versions of Internet Explorer, then Visual Studio .NET will position the controls using DHTML.

Compiled code. ASP.NET solves the problem of running interpreted script by compiling the server-side code into IL (Intermediate Language). IL code is significantly faster than interpreted script.

Early binding. ASP.NET also uses early binding when making calls to COM components, resulting in faster performance.

Security. ASP.NET has an enhanced security infrastructure that can be quickly configured and programmed to authenticate and authorize Web site users.

Performance. ASP.NET contains performance enhancements, such as page and data caching.

Diagnostics. ASP.NET offers an enhanced tracing and debugging option, which will save time when you are ready to get the system running.

Session state. ASP.NET has an improved session object. Session state can be configured to be shared among all servers in a Web farm.

.NET Framework. Since ASP.NET uses the .NET Framework, ASP.NET also inherits the features of the .NET Framework, such as:

- Automatic memory cleanup via garbage collection
- Cross-language inheritance
- A large object-oriented base class library
- The use of ADO.NET to access databases

Web services. ASP.NET also provides the Web service infrastructure. It is possible to create a Web service with very few lines of code.

What Language Should Be Used?

ASP.NET can be used with any of the .NET-compliant languages that are available. The release of Visual Studio .NET contains managed C++, Visual Basic .NET, and C# (C Sharp). Microsoft also released J# in June 2002. There are also many third-party languages. This means that you can use the language that you are the most comfortable with.

Listed below is a small Hello World program, written in Visual Basic .NET and saved to a file called hi-vb.aspx in the root Web directory (typically c:\inetpub\wwwroot\).

```
<% @Language="VB" %>
<html>
    <body>
        <%
            response.write("Hello World from VB")
```

```
            %>
      </body>
</html>
```

Here is the C# version of the same program, saved to a file called hi-cs.aspx in the root Web directory.

```
<% @Language="C#" %>
<html>
      <body>
            <%
                  Response.Write("Hello World from C#");
            %>
      </body>
</html>
```

So what's the difference? Notice the language directive on the first line. Also, notice that "response.write" is all lowercase in the Visual Basic .NET example. Visual Basic .NET is not case sensitive, which means that "RESPONSE.WRITE" could be typed and the program would still work. In the C# example, notice "Response.Write" is used. C# is case sensitive, and the response object was created with "Response", so "response" or "RESPONSE" or anything other than "Response" will fail. The same holds true for the "Write" method.

In Visual Basic .NET, a command terminates with a carriage return, but in C#, a command terminates with a semicolon.

There are indeed syntactical differences, but how about performance? All .NET languages will compile their source code to Microsoft Intermediate Language (MSIL or IL) before they are executed. The following is a snippet of the main part of the IL code that was produced from the Visual Basic .NET sample:

```
// Here is the Visual Basic .NET version snippet.
IL_0000: ldarg.1
IL_0001: ldstr "\r\n<html>\r\n <body>\r\n\t"
IL_0006: callvirt instance void
     [System.Web]System.Web.UI.HtmlTextWriter::Write(string)
IL_000b: ldarg.0
IL_000c: callvirt instance class
        [System.Web]System.Web.HttpResponse
        [System.Web]System.Web.UI.Page::get_Response()
IL_0011: ldstr "Hello World from VB"
IL_0016: callvirt instance void
        [System.Web]System.Web.HttpResponse::Write(string)
IL_001b: ldarg.1
IL_001c: ldstr " \r\n </body>\r\n</html>\r\n\r\n"
IL_0021: callvirt instance void
        [System.Web]System.Web.UI.HtmlTextWriter::Write(string)
IL_0026: ret
```

Here is the same code snippet, produced from the C# sample:

```
// Here is the C# version snippet.
IL_0000: ldarg.1
IL_0001: ldstr "\r\n<html>\r\n <body>\r\n\t"
IL_0006: callvirt instance void
      [mscorlib]System.IO.TextWriter::Write(string)
IL_000b: ldarg.0
IL_000c: call instance class
      [System.Web]System.Web.HttpResponse
      [System.Web]System.Web.UI.Page::get_Response()
IL_0011: ldstr "Hello World from C#"
IL_0016: callvirt instance void
      [System.Web]System.Web.HttpResponse::Write(string)
IL_001b: ldarg.1
IL_001c: ldstr " \r\n </body>\r\n</html>\r\n\r\n"
IL_0021: callvirt instance void
      [mscorlib]System.IO.TextWriter::Write(string)
IL_0026: ret
```

One might argue that since every .NET language compiles to IL code, they all run at the same speed. If you look at the two snippets of code, you will see that there are differences. Since the samples are different, they certainly won't run at the same speed. In reality, the faster language will be the language that creates the most optimized IL code. Although there are differences in code and performance between the .NET languages, the difference is usually not great enough to justify using one .NET language over another .NET language.

Although the older versions of ASP could be coded with VBScript, JScript, or other third-party scripting languages, most programmers used VBScript. This makes Web development with ASP.NET using Visual Basic .NET a natural migration path. Visual Basic .NET is considered by many to be the easiest of the .NET languages to learn, primarily due to its case-insensitive, easily read syntax. This book will use Visual Basic .NET exclusively.

Classroom Q & A

Q: Can Visual Basic .NET do everything that all of the other languages, such as C# can do?

A: Yes, with a few exceptions. Some .NET languages, such as C#, allow overloaded operators, but Visual Basic .NET does not. Also, Visual Basic .NET does not directly support unsigned integers. There are workarounds to accomplish similar functionality, and none of these items are used enough to warrant the move to another language.

Q: Is there a wizard that can be used to upgrade my ASP code to ASP.NET?

A: No, there isn't. In ASP, all variables are a special data type called a *variant*. When objects are created, they are assigned to a variant. Because a variant can hold anything, there is no easy way for a wizard to perform any type checking and correction. Also, in many cases, you will want to rewrite your code to take advantage of the new ASP.NET features.

Q: Does Visual Studio .NET have a way to restore a file to its original state, even if I have made lots of changes and saves during the day?

A: By itself, no, but Visual Studio .NET Developer and Enterprise Architect editions ship with Visual SourceSafe, which allows the tracking of changes to documents, and yes, the rollback of changes. In Lab 1, you will install Visual SourceSafe.

Choosing the Appropriate Development Environment

Before proceeding with ASP.NET development, it is important that the development environment be set up properly. There are certainly many ways to set up a computer, each having advantages and disadvantages. This section will look at the software requirements first, and then at installation locations for the software. Finally, this section will look at the permissions that are required for development work.

The Operating System

When choosing the version of Windows, it's best to select either the Professional (2000 or XP) or the Server (2000 or .NET) version. Windows 95 cannot be used, and although Widows 98, ME, and XP Home can be used, there will be limitations, especially in the area of security.

When developing a server product, it may be better to use the Windows Server product rather than the Professional version. This can help minimize the surprises that always seem to pop up when the product is released to production.

The Database Server

Microsoft has two database products, Access and SQL Server. SQL Server should always be used for Web applications because SQL Server is designed to be scalable and to perform well in a multiuser environment. Microsoft released Visual Studio .NET with a SQL Server provider that squeezes every ounce of performance and functionality from SQL Server.

SQL Server has several editions for production use, but there is also a developer edition, which is the edition that should be used. The SQL Server Developer Edition has all of the features that the SQL Server Enterprise Edition has, except that the licensing prohibits production deployment.

The Version Control Software

The need for a version control system is often overlooked. Even in a single-developer environment, it is important to have a version control system in place. If you haven't been using a version control system, this is a good time to bite the bullet and give it a try.

Microsoft's version control system is called Visual SourceSafe. Visual SourceSafe tracks changes that are made to documents, using its own database. The Visual SourceSafe database is efficient, storing only changes between document versions rather than complete copies of documents. The Visual SourceSafe database can be located on your machine, but is usually best to place the database on a server that is accessible to all of the developers.

Not only does Visual SourceSafe provide the version control for documents, it also provides an enhanced locking mechanism for use in a multideveloper environment.

Visual Studio .NET was released with version 6c of Visual SourceSafe. This version integrates nicely with Visual Studio .NET, and the use of this version or higher is recommended.

The Visual Studio .NET Edition

Visual Studio .NET needs to be installed, but which version should be installed? Visual Studio is available in the Professional, Enterprise Developer, and Enterprise Architect Edition. This section will look at the contents of each edition.

Visual Studio .NET Professional Edition

Visual Studio .NET Professional Edition contains the following:

- C#, Visual Basic .NET, Managed C++, J# .NET
- Web services
- Web Forms
- Windows Forms

- Mobile Web Forms
- Pocket PC and CE.NET-based applications
- .NET Framework and the common language runtime
- Visual Basic .NET Upgrade Wizard
- Visual Studio integrated development environment
- Rapid Application Development (RAD) for the server
- Visual Studio .NET Debugger
- Dynamic Help
- Task List
- HTML Designer
- SQL Server 2000 Desktop Engine
- Visual Database Tools
- XML Designer

Visual Studio .NET Enterprise Developer Edition

Visual Studio .NET Enterprise Developer Edition contains everything from Visual Studio .NET Professional, plus the following:

- Visual SourceSafe 6c
- Application Center Test
- Enterprise templates and frameworks
- Microsoft .NET-based reference applications
- Visual Studio Analyzer
- Licensed Development Versions of:
    - Windows 2000 Standard Server
    - SQL Server 2000
    - Microsoft Commerce Server
    - Microsoft Host Integration Server
    - Microsoft Exchange Server

Visual Studio .NET Enterprise Architect Edition Contents

Visual Studio .NET Enterprise Architect includes everything from Visual Studio .NET Enterprise Developer edition, plus the following:

- Microsoft Visio-based database modeling
- Microsoft Visio-based UML application modeling
- Enterprise template project type
- Licensed Developer Version of BizTalk Server

Software Selection Conclusions

The Enterprise Developer and Enterprise Architect editions of Visual Studio .NET contain licensed developer editions of Windows 2000 Server, SQL Server 2000, and Visual SourceSafe 6c. This software is needed for the computer setup. If you don't have licensed copies of this software, then obtaining a minimum of Visual Studio .NET Enterprise Developer Edition may make the most sense.

The recommended (not minimum) software requirements for this course are:

- Windows (2000 or .NET) Server
- Internet Information Server 5.0+ (included in Windows Pro and Server)
- Visual Studio .NET Enterprise Architect Edition
- SQL Server 2000+ Developer Edition
- Visual SourceSafe 6c+

Note that the focus of this section is on setting up the development environment, but other items that need to be considered are:

- Proper backup strategy
- Testing strategy
- Deployment strategy

The Software Installation Location

It's possible to install all of this software on one machine, but ideally you should install Visual SourceSafe (VSS) on its own server. When working in a team environment, a separate Visual SourceSafe server with the appropriate disaster recovery plan should always be implemented. Figure 1.1 shows a diagram of a typical development environment.

Previous versions of Visual Studio recommended running a shared version of Internet Information Server (IIS) on a central server. With Visual Studio .NET, it's preferable to install Internet Information Server on each developer's machine. This allows all the developers to debug their Web project at the same time, since Internet Information Server can only be debugged by one person at a time.

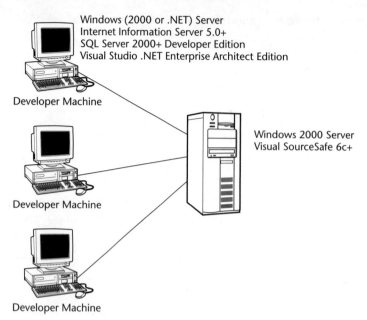

Windows (2000 or .NET) Server
Internet Information Server 5.0+
SQL Server 2000+ Developer Edition
Visual Studio .NET Enterprise Architect Edition

Developer Machine

Windows 2000 Server
Visual SourceSafe 6c+

Developer Machine

Developer Machine

Figure 1.1   Diagram of a typical development environment.

Running SQL Server on each developer's machine will allow each developer to have better control of schema updates. If SQL Server were on a single machine, one developer could make a schema change that would cause the other developers' code to break. The other developers would have to drop everything and fix their code. With SQL Server on each developer's machine, the developers can decide when the schema updates should be applied, so each developer has better control of the timing. The schema can be checked into VSS by generating a script from within SQL Enterprise Manager, or by writing code to extract the schema.

Developer Permission Assignments

There are many software packages on the market that work fine, as long as the user is logged on with an account that has administrative permissions. If the user is logged on with a standard user account, the software will not operate. This suggests that the developer wrote and tested this software while logged on with an administrative account.

If you are logged on with administrative permissions and someone finds a way to get you to unknowingly execute malicious code, the code will have the same permissions that you currently have. This means that the malicious code could also be running with administrative permissions. The solution to these problems is to do development with a standard user account, adding only those permissions that are required for you to do your job.

Use the administrator account for the initial machine setup, and as soon as that is done switch over to a standard user account. That's a good approach. Throughout this book, every attempt will be made to use a standard account for development work, using the minimum required security.

Setting up the Development Environment

This section will cover the important aspects setting up and configuring the development environment. You will actually perform the installation and configuration of this software in the lab at the end of this chapter.

Installing Windows

Consider performing a default installation of Windows, with one exception: the formatting of the hard drive. After the installation is complete, make any changes that are required.

When installing Windows, it's important that the drive(s) be formatted as NTFS (NT File System). This is best done during the initial install, but you can change to NTFS later by issuing the following command from the command prompt:

```
convert d: /fs:NTFS
```

where d: is the drive that you need to convert.

Why NTFS? Because NTFS is secure. If you use the FAT or FAT32 format, you cannot assign permissions to files and folders. You will also find that an NTFS drive is much more resistant to corruption than a FAT- or FAT32-formatted drive.

Configuring Internet Information Server

If you have chosen to install Windows (2000 or XP) Professional, Internet Information Services is not installed by default. Even if you are installing Windows (2000 or .NET) Server, you may want to select only the IIS components that you need. You can select Internet Information Services on the Windows Components screen and click the Details button. Notice that the only six components that are required are the Common Files, Documentation, Front Page Server Extensions, IIS Snap-In, SMTP Service (email), and World Wide Web Service. Figure 1.2 shows the components that are required.

Other Software

As soon as you finish installing Windows 2000, add any drivers that your system requires. If you were running on Windows 9x, you will need to obtain updated drivers for your new operating system.

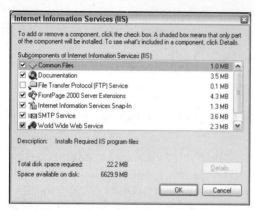

Figure 1.2   Required Internet Information Server components.

Be careful with the order in which you install your software. One problem that Windows has been plagued with is commonly called DLL hell. To experience DLL hell first hand, a user would do something like the following. *Don't actually perform these steps!*

1. Install all of your newest applications first and test them.
2. Next, install all of your oldest applications and test them.
3. Retest the newest applications, and note the applications that fail.

When the older software packages are installed, they overwrite some of the DLL files that were installed by the newer applications. The symptom is that the old software works, while the new software does not! It's best to always install your oldest software first, and work your way toward the newest software.

If you need Visual Studio 6 installed in order to work on existing projects, this is a good time to install it. Visual Studio 6 can run on the same machine as Visual Studio .NET without any problems. Be sure to apply the latest Visual Studio 6 service pack.

If you need to use Microsoft Office on your machine, this is a good time to install it, too.

Installing SQL Server 2000 Developer Edition

This first part of this section will cover the creation of a SQL Server Service Account, which will be assigned to the SQL services during the installation. After that, is the actual installation of SQL Server will be covered. After the installation has been completed, this section will cover the creation of a SQL Server account that you will use during development. The last part of this section deals with testing the installation in order to ensure that a SQL Server stored procedure can be debugged.

Creating the SQL Server Service Account

Before you install SQL Server, you should create an account that will be assigned to the SQL Server services. It's good to create a new account, maybe called ServiceAccount, and assign this account to any service that needs an account. If you are in a domain environment, this account should be a domain account. If you're not in a domain, create a local ServiceAccount. The created account needs to be placed into the local Administrators group. This account also needs Logon as a Service rights, but this right will be assigned automatically when you assign the account to the services.

Figure 1.3 shows the setup of the ServiceAccount in a nondomain environment, while Figure 1.4 shows the setup of the ServiceAccount in a domain environment using Active Directory.

SQL Server Installation

The SQL Server installer will prompt you for the following items:

Location of the Installation.   Settings are *Local Computer* or *Remote Computer*. It's usually better to perform Local Computer installations, because a Remote Computer installation will install the database engine, but the SQL Server Client Tools will not be installed. The last option is called Virtual Server (grayed out), which is available for clustered servers.

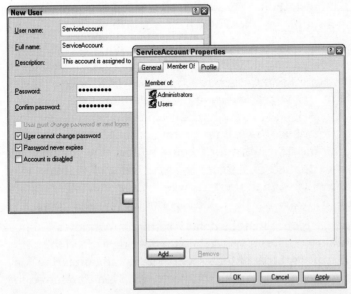

Figure 1.3   Local configuration of ServiceAccount in nondomain environment.

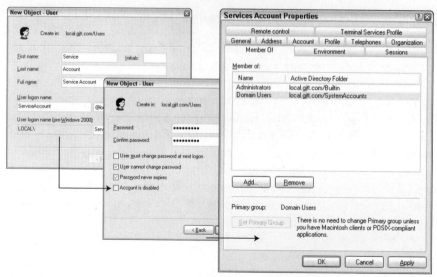

Figure 1.4   Domain configuration of ServiceAccount in domain environment.

Installation Selection.   Allows you to create a new instance of SQL Server
or upgrade or remove existing components. Installing an instance of SQL
Server is similar to creating an isolated copy of SQL Server on your
machine. After you install your first instance (Default instance), you can
install additional instances to have isolated copies of SQL Server on your
machine. The primary benefit of creating new instances of SQL Server is
to have isolated administration. There is a small performance hit associated with creating multiple instances of SQL Server on a machine.

Assign Service Account.   If you select the option for using the Local System account, you will not be able to debug SQL stored procedures. It's
good to assign an account to these services, because if SQL Server needs
to access any external resources, such as a file on a remote machine, or
an email system, the assigned account is the account that will be used
for authorization. Do not use the Administrator account because changing the password for the Administrator account will require you to
update the password on the SQL Server services. Figure 1.5 displays the
location where you will assign the ServiceAccount as previously
described. Be sure to always use the same account for both services.

Authentication Mode.   Notice that the default setting is Windows
Authentication mode (see Figure 1.6). While this setting is good for
client/server applications, Mixed Mode security is usually preferred for
Internet applications. Windows Authentication, which is also referred to

as *Trusted Security* or *Integrated Security*, uses your Windows account for SQL authentication. This means that you don't need to explicitly log on to SQL Server. This is a great feature, but when you are working with Internet and multitier applications, it's usually preferable to use a single standard SQL account for all user access to a database. Setting the authentication mode to Mixed Mode will allow you to use Windows accounts and standard SQL Server accounts. When Mixed Mode is selected, an account called *sa* (system administrator) is created. You need to assign a password to this account. Although you have the option to assign a blank password, the first password that a hacker would try is the blank password because this was the default password on previous versions of SQL Server, and many administrators neglected to change it.

Once the setup has been completed, you should apply the latest service packs for SQL Server.

Adding a SQL Server Login for Your Use

A new account needs to be added to SQL Server that will be used for developing and debugging. This can be done using the SQL Enterprise Manager. The security group called *Debugger Users* already exists on your machine. This group can be added to SQL Server, and assigned the appropriate permissions (see Figure 1.7). Later in this chapter, you will cover the creation of a standard Windows account for development use, and that account will be added to the Debugger Users group.

To debug stored procedures, the execute permission must be granted to the Debugger Users account for the sp_sdidebug extended stored procedure. This extended stored procedure is located in the master database (see Figure 1.8).

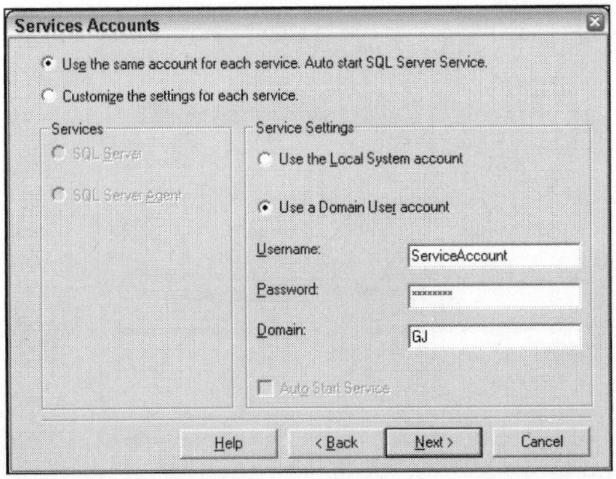

Figure 1.5 Assigning the service account to each SQL Server service.

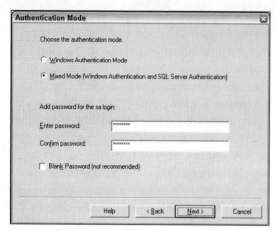

Figure 1.6   Configuring the authentication mode to mixed mode.

SQL Server Stored Procedure Debugging

In order to debug SQL stored procedures, the service account must have administrative permissions on your local machine. If you varied from the installation procedure previously described, and assigned the LocalSystem account to the SQL Server services, SQL Server debugging will fail.

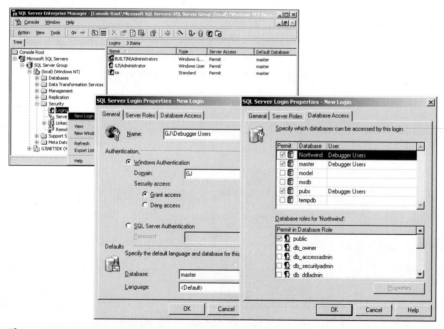

Figure 1.7   Creating the Debugger Users account.

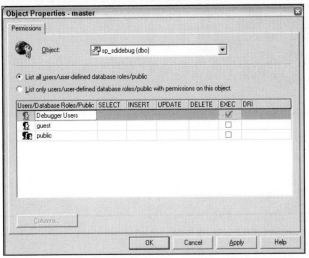

Figure 1.8   Granting EXEC permissions to Debugger Users.

The ADO.NET chapter will include instructions for debugging SQL stored procedures from within Visual Studio .NET, but it's a good idea to test the SQL Server debugger before installing Visual Studio .NET. This can be done by using the SQL Query Analyzer, and opening a stored procedure in debug mode. Figure 1.9 displays the SQL Query Analyzer in debug mode.

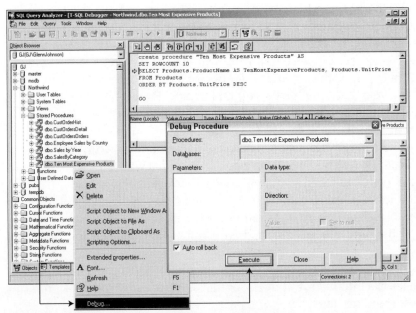

Figure 1.9   Verify SQL Server debugging capabilities.

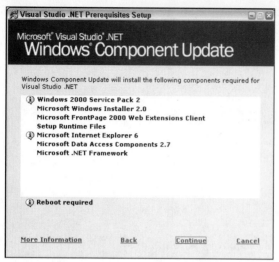

Figure 1.10 Component Update screen.

Installing Visual Studio .NET

To install Visual Studio .NET, you must be logged on with an account that has administrative permissions. The first thing that needs to be performed is a component update. This will check your system and install any necessary updates prior to installing Visual Studio .NET. See Figure 1.10.

The component update will give you the option of assigning a name and password for *automatic logon and continue* during the setup. The setup takes a while, and this option will keep you from waiting for each reboot.

Step 2 of the setup is the actual installation of Visual Studio .NET. The main screen for the Visual Studio .NET setup is shown in Figure 1.11. You can select which items you want to install, and which items should be run from the installation media. There is about 1 GB of documentation. If you lack space on your drive, you may want to change the documentation setting from *Local Source* to *From Source*. The *From Source* option requires you to make the installation media available when you need access to the documentation.

When the installation is complete, a summary page will be displayed. Be careful, because if there is an installation error, this screen will display a message stating that errors were reported. You can view the setup log from this screen.

The last item in the Visual Studio .NET installation is to check for updates. You can check the Internet for updates, or install the update from disk. You can also check for updates later.

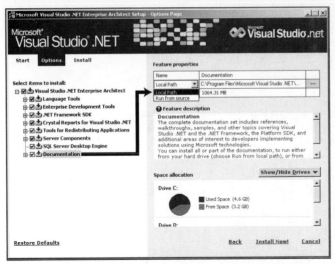

Figure 1.11 Selecting the Visual Studio .NET setup options.

Installing Visual SourceSafe Server

Visual SourceSafe is included with the Developer and Architect Editions of Visual Studio .NET, but it doesn't install by default. Insert the CD that has the VSS folder, navigate to that folder, and run the setup.exe program. You will have the option to install a stand-alone version of SourceSafe or a shared database version (Figure 1.12). You will install the shared database version. Looking back at the Development Environment diagram at the beginning of the chapter, you can see that this installation should be on a separate machine. If you don't have access to a separate server, it's okay to install Visual SourceSafe on your machine. Just remember that your disaster recovery plan for this machine is more important than ever.

The installation will search your drives, looking for an existing installation of Visual SourceSafe. If it finds an existing installation, you will be prompted to select this folder or select a different folder.

If you perform this installation on your computer, skip over the Visual SourceSafe Client installation, to the Windows Administration section.

Installing Visual SourceSafe Client

If you installed Visual SourceSafe on a separate machine, you now need to install the Visual SourceSafe client on your machine. First, share the folder on the server that Visual SourceSafe was installed into. Next, from your machine, navigate to the SourceSafe share, and run the NetSetup.exe program.

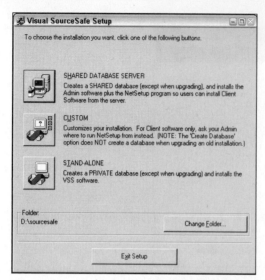

Figure 1.12 Selecting the Shared Database version in the Visual SourceSafe setup.

Next, Visual SourceSafe will search your drives for an existing installation. If Visual SourceSafe finds an existing installation, you will be prompted to select that folder or create a new folder. You will be able to select the desired folder and continue with the installation.

The Visual SourceSafe Client will need to be installed on each workstation that requires access to the Visual SourceSafe database.

Windows 2000 Administration

Your development should be done using the least possible permissions. This keeps any would-be hackers from doing damage to your machine while using your security context. This also helps to ensure that your code will operate with a standard user account when your application moves to a production environment. Depending on how you set up your computer, this account creation process will vary. If you are not in a domain environment, you will add a local user account using Local Users and Computers. This tool is accessible by right-clicking My Computer, and clicking Manage.

If you are in a domain environment, use Active Directory Users and Computers, which is available by clicking Start, Programs, Administrative Tools.

The new account needs to be added to the Debugger Users group and the VS Developers group. The Debugger Users group allows you to debug your applications. The VS Developers group gives you permissions to create ASP.NET Web projects.

You will need to make sure that this account has the right to log on locally to your development machine. If your policy setting includes the Users group, then you're all set. If you are on a domain controller, the Users group won't be in the list, so simply add your account to this list. Also, you should verify that your new account has the right to shutdown the system as well (see Figure 1.13).

Visual SourceSafe Administration

Before starting your first project, you will need to do a bit of administration to Visual SourceSafe. Assign a password to the default admin account and add accounts for each person who will be checking files in and out of Visual SourceSafe.

Visual SourceSafe has an option to perform an automatic login with the user's Windows account (see Figure 1.14). This is a good setting to keep selected, but you will need to make sure that each person who is doing development work has a unique name on the network, as opposed to everyone using the administrator account.

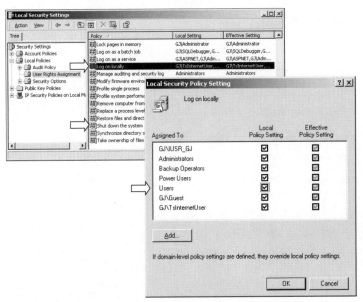

Figure 1.13 Adding rights to the user account.

Figure 1.14   Setting the Visual SourceSafe automatic login option.

When adding users, notice that the password is optional. If the password is left blank, the user will not be prompted for a password. Add an account for each user who will be accessing Visual SourceSafe. Be sure that the user account matches the Windows Logon account. If you are careful to add a unique account for each user who will be checking files into and out of Visual SourceSafe, you will be able to see who made the changes to file, and who has files checked out.

Lab 1.1: ASP.NET Development Environment Setup

In this lab, you will set up your development environment. This lab starts with the installation of the operating system, and includes the installation of the products (except Mobile Information Server, which we will install when we get to that chapter) that are necessary in order complete all of the labs in this book.

You may want to read this lab in its entirety, and then go back and perform the exercises that are required for your system. This is the longest lab in the book, but careful environment planning and configuration will make your development experience more enjoyable.

Install the Windows Operating System

1. Perform a default installation of the operating system, except format the drives using NTFS.

2. Install the latest Windows service pack.

Install Internet Information Server

If you have chosen to install Windows (2000 or XP) Professional, Internet Information Services is not installed by default. If you installed Windows Server, you will verify that Internet Information Server has been installed.

1. Click Start, Settings, Control Panel, Add/Remove Programs, Add/Remove Windows Components, Internet Information Services, Details.

2. Select the following six components:
   - Common Files
   - Documentation
   - Front Page Server Extensions
   - IIS Snap-In
   - SMTP Service (email)
   - World Wide Web Service

3. Click OK, Next to complete the installation.

Install Other Software

1. Add any drivers that your system requires.

2. Install Visual Studio 6, if required, and apply the latest Visual Studio 6 service pack.

3. Install Microsoft Office, if required, and apply the latest Office service pack.

Install SQL Server 2000 Developer Edition

In this section, you will create a service account, perform the SQL Server installation, add a SQL login for yourself, and verify that the SQL Debugger is operational.

Create the Service Account

You will create an account for the SQL services. The creation of this account will be done differently, depending on whether you are in a domain environment or not.

NONDOMAIN ENVIRONMENT

1. Right-click My Computer, and click Manage.

2. Expand Computer Management, System Tools, Local Users and Computers.

3. Right-click Users, and select New User.

4. Type in *ServiceAccount* for the name, assign a password, and enter any additional information. Uncheck the User must change password at next logon box, then click the Create button.

5. Place ServiceAccount into the local Administrators group.

DOMAIN ENVIRONMENT

1. Click Start, Programs, Administrative Tools, Active Directory Users and Computers.

2. Expand Active Directory Users and Computers, *domain name*, Users. Right-click Users, then click New, User.

3. Type in *ServiceAccount* for the name, assign a password, and enter any additional information. Be sure to clear the User must change password at next login check box.

4. Place ServiceAccount into the local Administrators group.

Install SQL Server

1. Start the SQL Server setup. Select SQL Server 2000 Components from the first setup screen, and then select Install Database Server. The next screen simply informs you that you are going to be installing an instance of SQL Server. Click Next.

2. On the Computer Name screen, verify that Local Computer is selected, and click Next.

3. On the Installation Selection screen, verify that *Create a new instance of SQL Server* is selected. Click Next.

4. The next screen is the License Agreement screen. If you agree with the licensing, click the Yes to continue.

5. On the next screen, verify that *Server and Client Tools* is selected and click Next.

6. The next screen prompts you for an instance name. Verify that the *Default* check box is selected, and click Next.

7. On the Setup Type screen, verify that *Typical* is selected. Before clicking Next, note that this is where you have the option to put the program and/or data in a different location. Click Next.

8. On the Services Accounts screen, verify that *Use the same account for each service* option is selected. Also, select Use a Domain User Account, type ServiceAccount as the name, type in the password for

the account, and type in the Domain Name. If you are not in a domain, use your machine name as the domain name.

9. On the Authentication Mode screen, enable Mixed Mode. Type in a password for the sa account, and click Next.

10. Finally, click the Next button again to install SQL Server.

11. Once the setup has been completed, apply the latest service packs for SQL Server.

Create the SQL Server Login

You will add an account to SQL Server called Debugger Users, and assign the appropriate permissions. This is the SQL account that you will use for development. Later, you will create a standard Windows account for development use and add that account to the Debugger Users group.

1. Open the SQL Enterprise Manager by clicking Start, Programs, Microsoft SQL Server, Enterprise Manager.

2. Expand Microsoft SQL Server, (local), Security. Right-click Logins, then click New Login.

3. In the Name field, type *Debugger Users*. Click the drop-down box for the domain, and select your computer. Be sure that the Grant Access option is selected.

4. Click the Database Access tab, and click the northwind, pubs, master, and any other database that you may need to edit. Note that master database must be selected in order to debug stored procedures.

5. Click OK to create the account.

6. Expand the master database, click Extended Stored Procedures, and then double-click the sp_sdidebug procedure.

7. In the Extended Stored Procedure dialog box, click Permissions. Grant the Debugger Users user account EXEC permissions.

8. Close SQL Enterprise Manager.

Verifying SQL Server Stored Procedure Debugger Operation

To debug SQL stored procedures, the service account must have administrative permissions on your local machine. If you varied from the installation procedure previously described, and assigned the LocalSystem account to the SQL Server services, SQL Server debugging will fail.

This section of the lab simply verifies that you are able to debug SQL Server stored procedures, prior to installing Visual Studio .NET.

1. Open the SQL Query Analyzer by clicking Start, Programs, Microsoft SQL Server, Query Analyzer.

2. When prompted for a logon, be sure to select Windows Authentication, and for the SQL Server machine, leave the period (for local machine).

3. Expand Northwind, Stored Procedures.

4. Right-click the dbo.Ten Most Expensive Products stored procedure, and click Debug.

The stored procedure will open in the T-SQL Debugger, and you should see a yellow arrow to the left of SET ROWCOUNT 10. Also, if you press the F11 function key, the program pointer will move to the next line, and so on.

If this didn't work, you may want to retrace the steps that are listed in this book. Also, you may want to search msdn.microsoft.com for articles on SQL Stored Procedure Debugging.

Install Visual Studio .NET

The installation of Visual Studio .NET will be done by performing a component update, then installing Visual Studio .NET, and finally installing updates. Make sure that you are logged in with an account that has administrator permissions.

Component Update

1. Start the Visual Studio .NET setup, and click Component Update.

2. The next screen is the Licensing screen. Click I Accept, and click Continue.

3. Next is the Component Update screen. Click Continue.

4. Type your name and password for *Automatic Logon and Continue* during the setup. Click Install Now.

5. When the component update is complete, you will see the status of the update. Be careful to read this screen. If there were any installation errors, they will be displayed here. Click Done.

Visual Studio .NET

1. Select Visual Studio .NET to continue.

2. The first screen will be the License Agreement screen for Visual Studio .NET. Click I Agree, type in the product key, and click Continue.

3. You are now on the main screen for the Visual Studio .NET setup. On this screen, click Install Now.

4. When the installation is complete, a summary page will be displayed. Be careful here, because if there is an installation error, this screen will display a message stating that errors were reported. Notice that you can view the setup log from this screen. Click Done.

Service Releases

The last item in the Visual Studio .NET installation is to check for updates. Check the Internet for updates, or install the updates from disk.

Install Visual SourceSafe Server

1. Insert the CD that has the VSS folder, navigate to that folder, and run the setup.exe program. Click Shared Database Server.

2. Enter the key code, and click OK.

3. Select the desired installation folder and continue.

4. If you installed VSS on your machine, skip over this section, and go to the Windows Administration section.

Install Visual SourceSafe Client

If you installed VSS on a separate machine, you now need to install the VSS client on your machine.

1. Share the folder on the server that Visual SourceSafe was installed on.

2. From your machine, navigate to the SourceSafe share, and run the NetSetup.exe program. NetSetup.exe will start the installation of the Visual SourceSafe client software.

3. Type your name and your company's name, and then the CD key.

4. Select the desired installation folder, and click the computer icon to continue with the installation.

5. Repeat the client installation for each workstation that requires access to the Visual SourceSafe database.

Windows 2000 Administration

In this section, you will create a standard Windows account with the minimum required permissions. This account will be placed into the Debugger Users and the VS Developers groups. The account will then be granted the right to log on locally and shut down the system. Follow the appropriate instructions, based on whether you are in a domain environment or not.

Nondomain Environment

1. Right-click My Computer, and click Manage.

2. Expand Computer Management, System Tools, Local Users and Computers.

3. Right-click Users, and select New User.

4. Type in the desired name and other information, uncheck the User must change password at next logon box, and then click the Create button.

5. Double-click the Debugger Users group. Click the Members tab. Add your new account to the group. The Debugger Users group allows you to debug your applications (remember that you added this group as a SQL Server account when you installed SQL Server).

6. Double-click the VS Developers group. Click the Members tab and add your account to the group. The VS Developers group gives you permissions to create ASP.NET Web projects.

7. Close Computer Management.

8. Click Start, Programs, Administrative Tools, Local Security Settings.

9. Expand Local Policy, User Rights Assignment.

10. Double-click Log on Locally. A window will be displayed, showing the users and groups who have permissions to log on locally to this machine. Make sure that your account belongs to one of the listed groups, or add or account to the list. In the diagram, my account has Log on locally permissions because the account is a member of the group called Users. If your policy setting includes the Users group, then you're done.

11. Double-click Shut Down the System. Verify that your account is in the list, or that a group that you are a member of is in the list (Users).

Domain Environment

1. Click Start, Programs, Administrative Tools, Active Directory Users and Computers.

2. Expand Active Directory Users and Computers, *domain name*, Users. Right-click Users, then click New, User.

3. Fill in the name and password information. Be sure to clear the User must change password at next login check box.

4. Double-click the Debugger Users group. Click the Members tab. Add your new account to the group. The Debugger Users group allows you to debug your applications (remember that you added this group as a SQL Server account when you installed SQL Server).

5. Double-click the VS Developers group. Click the Members tab, and add your account to the group. The VS Developers group gives you permissions to create ASP.NET Web projects.

6. Close Active Directory Users and Computers.

7. Click Start, Programs, Administrative Tools, Local Security Settings.

8. Expand Local Policy, User Rights Assignment.

9. Double-click Log on Locally. A window will be displayed, showing the users and groups who have permissions to log on locally to this machine. Make sure that your account belongs to one of the listed groups, or add the account to the list. In the diagram, my account has Log on locally permissions because the account is a member of the group called Users. If your policy setting includes the Users group, then you're all set.

10. Double-click Shut Down the System. Verify that your account is in the list, or that a group that you are a member of is in the list (Users).

Visual SourceSafe Administration

Before starting your first project, you need to do a little bit of administration to Visual SourceSafe. You will assign a password to the default admin account and add accounts for each person who will check files into and out of VSS.

1. Launch the Visual SourceSafe Administration tool by clicking Start, Programs, Microsoft Visual SourceSafe, Visual SourceSafe 6.0 Admin.

2. You will be immediately taken into the Administration tool, because there is no password assigned to the Admin account. Highlight the admin account, click Users, then click Change Password. Assign a password.

3. Before adding users, take a look at the options. Click Tools, Options. Notice that you have the ability to use the network name for automatic user login. This is a good setting to keep selected; make sure that each person that is doing development work has a unique name on the network, as opposed to everyone using the administrator account.

4. From the Users menu, add a new user. Notice that the password is optional. If the password is left blank, the user will not be prompted for a password. Add an account for each user who will be accessing Visual SourceSafe. Make sure that the user account matches the Windows Logon account.

Summary

From this point onward, you should be logged on with your personal account. When additional permissions are required, they will be added.

Review Questions

1. Name some benefits of using ASP.NET over ASP.

2. What are some of the .NET languages that are available?

3. You are planning on installing Visual Studio .NET, but you also need a Visual Source-Safe and SQL Server 2000. What edition(s) should you consider purchasing?

4. Name some benefits to using a standard user account for development instead of using an account that has administrative permissions.

5. Name some benefits of using Visual SourceSafe, even in a single-developer environment.

6. What Windows group allows you to debug programs?

7. What Windows group allows you to create Web projects?

Answers to Review Questions

1. Some benefits of ASP.NET are:
   a. The ASP.NET code behind page brings structure into Web development.
   b. ASP.NET uses compiled code, thereby delivering better performance.

2. Some .NET languages:
   a. Visual Basic .NET
   b. C# (C Sharp)
   c. J# (J Sharp)
   d. Managed C++
   e. COBOL (third party)
   f. Perl (third party)
   g. Eiffel (third party)
   h. Many more . . .

3. You should consider the purchase of either:
   a. Visual Studio .NET Enterprise Developer Edition
   b. Visual Studio .NET Enterprise Architect Edition

4. By using a standard user account:
   a. You will be able to identify potential security problems much earlier in the development process.
   b. Your exposure to would be hackers who may run code under your security context is minimized.

5. Visual SourceSafe allows you to:
   a. Track changes to your source documents.
   b. See who is currently working on documents.

6. Debugger Users.

7. VS Developers.

Solutions, Projects, and the Visual Studio .NET IDE

It is easy to launch Visual Studio .NET, create a project, and start coding. However a little planning should be considered to be sure you have the desired folder structure for the projects that will be created. This chapter starts by covering the creation of a folder structure, creation of projects within the folder structure, and storing these projects in Visual SourceSafe. The last part of this chapter covers the Visual Studio integrated development environment (IDE), its customization, and methods of getting Visual Studio .NET Help.

Planning and Creating the Visual Studio .NET Solution Structure

When working on many projects, these projects may be created as part of building a large system. Here are a few definitions that you need to understand for this chapter:

System.   A collection of one or more projects and applications to create a fully functional operating piece of production software. For example, an accounting system comprises many projects.

Project (or application). The source of the executable assembly that you will build using Visual Studio .NET. A project is also known as an application.

Solution. A group or projects that are loaded into Visual Studio at the same time for the purpose of development, debugging, and building.

Classroom Q & A

Q: Is it possible to include the same project in many solutions?

A: Yes. For example, you have an order entry solution, and a sales solution. In both of these solutions it may be desirable to include a customer project.

Q: I understand that Visual SourceSafe provides a locking mechanism for files when working in a multideveloper environment, but is there any benefit to using Visual SourceSafe when I am the only developer at my company?

A: Absolutely. The primary purpose of Visual SourceSafe is to track version history. Also, Visual SourceSafe isn't just for code; you can also place design documents and drawings under version control.

Q: One of the problems that I have with Visual Studio is that it always wants to create Web projects in the c:\inetpub\wwwroot\ folder. I like to keep all of my projects in a folder on my D: drive. Is there a way around this problem?

A: There is, and that's one of the topics of this chapter. If you create your folder structure and then create Web shares (also known as virtual directories), the logical location of the projects will still be in the c:\inetpub\wwwroot\ folder, but the physical locations will be on your D: drive.

Folder Structure

The examples in this chapter are built around an order entry system. This system comprises several projects. Before creating the first project, the folder structure needs to be created on the hard drive and in Visual SourceSafe. It is beneficial to have both folder structures match.

Carefully consider the naming of files and folders for your system. If you need to rename a file or folder, it's doable, but very much discouraged. Visual SourceSafe (VSS) provides a facility for renaming files without losing your document history, but keep in mind that renaming files outside your version control system will cause a break in the document's history in VSS. Also, the name of your Web project will be the name of the virtual directory that your users will navigate to. The name of non-Web projects, such as .exe projects, will become the name of the .exe file.

When a Web project is created in Visual Studio, the project files will be located under c:\inetpub\wwwroot\projectname. This location may be suitable for quick tests, but it's more beneficial to create a folder structure that is more solution-centric. A typical solution folder structure for an order entry system that can be built upon is shown in Figure 2.1.

Virtual Directory Creation

After the folder structure is created, a virtual directory needs to be created in IIS for the customer, order, and inventory projects. The creation of the virtual directory accomplishes two tasks. First, the virtual directory will map to the physical directories that have been created. Second, the creation of a virtual directory creates an IIS Web application. The files that are in this folder and its subfolders are considered part of a Web application. This means that if a global variable (also known as an application variable) is created on one Web page in the Customer folder, the variable will be available on any other page that is in the Customer folder, or a subfolder of Customer.

Virtual Directory via Web Sharing

The easiest method of creating a Virtual Directory is via the Web Sharing tab in Windows Explorer. Right-click the folder and click Properties, Web Sharing, as shown in Figure 2.2.

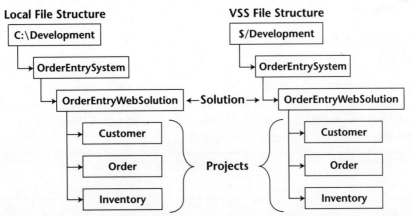

Figure 2.1 Folder structures for your hard drive and version control should match.

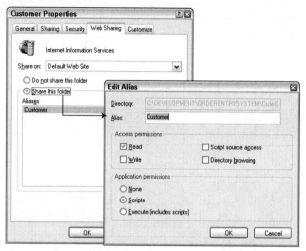

Figure 2.2   Adding a virtual directory via Windows Explorer.

The settings are as follows:

General Settings

Directory.   Location of the folder that is being shared.

Alias.   Name of the virtual directory to be created. Visual Studio .NET expects the Alias to be the same as the folder name.

 If you cannot see the Web Sharing tab, you don't have the proper permissions. Your account must be added to the VS Developers group.

Access Permissions

Read.   Allows users to read the files that are in this folder.

Write.   Allows users to make changes to the files that are in this folder.

Script Source Access.   If the Read option is selected, then selecting this option allows users to read the source code for the Web pages in the folder. If the Write option is selected, this allows users to write changes to the source code contained in this folder.

Directory Browsing.   Allows the user to see a listing of the files in this folder.

Selecting the Write option can reveal sensitive information to users, such as names and passwords that may be embedded in your code.

Application Permissions

None.   Does not allow running any script or executable code.

Scripts Allow.   Allows script code, such as VBScript on an ASP page, to run.

Execute (Includes Scripts).   Allows script and executable code, such as .exe files, to run.

 Selecting the Execute and Write options could be disastrous. This would allow someone to save executable code to the server and then run the code.

For most Web development, the default settings are appropriate when creating a virtual directory.

Virtual Directory via Internet Information Services (IIS)

Another method of creating a virtual directory is via the Internet Information Services snap-in. This may be available via Internet Service Manager from the Start menu (under Administrative Tools). Internet Information Services is also available by right-clicking My Computer, selecting Manage, and then selecting Services and Applications.

Under Internet Information Server, a virtual directory can be created by right-clicking the Default Web Site, selecting New, and then selecting Virtual Directory. This will launch the Virtual Directory Creation Wizard, as shown in Figure 2.3.

 Visual Studio requires matching folder and alias names, so be sure to share the Customer folder with the alias name Customer.

 If you couldn't open the computer icon to expose the default Web site, you may not have adequate permissions. You need to place yourself into the VS Developers group on your machine.

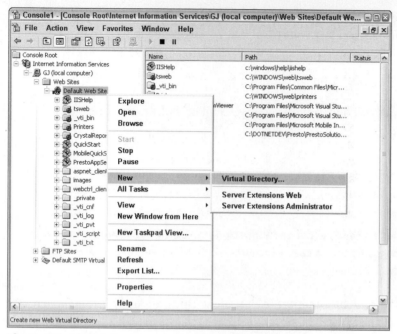

Figure 2.3 Virtual directory creation via Internet Information Services.

Visual Studio .NET Project Creation

Once the desired folder structure is created on your drive, the projects can be created. This can be done by starting Visual Studio .NET and creating a blank solution, as shown in Figure 2.4.

When the blank solution is created, a file with an .sln extension and a file with an .sou extension are created in the solution folder.

The .sln file contains:

- A list of the projects that are in this solution
- A list of project dependencies
- Visual SourceSafe information
- A list of Add-ins that will be available

The .sou file is user specific and contains settings such as:

- The task list
- Debugger breakpoints and watch window settings
- Visual Studio .NET window locations

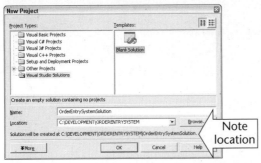

Figure 2.4   Create a blank solution, paying close attention to where the solution will be created.

After the solution is created, new projects can be added. The new project can be added by right-clicking the solution. When the Add New Project dialog box is displayed (see Figure 2.5), type in the location as *http://localhost/Customer*, since a virtual directory called Customer has already been created.

Visual Studio .NET will create the Customer project files in the folder that has been created and shared.

 If you get an error stating that the Web access failed (see Figure 2.6), you may not have the proper permissions to create this Web project. You need to make sure that you are a member of the VS Developers group on your local machine.

The same steps can be repeated to create the order project and the inventory project in the solution folder.

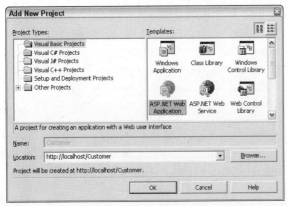

Figure 2.5   Adding a new project to the current solution.

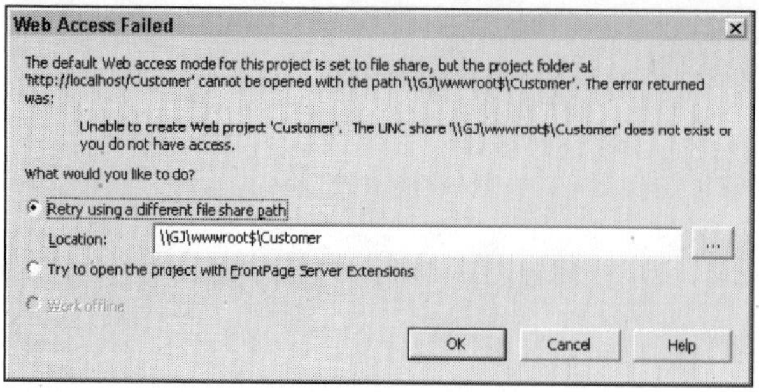

Figure 2.6   Error when trying to open a new project.

Adding the Solution to Visual SourceSafe

After the solution and its projects are created, they can be placed under source control using Visual SourceSafe (VSS). This can be done in Visual Studio .NET by clicking File, Source Control, Add Solution to Source Control.

A Source Control dialog box will be displayed, stating that if you add a file share Web access project to source control, you will no longer be able to access the project using Front Page Web access. Simply click Continue on this screen, because, by default, Front Page Server Extensions are not being used.

When using Front Page Server Extensions, Visual SourceSafe is required to be located on the Web server. Although you may have created the Web project as http://localhost/Customer, Visual Studio .NET resolved this to an UNC path. You are currently accessing your projects via a file share called www-root$ that is located on your machine. Visual Studio will use a combination of direct file access and HTTP access to get to the files.

The next screen prompts for the location of the solution. However, the folder structure has not been created in VSS yet, so you will be looking at nothing more than a root folder. To create the folder structure, type the name of the root development folder (C:\Development), and click the Create button. Type OrderEntrySystem, highlight the Development folder, and click the Create button. This is a good time to build the complete folder structure, as shown in Figure 2.7.

> **tip**   Be sure to select the desired parent folder prior to clicking Create. If you make a mistake, such as adding the Inventory project to the Customer project, you can correct the mistake after you're done by running the Visual SourceSafe program from the Start menu.

Now that you have the folder structure, remember that it's the solution that you wanted to store. Highlight the OrderEntrySolution, and click the OK button. There will be a prompt for each project location. Select the appropriate location, and click OK.

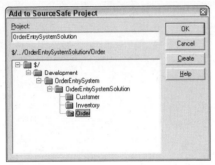

Figure 2.7   Creating the Visual SourceSafe folder structure.

 You should not see a dialog box that asks you if you want to create a new project folder. If you do, look closely at the path that Visual SourceSafe wants to use. Make sure that the path matches one of the folder paths that you have already created.

When you finish selecting the locations of the solution and the projects, VSS will begin adding all of the files to source control. After the copying has completed, Visual Studio .NET will have locks beside the solution, each project, and each file. The lock is an indicator that the file is in Visual SourceSafe, and the file is in Visual SourceSafe's safe. When a file is locked into the safe, the local copy of the file's read-only attribute is set to true.

Visual Studio has an automatic checkout feature that prompts you to check out a file if you start to edit it. If a file is opened by double-clicking it, the file will open in read-only mode. If you make an attempt to modify the file, Visual Studio .NET will display a Check Out for Edit dialog box. You can enter a comment and click the Check Out button to continue rather seamlessly. Notice that the Web form is now checked out. Figure 2.8 shows that styles.css is checked out, and the icon in the Solution Explorer has changed from a lock to a checkmark with an exclamation point, indicating that you have the file checked out of Visual SourceSafe.

An attempt to check out a file that is already checked out will cause a message to be displayed stating that the file is already checked out by another user. Figure 2.8 shows how the icon for the Web.config file has changed to indicate that the file is not available.

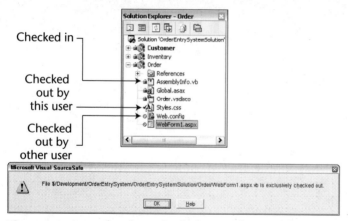

Figure 2.8 Icons showing a checked-out and unavailable status.

To see who has files checked out, launch Visual SourceSafe either from the Start menu or from the Visual Studio by clicking File, Source Control. Figure 2.9 shows the files that are checked out. You can also see the identity of the user who checked out the file. Right-clicking the file will display a menu with options to undo a checkout, view the document history, and compare versions to see the differences.

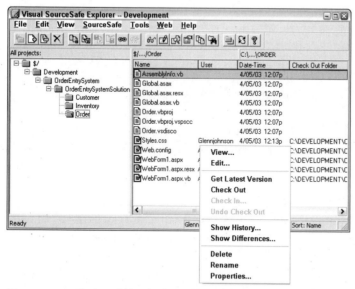

Figure 2.9 Display of checked out files and the options.

Lab 2.1: Creating the OrderEntrySystem Solution

In this lab, you will create a Visual Studio .NET solution for an order entry system that has file and folder structures on your hard drive that match the file and folder structures that you will create in Visual SourceSafe (VSS).

Create the Folder Structure and Virtual Directories
Open Windows Explorer and create the following folder structure:

```
C:\Development
    \OrderEntrySystem
        \OrderEntrySystemSolution
            \Customer
            \Order
            \Inventory
```

Right-click the folder, click Properties, click the Web Sharing tab, and then click Share This Folder. A dialog box will be displayed, prompting for the folder settings. Click OK to create the virtual directory. Repeat this step for the Customer, Order, and Inventory folders.

Create the Visual Studio Solution and Projects
Instead of creating a Web development project, create a Blank Solution called OrderEntryWebSolution located at C:\Development\OrderEntrySystem, as shown in Figure 2.4. After the solution is created, the new projects can be added to the solution.

1. Click File, New, Blank Solution.

2. Change the name to OrderEntrySystemSolution, change the location to C:\Development\ OrderEntrySystem, and click OK.

3. Click File, AddProject, New Project.

4. In the Add New Project dialog box, click Visual Basic Projects, and then click ASP.NET Web Application. In the Location box, type http://localhost/Customer, and click OK. Repeat this step for the Order and Inventory projects.

5. Save the solution.

Add the Solution to Visual SourceSafe
The solution has been created in Visual Studio .NET, but not in Visual SourceSafe. Create the folder structure in Visual SourceSafe, and then add the solution and projects.

1. In Visual Studio .NET, click File, Source Control, Add Solution To Source Control.

2. When prompted for a VSS location, create the following folder structure:

   $\Development
       \OrderEntrySystem
           \OrderEntrySystemSolution
               \Customer
               \Order
               \Inventory

3. Click the OrderEntrySystemSolution folder for the solution location. When prompted for each project location, you can select the appropriate project folder.

 Creating the folder structure in Visual SourceSafe before clicking the OK button will keep you from making mistakes when setting up your new project. After the folder structure has been created, you should not see a dialog box stating that the folder you are selecting does not exist. If you do, look carefully at the path that Visual SourceSafe wants to create and find the mistake. You may need to clear the Project text box to keep Visual SourceSafe from creating two folders with the same name.

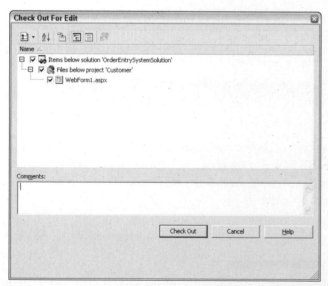

Figure 2.10 The automatic Visual SourceSafe file checkout window is displayed to allow the checking out of the file when an attempt is made to edit a file that is currently locked.

Test Your Work

Open the WebForm1.aspx page that is located in the Customer project. Notice that the Web page still has a lock icon and that the title bar shows that the page is opened in read-only mode. Hover your mouse over the Toolbox; the Toolbox will slide out and expose all of the controls that can be added to the form. Double-click the button control. This would normally place a button on the Web Form, but the Web Form must be checked out first. Notice that the Check Out For Edit dialog box is displayed, as shown in Figure 2.10. You can enter any comment and then click the Check Out button. The Web Form will be checked out and the button will be placed on the Web Form.

Close WebForm1.aspx. Check the page back into VSS by right-clicking the page and clicking Check In. Alternately, you can right-click the project or the solution to check in all files within that item.

 The default location of the Tooblox window is on the left side of the screen. If the Toolbox has been closed, you click View, Toolbox to open it.

The Visual Studio .NET Integrated Development Environment (IDE)

This section will look at the Visual Studio .NET Integrated Development Environment in detail by first presenting the windows in the IDE and then exploring the possible customization options.

Classroom Q & A

Q: With Visual Studio 6, each language had its own set of keystrokes for performing tasks. This was rather cumbersome when working with Visual InterDev and Visual Basic 6. Do I need to learn a new set of keystrokes for each of these new languages?

A: This is one area where Visual Studio .NET really shines. Out of the box, every language uses the same keystrokes for each task. In addition, you have the option of remapping the keys yourself. When you start Visual Studio .NET, the Start page has an option called My Profile, which allows you to set up the keyboard, windows, and Help filters with a couple of mouse clicks.

Q: There is a line and column indicator at the bottom of the screen, but is there a way to see line numbers beside each line of code?

A: Absolutely. Click Tools, Options, Text Editor, and you will see a list of the languages. You have the ability to control line numbering for each language individually. There is also an option called All Languages that allows you to globally control the line numbering for all languages.

Q: Is there a way to use the debugger to step through a solution that may have projects that are written in different languages?

A: Yes. The Visual Studio .NET debugger is robust. Not only can you step between applications that are written in different languages, but you can also step into SQL Server stored procedures. As a side note, the Visual Studio .NET debugger gives you even more functionality when debugging script files (.vbs and .js files).

The Visual Studio .NET Windows

Visual Studio .NET provides a large amount of information and components via numerous windows. Some of the windows covered in this section will not be visible by default. If the window that you are looking for is not visible, access it by clicking the related View menu option.

Each window can be configured by right-clicking its title bar. The following selections are available:

Dockable. Causes the window to stick to the edge of the IDE.

Hide. Hides the window.

Floating. Allows positioning the window anywhere on the screen. This option can be useful on systems with multiple monitors.

Auto Hide. Automatically displays the window when the mouse cursor moves on top of the window title, and hides the window when the mouse cursor is moved off the window.

A window can be moved by placing the mouse cursor on the title bar of the window, holding down the mouse button, and then dragging the window. When multiple windows are docked on top of each other, they will be displayed with tabs. To move only one of the tabbed windows, place the mouse cursor on the tab of the window, hold the mouse button down, and then drag. The positioning of the window is based on the location of the mouse cursor.

Docked window　　　Auto Hide window

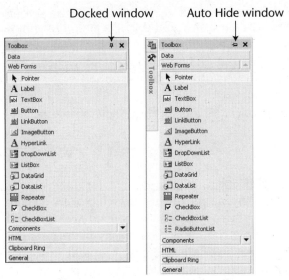

Figure 2.11　Docked (pinned) and auto hide (unpinned) window examples are illustrated. Notice that the auto hide window includes an icon to the left of the window over which the mouse can be hovered to show the window.

A window can be freely moved around the screen without becoming docked by holding down the Ctrl button while dragging the window.

Each window has a pushpin on the title bar. If the pointy part of the pin is pointing downward, then the window is docked. If it's pointing to the left, the window is set to auto hide. (See Figure 2.11.)

　The IDE remembers the docked and undocked settings of your windows. If you accidentally undock a window, simply double-click the title bar to pop the window back into its docked state, and vice versa. A quick way of resetting all windows to their original state, is to click Tools, Environment, General, Reset Window Layout.

Start Window

The Start window is the first window that is displayed when you start Visual Studio .NET. This window is an HTML page that is displayed using the Visual Studio .NET built-in browser.

The first time Visual Studio .NET is started, the My Profile tab is selected. The My Profile tab contains options for changing the IDE behavior to match your preferences. For example, the keyboard behavior can be changed to match the existing Visual Basic 6 keyboard behavior. It is also possible to map any key to an action by clicking Tools, Options, Environment, Keyboard.

After the first time Visual Studio .NET is started, the Get Started tab will be selected. The Get Started tab displays a list of recent projects and allows new and existing projects to be opened. The quantity of recent projects that are displayed can be changed by clicking Tools, Options, Environment, General and changing the View <n> Items in Most Recently Used Lists option.

 The Start window can be displayed by clicking Help, Show Start Page.

Solution Explorer

The Solution Explorer is a view of the current solution, which can contain many project, folders, and files. Only one solution can be opened at a time, and each solution may have many projects. The same project may be included in many solutions. The Solution Explorer supports file dragging and dropping from project to project, as well as from Windows Explorer to a project. A context-sensitive menu is displayed by right-clicking any item in the Solution Explorer. The upper part of the Solution Explorer (Figure 2.12) contains a button bar menu with the following items:

View Code.   Opens the currently selected file in code-editing mode. For a Web page, this allows you to modify the code that is associated with the Web page.

View Designer.   Opens the currently selected file in the graphical designer. For a Web page, this allows Web controls to be dragged and dropped onto the Web page.

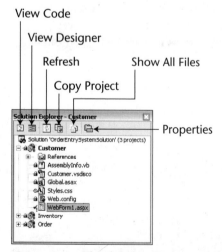

Figure 2.12   The Solution Explorer contains a single solution that can contain multiple projects. The Solution Explorer also contains command buttons, as shown.

Refresh.   Rereads the solution file and folder structure from the file system. The Refresh option may be needed when files are added to the folder structure via a program other than Visual Studio .NET.

Copy Project.   Makes a copy of the current project in a new location. The Copy Project dialog box has options to select the destination, which can be a new folder on the local machine or a remote machine. Front Page or file share may be selected as the method of copying the files. Front Page requires Front Page Server Extensions on the destination server. The Copy Project dialog box also has an option for selecting that files will be copied. The choices are:

- Only files needed to run the application
- All project files
- All files in the source project location

Show All Files.   Displays all files that are located in the physical folder structure. This is handy way of viewing the files that are produced by the compiler.

Properties.   Displays the properties of the currently selected item. This option can be useful when looking for the full path to a file, project, or solution.

If Visual SourceSafe is being used, the icons to the left of each item will display the Visual SourceSafe status, as shown in Figure 2.10.

Class View

The Class View displays an object-oriented view of your solution, projects, and classes. This window is updated dynamically as you edit your code. Right-clicking an item in the Class View window displays a context-sensitive menu. This menu allows you to jump to the code definition of the currently select item. When using Visual Basic .NET, this window is primarily a read-only view; however other languages such as C# and Managed C++ offer the ability to add classes, methods, properties, and more from this window.

Toolbox

The Toolbox is a context sensitive window that offers a list of components that are available to be placed on the current form. The Toolbox offers the ability to add and delete items by right-clicking the Toolbox and selecting the Customize Toolbox option. COM and .NET components can be added using this option.

One appealing feature of the Toolbox is the ability to add code snippets by simply selecting a section of code, and dragging and dropping it onto the Toolbox. The code snippet can be renamed by right-clicking it and clicking Rename. The Toolbox also allows new tabs to be added. Adding new tabs will add user-defined areas to the Toolbox. Code and other menu items can be dragged and dropped into the user-defined areas to provide categorized tabs to help manage code and components libraries.

The Server Explorer

The Server Explorer provides an extensible mechanism for discovering and utilizing server data (see Figure 2.13). By default, the Server Explorer has the following nodes:

- Crystal Decisions
- Event Logs
- Message Queues
- Performance Counters
- Services
- SQL Servers

One of the primary uses of the Server Explorer is to access SQL Server. Many SQL Server development functions can be performed without leaving Visual Studio .NET. The Server Explorer can also be used to start and stop services, view event logs, manage message queues, and monitor performance.

The Server Explorer supports drag-and-drop functionality. Some of the things that you can drag are:

- Drag an event log and drop it onto a form. This creates an event log object that can be used to access the log.

- Drag a service and drop it onto a form. This creates a service controller object that can be used to monitor and control the service.

Figure 2.13   The Server Explorer window contains nodes that allow server management and the ability to drag and drop from node to code.

- Drag a performance monitor counter and drop it onto a form. This creates a PerformanceCounter object that can be used to monitor an existing counter.

- Drag a SQL Server table or view and drop it onto a form. This creates a connection and data adapter object that can be used to access the table.

- Drag a SQL Server stored procedure and drop it onto a form. This creates a connection and command object, and all of the parameters that are required to execute the command.

Shortly after the release of Visual Studio .NET, Microsoft released a new component for Windows Management Instrumentation (WMI). The installation of this component adds two new nodes, Management Data and Management Events. This component supports drag-and-drop functionality as well as data exploration and method invoking. This component is available for downloading from Microsoft's MSDN Web site at www.microsoft.com/downloads/ release.asp?ReleaseID=31155.

Task List

The task list contains a list of tasks that may be categorized as comments, errors, reminders, and shortcuts to code. Some of the items that are displayed in the Task List appear dynamically, while other items are manually placed into the Task List.

The Task List stores its contents in the .sou file. The .sou file is a user-based file, which means that each user will have an individual Task List. Figure 2.14 has a list of the icons and associated descriptions for each task.

One method of adding items to the Task List is by using comment tokens in your code. Comment tokens are words that can be placed in a comment to tell the Task List to create a task that has a shortcut back to the token. Visual Studio .NET has built-in comment tokens, such as TODO, UNDONE, and HACK, but custom comment tokens can also be added. Click Tools, Options, Environment, Task List to access the Task List options.

Output Window

The Output window displays messages from many of the IDE functions. Some of the messages include compiler errors as well as diagnostic information that may be sent to this window from your program.

Icon	Description
◆	Comment link that is dynamically added to the Task List, which point to lines in your code that contain a comment token such as TODO, HACK, and UNDONE. These links are definable under Tools|Options|Environment|Task List.
🖘	Build Error link that is dynamically added to the Task List when you build you project. This is a link that you can double-click to go to the error line. To remove the link, you need to fix the problem.
🖘	Reminder link that is entered manually. The item can be deleted, but it is better to click the completed check box when finished with the task.
✱	Bookmark link to a line of code that is entered manually. You can add and delete items of this type.
{	Intellisense Code Validation Error link to a error that Intellisense detected in your code as you are typing. Fix the error to remove the icon.

Figure 2.14   Task List items include these icons.

Command Window

The Comment window has two modes, Command and Immediate. Command mode allows the execution of any Visual Studio .NET command, bypassing the menu system. An example follows:

```
File.SaveAll
```

This will save all files. Many commands can be accessed simply by typing the first character; the IntelliSense menu will then be displayed. You are in Command mode when you see the greater than sign (>) prompt.

 The autocompletion setting can be changed by clicking Tools, Options, Environment, General.

You can switch to Command mode by typing:

```
>cmd
```

Temporarily switch to Immediate mode to evaluate a single expression by typing:

```
?myVariable
```

Immediate mode allows evaluation of expressions, prints the values of variables and executes statements while in debugging mode. An example follows:

```
?EmpName
```

You are in Immediate mode when you don't have a > prompt.

Switch to Immediate mode by typing:

```
immed
```

Temporarily switch to Command mode to execute a single command by typing > followed by the command:

```
>shell notepad.exe
```

Object Browser

The Object Browser is a powerful tool that displays all of the data types that are available to your application. This tool can be used to view and discover the data types in any assembly. By default the Object Browser only displays the data types that are available to your application, but this can be changed via the Customize menu option. An example of the Object Browser displaying some data types is shown in Figure 2.15.

Icon	Description
	Assembly
	Project
{}	Namespace
	Private Method
	Public Method
	Friend Method
	Protected Method
	Public Property
	Protected Variable
	Public Variable
	Event
	Delegate

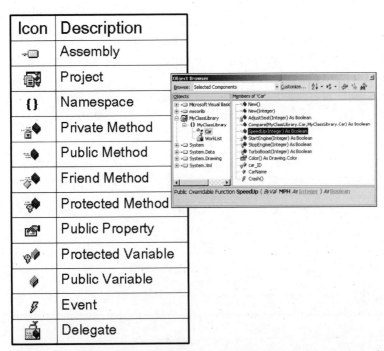

Figure 2.15 This Object Browser window displays a list of most data types that are available within Visual Basic .NET. Notice the different icons for each data type as well as the visibility modifier (public, private, and so on). Chapter 4 covers visibility modifiers in detail.

Macro Explorer

Visual Studio .NET provides the ability to create macros, which can be run in the development environment. This allows complete automation of the Visual Studio .NET development environment. Macro projects can be created, saved, and loaded while in the Macro Explorer.

Macros can be saved as either binary (default) or text. Macros have a .VSmacros extension and are stored in the Visual Studio project location that is specified under Tools, Options, Environment, Projects, Solutions.

Code or Text Editor

The Code Editor (also known as the Text Editor) window is accessible by clicking a file and then clicking the View Code button in the Server Explorer. The Code Editor is language aware, delivering language-specific IntelliSense statement and word completion.

The Code Editor window contains a gray bar down the left side of the window, called the Margin Indicator Bar (Figure 2.16). This is where breakpoints, bookmarks, and shortcuts are displayed. Breakpoints can be set in a program by clicking the Margin Indicator Bar. A red dot appears in the Margin Indicator Bar to indicate that the breakpoint has been set.

There is a column of white space between the Margin Indicator Bar and the code. This white space is called the Selection Margin. You can select a complete line of code by clicking in the Selection Margin.

Another Code Editor feature is the ability to create collapsible regions in your code. Use the #*Region* and #*End Region* tags to create the collapsible region.

The fonts and colors of the Code Editor window can be changed by clicking Tools, Environment, Fonts and Colors.

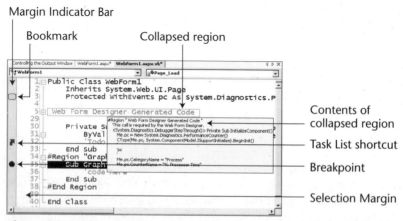

Figure 2.16   The Code Editor window shows the location of the Margin Indicator Bar and the Selection Margin. Also notice that the contents of a collapsed region can be displayed by hovering the mouse over the collapsed region.

A section of the settings is devoted entirely to the Code Editor and can be accessed by clicking Tools, Options, Text Editor. This section contains individual settings for each language. Options such as line numbering and statement completion can be turned on here.

 Global language setting changes can be accessed by clicking Tools, Options, Text Editor, All Languages. This allows you to make changes quickly, such as turning on line numbering, in all languages.

Getting Help

Visual Studio .NET provides tight Help integration within the development environment. This section covers the Help that is contained in Visual Studio .NET as well as several ways to get help on the Web.

Visual Studio .NET Help

Help can be obtained in Visual Studio .NET by simply pressing the F1 key. The F1 key is context sensitive, so if your cursor is placed within the word *Print*, pressing the F1 key will display Help for the print command.

Visual Studio .NET supports Dynamic Help, which is available by clicking Help, Dynamic Help. The Dynamic Help window displays a context-sensitive list of links to topics that are related to the cursor location as well as links to sample code and related training topics. The topics that are displayed in the Dynamic Help window can be configured by clicking Tools, Options, Environment, Dynamic Help.

It is possible to add topics to Dynamic Help. This feature can be used by vendors to add Help on their product and by information technology (IT) managers to display standard company coding practices. For more information, search the Help for "Creating Basic XML Help Files" (use the quotation marks in the search).

Visual Studio .NET also contains a Full-Text Search feature, which allows you to enter a keyword or phrase to search for Help on. The Full-Text Search contains built-in filters, which help reduce the scope of your search. The Help filter list can be edited by clicking Help, Edit Filters, as shown in Figure 2.17. Previous versions of Visual Studio only allowed the creation of filters by sets of Help documentation, while Visual Studio .NET allows creation of help on a topic-by-topic basis. Searching topic by topic across sets of Help documentation is possible. Every topic contains a set of attributes relating to programming language, locale, status, target operating system, technology covered, information type, and document set. An example of a Help filter for use when developing software for WML-based cell phones is

```
("Technology"="kbWML") OR ("DevLang"="WML")
```

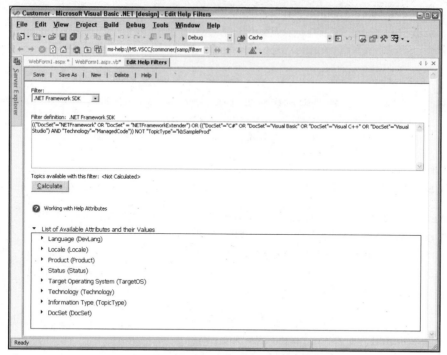

Figure 2.17 When creating a Help filter, the filter definition (top) can be edited directly in its window or indirectly by selecting attributes and values from the lower window section.

Help on the Web

The following is a small list of the many Web sites that may help you find additional information about Visual Studio .NET:

- http://msdn.microsoft.com
- http://msdn.microsoft.com/vstudio
- www.GotDotNet.com
- www.asp.net
- www.ibuyspy.com
- www.ibuyspyportal.com
- www.aspalliance.com
- www.dotnetjunkies.com
- www.c-sharpcorner.com
- www.4guysfromrolla.com
- www.123aspx.com
- www.aspfree.com

- www.dotnet247.com
- www.411asp.net
- www.angrycoder.com

Lab 2.2: Customizing Windows and Help Filters

In this lab, you will start by customizing several windows to discover some of the options that are available in Visual Studio .NET. In the second part of the lab, you will create a custom Help filter.

Window Customization

In this section, you will turn on line numbering, set the quantity of recent projects to display to 10, configure a comment token called CleanupRequired, and explore the Show All Files button behavior.

To start this lab, open the OrderEntrySolution from Lab 2.1.

Turn on Line Numbers

You will turn on line numbering for all languages.

1. Click Tools, Options, Text Editor, All Languages, General.
2. Click the Line Numbers check box until there is a checkmark with a white background, then click OK.
3. Open the one of the Web pages in code view mode.

Notice that line numbers are now displayed. This will help you locate an error when the error and its line number are displayed.

Setting the Quantity of Recent Projects

You will set up the quantity of recent project that are displayed on the Start page.

1. Click Tools, Options, Environment, General.
2. Locate the Display <n> Items in the Most Recently Used List option.
3. Change <n> to 10, and then click OK.
4. Refresh the Start page by clicking Help, Show Start Page.

You should see the last 10 projects that you have worked with. If you haven't worked with 10 projects, you will only see the projects that you have worked with.

Configure a CleanupRequired Comment Token

You will create a comment token and test it.

1. Click Tools, Options, Environment, Task List.

2. In the Name text box, type CleanupRequired.

3. Set the priority to High.

4. Click Add, and then click OK.

5. Test your comment token by opening one of your Web pages in Code View mode and typing a comment like the following:

   ```
   'CleanupRequired - Need to replace magic numbers with constants.
   ```

6. Open the Task List by clicking View, Show Tasks, All.

   You should see your new task in the Task List.

Exploring the Show All Files Button

You will use the Show All Files button to see the files that are normally hidden.

1. If the Solution Explorer is not visible, open it by clicking View, Solution Explorer.

2. Try to locate the bin folder. Notice that it is not visible.

3. Click the Show All Files button in the Solution Explorer. If you don't know which button this is, move the mouse over each button to see its ToolTip.

4. Locate the bin folder. It is visible.

5. If there are no files in the bin folder, click Build, Build Solution.

   You should see the DLL that is created for your project and its .pdb (debugger) file.

Creating an ASP.NET with Visual Basic .NET Help Filter

In this section, you will try searching with no Help filter. You will then create an ASP.NET with Visual Basic Help filter that you can use. Finally, you will try the original search using your new Help filter.

1. Search for Cache topics. Click Help, Search.

2. Type *Caching* in the *Look For* text box.

3. Verify that the filter is set to (no filter), and click OK. Notice that more than 500 topics are returned, relating to many different subjects that have the Caching keyword. If you look at the first 10 topics, they relate to SQL Server, Proxy Server, and ASP.NET.

4. Click Help, Edit Filters to create a new filter.

5. Click New to create a new Help filter. Notice that the filter definition is empty.

6. Update the topics that are available by clicking Calculate.

7. Locate and click the option called List of Available Attributes and their Values, to view the list.

8. Click Language, Visual Basic (VB).

9. Click Product, Visual Studio (VS).

10. Click Technology, ASP.NET. Your filter definition should look like this:

    ```
    ("Technology"="ASPNET") OR ("Product"="VS") OR ("DevLang"="VB")
    ```

11. Click Save, and label the filter ASP.NET Using VB.

12. Search for *Caching* again, but set the Help filter to your new Help filter. Notice that less than 200 topics are displayed. Notice that the first 10 (and more) topics are all related to ASP.NET.

You can increase your productivity by creating many Help filters in Visual Studio .NET.

Summary

- The creation of solutions and projects using the default settings will place Web projects in the c:\inetpub\wwwroot folder, which does not lend itself to creating a directory structure that can be built upon.

- A custom directory structure can be created manually, and the project directories can be Web shared through Windows Explorer or Internet Information Services. After the Web shares are created, you can use Visual Studio .NET to create your projects.

- After the solution and projects are created in Visual Studio .NET, they can be added to Visual SourceSafe. It is best to create the Visual SourceSafe folder structure before adding the projects to ensure their proper creation.

- Visual Studio .NET provides a large amount of information and components via numerous windows.

- Many of the windows are customizable, and support drag-and-drop functionality.

- Visual Studio .NET provides a great amount of Help, which can become intimidating. With custom Help filters, you can narrow the scope of your searches to topic-by-topic responses. Searching topic by topic across sets of Help documentation is possible because every topic contains a set of attributes relating to programming language, locale, status, target operating system, technology covered, information type, and document set.

Review Questions

1. What is a Visual Studio .NET project?

2. What is the benefit of creating your own folder structure instead of letting Visual Studio .NET create the folder structure for you?

3. How do you get Visual Studio .NET to see a folder that you have created that is not in the C:\inetpub\wwwroot folder?

4. You are trying to create a Web share for a folder in Windows Explorer, but the Web Share tab is not available. What is the most probable cause and solution?

5. What is an easy way to get access to the event log objects?

6. Which window can be used to discover the data types that are defined within an assembly?

7. What is a method of narrowing the scope of your searches to get more accurate results?

Answers to Review Questions

1. A project is the source of the executable assembly that you will build using Visual Studio .NET. It is also known as an application.

2. If you create your own folder structure, it can be created in more organized format for the system that you are building.

3. After you create your folder, you must create a Web share for the folder, which creates a virtual directory in Internet Information Services.

4. You are not a member of the VS Developers group. You must be placed into this group to be able to create Web shares.

5. Drag-and-drop the event log from the Server Explorer to your form. This will create an EventLog component that you can use in your code.

6. The Object Browser window.

7. Create and use a Help filter.

CHAPTER

3

Exploring ASP.NET and Web Forms

The last chapter covered the setup and configuration of the development environment. The development environment is an important necessity and will make the rest of your development more enjoyable.

This chapter explores Web Forms. Web Forms bring the structure and fun back to Web development. This chapter starts by looking at the two programming models for ASP.NET. It then looks at how ASP.NET uses server controls and at the HTML (HyperText Markup Language) and Web server controls. It finishes by looking at view state and post back.

Web Forms

Web Forms are an exciting part of the ASP.NET platform. Web Forms give the developer the ability to drag and drop ASP.NET server controls onto the form and easily program the events that are raised by the control. Web Forms have the following benefits:

Rendering. Web Forms are automatically rendered in any browser. In addition, Web Forms can be tweaked to work on a specific browser to take advantage of its features.

Programming.   Web Forms can be programmed using any .NET language, and Win32 API calls can be made directly from ASP.NET code.

.NET Framework.   Web Forms are part of the .NET Framework, therefore Web Forms provide the benefits of the .NET Framework, such as performance, inheritance, type safety, structured error handling, automatic garbage collection, and xcopy deployment.

Extensibility.   User controls, mobile controls, and other third-party controls can be added to extend Web Forms.

WYSIWYG.   Visual Studio .NET provides the WYSIWYG (what you see is what you get) editor for creating Web Forms by dragging and dropping controls onto the Web Form.

Code Separation.   Web Forms provide a code-behind page to allow the separation of HTML content from program code.

State Management.   Provides the ability to maintain the view state of controls across Web calls.

Classroom Q & A

Q: I am currently developing my entire Web page by typing the HTML and client-side script into an ASCII editor. Are standard HTML tags with client-side script still available? Also, can I still use JavaScript for client-side code?

A: Yes. ASP.NET is focused around the added functionality of server controls, but you can still use standard HTML tags with client-side script as you have done in the past. As you become more familiar with the Visual Studio .NET environment, you may choose to change some of your controls to server controls to take advantage of the benefits that server controls provide.

Q: Can I use ASP and ASP.NET pages on the same Web site? Can I use Session and Application variables to share data between the ASP and ASP.NET pages?

A: Yes and no. You can run ASP and ASP.NET Web pages on the same Web site; in order words, the pages can coexist. You cannot share application and session data between the ASP and ASP.NET pages, because the ASP and ASP.NET run under separate contexts. What you will find is that you will have one set of Session and Application variables for the ASP pages and a different set of Session and Application variables for the ASP.NET pages.

Q: It's my understanding that there are two types of server controls. Can both types of server controls be used on the same Web page?

A: Yes. Visual Studio .NET provides HTML and Web server controls. You can provide a mixture of these controls on the same page. These controls will be covered in this chapter.

Q: I currently use VBScript and JavaScript to write my server-side code. Basically, if I am writing the ASP page and a function is easier to accomplish in JavaScript, I write it in JavaScript. For all other programming, on the page, I use VBScript. Can I continue to mix Visual Basic .NET and JavaScript on the same page?

A: No. ASP.NET requires server-side script to be written in the same language on a page-by-page basis. In addition, Visual Studio .NET requires a project to be written in a single server-side language.

Two ASP.NET Programming Models

People who are familiar with traditional ASP are accustomed to creating a single file for each Web page. ASP.NET supports the single-file programming model. Using the single-page programming model, the server code and the client-side tags and code are placed in the same file with an .aspx file extension. This doesn't do anything to help clean up spaghetti code, but the single-file model can be especially useful to ease the pain of migrating ASP code to ASP.NET.

The two-page model provides a separation of the server-side code and client-side HTML and code. The model offers the ability to use an .aspx page for the client-side presentation logic and a Visual Basic *code-behind* file with a .vb file extension for the server-side code.

This chapter starts by using the single-page model due to its simplicity. After most of the basic concepts are covered, the chapter switches to the two-page model. The two-page, or code-behind, model is used exclusively throughout the balance of the book due to the benefits it provides.

Simple ASP.NET Page

Using the single-page programming model, a simple Hello World page using ASP.NET can be written and saved to a file called vb.aspx containing the following:

```
<%@ Page Language="vb" %>
<HTML>
    <HEAD><title>Hello World Web Page</title></HEAD>
```

```
<body>
    <form id="Form1" method="post" runat="server">
        <asp:TextBox id="Hi" runat="server">
            Hello World
        </asp:TextBox>
        <asp:Button id="Button1" runat="server" Text="Say Hi">
        </asp:Button>
    </form>
</body>
</HTML>
```

The first line of code contains the page directive, which contains the compiler language attribute. The compiler language attribute can only be used once on a page. If additional language attributes are on the page, they are ignored. Some language identifiers are shown in Table 3.1. If no language identifier is specified, the default is vb. The page directive has many other attributes, which will be covered throughout this book.

 The language identifiers that are configured on your machine may be found by looking in the machine.config file, which is located in the %systemroot%\\Microsoft.NET\Framework*version*\CONFIG folder. The machine.config file is an xml configuration file, which contains settings that are global to your machine. A search for *compilers* will expose all of the language identifiers that are configured on your computer. Always back up the machine.config file before making changes, as this file affects all .NET applications on the machine.

The rest of the page looks like standard HTML, except that this page contains three server controls: the form, the asp:TextBox, and the asp:Button. Server controls have the run="server" attribute. Server controls automatically maintain client-entered values across round trips to the server. ASP.NET automatically takes care of the code that is necessary to maintain state by placing the client-entered value in an attribute. In some cases, no acceptable attribute is available to hold the client-entered values. In those situations, the client-entered values are placed into a *<input type="hidden">* tag.

Table 3.1   ASP.NET Language Identifiers

LANGUAGE	ACCEPTABLE IDENTIFIERS
Visual Basic .NET	vb; vbs; visualbasic; vbscript
Visual C#	c#; cs; csharp
Visual J#	VJ#; VJS; VJSharp
Visual JavaScript	js; jscript; javascript

When the page is displayed in the browser, the text box displays the initial Hello World message. A look at the client-side source reveals the following:

```
<HTML>
<HEAD><title>Hello World Web Page</title></HEAD>
    <body>
            <form name="Form1" method="post" action="vb.aspx" id="Form1">
                <input type="hidden"
                    name="__VIEWSTATE"
        value="dDwtMTc2MjYxNDA2NTs7Pp6EUc0BOodWTOrpqefKJJjg3yEt"/>
                <input type="text"
                    name="Hi"
                    value="Hello World" id="Hi" />
                <input type="submit"
                    name="Button1"
                    value="Say Hi" id="Button1" />
            </form>
    </body>
</HTML>
```

The form server control was rendered as a standard HTML form tag with the action (the location that the data is posted to) set to the current page. A new control has been added automatically, called the __VIEWSTATE control. (More on the __VIEWSTATE control is provided in this chapter.) The asp:TextBox Web server control was rendered as an HTML text box and has its value set to "Hello World." The asp:button Web server control was rendered as an HTML Submit button.

If *Hi Universe* is typed into the text box and the button is clicked, the button will submit the form data to the server and return a response. The response simply redisplays the page, but *Hi Universe* is still in the text box, thereby maintaining the state of the text box automatically.

A glimpse at the client-side source reveals the following:

```
<HTML>
    <HEAD><title>Hello World Web Page</title></HEAD>
    <body>
            <form name="Form1" method="post" action="vb.aspx" id="Form1">
                <input type="hidden"
                    name="__VIEWSTATE"
        value="dDwtMTc2MjYxNDA2NTs7Pp6EUc0BOodWTOrpqefKJJjg3yEt"/>
                <input type="text"
                    name="Hi"
                    value="Hi Universe" id="Hi" />
                <input type="submit"
                    name="Button1"
                    value="Say Hi" id="Button1" />
            </form>
    </body>
</HTML>
```

Table 3.2   ASP.NET Server Tags

SERVER TAG	MEANING
<%@ Directive %>	Directives no longer need to be the first line in the code, and many new directives may be used in a single ASP.NET file.
<tag runat="server" >	Tags that have the runat="server" attribute are server controls.
<script runat="server" >	ASP.NET subs and functions must be placed inside the server-side script tag and cannot be placed inside the <% %> tags.
<%# DataBinding %>	This is a new tag in ASP.NET. It is used to connect, or bind, to data. This will be covered in more detail in Chapter 8, "Data Access with ADO.NET."
<%-- Server Comment --%>	Allows a server-side comment to be created.
<!-- #include -->	Allow a server-side file to be included in a document.
<%= Render code %> and <% %>	Used as in-line code sections, primarily for rendering a snippet of code at the proper location in the document. Note that no functions are permitted inside <% %> tags.

The only change is that the text box now has a value of *Hi Universe*. With traditional ASP, additional code was required to get this functionality that is built into ASP.NET server controls.

Many changes have been made in the transition from ASP to ASP.NET. Table 3.2 shows server tags that are either new or have a different meaning in ASP.NET. Understanding these changes will make an ASP to ASP.NET migration more palatable.

Server Controls

A server control is a control that is programmable by writing server-side code. Server controls automatically maintain their state between calls to the server. Server controls can be easily identified by their *runat="server"* attribute. A server control must have an ID attribute to be referenced in code. ASP.NET provides two types of server controls; HTML and Web. This section looks at these controls.

HTML Server Controls

HTML server controls resemble the traditional HTML controls, except they have a *runat="server"* attribute. There is typically a one-to-one mapping of an HTML server control and the HTML tag that it renders. HTML server controls are primarily used when migrating older ASP pages to ASP.NET. For example, the following ASP page needs to be converted to ASP.NET:

```
<HTML>
    <HEAD><title>Employee Page</title></HEAD>
    <body>
        <form name="Form1" method="post" action="vb.asp" id="Form1">
            <input type="text"
                name="EmployeeName"
                id=" EmployeeName " >
            <input type="submit"
                name="SubmitButton"
                value="Submit" id=" SubmitButton " >
        </form>
    </body>
</HTML>
```

This sample page can be converted by adding the *runat="server"* attribute to the form and input tags, and removing the action="*vb.asp*" attribute on the form. The filename needs an .aspx extension. The modified Web page looks like this:

```
<HTML>
    <HEAD><title>Employee Page</title></HEAD>
    <body>
        <form name="Form1" method="post" id="Form1" runat="server">
            <input type="text"
                name="EmployeeName"
                id="EmployeeName" runat="server" >
            <input type="submit"
                name="SubmitButton"
                value="Submit" id="SubmitButton" runat="server">
        </form>
    </body>
</HTML>
```

This example shows how the use of HTML controls can ease a conversion process. If the existing tags had JavaScript events attached, those client-side events would continue to operate.

This ease of migration benefit can also be a drawback. Being HTML-centric, the object model for these controls is not consistent with other .NET controls. This is where Web server controls provide value.

Web Server Controls

Web server controls offer more functionality than HTML controls, their object model is more consistent, and more elaborate controls are available. Web server controls are designed to provide an object model that is heavily focused on the purpose of the object rather that the HTML that is generated. In fact, the Web server control's source code will typically be substantially different from the HTML it generates. Some Web server controls, such as the Calendar and DataGrid, produce complex tables with JavaScript client-side code.

Web server controls have the ability to detect the browser capabilities and generate HTML that uses the browser to its fullest potential.

During design, a typical Web server control's source code will look like the following:

```
<asp:button attributes runat="server"/>
```

The attributes of the Web server control are properties of that control, and may or may not be attributes in the generated HTML.

Server Control Recommendations

Consider using HTML server controls when:

- Migrating existing ASP pages to ASP.NET.
- The control needs to have custom client-side script attached to the control's events.
- The Web page requires a great amount of client-side code, where client-side events need to be programmed extensively.

In all other situations, it's preferable to use Web server controls.

Server Control Event Programming

An important feature of server controls is the ability to write code that executes at the server in response to an event from the control.

ViewState

When a Web Form is rendered to the browser, a hidden HTML input tag is dynamically created, called __VIEWSTATE (ViewState). This input contains base64-encoded data that can be used by any object that inherits from System.Web.UI.Control, which represents all of the Web controls and the

Web Page object itself. ViewState is a property tag that is optimized to hold primitive type, strings, HashTables, and ArrayLists, but can also hold any object that is serializable or data types that provide a custom TypeConverter.

An object may use ViewState to persist information across calls to the server when that information cannot easily be persisted via traditional HTML attributes. In some instances, ViewState is not necessary, because the content of a control may automatically be persisted across calls to the server. For example, a TextBox automatically sends its contents back to the server via its value property, and the server can repopulate the value property when rendering it back to the browser. If, however, additional information is needed that cannot easily be represented with traditional HTML attributes, ViewState comes to the rescue.

One example of using ViewState would be a scenario where a ListBox is populated by querying a database. It may not be desirable to requery the database everytime the page is posted to the server. The ListBox uses ViewState to hold the complete list of items that are placed in the ListBox. ViewState stores the list of items that were programmatically placed into the ListBox. By placing the list of items in ViewState, the ListBox will be repopulated automatically. The server will not need to requery the database to repopulate the ListBox, because the ListBox is maintaining its own state. In the following code sample, an asp:ListBox server control has been added, as has been a subroutine to simulate loading the ListBox programmatically from a database.

```
<HTML>
    <script runat="server">
        sub Form_Load(sender as object, e as System.EventArgs) _
            handles MyBase.Load
            'simulate loading the ListBox from a database
            ListBox1.Items.Add(New ListItem("apple"))
            ListBox1.Items.Add(New ListItem("orange"))
        end sub
    </script>
    <HEAD><title>Hello World Web Page</title></HEAD>
    <body>
        <form id="Form1" method="post" runat="server">
            <asp:TextBox id="Hi" runat="server">
                Hello World
            </asp:TextBox>
            <asp:Button id="Button1" runat="server" Text="Nothing">
            </asp:Button>
            <asp:ListBox id="ListBox1" runat="server">
            </asp:ListBox>
        </form>
    </body>
</HTML>
```

After the ListBox and code have been added, browsing to this sample page will show the ListBox, which will contain the Apple and Orange items that were added by the form load procedure. Viewing the source reveals a much larger ViewState as shown next.

```
<input type="hidden" name="__VIEWSTATE"
 value="dDwtMzE3ODYxNTUzO3Q8O2w8aTwyPjs+O2w8dDw7bDxpPDU+Oz47bDx
0PHQ8O3A8bDxpPDA+O2k8MT47PjtsPHA8YXBwbGU7YXBwbGU+O3A8b3Jhbmdl02
9yYW5nZT47Pj47Pjs7Pjs+Pjs+Gyn1i+uQFP6LoU14/8djhigkR4Q=" />
```

Correcting Multiple Entries

This page contains a button, which has not been programmed to do anything, but will cause all of the form data to be posted back to the server. If the button is clicked, the ListBox will contain Apple, Orange, Apple, and Orange. What happened?

ASP.NET will automatically rebuild the ListBox using the items that are in ViewState. Also, the form load subroutine contains code that simulates loading the ListBox from a query to a database. The result is that we end up with repeated entries in the ListBox. One of the following solutions can be applied.

Use the IsPostBack Property

ASP.NET provides the IsPostBack property of the Page object to see if the page is being requested for the first time. The first time that a page is requested, its IsPostBack property will be false. When data is being sent back to the server, the IsPostBack property will be true (see Figure 3.1).

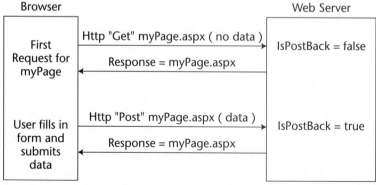

Figure 3.1   The first time that a page is requested, the IsPostBack property of the page is equal to false. When the page data is submitted back to the server, the IsPostBack property will be true.

Change the form load subroutine by adding a condition that checks to see if the page is being loaded for the first time, and if so, load the TextBox from the database. If not, use the ViewState to populate the ListBox. Here is a sample:

```
sub Form_Load(sender as object, e as System.EventArgs) _
    handles MyBase.Load
    'simulate loading the ListBox from a database
    If not IsPostBack then
        ListBox1.Items.Add(New ListItem("apple"))
        ListBox1.Items.Add(New ListItem("orange"))
    End if
end sub
```

This routine uses the IsPostBack method to see if the page is being posted back. If true, then there is no need to load the information from the database.

Turn off ViewState

It may more desirable to requery the database, especially if the data changes regularly. In this example, instead of turning off the query to the database, the ViewState can be turned off. Here is a sample:

```
<asp:ListBox id="ListBox1" EnableViewState="False">
</asp:ListBox>
```

Turning off ViewState for this control reduces the size of the data that ViewState passes to and from the server.

Post Back

In the previous examples, all ASP.NET server controls were encapsulated in a form that has the *runat="server"* attribute. This is a requirement. Also notice that the original form tag in the source code is:

```
<form id="Form1" method="post" runat="server">
```

A view of the client source reveals that the form tag was transformed to:

```
<form name="Form1" method="post" action="vb.aspx" id="Form1">
```

Notice that the action attribute is not valid in the original source, but ASP.NET adds the *action="vb.aspx"* attribute, where vb.aspx is the name of the current page. In essence, the page will always post back to itself.

Each server control has the ability to be configured to submit, or post, the form data back to the server. For the TextBox, AutoPostBack is set to false by default, which means that the text is not sent back to the server until a different control posts the data back to the server. If AutoPostBack is set to true and the text is changed, then the text box will automatically post the form data back to the server when the text box loses focus. The following line shows how to turn on the AutoPostBack feature for the text box.

```
<asp:TextBox id="Hi" runat="server" AutoPostBack="True">
```

In many cases, the default behavior for the TextBox is appropriate. The List-Box and DropDownList also have their AutoPostBack set to false. But it may be desirable to change AutoPostBack to true. When set to true, the ListBox and DropDownList will post back to the server when a selection is made.

Responding to Events

AutoPostBack is great, but usually something needs to be accomplished with the data that is posted back to the server. This is where events come in. Using the single-page model, event-handling code can be added into the .aspx page to respond to an event such as the click of a button or the changing of a selection in a ListBox. The following syntax is used:

```
<control id="myctl" runat="server" event="ProcName">
```

The *event="ProcName"* attribute defines the name of a procedure that will be executed with the event is raised. The attribute creates a link, or Event Handler, to connect the control to the procedure that will be executed.

In the following example, the lblDateTime label control is populated with the current date and time when btnSelect is clicked.

```
<HTML>
    <HEAD>
        <title>Hello World Web Page</title>
        <script runat="server">
            sub ShowDateTime(sender as object, e as System.EventArgs)
                lblDateTime.Text = DateTime.Now
            end sub
        </script>
    </HEAD>
<body>
        <form id="Form1" method="post" runat="server">
            <asp:label id="lblDateTime"
                runat="server">
            </asp:label>
```

```
        <asp:button id="btnSelect" Text="Select"
                Runat="server"
                OnClick="ShowDateTime">
        </asp:button>
    </form>
</body>
</HTML>
```

The previous example works exactly as expected, because AutoPostBack defaults to true for buttons. Controls that do not have their AutoPostBack attribute set to true will not execute their event handler code until a control posts back to the server. In the following example, lstFruit has been programmed to populate txtSelectedFruit when SelectedIndexChanged has occurred.

```
<HTML>
    <HEAD>
        <title>Hello World Web Page</title>
        <script runat="server">
            sub ShowDateTime(sender as object, e as System.EventArgs)
                lblDateTime.Text = DateTime.Now
            end sub
            sub FruitSelected(sender as object,
                    e as System.EventArgs)
                txtSelectedFruit.Text = lstFruit.SelectedItem.Value
            end sub
            sub Form_Load(sender as object, e as System.EventArgs) _
                handles MyBase.Load
                if not IsPostBack then
                    'simulate loading the ListBox from a database
                    lstFruit.Items.Add(New ListItem("apple"))
                    lstFruit.Items.Add(New ListItem("orange"))
                end if
            end sub
        </script>
    </HEAD>
    <body>
        <form id="Form1" method="post" runat="server">
            <asp:label id="lblDateTime"
                runat="server">
            </asp:label>
            <asp:textbox id="txtSelectedFruit"
                runat="server">Hello World
            </asp:textbox>
            <asp:listbox id="lstFruit" Runat="server"
                OnSelectedIndexChanged="FruitSelected">
            </asp:listbox>
            <asp:button id="btnSelect" Text="Select"
                Runat="server"
```

```
                        OnClick="ShowDateTime">
                </asp:button>
            </form>
        </body>
    </HTML>
```

In the previous example, selecting a fruit did not update the txtSelectedFruit TextBox. If the button is clicked, the txtSelectedFruit TextBox will be updated, because the button will post all of the Web Form's data back to the server, and the server will detect that the selected index has changed on the lstFruit ListBox.

Although this behavior may be okay in some solutions, in other solutions it may be more desirable to update the txtSelectedFruit TextBox immediately upon change of the lstFruit selection. This can be done by adding *AutoPost-Back="true"* to the lstFruit control.

Event Handler Procedure Arguments

All events in the Web Forms environment have been standardized to have two arguments. The first argument, *sender as object*, represents the object that triggered, or raised, the event. The second argument, *e as EventArgs*, represents an EventArgs object or an object that derives from EventArgs. By itself, the EventArgs object is used when there are no additional arguments to be passed to the event handler. In essence, if EventArgs is used as the second argument, then there is no additional data being sent to the event handler. If custom arguments need to be passed to the event handler, a new class is created that inherits the EventArgs class and adds the appropriate data.

Examples of some of the custom argument classes that already exist are ImageClickEventArgs, which contains the x and y coordinates of a click on an ImageButton control, and DataGridItemEventArgs, which contains all of the information related to the row of data in a DataGrid control. Events will be looked at more closely in Chapter 4, "The .NET Framework and Visual Basic .NET Object Programming."

Code-Behind Page

The two page model for designing Web Forms uses a *Web Forms page* (with an .aspx extension) for visual elements that will be displayed at the browser, and a *code-behind page* (with the .vb extension for Visual Basic .NET) for the code that will execute at the server. When a new WebForm is added to an ASP.NET project using Visual Studio .NET, it will always be the two-page model type.

With the two-page model, all of the code-behind pages must be compiled into a single .dll file for the project. Each code-behind page contains a class that derives from System.Web.UI.Page. The System.Web.UI.Page class contains the functionality to provide context and rendering of the page.

The Web Form page is not compiled until a user requests the page from a browser (see Figure 3.2).

The Web Form page is then converted to a class that inherits from the code-behind class. Then, the class is compiled, stored to disk, and executed. Once the Web Form page has been compiled, additional requests for the same Web Form page will execute the page's .dll code without requiring another compile. If the .aspx file has been changed, the .aspx file will be reparsed and recompiled.

The connection of the Web Form page and the code-behind page is accomplished by adding additional attributes to the Web Form page's Page directive, as in the following:

```
<%@ Page Language="vb" Codebehind="myPage.aspx.vb"
     Inherits="ch3.myPage"%>
```

The *Codebehind* attribute identities the filename of the code-behind page. The *Inherits* attribute identifies the class that the Web Form page will inherit from, which is in the code-behind page.

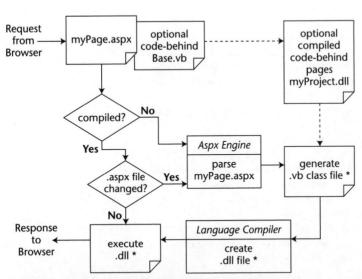

* Files created within the following folder structure:
%SystemRoot%\Microsoft.NET\Framework*version*\Temporary ASP.NET Files\

Figure 3.2   A Web page is dynamically compiled, as shown in this diagram, when a user navigates to the page for the first time.

In Visual Studio .NET, when a Web Form is created, Visual Studio .NET automatically creates the Web Form page, which has the .aspx extension, and the code-behind page, which has the aspx.vb extension. The code-behind page will not be visible until the Show All Files button is clicked in the Solution Explorer.

Accessing Controls and Events on the Code-Behind Page

In Visual Studio .NET, when a control is dragged and dropped onto the Web Form page, a matching control variable is defined inside the code-behind class. This control contains all of the properties, methods, and events that belong to the control that is rendered on to the Web Form page (see Figure 3.3).

The following code is created in the Web Form page when a new page is created in Visual Studio .NET called myPage. A TextBox and Button are added, and code is added that displays the current date and time in the TextBox when the button is clicked.

```
<%@ Page Language="vb" AutoEventWireup="false"
Codebehind="myPage.aspx.vb"
     Inherits="ch3.myPage"%>
<!DOCTYPE HTML PUBLIC "-//W3C//DTD HTML 4.0 Transitional//EN">
<HTML>
     <HEAD>
          <title>myPage</title>
          <meta name="GENERATOR"
              content="Microsoft Visual Studio .NET 7.0">
          <meta name="CODE_LANGUAGE" content="Visual Basic 7.0">
          <meta name="vs_defaultClientScript" content="JavaScript">
          <meta name="vs_targetSchema"
              content="http://schemas.microsoft.com/intellisense/ie5">
     </HEAD>
     <body MS_POSITIONING="GridLayout">
          <form id="Form1" method="post" runat="server">
          'positioning style elements removed for clarity
               <asp:TextBox id="TextBox1"
                    runat="server">
               </asp:TextBox>
               <asp:Button id="Button1"
                    runat="server" Text="Button">
               </asp:Button>
          </form>
     </body>
</HTML>
```

Notice that there is no server-side code in this page. All server-side code is packed into the code-behind page. The following is a code listing of the code-behind class.

```
Public Class myPage
     Inherits System.Web.UI.Page
     Protected WithEvents TextBox1 As System.Web.UI.WebControls.TextBox
     Protected WithEvents Button1 As System.Web.UI.WebControls.Button
     #Region " Web Form Designer Generated Code "
     'This call is required by the Web Form Designer.
     <System.Diagnostics.DebuggerStepThrough()> _
     Private Sub InitializeComponent()
     End Sub
     Private Sub Page_Init(ByVal sender As System.Object, _
          ByVal e As System.EventArgs) Handles MyBase.Init
          'CODEGEN: This method call is required by the
          'Web Form Designer
          'Do not modify it using the Code Editor.
          InitializeComponent()
     End Sub
     #End Region
     Private Sub Page_Load(ByVal sender As System.Object, _
          ByVal e As System.EventArgs) Handles MyBase.Load
          'Put user code to initialize the page here.
     End Sub
     Private Sub Button1_Click(ByVal sender As System.Object,
          ByVal e As System.EventArgs) Handles Button1.Click
          TextBox1.Text = DateTime.Now
     End Sub
End Class
```

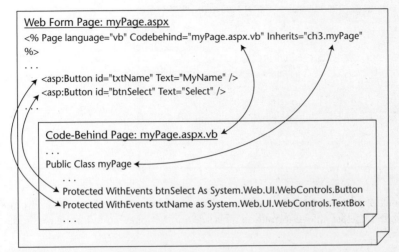

Figure 3.3 The code-behind page contains matching objects, which gives the code the ability to access the control from within the code-behind page.

Button1's event handler code is connected to Button1's click event by the *Handles Button1.Click* tag at the end of the Button1_Click subprocedure. The Button1_Click subprocedure can be renamed without losing the connection between the Web Form page and the code-behind page. For example, if two buttons are programmed to execute the subprocedure, it may be more beneficial to rename the subprocedure to something that is more generic. Additional events can be added to the Handles keyword, separated by commas. The following code snippet shows how Button2's click event can execute the same procedure.

```
Private Sub Clicked(ByVal sender As System.Object,
    ByVal e As System.EventArgs) _
    Handles Button1.Click, Button2.Click
```

Visual Studio .NET also exposes all events that are available for a given control. Figure 3.4 shows the code window, which has a class selection drop-down list and an event method drop-down list. Selecting an event will generate template code inside the code-behind page for the event.

Web Form Designer Generated Code

The code-behind page contains a region called Web Form Designer Generated Code. This region is controlled by the Web Form Designer, which can be opened to reveal the code that the Web Form Designer generates. Exploring and understanding this region can be beneficial. If changes to the code that is in the region are required, it is best to make the changes through the Web Form Designer.

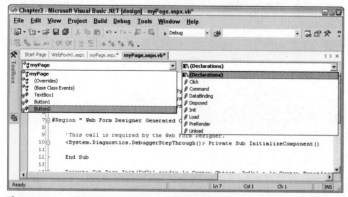

Figure 3.4 The class and event method selection lists are shown. First select an item from the class list and then select an event method. This will add template code for the method, if it doesn't exist.

Life Cycle of a Web Form and Its Controls

It's important to understand the life cycle of a Web Form and its controls. Every time a browser hits a Web site, the browser is requesting a page. The Web server constructs the page, sends the page to the browser, and destroys the page. Pages are destroyed to free up resources. This allows the Web server to scale nicely, but poses problems with maintaining state between calls to the server. The use of ViewState allows the state to be sent to the browser. Posting the entire Web Form's data, including ViewState, back to the server allows the previous state to be reconstructed to recognize data that has changed between calls to the server.

All server controls have a series of methods and events that execute as the page is being created and destroyed. The Web page derives from the Control class as well, so the page also executes the same methods and events as it is being created and destroyed. Table 3.3 contains a description of the events that take place when a page is requested, paying particular attention to ViewState and its availability.

Table 3.3   Page/Control Life Cycle Method and Events

PAGE/CONTROL METHOD AND (EVENT)	DESCRIPTION
OnInit (Init)	Each control is initialized.
LoadViewState	Loads the ViewState of the control.
LoadPostData	Retrieves the incoming form data and updates the control's properties accordingly.
Load (OnLoad)	Actions that are common to every request can be place here.
RaisePostDataChangedEvent	Raises change events in response to the postback data changing between the current postback and the previous postback. For example, if a TextBox has a TextChanged event and AutoPostBack is turned off, clicking a Button causes the TextChanged event to execute in this stage before handling the click event of the button (next stage).
RaisePostBackEvent	Handles the client-side event that caused the postback to occur.
PreRender (OnPreRender)	Allows last minute changes to the control. This event takes place after all regular postback events have taken place. Since this event takes place before saving ViewState, any changes made here will be saved.

(continued)

Table 3.3   *(continued)*

PAGE/CONTROL METHOD AND (EVENT)	DESCRIPTION
SaveViewState	Saves the current state of the control to ViewState. After this stage, any changes to the control will be lost.
Render	Generates the client-side HTML, DHTML, and script that are necessary to properly display this control at the browser. In this stage, any changes to the control are not persisted into ViewState.
Dispose	Cleanup code goes here. Releases any unmanaged resources in this stage. Unmanaged resources are resources that are not handled by the .NET common language runtime, such as file handles and database connections.
UnLoad	Cleanup code goes here. Releases any managed resources in this stage. Managed resources are resources that are handled by the runtime, such as instances of classes created by the .NET common language runtime.

Page Layout

Each Web Form has a pageLayout property, which can be set to GridLayout or FlowLayout. These layouts have different control positioning behaviors. This setting can be set at the project level, which will affect new pages that are added. The setting can also be set on each Web Form.

FlowLayout

FlowLayout behavior is similar to traditional ASP/HTML behavior. The controls on the page do not have dynamic positioning. When a control is added to a Web Form, it is placed in the upper-left corner. Pressing the Spacebar or Enter can push the control to the right, or downward, but this model usually uses tables to control the positioning of controls on the page.

GridLayout

GridLayout behavior uses dynamic positioning to set the location of a control on the page. A control can be placed anywhere on the page. This mode also allows controls to be snapped to a grid. Behind the scenes, GridLayout is accomplished by adding the attribute *ms_positioning="GridLayout"* to the body tag of a Web Form.

Selecting the Proper Layout

GridLayout can save lots of development time, since positioning of controls does not require an underlying table structure. GridLayout is usually a good choice for a fixed-size form.

Since FlowLayout does not use absolute positioning, it can be an effective choice when working with pages that are resizable. In many cases, it is desirable to hide a control and let the controls that follow shift to move into the hole that was created.

The benefits of both layout types can be implemented on the same page by using panel controls. The panel control acts as a container for other controls. Setting the visibility of the panel to false turns off all rendered output of the panel and its contained controls. If the panel is on a page where FlowLayout is selected, any controls that follow the panel are shifted to fill in the hole that was created by the absence of the panel.

Figure 3.5 shows an example of a FlowLayout page that has two HTML Grid Layout Panels that are configured to run as HTML server controls. Web server controls were added for the Button, Labels, and TextBoxes. The Page_Load method is programmed to display the top Grid Layout Panel if this is the first request for the page. If data is being posted to this page, the lower Grid Layout Panel is displayed. The .aspx page contains the following HTML code:

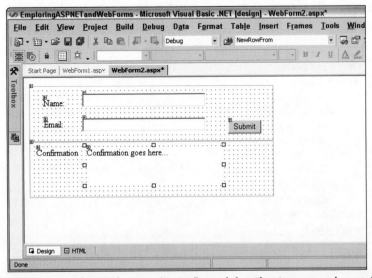

Figure 3.5 This Web page is configured for FlowLayout and contains two HTML Grid Layout Panels.

```
<%@ Page
    Language="vb"
    AutoEventWireup="false"
    Codebehind="WebForm1.aspx.vb"
    Inherits="chapter3.WebForm1"%>
<!DOCTYPE HTML PUBLIC "-//W3C//DTD HTML 4.0 Transitional//EN">
<html>
  <head>
    <title>WebForm1</title>
    <meta name="GENERATOR"
          content="Microsoft Visual Studio .NET 7.0">
    <meta name="CODE_LANGUAGE"
          content="Visual Basic 7.0">
    <meta name=vs_defaultClientScript
          content="JavaScript">
    <meta name=vs_targetSchema
          content="http://schemas.microsoft.com/intellisense/ie5">
  </head>
  <body>
    <form id="Form1" method="post" runat="server">
        <div                    style="WIDTH: 450px;
            POSITION: relative;
            HEIGHT: 100px"
            ms_positioning="GridLayout"
            id=TopPanel
            runat="server">
            <asp:TextBox
                id=txtName
                style="Z-INDEX: 101;
                LEFT: 98px;
                POSITION: absolute;
                TOP: 13px"
                runat="server"
                Width="228"
                height="24">
            </asp:TextBox>
            <asp:TextBox
                id=txtEmail
                style="Z-INDEX: 102;
                LEFT: 98px;
                POSITION: absolute;
                TOP: 57px"
                runat="server"
                Width="228"
                height="24">
            </asp:TextBox>
            <asp:Label
                id=Label1
                style="Z-INDEX: 103;
                LEFT: 25px;
```

```
            POSITION: absolute;
            TOP: 21px"
            runat="server">
            Name:
        </asp:Label>
        <asp:Label
            id=Label2
            style="Z-INDEX: 104;
            LEFT: 26px;
            POSITION: absolute;
            TOP: 59px"
            runat="server">
            Email:
        </asp:Label>
        <asp:Button
            id=btnSubmit
            style="Z-INDEX: 105;
            LEFT: 367px;
            POSITION: absolute;
            TOP: 63px"
            runat="server"
            Text="Submit">
        </asp:Button>
    </div>
    <div
        style="WIDTH: 450px;
        POSITION: relative;
        HEIGHT: 100px"
        ms_positioning="GridLayout"
        id=BottomPanel
        runat="server">
        <asp:Label
            id=lblConfirmation
            style="Z-INDEX: 101;
            LEFT: 105px;
            POSITION: absolute;
            TOP: 10px"
            runat="server"
            Width="249px"
            Height="66px">
            Confimarion goes here...
        </asp:Label>
        <asp:Label
            id=Label3
            style="Z-INDEX: 102;
            LEFT: 12px;
            POSITION: absolute;
            TOP: 10px"
            runat="server"
            Width="76px">
```

```
                              Confirmation
                        </asp:Label>
                  </div>
            </form>
      </body>
</html>
```

Notice that the HTML Grid Layout Panels are nothing more that DIV tags with the *ms_positioning="GridLayout"* attribute. The other controls are contained in the DIV tags.

The code-behind page contains the following code:

```
Public Class WebForm1
    Inherits System.Web.UI.Page
    Protected WithEvents Label1 As _
        System.Web.UI.WebControls.Label
    Protected WithEvents Label2 As _
        System.Web.UI.WebControls.Label
    Protected WithEvents lblConfirmation As _
        System.Web.UI.WebControls.Label
    Protected WithEvents txtName As _
        System.Web.UI.WebControls.TextBox
    Protected WithEvents txtEmail As _
        System.Web.UI.WebControls.TextBox
    Protected WithEvents Label3 As _
        System.Web.UI.WebControls.Label
    Protected WithEvents TopPanel As _
        System.Web.UI.HtmlControls.HtmlGenericControl
    Protected WithEvents BottomPanel As _
        System.Web.UI.HtmlControls.HtmlGenericControl
    Protected WithEvents btnSubmit As _
        System.Web.UI.WebControls.Button
#Region " Web Form Designer Generated Code "
    'This call is required by the Web Form Designer.
    <System.Diagnostics.DebuggerStepThrough()> _
    Private Sub InitializeComponent()
    End Sub
    Private Sub Page_Init(ByVal sender As System.Object, _
        ByVal e As System.EventArgs) Handles MyBase.Init
        'CODEGEN: This method call is required by the Web Form Designer
        'Do not modify it using the code editor.
        InitializeComponent()
    End Sub
#End Region
    Private Sub Page_Load(ByVal sender As System.Object, _
        ByVal e As System.EventArgs) Handles MyBase.Load
```

```
      If Page.IsPostBack Then
          TopPanel.Visible = False
          BottomPanel.Visible = True
      Else
          TopPanel.Visible = True
          BottomPanel.Visible = False
      End If
    End Sub
    Private Sub btnSubmit_Click(ByVal sender As System.Object, _
        ByVal e As System.EventArgs) Handles btnSubmit.Click

        lblConfirmation.Text = "Hello " & txtName.Text & "<br>"
        lblConfirmation.Text &= "Your email address is " & txtEmail.Text
    End Sub
End Class
```

When the page is viewed for the first time (see Figure 3.6), only the top panel is displayed. When data is entered and submitted, the top panel is hidden and the bottom panel is displayed. Since the page layout is set to FlowLayout, the bottom panel will shift to the top of the page to fill in the hole that was created by setting the top panel's visible property to false.

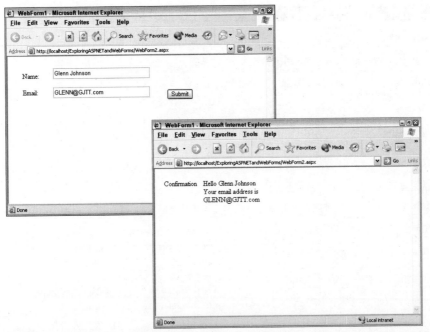

Figure 3.6 Only one panel is displayed at a time. When the first panel is hidden, the second panel moves into the space that was originally occupied by the first panel.

Lab 3.1: Web Forms

In this lab, you will create a Web Form using Visual Studio .NET and then explore the life cycle of the Web Form and its controls.

Create the Web Form

In this section, you will create a Web Form called NewCustomer.aspx, which allows you to collect customer information. Later, you will store this information in a database.

1. To start this lab, open the OrderEntrySolution from Lab 2.1 or Lab 2.2.

2. Right-click the Customer project, click Add, Add Web Form, and type NewCustomer.aspx for the name of the new Web Form. When prompted to check out the project, click the Check Out button.

3. Add the Web server controls in Table 3.4 to the Web Form. Figure 3.7 shows the completed page. Save your work.

Table 3.4   NewCustomer.aspx Web Server Controls

ID	TYPE	PROPERTIES	
lblCustomer	asp:Label	Text=Customer Name	
txtCustomerName	asp:TextBox	Text=	
lblAddress	asp:Label	Text=Address	
txtAddress1	asp:TextBox	Text=	
txtAddress2	asp:TextBox	Text=	
lblCity	asp:Label	Text=City	
txtCity	asp:TextBox	Text=	
lblState	asp:Label	Text=State	
drpState	asp:DropDownList	Items = Enter the states below plus an empty entry as the default.	
		Text=	Value=
		Text=FL	Value=FL
		Text=MA	Value=MA
		Text=OH	Value=OH
		Text=TX	Value=TX
lblZipCode	asp:Label	Text=Zip	
txtZipCode	asp:TextBox	Text=	
btnAddCustomer	asp:Button	Text=Add Customer	
lblConfirmation	asp:Label	Text=	

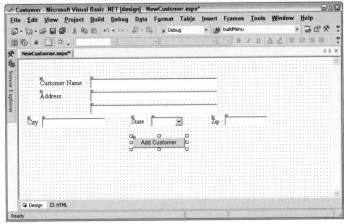

Figure 3.7   The completed Web page after entering the Web server controls in Table 3.4.

Test Your Work

Test your work by performing the following steps:

1. Compile your project. Click Build, Build Solution. You should see an indication in the output window that all three projects compiled successfully.

2. Select a startup page for the Visual Studio .NET Debugger. Locate the NewCustomer.aspx page in the Solution Explorer. Right-click NewCustomer.aspx, and then click Set As Start Page.

3. Press F5 to launch the Visual Studio .NET debugger, which will display your page in your browser.

4. Test ASP.NET's ability to maintain state. Type some text into each TextBox, select a state from the DropDownList, and click the Add Customer button.

What happened? When the button was clicked, the data was posted back to the server. If your page functioned properly, the server received the data that was entered into the Web Form. No code has been assigned to the Add Customer button's click event, so the server simply returns the page to the browser.

What is most interesting is that the data is still on the form; the TextBoxes still have the data that you typed in, and the DropDownList still has the selected state. This demonstrates ASP.NET's ability to maintain state.

Adding Code to Process the Data

In this section, you will add some code to the Add Customer's click event. The code simply displays a summary message on the current page. This data will be put into a database in a later lab.

Double-click the Add Customer button. This opens the code-behind page and adds template code for the button's click event. Add code to the button's click event procedure so that it looks like this:

```
Private Sub btnAddCustomer_Click(ByVal sender As System.Object, _
    ByVal e As System.EventArgs) Handles btnAddCustomer.Click
    Dim s As String
    s = "<font size='5'>Confirmation Info:</font>" & "<BR>"
    s += txtCustomerName.Text & "<BR>"
    s += txtAddress1.Text & "<BR>"
    If txtAddress2.Text.Length > 0 Then
        s += txtAddress2.Text & "<BR>"
    End If
    s += txtCity.Text & ", "
    s += drpState.SelectedItem.Text & " "
    s += txtZipCode.Text & "<BR>"
    lblConfirmation.Text = s
End Sub
```

Test Your Work

1. Save your work.

2. Press F5 to launch the Visual Studio .NET debugger, which will display your page in your browser.

3. Test ASP.NET's ability to process the data on the Web Form by entering data and then clicking the Add Customer button.

4. When the Add Customer button is clicked, the confirmation label will be populated with data from the Web Form.

Exploring ViewState

In this section, you will explore the ViewState to appreciate the need for this hidden object.

1. Add a Web server control button to the NewCustomer.aspx page. Change its ID to "btnViewState" and its Text to "ViewState Test." Don't add any code to this button's click event.

2. Press F5 to view the page.

3. View the size of the ViewState hidden object. When the page is displayed, click View, Source. Note the size of the ViewState, which should be approximately 50 characters.

4. Enter data into the Web Form, and click the Add Customer button. Note the change in the ViewState, which should be significantly larger, depending on the amount of data that was entered on the Web Form.

5. Click the ViewState Test button. Notice that the data is posted back to the server, and the information that is in the Confirmation label has not been not lost.

6. View the size of the ViewState hidden object. When the page is displayed, click View, Source. Note the size of the ViewState, which is much larger that before. ASP.NET stores the value of the Confirmation label in ViewState.

Identifying ViewState Contributors

As ViewState grows, you will need to identify the controls that are placing data into ViewState. This section will use the ASP.NET trace function to identify the objects that are using ViewState.

1. Open the Web.Config file. This is an XML file that contains settings for the Web site.

2. Locate the following trace element:

```
<trace
    enabled="false"
    requestLimit="10"
    pageOutput="false"
    traceMode="SortByTime"
    localOnly="true"
/>
```

3. Make the following changes:

```
<trace
    enabled="true"
    requestLimit="100"
    pageOutput="false"
    traceMode="SortByTime"
    localOnly="true"
/>
```

4. Save the Web.Config file.

5. Press F5 to view the page.

6. Enter data into the Web Form, and click the Add Customer button. Note the change in the ViewState, which should be significantly larger, depending on the amount of data that was entered on the Web Form.

7. Click the ViewState Test button. Notice that the data is posted back to the server, and the information that is in the Confirmation label has not been not lost.

8. Change the URL from http://localhost/Customer/NewCustomer .aspx to http://localhost/Customer/trace.axd and press Enter. The trace page is displayed. The trace page has an entry for each time you requested the NewCustomer.aspx page. Notice that the first time the page was requested, a GET was performed. Each additional page request resulted in a POST of data back to the page.

9. Click the View Details link of the first page request. This page contains lots of information. Locate the Control Tree section, which shows all of the controls that are on the page and the quantity of bytes that each control has placed into ViewState. On the first request for the page, only the page itself has contributed to View-State (typically 20 bytes). The page automatically stores globalization information in ViewState.

10. Click the Back button in the browser, and then click the View Details link of the second request. Locate the Control Tree section. Notice that the page still contributes the same quantity of bytes to View-State, and the lblConfirmation (Confirmation Label) contributes many bytes of data to ViewState, depending on the size of the data that needed to be remembered (see Figure 3.8).

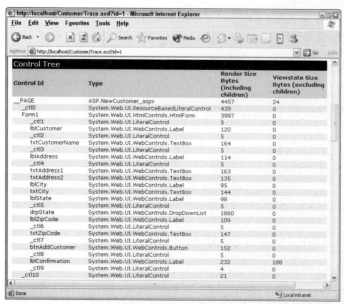

Figure 3.8 Use Trace to identify ViewState contributors. Notice that the page always contributes approximately 20 bytes, and that the confirmation label contributes many bytes to ViewState, depending on the amount of data that is in the label.

Understanding the Page Life Cycle (Optional)

This section will help you understand the page's life cycle by adding code to some of the page's significant events.

1. Close all open files.

2. Open the WebForm1.aspx file that is located in the Customer project.

3. Add a TextBox and a Button to the page from the Web Forms tab of the ToolBox. When prompted to check out files from Visual Source-Safe, click the Check Out button.

4. Double-click the button to go to the code-behind page.

5. Add the following code to the Button1_Click event method.

   ```
   Response.Write("Button Clicked<br>")
   ```

6. The upper part of the code window contains two drop-down boxes. The first drop-down box is used to select a class, and the second drop-down box is used is to select an event method. Select TextBox1 from the class drop-down list, and select TextChanged from the event method drop-down list.

7. Add the following code to the TextBox1_TextChanged event method.

   ```
   Response.Write("Text Changed<br>")
   ```

8. In the Page_Load subroutine, add the following code:

   ```
   Response.Write( "Page_Load")
   ```

9. With WebForm1 selected from the class drop-down list, select the Page_Init event method. Add a Response.Write method as you did in the previous steps.

10. Select Base Class Events from the class drop-down list and select the PreRender event method. Add Response.Write code as you did in the previous steps.

11. In the Solution Explorer, right-click WebForm1.aspx and click Set as Start Page. Press F5 to see the page. The page will display a message indicating that the Page Init, Page Load, and PreRender events took place.

12. Enter some information into the TextBox, and click the Button. The page will display a message indicating that the Page Init, Page Load, Text Changed, Button Clicked, and PreRender events took place. Although AutoPostBack is set to false on the TextBox, the TextChanged still executes, but not until a posting control, such as the Button, caused the data to be posted back to the server.

Summary

- ASP.NET supports the traditional single-page programming model. It also provides the two-page coding model, which utilizes the code-behind page for the separation of client-side and server-side code.

- ASP.NET provides two types of server controls: HTML server controls and Web server controls.

- HTML server controls are used when migrating existing ASP pages to ASP.NET because a runat="server" attribute can be easily added to an HTML tag to convert it to an HTML server control.

- Web server controls are the preferred controls for new projects because of their consistent programming model and their ability to provide browser-specific code. ASP.Net provides Web server controls that can produce many lines of complex HTML output to accomplish a task rather that the one-to-one mapping that exists when using Web server controls.

- Use the Page.IsPostBack property to see if this is the first time that the page has been requested.

- Controls such as the DropDownList and the ListBox have their Auto-PostBack property set to false. This setting can be changed to true to post back to the server each time a new item is selected.

- Events in ASP.NET pass two arguments: the sender and the EventArgs. The sender is the object that raised the event and the EventArgs may contain extra data, such as the x and y coordinates of the mouse.

Review Questions

1. What are the two types of controls that ASP.NET provides?

2. What would be the best controls to use when migrating an existing ASP page to ASP.NET?

3. What is the best control to use when client-side JavaScript code will be executing from a control's events?

4. Name some benefits to using Web server controls.

5. A user complains that each time a button is pressed on the Web page, another copy of the data in a ListBox is being added to the ListBox. What is the problem? How can it be corrected?

6. You added a DropDownList to a Web page. You programmed the DropDownList to do a database lookup as soon as a new item is selected from the list. Although you wrote the code to do the lookup, selecting a new item from the list doesn't appear to work. After investigating further, you find that the lookup works, but not until a button on the form is clicked. What is the most likely problem?

7. What is the key benefit to using code-behind pages?

Answers to Review Questions

1. HTML server controls and Web server controls.

2. HTML server controls, because existing HTML tags can be converted to HTML server controls by adding the runat="server" attribute.

3. HTML server contols, because it is simple to attach client-side code to these controls using traditional HTML and DHTML methods.

4. Web server controls have the following benefits:

   a. A more consistent programming model.

   b. A single control can create complex HTML output.

   c. They produce browser-specific HTML code, taking advantage of the browser's capabilities.

5. The data is being programmatically added to the ListBox, using code that is in the Page_Load event method. Since the ListBox remembers its data (via ViewState) between calls to the server, each time the page is requested, another copy of the data is added to existing data. To solve the problem, check to see if the page is being posted back to the server using the Page.IsPostBack property. If so, there is no need to repopulate the ListBox.

6. The default setting of AutoPostBack is set to false on the DropDownList control.

7. Code-behind pages provide the ability to separate client-side and server-side code.

The .NET Framework and Visual Basic .NET Object Programming

The last chapter introduced code-behind pages. The aspx page inherited from the code-behind page, which inherited from System.Web.UI.Page. This is one of many examples of the power of inheritance in the .NET Framework.

After looking at a couple of definitions, this chapter covers the .NET Framework as well as many aspects of object programming, such as inheritance with Visual Basic .NET. This chapter can be especially useful for traditional Visual Basic programmers, who may be accustomed to using objects, but may not have experience creating objects.

Definitions

Before getting too deeply into this chapter, there are a couple of words that need to be defined in order to establish a baseline for this chapter. These words, and others, will be further defined as the chapter progresses.

Class.   A class is a blueprint for the construction of objects. Just as an architect creates a blueprint, which contains the instructions for building a house, a developer creates a class, which contains the instructions for building an object.

Object.   An object is an instance of a constructed class. The *New* keyword instantiates (construct an instance of) a class.

Field.   A field is a variable that has been defined at the class level. This variable is typically used to describe the class. A house class might have a color field, which refers to the color of the house.

Method.   A method is a procedure (either sub or function) that has been created within a class. The method typically performs an action that relates to the class. A car class might have a StartEngine method.

Event.   An event is something that takes place within the class at a point in time. When an event is *raised* (takes place), the event executes code that was created to handle the event. If events and methods are looked at from a messaging perspective, methods handle inbound messages to a class, while events generate outbound messages from the class that can be handled by other classes.

Property.   A property looks and feels like a field. The problem with a field is that there is no easy way to keep someone from placing invalid data into it. A property provides a mechanism for encapsulating the field so any data changes must go through a routine to enforce data integrity.

Member.   *Member* is a generic term that refers to a field, property, method, or event of a class. If members of a car class are public, then the fields, properties, methods, and events of the car class are public.

Inheritance.   Inheritance is the ability to define a class that is based on another class. Classical inheritance involves an *"is-a"* relationship between entities. For example, a car is a vehicle.

Classroom Q & A

Q: I read that System.Object is the root object for all .NET data type. Does that mean that all data types expose the methods and properties of System.Object?

A: They sure do. For example, System.Object has a ToString( ) method. Any new class that you create automatically has a ToString( ) method.

Q: It's nice to be able to receive all of the base class members, but is it possible to change the behavior of these methods in a derived class?

A: Absolutely. You have the ability to override a method that is in the base class. In addition, you can still make a call to the base class's method by using the *MyBase* keyword.

Q: Does Visual Basic .NET support overloading?

A: Yes and no. Visual Basic .NET supports method overloading, but not operator overloading. This means that you can create several versions of a method, each having a different method signature (different argument count and argument data types). Visual Basic .NET does not allow operators to be overloaded. This means that operators such as the plus and minus sign cannot be overloaded. This is usually not a problem, since operator overloading is more of an aesthetic language feature.

Q: Is it possible to retrieve an enumeration's text labels as well as its values from a Visual Studio .NET project?

A: Yes. This is a nice feature. It may be desirable to populate a ListBox with the text labels of an enumeration. This was extremely difficult in Visual Basic 6, but it's easy in Visual Basic .NET. Enumerations will be covered later in this chapter.

The .NET Framework

The .NET Framework is a computing platform that offers a simplified, consistent development and runtime environment. The .NET Framework provides a consistent programming model across all .NET languages. This makes the challenge of learning new development languages much easier. For example, since the Base Class Libraries are the same for all languages, learning a new language can be as easy as learning the new syntax.

There are two key components to the .NET Framework; the common language runtime and the Base Class Libraries. The common language runtime is the .NET Framework's execution engine and provides an environment that guarantees safe execution of code. Items that are part of the common language runtime include (see Figure 4.1):

Thread support.   Provides a framework for enabling multithreaded programming.

COM Marshaler.   Provides the ability to marshal data to and from COM components.

Debug Engine.   Is used to debug and trace a program's execution.

Security Engine.   Provides evidence-based code, based on the user identity and the location of the code.

Exception Manager.   Provides Structured Exception Handling (SEH), which is a major improvement to error (On Error) handling using Visual Basic 6.

Garbage Collector. Provides object cleanup support that can be used on multiprocessor machines.

Class Manager. Manages all code execution and controls the JIT compiler and the Class Loader.

Type Checker. Does not allow unsafe casts; ensures that all objects are initialized.

Class Loader. Loads classes by reading the metadata in the assembly.

JIT Compiler. Compiles MSIL code to native machine code.

Applications that are hosted by the .NET Framework do not require entries into the registry. This means that deployment of most .NET applications can be done by simply copying the executable files to the new location.

Application code that targets the common language runtime is called *managed code*. Figure 4.2 shows how the common language runtime is used to host managed applications and managed Web applications.

Assemblies

An assembly is produced when a Visual Studio .NET project is compiled. Although the assembly is conceptually similar to the .exe or .dll of the past, it is important to know that it is possible to create multimodule (multifile) assemblies.

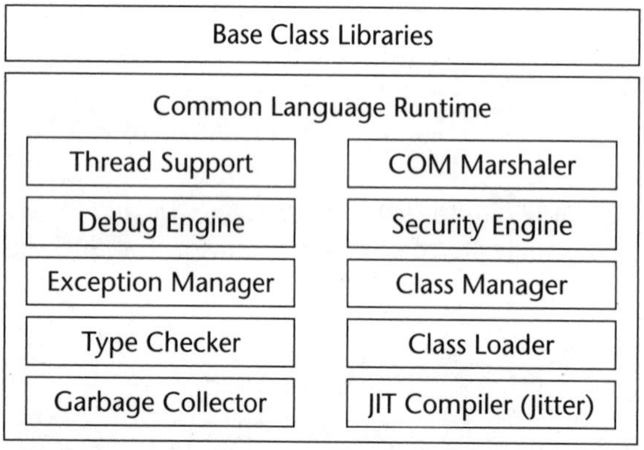

Base Class Libraries	
Common Language Runtime	
Thread Support	COM Marshaler
Debug Engine	Security Engine
Exception Manager	Class Manager
Type Checker	Class Loader
Garbage Collector	JIT Compiler (Jitter)

Figure 4.1 The .NET Framework consists of two primary items; the Base Class Library and the common language runtime.

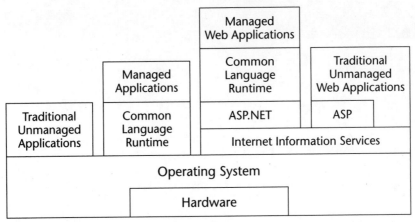

Figure 4.2 The common language runtime runs managed code. It provides a consistent layer above the operating system and ASP.NET.

Multimodule assemblies may be desirable when you want to combine modules that were written in different languages or when it is necessary to optimize an application download by placing seldom-used types into modules that can be downloaded on demand. This book is primarily focused on single-module assemblies.

There is no option to create a multimodule assembly from within Visual Studio .NET. The Visual Basic .NET command-line compiler can be used to compile code into modules and then create an assembly with the modules. Use the following commands:

```
vbc /target:module SeldomUsedCode.vb
vbc MainCode.vb /addmodule:SeldomUsedCode.netmodule
```

The first command creates a module called SeldomUsedCode.netmodule, while the second command creates an executable called MainCode.exe. Both output files are collectively called an assembly. Use vbc /? to see a list of compiler switches.

An assembly is a version boundary. Regardless of the quantity of data types that are defined within an assembly, all of them are versioned within the assembly as a unit. When a project is compiled, all dependent assemblies and their versions are recoded in the compiled assembly's manifest.

The assembly forms a security boundary. Permissions may be requested and granted at the assembly level.

The assembly contains the Microsoft Intermediate Language and metadata. The following sections describe these items in detail.

◆ Intermediate Language Disassembler

The IL Disassember (ILDasm.exe) is included in the .NET Framework SDK, which is part of the default installation of Visual Studio .NET. ILDasm can be used to look at the contents of an assembly. ILDasm will be used throughout this book to understand what's inside an assembly. Figure 4.3 shows ILDasm and the legend describing its symbols.

Symbol	Description
▶	More Information
🛡	Namespace
▤	Class
▨	Structure
🄸	Interface
■	Method
Ⓢ	Static Method
◈	Field
Ⓢ	Static Field
▽	Event
▲	Property

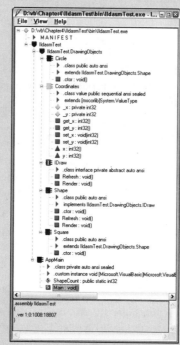

Figure 4.3   IL Disassembler (ILDasm.exe) with symbol legend.

The IL code can be viewed by double-clicking any method. The manifest can be viewed by double-clicking it. To see the type metadata, press Ctrl+M. To dump the complete contents of the assembly to disk, click File, Dump, OK, and then select a location for the files that will be stored.

A companion tool is called ILAsm.exe, which can be used to assemble an IL source file into an assembly. ILAsm is part of the .NET Framework.

Microsoft Intermediate Language

An assembly does not contain executable machine code. Instead, it contains Microsoft Intermediate Language (MSIL or IL) code. MSIL (pronounced like the word *missile*) code may be thought of as being platform-independent assembly language. All .NET language compilers produce MSIL code, which means that there is not a significant difference in performance between .NET languages. The following Hello program is an example of IL code:

```
Module Hello
    Sub Main()
        Dim s As String
        Console.Write("Enter Your Name: ")
        s = Console.ReadLine()
        Console.WriteLine("Hello " & s)
    End Sub
End Module
```

This little console application simply prompts for a user's name, then displays Hello plus the name on the screen. Figure 4.4 shows the hello.exe application loaded into ILDasm.

The IL code is displayed by double-clicking Main. The IL code functions as follows:

```
IL_0000: No Operation.
IL_0001: Load a pointer to "Enter Your Name" on to the stack.
IL_0006: Call the Console.Write method, passing a string pointer.
IL_000b: No Operation.
IL_000c: Make call to Console.ReadLine, placing a return
                string pointer on to the stack.
IL_0011: Store the string point from the stack to location 0
                (variable s).
IL_0012: Load a pointer to "Hello" on to the stack.
IL_0017: Load the pointer from location 0 (variable s) onto the stack.
IL_0018: Call the String.Concat method to concatenate the
                contents of the string pointers that have
                been pushed on to the stack. Place a string
                pointer to the result onto the stack.
IL_001d: Call the Console.WriteLine method, passing a string pointer.
IL_0022: No Operation.
IL_0023: No Operation.
IL_0024: Return to the caller, which ends this application.
```

This code is quite readable. But in many cases, viewing the IL code can reveal many facts about a component's behavior that would have been much harder to see by simple testing.

tip Some people are shocked to see how easy it is to read the IL code that is inside an assembly. Although there is no way to encrypt the IL code, the code can be made more difficult to read by using a tool called an *obfuscator*. Obfuscators have been used in the Java market for some time. Several vendors offer an obfuscator for .NET assemblies. Visual Studio 2003 also contains an obfuscator that can be used to make the IL code less readable.

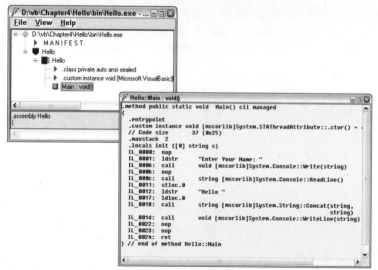

Figure 4.4   IL code in the Hello application as viewed in ILDasm.

Metadata

Assemblies are completely *self-describing*, which means that is possible to query an assembly for all its information, or metadata. Two types of metadata are provided within an assembly: the manifest and the type metadata.

Manifest

The manifest contains metadata that is global to the assembly (see Figure 4.5). Assembly information includes the following:

External references.   List of assemblies (dependencies) that this assembly needs to operate.

General assembly information.   Contains information such as Assembly Title, Assembly Description, and Assembly Copyright Information. This information is located in the AssemblyInfo.vb file in a Visual Studio .NET project.

Assembly version.   Contains the version number for the complete assembly. The assembly version information is located in the AssemblyInfo.vb file in a Visual Studio .NET project. New Visual Studio .NET projects have a version number of 1.0.*, and Visual Studio .NET automatically generates the last two digits of the version. The third digit is equal to the number of days since January 1, 2000, and the fourth digit is the number of seconds since midnight (or 1:00 A.M., depending on daylight savings time setting) divided by 2, resulting in a number between 0 and 43199.

Module definitions.   Contains a list of the modules (files) and settings that compose the assembly.

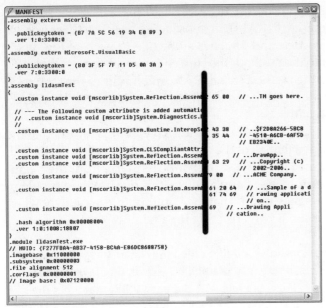

Figure 4.5 Viewing a manifest using ILDasm. The information in the center has been extracted to reveal the data at each end of the lines.

Type Metadata

The type metadata contains information to fully describe all data types in the assembly. This metadata is used by Visual Studio .NET to display the list of available members in IntelliSense.

 Type metadata is viewable in the IL Disassembler (ILDasm.exe) by pressing Ctrl+M.

Common Language Runtime

The common language runtime manages thread execution, memory, code safety, compilation, code access security, and many other services. This section covers some of the key components that the common language runtime uses when executing code.

Core Execution Engine

The Core Execution Engine comprises the Class Manager, the Class Loader, and the just-in-time (JIT or Jitter) compiler. An executable file contains MSIL code. When an application runs, the MSIL code must be compiled to native machine code. Some of the code in an application may not be called; so rather than compile the complete application, the MSIL is compiled as needed and stored in random access memory (RAM) for subsequent use. The Class Loader loads each data type as needed and attaches stub code to each of the type's methods. On the first call to the method, the stub code passes control to the JIT compiler, which compiles the method tree in RAM and modifies the stub code to point to the compiled code. Subsequent calls to the method result in direct execution of the compiled native code. (See Figure 4.6.)

When an application has ended, the application's memory is returned to the operating system. This means that all of the compiled native code is destroyed. If the application is restarted, the JIT compiler process starts from the beginning. For most small to medium-sized applications, this may not be a problem. For large applications, users may report that the application runs slowly when it starts, but get faster after it has been running for a while.

 The .NET Framework includes a utility called the Native Image Generator (ngen.exe), which can be used to compile an .exe or .dll file into a native image file. When you are compiling with the ngen utility, note that the original .exe or .dll file remains unchanged. The compiled image is stored in the Native Image Cache, which is located in the %SystemRoot%\ Assembly\NativeImages1_version folder. It's not easy to see this folder via Windows Explorer or MyComputer, because a COM component called shfusion.dll intercepts the call, but this folder can be viewed via the command prompt. Note that the ngen utility must be run on the machine that will be running the compiled image.

Namespaces

How many readme.txt files are on a typical computer? How can many files with the same name reside on a disk drive? That's simple: The files are in different folders. Providing different folders prevents filename collisions on the hard drive.

The .NET Framework provides a method to prevent data type name clashes, called namespaces. It's relatively easy to imagine many vendors creating a Customer or Employee class in the code that they provide. To avoid name clashes between vendors, each vendor might create a namespace, using their company name as their root namespace. This concept is similar to using folders on your hard drive.

When creating a Visual Basic .NET application, a default namespace is created that matches the name of the project. To change the default namespace for a project, close all open files within the project, click the project, then click Project, Properties, Common Properties, General. This window displays the namespace option.

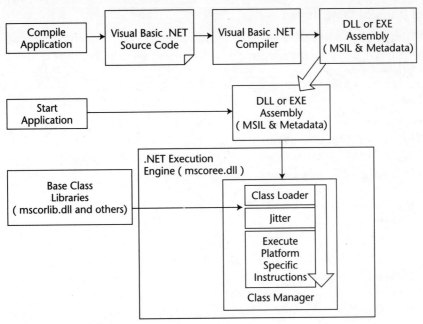

Figure 4.6   The just-in-time compiler compiles methods as they are called.

Namespaces are hierarchical, with each level being separated by a period. The recommend namespace should start with the company name, then the technology name, and then the data type, as in the following example:

```
CompanyName.TechnologyName.DataType
```

The root namespace for most .NET data types is called System. Be careful when using namespaces that are not under the system namespace, because these namespaces will not be platform independent. An example of a non-System namespace is the Microsoft.Win32 namespace, which contains the registry classes.

Common Type System

The common language runtime also contains the common type system (CTS), which defines how types are declared, used, and managed in the runtime. The common type system also defines syntactical constructs, such as operators and overloads.

The common type system plays an important role in ensuring cross-language integration. The common type system defines rules that all .NET languages must follow.

Classifications of Data Types

The common type system defines to general categories of data types: value types and reference types. (See Figure 4.7.) The next section looks at both of these categories in detail.

Value Types

Value types are structures. Variables that are value types hold their own copy of data. This means that operations on one variable will not affect other variables. Value types are either created on the stack or allocated inline as a structure. The following code demonstrates value types:

```
Dim x as integer
Dim y as integer
x = 100
y=x
y=200
Console.WriteLine( "x = " + x.ToString( ))
Console.WriteLine("y = " + y.ToString( ))
'Result: x=100, y=200
```

Notice that changing the value of y has no impact on the value of x, because the assignment *y=x*, placed a copy of the data from x into y.

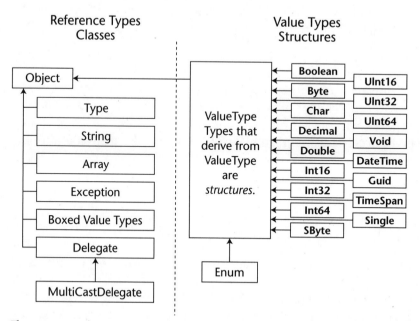

Figure 4.7 Value types are classes, while reference types are structures and inherit from System.ValueType.

Reference Types

Reference types are classes. Variables that are reference types that reference an address to an object in memory. Multiple variables can reference the same memory address, so changes to one variable can affect other variables. Reference types are created on the garbage collected heap. Reference types are not destroyed immediately; they are destroyed when garbage collection takes place. The following code demonstrates reference types:

```
Class reftest
    Public test As Integer
End Class
Dim x As New reftest()
Dim y As New reftest()
x.test = 100
y = x
y.test = 200
Console.WriteLine("x = " + x.test.ToString())
Console.WriteLine("y = " + y.test.ToString())
'Result: x.test=200, y.test=200
```

Notice that changing the value of y also changes x. This is because x and y are reference types. With reference types, the assignment *y=x* causes y to reference the same memory location that x references.

Everything Is an Object

System.Object is the root type for all types in the .NET Framework. This means that all of the members of System.Object are available on any data type that is created. System.Object contains the following methods:

Equals.   Compares two object variables. This method is also called when the equal sign is used to compare objects.

Finalize.   Performs cleanup operations before an object is automatically reclaimed.

GetHashCode.   Generates a number corresponding to the value of the object to support the use of a hash table.

ToString.   Creates a string that represents the fully qualified name of the data type.

Common Language Specification

Although the common type system defines the rules for data types and syntactical constructs, it may not be desirable for a language developer to implement every feature of the common type system. The Common Language Specification (CLS) is a subset of the common type system, which defines a set of rules that every .NET language must adhere to.

When writing reusable components, it is important to make sure that the components can be used by all .NET languages. This is done by writing Common Language Specification Compliant (CLSCompliant) code.

The first rule of writing CLSCompliant code is that CLSCompliant rules only apply to the parts of a type that are exposed outside its assembly. A language like C# can use unsigned integers in a code component, but the code should not expose unsigned integers, since unsigned integers are not CLSCompliant.

Base Class Library

In addition to the common language runtime, the .NET Framework contains a large Base Class Library (BCL). The Base Class Library provides many data types within many namespaces. Figure 4.8 shows some of the key namespaces in the Base Class Library.

For many people, the hardest part of learning the .NET Framework is learning the data types in the Base Class Library. After the Base Class Library is mastered, moving to a different .NET language is not all that difficult.

This book covers many of the key namespaces in the Base Class Library, but it's important to continue exploring these namespaces and data types.

System Data Types

The System namespace is the root namespace for the .NET Framework. The System namespace contains many of the fundamental classes and structures that correspond to primitive data types for most .NET languages. Table 4.1 lists some of the common data types in the System namespace and the Visual Basic .NET data type that the type maps to. Notice that Visual Basic .NET does not have a primitive data type to match all of the .NET data types.

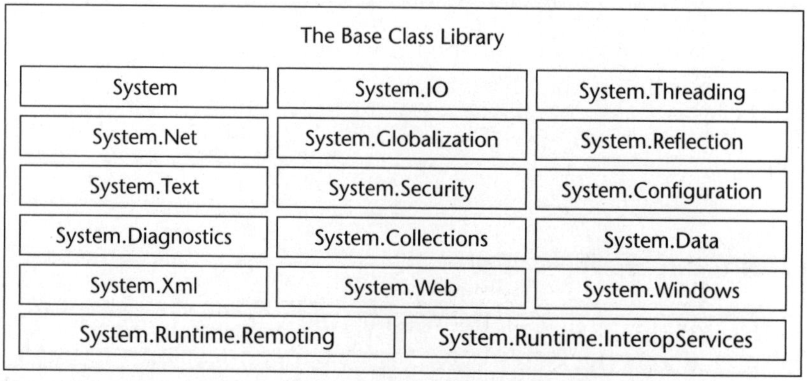

The Base Class Library		
System	System.IO	System.Threading
System.Net	System.Globalization	System.Reflection
System.Text	System.Security	System.Configuration
System.Diagnostics	System.Collections	System.Data
System.Xml	System.Web	System.Windows
System.Runtime.Remoting		System.Runtime.InteropServices

Figure 4.8   Key namespaces in the Base Class Library.

Table 4.1   System Namespace Data Types, with Visual Basic .NET Mapping

.NET TYPE	DESCRIPTION	VISUAL BASIC .NET TYPE
Byte	8-bit unsigned integer	Byte
Sbyte	8-bit signed integer—not CLSCompliant	
Int16	16-bit signed integer	Short
Int32	32-bit signed integer	Integer
Int64	64-bit signed integer	Long
UInt16	16-bit unsigned integer—not CLSCompliant	
UInt32	32-bit unsigned integer—not CLSCompliant	
UInt64	64-bit unsigned integer—not CLSCompliant	
Single	32-bit, single-precision floating point number	Single
Double	64-bit, double-precision floating point number	Double
Decimal	96-bit decimal number	Decimal
IntPtr	Signed integer pointer whose size depends on the underlying platform	
UIntPtr	Unsigned integer pointer whose size depends on the underlying platform—not CLSCompliant	
Object	The root of the .NET type hierarchy	Object
String	Immutable fixed length string of Unicode characters	String

System Data Type or Visual Basic .NET Data Type?

One question that commonly arises is whether to use the .NET data type or the Visual Basic .NET data type. For example, which of the following lines of code is correct?

```
Dim x as Long ' Use the Visual Basic .NET data type.
Dim x as System.Int64 ' Use the .NET data type.
```

Either of these lines could be used, since a Long is an Int64. When the code is compiled to an assembly, a quick look at the IL reveals that the Visual Basic .NET compiler converted the Long to a System.Int64 anyway. Since both of these lines become System.In64 types in IL code, there is no difference in runtime performance.

It may be best to look at history to decide which data type to use. Visual Basic 6 had a data type called Long, which was a 32-bit signed integer. When a project was upgraded from Visual Basic 6 to Visual Basic .NET, the Long data type was mapped to the Int64. This automatically gave old code the ability to take advantage of the larger data type. By using Long, the Visual Basic .NET compiler can map to the largest signed integer that is available, which is an Int64 today, but may be an Int128 tomorrow.

This behavior may, or may not, be desirable. If it is, use the Long Visual Basic .NET data type. If a 64-bit signed integer is mandatory, use the Int64 .NET data type. As a general rule though, it's probably best to use the specific language's data type. This allows the compiler to make mapping changes in the future.

Visual Basic .NET Object-Oriented Programming

The .NET Framework consists of many classes, but there is always a need to develop classes that are specific to the solution that is being created. This section takes a look at object-oriented programming using Visual Basic .NET.

Classes

A class represents a grouping of behaviors and attributes that make up an entity. Classifying items is something that human beings do all the time. This involves looking at common attributes and behaviors. For instance, a car is an item that has four wheels, an engine, and an enclosure (body), and that transports people on a road. When creating a classification, or a class, you must think about the attributes and behaviors that are important to the solution that is being created. This is done through the concept of abstraction.

Abstraction

The concept of abstraction involves making the decision on what attributes and behaviors are important. This is done through the process of selective cognizance—or selective ignorance. What is important to the solution that is being created?

If the solution that is being created is a race car game, a car class may contain current speed and Revolutions per Minute (RPM) attributes. If, however, the solution that is being provided is a maintenance tracking program for cars, current speed and RPM are not required, but last oil change date and odometer readings are required.

When creating new classes, decide what attributes and behaviors are important, and add them to them class. There is no need to have an attribute if the solution never uses it.

Class Creation

In its simplest form, a class can be created in Visual Basic .NET by using the following syntax:

```
Class Car
End Class
```

This class has no apparent behavior or attributes, but it is a class. Some languages, including older versions of Visual Basic, required each class to be in its own file. This is not the case with Visual Basic .NET. Many classes can be created in the same file. From a maintenance perspective, it's usually good to place each major class and its helper classes in the same file.

Class Visibility Modifiers

When a class is created, it is usually desirable to place a constraint on the visibility of the class. Table 4.2 contains a list of the visibility modifiers, or access modifiers, that can be placed on a class.

 Classes that are created with no visibility modifier default to Friend.

Table 4.2   Entity Visibility Modifiers

VISIBILITY MODIFIER	DESCRIPTION
Public	The entity is globally available. There are no restrictions on the use of public entities.
Private	A private entity is only accessible from within the block of code in which it was declared, including nested entities. Private can only be used as a class visibility modifier when working with nested classes.
Protected	A protected entity is accessible only from within its own class or from a derived class. Protected access can be specified only on members of classes. It is not a superset of Friend access. Protected can only be used as a class visibility modifier when working with nested classes.
Friend	An entity that is accessible only within the program that contains the entity declaration.
Protected Friend	An entity that has the union of Protected and Friend accessibility. Protected Friend can only be used as a class visibility modifier when working with nested classes.

Notice that there are only two visibility modifier selections for classes that are not nested: Public and Friend. An example of a class that uses a visibility modifier follows:

```
Public Class Car
End Class
```

Working with Class Members

When creating classes, class members such as events, methods, fields, and properties need to be defined for a class to be a meaningful entity.

Fields

A field is a memory variable that is defined at the class level. The field can be created with the same visibility modifiers as the class, as shown in Table 4.2.

 Fields that are created with no visibility modifier default to Private.

If a visibility modifier is used, the word *Dim* is optional. An example of fields that are created inside a class is as follows:

```
Public Class Car
      Public CarMake as string
      Public CarModel as string
End Class
```

It is also possible to declare many fields of the same type in one command. The following code shows an example:

```
Public Class Car
      Public CarMake, CarModel as string
End Class
```

It is also possible to initialize the fields, but this requires the fields to be on their own line, as shown:

```
Public Class Car
      Public CarMake as string = "Volkswagen"
      Public CarModel as string = "Beetle"
End Class
```

Methods

A method is a sub or function that is defined at the class level. Methods may be assigned a visibility modifier, as shown in Table 4.2.

 Methods that are created with no visibility modifier default to Public.

An example of a public method that returns a value follows:

```
Public Class Car
    Public CarMake As String = "Volkswagen"
    Public CarModel As String = "Beetle"
    Public Function StartEngine(ByVal CarKey As Integer) As Boolean
        If CarKey = 5 Then 'correct key
            Return True
        Else
            Return False
        End If
    End Function
End Class
```

Arguments are passed ByVal by default. Previous versions of Visual Basic passed arguments ByRef by default. Also, notice that the *return* statement is used to return a value from a function.

Overloaded Methods

In Visual Basic .NET, a method can be overloaded. An overloaded method is a method that has the same name as an existing method, but the arguments are different. An example of an overloaded StartEngine method follows:

```
Public Class Car
    Dim CarMake As String = "Volkswagen"
    Public CarModel As String = "Beetle"
    Public Overloads Function StartEngine(ByVal CarKey As Integer) _
            As Boolean
        If CarKey = 5 Then 'correct key
            Return True
        Else
            Return False
        End If
    End Function
    Public Overloads Function StartEngine(ByVal SecretWord As String) _
            As Boolean
        If SecretWord = "Please" Then 'correct key
            Return True
        Else
            Return False
        End If
    End Function
End Class
```

In this example, StartEngine accepts either an integer or a string. The proper method will execute, based on the data type that is passed to the method. Figure 4.9 shows how IntelliSense handles the overloaded method. The up and down arrows can be used to scroll through the overloads.

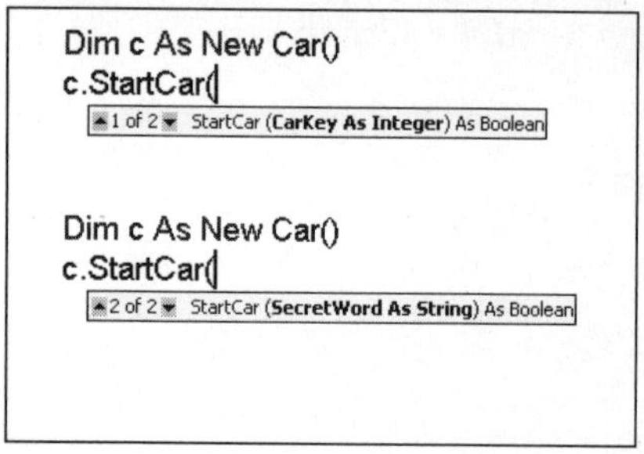

Figure 4.9 Using IntelliSense to view the method overloads. Code is being added to execute the StartEngine method. When the opening parenthesis is typed, IntelliSense displays a list of the available overloads for the StartEngine method.

Encapsulation

The problem with using public fields is that changes can be made to the data, and there is no easy way to protect the data's integrity. Encapsulation is the solution to this problem. Encapsulation can be accomplished via public accessor/mutator methods or by using properties.

Accessor/Mutator Methods

To encapsulate a field via accessor/mutator methods, the visibility modifier must be changed to private. A method is provided to retrieve the value of the private field, called the accessor method. This method is sometimes called a *getter*. Another method is provided to assign a value to the private field, called the mutator method. This method is sometimes called a *setter*. An example of an accessor/mutator is as follows:

```
Public Class Car
    Private CarMake As String = "Volkswagen"
    Public Function GetMake() As String
        'Make any change to CarMake before
        'returning it.
        Return CarMake
    End Function
    Public Sub SetMake(ByVal Make As String)
        'Test Make for proper data
        'then assign to CarMake.
        CarMake = Make
    End Sub
End Class
```

Properties

Although accessor/mutator methods provide encapsulation, IntelliSense makes no differentiation between these methods and regular methods. Also, since two methods are required for each field, the quantity of methods grows substantially.

The use of properties is another method of accomplishing encapsulation. A property can be as follows.

```
Public Class Car
    Private _CarMake As String = "Volkswagen"
    Public Property CarMake() As String
        Get
            Return _CarMake
        End Get
        Set(ByVal Value As String)
            _CarMake = Value
        End Set
    End Property
End Class
```

Figure 4.10 shows an example of how IntelliSense differentiates properties from methods. Also notice that when an assembly that has a property is viewed with ILDasm, the property can be seen, but in addition to the property there are two additional methods: a get_method and a set_method.

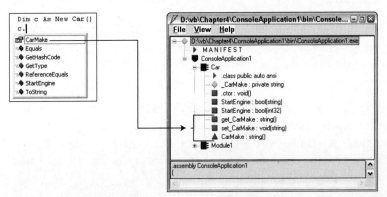

Figure 4.10 The CarMake property has a property icon. The property is also shown in ILDasm. Notice that two hidden methods were created to support the property.

Events

When a class is created, it's not always known exactly how the class will be used in the solution. For example, the Car class may have *Started*, *Stalled*, and *SpeedChanged* events. The writer of the class does not know how these events will be used, but the writer knows that there is a requirement for solution code to execute when any of these events takes place. An example of a class with the Started, Stalled, and SpeedChanged events is as follows:

```
Public Class Car
    Public Event Started()
    Public Event Stalled()
    Public Event SpeedChanged(NewSpeed as integer)
    Private _CurrentSpeed As Integer = 0
    Public Overloads Function StartEngine(ByVal CarKey _
                As Integer) As Boolean
        If CarKey = 5 Then 'correct key
            RaiseEvent Started()
            Return True
        Else
            Return False
        End If
    End Function
    Public Sub SpeedUp(ByVal Amount As Integer)
        _CurrentSpeed += Amount
        If _CurrentSpeed > 65 Then
            _CurrentSpeed = 0
            RaiseEvent Stalled()
        End If
        RaiseEvent SpeedChanged( _CurrentSpeed )
    End Sub
End Class
```

In the previous code sample, the Started, Stalled, and SpeedChanged events were created at the top of the class. The writer of the class knows that some code should execute when these events take place, but since the code will vary depending on the user of this class, creating events allows the user to hook into this code.

In the next code snippet, a small console application is using the Car class to demonstrate the events:

```
Module Module1
    Dim WithEvents c As New Car()
    Sub Main()
        Dim x As Integer
        For x = 1 To 10
            c.SpeedUp(15)
        Next
    End Sub
    Public Sub ItStalled() Handles c.Stalled
```

```
            Console.WriteLine("Car Stalled")
        End Sub
        Public Sub DifferentSpeed(ByVal NewSpeed As Integer) _
            Handles c.SpeedChanged
            Console.WriteLine("Speed is now: " & NewSpeed.ToString())
        End Sub
    End Module
```

To use events, the *WithEvents* keyword is required in the variable declaration. This is effectively telling Visual Basic .NET to listen for events that may be raised from this instance of a Car.

To hook into an event, a method is created for the events that need additional code. In the previous example, Started is not used. The method signature must match the method signature that is required by the event. Each event must be a sub (a function is not allowed), the name can be any name you choose, and the arguments must match the arguments defined in the event definition. The Started and Stalled events have no arguments, but the SpeedChanged has an integer argument containing the new speed. Finally, the event methods need to be connected to one or more events via the *Handles* statement. Notice that the ItStalled method Handles c.Stalled, and the DifferentSpeed method handles c.SpeedChanged.

Sometimes is it desirable to use the same method to handle events from many objects. This can also be done by adding additional events after the Handles statement, separated by commas.

What Is a Constructor?

When a new instance of a class is being created, a special method is executed, called the constructor. If a class has been created with no constructors, the Visual Basic .NET compiler will create a default constructor, which will allow the object to be created.

In many cases, variables are required to be initialized when the instance of the class is created. This can be done by creating a custom constructor for the class. A custom constructor is created by creating a method called *New*. For example, using the Car class, the requirement might be to construct a new instance of a Car, passing the VIN (vehicle identification number) to the constructor. After the instance of the Car has been constructed, the VIN may be readable, but not writeable. The following listing shows such an example:

```
Public Class Car
    Public ReadOnly VIN As String
    Public Sub New(ByVal VIN As String)
        Me.VIN = VIN
    End Sub
End Class
'Create a new Car instance
Dim c as new Car("123-ABC-456")
```

The constructor is always a sub and has the name *New*. In this example, the only way to create an instance of the Car class is to pass a VIN into the constructor.

This example fulfills the requirements of encapsulation (protecting data integrity) without using a property. If a variable is created as ReadOnly, the variable can only be changed on the same line as the variable declaration or in the constructor. After the constructor executes, the variable becomes ReadOnly.

Overloaded Constructors

Just as methods may be overloaded, constructors may be overloaded. Overloading constructors does not require the use of the *overloads* keyword. For example, in addition to the custom constructor shown in the previous example, there could also be a requirement for a custom constructor that allows the VIN and Model to be assigned when Car is being instantiated.

```
Public Class Car
    Public ReadOnly VIN As String
    Public ReadOnly Model As String
    Public Sub New(ByVal VIN As String)
        Me.VIN = VIN
    End Sub
    Public Sub New(ByVal VIN As String, ByVal Model As String)
        Me.VIN = VIN
        Me.Model = Model
    End Sub
End Class
'Create a new Car instance
Dim c As New Car("123-ABC-335", "Corvette")
```

Me Keyword

The last two code examples used the keyword Me. *Me* refers to the current instance of the class whose code is currently running. In the previous examples, Me is required because the variables called VIN and Model are defined in two locations: at the class level and at the constructor argument level. When VIN is referred to inside the constructor, the closest VIN variable (constructor argument) is used. To access the VIN that is defined at the class level, Me.VIN is used.

Shared Methods and Variables

When working with classes, it's common to create a variable and assign a new instance of a class to the variable as follows:

```
Dim x as new Car()
```

As each instance of a Car class is created, there is an isolated copy of instance data, such as VIN, Make, Model, Year, and Mileage.

There are some situations in which common data is required, such as a data element that represents the count of Car instances. The count is related to the Car class, so placing a variable inside that Car class makes sense.

Common data may be represented in the Car class by creating a shared variable. The follow code is an example of a private shared variable called _count, a public shared property called Count, and a public shared method called IncrementCount.

```
Public Class Car
    Private Shared _count As Integer
    Public Shared Property Count() As Integer
        Get
            Return _count
        End Get
        Set(ByVal Value As Integer)
            _count = Value
        End Set
    End Property
    Public Shared Sub IncrementCount()
        _count += 1 'add 1 to the count
    End Sub
End Class
```

The public shared members are accessible by using the class name, for example Car.Count and Car.IncrementCount( ), since shared members do not belong to a Car instance.

Inheritance

A class that inherits from another class receives the members of the base class. Figure 4.11 shows an example of inheritance using Unified Modeling Language (UML) with a Vehicle class that inherits from the Object class, and a Motorcycle class that inherits from the Vehicle class. After creating a Motorcycle instance called m, the variable m has all of the derived members. Microsoft IntelliSense is smart enough to display all available members.

This type of inheritance is sometime referred to as *is-a* inheritance. In this example, a Vehicle *is-a* Object, and a Motorcycle *is-a* Vehicle. The Vehicle class contains all of the members that are common to a vehicle. When Motorcycle is derived from the Vehicle class, the only extra members that are needed are the members that are unique to the Motorcycle class.

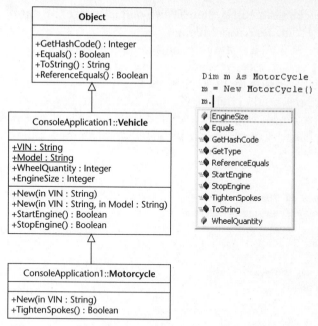

Figure 4.11 Vehicle inherits from Object, Motorcycle inherits from Vehicle. All public members of each class are available as shown when using Visual Basic .NET. The left side is a UML representation of the inheritance. VIN and Model are underlined to denote they are read-only fields.

 The .NET Framework only supports single inheritance. Some languages, such as unmanaged C++, support multiple inheritance, but managing multiple inheritance can become a quandary, especially when multiple base classes have members with the same names. Single inheritance was a design decision across all .NET languages, and there are methods of accomplishing the intent of multiple inheritance, such as the implementation of interfaces (discussed in the *Interfaces* section later in this chapter).

Overriding Methods

In many situations, it may be desirable to override one or more methods in a base class. A common example is the System.Object.ToString method. The default behavior of the ToString method is that it returns the fully qualified name of the current object (Me). In the case of the Motorcycle from Figure 4.11, m.ToString( ) will return *ConsoleApplication1.Motorcycle*.

The Vehicle class can override the ToString method to display the VIN and the Model instead with the following code:

```
Public Class Vehicle
    Inherits Object
    Public ReadOnly VIN As String
    Public ReadOnly Model As String
    Public WheelQuantity As Integer
    Public EngineSize As Integer
    Public Sub New(ByVal VIN As String)
        Me.VIN = VIN
    End Sub
    Public Sub New(ByVal VIN As String, ByVal Model As String)
        Me.VIN = VIN
        Me.Model = Model
    End Sub
    Public Function StartEngine() As Boolean
    End Function
    Public Function StopEngine() As Boolean
    End Function
    Public Overrides Function ToString() As String
        Return "VIN: " & VIN & " - Model: " & Model
    End Function
End Class
```

The ToString method in the Vehicle returns a string with the VIN and the Model. Now that the ToString method is overridden in the Vehicle class, the Vehicle class and any class that derives from Vehicle automatically inherits this new behavior. Using the Motorcycle in Figure 4.11, executing m.ToString( ) returns "VIN: 123 – Model: ". There is no Model because Motorcycle was allowed to be created without a Model.

 To override a method, the base class method must use the *overridable* keyword.

MyBase Keyword

In the previous example, it may have been desirable to return the VIN and Model as well as the fully qualified name of the class. Calls can be made to the original ToString method by using the MyBase keyword as follows:

```
Public Overrides Function ToString() As String
    Dim s as string
    s = "VIN: " & VIN & " - Model: " & Model
    s = s & " - " & MyBase.ToString( )
    Return s
End Function
```

Abstract Methods and Classes

Quite often, a class writer must provide program specification where implementation may vary depending on the class that derives from the class. Abstract methods and classes allow for the separation of the specification from implementation.

Abstract methods may be created in Visual Basic .NET by using the MustOverride keyword, as follows:

```
'part of a class called DrawingShape
Public MustOverride Sub Print( )
```

In this example, a method signature is provided, but there is no implementation code and no End Sub. The idea is that the writer of this class knows that a Print method needs to be called by the application, but does not know the printing requirements for each class. Any class that derives from this class must provide implementation code for this method, even if a simple, empty code block is provided, such as the following:

```
Public class Circle
      Inherits DrawingShape
      Public Overrides Sub Print()
            'provide implementation code
            'here, but just having this code
            'block is good enough.
End Sub
End class
```

The only way that implementation code can be provided for the Print method is to derive a new class from the DrawingShape class. This means that it is no longer possible to create an instance of the DrawingShape. To ensure this functionality, Visual Basic .NET requires the class to be labeled as MustInherit as soon as a single method is labeled as MustOverride. The DrawingShape class must be written as follows:

```
Public MustInherit Class DrawingShape
    Public x As Integer = 0
    Public y As Integer = 0
    Public MustOverride Sub Print()
    Public Overrides Function ToString() As String
        Dim s As String
        s = String.Format("{0} x={1} y={1}", MyBase.ToString(), x, y)
        Return s
    End Function
End Class
```

Notice that the DrawingShape class contains concrete and abstract code. A class does not need to be completely abstract when it is labeled as MustInherit.

Polymorphism

From Greek roots, polymorphism means many forms or many faces. Polymorphism is often required when a general routine, such as a Print method, needs to be executed across many objects, but each object implements its print method differently.

Polymorphism can be accomplished via the following methods:

1. Overriding methods that are labeled as overridable.

2. Overriding methods that are labeled as abstract.

3. Implementing interfaces (discussed in the *Interfaces* section later in this chapter).

Modules

A module is a class that only contains shared members. Members do not need the shared keyword, as they are implicitly shared. Public module members are essentially global members. Modules are not inheritable, and instances of modules cannot be created. Interfaces, which are covered later in this chapter, cannot be implemented on modules. The following is an example of a module:

```
Public Module Utilities
    Public Sub CopyFile(ByVal Src As String, ByVal Dest As String)
        'copy code
    End Sub
    Public Function ReadKeys() As String
        'Read keystrokes from keyboard
    End Function
End Module
```

Notice that the Shared keyword is not used, although both methods are implicitly shared. These methods can be executed from another part of the application by simply using the method name. The following code will work:

```
CopyFile( "C:\Test.txt", "D:\abc.txt" )
```

Structures

Structures are light classes. All structures are derived from System.ValueType. When an instance of a structure is created, memory is allocated onto the stack. When making an assignment, a *deep copy* is done, which means that all data is copied; not just the reference.

Structures support properties, fields, methods, and interfaces. Structures cannot be inherited and cannot have events. The *no parameter* constructor for a structure is automatically created by the Visual Basic .NET compiler and cannot be overridden, which allows the following syntax:

```
Dim z as myStructure 'automatically creates instance
```

Structures can have parameterized constructors, as shown in the following code:

```
Public Structure myStructure
    Public x As Integer
    Public y As Integer
    Public Sub New(ByVal x As Integer, ByVal y As Integer)
        Me.x = x
        Me.y = y
    End Sub
End Structure
```

This example shows a structure called myStructure and its parameterized constructor. An instance of this structure may be created by issuing any of the following commands:

```
Dim z as myStructure 'use the default constructor
Dim z as new myStructure 'also uses the default constructor
Dim z as new myStructure(5,9) 'use parameterized constructor
```

Since structure assignment is done by performing a deep copy, keep a structure limited in size. Depending on how the structure is used, there could be a performance gain to converting structures over 50 bytes in size to classes.

Interfaces

Interfaces can be created and used when it is necessary to separate specification from implementation, which is the basis for polymorphism. In many respects, an interface is similar to an abstract class (a class labeled as MustInherit) that has no concrete members (all methods are labeled as MustOverride). The differences between interfaces and abstract classes are shown in Table 4.3.

The last item in Table 4.3 is probably the most compelling reason to use an interface. Consider the scenario in which an application is being written to maintain a list of cars, and two vendors have written car classes for this application. VendorA supplied a class called GeneralCar and VendorB supplied a class called SportsCar. At some point, a complete list of cars must be printed, based on properties that are unique in each of the car classes. Assumptions are that the source code is unavailable for GeneralCar and SportsCar, and these classes don't derive from a common class that has its source code available.

In this scenario, a new class is created for each of the car classes, called PrintableGeneralCar, which derives from GeneralCar, and PrintableSportsCar, which derives from SportsCar. In addition, an interface has been created called Ireport. (See Figure 4.12).

Table 4.3 Differences between Interfaces and Abstract Classes

INTERFACE	ABSTRACT CLASS
Cannot contain data	Can contain data members, such as variables.
Supports multiple inheritance	Only supports single inheritance.
Cannot provide concrete methods	Can provide concrete methods along with abstract methods.
Does not require a common base class to separate specification from implementation	Requires a common base class to separate specification from implementation.

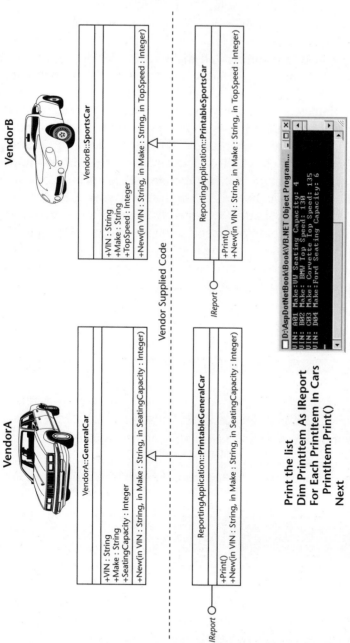

Figure 4.12 Both VendorA and VendorB provide code. A method is needed to print each item, so an interface is created called IReport. Notice that IReport is the data type that is used by PrintItem when moving through the loop. This allows the Print method to be executed, which will have a different output based on the object that executes the Print method.

The code listing is as follows:

```
'VendorA
Public Class GeneralCar
    Public VIN, Make As String
    Public SeatingCapacity As Integer
    Public Sub New(ByVal VIN As String, ByVal Make As String, _
        ByVal SeatingCapacity As Integer)
        Me.VIN = VIN : Me.Make = Make
        Me.SeatingCapacity = SeatingCapacity
    End Sub
End Class
'VendorB
Public Class SportsCar
    Public VIN, Make As String
    Public TopSpeed As Integer
    Public Sub New(ByVal VIN As String, ByVal Make As String, _
        ByVal TopSpeed As Integer)
        Me.VIN = VIN : Me.Make = Make
        Me.TopSpeed = TopSpeed
    End Sub
End Class
'The assumption is that we did not have the above
'code. If we did, we could simply add a Print method
'to the classes.
'
'Here is our code.
Interface IReport
    Sub Print()
End Interface
Public Class PrintableGenerlCar
    Inherits GeneralCar
    Implements IReport
    Public Sub New(ByVal VIN As String, ByVal Make As String, _
        ByVal SeatingCapacity As Integer)
        MyBase.New(VIN, Make, SeatingCapacity)
    End Sub
    Public Sub Print() Implements IReport.Print
        Console.WriteLine("VIN: {0} Make:{1} Seating Capacity: {2}", _
            VIN, Make, SeatingCapacity)
    End Sub
End Class
Public Class PrintableSportsCar
    Inherits SportsCar
    Implements IReport
    Public Sub New(ByVal VIN As String, ByVal Make As String, _
        ByVal TopSpeed As Integer)
        MyBase.New(VIN, Make, TopSpeed)
    End Sub
```

```
        Public Sub Print() Implements IReport.Print
            Console.WriteLine("VIN: {0} Make: {1} Top Speed: {2}", _
                VIN, Make, TopSpeed)
        End Sub
    End Class
```

The following code is an example of using these new classes and the interface. An array of cars is created manually. Next, a loop moves through each item in the loop.

```
Sub Main()
    'Create a list and fill it manually.
    Dim Cars(3) As Object
    Cars(0) = New PrintableGenerlCar("A01", "VW", 4)
    Cars(1) = New PrintableSportsCar("B02", "BMW", 130)
    Cars(2) = New PrintableSportsCar("C03", "Corvette", 135)
    Cars(3) = New PrintableGenerlCar("D04", "Ford", 6)
    'Print the list
    Dim PrintItem As IReport
    For Each PrintItem In Cars
        PrintItem.Print()
    Next
End Sub
```

Since each object in the array has implemented the IReport interface, the code works properly. If an object were placed into the Cars array that did not implement the IReport interface, an exception would be thrown. The better way to write the print loop might be as follows:

```
'Print the list
Dim o As Object
Dim PrintItem As IReport
For Each o In Cars
    If TypeOf (o) Is IReport Then
        PrintItem = CType(o, IReport)
        PrintItem.Print()
        'quicker method...
        'CType(o, IReport).Print()
    End If
Next
```

The *typeof-is* statement tests an object to see if it is, derived from, or implements a particular data type. This example contains a check to see if the variable called *o* implements the IReport interface.

The *CType* statement converts object o to an IReport data type. This can only happen if the original object that was created with the *New* statement supported the IReport interface. In this scenario, both the PrintableGenericCar and the PrintableSportsCar implement the IReport interface.

Enumerations

An enumeration is a name and value collection. Enumerations can be used to eliminate *magic numbers* from your code. The term *magic numbers* refers to the use of numbers as attributes. For example, rather than assigning the word Manager to an employee's position, the number 5 might indicate that the employee is a manager. This saves space in memory and in the database. It also makes comparisons much easier. If a word such as Manager were used, looking for a manager (lower case m) would require conversions before the comparison could take place. The problem with the usage of numbers in code is that the code becomes much less readable. In the following code, the meaning of the number 2 is not very apparent.

```
Dim c as New SportsCar( )
c.DriverType=2 'magic number!
```

If an enumeration were created called DriverTypeEnum, the code could be rewritten with an enumeration name instead of a value as follows:

```
Public Enum DriverTypeEnum
    HighRisk=0
    MediumRisk=1
    LowRisk=2
    NoRisk=9
End Enum
Dim c as New SportsCar( )
c.DriverType=DriverTypeEnum.LowRisk 'no magic number!
```

Notice that the enumeration values do not need to be consecutive numbers. In fact, the numbers do not need to be in any order. If the numbers are omitted, the names will be sequentially numbered, starting from zero.

Working with Collections

The .NET Framework provides several collection types and the ability to create custom collection. Table 4.4 lists some of the common collection types that are available. The .NET collections are located in the System.Collections namespace.

Table 4.4 Common Collection in the .NET Framework

COLLECTION	DESCRIPTION
ArrayList	General purpose, dynamically sized collection.
HashTable	A collection of associated keys and values that are organized based on the hash code of the key. Types stored in HashTable should always override System.Object.GetHashCode( ).
SortedList	Like a dictionary, but the elements can also be accessed by ordinal position (index).
Queue	Represents a standard first-in-first-out (FIFO) queue.
Stack	A last-in-first-out (LIFO) queue that provides push, pop, and peek functionality.
BitArray	Provides a collection of bit values, where *true* indicates that the bit is on (1) and *false* indicates the bit is off (0).

Most collections in .NET are nontyped, which means that they are a collection of System.Object instances. The following code creates a new ArrayList and places a couple of SportsCar objects into it.

```
Dim a As New ArrayList()
Dim bmw As New SportsCar("A01", "BMW", 130)
Dim porsche As New SportsCar("B02", "Porsche", 140)
Dim myCar As SportsCar
a.Add(bmw)
a.Add(porsche)
mycar=a(1) ' get the second one
```

When retrieving an item from a collection, the item will be retrieved as an object. If the project's *Option Strict* setting is set to off, the preceding code will function, because Visual Basic .NET automatically converts the object back to a SportsCar. If the Option Strict setting is set to on, the code must be as follows.

```
mycar= CType(a(1), SportsCar) ' get the second one
```

Referencing External Code Libraries

When writing an application, many times it will be necessary to tell Visual Studio .NET that the application is going to be using code that is in an external .dll file. This code won't be available until a reference is set to the appropriate

.dll file. To set a reference to an external .dll file, click Project, Add Reference. A window will appear with tabs as follows:

.NET. Contains a list of .NET .dll files, where the list is generated by looking into the registry for a folder list and then retrieving a list of files in each folder. Additional folder keys can be placed in the registry at the following location (see Figure 4.13).

```
HKEY_LOCAL_MACHINE\SOFTWARE\Microsoft\.NETFramework\AssemblyFolders\
```

There are existing keys in that location, plus new keys can be added. The new key name doesn't matter; just make sure that the default value of the key points to the folder that will contain .dll files. After adding a registry key, Visual Studio .NET must be restarted for the change to be seen. This tab also provides a browse button that can be used to browse for a .NET .dll file.

COM. Contains a list of COM components that are available. Visual Studio .NET automatically creates proxy class wrappers for each COM component to give .NET code the ability to talk to COM components.

Project. Contains a list of open projects. This option can be used to tell Visual Studio .NET that the current .NET project should be dependent on the project that is selected form this list. When projects are referenced, Visual Studio .NET automatically compiles the projects in the proper order.

After a reference has been set, IntelliSense will be available for all data types, and the .dll will be accessible from the Object Browser.

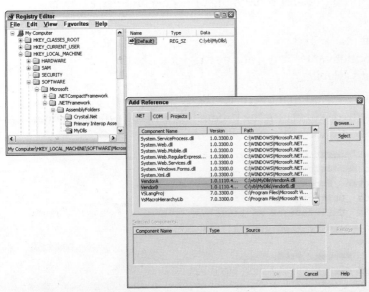

Figure 4.13 To add files to the .NET list, a registry entry called MyDlls was added to point to c:\vb\MyDlls. Visual Studio .NET was restarted and the files are available.

Lab 4.1: Working with Classes

In this lab, you will create a class hierarchy for product of different types. These classes will explore inheritance, encapsulation, and polymorphism.

First, you will create a product class hierarchy in an Inventory project. You will start by creating a base product class and then add two derived product types.

1. Open the OrderEntrySolution from Lab 3.1.

2. Right-click the OrderEntrySolution in the Solution Explorer, and click Check Out. This checks out the complete solution.

3. Add a class file. Right-click the Inventory project in the Solution Explorer, click Add, Add New Item, Class. Type *ProductClasses.vb*, and click Open.

4. Delete the contents of the new class file.

5. You will create a base class called BaseProduct. This class will contain the following data members:

   a. _ProductID, Integer, Public ReadOnly

   b. _ProductName, String, Protected

   c. _UnitPrice, Decimal, Private

   d. _UnitsInStock, Integer, Private

6. Add public properties for each of the protected and private data members.

7. Create a parameterized constructor with arguments called ProductID and ProductName. These arguments initialize the corresponding member variables.

8. Add a public method that overrides the ToString method. The new ToString method will return the product ID and the product name. Your code should look like the following:

```
Public MustInherit Class BaseProduct
    Public ReadOnly ProductID As Integer
    Protected _ProductName As String
    Private _UnitPrice As Decimal
    Private _UnitsInStock As Integer
    Public Property ProductName() As String
        Get
            Return _ProductName
        End Get
```

```
            Set(ByVal Value As String)
                _ProductName = Value
            End Set
        End Property
        Public Property UnitPrice() As String
            Get
                Return _UnitPrice
            End Get
            Set(ByVal Value As String)
                _UnitPrice = Value
            End Set
        End Property
        Public Property UnitsInStock() As String
            Get
                Return _UnitsInStock
            End Get
            Set(ByVal Value As String)
                _UnitsInStock = Value
            End Set
        End Property
        Public Sub New(ByVal ProductID As Integer, _
                ByVal ProductName As String)
            Me.ProductID = ProductID
            _ProductName = ProductName
        End Sub
        Public Overrides Function ToString() As String
            Dim s As String
            s = String.Format("Product ID: {0} Name: {1}", _
                ProductID, _ProductName)
            Return s
        End Function
    End Class
```

9. Add another class called Beverage to this file. This class inherits from the BaseProduct class.

10. Add a parameterized constructor to the Beverage class. The parameterized constructor contains the ProductID and ProductName arguments, and calls the BaseProduct's constructor with these arguments.

11. Add code to override the ToString method of the BaseProduct class. This adds the word Beverage before the output of the BaseProduct's ToString method. Your code should look like the following:

```
Public Class Beverage
    Inherits BaseProduct
    Public Sub New(ByVal ProductID As Integer, _
            ByVal ProductName As String)
        MyBase.New(ProductID, ProductName)
    End Sub
```

```
Public Overrides Function ToString() As String
    Return "Beverage " & MyBase.ToString()
End Function
End Class
```

12. Create a copy of the Beverage class. Rename the class to Confection and change the ToString method to return the word Confection and the output of the BaseProduct ToString method. Your code should look like the following:

```
Public Class Confection
    Inherits BaseProduct
    Public Sub New(ByVal ProductID As Integer, _
            ByVal ProductName As String)
        MyBase.New(ProductID, ProductName)
    End Sub
    Public Overrides Function ToString() As String
        Return "Confection " & MyBase.ToString()
    End Function
End Class
```

13. Save your work.

Next, to test the classes that you just created, you will add a Web page to the Inventory project. On the new page, you will hard-code the creation of several instances of the Beverage and Confection classes, and place the instances into a collection. Finally, you will test the ToString method by displaying the contents of the collection on the page using a label control.

1. Add a Web Form. Right-click the Inventory project in the Solution Explorer and click Add, Add Web Form. *Type ProductList.aspx*, and click Open.

2. Right-click the Form and click View Code.

3. In the Page_Load event method, add code to create a new ArrayList.

4. Add code to create three Beverage instances and three Confection instances and add them to the ArrayList.

5. Add code to loop through the ArrayList, executing the ToString method of System.Object to retrieve the product information. Use the Response.Write to send the output to the browser and be sure to

concatenate an HTML linefeed to each line. Your code should look like the following:

```
Private Sub Page_Load(ByVal sender As System.Object, _
            ByVal e As System.EventArgs) Handles MyBase.Load
        'Put user code to initialize the page here.
        Dim Products As New ArrayList()
        Products.Add(New Beverage(1, "Milk"))
        Products.Add(New Beverage(2, "Juice"))
        Products.Add(New Beverage(3, "Cola"))
        Products.Add(New Confection(4, "Ice Cream"))
        Products.Add(New Confection(5, "Cake"))
        Products.Add(New Confection(6, "Candy"))
        Dim o As Object
        For Each o In Products
            Response.Write(o.ToString() & "<BR>")
        Next
    End Sub
```

6. Right-click the Inventory project in the Solution Explorer. Click Set As Startup Project. Right-click the ProductList.aspx page. Click Set As Start Page.

7. Save your work.

Run the application by pressing F5. Figure 4.14 displays the browser output.

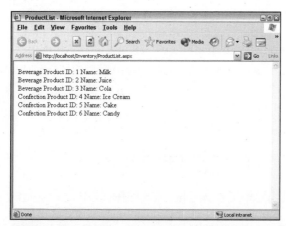

Figure 4.14   Browser output showing the Products collection.

Summary

- The .NET Framework contains the common language runtime and the Base Class Libraries (BCL).

- An assembly is created by compiling a Visual Studio .NET project, and is conceptually similar to the .dll and .exe files of the past, except that it is possible to create a multimodule (file) assembly by using the command-line compiler.

- The assembly contains MSIL code and metadata. The assembly is completely self-describing via the manifest, which is global metadata. In addition to the manifest metadata, the assembly contains type metadata, which describes every data type that has been defined in the assembly.

- MSIL code is compiled to machine code as needed by the JIT compiler.

- Namespaces are used to prevent data type naming collisions.

- The Common Language Specification is a subset of the common type system. All .NET languages must be Common Language Specification-compliant.

- System.Object is the root class for all .NET classes.

- The .NET data types are either reference or value types. Reference types are allocated on the garbage collected heap and assignments create a shallow (reference) copy. Value types are allocated on the stack and assignments create a deep (full bitwise) copy.

- Classes are reference types. Structures are value types.

- To access the current instance of an object, use the keyword *Me*.

- To access the parent, or base class of the current class, use the keyword *MyBase*.

- Interfaces, overridden methods, and abstract methods may be used to achieve polymorphism.

- Enumerations should be used in an application instead of hard-coded numbers.

- The .NET Framework provided several types of collection, which are located in the System.Collections namespace.

- To access code in an external .dll file, a reference must be assigned to the file.

Review Questions

1. What class is the root to all .NET classes?

2. What is the benefit of using enumerations in your code?

3. Where are value types created?

4. Where are reference types created?

5. How can you get access to the current instance of the class that code is running?

6. How can you get access to the current class's parent class?

7. Name three ways of achieving polymorphic behavior.

8. What keyword is used to create a variable that belongs to a class instead of an instance of the class?

9. What is the subname of a class' constructor?

Answers to Review Questions

1. System.Object.
2. They eliminate magic numbers in code.
3. On the stack.
4. On the garbage collected heap.
5. Use the keyword Me.
6. Use the keyword MyBase.
7. Interfaces, overridden methods, and abstract (using MustOverride) methods.
8. Shared.
9. New.

CHAPTER

5

Working with Web Server Controls

The previous chapters focused heavily on creating a foundation for ASP.NET development. It's now time to use that knowledge to look at Web Server controls. Web Server Controls are widgets that may be added to an ASP.NET Web page to give the user the ability to interact with the Web application. Previous versions of ASP contained controls that could be dropped onto a Web page, but these controls didn't offer much functionality. The new ASP.NET Web controls offer lots of functionality. Some of the new ASP.NET Web Server Controls include the calendar, ad rotators, validators, data grids, and data list controls.

All of the Web server controls are derived, or inherited from, the System .Web.UI.WebControls.WebControl class. This class is derived from the System .Web.UI.Control class. Each of these classes has a number of properties. This chapter starts by identifying many of the common properties that are available through inheritance. After that, it looks in detail at many of the server controls that are available in Visual Studio .NET.

Classroom Q & A

Q: Our company standard requires the use of an external Cascading Style Sheet to set the appearance of our Web pages. Are Cascading Style Sheets still usable in ASP.NET?

A: Yes. Cascading Style Sheets are still useable in ASP.NET. The Web server controls even expose a CssClass property, which allows you to easily assign a named style to the control.

Q: I tried setting the tab order of my Web server controls, and although the controls seemed to be in order, I couldn't find a way of setting the control that will initially have focus when the page is displayed. Is there a way to accomplish this?

A: Yes there is, although it's not as straightforward as simply setting the tab order. See the TabIndex information in this chapter for a small JavaScript snippet that will set the initial focus to a control of your choice.

Q: It's my understanding that ASP.NET provides validator controls. I can use them for most pages, but I have one control that needs special validation. Is there a way to link this special validation routine into the ASP.NET validation?

A: Yes. The CustomValidator control provides a link between the ASP.NET validation and your special routine. There are several code samples in this chapter.

The Web Server Control Hierarchy

All of the Web server controls that are covered in this chapter inherit from System.Web.UI.WebControls.WebControl, which inherits from System.Web.UI.Control. Figure 5.1 shows the Web server control hierarchy. This chapter views the members of Control and WebControl first. After these members are covered, this chapter will look at the individual controls.

System.Web.UI.Control

This System.Web.UI.Control class provides the base functionality for all of the HTML server controls, Web server controls, and the Web page itself. This section looks at each of the members of this class.

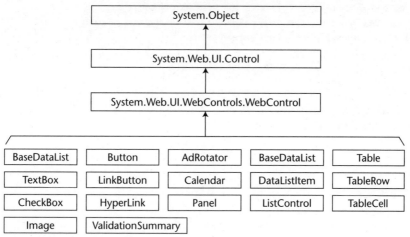

Figure 5.1   The Web server control hierarchy.

ClientID

A client identifier is automatically generated by ASP.NET for every server control. This identifier can be used for client-side scripting operations. If a name is assigned to the ID property, the ID property will override the value of this property. The following code will display a list of the controls with their corresponding ClientID property.

```
Private Sub Page_Load(ByVal sender As System.Object, _
        ByVal e As System.EventArgs) Handles MyBase.Load
    Response.Write("<h3>Control ClientID</h3>")
    ' Get the list of all controls.
    Dim c As Control
    For Each c In Me.Controls
        Response.Write("The ClientID is: " & c.ClientID & "<BR>")
    Next
End Sub
```

Controls

The Controls property gets the collection of child controls that belong to the current control. For the Web page, this is a collection of the controls on the page. This property can be used to add and delete controls, as well as to iterate through the child control collection. The following code adds a TextBox and a Button to the page's form control.

```
Private Sub Page_Load(ByVal sender As System.Object, _
        ByVal e As System.EventArgs) Handles MyBase.Load
    Dim c As Control = Me.FindControl("Form1")
    Dim t As New TextBox()
    t.Text = DateTime.Now.ToShortDateString()
    Dim b As New Button()
    b.Text = "Submit"
    c.Controls.Add(t)
    c.Controls.Add(b)
End Sub
```

EnableViewState

The EnableViewState property must be enabled to maintain its state across HTTP requests. If it is not necessary to save state, set this property to false. The following is an example of a TextBox that loads data from a database every time the page is loaded, so ViewState is not required. The example also has an example of a TextBox that only loads data from a database on the first time that the page is requested, so ViewState is required.

```
Private Sub Page_Load(ByVal sender As System.Object, _
        ByVal e As System.EventArgs) Handles MyBase.Load
    'TextBox1 is loaded from the database
    'on every page load, so there is no need for ViewState.
    TextBox1.Text = LoadTextBox1FromDB()
    TextBox1.EnableViewState = False
    'TextBox2 is only loaded from the database
    'on the first time to the page,
    'so ViewState is required.
    TextBox2.EnableViewState = True
    If Not IsPostBack Then
        TextBox2.Text = LoadTextBox2FromDB()
    End If
End Sub
```

ID

The ID is a changeable property that is used as the programmatic identifier that the Web developer assigns to a control. Note that placing spaces in this property will cause an ASP.NET parser error. If a control does not have an ID, it is still available in code from its parent controls collection or the FindControl method of the parent. The following code recursively writes the ID of all controls to the page.

```
Private Sub Page_Load(ByVal sender As System.Object, _
        ByVal e As System.EventArgs) Handles MyBase.Load
```

```
        RecurseControls(Me, "")
    End Sub
    Public Sub RecurseControls(ByVal c As Control, ByVal f As String)
        Dim ch As Control
        Dim i As String
        i = IIf(c.ID = "", "-undefined", c.ID)
        Response.Write(f & i & "<BR>")
        For Each ch In c.Controls
            'recurse, and add 3 spaces for
            'formatted output
            RecurseControls(ch, f & "   ")
        Next
    End Sub
```

NamingContainer

The NamingContainer property for a control contains a reference to the parent control above it in the control hierarchy that created a unique namespace. The unique namespace ensures unique ID values, especially with list controls, such as the DataGrid. A control can create a unique namespace by implementing the INamingContainer interface.

The following code recursively writes the NamingContainer control's ID for all controls on the page. The page contains a DataGrid called DataGrid1, which is the NamingContainer for all of the controls that it creates when populating the grid.

```
    Private Sub Page_Load(ByVal sender As System.Object, _
            ByVal e As System.EventArgs) Handles MyBase.Load
        Dim evlog As New Diagnostics.EventLog("Application")
        DataGrid1.DataSource = evlog.Entries
        DataGrid1.DataBind()
        RecurseControls(Me, "")
    End Sub
    Public Sub RecurseControls(ByVal c As Control, ByVal f As String)
        Dim ch As Control
        Dim i As String
        If c.NamingContainer Is Nothing Then
            i = "-undefined container"
        Else
            If c.NamingContainer.ID = "" Then
                i = "-undefined ID"
            Else
                i = c.NamingContainer.ID
            End If
        End If
        Response.Write(f & i & "<BR>")
        For Each ch In c.Controls
            'recurse, and add 3 spaces for
```

```
                    'formatted output
                    RecurseControls(ch, f & "   ")
        Next
    End Sub
```

Page

The Page property contains a reference to the .aspx page that hosts the control. This property can be used by a control developer to get access to current page properties. Although this is a changeable property, it's better to change the Page property indirectly by adding the control to the Page's form controls collection. The following code displays the Page name of a TextBox called TextBox1.

```
Private Sub Page_Load(ByVal sender As System.Object, _
        ByVal e As System.EventArgs) Handles MyBase.Load
    'This code is on a page called WebForm1.aspx.vb.
    'The output is WebForm1_aspx.
    Response.Write(TextBox1.Page.ToString())
End Sub
```

Parent

The Parent property returns a read-only reference to the parent of the current control. Every control has a controls collection, which allows controls to be added to and removed from it. Since all ASP.NET controls must be located in a form, the form will be the parent to any control that is dropped onto a page. The following code displays the parent ID of a TextBox called TextBox1 that has been placed on a page.

```
Private Sub Page_Load(ByVal sender As System.Object, _
        ByVal e As System.EventArgs) Handles MyBase.Load
    Dim c As Control = FindControl("TextBox1")
    Dim p As Control = c.Parent
    Response.Write("Parent: " & p.ID)
End Sub
```

Site

The Site property contains a reference to the ISite information, which provides a communication mechanism between components and their container. This also provides a way for a container to manage its controls.

TemplateSourceDirectory

The Template Source Directory property returns the name of the virtual directory that the page or control is in. This can be converted to the actual path by using the MapPathSecure function. The following code displays the full path to the virtual directory that the current page is in.

```
Private Sub Page_Load(ByVal sender As System.Object, _
        ByVal e As System.EventArgs) Handles MyBase.Load
    Response.Write("The full path of the virtual directory is " & _
    MapPathSecure(Me.TemplateSourceDirectory) & "<BR>")
End Sub
```

UniqueID

This property returns the fully qualified name of the control. The difference between this property and the ID property is that the UniqueID property is generated automatically and contains the NamingContainer information.

The following code recursively writes the control's UniqueID and ID for all controls on the page. The page contains a DataGrid called DataGrid1, which is the NamingContainer for all of the controls that it creates when populating the grid.

```
Private Sub Page_Load(ByVal sender As System.Object, _
        ByVal e As System.EventArgs) Handles MyBase.Load
    Dim evlog As New Diagnostics.EventLog("Application")
    DataGrid1.DataSource = evlog.Entries
    DataGrid1.DataBind()
    RecurseControls(Me, "")
End Sub
Public Sub RecurseControls(ByVal c As Control, ByVal f As String)
    Dim ch As Control
    Response.Write(f & c.UniqueID & " - " & c.ID & "<BR>")
    For Each ch In c.Controls
        'recurse, and add 3 spaces for
        'formatted output
        RecurseControls(ch, f & "   ")
    Next
End Sub
```

Visible

The Visible property is a changeable property that indicates whether a control should be rendered on the page. If this property is set to false, the control will not generate any client-side code. If the Layout property of a page is configured for FlowLayout, the missing control may cause any following controls to shift upward on the page.

The following code sets the visible property of a Panel control called Panel1, to false when Button1 is clicked. This will hide Panel1 and all of the controls that it contains.

```
Private Sub Button1_Click(ByVal sender As System.Object, _
    ByVal e As System.EventArgs) Handles Button1.Click
    Panel1.Visible = False
End Sub
```

System.Web.UI.WebControls.WebControl

This class inherits from the System.Web.UI.Control class and provides base functionality all of the controls in the System.Web.UI.WebControls namespace. Most of the properties that are exposed by this control affect the appearance of the control. This section will look at the WebControl members.

AccessKey

The AccessKey property sets the hotkey for quick access to the control. For example, if the letter D is assigned to the AccessKey property of a TextBox, pressing Alt+D will set the focus to that control. This property may only be set to a single character or left empty. If an attempt is made to assign multiple characters to the property, an exception will be thrown. The following code assigns AccessKey values to Button and TextBox controls.

```
Private Sub Page_Load(ByVal sender As System.Object, _
    ByVal e As System.EventArgs) Handles MyBase.Load
    Button1.AccessKey = "1"
    Button2.AccessKey = "2"
    TextBox1.AccessKey = "C"
    TextBox2.AccessKey = "D"
End Sub
```

Attributes

The Attributes property is a changeable collection of all of the attributes that are included in the control's opening HTML tag. This property can be used to assign and retrieve the attributes of a control. This can provide another method of persisting data between calls to the Web server.

♦ Cascading Style Sheets

Many of the WebControl properties are styles that are applied directly to the control. Rather than set the styles of each control separately, it's usually better to create an external Cascading Style Sheet (CSS) to obtain a consistent look and feel across the Web site.

Styles can be created for each HTML tag. For example, a style can be created for the <H1> tag to give the header tag a completely new look. For Web server controls that often generate many HTML tags as they are created, it may be more desirable to create a named style for each Web server control and nest the tag styles within the name style. This keeps the style of a table from interfering with the style of a DataGrid, which produces an HTML table. A named style is called a *css class*.

When a new ASP.NET project is created in Visual Studio .NET, a file called Styles.css is added to the project. By default, this is not used, but can be implemented with minimum effort. Open the Styles.css page, add the desired styles, and then save the file. Open each .aspx file, and drag and drop the Sytes.css onto the .aspx page.

This will add the following <link> tag into the <head> tag of the .aspx page.

```
<LINK href="Styles.css" type=text/css rel=stylesheet>
```

Close and reopen the .aspx page to see the effect of adding the Styles.css link. The same external style sheet can be applied to many .aspx pages.

Note that styles that are assigned directly to a Web server control will override any styles that are in the Styles.css page.

In the following code, a TextBox called TextBox1 has been placed in the upper corner of the page. A Button called Button1 is also on the page. When TextBox1 is clicked, a client-side script will generate a pop-up message. When Button1 is clicked, the style of TextBox1 is altered, which moves the control down on the page.

```
Private Sub Page_Load(ByVal sender As System.Object, _
    ByVal e As System.EventArgs) Handles MyBase.Load
    TextBox1.Attributes("onclick") = _
        "javascript:alert('TextBox1 Clicked');"
End Sub
Private Sub Button1_Click(ByVal sender As System.Object, _
    ByVal e As System.EventArgs) Handles Button1.Click
    TextBox1.Attributes("style") = _
        "LEFT: 200px; POSITION: absolute; TOP: 300px"
End Sub
```

BackColor, BorderColor, and ForeColor

The BackColor, BorderColor, and ForeColor properties set the color of the control by using the Color class, which is located in the System.Drawing namespace. The client-side code will contain a style attribute that sets the *background-color* as required.

The following code assigns a BackColor to TextBox1 and TextBox2, and then clears the BackColor of TextBox1.

```
Private Sub Page_Load(ByVal sender As System.Object, _
    ByVal e As System.EventArgs) Handles MyBase.Load
    'Set color to Red using well-known color
    TextBox1.BackColor = Color.Red
    'Set color to Green using R,G,B settings
    TextBox2.BackColor = Color.FromArgb(0, 255, 0)
    'Clear the color setting.
    TextBox1.BackColor = Color.Empty
End Sub
```

BorderStyle

The BorderStyle property is used to view and change the style of the border to a setting from the BorderStyle enumeration. Table 5.1 contains a list of the BorderStyle enumeration members.

Table 5.1 BorderStyle Enumeration Members

BORDERSTYLE MEMBER	DESCRIPTION
NotSet	The style is not set. This is the default.
None	No border.
Dotted	Provide a dotted-line border.
Dashed	Provide a dashed-line border.
Solid	Provide a solid-line border.
Double	Provide a solid double-line border.
Groove	Provide a grooved border, which gives a sunken border appearance.
Ridge	Provide a ridged border for a raised border appearance.
Inset	Provide an inset border for a sunken control appearance.
Outset	Provide an outset border for a raised control appearance.

The following code shows an example of setting TextBox1 to a Dotted Border-Style and TextBox2 to a Double BorderStyle.

```
Private Sub Page_Load(ByVal sender As System.Object, _
    ByVal e As System.EventArgs) Handles MyBase.Load
    TextBox1.BorderStyle = BorderStyle.Dotted
    TextBox2.BorderStyle = BorderStyle.Double
End Sub
```

Note that when using Windows XP, the default theme overrides these settings. If the desktop theme is set to Windows Classic, the different border styles can be seen in the browser.

BorderWidth

The BorderWidth property displays and changes the width of the Web server control border. This property uses the unit class when making setting changes. An exception will be thrown if the unit contains a negative number. The following code sets the BorderWidth of TextBox1 and displays *4 - Pixel* in TextBox1.

```
Private Sub Page_Load(ByVal sender As System.Object, _
    ByVal e As System.EventArgs) Handles MyBase.Load
    TextBox1.BorderWidth = New Unit(4, UnitType.Pixel)
    Dim u As Unit
    u = TextBox1.BorderWidth
    TextBox1.Text = u.Value.ToString() & " - " & u.Type.ToString()
End Sub
```

ControlStyle and ControlStyleCreated

The ControlStyle property is a read-only property that retrieves the current style settings of a control. This property returns a Style object. Note that this property does not take external styles that are applied to a page into account.

The ControlStyleCreated property is a read-only property that returns a Boolean value that indicates whether a ControlStyle has been created for the current contol.

The following code displays *Green 4 - Pixel* in TextBox1 if the ControlStyle Created is true.

```
Private Sub Page_Load(ByVal sender As System.Object, _
    ByVal e As System.EventArgs) Handles MyBase.Load
    TextBox1.BackColor = Color.Green
```

```
    TextBox1.BorderWidth = New Unit(4, UnitType.Pixel)
    'Get the style from TextBox1.
    Dim s As Style = TextBox1.ControlStyle
    If TextBox1.ControlStyleCreated Then
            'Display the BackColor and the Borderwidth info
            TextBox1.Text = s.BackColor.Name & " " _
            & s.BorderWidth.Value.ToString() & " - " _
            & s.BorderWidth.Type.ToString()
        End If
    End Sub
```

CssClass

The CssClass Property is a changeable property that assigns a class name (a named style) to the current control. Cascading style sheet classes can be created in an external style sheet file or in the Web page by placing <style> tags in the <head> of the Web page.

The following code sets the CssClass of TextBox1 to a class called *TextBox* in an external style sheet.

```
Private Sub Page_Load(ByVal sender As System.Object, _
    ByVal e As System.EventArgs) Handles MyBase.Load
    TextBox1.CssClass = "TextBox"
End Sub
```

Enabled

Enabled is a changeable property that enables or disables a control. Setting this property to false locks and dims the control. Not all Web server controls support this property.

Changing this setting will cause the setting to propagate down to the child controls.

The following code toggles the enabled state of TextBox1.

```
Private Sub Button1_Click(ByVal sender As System.Object, _
        ByVal e As System.EventArgs) Handles Button1.Click
    TextBox1.Enabled = Not TextBox1.Enabled
End Sub
```

Font

The Font property returns a reference to a FontInfo object, which contains the font attribute for the current control. Table 5.2 contains a list of the FontInfo members. Note that the overlined member does not work properly on pre-Internet Explorer 4.0 browsers.

Table 5.2   FontInfo Members That Can be Assigned to a WebControl

FONTINFO MEMBERS	DESCRIPTION
Bold	Gets or sets the bold setting
Italic	Gets or sets the italic setting
Name	Gets or sets the primary font name
Names	Gets or sets an ordered array of font names
Overline	Gets or sets the overlined setting
Size	Gets or sets the font size
Strikeout	Gets or sets the strikethrough setting
Underline	Gets or sets the underlined setting

The following code assigns new font settings to TextBox1 and then displays the settings in the TextBox.control called Label1.

```
Private Sub Page_Load(ByVal sender As System.Object, _
        ByVal e As System.EventArgs) Handles MyBase.Load
    With TextBox1.Font
        .Bold = True
        .Name = "Arial"
        .Size = New FontUnit(FontSize.XXSmall)
        TextBox1.Text = "Bold: " & .Bold.ToString() & _
        " - Name: " & .Name & _
        " - Size: " & .Size.ToString()
    End With
End Sub
```

Height, Width

The Height and Width properties are changeable settings that set the Height and Width of a control. These properties are nonstandard HTML properties and some controls, such as the Label, HyperLink, and LinkButton, will not be rendered properly with pre-Internet Explorer 4.0 browsers.

The following code assigns a new Height and Width to TextBox1.

```
Private Sub Page_Load(ByVal sender As System.Object, _
    ByVal e As System.EventArgs) Handles MyBase.Load
    TextBox1.Height = New Unit(40, UnitType.Pixel)
    TextBox1.Width = New Unit(50, UnitType.Percentage)
End Sub
```

Style

The Style property returns a reference to a collection of text attributes that will be rendered as a style attribute on the outermost tag of the WebControl. Note that style settings that are explicitly placed on the WebControl, such as Back-Color and BorderColor, will not be included in this collection and will override the items in this collection.

The following code moves TextBox1 by 10 units when Button1 is clicked and then displays all of the items in the Style collection in Label1.

```
Private Sub Button1_Click(ByVal sender As System.Object, _
        ByVal e As System.EventArgs) Handles Button1.Click
    Dim u As New Unit(TextBox1.Style("LEFT"))
    u = New Unit(u.Value + 10, u.Type)
    TextBox1.Style("LEFT") = u.ToString()
    Dim s As String
    Label1.Text = ""
    For Each s In TextBox1.Style.Keys
        Label1.Text &= s & ": " & TextBox1.Style(s) & "<BR>"
    Next
End Sub
```

TabIndex

The TabIndex property sets and gets the tab order of controls on the page. When a page is rendered, the address bar will be the fist item to have the focus. Each time the tab key is pressed, the focus will move from control to control, starting from the lowest, positive, nonzero number.

It is often desirable to set a control to have the focus when the page is loaded. The following code sets the tab order and then sets the initial focus to TextBox1 by emitting a small JavaScript routine that will execute at the browser when the page is first loaded.

```
Private Sub Page_Load(ByVal sender As System.Object, _
        ByVal e As System.EventArgs) Handles MyBase.Load
    'Set tab order
    TextBox1.TabIndex = 1
    TextBox2.TabIndex = 2
    Button1.TabIndex = 3
    'This code sets the initial focus to TextBox1.
    Dim s As String
    s = "<script type='text/javascript'>"
    s += "document.getElementById('TextBox1').focus();"
    s += "</script>"
    Me.Page.RegisterStartupScript("FocusController", s)
End Sub
```

ToolTip

The ToolTip property creates a ToolTip for the current control. The ToolTip will be displayed when the mouse cursor hovers over the control.

The following code adds a ToolTip to TextBox1, which will be displayed when the mouse cursor is hovered over TextBox1.

```
Private Sub Page_Load(ByVal sender As System.Object, _
    ByVal e As System.EventArgs) Handles MyBase.Load
    TextBox1.ToolTip = "Enter your full name."
End Sub
```

Label Control

The Label control is a placeholder for text that will be displayed on the Web page. The primary property for this control is the Text property. This control renders text and HTML tags that are placed into the Text property.

TextBox Control

The TextBox control allows data entry and retrieval. Table 5.3 shows a list of attributes for this control.

Table 5.3   TextBox Control Member Properties

TEXTBOX MEMBER	DESCRIPTION
AutoPostBack	Changeable value indicating whether an automatic postback to the server will occur when the user changes the content of the text box. The default is false.
Columns	Changeable value containing the display width of the text box in characters. The default is 0 (not set).
MaxLength	Changeable value containing the maximum number of characters allowed.
ReadOnly	Changeable value indicating whether the Text property can be changed.
Rows	Changeable value containing the display height of a multiline text box.

(continued)

Table 5.3 *(continued)*

TEXTBOX MEMBER	DESCRIPTION
Text	Changeable value that displays the text content.
TextMode	Changeable value that controls the behavior mode of the text box. This can be set to SingleLine, MultiLine, or Password. The default is SingleLine.
Wrap	Changeable value that controls the word wrapping in the text box.

The only event that is exposed by the TextBox is the TextChanged Event. This event will be raised when the TextBox loses focus if AutoPostBack is set to true. If AutoPostBack is set to false (default), this event will be raised when a control causes a postback to the server.

The following code set the TextMode of TextBox1 to TextMode.Password. In addition, the TextMode of TextBox2 is set to TextMode.MultiLine, and the Rows are set to display 3 rows.

```
Private Sub Page_Load(ByVal sender As System.Object, _
    ByVal e As System.EventArgs) Handles MyBase.Load
    TextBox1.TextMode = TextBoxMode.Password
    TextBox2.TextMode = TextBoxMode.MultiLine
    TextBox2.Rows = 3
End Sub
```

Button and LinkButton Control

The Button control creates a push button on the page. The LinkButton creates a button that looks like a hyperlink, but has the same functionality as the Button control. These controls can be used as a submit or command button. Table 5.4 shows the properties of the Button.

Table 5.4 Button and LinkButton Control Properties

CONTROL MEMBERS	DESCRIPTION
CausesValidation	Changeable value indicating whether validation is performed when the button is clicked.
CommandArgument	Changeable value that defines an optional parameter passed to the Command event along with the associated CommandName.

Table 5.4 *(continued)*

CONTROL MEMBERS	DESCRIPTION
CommandName	Changeable value that contains the command name associated with the button that is passed to the Command event.
Text	Changeable value that displays the text on the face of the button.

As a submit button, the click event submits the page data back to the server. The Click event method can contain executable code.

It may be desirable to configure a control as a command button when the page has many buttons being dynamically created on the page. Each command button can have its own command name and command event arguments. All of the command buttons will have a Command event, which calls the same event method procedure. Table 5.5 lists the events that are available.

The following code dynamically adds three Button controls into a Label control and attaches to the ButtonCommand event method. Instead of a for loop, this may be a loop that iterates a customer table, adding buttons for each customer. When any button is pressed, the ButtonCommand executes, which populates TextBox1 with the CommandName and CommandArgument.

```
Private Sub Page_Load(ByVal sender As System.Object, _
    ByVal e As System.EventArgs) Handles MyBase.Load
    Dim x As Integer
    For x = 1 To 3
        Dim b As New Button()
        b.Text = "Add " & x.ToString()
        b.CommandName = "NewOrder"
        b.CommandArgument = "CustomerID=" & x.ToString()
        AddHandler b.Command, AddressOf ButtonCommand
        Label1.Controls.Add(b)
    Next
End Sub
Private Sub ButtonCommand(ByVal sender As Object, _
    ByVal e As System.Web.UI.WebControls.CommandEventArgs)
    TextBox1.Text = e.CommandName & " - " & e.CommandArgument
End Sub
```

Table 5.5 Button and LinkButton Events

CONTROL EVENTS	DESCRIPTION
Click	Occurs when the button is clicked.
Command	Occurs when the button is clicked.

Notice the use of the AddHandler command to attach an event to a method. This allows the events from many object to be dynamically added to a single method.

HyperLink Control

The HyperLink control allows page navigation through the HyperLink's NavigateURL property. The NavigateURL property can be set from the code-behind page and may contrain a constructed URL. Table 5.6 contains a list of the HyperLink control properties. The difference between the HyperLink control and the LinkButton is that when the HyperLink is clicked, the NavigateURL is immediately executed without posting data back to the server. The HyperLink control is usually the better solution when the NavigateURL is an off-site URL.

Another interesting feature of the HyperLink control is the Target property. The use of _blank_ opens a new browser window. This can allow detail or help pages to display in a separate window, while keeping the existing page open in the original browser window.

The following code sample shows how to program the Page_Load method of the code-behind page. This sample assumes that the Web Form page contains a HyperLink control called HyperLink1.

```
Private Sub Page_Load(ByVal sender As System.Object, _
        ByVal e As System.EventArgs) Handles MyBase.Load
    'Put user code to initialize the page here
    Dim OrderID as Integer
    'Assign OrderID to a value obtained from the database.
    HyperLink1.NavigateUrl = _
        "OrderDetails.aspx?OrderID=" & OrderID
    HyperLink1.Target = "_blank"
End Sub
```

This code builds and sets the NavigateURL, typically based on database query results. The Hyperlink also has a Target property, which is the type HTML target attribute. When set to _blank_, a new browser window is opened to contain the OrderDetails page.

Table 5.6   HyperLink Control Properties

HYPERLINK PROPERTIES	DESCRIPTION
ImageURL	Changeable value containing the URL to an optional image to display in lieu of the text.
NavigateURL	Changeable value containing the URL to go to when the link is clicked.

Table 5.6 *(continued)*

HYPERLINK PROPERTIES	DESCRIPTION
Target	Changeable value containing the name of the window or frame to display the NavigateURL in. This property also supports the following special names. **_blank.** Open new browser window. **_parent.** Open in parent frame. **_self.** Open in same window (default). **_top.** Open in browser window with no frames.
Text	Changeable value containing the text to display at the browser.

Image and ImageButton Controls

The Image control is capable of displaying an image on the page. The Image-Button control inherits from the Image control and adds button click functionality to the Image control. Table 5.7 lists the properties of these controls.

Table 5.7 Image and ImageButton Properties

MEMBERS	IMAGE	IMAGEBUTTON	DESCRIPTION
AlternateText	X	X	Displays alternate text when the image cannot be displayed. Browsers that support ToolTips will display this in the ToolTips.
CausesValidation		X	Changeable value indicating whether validation is performed when the button is clicked.
CommandArgument		X	Changeable value that defines an optional parameter passed to the Command event along with the associated CommandName.
CommandName		X	Changeable value that contains the command name associated with the button that is passed to the Command event.

(continued)

Table 5.7   *(continued)*

MEMBERS	IMAGE	IMAGEBUTTON	DESCRIPTION
ImageAlign	X	X	Changeable value that contains the alignment of the Image control in relation to other elements on the Web page.
ImageUrl	X	X	Changeable value that contains the address of the image to be displayed.

The ImageButton control raises the same events as the Button control, but the ImageButton control passes the x and y coordinates as part of the System .Web.UI.ImageClickEventArgs in the Click event.

The following code sets the ImageButton control's ImageUrl property and places the x and y coordinates of the mouse click into TextBox1.

```
Private Sub Page_Load(ByVal sender As System.Object, _
    ByVal e As System.EventArgs) Handles MyBase.Load
    ImageButton1.ImageUrl = "myLogo.gif"
    ImageButton1.ImageAlign = ImageAlign.Middle
End Sub
Private Sub ImageButton1_Click(ByVal sender As System.Object, _
        ByVal e As System.Web.UI.ImageClickEventArgs) _
    Handles ImageButton1.Click
    TextBox1.Text = "X: " & e.X.ToString() & _
        " Y: " & e.Y.ToString()
End Sub
```

CheckBox and RadioButton Controls

The CheckBox control displays a check box that returns a true or false value. The RadioButton inherits from CheckBox and places a radio button on the page. RadioButtons are intended to be placed into a group where only one RadioButton is true in the group. Table 5.8 show the properties of these controls.

The only event that is exposed by the CheckBox and RadioButton is the CheckChanged Event. This event will be raised when the control changes state if AutoPostBack is set to true. If AutoPostBack is set to false (default), this event will be raised when a control causes a postback to the server.

The following code tests three RadioButtons to see which one is checked and places the result into a Label control.

```
Private Sub Button1_Click(ByVal sender As System.Object, _
    ByVal e As System.EventArgs) Handles Button1.Click
    If RadioButton1.Checked Then
        Label1.Text = "1"
    ElseIf RadioButton2.Checked Then
        Label1.Text = "2"
    ElseIf RadioButton3.Checked Then
        Label1.Text = "3"
    End If
End Sub
```

The next code snippet tests three CheckBoxes to see which ones are checked and places the result into a Label control.

```
Private Sub Button1_Click(ByVal sender As System.Object, _
    ByVal e As System.EventArgs) Handles Button1.Click
    Label1.Text = ""
    If CheckBox1.Checked Then Label1.Text &= "1"
    If CheckBox2.Checked Then Label1.Text &= "2"
    If CheckBox3.Checked Then Label1.Text &= "3"
End Sub
```

Table 5.8 CheckBox and RadioButton Properties

CONTROL MEMBER	CHECKBOX	RADIOBUTTON	DESCRIPTION
AutoPostBack	X	X	Changeable value indicating whether an automatic postback to the server will occur when the user changes the content of the text box. The default is false.
Checked	X	X	Changeable value that indicates if the control is checked.
GroupName		X	Changeable value that contains the name of the group to which the radio button belongs.
Text	X	X	Changeable value that displays the text beside the control.
TextAlign	X	X	Changeable value that contains the alignment of the text label associated with the control.

ListControl Abstract Class

The ListControl is an abstract control class that provides most of the base functionality for ListBox, DropDownList, RadioButtonList, and CheckBoxList. (See Figure 5.2.) The ListControl contains a property called Items, which is used by the derived classes. The Items property is a collection of ListItems. The Items can be manually populated within Visual Studio .NET, or programmatically, and the list can be data bound (connected to data). Table 5.9 displays a list of properties that the ListControl provides.

Table 5.9 ListControl Properties

LISTCONTROL PROPERTY	DESCRIPTION
AutoPostBack	Changeable value indicating whether an automatic postback to the server will occur when the user changes the content of the text box. The default is false.
DataMember	Changeable value containing the specific table in the DataSource to bind (connect) to the control.
DataSource	Changeable value containing the data source that populates the items of the list control.
DataTextField	Changeable value containing the field from the data source that will provide the Text property of the list items.
DataTextFormatString	Changeable value containing the formatting string used to control how data bound to the list control is displayed.
DataValueField	Changeable value containing the field of the data source that will populate the Value property of the list items.
Items	Changeable collection of ListItem objects that will be displayed in the control. See Table 5.10 for ListItem properties.
SelectedIndex	Changeable value containing the lowest ordinal index of the selected items in the list. If no items are selected, this property will contain -1. When assigning a value to this property, all other selections will be cleared. When using the CheckBoxList, it may be more desirable to change the Selected state of the ListItem.
SelectedItem	Changeable value containing the selected item with the lowest index in the list control. When using the CheckBoxList, it may be more desirable to iterate through the ListItems to get each item's selected state.

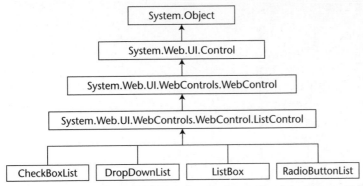

Figure 5.2 The ListControl hierarchy. The items that inherit from ListControl automatically contain the ListControl's behavior.

The ListControl provides an event called SelectedIndexChanged. Since AutoPostBack is set to false by default, this event will not be raised until a different control posts back to the server. If AutoPostBack is enabled, everytime a new item is selected, this event will post back to the server.

Each of the list controls contains an Items collection, which is a collection of ListItem objects. Table 5.10 has a list of the properties that are available on the ListItem class.

The RadioButtonList and CheckBoxList Controls

RadioButtonList and CheckBoxList are derived from ListControl and share most of its properties. Although RadioButton and CheckBox offer more layout flexibility than RadioButtonList and CheckBoxList, the list controls defined here can be much easier to use when many items are being displayed. Figure 5.3 shows several examples of the automatic layout options, such as vertical and horizontal layout.

Table 5.10 ListItem Properties

LISTITEM PROPERTY	DESCRIPTION
Attributes	Contains a collection of attribute name and value pairs for the ListItem that are not directly supported by the class.
Selected	Changeable value indicating whether the item is selected.
Text	Changeable text displayed in a list control for the item represented by the ListItem.
Value	Changeable value associated with the ListItem.

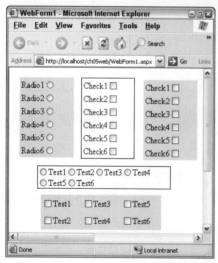

Figure 5.3   The RadioButtonList and CheckBoxList offer various automatic layout options as shown.

Table 5.11 displays a list of properties that are available with these controls. Also be sure to see the ListControl base class and ListItem class for additional properties (Tables 5.9 and 5.10).

Table 5.11   RadioListButton and CheckBoxList Properties (See Preceding Tables for Inherited Properties)

CONTROL PROPERTY	DESCRIPTION
CellPadding	Changeable value containing the pixel distance between the border and contents of each cell.
CellSpacing	Changeable value containing the pixel distance between each cell.
RepeatColumns	Changeable value containing the number of columns to display in the control. The default is 0. The column count is equal to the number in this property when the property is set to any positive integer. When set to 0, an unlimited amount of columns can be displayed.
RepeatDirection	Changeable value that indicates whether the control is displayed vertically or horizontally.

Table 5.11 *(continued)*

CONTROL PROPERTY	DESCRIPTION
RepeatLayout	Changeable value that indicates whether the layout of the items will be Flow or Table. When this is set to Flow layout and RepeatColumns is set to 0, the quantity of columns changes based on the width of the control, essentially wrapping to the next line until the complete list has been displayed.
TextAlign	Changeable value indicating the location of the text. This can be set to Left or Right. The default is Right.

In the following code sample, the WebForm contains Button1, TextBox1, and RadioButtonList1. When Button1 is clicked, the SelectedItem's Text and Value are placed in TextBox1. This code works with all of the classes that inherit from ListControl. With classes that allow multiple selections, the SelectedItem will be the lowest numbered item.

```
Private Sub Button1_Click(ByVal sender As System.Object, _
        ByVal e As System.EventArgs) Handles Button1.Click
    If RadioButtonList1.SelectedIndex >= 0 Then
        TextBox1.Text = RadioButtonList1.SelectedItem.Text _
            & " " & RadioButtonList1.SelectedItem.Value
    Else 'SelectedIndex = -1 if nothing is selected
        TextBox1.Text = "Nothing selected"
    End If
End Sub
```

In the following code sample, the WebForm contains Label1, Button1, and CheckBoxList1. When Button1 is clicked, Label1 is populated with all of the selected items. This code works with all of the classes that inherit from List-Control.

```
Private Sub Button1_Click(ByVal sender As System.Object, _
        ByVal e As System.EventArgs) Handles Button1.Click
    Label1.Text = ""
    Dim i As ListItem
    For Each i In CheckBoxList1.Items
        If i.Selected Then
            Label1.Text &= i.Text & " - " & i.Value & "<BR>"
        End If
    Next
End Sub
```

DropDownList and ListBox Controls

DropDownList and ListBox are similar controls. They inherit from the List-Control abstract class. The DropDownList only allows a single selection, while the ListBox control has a SelectionMode property, which allows the ListBox to be configured as single or multiple selection. The DropDownList doesn't offer any additional properties. Table 5.12 contains a list of the additional properties that are available with the ListBox.

In the following code sample, the WebForm contains Button1, TextBox1, and DropDownList1. When Button1 is clicked, the SelectedItem's Text and Value are placed into TextBox1. This code works with all of the classes that inherit from ListControl. With classes that allow multiple selections, such as ListBox, the SelectedItem will be the lowest numbered item.

```
Private Sub Button1_Click(ByVal sender As System.Object, _
    ByVal e As System.EventArgs) Handles Button1.Click
    If DropDownList1.SelectedIndex >= 0 Then
        TextBox1.Text = DropDownList1.SelectedItem.Text _
        & " " & DropDownList1.SelectedItem.Value
    Else 'SelectedIndex = -1 if nothing is selected
        TextBox1.Text = "Nothing selected"
    End If
End Sub
```

In the following code sample, the WebForm contains Label1, Button1, and ListBox1. When Button1 is clicked, Label1 is populated with all of the selected items. This code works with all of the classes that inherit from ListControl.

```
Private Sub Button1_Click(ByVal sender As System.Object, _
    ByVal e As System.EventArgs) Handles Button1.Click
    Label1.Text = ""
    Dim i As ListItem
    For Each i In ListBox1.Items
        If i.Selected Then
            Label1.Text &= i.Text & " - " & i.Value & "<BR>"
        End If
    Next
End Sub
```

Table 5.12 Properties of the ListBox

PROPERTY	DESCRIPTION
Rows	Changeable value containing the quantity of rows to be displayed in the ListBox. If this property is set to 1 and the SelectionMode is set to Single, this control will look like a DropDownList.
SelectionMode	Changeable value indicating the ability to select Single or Multiple rows.

Validation Controls

One of the problems with writing Web pages is making sure that all data is valid. Data validation requires checking required fields to verify that they contain values and checking all values to see if they are within a valid range. Also, all fields must be confined to an acceptable length. There may be business rules that affect validation as well.

Doing validation at the server allows the ability to write standard Visual Basic .NET code. But the problem with server-side validation is that the user gets no error feedback until the data is posted back to the server.

Doing validation at the browser (client) allows the ability to check the data before it is posted back to the server. The problem with client-side validation is that someone could spoof the page (create a page that contains the data that they want to pass to the server), thereby bypassing the validation. Also, client-side validation requires writing JavaScript code.

The best answer to the problems associated with validation is to provide validation at both the client and the server.

ASP.NET provides several validation controls. These controls automatically provide server-side and client-side validation. Figure 5.4 shows the validation control hierarchy, which shows how all of the validators are derived from the System.Web.UI.WebControls.WebControl.BaseValidator class. The BaseValidator is derived from the System.Web.UI.WebControls.WebControl.Label class. This makes sense because the visual element of a validator is a Label that indicates a user input error.

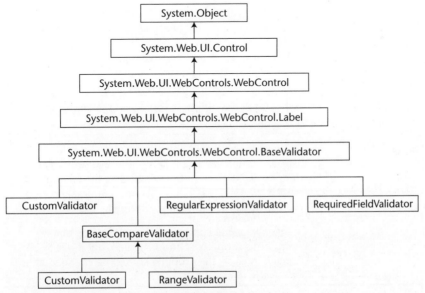

Figure 5.4   The validation control hierarchy.

BaseValidator Class

All of the validation controls inherit from the BaseValidator abstract class. The BaseValidator contains most of the validation functionality and is derived from Label and WebControl. Table 5.13 lists the properties that the BaseValidator provides.

 Setting the Enabled property to false will completely disable the control. If a validation control is intended to supply information to the ValidationSummary control and not display its own information, set the Display property of the control to *None*.

RequiredFieldValidator

The RequiredFieldValidator verifies that the user has not skipped over entries. This control can be used by dragging it onto a form, selecting a control to validate, and assigning an error message.

None of the other controls checks an empty field, so it's common to use a different validator control with the RequiredFieldValidator on the same control.

Table 5.13 BaseValidator Properties

BASEVALIDATOR PROPERTY	DESCRIPTION
ControlToValidate	Changeable value of the control that is to be validated.
Display	Changeable value containing the display behavior of the error message. This property can be set to any of the following settings: **None.** Does not display anything. **Static.** Displays the error message. **Dynamic.** Displays the error message.
EnableClientSideScript	Changeable value that indicates whether client-side validation will occur.
ErrorMessage	Changeable value containing the text that will be displayed when validation fails. If the Text property is used, the validation control will display the contents of the Text property, while the ValidationSummary control will display the ErrorMessage contents.
IsValid	Changeable value containing the valid status of a control. This property is normally read, but if it is to be changed in code, the property should be changed after the page load event.

The RequiredField validator provides an additional property called Initial-Value, which allows the field to be initialized with this value.

BaseCompareValidator

The BaseCompareValidator inherits from the BaseValidator class and offers comparable functionality. RangeValidator and CompareValidator inherit from this control.

The BaseCompareValidator contains a property called Type, which contains the data type that the text will be converted to before the comparison is made. The data types that are available are as follows:

Currency. The data is treated as a System.Decimal, but currency symbols and grouping characters, such as the comma, are still allowed.

Date. Only numeric dates are allowed, and times are not allowed.

Double. The data is treated as a System.Double, which is a double-precision floating point number.

Integer. The data is treated as a System.Int32.

String. The data is treated as a System.String.

This control also contains some static helper members. There is a public static method called CanConvert, which can test a value to see if it can be converted to a specified type as listed here. There is also a protected static property called CutoffYear, which contains the largest two-digit year that can be represented in this control. Finally, there is a protected static method called GetFullYear that returns the four-digit year for any two-digit year.

CompareValidator

CompareValidator inherits from the BaseCompareValidator class. The Compare-Validator uses comparison operators such as *greater than* and *less than* to compare the user's entry with either a constant or a value in a different control. The CompareValidator can also be used to verify that the user's entry is a certain data type, such as an integer.

Table 5.14 lists the additional properties that are included with the CompareValidator control.

RangeValidator

The RangeValidator control verifies that the user's entry is within a required range. The control has MinimumValue and MaximumValue properties. These properties are used with the Type property to convert the user's entry to the proper data type prior to checking the range.

Table 5.14   CompareValidator Properties

COMPAREVALIDATOR PROPERTY	DESCRIPTION
ControlToCompare	Changeable value containing the control to be used in the comparison. This property takes precedence if this property and the ValueToCompare properties are both set.
Operator	Changeable value that can be set to Equal, Not Equal, GreaterThan, GreaterThanEqual, LessThan, LessThanEqual, or DataTypeCheck.
ValueToCompare	Changeable value containing a constant to be used in the comparison.

 The Type property defaults to string. For other data types, be sure to set the Type property accordingly. For example, if the Type is still set to string and numeric range is being checked from 1 to 10, only strings that begin with the string letter 1 are valid.

RegularExpressionValidator

The RegularExpressionValidator control checks a control based on a regular expression. Regular expressions offer powerful pattern matching capabilities that might normally require writing code to accomplish. This control contains a property called ValidationExpression, which is a changeable value that contains the regular expression to be applied. If the regular expression is matched, validation succeeds.

 When setting the ValidationExpression property in Visual Studio .NET, click the ellipse button to display the regular expression editor, which contains many common regular expressions. There are also many Web sites that offer regular expression libraries, such as www.regxlib.com.

CustomValidator

The CustomValidator control is used when is it necessary to create a custom validation script for a control. A custom validation script can be written using client-side or server-side code.

Client-Side Validation Examples

To setup client-side validation, the ClientValidationFunction property must be assigned to the name of a function that has the following method signature:

```
function ClientFunctionName(source, arguments)
```

Function is a JavaScript function, ClientFunctionName is a function name of your choosing, source is a reference to the CustomValidator that called the function, and arguments contains two properties, Value, which is the value to be validated, and IsValid, which is initialized as true, but the custom validation script should assign a true or false to this argument before exiting.

In the following code example, the Web page contains a TextBox called TextBox1, with an associated CustomValidator called CheckTime. If the current hour is greater than 12 (after noon) TextBox1 must contain the phrase *Deliver Tommorrow*.

```
<script language=javascript>
<!--
function CheckTime(object, arguments)
{
    arguments.IsValid=true;
    var t = new Date();
    var h = t.getHours();
    //if after noon, TextBox1 must have the correct entry
    if( h >= 12 )
    {
        //Check value in TextBox1
        if (arguments.Value != "Deliver Tommorrow")
        {
            arguments.IsValid=false;
        }
    }
}
//-->
</script>
```

In the following code sample, the Web page contains DropDownList1, which contains three items called Item1-3, with values of Value1-3. DropDownList1 also has an associated CustomValidator, called CustomValidator1, with its ClientValidationFunction set to a function named ValidateText. The page also has a TextBox called TextBox1, with an associated RequiredFieldValidator. The following code will turn off TextBox1's validators if DropDownList1's value is not equal to Value1, otherwise TextBox1's validators are turned on. In this function, the IsValid argument always returns true.

```
<script language=javascript>
<!--
function ValidateText(object, arguments)
{
      //object is ref to the custom validator
      //arguments has a Value and IsValid
      //property.
      //
      //check the value to see if
      //it is equal to "Value1".
      if(arguments.Value != "Value1")
      {
            alert("Turning off validation");
            //turn off TextBox1 validators
            var e=document.getElementById("TextBox1").Validators;
            for(var x =0;x < e.length;x++)
            {
                  var el = e[x];
                  //hide the validator cause it my
                  //be visible
                  el.style.visibility="hidden";
                  el.enabled=false;
            }
      }
      else
      {
            alert("Turning on validation");
            var e=document.getElementById("TextBox1").Validators;
            for(var x =0;x < e.length;x++)
            {
                  var el = e[x];
                  //Make the validator visible
                  //if the TextBox1 is not valid.
                  el.style.visibility=el.isvalid?"hidden":"visible";
                  el.enabled=true;
            }
      }
      //always returns true
      arguments.IsValid=true;
}
//-->
</script>
```

Server-Side Validation Examples

The CustomValidator control raises an event called ServerValidate, which can be assigned to an event method handler. To setup server-side validation, the ServerValidate event must be assigned to a method that has the following method signature:

```
Sub ServerSubName( _
    ByVal source As System.Object, _
    ByVal args As System.Web.UI.WebControls.ServerValidateEventArgs) _
    Handles CustomValidator1.ServerValidate
```

Function is a JavaScript function, ServerSubName is a function name of your choice, source is a reference to the CustomValidator that called the method, and args contains two properties, Value, which is the value to be validated, and IsValid, which should be assigned to true of false before exiting.

The following code example is the server-side match for the first client-side example.

```
Private Sub CustomValidator1_ServerValidate( _
    ByVal source As System.Object, _
    ByVal args As System.Web.UI.WebControls.ServerValidateEventArgs) _
    Handles CustomValidator1.ServerValidate
    args.IsValid = True
    Dim t As DateTime = DateTime.Now
    Dim h As Integer = t.Hour
    'If after noon, TextBox1 must have an entry
    If h >= 12 Then
        'Check value in TextBox1
        If args.Value <> "Deliver Tommorrow" Then
            args.IsValid = False
        End If
    End If
End Sub
```

ValidationSummary

Many times a Web page simply doesn't have the space for validation messages. This is where the ValidationSummary Control can be useful. The Validation Summary displays a list of all ValidationErrors in one place, maybe at the top or bottom of the Web page.

The ValidationSummary control inherits directly from WebControl. Table 5.15 contains a list of properties.

 The validation controls have Text and ValidationError properties. ValidationSummary displays the list of ValidationErrors, while the individual validation control display the Text property, if it has been set. A typical scenario would be to place a verbose message in the ValidationError and very short message or a simple asterisk into the Text property.

Table 5.15　ValidationSummary Properties

PROPERTY	DESCRIPTION
DisplayMode	Changeable value containing the type of display. The value must be BulletList, List, or SingleParagraph.
EnableClientSideScript	Changeable value that indicates whether client-side validation will occur.
HeaderText	Changeable value containing the text to be displayed at the top of the summary.
ShowMessageBox	Changeable Boolean value to direct the control to display a message box with the summary report.
ShowSummary	Changeable Boolean value to direct the control to display the summary report on the Web page.

Using Cancel Buttons with Validation

The benefit of client-side validation is that the page is not allowed to be posted until all client-side validation has successfully occurred. This benefit can also become a problem when the user wants to press a cancel button, and the page is not valid. The problem is that the cancel button will try to post a cancel message to the server, but the page is not valid, so clicking on the button won't post anything back to the server.

This problem can be solved by changing the CausesValidation property of the cancel button to false. This property typically defaults to true. It may also be desirable to change this property to false when implementing Help buttons.

Lab 5.1: Validating Web Controls

In this lab, you will add validation to the existing NewCustomer page. RequiredFieldValidator controls will be added and then a RegularExpressionValidator will be added. Finally, client-side and server-side validation will be tested.

Add Validation to the NewCustomer Page

In this section, you will add validation controls to the NewCustomer page.

1. Start this lab by opening the OrderEntrySolution from Lab 4.1.

2. Right-click the OrderEntrySolution in the Solution Explorer and click Check Out. This will check out the complete solution.

3. Add a RequiredFieldValidator control just to the right of the txtCustomerName TextBox. Assign the following properties to the validator control.

PROPERTY	VALUE
ID	valReqCustomerName
ControlToValidate	txtCustomerName
ErrorMessage	Customer Name is Required
Text	Error
ToolTip	Customer Name is Required

4. Add a RequiredFieldValidator control just to the right of the txtAddress1 TextBox. Assign the following properties to the validator control.

PROPERTY	VALUE
ID	valReqAddress1
ControlToValidate	txtAddress1
ErrorMessage	Address Line 1 is Required
Text	Error
ToolTip	Address Line 1 is Required

5. As you add each of the next series of validator controls, reposition existing controls as necessary. Add a RequiredFieldValidator control just to the right of the txtCity TextBox. Assign the following properties to the validator control.

PROPERTY	VALUE
ID	valReqCity
ControlToValidate	txtCity
ErrorMessage	City Is Required
Text	Error
ToolTip	City Is Required

6. Add a RequiredFieldValidator control just to the right of the txtState TextBox. Assign the following properties to the validator control.

PROPERTY	VALUE
ID	valReqState
ControlToValidate	drpState

ErrorMessage	State Is Required
Text	Error
ToolTip	State Is Required

7. Add a RequiredFieldValidator control just to the right of the txtZipCode TextBox. Assign the following properties to the validator control.

PROPERTY	VALUE
ID	valReqZipCode
ControlToValidate	txtZipCode
ErrorMessage	Zip Code Is Required
Text	Error
ToolTip	Zip Code Is Required

8. Add a RegularExpressionValidator control on top of the valReqZip-Code validator. You may find that you can't completely cover the valReqZipCode control. If that's the case, cover the control as much as possible, and then click the HTML tab on the bottom of the designer window, locate the valReqZipCode validator, and copy the location information to the location information of the ReqularExpression. Click the Design tab to go back to the designer window, which should show the RegularExpressionValidator's new position. Assign the following properties to the validator control.

PROPERTY	VALUE
ID	valExpZipCode
ControlToValidate	txtZipCode
ErrorMessage	Zip Code Must Be 99999 or 99999-9999
Text	Error
ToolTip	Zip Code Must Be 99999 or 99999-9999
ValidationExpression	\d{5}(-\d{4})?

9. If you still have a ViewState Test button on your page from Lab 3.1, delete it.

10. Add a new Button control to the page, which allows the user to cancel the addition of a new customer. Assign the following properties to the Button control.

PROPERTY	VALUE
ID	btnCancel
CausesValidation	False
Text	Cancel

11. Add a ValidationSummary control to the page. This control will be used to display a message box containing all validation errors. This control will not be displayed on the page, so placement is not important. Assign the following properties to the ValidationSummary control. Figure 5.5 shows the completed page.

PROPERTY	VALUE
ID	valSummary
ShowMessageBox	True
ShowSummary	False

12. Double-click the Cancel button to go to the code-behind window. Add code to the btnCancel_Click method to display a Cancelled message in the lblConfirmation. Your code should look like the following:

```
Private Sub btnCancel_Click(ByVal sender As System.Object, _
        ByVal e As System.EventArgs) Handles btnCancel.Click
    lblConfirmation.Text = "Cancelled"
End Sub
```

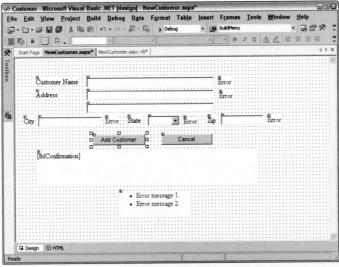

Figure 5.5 Completed NewCustomer.aspx page with validation controls added.

13. Add code to the btnAddCustomer_Click method to only display a confirmation if the page is valid. Your code should look like the following:

```
Private Sub btnAddCustomer_Click(ByVal sender As System.Object, _
        ByVal e As System.EventArgs) Handles
btnAddCustomer.Click
    If Page.IsValid Then
        Dim s As String
        s = "<font size='5'>Confirmation Info:</font>" & "<BR>"
        s += txtCustomerName.Text & "<BR>"
        s += txtAddress1.Text & "<BR>"
        If txtAddress2.Text.Length > 0 Then
            s += txtAddress2.Text & "<BR>"
        End If
        s += txtCity.Text & ", "
        s += drpState.SelectedItem.Text & " "
        s += txtZipCode.Text & "<BR>"
        lblConfirmation.Text = s
    Else
        'Make sure that confirmation is empty
        lblConfirmation.Text = ""
    End If
End Sub
```

14. Locate the Customer project in the Solution Explorer. Right-click the Customer project, and click Set As Startup Project.

15. Locate the NewCustomer.aspx page in the Solution Explorer. Right-click the NewCustomer.aspx page, and click Set As Start Page.

16. Save your work.

Test Client Validation

Client-side validation will be tested by trying to post empty fields back to the server and then trying to post a badly formed Zip Code back to the server.

1. Press F5 to start the Web application. The NewCustomer.aspx page appears.

2. Before typing into any field, click Add Customer. A message box showing all validation errors should be displayed, as shown in Figure 5.6. Notice that valExpZipCode did not generate an error. Only the RequiredValidation control can generate an error when a field is empty.

3. Click OK to dismiss the message box. Move the mouse over the error messages to reveal the ToolTip of each validation control.

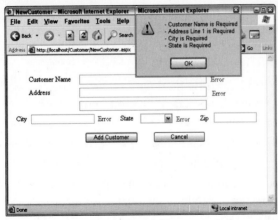

Figure 5.6 When validation fails, a message box containing the validation errors appears.

4. Press the Cancel button. This should post information back to the server. All error messages are cleared, and the lblConfirmation contains the word Canceled.

5. Fill in all of the fields. In the Zip Code field, enter 000 and click Add Customer. A message box should appear, showing the Zip Code validation error.

6. Click OK to dismiss the message box. Move the mouse over the error message to see the ToolTip.

7. Correct the Zip Code and click Add Customer. The contents of lblConfirmation are updated to show the new customer information.

8. Close the browser window.

Test Server Validation

Server-side validation will be tested by temporarily disabling client-side validation on the Zip Code field and then trying to post a badly formed Zip Code back to the server.

1. Select both of the Zip Code validators by using your mouse to select a rectangular area around the validators. If both validators are selected, the properties window should not contain a name in the current object DropDown, and there should not be an ID property in the property list.

2. Change the EnableClientScript property to false.

3. Press F5 to start the Web application. The NewCustomer.aspx page appears.

4. Enter all information except the Zip Code, and then click Add Customer. This will post back to the server, but the server will detect the missing entry and display an error message. Move the mouse over the error to reveal the ToolTip.

5. Fill in all of the fields. In the Zip Code field, enter 000, and click Add Customer. Notice that no message box is displayed, but an error message is displayed beside the Zip Code field.

6. Move the mouse over the error message to see the regular expression ToolTip.

7. Correct the Zip Code and click Add Customer. The contents of lblConfirmation are updated to show the new customer information. Close the browser window.

8. Change the EnableClientScript of both Zip Code validators back to true.

9. Save your work.

Summary

- System.Web.UI.Control class provides the base functionality for all of the HTML server controls, Web server controls, and the Web page itself.

- If the Visible property of a control is set to false, the control will not generate any client-side code.

- System.Web.UI.WebControls.WebControl provides the base functionality for all of the Web server controls in the System.Web.UI.WebControls namespace.

- A Cascading Style Sheet may be created and linked to all of the pages in the Web site. A named style, called a CSS class, can be created for each type control to create a uniform look and feel across the Web site.

- If a control is being used as a Cancel or Help button, the CausesValidation property should be set to false.

- Controls that inherit from ListControl have a property called Items, which is a collection of ListItem object. The Items collection can be enumerated to identify selected items.

- Many validation controls may be assigned to a single control to perform different types of validation.

- The RequiredFieldValidator control must be used to verify that an entry has been placed into a field. Other controls will not validate an empty field.

- CustomValidator controls may be used to provide customized client-side and server-side validation.

Review Questions

1. How do you create a Web server control for entering a password?

2. How can you retrieve a list of selected items from a MultiSelect ListBox control?

3. What will the SelectedIndex property contain if no item is selected?

4. How can a control be validated to see if it contains a valid data type?

5. How can a Cancel button post back to the server when none of the data on the page is valid?

6. How can the ValidationSummary be used to create a pop-up message with a list of all ValidationErrors?

7. A DropDownList control was added to the Web page, which displays a list of customers. It is intended to get a list of the customer's orders from the server when a customer is selected. The code does not appear to have any problems, but it seems as though the selection of a customer does not post data back to the server. How can this be corrected?

Answers to Review Questions

1. Use the TextBox control and set the TextMode property to Password.

2. Use a foreach loop to enumerate the Items collection, checking the Selected property of each item to see if it is true.

3. -1.

4. Use the CompareValidator, set the Operator property to DataTypeCheck, and assign the Type property to the data type to check for.

5. Cancel buttons should have the CausesValidation property set to false.

6. Set the ShowMessageBox property to true and optionally set the ShowSummary to false.

7. Change the AutoPostBack property to true.

CHAPTER

6

Using Data-Bound Web Controls

The previous chapter covered lots of controls and control hierarchies. But one thing that was not covered was the ability to connect, or bind, to data.

This chapter looks at methods of binding data for the purpose of presenting the data to the user. Since database access hasn't been covered yet, the data in this chapter will primarily come from an ArrayList. It's important to understand the data-binding basics, which will be somewhat consistent, regardless of whether the data source is an ArrayList, an XML file, or a database. Completion of this chapter will allow the data chapters to focus on data access.

Questions Q & A

Q: Is it possible to edit the data that is being displayed in a DataGrid control?

A: Yes. The DataGrid will be covered in detail in this chapter.

Q: Is there a way to present data, like catalog items, in a left-to-right format instead of a top-down format?

A: Yes. The DataList is the control for you. The DataList has Repeat-Layout and RepeatDirection properties that can help you achieve a left-to-right display of data. This will be covered in this chapter.

Q: I have a collection of Cars, and I noticed that the DataGrid only displays the properties, but not the public member variables. Is there a way to display the public member variables as well?

A: Absolutely. This chapter will cover some of the methods of getting to this data.

Data-Binding Basics

Data binding refers to connecting to data. Data binding typically defines a method of connecting presentation controls to a data object without having to write code that moves data back and forth to and from the data object to the presentation control and vice versa.

When the term data binding is used with ASP.NET, it typically refers to connecting a server control to a data object. Binding is still done between the server control and the data, but the server control will be responsible for moving data between the presentation element, which may be a browser or other Web device, and the server.

Two types of binding will be covered in this chapter, single value binding and repeated value binding. Single value binding refers to connecting a single data element, such as a variable, to a property of a control, such as the Text property. Repeated value binding refers to connecting a data source that has more than one value, such as a collection, to a list control such as a DataGrid.

Single Value Data Binding

Single value data binding in ASP.Net can be done in an ASP.NET page using the following statement:

```
<%# DataSourceExpression %>
```

This statement may look much like a server-side code block, but no code can be placed in the data binding block. An example of this is a page that contains a TextBox, Label, and Button. The Label may be bound to the TextBox as follows:

```
<asp:Label id=Label1 runat="server"
Text="<%# TextBox1.Text %>" />
```

To activate the binding, a line of code needs to be added to the Page_Load method as follows:

```
Private Sub Page_Load(ByVal sender As System.Object, _
    ByVal e As System.EventArgs) Handles MyBase.Load
    'Activate the binding
    DataBind()
End Sub
```

In addition to binding to a property of another control, binding can be done to a method or expression as follows:

```
<asp:Label id=Label1 runat="server"
Text="<%# DateTime.Now.AddDays(1) %>" />

<asp:Label id=Label1 runat="server"
Text="<%# &quot;Date/Time: &quot; &amp; DateTime.Now.ToString() %>" />
```

The first example adds a day to the current date and returns the result, which is bound to the Label control. The second example evaluates the expression and places the result into the Label control. The use of " allows quotation marks to be embedded into the HTML tag.

Many data binding statements may be placed on a Web page, but the data-binding statements will not operate until the binding is activated. This is done by issuing a call to the Page.DataBind() or simply DataBind() method. The Page.DataBind method will call the DataBind method of all controls that are on the page. The DataBind method is implemented on System.Web.UI.Control, from which all Web controls are derived.

It is sometimes desirable to only activate the binding on selective controls. This can be done by simply making a call to the DataBind method of these controls instead of calling the Page.DataBind method.

In many respects, single value data binding simply reflects a different way of placing a piece of data into a server control. It is just as easy to place the following code into the page's load method.

```
Private Sub Page_Load(ByVal sender As System.Object, _
    ByVal e As System.EventArgs) Handles MyBase.Load
    Label1.Text = TextBox1.Text
    Label2.Text = DateTime.Now.AddDays(1)
    Label3.Text = "Date/Time: " & DateTime.Now.ToString()
End Sub
```

So where is the value? The real value of data binding can be realized when performing repeated value binding.

Repeated Value Data Binding

Repeated value data binding is where ASP.NET data binding shines. This is where repeating values from a database table, an XML file, an array or collection, or other data source can be displayed with a few lines of code. For an ASP.NET server control to bind to repeated data, the data source must provide an implementation of the IEnumerable, ICollection, or IListSource interface.

ASP.NET contains the following controls that have been designed specifically to bind to repeated value data:

- HTMLSelect
- ListBox
- DropDownList
- CheckBoxList
- RadioButtonList
- Repeater
- DataList
- DataGrid

Before covering any of these controls in detail, the next sections will cover the properties, methods, and events that are common to all of these controls.

Repeated Binding Control Properties

This section covers the properties that are common to all of the repeated binding controls.

DataSource

The DataSource is a changeable value that will accept any data type that implements the IEnumerable, Icollection, or IListSource interface. Some of the data types that meet this requirement are listed below.

Array.   This includes user-defined arrays and data types that are derived from Array.

Collection.   This includes most of the collection data types in the System.Collections namespace, which include ArrayList, HashTable, BitArray, Queue, SortedList, Stack, and many of the collection data types in the System.Collections.Specialized namespace.

ADO.NET DataTable. This is an in-memory data table containing Data-Columns, DataRows, and Constraints. The DataTable can be created dynamically in memory and assigned to a DataSource.

ADO.NET DataView. This is a window into the DataTable. The DataView can be set up to provide a sorted and filtered data. The DataView can also be set up to view only added, deleted, changed, or unchanged rows.

ADO.NET DataSet. This is an in-memory relational database. The DataSet contains DataTables, DataViews, and DataRelations.

ADO.NET DataReader. This is an object that returns a forward-only, read-only stream of data from a database. This object has limited functionality, but has the best performance when retrieving data.

DataMember

The DataMember is a changeable value containing the specific rowset in the DataSource to bind to the control. If a DataSource only contains a single rowset, the DataMember is not required. For objects like the DataSet, which contain multiple rowsets (DataTables), the DataMember is required to select the appropriate DataTable.

DataTextField

The DataTextField is a changeable value containing the field or column from the data source that will provide the Text property of list items, such as the DropDownList control. This property is not necessary when the repeating data contains a single column. When the data contains multiple columns, this property must be set to the name of the desired column.

DataTextFormatString

The DataTextFormatString is a changeable value containing the formatting string used to control how data bound to the list control is displayed. Table 6.1 contains a list of available formatting characters. A format string must be provided that contains placeholder zero only. A format string can contain literals and can contain placeholder zero multiple times. Placeholder zero must be in the format {0:Cn}, where C is a valid format character and n is an integer representing the quantity of digits. The following format string is valid:

```
"Order Number: {0:D6} Original Order Number: {0}"
```

For order number 123, this format string will display the following:

```
Order Number: 000123 Original Order Number: 123
```

Table 6.1 Formatting Characters for Numeric Values

FORMAT CHARACTER	DESCRIPTION
C or c	Used to format currency. By default, the flag will prefix a dollar sign ($) to the value, but this can be changed using the NumberFormatInfo object. "{0:C}",99989.987 = $99,989.99 "Total: {0:C}",9989.987 = Total: $9,989.99
D or d	Formats decimal numbers. Also specifies the minimum number of digits to pad the value. "{0:D9}",99999 = 000099999
E or e	Exponential notation. "{0:E}",99999.76543 = 9.999977E+004
F or f	Fixed point formatting. "{0:F3}",99999.9999 = 100000.000
G or g	General. Used to format a number to fixed or exponential format. "{0:G}",999.99999 = 999.99999 "{0:G4}",999.99999 = 1E+03
N or n	Basic numerical formatting with commas (two decimal places by default). "{0:N}",99999 = 99,999.00 "{0:N1}", 99999 = 99,999.0
X or x	Hex formatting. Uppercase X displays uppercase letters. "{0:X}",99999 = 1869F "{0:x}",99999 = 1869f

There is also a set of formatting characters for date and time values. Table 6.2 lists these formatting characters. Some of these characters are the same as the numeric characters, but the runtime will check the data type of the object that is being displayed, and if it is a date or time, the format character in this table will be used.

Table 6.2 Date and Time Formatting Characters

FORMAT CHARACTER	DESCRIPTION
D	Short date. "{0:d}", #1/2/03 4:56:07# =1/2/2003
D	Long date. "{0:D}", #1/2/03 4:56:07# =Thursday, January 02, 2003
F	Full, long date and short time. "{0:f}", #1/2/03 4:56:07# =Thursday, January 02, 2003 4:56 AM
F	Full, long date and long time. "{0:F}", #1/2/03 4:56:07# =Thursday, January 02, 2003 4:56:07 AM
G	General, short date and short time. "{0:g}", #1/2/03 4:56:07# =1/2/2003 4:56 AM
G	General, short date and long time. "{0:G}", #1/2/03 4:56:07# =1/2/2003 4:56:07 AM
M or m	Month and day. "{0:M}", #1/2/03 4:56:07# =January 02
R or r	RFC1123 format. "{0:R}", #1/2/03 4:56:07# =Thu, 02 Jan 2003 04:56:07 GMT
S	ISO 8601 sortable using universal time. "{0:s}", #1/2/03 4:56:07# =2003-01-02T04:56:07
T	Short time. "{0:t}", #1/2/03 4:56:07# =4:56 AM
T	Long time. "{0:T}", #1/2/03 4:56:07# =4:56:07 AM
U	ISO 8601 sortable using universal time. "{0:u}", #1/2/03 4:56:07# =2003-01-02 04:56:07Z
U	Universal sortable date/time. "{0:U}", #1/2/03 4:56:07# =Thursday, January 02, 2003 9:56:07 AM
Y or y	Year and month. "{0:Y}", #1/2/03 4:56:07# =January, 2003

There is also a set of formatting characters for use when creating the traditional picture clause for numeric value. The picture clause can contain a format for positive;negative;zero formats, each having a semicolon separator. Table 6.3 contains a list of these characters.

Table 6.3   Formatting Characters When Creating a Traditional Picture Clause

FORMAT CHARACTER	DESCRIPTION
0	Displays a zero if no other number is being placed at this location. This is usually used when leading or trailing zeros are required. "{0:000.00}",12345.678=12345.68 "{0:000000.0000}",12345.678=012345.6780
#	This is a placeholder for a digit; but if no number is being placed at this location, the formatting character is ignored. "{0:###.##}",12345.678=12345.68 "{0:######.####}",12345.678=12345.678
.	Display the decimal point of the current culture.
,	Display the repeating number separator that is used in the current culture. "{0:#,####.00}",12345678.5678=12,345,678.57
%	Displays the percent symbol of the current culture. "{0:#.00%}",1.456=145.60%
E+0,E-0,e+0 or e-0	Displays the output as exponential notation. "{0:#.00E+0}",123456.789=1.23E+5
\	Displays the character that follows as a literal. "{0:\'#,####.00\'}",123456.789='123,456.79'
" or '	A character that is enclosed in single or double quotes is treated as a literal.
{ and }	Double curly braces, {{, are used to display a curly brace {.
;	Separates the sections of the format string. The sections are composed of positive;negative;zero formats. For the format string. "{0:#,####.00;(#,###.00);empty}" 12345.6789=12,345.68 -12345.6789=(12,345.68) 0=empty

DataValueField

The DataValueField is a changeable value containing the column or field name of the data source that will populate the Value property of the list items. If the repeating data contains a single column, both the Text and the Value will contain the same value, and setting this property is not necessary. When the data contains multiple columns, this property must be set to the name of the desired column.

Repeated Binding Control Methods

This section covers the methods that are common to all of the repeated binding controls. These methods are defined in System.Web.UI.Control and may be overridden by the data bound controls.

DataBind.   The DataBind method binds the data source to the current server control and its child controls. When DataBind is called at the page level, all controls on the page are bound.

FindControl.   The FindControl method is a utility method that can locate a child control when a control, such as a table cell, contains child controls such as TextBox and Button controls.

Repeated Binding Control Events

This section covers the events that are common to all of the repeated binding controls. These events are provided by various base class controls.

DataBinding.   The DataBinding event is provided by the System.Web.UI.Control and is raised by a control when data is bound to it. The event will be raised by the control for each row that is being created in the control.

SelectedIndexChanged.   The SelectedIndexChanged event is provided by the System.Web.UI.WebControls.ListControl and is raised by the control when the current selection changes. This event may not operate as expected until the AutoPostBack property is set to true.

Mapping Fields to the Control

When a data source contains multiple fields, it is necessary to tell the control what fields the control should bind to. There are two methods of mapping fields to a control: The mappings can be done dynamically by setting the properties at runtime, or if the control supports templates, a template can be declaratively created, which defines the contents of each item of each row.

Dynamic Field Mapping

Dynamic binding involves setting the DataSource, DataMember, Data-TextField, DataTextFormat, and DataValueField through code, which means that the values are resolved at run time. The following is a sample of binding a ListBox to a HashTable.

```
Private Sub Page_Load(ByVal sender As System.Object, _
        ByVal e As System.EventArgs) Handles MyBase.Load
    Dim h As New Hashtable()
    h.Add("Glenn", 45)
    h.Add("Joe", 20)
    h.Add("Mary", 32)
    h.Add("Frank", 46)
    h.Add("Anne", 25)
    ListBox1.DataSource = h
    ListBox1.DataTextField = "key"
    ListBox1.DataValueField = "value"
    DataBind()
End Sub
```

In this example, the sorted list object has two fields, key and value. The DataTextField and DataValueField are bound to the key and value fields. Although *key* and *value* are hard-coded in the example, they could have been variables and the binding would be evaluated at run time.

Templated Field Mapping

Templated binding is used on controls that support templates. A template control is a control that has no user interface. The control simply provides the mechanism for binding to data. The user interface is supplied by the developer in the form of inline templates. The template can contain presentation code such as HTML and DHTML. The template can also contain ASP.NET data binding syntax to insert data from the data source. Controls that support templates include the DataList, Repeater, and DataGrid. A control may allow the following templates to be programmed:

HeaderTemplate.   This is an optional header, which will be rendered at the top of the control.

FooterTemplate.   This is an optional footer, which will be rendered at the bottom of the control.

ItemTemplate.   The item template is rendered for each row in the data source.

AlternatingItemTemplate.   (Optional) If the alternating item template is implemented, every other row will be rendered using this template.

SelectedItemTemplate.   (Optional) The selected item template will be used to render a row that has been selected.

SeparatorTemplate.   (Optional) The separator template will define the separation of each item and alternate item.

EditItemTemplate.   (Optional) The edit item template will be used to render a row that is in edit mode. This usually involves displaying the data in a TextBox instead of a Label control.

A simple Repeater control example follows:

```
<asp:repeater id=Repeater1 runat="server">
    <itemtemplate>
    Hello <%# Container.DataItem.Key %><br>
    You are <%# Container.DataItem.Value %> years old<br>
    </itemtemplate>
</asp:repeater>
```

The code-behind page for this example might look like the following:

```
Private Sub Page_Load(ByVal sender As System.Object, _
    ByVal e As System.EventArgs) Handles MyBase.Load
    Dim h as new HashTable()
    h.Add("Glenn", 45)
    h.Add("Joe", 20)
    h.Add("Mary", 32)
    h.Add("Frank", 46)
    h.Add("Anne", 25)
    Repeater1.DataSource = h
    DataBind()
End Sub
```

A templated control exposes itself as a Container object, which is available from within the template when using the data binding syntax. The DataItem represents a row of data to be processed. The HashTable's row is exposed as an instance of a DictionaryEntry, which contains a Key and Value property for each row. These fields are available within the template by using the following format:

```
<%# Container.DataItem.Key %> and <%# Container.DataItem.Value %>
```

In some cases, the DataItem may be a collection that requires the column name to be included in parentheses. A DataTable is one such example. Each row of the DataTable is exposed as a DataRowView, which allows access to the columns by an index number or column name. To retrieve the value of the price column, the following data binding code is used.

```
<%# Container.DataItem("price") %> or <%# Container.DataItem(4) %>
```

Using the Eval Method

The DataBinder class offers a static method called Eval, which can simplify access to data. The Eval method uses reflection to perform a lookup of the DataItem's underlying type by looking at the type metadata that is stored in the underlying type's assembly. Once the metadata is retrieved, the Eval method determines how to connect to the given field.

The end result is that Eval provides a consistent method of binding to the data. The following code shows the binding to the Key property of the HashTable and the binding of the price column to the DataTable.

```
<%# DataBinder.Eval(Container.DataItem, "Key") %>
<%# DataBinder.Eval(Container.DataItem, "price" %>
```

 The consistent behavior that DataBinder.Eval provides comes at a high performance cost.

The Eval method provides an overloaded method that allows a format string to be assigned. Tables 6.1, 6.2, and 6.3 contain lists of formatting characters that can be used in a format string. The price can be modified to provide currency formatting as shown in the following code.

```
<%# DataBinder.Eval(Container.DataItem, "price", "{0:C}" %>
```

Data Bound Controls

This section covers several of the data bound controls in more detail. Some of these controls, such as the ListBox and DropDownList control, were covered in the previous chapter. This chapter covers these controls and other controls with a strong focus on data binding.

ListBox and DropDownList Control

The ListBox and DropDownList controls are similar. Both provide the following properties that can be set in the Visual Studio .NET designer or in code:

- DataSource
- DataMember
- DataTextField

- DataTextFormat
- DataValueField

The following code can be used to bind a HashTable to the ListBox:

```
Private Sub Page_Load(ByVal sender As System.Object, _
        ByVal e As System.EventArgs) Handles MyBase.Load
    Dim h As New Hashtable()
    h.Add("Glenn", 0)
    h.Add("Joe", 2)
    h.Add("Mary", 3)
    h.Add("Frank", 1)
    h.Add("Anne", 2)
    ListBox1.DataSource = h
    ListBox1.DataTextField = "Key"
    ListBox1.DataValueField = "Value"
    DataBind()
End Sub
```

When the ListBox is rendered to the browser, the browser source looks like
the following code:

```
<select name="ListBox1" id="ListBox1" size="5"
    <option value="0">Glenn</option>
    <option value="2">Anne</option>
    <option value="2">Joe</option>
    <option value="3">Mary</option>
    <option value="1">Frank</option>
</select>
```

The ListBox rendered as an HTML ListBox, which is a simple select tag with
option tags containing the value attribute and the inner HTML of the option
containing the text to be displayed.

Repeater Control

The Repeater control is probably the simplest of the template controls. It's simple because the Repeater control does not provide any styles or layout options.
Presentation is purely the developer's job. The Repeater control simply provides the calls to the appropriate templates. The Repeater provides the following properties, which can be set in the Visual Studio .NET designer or in code:

- DataSource
- DataMember

In addition, the Repeater allows assignment of the following template types:

- HeaderTemplate
- FooterTemplate
- ItemTemplate
- AlternatingItemTemplate
- Separator Template

The Repeater control is the only template control that allows HTML tags to span across templates. This means that a <table> tag can be placed into the header template, each table row <tr> tag with its table data <td> tags and end tags can be placed into the item template and alternating item template. The end of the table tag may be placed into the footer template.

In the next series of Repeater examples the follow code will be assigned to the Page_Load method. Entries are placed into a HashTable and the HashTable has been assigned to Repeater1's DataSource.

```
Private Sub Page_Load(ByVal sender As System.Object, _
        ByVal e As System.EventArgs) Handles MyBase.Load
    Dim h As New Hashtable()
    h.Add("Glenn", 46)
    h.Add("Joe", 42)
    h.Add("Mary", 31)
    h.Add("Frank", 36)
    h.Add("Anne", 24)
    Repeater1.DataSource = h
    DataBind()
End Sub
```

At a minimum, the item template must be supplied. The item template is assigned in the HTML. The following example implements the item template:

```
<asp:Repeater id=Repeater1 runat="server">
    <itemtemplate>
    User Name: <%# DataBinder.Eval(container.dataitem,"Key") %>
    has <%# DataBinder.Eval(container.dataitem,"Value","{0:C}") %><hr>
    </itemtemplate>
</asp:Repeater>
```

Figure 6.1 shows the browser output. The username is the Key property of the HashTable, while the amount is the Value property of the HashTable. An HTML horizontal rule tag has been added to place each user on a different line. The Value has been formatted as currency with the "{0:C}" format string.

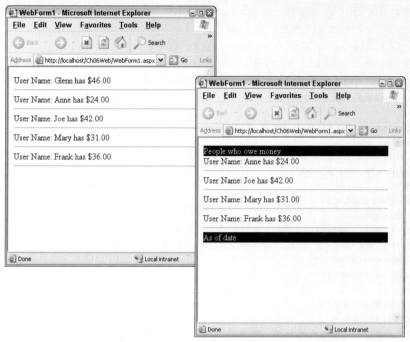

Figure 6.1 Browser output without header and footer, then with the header and footer.

In the next example, a header and footer are added to Repeater1 as follows. Figure 6.1 shows the browser output.

```
<asp:Repeater id=Repeater1 runat="server">
    <headertemplate>
    <div style="color: white; background-color: black">
    People who owe money
    </div>
    </headertemplate>
    <itemtemplate>
    User Name: <%# DataBinder.Eval(container.dataitem,"Key") %>
    has <%# DataBinder.Eval(container.dataitem,"Value","{0:C}") %><hr>
    </itemtemplate>
    <footertemplate>
    <div style="color: white; background-color: black">
    As of date.
    </div>
    </footertemplate>
</asp:Repeater>
```

Notice that the output has the header and footer, but the footer looks especially ugly with that extra horizontal rule tag. This is where the separator template comes in. The separator template can be used place a separator only between items, and will not place a separator between the last item and the footer. In the next example, the horizontal rule has been moved from the item template to the separator template.

```
<asp:Repeater id=Repeater1 runat="server">
    <headertemplate>
    <div style="color: white; background-color: black">
    People who owe money
    </div>
    </headertemplate>
    <itemtemplate>
    User Name: <%# DataBinder.Eval(container.dataitem,"Key") %>
    has <%# DataBinder.Eval(container.dataitem,"Value","{0:C}") %>
    </itemtemplate>
    <separatortemplate>
    <hr>
    </separatortemplate>
    <footertemplate>
    <div style="color: white; background-color: black">
    As of date.
    </div>
    </footertemplate>
</asp:Repeater>
```

The output of this example is shown in Figure 6.2. Notice that the horizontal rule tag is omitted between the last item and the footer.

As the number of users grows, it may be more desirable to shade every other line to make it easier to read the report. The alternating item template can be used to accomplish this. The alternating item template can contain different styles and different text. The following example implements the alternating item template, which shades the alternating items and has different text (a plus sign at the start of the line). The results are shown in Figure 6.2.

```
<asp:Repeater id=Repeater1 runat="server">
    <headertemplate>
    <div style="color: white; background-color: black">
    People who owe money
    </div>
    </headertemplate>
```

```
        <itemtemplate>
        -User Name: <%# DataBinder.Eval(container.dataitem,"Key") %>
        has <%# DataBinder.Eval(container.dataitem,"Value","{0:C}") %>
        </itemtemplate>
        <alternatingitemtemplate>
        <div style="background-color: silver">
        +User Name: <%# DataBinder.Eval(container.dataitem,"Key") %>
        has <%# DataBinder.Eval(container.dataitem,"Value","{0:C}") %>
        </div>
        </alternatingitemtemplate>
        <separatortemplate>
        <hr>
        </separatortemplate>
        <footertemplate>
        <div style="color: white; background-color: black">
        As of date.
        </div>
        </footertemplate>
    </asp:Repeater>
```

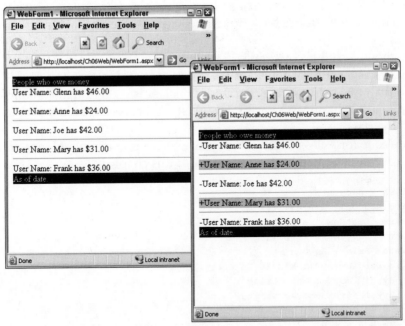

Figure 6.2 The browser output, which displays the implemented separator template and the alternating item template.

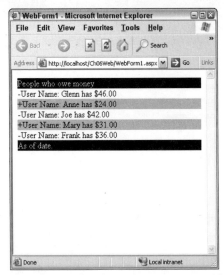

Figure 6.3 The cleaned-up repeater with the separator template removed.

Now that the alternate items are shaded, there is no need for the separator. Figure 6.3 shows the cleaned-up repeater with the separator template removed.

In the previous examples, a simple HashTable was used to display name and value pairs as a series of rows with two columns. There are many cases where more than two columns are required. If a class is created that contains properties for each column, an array or ArrayList can be used to hold multiple instances of the class.

Here is the code for a class called Employee, which contains several properties. The Employee class will be used throughout this chapter.

```
Public Class Employee
    Public ReadOnly EID As Integer
    Private _LastName As String
    Private _FirstName As String
    Private _Salary As Decimal
    Public Sub New(ByVal EID As Integer, _
        ByVal LastName As String, _
        ByVal FirstName As String, _
        ByVal Salary As Decimal)
        Me.EID = EID
        Me._LastName = LastName
        Me._FirstName = FirstName
        Me._Salary = Salary
    End Sub
    Public Property LastName() As String
        Get
```

```
            Return _LastName
        End Get
        Set(ByVal Value As String)
            _LastName = Value
        End Set
    End Property
    Public Property FirstName() As String
        Get
            Return _FirstName
        End Get
        Set(ByVal Value As String)
            _FirstName = Value
        End Set
    End Property
    Public Property Salary() As Decimal
        Get
            Return _Salary
        End Get
        Set(ByVal Value As Decimal)
            Salary = Value
        End Set
    End Property
End Class
```

The Page_Load code has been changed to use the Employee class. This example uses an ArrayList to hold the employees as shown in the following code:

```
Private Sub Page_Load(ByVal sender As System.Object, _
        ByVal e As System.EventArgs) Handles MyBase.Load
    Dim a As New ArrayList()
    a.Add(New Employee(1, "GlennLast", "Glenn", 50000))
    a.Add(New Employee(2, "JoeLast", "Joe", 42000))
    a.Add(New Employee(3, "MaryLast", "Mary", 31000))
    a.Add(New Employee(4, "FrankLast", "Frank", 36000))
    a.Add(New Employee(5, "AnneLast", "Anne", 24000))
    Repeater1.DataSource = a
    DataBind()
End Sub
```

With four values displayed, it may be more desirable to create an HTML table to display this information. This requires a header template for the initial table tag, a footer template for the table ending tag, and an item template for the table rows. Optionally, an alternating item template may be included. The following code shows the Repeater with its templates:

```
<asp:Repeater id=Repeater1 runat="server">
    <headertemplate>
    <table width="100%" border="1px" cellpadding="3px" >
```

```
        <tr style="color: white; background-color: black">
            <th>ID</th>
            <th>Last</th>
            <th>First</th>
            <th>Salary</th>
        </tr>
        </headertemplate>
        <itemtemplate>
        <tr>
        <td align="right">
            <%# string.Format("{0:D4}",Container.DataItem.EID ) %>
        </td>
        <td align="left">
            <%# DataBinder.Eval(Container.DataItem,"LastName") %>
        </td>
        <td align="left">
            <%# DataBinder.Eval(Container.DataItem,"FirstName") %>
        </td>
        <td align="right">
            <%# DataBinder.Eval(Container.DataItem,"Salary", "{0:C}") %>
        </td>
        </tr>
        </itemtemplate>
        <alternatingitemtemplate>
        <tr style="background-color: silver">
        <td align="right">
            <%# string.Format("{0:D4}",Container.DataItem.EID ) %>
        </td>
        <td align="left">
        <%# DataBinder.Eval(Container.DataItem,"LastName") %>
        </td>
        <td align="left">
            <%# DataBinder.Eval(Container.DataItem,"FirstName") %>
        </td>
        <td align="right">
            <%# DataBinder.Eval(Container.DataItem,"Salary", "{0:C}") %>
        </td>
        </tr>
        </alternatingitemtemplate>
        <footertemplate>
        </table>
        </footertemplate>
    </asp:Repeater>
```

Notice that the data binding for the EID is different from the others. This is because the EID was not created as a property. In the class, the EID was created as a public, read-only variable. If an attempt were made to use the same syntax as the LastName, FirstName, and Salary properties, an error would be generated, stating that the Employee class does not have an EID property. The output is shown in Figure 6.4.

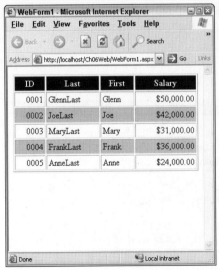

Figure 6.4 Creating a table with the Repeater control.

The previous Repeater examples have shown how the use of templates can give the Repeater control lots of flexibility. The biggest problem is that the programmer is doing most of the work.

DataList Control

The DataList control offers more functionality than the Repeater control. The DataControl has a property called RepeatLayout that can be set to Flow or Table. When this property is set to Table (the default), the DataList displays items from a data source by automatically creating a table with a cell for each item. The item refers to a repeating row in the data source. The cells can be configured to display horizontally or vertically, with a configurable quantity of column cells per row. The developer's job is to provide the presentation of the cell, which will hold one of the repeating items from the data source. The DataList control provides the calls to the appropriate templates.

If the RepeatLayout property is set to Flow, the DataList displays items from the data source by creating a span element to hold each item. The items can still be configured to be displayed horizontally or vertically with a configurable quantity of columns per row.

The DataList provides the following properties that have already been defined in this chapter and can be set in the Visual Studio .NET designer or in code:

- DataSource
- DataMember

In addition, the DataList contains several properties that have not yet been defined. Table 6.4 contains a list of each of the properties along with their description.

Table 6.4 Additional DataList Properties

PROPERTY	DESCIPTION
DataKeyField	Changeable value that contains the name of the field that will contain the unique identifier of the row. In database terminology, this would be the primary key.
CellPadding	Changeable value that contains the amount of space between the content of the table cell and the border of the cell.
CellSpacing	Changeable value that contains the space between cells.
EditItemIndex	Changeable value that contains the index number of the current item that is being edited. This property will contain -1 if no item is being edited.
ExtractTemplateRows	Changeable value used to determine if the asp:tables should be merged into the table that is created by the DataList. This only works with asp:tables. When this setting is true, every template that is implemented must contain a well formed asp:table. All of the asp:tables will be merged together. Any other content will be disposed. When true, The RepeatColumns, RepeatDirection, and RepeatDirection properties are disabled.
GridLines	Changeable value containing the grid settings for the table. Possible values are none, Horizontal, Vertical, or both.
RepeatColumns	Changeable value containing the quantity of columns to be displayed. The default is zero, which means that repeating columns is turned off.
RepeatDirection	Changeable value that indicates whether the repeating items in the data source displays horizontally or vertically.
RepeatLayout	Changeable value indicating whether the output of each item should treated as a table or flow. When set to table, the DataList automatically builds a table for displaying its output. When set to flow, the DataList builds its output without a table.

Table 6.4 *(continued)*

PROPERTY	DESCIPTION
SelectedIndex	Changeable value containing the index number of the currently selected item in the DataList. This property contains -1 if no item is currently selected.
ShowHeader	Changeable Boolean value indicating whether the header should be displayed.
ShowFooter	Changeable Boolean value indicating whether the footer should be displayed.

The DataList allows assignment of the following template types:

- AlternatingItemTemplate
- EditItemTemplate
- FooterTemplate
- HeaderTemplate
- ItemTemplate
- SelectedItemTemplate
- Separator Template

The DataList also supports style elements, which allows the style to change without repeating the same code. For example, the Repeater control examples that were previously covered had the same code for the ItemTemplate and the AlternatingItemTemplate. The only thing that was different was the style. The DataList solves the problem with these special style elements. The following is a list of style elements that are supported by the DataList. Figure 6.5 shows the style hierarchy.

- AlternatingItemStyle
- EditItemStyle
- FooterStyle
- HeaderStyle
- ItemStyle
- SelectedItemStyle
- SeparatorStyle

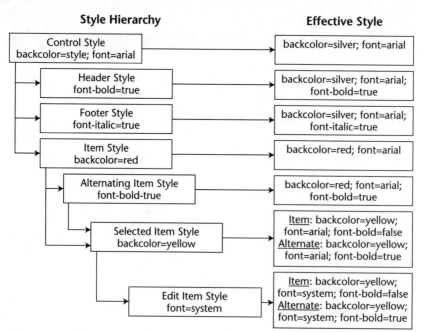

Figure 6.5   The style hierarchy for the DataList and the DataGrid controls. Styles are applied from the top to the bottom.

In the next series of DataList examples, the following code will be assigned to the Page_Load method:

```
Private Sub Page_Load(ByVal sender As System.Object, _
        ByVal e As System.EventArgs) Handles MyBase.Load
    Dim a As New ArrayList()
    a.Add(New Employee(1, "GlennLast", "Glenn", 50000))
    a.Add(New Employee(2, "JoeLast", "Joe", 42000))
    a.Add(New Employee(3, "MaryLast", "Mary", 31000))
    a.Add(New Employee(4, "FrankLast", "Frank", 36000))
    a.Add(New Employee(5, "AnneLast", "Anne", 24000))

    DataList1.DataSource = a
    DataBind()
End Sub
```

This code uses the Employee class that was used in the previous Repeater examples, and five Employee instances are being added to an ArrayList. In this example, the DataList is placed on to the Web page and the fields are placed into the item template as follows.

```
<asp:DataList id=DataList1 runat="server">
<itemtemplate>
    <%# string.Format("{0:D4}",Container.DataItem.EID ) %>
    <%# DataBinder.Eval(Container.DataItem, "LastName")%>
    <%# DataBinder.Eval(Container.DataItem, "FirstName")%>
    <%# DataBinder.Eval(Container.DataItem, "Salary","{0:C}")%>
</ItemTemplate>
</asp:DataList>
```

The browser output (see the left window in Figure 6.6) shows a line for each employee. Taking a peek at the browser's source code reveals that the DataList generated a table with one cell for each of the employees.

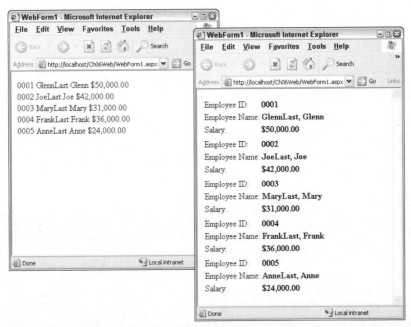

Figure 6.6 Shows a line (left) for each employee and then (right) shows a cleaner version, with a table embedded into the item template.

In the next example, some formatting is added by placing a table inside the item template, as shown in the following code:

```
<asp:DataList id=DataList1 runat="server">
<itemtemplate>
     <table>
     <tr><td>Employee ID:</td>
     <td><b><%# string.Format("{0:D4}",Container.DataItem.EID ) %></b>
     </td></tr>
     <tr><td>Employee Name: </td>
     <td><b><%# DataBinder.Eval(Container.DataItem, "LastName")%>,
     <%# DataBinder.Eval(Container.DataItem, "FirstName")%></b>
     </td></tr>
     <tr><td>Salary: </td>
     <td><b>
     <%# DataBinder.Eval(Container.DataItem, "Salary","{0:C}")%>
     </b></td></tr>
     </table>
</ItemTemplate>
</asp:DataList>
```

This code will nest a table inside each of the cells that the DataList originally produced. The browser output (see the right window in Figure 6.6) shows a much cleaner appearance.

Although the last example was cleaner looking, it lacks a header, and it can be difficult to see where one employee ends and another employee starts. In the following example, an alternate item style is created. This is better than the Repeater, because the layout from the item template does not need to be copied. A header and footer are supplied here as well.

```
<asp:DataList id=DataList1 runat="server">
<headerstyle backcolor="black"
     forecolor="white"
     font-bold="True"
     horizontalalign="Center">
</headerstyle>
<alternatingitemstyle backcolor="silver">
</alternatingitemstyle>
<footerstyle backcolor="black"
     forecolor="white"
     font-bold="True"
     horizontalalign="Center">
</footerstyle>
<headertemplate>
     Employee List
</headertemplate>
<itemtemplate>
     <table>
```

```
<tr><td>Employee ID:</td>
<td><b>
<%# string.Format("{0:D4}",Container.DataItem.EID ) %>
</b>
</td></tr>
<tr><td>Employee Name: </td>
<td><b>
<%# DataBinder.Eval(Container.DataItem, "LastName")%>,
<%# DataBinder.Eval(Container.DataItem, "FirstName")%>
</b>
</td></tr>
<tr><td>Salary: </td>
<td><b>
<%# DataBinder.Eval(Container.DataItem, "Salary","{0:C}")%>
</b></td></tr>
</table>
</ItemTemplate>
<footertemplate>
     End of List
</footertemplate>
</asp:DataList>
```

The browser output (see Figure 6.7) shows a very readable list of employees. The data is in the item template, and the formatting is in the style elements.

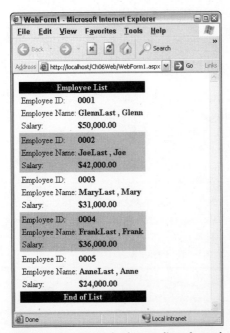

Figure 6.7 A much cleaner list of employees, with a header, a footer, and an alternating style.

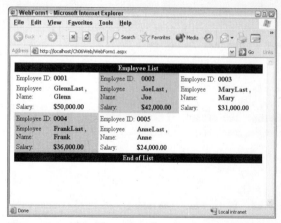

Figure 6.8 The effect of setting the RepeatColumns to 3, the RepeatDirection to Horizontal, the GridLines to Both, and the BorderColor to Black.

As the list of employees gets longer, it will be necessary to come up with a way to fill the screen with employees instead of having a narrow column of employees. That is where the RepeatColumns and RepeatDirection come into play.

Figure 6.8 shows an example of setting the RepeatColumns to three and the RepeatDirection to Horizontal. In this example, the GridLines property is set to Both and the BorderColor is set to Black. Notice that the RepeatDirection can also be set to Vertical, which will cause the employee list to be rendered downward in vertical columns.

Selecting an Item

The DataList can allow a user to select an item. This is usually desirable when only a small amount of data is being displayed and more details are desired.

Making a selection involves setting the SelectedIndex to a number other than minus one (-1), which is the default. This can be done by creating an Item-Command method, which will change the selection number.

There is one small problem, which is that the SelectedIndex must be set before the data is bound to the DataList. Currently, our data is being bound in the Page_Load method. This is only acceptable when the data is not being posted to the server (the first time to the page). The code to create the employees will be placed into a procedure called BindEmployees as follows:

```
Private Sub Page_Load(ByVal sender As System.Object, _
     ByVal e As System.EventArgs) Handles MyBase.Load
     If Not IsPostBack() Then
          BindEmployees()
     End If
End Sub
```

```
Public Sub BindEmployees()
    Dim a As New ArrayList()
    a.Add(New Employee(1, "GlennLast", "Glenn", 50000))
    a.Add(New Employee(2, "JoeLast", "Joe", 42000))
    a.Add(New Employee(3, "MaryLast", "Mary", 31000))
    a.Add(New Employee(4, "FrankLast", "Frank", 36000))
    a.Add(New Employee(5, "AnneLast", "Anne", 24000))
    DataList1.DataSource = a
    DataList1.DataBind()
End Sub
```

An event method must be created in the code-behind page to set the Selected-Index of the DataList when a button is clicked. Do this by clicking the Class Name drop-down list and clicking DataList1. In the Method drop-down list, click ItemCommand, which inserts code for this event. In this method, add code to set the SelectedIndex and call the BindEmployees method as follows:

```
Private Sub DataList1_ItemCommand(ByVal source As Object, _
    ByVal e As System.Web.UI.WebControls.DataListCommandEventArgs) _
    Handles DataList1.ItemCommand
    DataList1.SelectedIndex = e.Item.ItemIndex
    BindEmployees()
End Sub
```

Another event method must be added in the code-behind page to clear the SelectedIndex when no details are desired. Do this by clicking the Class Name drop-down list and then clicking DataList1. In the Method drop-down list, click CancelCommand, which inserts code for the event. In this method, add code to set the SelectedIndex to minus one (-1) and call the BindEmployees method as follows:

```
Private Sub DataList1_CancelCommand(ByVal source As Object, _
    ByVal e As System.Web.UI.WebControls.DataListCommandEventArgs) _
    Handles DataList1.CancelCommand
    DataList1.SelectedIndex = -1
    BindEmployees()
End Sub
```

Finally, the item template is modified to display a Display Details button and the employee's full name. The selected item template contains all the details plus a Hide Details button. The following code contains the completed DataList1 control:

```
<asp:datalist id=DataList1 runat="server"
    GridLines="Both"
    bordercolor="black" >
<headertemplate>
    Employee List
</HeaderTemplate>
```

```
<alternatingitemstyle backcolor="Silver">
</AlternatingItemStyle>
<selecteditemstyle backcolor="yellow">
</selecteditemstyle>
<footertemplate>
      End of List
</FooterTemplate>
<selecteditemtemplate>
      <table>
      <tr><td colspan="2">
      <asp:linkbutton id="Linkbutton2" runat="server"
      text="Hide Details" commandname="cancel" />
      </td></tr>
      <tr><td>Employee ID:</td>
      <td><b>
      <%# string.Format("{0:D4}",Container.DataItem.EID ) %>
      </b>
      </td></tr>
      <tr><td>Employee Name: </td>
      <td><b>
      <%# DataBinder.Eval(Container.DataItem, "LastName")%>,
      <%# DataBinder.Eval(Container.DataItem, "FirstName")%>
      </b>
      </td></tr>
      <tr><td>Salary: </td>
      <td><b>
      <%# DataBinder.Eval(Container.DataItem, "Salary","{0:C}")%>
      </b></td></tr>
      </table>
</selecteditemtemplate>
<itemtemplate>
      <table>
      <tr><td colspan="2">
      <asp:linkbutton id="LinkButton1" runat="server"
      text="Show Details" commandname="select" />
      </td></tr>
      <tr><td>Employee Name: </td>
      <td><b>
      <%# DataBinder.Eval(Container.DataItem, "LastName")%>,
      <%# DataBinder.Eval(Container.DataItem, "FirstName")%>
      </b>
      </td></tr>
      </table>
</ItemTemplate>
<footerstyle font-bold="True" horizontalalign="Center"
      forecolor="White" backcolor="Black">
</FooterStyle>
<headerstyle font-bold="True" horizontalalign="Center"
      forecolor="White" backcolor="Black">
</HeaderStyle>
</asp:datalist>
```

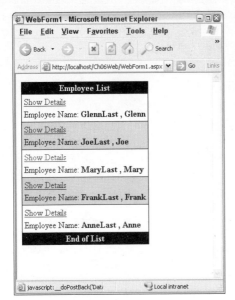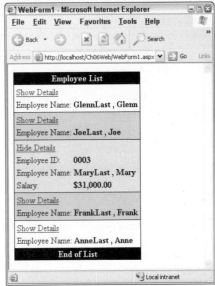

Figure 6.9 Employee list with no employee details selected (left) and with employee 0003 selected (right).

The browser output (see Figure 6.9) shows the items without and with an employee selected. If the Show Details is clicked on a different employee, that employee's details are exposed.

Editing an Item

The DataList can allow a user to edit an item. Editing an item involves setting the EditItemIndex to a number other than minus one (-1), which is the default. This can be done by creating an EditCommand method, which will change the edit item number.

There is one small problem: Our data in the ArrayList is not persisted, so the ArrayList is being recreated every time that data is posted back to the server. The BindEmployee method has been changed to store the ArrayList in a Session variable. Session variables are available throughout the browser session and will be covered in more detail in Chapter 12, "ASP.NET Applications." The following is the revised BindEmployees method:

```
Public Sub BindEmployees()
    'create employee list if it
    'does not exist
    If Session("Employees") Is Nothing Then
        Dim a As New ArrayList()
        a.Add(New Employee(1, "GlennLast", "Glenn", 50000))
        a.Add(New Employee(2, "JoeLast", "Joe", 42000))
        a.Add(New Employee(3, "MaryLast", "Mary", 31000))
        a.Add(New Employee(4, "FrankLast", "Frank", 36000))
        a.Add(New Employee(5, "AnneLast", "Anne", 24000))
```

```
              Session("Employees") = a
          End If
          DataList1.DataSource = Session("Employees")
          DataList1.DataBind()
      End Sub
```

An event method must be created in the code-behind page to set the Edit-ItemIndex of the DataList when a button is clicked. Do this by clicking the Class Name drop-down list and then clicking DataList1. In the Method drop-down list, click EditCommand, which inserts code for this event. In this method, add code to set the EditItemIndex, and call the BindEmployees method as follows:

```
Private Sub DataList1_EditCommand(ByVal source As Object, _
    ByVal e As System.Web.UI.WebControls.DataListCommandEventArgs) _
    Handles DataList1.EditCommand
    DataList1.EditItemIndex = e.Item.ItemIndex
    BindEmployees()
End Sub
```

The CancelCommand must be modified to set the EditItemIndex to minus one (-1) if editing is cancelled:

```
Private Sub DataList1_CancelCommand(ByVal source As Object, _
    ByVal e As System.Web.UI.WebControls.DataListCommandEventArgs) _
    Handles DataList1.CancelCommand
    If DataList1.EditItemIndex = -1 Then
        DataList1.SelectedIndex = -1
    Else
        DataList1.EditItemIndex = -1
    End If
    BindEmployees()
End Sub
```

The selected item template has been changed to have an Edit button beside the Hide Details button. Also, an edit item template needs to be added to the DataList. The following is the revised selected item template and the new edit item template:

```
<selecteditemtemplate>
    <table>
    <tr>
    <td>
    <asp:linkbutton id="itemCancel" runat="server"
    text="Hide Details" commandname="cancel" />
    </td>
    <td>
    <asp:linkbutton id="itemEdit" runat="server"
    text="Edit" commandname="edit" />
    </td>
    </tr>
```

```
    <tr><td>Employee ID:</td>
    <td><b>
    <%# string.Format("{0:D4}",Container.DataItem.EID ) %>
    </b>
    </td></tr>
    <tr><td>Employee Name: </td>
    <td><b>
    <%# DataBinder.Eval(Container.DataItem, "LastName")%>,
    <%# DataBinder.Eval(Container.DataItem, "FirstName")%>
    </b>
    </td></tr>
    <tr><td>Salary: </td>
    <td><b>
    <%# DataBinder.Eval(Container.DataItem, "Salary","{0:C}")%>
    </b></td></tr>
    </table>
</SelectedItemTemplate>
<edititemtemplate>
    <table>
    <tr>
    <td>
    <asp:linkbutton id="editCancel" runat="server"
    text="Cancel" commandname="cancel" />
    </td>
    <td>
    <asp:linkbutton id="editUpdate" runat="server"
    text="Update" commandname="update" />
    </td>
    </tr>
    <tr><td>Employee ID:</td>
    <td><b>
    <asp:label id="empID" runat="server"
    Text='<%# string.Format("{0:D4}",Container.DataItem.EID ) %>' />
    </b>
    </td></tr>
    <tr><td>Last: </td>
    <td>
    <asp:textbox id="empLast" runat="server"
    Text='<%# DataBinder.Eval(Container.DataItem, "LastName")%>' />
    </td></tr>
    <tr><td>First: </td>
    <td>
    <asp:textbox id="empFirst" runat="server"
    Text='<%# DataBinder.Eval(Container.DataItem, "FirstName")%>' />
    </td></tr>
    <tr><td>Salary: </td>
    <td>
    <asp:textbox id="salary" runat="server"
    Text='<%# DataBinder.Eval(Container.DataItem, "Salary")%>' />
    </td></tr>
    </table>
</edititemtemplate>
```

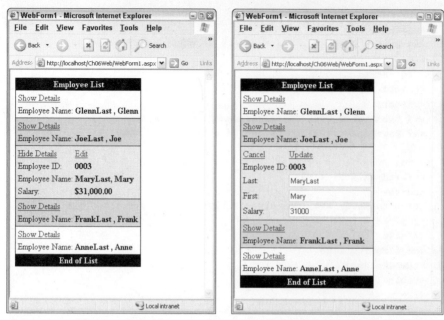

Figure 6.10 The DataList with an employee selected (left) and with the employee in edit mode (right).

The browser output is shown in Figure 6.10. Notice that the edit item template contains TextBoxes for the editable fields. The employee ID field is a read-only field, so it is displayed in a Label control.

The last thing to do is to update the data. The update will be very different, based on the data source. To do any update, the data must be retrieved from the edit template. This can be done with the FindControl method. The following code demonstrates the extraction of data from the edit template and the updating of the employee data.

```
Private Sub DataList1_UpdateCommand(ByVal source As Object, _
    ByVal e As System.Web.UI.WebControls.DataListCommandEventArgs) _
    Handles DataList1.UpdateCommand
    Dim empID As Label = e.Item.FindControl("empID")
    Dim empLast As TextBox = e.Item.FindControl("empLast")
    Dim empFirst As TextBox = e.Item.FindControl("empFirst")
    Dim salary As TextBox = e.Item.FindControl("salary")
    'This would normally be an
    'update statement to the database
    Dim emp As Employee
    For Each emp In Session("Employees")
        If emp.EID = Integer.Parse(empID.Text) Then
            emp.LastName = empLast.Text
            emp.FirstName = empFirst.Text
            emp.Salary = Decimal.Parse(salary.Text)
            Exit For
        End If
```

```
        Next
        DataList1.EditItemIndex = -1
        BindEmployees()
    End Sub
```

 The DataList can also be set up by using the GUI menus. These menus are available by right-clicking the DataList, and then clicking Auto Format, Property Builder, or Edit Template.

DataGrid Control

The DataGrid control is the most powerful of the data bound controls provided with ASP.NET. The DataGrid is designed to display the fields of a data source in an HTML table. Each row in the HTML table represents one of the repeating items in the data source.

The DataGrid supports item selection, editing, deleting, sorting, and paging. The DataGrid has many properties, but can be quickly set up to display data by using its default settings. The DataGrid provides the following properties that have already been defined in this chapter and can be set in the Visual Studio .NET designer or in code:

- DataSource
- DataMember

In addition, the DataGrid contains several properties that have not yet been defined. Table 6.5 contains the list of new properties.

Table 6.5 Additional DataGrid Properties

PROPERTY	DESCRIPTION
AllowCustomPaging	Changeable Boolean value indicating whether custom paging is used. If custom paging is used, the assumption is that the data source does not contain all of the data. The data source instead contains only one page of data.
AllowPaging	Changeable Boolean value indicating whether paging is allowed. Paging allows data to be split into smaller segments based on the PageSize property.
AllowSorting	Changeable Boolean value indicating whether sorting is enabled. If the value is true, LinkButtons controls are rendered in the header of each column that has its SortExpression property set.

(continued)

Table 6.5   *(continued)*

PROPERTY	DESCRIPTION
AutoGenerateColumns	Changeable Boolean property indicating whether columns will be automatically generated and rendered. If true, a column will be created for each field in the data source. Columns may also be explicitly added, and they will appear before the autogenerated columns.
BackImageUrl	Changeable value containing the location of the image that is used as a background for the DataGrid. The image will tile as necessary to fill the DataGrid.
Columns	Changeable value containing a DataGridColumnCollection. Note that autogenerated columns will not be added to this collection.
CurrentPageIndex	Changeable value containing the page of data that will display in the DataGrid.
EditItemIndex	Changeable value indicating which item in the DataGrid is being edited. This value is set to -1 when no item is being edited.
Items	Changeable value containing the items from the data source that are included in the DataGrid.
PageCount	Read-only count of the quantity of pages that are required to display all of the data.
PagerStyle	Changeable value indicating the type of paging controls that will be rendered onto the DataGrid. The PageStyle mode can be set to Numeric, to display page number links for each page, or to PrevNext to display previous and next links to move between pages.
PageSize	Changeable value containing the count of rows per DataGrid page.
SelectedIndex	Changeable value indicating the currently selected item in the DataGrid. This value is set to -1 when no item is selected.
SelectedItem	Read-only value that contains the row that is currently selected in the DataGrid.
ShowHeader	Changeable Boolean value indicating whether the header should be displayed.
ShowFooter	Changeable Boolean value indicating whether the footer should be displayed.
VirtualItemCount	Changeable value containing the virtual quantity of items for use when using custom paging.

In the next series of DataGrid examples, the following code will be assigned to the Page_Load method and the BindEmployees method:

```
Private Sub Page_Load(ByVal sender As System.Object, _
    ByVal e As System.EventArgs) Handles MyBase.Load
    If Not IsPostBack() Then
        BindEmployees()
    End If
End Sub
Public Sub BindEmployees()
    'Create employee list if it
    'does not exist.
    If Session("Employees") Is Nothing Then
        Dim a As New ArrayList()
        a.Add(New Employee(1, "GlennLast", "Glenn", 50000))
        a.Add(New Employee(2, "JoeLast", "Joe", 42000))
        a.Add(New Employee(3, "MaryLast", "Mary", 31000))
        a.Add(New Employee(4, "FrankLast", "Frank", 36000))
        a.Add(New Employee(5, "AnneLast", "Anne", 24000))
        Session("Employees") = a
    End If
    DataGrid1.DataSource = Session("Employees")
    DataGrid1.DataBind()
End Sub
```

The code is using the Employee class that was used in the previous Repeater and DataList examples, and five Employee instances are added to an ArrayList. In this example, the DataGrid is placed on to the Web page.

When the page is displayed (see Figure 6.11), the DataGrid created and rendered three columns. Notice that the employee ID (EID) of the employees has not been rendered, because the DataGrid is not looking for public fields; it's only looking for public properties.

Assigning a Style to the DataGrid

The DataGrid supports style elements, which allows the style to change without repeating the same code. For example, the Repeater control examples in this chapter had the same code for the ItemTemplate and the AlternatingItem-Template. The only thing that was different was the style.

The DataGrid solves the problem with these special style elements. The following is a list of style elements that are supported by the DataGrid. Figure 6.5 shows the style hierarchy.

- AlternatingItemStyle
- EditItemStyle
- FooterStyle
- HeaderStyle

- ItemStyle

- SelectedItemStyle

In addition to these styles, a quick way to assign a style is to right-click the DataGrid and then click Auto Format. The Auto Format window displays many options that allow the DataGrid to be quickly formatted. Professional 3 will be used in the following examples, as shown in Figure 6.11.

Adding Columns to the DataGrid

You can add columns to the DataGrid via HTML, code, or the Property Builder. The following types of columns may be added to the DataGrid:

BoundColumn.   A column that can be bound to a field in the data source.

ButtonColumn.   A column that contains a command button. This button can be used with the item on the current row (for example, Add or Delete).

EditCommandColumn.   A column that displays an Edit button until a row is being edited. When a row is being edited, Cancel and Update buttons will be placed in the column on the edited row.

HyperLinkColumn.   A column that displays a hyperlink button, which can be configured to provide a URL and a querystring that contains information about the current item.

TemplateColumn.   A column with the ability to be completely customized with templates.

In the previous example, the employee ID column was missing. The following code adds the employee ID to the DataGrid.

```
Private Sub DataGrid1_Init(ByVal sender As Object, _
    ByVal e As System.EventArgs) _
    Handles DataGrid1.Init
        Dim col As New BoundColumn()
        col.HeaderText = "Employee ID"
        DataGrid1.Columns.Add(col)
End Sub
```

It is important to add the column as early as possible in the DataGrid control's life cycle. Adding the column in the Init event method of the DataGrid means that the column will be available to work with ViewState and be assigned data.

Although a bound column was used, a DataField could not be provided because the EID is a public variable instead of a property. Although this column will be displayed, there will not be any data.

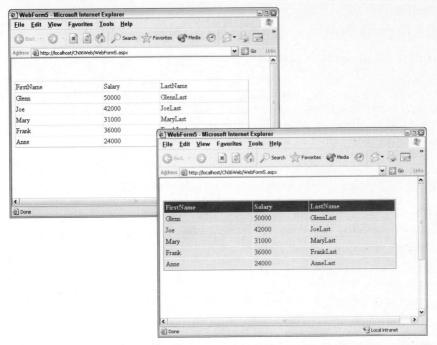

Figure 6.11 DataGrid rendered with default settings (left), and with Professional 3 style selected (right).

An easy way to populate the data would be to add code to the DataGrid's ItemDataBound event method. This method executes every time that a row needs to be rendered. One problem is that this will execute on the header and footer rows, so a check needs to be done to verify that there is data available for a row before attempting to extract the EID. The following code will get the EID and populate column 0, which is the Employee ID column.

```
Private Sub DataGrid1_ItemDataBound(ByVal sender As Object, _
    ByVal e As System.Web.UI.WebControls.DataGridItemEventArgs) _
    Handles DataGrid1.ItemDataBound
    If TypeOf e.Item.DataItem Is Employee Then
        Dim currentEmployee As Employee = _
            CType(e.Item.DataItem, Employee)
        e.Item.Cells(0).Text = _
            string.Format("{0:D3}",currentEmployee.EID)
    End If
End Sub
```

◆ Object-Oriented Method to Display Hidden Data in a DataGrid

The Employee class was created with the EID, which is a public read-only member variable. In the DataList and DataGrid examples, the public properties were displayed, while a more creative method was required to get to the EID. In these examples, the source code for the Employees class was available, so a simple way to get access to the EID would be to add another public property to the Employee class.

How is this problem solved if the source code is unavailable? If the Employee class was provided as a compiled .dll file with no source code, it's not possible to simply add the property. Instead, a new class can be created that inherits from the Employee class. The following code is an example of a new class called EmployeeData, which inherits from Employee. This class has the additional read-only property called EmployeeID. The rest of the properties are available through inheritance.

```
Public Class EmployeeData
    Inherits Employee
    Public Sub New(ByVal EID As Integer, _
        ByVal LastName As String, _
        ByVal FirstName As String, _
        ByVal Salary As Decimal)
            MyBase.New(EID, LastName, FirstName, Salary)
    End Sub
    Public ReadOnly Property EmployeeID() As Integer
        Get
            Return EID
        End Get
    End Property
End Class
```

This class could be used to create an EmployeeData collection instead of the Employee collection. The EmployeeData collection could be assigned to the data source of the DataGrid.

This is one example method of populating the Employee ID column. Another method of populating the Employee ID column is to use an object-oriented approach as described in the sidebar titled *Object-Oriented Method to Display Hidden Data in a DataGrid*.

With the HTML page, the DataGrid tag can contain a columns collection. Another method of adding the EID column is by adding a template column tag in the DataGrid HTML tag. The following code is an example of the added template column. This code is similar to the DataList template code:

```
<asp:DataGrid id="DataGrid1" runat="server">
    <columns>
        <asp:TemplateColumn HeaderText="Employee ID">
            <itemtemplate>
            <%# string.Format("{0:D4}",Container.DataItem.EID ) %>
            </ItemTemplate>
        </asp:TemplateColumn>
    </Columns>
</asp:DataGrid>
```

Visual Studio .NET also provides a property builder that can be used to insert columns via GUI windows. The property builder can be accessed by right-clicking the DataGrid and then clicking Property Builder. Figure 6.12 shows the Property Builder screen.

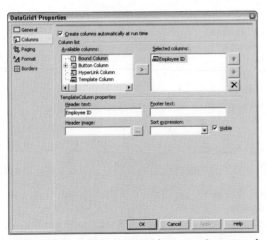

Figure 6.12 Most DataGrid properties may be assigned with the DataGrid Property Builder.

Ordering Columns

Although all columns may be displayed, the order of the fields may not be appropriate. In addition, different header text may be required. In the previous example, the fields were automatically added, but it's usually better to manually create the columns and set their properties. Once again, the columns may be added manually via code, the HTML window, or the Property Builder. All of the examples that follow are done in code.

The columns need to be added to the DataGrid's Init event method. In the following code example, all four columns are manually added in the appropriate order and with the desired header text.

```vb
Private Sub DataGrid1_Init(ByVal sender As Object, _
  ByVal e As System.EventArgs) _
  Handles DataGrid1.Init
    DataGrid1.AutoGenerateColumns = False
        Dim col As New BoundColumn()
        col.HeaderText = "Employee<BR>ID"
        col.ItemStyle.HorizontalAlign = HorizontalAlign.Right
        col.HeaderStyle.HorizontalAlign = HorizontalAlign.Center
        col.ItemStyle.Width = New Unit(75, UnitType.Pixel)
        DataGrid1.Columns.Add(col)
        'Store this info for later use.
        DataGrid1.Attributes("EidCol") = DataGrid1.Columns.Count - 1
        col = New BoundColumn()
        col.HeaderText = "Last<BR>Name"
        col.DataField = "LastName"
        col.HeaderStyle.HorizontalAlign = HorizontalAlign.Center
        col.ItemStyle.Width = New Unit(200, UnitType.Pixel)
        DataGrid1.Columns.Add(col)
        DataGrid1.Attributes("LastNameCol") = _
            DataGrid1.Columns.Count - 1
        col = New BoundColumn()
        col.HeaderText = "First<BR>Name"
        col.DataField = "FirstName"
        col.HeaderStyle.HorizontalAlign = HorizontalAlign.Center
        col.ItemStyle.Width = New Unit(200, UnitType.Pixel)
        DataGrid1.Columns.Add(col)
        DataGrid1.Attributes("FirstNameCol") = _
            DataGrid1.Columns.Count - 1
        col = New BoundColumn()
        col.HeaderText = "Salary"
        col.DataField = "Salary"
        col.DataFormatString = "{0:C}"
        col.ItemStyle.HorizontalAlign = HorizontalAlign.Right
        col.HeaderStyle.HorizontalAlign = HorizontalAlign.Center
        col.ItemStyle.Width = New Unit(150, UnitType.Pixel)
        DataGrid1.Columns.Add(col)
        DataGrid1.Attributes("SalaryCol") = _
            DataGrid1.Columns.Count - 1
End Sub
```

```
Private Sub DataGrid1_ItemDataBound(ByVal sender As Object, _
    ByVal e As System.Web.UI.WebControls.DataGridItemEventArgs) _
    Handles DataGrid1.ItemDataBound
    Dim EidCol As Integer
    EidCol = Integer.Parse(DataGrid1.Attributes("EidCol"))
    If TypeOf e.Item.DataItem Is Employee Then
        Dim currentEmployee As Employee = _
         CType(e.Item.DataItem, Employee)
        e.Item.Cells(EidCol).Text = _
         String.Format("{0:D3}", currentEmployee.EID)
    End If
End Sub
```

Figure 6.13 shows the browser output. The first statement in this code turned off the automatic generation of the columns. If this setting were not set to false, the manual columns and the autogenerated columns would be displayed. The statements that follow set up each of the columns in order. Each column has additional formatting to set the width of the column and the alignment of the text. The last part of the code is the ItemDataBound event method. This only contains code to assign the employee ID, because the other columns were easily bound by their field name in the InitDataBind method.

Another interesting item is the persistence of the column numbers. After the column was added, the column number is persisted to an attribute in the DataGrid. This means that a peek at the browser source will reveal these attributes on DataGrid1's table. This attributes can be retrieved when binding, selecting, editing, and updating the data. The benefit of this approach is realized when more columns are added. There is no need to update the column numbers throughout the code.

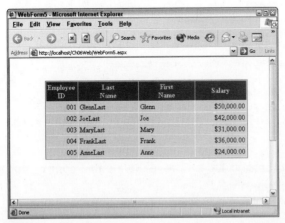

Figure 6.13 The browser output showing the DataGrid with its columns defined in the code-behind page.

Selecting an Item

The DataGrid can allow a user to select an item. This is usually desirable when only a small amount of data is being displayed and more details are desired. A common requirement is to cause a child DataGrid to refresh and display information about the item that was selected in the parent DataGrid. For example, selecting a customer may cause that customer's orders to be displayed in a child DataGrid.

Making a selection involves setting the SelectedIndex to a number other than minus one (-1), which is the default. This can be done by creating an Item-Command method, which will change the selection number. The SelectedIndex must be set before the data is bound to the DataList. After the SelectedIndex is set, a call will be made to bind the data.

The following code shows the addition of a column to the top of the Data-Grid1 Init method and the added ItemCommand event method:

```
Private Sub DataGrid1_Init(ByVal sender As Object, _
    ByVal e As System.EventArgs) _
    Handles DataGrid1.Init
    DataGrid1.AutoGenerateColumns = False
    Dim colSelect As New ButtonColumn()
    colSelect.ButtonType = ButtonColumnType.PushButton
    colSelect.Text = "Select"
    colSelect.CommandName = DataGrid.SelectCommandName
    DataGrid1.Columns.Add(colSelect)
    'additional columns here as shown in
    'the previous example
End Sub
Private Sub DataGrid1_ItemCommand(ByVal source As Object, _
    ByVal e As System.Web.UI.WebControls.DataGridCommandEventArgs) _
    Handles DataGrid1.ItemCommand
    DataGrid1.SelectedIndex = e.Item.ItemIndex
    'Get EID and simply display it.
    Dim EidCol As Integer
    EidCol = Integer.Parse(DataGrid1.Attributes("EidCol"))
    Dim EID As Integer
    EID = Integer.Parse(e.Item.Cells(EidCol).Text)
    Label1.Text = "Employee ID Selected: " & EID.ToString()
    BindEmployees()
End Sub
```

This code displays the EID of the selected employee in a Label control that is placed on the page as shown in Figure 6.14.

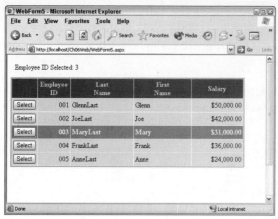

Figure 6.14 The ItemCommand event has been used to retrieve the current employee ID and display it in a Label control.

Editing an Item

The DataGrid can allow a user to edit an item. Editing an item involves setting the EditItemIndex to a number other than minus one (-1), which is the default. This is done by clicking the Class Name drop-down list and then clicking DataGrid1. In the Method drop-down list, click EditCommand, which inserts code for this event. In this method, add code to set the EditItemIndex and call the BindEmployees method as follows:

```
Private Sub DataGrid1_EditCommand(ByVal source As Object, _
    ByVal e As System.Web.UI.WebControls.DataGridCommandEventArgs) _
    Handles DataGrid1.EditCommand
    DataGrid1.EditItemIndex = e.Item.ItemIndex
    BindEmployees()
End Sub
```

The CancelCommand must be modified to set the EditItemIndex to minus one (-1) if editing is cancelled.

```
Private Sub DataGrid1_CancelCommand(ByVal source As Object, _
    ByVal e As System.Web.UI.WebControls.DataGridCommandEventArgs) _
    Handles DataGrid1.CancelCommand
    DataGrid1.EditItemIndex = -1
    BindEmployees()
End Sub
```

The following code shows the addition of the Edit button column to the DataGrid1 Init method. The Edit button turns into an Update and Cancel button pair when the Edit button is clicked. Figure 6.15 shows the new Edit column and the browser in edit mode.

```
Dim colEdit As New EditCommandColumn()
colEdit.ButtonType = ButtonColumnType.PushButton
colEdit.EditText = "Edit"
colEdit.CancelText = "Cancel"
colEdit.UpdateText = "Update"
colEdit.ItemStyle.Width = New Unit(200, UnitType.Pixel)
DataGrid1.Columns.Add(colEdit)
```

The Edit and Cancel code has been added. The last item to be added to the program is the Update method. This is done by clicking the Class Name drop-down list and then clicking DataGrid1. In the Method drop-down list, click UpdateCommand, which inserts code for this event. The following code updates the ArrayList that is stored in Session("Employees").

```
Private Sub DataGrid1_UpdateCommand(ByVal source As Object, _
    ByVal e As System.Web.UI.WebControls.DataGridCommandEventArgs) _
    Handles DataGrid1.UpdateCommand
    Dim LastName As TextBox
    Dim FirstName As TextBox
    Dim Salary As TextBox
    LastName = CType(e.Item.Cells(DataGrid1.Attributes( _
      "LastNameCol")).Controls(0), TextBox)
    FirstName = CType(e.Item.Cells(DataGrid1.Attributes( _
      "FirstNameCol")).Controls(0), TextBox)
    Salary = CType(e.Item.Cells(DataGrid1.Attributes( _
      "SalaryCol")).Controls(0), TextBox)
    'Get the row index from the DataGrid.
    Dim di As Integer = e.Item.DataSetIndex
    'Get the Data from the DataGrid.
    Session("Employees")(di).LastName = LastName.Text
    Session("Employees")(di).FirstName = FirstName.Text
    Session("Employees")(di).Salary = Salary.Text
    'Get EID and display it
    Dim EidCol As Integer
    EidCol = Integer.Parse(DataGrid1.Attributes("EidCol"))
    Dim EID As Integer
    EID = Integer.Parse(e.Item.Cells(EidCol).Text)
    Label1.Text = "Employee ID Updated: " & EID.ToString()

    DataGrid1.EditItemIndex = -1
    BindEmployees()
End Sub
```

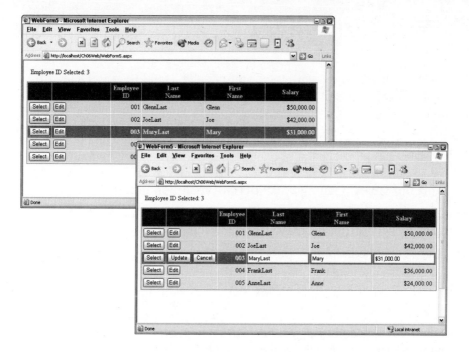

Figure 6.15 The new edit column (left) and the browser in edit mode (right).

In this code, references are first obtained to each of the TextBoxes that were displayed. The attributes that were saved when the columns were added can be used to select the appropriate cell. Retrieving Controls(0) gets the first control in the call, but it must be cast to a TextBox data type by using the CType function. This allows access to the Text property.

Another interested property of the Item is the DataSetIndex, which contains the row number of the data source. This can easily be used to assign the modified values to Session("Employees"). The Item also contains an ItemIndex property, which contains the index number of the current item in the Data-Grid. This may not be equal to the DataSetRow, especially when paging is used in the DataGrid.

The last piece of the update code retrieves the EID and places its value in Label1. In these examples, the EID is considered read-only, so no attempt is made to edit or update this field.

Lab 6.1: Data Bound Web Controls

In this lab, you will work with the DataRepeater, DataList, and DataGrid to display a collection of categories from the category classes that were created in Lab 4.1.

Displaying the Categories in a Repeater

In this section, you will add a Repeater to the ProductList page.

1. Start this lab by opening the OrderEntrySolution from Lab 5.1.

2. Right-click the OrderEntrySolution in the Solution Explorer, and then click Check Out. This will check out the complete solution.

3. Right-click the Inventory project, and then click Set as Startup Project.

4. Right-click the ProductList.aspx page, and then click Set As Start Page.

5. Open the ProductList.aspx page. Add a Repeater control to the page. Rename the repeater to ProductGrid.

6. Click the HTML tab and add a header template to the ProductGrid that displays *Product List* with a silver background. The font should be in a large size and centered.

7. Add an item template to the ProductGrid to display the product name, price, and quantity on hand. These items should be listed on a separate line. Be sure to use the DataBinder.Eval method to display the price as a formatted currency value.

8. Add a separator template. In the separator template, add a horizontal line.

9. Add a footer template that displays End of List with a silver background. The font should be xx-small size and centered. Your HTML for the ProductsGrid should look like the following:

```
<asp:repeater id=ProductGrid runat="server">
<headertemplate >
    <div style="font-size: large;
        background-color: silver; text-align: center">
    Product List
```

```
        </div>
    </headertemplate>
    <itemtemplate>
        Product Name: <%# Container.DataItem.ProductName %><br>
        Price: <%# DataBinder.Eval(
            container.dataitem,"UnitPrice","{0:C}") %><br>
        Quantity in Stock <%# Container.DataItem.UnitsInStock %><br>
    </itemtemplate>
    <separatortemplate>
        <hr>
    </separatortemplate>
    <footertemplate>
    <div style="font-size: xx-small;
        background-color: silver; text-align: center">
        End of List
    </div>
    </footertemplate>
    </asp:Repeater>
```

10. Right-click the page, and click View Code. Locate the Page_Load method. This method contains a loop that is currently used to display the categories. Remove the loop.

11. At the bottom of the Page_Load method, add code to assign 100 to the price and a random value between 1 and 10 to the UnitsInStock of all items in the Products ArrayList. Next, assign the Products ArrayList to the ProductGrid and bind the data. The code should look like the following:

```
Dim b As BaseProduct
For Each b In Products
    b.UnitPrice = 100
    b.UnitsInStock = Rnd() * 10
Next
ProductGrid.DataSource = Products
DataBind( )
```

12. Save your work.

The repeater can be tested by viewing the page. Press F5 to start the Web application. The ProductList.aspx page is displayed. Figure 6.16 shows an example of the completed page.

Figure 6.16   The completed Repeater control.

Displaying Data in the DataGrid

In this section, the Repeater control will be removed and a DataGrid will be placed on the page. The Page_Load method contains code to populate an ArrayList every time the page is loaded. In this example, the ArrayList will only be populated at the beginning of the session, and the ArrayList will be saved to a session variable. This approach can be used to test the ability to edit with the DataGrid control.

1. Remove the Repeater control from the Web page.

2. Add a DataGrid control to the page, and rename the DataGrid to ProductGrid.

3. Right-click the page, and click View Code. Locate the Page_Load method. Cut all of the code from the Page_Load method and paste it into a new method called BindProducts.

4. In the Page_Load method, add code to call the BindProducts method if the data is not being posted back to the server.

5. In the BindProducts method, change the code to use a session variable called Session("Products"). This variable will be populated if it is currently empty. Your code should look like the following:

```
Private Sub Page_Load(ByVal sender As System.Object, _
    ByVal e As System.EventArgs) _
    Handles MyBase.Load
    If Not IsPostBack Then
        BindProducts()
    End If
End Sub
Public Sub BindProducts()
    If Session("Products") Is Nothing Then
        Dim Products As New ArrayList()
        Products.Add(New Beverage(1, "Milk"))
        Products.Add(New Beverage(2, "Juice"))
        Products.Add(New Beverage(3, "Cola"))
        Products.Add(New Confection(4, "Ice Cream"))
        Products.Add(New Confection(5, "Cake"))
        Products.Add(New Confection(6, "Candy"))
        Dim b As BaseProduct
        For Each b In Products
            b.UnitPrice = 100
            b.UnitsInStock = Rnd() * 10
        Next
        Session("Products") = Products
    End If
    ProductGrid.DataSource = Session("Products")
    DataBind()
End Sub
```

6. Save your work.

The DataGrid can be tested by viewing the page. Press F5 to start the Web application. The ProductList.aspx page displays. Figure 6.17 shows an example of the completed page.

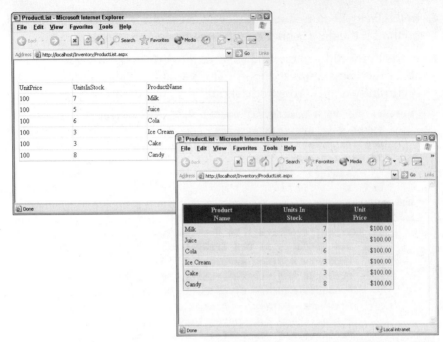

Figure 6.17 The basic DataGrid (upper left) and the enhanced DataGrid (lower right).

Enhancing the DataGrid Output

In this section, you will assign a style format to the DataGrid. You will also add the columns manually, setting their properties as you go.

1. Right-click the ProductGrid, and click Auto Format, Colorful 2, OK.

2. Go to the code-behind page and add code to create each column of the DataGrid. This code will be added into the DataGrid Init event method. The columns will be created using the properties shown in Table 6.6.

Table 6.6 New Column Properties

COLUMN	PROPERTY	VALUE
ProductName	HeaderText	Product Name
ProductName	HeaderStyle.HorizontalAlign	HorizontalAlign.Center
ProductName	ItemStyle.HorizontalAlign	HorizontalAlign.Left
ProductName	DataField	ProductName
UnitsInStock	HeaderText	Units In Stock
UnitsInStock	HeaderStyle.HorizontalAlign	HorizontalAlign.Center

Table 6.6   *(continued)*

COLUMN	PROPERTY	VALUE
UnitsInStock	ItemStyle.HorizontalAlign	HorizontalAlign.Right
UnitsInStock	DataField	UnitsInStock
UnitPrice	HeaderText	Unit Price
UnitPrice	HeaderStyle.HorizontalAlign	HorizontalAlign.Center
UnitPrice	ItemStyle.HorizontalAlign	HorizontalAlign.Right
UnitPrice	DataField	UnitPrice
UnitPrice	DataFormatString	{0:C}

3. Be sure to add code to store the field number in an attribute. This will help you retrieve the column later.

4. Add code to turn off the automatic generation of the fields. Your finished code should look like the following:

```
Private Sub ProductGrid_Init(ByVal sender As Object, _
    ByVal e As System.EventArgs) _
    Handles ProductGrid.Init
        ProductGrid.AutoGenerateColumns = False
        Dim col As New BoundColumn()
        col.HeaderText = "Product<BR>Name"
        col.HeaderStyle.HorizontalAlign =
            HorizontalAlign.Center
        col.ItemStyle.HorizontalAlign = HorizontalAlign.Left
        col.DataField = "ProductName"
        ProductGrid.Columns.Add(col)
        'Store this info for later use.
        ProductGrid.Attributes("ProductNameCol") = _
         ProductGrid.Columns.Count - 1
        col = New BoundColumn()
        col.HeaderText = "Units In<BR>Stock"
        col.HeaderStyle.HorizontalAlign =
            HorizontalAlign.Center
        col.ItemStyle.HorizontalAlign = HorizontalAlign.Right
        col.DataField = "UnitsInStock"
        ProductGrid.Columns.Add(col)
        'Store this info for later use
        ProductGrid.Attributes("UnitsInStockCol") = _
         ProductGrid.Columns.Count - 1
        col = New BoundColumn()
        col.HeaderText = "Unit<BR>Price"
        col.HeaderStyle.HorizontalAlign =
            HorizontalAlign.Center
        col.ItemStyle.HorizontalAlign = HorizontalAlign.Right
        col.DataField = "UnitPrice"
        col.DataFormatString = "{0:C}"
```

```
            ProductGrid.Columns.Add(col)
            'Store this info for later use.
            ProductGrid.Attributes("UnitPriceCol") = _
                ProductGrid.Columns.Count - 1
    End Sub
```

5. Save your work.

The DataGrid can be tested by viewing the page. Press F5 to start the Web application. The ProductList.aspx page should be displayed. Figure 6.17 shows an example of the completed page.

Summary

- This chapter covered many of the basics of displaying data on a Web page. More DataGrid features will be presented throughout the book.
- The DataSource property can be set to an Array, Collection, ADO.NET DataTable, ADO.NET DataView, ADO.NET DataSet, or ADO.NET DataReader.
- The DataMember property only needs to be assigned when the Data-Source contains multiple rowsets.
- DataBind will connect to control to the DataSource.
- There are many formatting characters that you can use to modify the look of a numeric field.
- A template control has no user interface. The control simply provides the mechanism for binding to data. The user interface is supplied by the developer in the form of inline templates.
- The Eval method uses reflection to perform a lookup of the DataItem's underlying type by looking at the type metadata that is stored in the underlying type's assembly. Once the metadata is retrieved, the Eval method determines how to connect to the given field.
- Assigning an index number to the EditItemIndex causes the DataGrid row to switch to edit mode. Assigning minus one (-1) to the Edit-ItemIndex cancels the Edit mode.
- Columns may be added to a DataGrid by using the <columns> tag in the HTML of the .aspx page. Columns may also be added to a DataGrid by placing code into the code-behind page in the Init event method of the DataGrid.
- Repeater controls are very flexible, but they require the developer to write most of the code to implement any desired functionality.

Review Questions

1. What is a key benefit of using the DataList control over using the Repeater control?

2. What are some of the items that can be bound to a DataGrid?

3. If an Edit column is added to a DataGrid, how are TextBoxes automatically placed in DataGrid to allow editing?

4. You added code to create the columns that you want to see in the DataGrid. When you display the DataGrid, you see the columns you added, plus you see a copy of all columns as well. How can this be corrected?

Answers to Review Questions

1. The DataList has a separate style element, which allows the developer to assign a different style to the alternating items without requiring the code to be repeated.

2. An Array, an ArrayList, a HashTable, a SortedList, a DataTable, and a DataView.

3. The EditItemIndex must be assigned to the index number of the column to be edited.

4. Set the DataGrid's AutoGenerateColumns property to false.

CHAPTER

7

Building User Controls and Custom Web Controls

The previous chapters covered many controls in great detail. Many of the properties were covered, including data access properties. Although there are many controls, there are many occasions when it may be desirable to create a new control with different functionality, new functionality, or the combined functionality of several controls.

This chapter starts by covering user controls. After that, the chapter looks at creating custom Web controls from scratch and finishes by exploring the ability to inherit from existing Web server controls.

Classroom Q & A

Q: I want to be able to combine several TextBoxes and Labels on to a single control that can be simply dragged on to my Web page without writing much code. Can this be done?

A: Sure. If you want a quick way to combine multiple controls, then user controls may be the answer for you.

Q: Every time I drag a DataGrid onto a Web page, I need to make many settings to set up this control. Is there a way to change the default properties of a control so I can simply drag it out and the settings will be applied automatically?

A: Yes. One option is to create a new DataGrid control that inherits from the existing DataGrid. You can simply place all of the default settings into the constructor of the new DataGrid.

User Controls

Many times pages contain similar controls. For example, when prompting a user for a billing address and a shipping address, the controls to retrieve the name, address, city, state, and zip code are duplicated. This is where user controls can be very handy. A user control containing the name, address, city, state, and zip code can be created and dropped onto a Web page where needed.

It's also common to have the same header, footer, and menu on every page. This is another place where user controls could be implemented. Although ASP.NET still supports the #INCLUDE directive, a user control offers many more benefits, such as the ability to include code and server controls.

User controls are built using similar procedures to those that are required to build a standard Web page. Web pages can even be converted to user controls with little effort.

Creating a User Control

User controls have a standard naming convention, which uses an .ascx extension to ensure that the control is not executed in a stand-alone fashion. A user control can be created in Visual Studio .NET by clicking Project, Add New Web User Control. On the surface, it appears that a new Web page was added, except that the default layout is set to FlowLayout. A quick glance at the HTML reveals a Control directive instead of a Page directive as shown:

```
<%@ Control Language="vb"
    AutoEventWireup="false"
    Codebehind="MyControl.ascx.vb"
    Inherits="Ch07Web.MyControl"
    TargetSchema="http://schemas.microsoft.com/intellisense/ie5" %>
```

All text and controls that are added to this page will be rendered on the page that the control is added to. For example, if a Label called lblName and a

TextBox called txtName are placed on the user control, the user control could be added to any Web page where required.

Adding a User Control to a Page

The user control can be added to a Web page by simply dragging it from the Solution Explorer and dropping it on a Web page. When the user control is added to the page, a look at the HTML reveals the following additions to the page:

```
<%@ Page Language="vb" AutoEventWireup="false"
    Codebehind="WebForm1.aspx.vb" Inherits="Ch07Web.WebForm1"%>
<%@ Register TagPrefix="uc1" TagName="MyControl" Src="MyControl.ascx" %>
<!DOCTYPE HTML PUBLIC "-//W3C//DTD HTML 4.0 Transitional//EN">
<html>
    <head>
    <title>WebForm1</title>
    <meta name="GENERATOR" content="Microsoft Visual Studio.NET 7.0">
    <meta name="CODE_LANGUAGE" content="Visual Basic 7.0">
    <meta name=vs_defaultClientScript content="JavaScript">
    <meta name=vs_targetSchema
        content="http://schemas.microsoft.com/intellisense/ie5">
    </head>
    <body MS_POSITIONING="GridLayout">
    <form id="Form1" method="post" runat="server">
        <uc1:MyControl id="MyControl1" runat="server"></uc1:MyControl>
    </form>
    </body>
</html>
```

Notice the @Register directive at the top of the page. This is a requirement to place the controls on the page. The TagPrefix attribute is a namespace identifier for the control. The default TagPrefix is uc1 (as in User Control One), and is changeable. The TagName attribute is the name of the control to use. The Src attribute is the location of the user control.

The instance of MyControl is in the form tag. Notice that the ID is automatically created as MyControl1, the next instance will be called MyControl2, and so on.

Accessing Data from the User Control

If this user control is placed on a Web page, the TextBox and Label will be visible, but how can the name be retrieved? In the code-behind page, the TextBox and Label controls are declared as protected members, which mean that they are only available to classes that inherit from the control. Although the controls could be changed to public, the better approach would be to expose only the properties that are required, such as the Text property of the txtName TextBox.

The user control is a class, and can contain properties and methods. A property can be added to the user control called UserName, which exposes the Text property of the txtName TextBox as follows:

```
Public Property UserName() As String
    Get
            Return txtName.Text
    End Get
    Set(ByVal Value As String)
            txtName.Text = Value
    End Set
End Property
```

After the user control, a button, and a label are added to the Web page, code can be added to the code-behind page of the Web page to retrieve the User-Name as follows:

```
Public Class WebForm1
    Inherits System.Web.UI.Page
    Protected WithEvents Label1 As System.Web.UI.WebControls.Label
    Protected WithEvents Button1 As System.Web.UI.WebControls.Button
    Protected WithEvents MyControl1 As MyControl
    'Web form designer generated code is hidden.
    Private Sub Page_Load(ByVal sender As System.Object, _
        ByVal e As System.EventArgs) Handles MyBase.Load
        'Put theuser code to initialize the page here.
    End Sub
    Private Sub Button1_Click(ByVal sender As System.Object, _
        ByVal e As System.EventArgs) Handles Button1.Click
        Label1.Text = MyControl1.UserName
    End Sub
End Class
```

 When dragging and dropping user controls onto a Web page, Visual Studio .NET does not automatically create the code-behind object variable. In the previous example, the following line was manually typed into the code:

```
Protected WithEvents MyControl1 As MyControl.
```

Positioning User Controls

When a user control is dropped onto a Web page, it is always positioned at the top-left corner of the page. Positioning the user control on a Web page that uses FlowLayout requires using a table and placing the user control into the desired cell of the table.

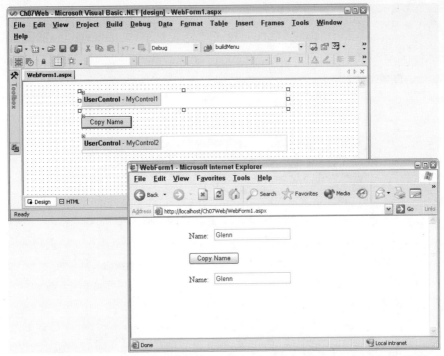

Figure 7.1 The Web page with user controls placed inside panel controls (left) and the rendered page (right).

When using GridLayout, the user control can be positioned by placing a panel control at the desired position on the Web page and adding the user control into the panel.

For example, Figure 7.1 shows a Web page with two user controls and a button. The user controls were placed by adding panel controls to the page and then adding the user controls into the panel controls.

User Control Events

User controls can have their own events, and cause a post back of the Web page's form data. It's interesting to note that user controls do not contain a form server control, since there can only be one form server control on a Web page. User controls are aware of the life cycle of the page and the user control has many of the same events that the page has, such as the Init and Load events.

A user control can also handle its own events. In the following example, a button called bthHi and Label called lblHi are added to the user control. When the button is clicked, the user control handles the button click event to populate lblHi with a hello message.

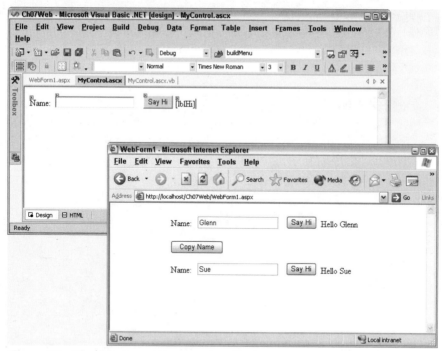

Figure 7.2 The user control encapsulated other controls as well as code (left). The rendered output is displayed using a page with two user controls (right).

```
Public MustInherit Class MyControl
        Inherits System.Web.UI.UserControl
    Protected WithEvents lblName As System.Web.UI.WebControls.Label
    Protected WithEvents lblHi As System.Web.UI.WebControls.Label
    Protected WithEvents btnHi As System.Web.UI.WebControls.Button
    Protected WithEvents txtName As System.Web.UI.WebControls.TextBox
    'Web form designer code
Private Sub Page_Load(ByVal sender As System.Object, _
        ByVal e As System.EventArgs) Handles MyBase.Load
    'Put the user code to initialize the page here.
End Sub
    Public Property UserName() As String
        Get
            Return txtName.Text
        End Get
        Set(ByVal Value As String)
            txtName.Text = Value
        End Set
    End Property
    Private Sub btnHi_Click(ByVal sender As System.Object, _
            ByVal e As System.EventArgs) Handles btnHi.Click
        lblHi.Text = "Hello " & txtName.Text
    End Sub
End Class
```

It's interesting to note that the code for btnHi has been encapsulated into the user control. Figure 7.2 shows the user control and the rendered output. This can help to simplify the page.

Dynamically Loading Controls

Like other server controls, user control can be loaded dynamically. Loading controls dynamically can be useful in situations where a variable quantity of user controls may be displayed on the page.

In the following example, the Web page loads two instances of MyControl on to the page. The UserName of the first instance will be initialized.

```
Private Sub Page_Load(ByVal sender As System.Object, _
        ByVal e As System.EventArgs) Handles MyBase.Load
    'Locate the form control on the page.
    Dim f As Control = Page.FindControl("Form1")
    'Populate the form.
    Dim c1 As MyControl = CType(LoadControl("MyControl.ascx"), _
        MyControl)
    c1.UserName = "Glenn"
    f.Controls.Add(c1)
    Dim c2 As MyControl = CType(LoadControl("MyControl.ascx"), _
        MyControl)
    f.Controls.Add(c2)
End Sub
```

The LoadControl method loads the control into memory, but this method returns a System.Web.UI.WebControl. To see the properties of MyControl, the returned WebControl object must be cast as a MyControl object. This is done using the CType function. The user control contains server controls, so it must be loaded in the controls collection of the form as shown.

User controls only need to be loaded into the controls collection of the form if they are taking part in view state or they contain server controls. If a user control contains simple HTML, it may be added to the controls collection of the page.

The following code dynamically loads a user control called Header.ascx into the page's controls collection. The header control only contains the Web site name with large, centered font. Since this header will be placed at the top of the page, it is important to add the Header control after the body tag has been rendered, but before the form has been rendered, as follows:

```
Dim f As Control = Page.FindControl("Form1")
Dim h As Header = _
    CType(LoadControl("Header.ascx"), Header)
Controls.AddAt(Controls.IndexOf(f), h)
```

The header is loaded into variable h. After that, the control is added using the AddAt method, which takes a location as the first parameter. The header is loaded into the controls collection at the form's current location. In effect, this pushes the form and everything after the form down in the list of controls. The net effect is that the header is inserted in the Web page after the body tag and before the form tag.

Raising Events to the Page

There may be times when a control is required to be placed on the user control, but it's not known how the control will be implemented when the developer is creating the user control. This problem can be solved by raising the event to the Web page.

For example, there may be a button on a user control that sends a message to the user. The type of message and the content of the message are not known to the developer when the user control is created, so the click event of the button is programmed to raise an event to the page. The following code shows a user control with a button called btnMessage that raises an event called SendMessage. The SendMessage event also passes the name that was typed into the TextBox.

```
Public MustInherit Class MyControl
  Inherits System.Web.UI.UserControl
      Protected WithEvents lblName As System.Web.UI.WebControls.Label
      Protected WithEvents btnMessage As System.Web.UI.WebControls.Button
      Protected WithEvents txtName As System.Web.UI.WebControls.TextBox
      Public Event SendMessage(ByVal UserName As String)
      'Web form designer code
      Private Sub Page_Load(ByVal sender As System.Object, _
        ByVal e As System.EventArgs) Handles MyBase.Load
          'Put the user code to initialize the page here.
      End Sub
      Public Property UserName() As String
          Get
                Return txtName.Text
          End Get
          Set(ByVal Value As String)
                txtName.Text = Value
          End Set
      End Property
      Private Sub btnMessage_Click(ByVal sender As System.Object, _
        ByVal e As System.EventArgs) Handles btnMessage.Click
            RaiseEvent SendMessage(txtName.Text)
      End Sub
  End Class
```

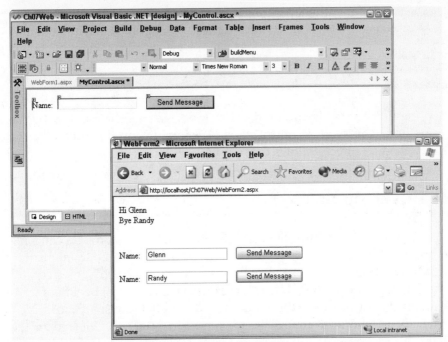

Figure 7.3 The user control with the Send Message button (left). The rendered output displays a different message for each of the dynamically created controls (right).

The event must always be declared as public at the top of the user control class. The btnMessage's click event method has been programmed to raise the event, passing the contents of txtName.Text.

The Web page contains a Label control. The user controls are being dynamically created and the AddHandler command attaches the SendMessage event to the appropriate method. The following code snippet shows how this can be done.

```
Private Sub Page_Load(ByVal sender As System.Object, _
    ByVal e As System.EventArgs) Handles MyBase.Load
    'Locate the form control on the page.
    Dim f As Control = Page.FindControl("Form1")
    'Populate the form.
    Dim c1 As MyControl = _
     CType(LoadControl("MyControl.ascx"), MyControl)
    c1.UserName = "Glenn"
    f.Controls.Add(c1)
    AddHandler c1.SendMessage, AddressOf SayHi
    Dim c2 As MyControl = _
     CType(LoadControl("MyControl.ascx"), MyControl)
    f.Controls.Add(c2)
    AddHandler c2.SendMessage, AddressOf SayBye
End Sub
```

```
Public Sub SayHi(ByVal msg As String)
      Label1.Text &= "Hi " & msg & "<br>"
End Sub
Public Sub SayBye(ByVal msg As String)
      Label1.Text &= "Bye " & msg & "<br>"
End Sub
```

When the first control is added, the SendMessage event is handled by the SayHi method. The second control's SendMessage event is handled by the SayBye method. Figure 7.3 shows the output.

Web Server Controls

Building a Web server control that can be reused on many projects can save many hours. Writing Web server controls may take more time than creating user controls due to their lower-level nature. Writing a Web server control involves writing code to send HTML to the browser. One major benefit of writing Web server controls is that the control will render in the Visual Studio .NET Designer, where the user control is not rendered until it is viewed in the browser. This section starts by creating a simple control and then adds more functionality.

Creating and Compiling a Control Library

Creating custom server controls that can be reused in many projects involves creating a separate project for the server controls. This can be done by creating a new project in Visual Studio .NET. The project type should be a Visual Basic Web Control Library, as shown in Figure 7.4. This project compiles to a .dll file, which needs to reside in the same folder as the Web application. Simply copying the .dll file suffices. If Visual Studio .NET is used to add the control to the Toolbox, a reference is automatically created to the .dll file and Visual Studio .NET automatically copies the file to the bin directory of the Web project.

Before the compiled control can be used on a Web page, a reference to the control must be defined at the top of the Web page. This can be done as follows:

```
<%@ Register TagPrefix="cc" Namespace="myControl"
Assembly="HelloWorld" %>
```

The TagPrefix will be used at the beginning of the tag, followed by the name of the control, as follows:

```
<cc:MyCustomControl id="MyCustomControl1" runat="server"/>
```

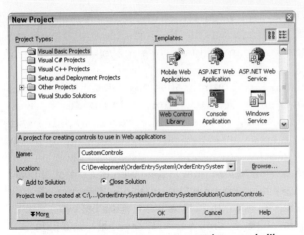

Figure 7.4   Creating a new custom Web controls library project.

Creating a Simple Control

Custom Web server controls can be created by creating a new class that inherits from the System.Web.UI.Control class and overrides the Render method. The Render method is passed an instance of the System.Web.UI.HTML-TextWriter class, which has a Write method that can be used to send HTML to the browser to render your control. The following code shows an example of a Hello World control.

```
'This is the Web page.
Public Class CustomWebControlApp
     Inherits System.Web.UI.Page
     Private Sub Page_Load(ByVal sender As System.Object, _
         ByVal e As System.EventArgs) Handles MyBase.Load
         Dim f As Control
         f = Page.FindControl("Form1")
         Dim m As New MyWebControl()
         f.Controls.Add(m)
     End Sub
End Class
'Here is the Custom Web control.
Public Class MyWebControl
     Inherits System.Web.UI.Control
     Protected Overrides Sub Render( _
         ByVal w As System.Web.UI.HtmlTextWriter)
         w.Write("Hello World")
     End Sub
End Class
```

The first class in this code is the Web page, which creates an instance of the control called MyWebControl and places it into the form control. This is the same code that would be used to dynamically create any Web server control and place it on the page.

The second class is the custom Web control called MyWebControl. Notice that this control inherits from System.Web.UI.Control and provides an override for the Render method. This simply displays Hello World on the browser screen.

 Instead of having your control inherit from System.Web.UI.Control, it may be more desirable to have it inherit from System.Web.UI.WebControls .WebControl, because this base control offers much more built-in functionality, such as the ability to drop a control anywhere on a page in GridLayout mode. We will look at this in more detail later in this chapter.

The HTMLTextWriter

The HTMLTextWriter is a class that provides that ability to send a sequence of bytes, called the output stream, to the browser. Understanding the HTMLTextWriter is an important key to creating Web server controls, since this is the class that is used to send data to the browser. This section looks at many of the methods that are available with this class.

Write

The Write method sends an object to the output stream. This method has 17 overloads, which provide lots of flexibility with regard to how the Write method is called. The overloads may be viewed using the Object Browser (Ctrl+Alt+J). The following code demonstrates examples of using this method.

```
Protected Overrides Sub Render( _
  ByVal writer As System.Web.UI.HtmlTextWriter)
     Dim name As String = "Glenn"
     Dim msg As String = "World"
     writer.Write("Hello World!")
     writer.Write("Hello {0}, Welcome to the {1}, Bye {0}", name, msg)
End Sub
```

When viewing the browser source code, the output of the preceding code is as follows:

```
Hello World! Hello Glenn, Welcome to the World, Bye Glenn
```

WriteLine and WriteLineNoTabs

The WriteLine method is similar to the Write method in that both of them send an object to the output stream. The difference is that this method adds a new line to the output, which helps to format the source of the HTML, not the rendered output. This means that viewing the source will reveal new lines, but this method does not generate HTML break or paragraph tags. The method has 18 overloads, which provide many options. The following code demonstrates examples of this method.

```
Protected Overrides Sub Render( _
  ByVal writer As System.Web.UI.HtmlTextWriter)
      Dim name As String = "Glenn"
      Dim msg As String = "World"
      writer.WriteLine("Hello World!")
      writer.WriteLine("Hello {0}, Welcome to the {1}, Bye {0}", _
          name, msg)
      writer.WriteLine("Testing 1,2,3")
  End Sub
```

When viewing the browser source code, the output of the preceding code is as follows:

```
Hello World!
Hello Glenn, Welcome to the World, Bye Glenn
Testing 1,2,3
```

This is the source of the browser output. Notice that there are no HTML break tags, so this text is rendered on the browser as one long line.

The WriteLine method and the WriteLineNoTabs are the same, except that the WriteLine method includes tabs to neatly format the HTML output. Use WriteLineNoTabs to suppress writing tabs to the output stream.

WriteBeginTag and WriteAttribute

The WriteBeginTag method writes the beginning HTML tag, omitting the tag's right character (>). Attributes can be added using the WriteAttribute method before the final tag right character is written. The following example uses the WriteBeginTag, followed by the WriteAttribute.

```
Protected Overrides Sub Render( _
        ByVal writer As System.Web.UI.HtmlTextWriter)
        Dim name As String = "Glenn"
        Dim msg As String = "World"
        writer.WriteBeginTag("font")
        writer.WriteAttribute("size", "6")
        writer.WriteAttribute("color", "red")
```

```
    writer.Write(HtmlTextWriter.TagRightChar)
    writer.WriteLine("Hello {0}, Welcome to the {1}, Bye {0}", _
        name, msg)
    writer.WriteLine("Testing 1,2,3")
    writer.WriteEndTag("font")
End Sub
```

When viewing the browser source code, the output of the preceding code is as follows. Notice that the TagRightChar needed to be written to close the font's tag.

```
<font size="6" color="red">Hello Glenn, Welcome to the World, Bye Glenn
Testing 1,2,3
</font>
```

WriteFullBeginTag

The WriteFullBeginTag writes a begin tag to the output stream when the tag has no attributes. The following code uses the WriteFullBeginTag to display text in italics by executing the WriteBeginFullTag.method with an "i".

```
Protected Overrides Sub Render( _
    ByVal writer As System.Web.UI.HtmlTextWriter)
    Dim name As String = "Glenn"
    Dim msg As String = "World"
    writer.WriteFullBeginTag("i")
    writer.WriteLine("Hello {0}, Welcome to the {1}, Bye {0}", _
        name, msg)
    writer.WriteLine("Testing 1,2,3")
    writer.WriteEndTag("i")
End Sub
```

When viewing the browser source code, the output of the above code is as follows:

```
<i>Hello Glenn, Welcome to the World, Bye Glenn
Testing 1,2,3
</i>
```

WriteStyleAttribute

The WriteStyleAttribute sends style attributes to the output stream. The writing of the style attribute must still be done, but this method can make it easier to output the name and value pairs that are associated with each style. The follow code shows an example of using the WriteStyleAttribute.

```
Protected Overrides Sub Render( _
     ByVal writer As System.Web.UI.HtmlTextWriter)
     Dim name As String = "Glenn"
     Dim msg As String = "World"
     writer.WriteBeginTag("p")
     writer.Write(HtmlTextWriter.SpaceChar)
     writer.Write("style")
     writer.Write(HtmlTextWriter.EqualsDoubleQuoteString)
     writer.WriteStyleAttribute("font-size", "14pt")
     writer.WriteStyleAttribute("color", "blue")
     writer.Write(HtmlTextWriter.DoubleQuoteChar)
     writer.WriteLine(HtmlTextWriter.TagRightChar)
     writer.WriteLine("Hello {0}, Welcome to the {1}, Bye {0}", _
          name, msg)
     writer.WriteLine("Testing 1,2,3")
     writer.WriteEndTag("p")
End Sub
```

Notice the use of HtmlTextWriter's static fields to retrieve some of the special characters. When viewing the browser source code, the output of the above code is as follows:

```
<p style="font-size:14pt;color:blue;">
Hello Glenn, Welcome to the World, Bye Glenn
Testing 1,2,3
</p>
```

RenderBeginTag and RenderEndTag

The RenderBeginTag writes an opening HTML tag to the output stream, while the RenderEndTag writes the ending HTML tag. The following code writes a simple italic tag and text.

```
Protected Overrides Sub Render( _
     ByVal writer As System.Web.UI.HtmlTextWriter)
     Dim name As String = "Glenn"
     Dim msg As String = "World"
     writer.RenderBeginTag("i")
     writer.WriteLine("Hello {0}, Welcome to the {1}, Bye {0}",
          name, msg)
     writer.WriteLine("Testing 1,2,3")
     writer.RenderEndTag()
End Sub
```

When viewing the browser source code, the output of the preceding code is as follows:

```
<i>Hello Glenn, Welcome to the World, Bye Glenn
Testing 1,2,3
</i>
```

AddAttribute and AddStyleAttribute

The AddAttribute and AddStyleAttribute methods create an HTML attribute with its value and add it to the output stream. This method is primarily used with the RenderBeginTag method, as shown:

```
Protected Overrides Sub Render( _
     ByVal writer As System.Web.UI.HtmlTextWriter)
     Dim name As String = "Glenn"
     Dim msg As String = "World"
     writer.AddAttribute(HtmlTextWriterAttribute.Id, "MyPara")
     writer.AddStyleAttribute(HtmlTextWriterStyle.Color, "blue")
     writer.AddStyleAttribute(HtmlTextWriterStyle.FontSize, "14pt")
     writer.RenderBeginTag("p")
     writer.WriteLine("Hi")
     writer.WriteLine("Hello {0}, Welcome to the {1}, Bye {0}",
          name, msg)
     writer.WriteLine("Testing 1,2,3")
     writer.RenderEndTag()
End Sub
```

Notice that the AddAttribute and AddStyleAttribute methods are executed prior to executing the BeginRenderTag. When viewing the browser source code, the output of the preceding code is as follows:

```
<p id="MyPara" style="color:blue;font-size:14pt;">Hi
Hello Glenn, Welcome to the World, Bye Glenn
Testing 1,2,3
</p>
```

Adding Properties to the Server Control

Properties can be added to the Web server control in the same manner as properties are added to any class. Using properties enforces encapsulation of data in the control. If the property is being set to an invalid value, an ArgumentException can be thrown. The following is an example of a property called User-Name, which has a maximum limit of 20 characters.

```
Public Class MyWebControl
     Inherits System.Web.UI.Control
     Dim _UserName As String = ""
```

```
Const MaxUserLength As Integer = 20
Public Property UserName() As String
    Get
        Return _UserName
    End Get
    Set(ByVal Value As String)
        If Value.Length > MaxUserLength Then
            Throw New ArgumentException( _
            "UserName length cannot be greater than " _
            & MaxUserLength)
        Else
            _UserName = Value
        End If
    End Set
End Property
Protected Overrides Sub Render( _
 ByVal writer As System.Web.UI.HtmlTextWriter)
    writer.RenderBeginTag("i")
    writer.WriteLine("Hello {0}, Bye {0}", _UserName)
    writer.RenderEndTag()
End Sub
End Class
```

Figure 7.5 shows the output when an attempt is made to place a large amount of text into the UserName. Properties should always be implemented to enforce data integrity and maintain encapsulation.

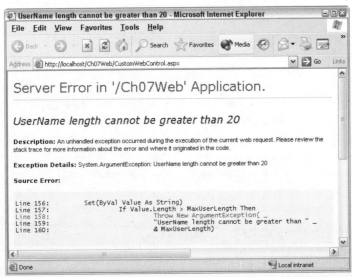

Figure 7.5 An exception is thrown when an attempt is made to place a large amount of text into the UserName property.

Working with ViewState Data

Although the previous code example demonstrates the creation of a property, the variable called _UserName is not persisted. In many cases, it's important to persist this data over calls to the server. To persist the UserName, place the data into ViewState instead of placing the data in a local variable. The following code snippet shows the property implemented using ViewState to hold the data between server calls.

```
Public Class MyWebControl
    Inherits System.Web.UI.Control
    Const MaxUserLength As Integer = 20
    Public Property UserName() As String
        Get
            If ViewState("UserName") Is Nothing Then
                Return String.Empty
            Else
                Return ViewState("UserName").ToString()
            End If
        End Get
        Set(ByVal Value As String)
            If Value.Length > MaxUserLength Then
                Throw New ArgumentException( _
                "UserName length cannot be greater than " _
                & MaxUserLength)
            Else
                ViewState("UserName") = Value
            End If
        End Set
    End Property
End Class
```

 When adding controls dynamically, be sure to add the control to the form's control collection before assigning any property values to it. A dynamically added control does not participate in the page's ViewState until the control is added, so any property changes that are made prior to placing the control into the form's control collection will be lost.

Adding Methods to the Server Control

Methods can be added to the Web server control using the same techniques as adding a method to any other class. The following example contains a method that changes the case of the _UserName based on the case of the first character.

```
Public Sub ChangeCase()
    If _UserName.Length > 0 Then
        If _UserName.Substring(0, 1).ToUpper() = _
        _UserName.Substring(0, 1) Then
            'make lowercase
            _UserName = _UserName.ToLower()
        Else
            _UserName = _UserName.ToUpper()
        End If
    End If
End Sub
```

Since this method is public, it can be executed from the Web page with the following code in the Web page.

```
Public Class CustomWebControl
  Inherits System.Web.UI.Page
    Protected WithEvents Button1 As System.Web.UI.WebControls.Button
    Dim m As New MyWebControl()
    'designer generated code here...
    Private Sub Page_Load(ByVal sender As System.Object, _
        ByVal e As System.EventArgs) Handles MyBase.Load
        'Put the user code to initialize the page here.
        Dim f As Control
        f = Page.FindControl("Form1")
        f.Controls.Add(m)
        If Not IsPostBack Then
            m.UserName = "Glenn"
        End If
    End Sub
    Private Sub Button1_Click(ByVal sender As System.Object, _
      ByVal e As System.EventArgs) Handles Button1.Click
        m.ChangeCase()
    End Sub
  End Class
```

Notice that the control is added to the form's control collection before the UserName is initialized. Also, the UserName is only initialized on the first request for the page. On subsequent calls to the page, the current value of UserName is extracted from ViewState.

Adding Child Controls to the Server Control

Many times it is desirable to create a control that contains other controls. The DataGrid, Calendar, and ListBox are examples of existing controls that contain many other controls. When working with the ListBox control, the items that are inside the ListBox are instances of the ListItem class. They are added to the ListBox either by HTML or code, as follows:

```
<!--Adding ListItems via HTML →
<asp:ListBox runat="server">
    <asp:ListItem Text="Item 1" />
    <asp:ListItem Text="Item 2" />
    <asp:ListItem Text="Item 3" />
</asp:ListBox>
'Adding the ListItems via code
Private Sub Page_Load(ByVal sender As System.Object, _
ByVal e As System.EventArgs) Handles MyBase.Load
Dim f As Control = FindControl("Form1")
    Dim lst As New ListBox()
    f.Controls.Add(lst)
    lst.Items.Add(New ListItem("Item 1"))
    lst.Items.Add(New ListItem("Item 2"))
    lst.Items.Add(New ListItem("Item 3"))
End Sub
```

Creating a control that can have child controls involves creating a second control to hold each item. In the following example, a second control called HiItem is created. The UserName has been removed from the original control and is placed inside the HiItem control.

```
Public Class MyWebControl
    Inherits System.Web.UI.Control
    Protected Overrides Sub Render( _
     ByVal writer As System.Web.UI.HtmlTextWriter)
        writer.RenderBeginTag("b")
        Dim c As Control
        For Each c In Me.Controls
            writer.WriteLine("{0}<br>", c)
        Next
        writer.RenderEndTag()
    End Sub
End Class
Public Class HiItem
    Inherits System.Web.UI.Control
    Const MaxUserLength As Integer = 20
    Public Property UserName() As String
        Get
            If ViewState("UserName") Is Nothing Then
                Return String.Empty
            Else
                Return ViewState("UserName").ToString()
            End If
        End Get
        Set(ByVal Value As String)
            If Value.Length > MaxUserLength Then
                Throw New ArgumentException( _
                "UserName length cannot be greater than " _
                & MaxUserLength)
            Else
```

```
                    ViewState("UserName") = Value
            End If
        End Set
    End Property
End Class
```

The Render method loops through all of the child controls and writes them to the output stream. This writes the fully qualified type name to the output stream. What should the browser see if the following HTML is added to the page to create four HiItems?

```
<cc:MyWebControl runat="server" id=MyWebControl1 >
    <cc:hiitem id="Hiitem1" runat="server" username="Glenn" />
    <cc:hiitem id="Hiitem2" runat="server" username="Sue" />
    <cc:hiitem id="Hiitem3" runat="server" username="Gary" />
    <cc:hiitem id="Hiitem4" runat="server" username="Randy" />
</cc:MyWebControl>
```

One would assume that four lines would be output, showing the fully qualified type for each of the HiItems controls. The output is shown in Figure 7.6. Further investigation shows that MyWebControl1 is storing the white space between each of its child controls as LiteralControls (Figure 7.6). If all of the HiItems were placed on the same line with MyWebControl's start and end tags, only the HiItem controls would be in the MyWebControl's control collection.

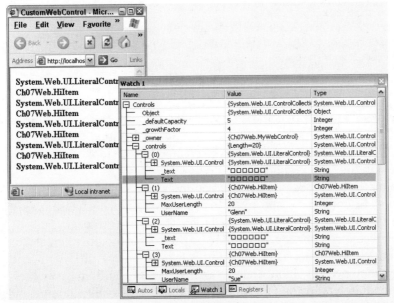

Figure 7.6 The rendered output of MyWebControl1 (left). A breakpoint was placed in the render method; when the break point was reached, the debugger watch window revealed nonviewable characters in the LiteralControls (right).

This could be a serious problem, because it is usually preferable to render only the HiItems and not any text or white space that a user types between the begin and end tags of the control.

This problem can be solved by adding a filter to ensure that only HiItems are rendered. The following code shows how this can be accomplished.

```
Public Class MyWebControl
    Inherits System.Web.UI.Control
    Private _Items As New ArrayList()
    Public Sub AddHiItem(ByVal obj As HiItem)
        _Items.Add(obj)
        Controls.Add(obj)
    End Sub
    Public Sub RemoveHiItem(ByVal obj As HiItem)
        _Items.Remove(obj)
        Controls.Remove(obj)
    End Sub
    Protected Overrides Sub AddParsedSubObject(ByVal obj As Object)
        If TypeOf (obj) Is HiItem Then
            _Items.Add(obj)
        End If
        Controls.Add(Ctype(obj,Control))
    End Sub
    Protected Overrides Sub Render( _
     ByVal writer As System.Web.UI.HtmlTextWriter)
        writer.RenderBeginTag("b")
        Dim c As HiItem
        For Each c In Me._Items
            writer.WriteLine("Hi {0}<br>", c.UserName)
        Next
        writer.RenderEndTag()
    End Sub
End Class
```

In the previous code snippet, the AddParsedSubObject method is implemented, which is executed each time that a new control is added to the control collection via HTML. This allows a filter to be created, which looks for HiItems and stores them in the _Items collection.

The Render method has been modified to enumerate the controls collection, looking for only HiItem objects, and to write a Hi message for each UserName. The browser output (Figure 7.7) shows the Hi message for each user.

The _Items collection is private, but it may be preferable to allow items to be dynamically added via code. This is done by exposing an AddHiItem and RemoveHiItem method, which only accept an instance of a HiItem as an argument, and immediately add the HiItem to both the _Items collection and the controls collection. Remember that the HiItem must be a member of the controls collection in order to participate in ViewState.

```
<cc:MyWebControl runat="server" id="MyWebControl1">
    <cc:hiitem id="Hiitem1" runat="server" username="Glenn"></cc:hiitem>
    <cc:hiitem id="Hiitem2" runat="server" username="Sue"></cc:hiitem>
    <cc:hiitem id="Hiitem3" runat="server" username="Gary"></cc:hiitem>
    <cc:hiitem id="Hiitem4" runat="server" username="Randy"></cc:hiitem>
</cc:MyWebControl>
```

Figure 7.7 The HTML page contents (top) with each item. The browser output for is shown for the users who were added as HiItems in MyWebControl1 (bottom).

Adding the Custom Control Builder

In the previous example, each one of the HiItem controls was added using the TagPrefix and the runat="server" attribute. A custom control builder can be created to minimize the typing that is required for each of the HiItem controls that is added. The following HTML represents the minimum typing that is desired.

```
<form id=Form1 method=post runat="server">
    <cc:mywebcontrol id=MyWebControl1 runat="server">
        <HiItem username="Glenn" />
        <HiItem username="Sue" />
        <HiItem username="Gary" />
        <HiItem username="Randy" />
    </cc:mywebcontrol>
</form>
```

The control builder is responsible for adding nested controls to the parent's control collection. Every control is associated with a default control builder, but a new control builder can be implemented to help locate the proper data type of a control based on its HTML tag. The following code shows the implementation of a custom control builder for the MyWebControl class.

```
Public Class MyWebControlBuilder
    Inherits ControlBuilder
    Public Overrides Function GetChildControlType( _
    ByVal TagName As String, _
```

```
          ByVal Attributes As IDictionary) As Type
              If String.Compare(TagName, "hiitem", True) = 0 Then
                  Return GetType(HiItem)
              End If
              Return Nothing
          End Function
    End Class
    <ControlBuilderAttribute(GetType(MyWebControlBuilder))> _
    Public Class MyWebControl
          Inherits System.Web.UI.Control
          'cool code here from previous examples....
    End Class
```

The custom control builder class is called MyWebControlBuilder and inherits from ControlBuilder. This class has a single function called GetChildControlType, which returns a Type object when the TagName is HiItem (with case insensitive compare, which means that this method can be called with hiitem or HIITEM as the first parameter, and the HiItem type will be returned). The control builder is attached to MyWebControl class by using an attribute. The end result is that the HTML code is much cleaner.

Raising Events

Often, a custom control contains items, such as buttons, but the exact implementation of the functionality of the button is not known at design time. Using events allows the control developer to provide a way to hook into the control, thereby giving the control much more power than a control that has been programmed for a single use.

Raising events in the control is as easy as declaring a public event and then raising the event from a code block. The following code adds a SaidHi event to the MyWebControl class.

```
<ControlBuilderAttribute(GetType(MyWebControlBuilder))> _
Public Class MyWebControl
      Inherits System.Web.UI.Control
      Public Event SaidHi(ByVal UserName As String)
      Private _Items As New ArrayList()
      Public Sub AddHiItem(ByVal obj As HiItem)
          _Items.Add(obj)
          Controls.Add(obj)
      End Sub
      Public Sub RemoveHiItem(ByVal obj As HiItem)
          _Items.Remove(obj)
          Controls.Remove(obj)
      End Sub
```

```
Protected Overrides Sub AddParsedSubObject(ByVal obj As Object)
    If TypeOf (obj) Is HiItem Then
        _Items.Add(obj)
    End If
    Controls.Add(CType(obj, Control))
End Sub
Protected Overrides Sub Render( _
 ByVal writer As System.Web.UI.HtmlTextWriter)
    writer.RenderBeginTag("b")
    Dim c As HiItem
    For Each c In Me._Items
        writer.WriteLine("Hi {0}<br>", c.UserName)
        RaiseEvent SaidHi(CType(c, HiItem).UserName)
    Next
    writer.RenderEndTag()
End Sub
End Class
```

When using the control, the code-behind page must have MyWebControl defined using the WithEvents keyword, or the AddHandler command can be used to dynamically connect events to event handler methods. The first example will use the WithEvents keyword, as follows:

```
Public Class CustomWebControl
        Inherits System.Web.UI.Page
    Protected WithEvents ListBox1 As System.Web.UI.WebControls.ListBox
    Protected WithEvents MyWebControl1 As Ch07Web.MyWebControl
    'Web Form Designer Generated Code
    Private Sub MyWebControl1_SaidHi(ByVal UserName As String) _
     Handles MyWebControl1.SaidHi
        Response.Write("* " & UserName & " Rendered *<BR>")
    End Sub
End Class
```

The WithEvents keyword is used when declaring the control. The SaidHi event is connected to the MyWebControl1_SaidHi method by using *Handles MyWebControl1.SaidHi* at the end of the method definition. This code outputs each name to the browser, using the response.write method as the SaidHi event is raised (Figure 7.8).

The second example allows the use of the AddHandler command to dynamically attach to a method. This method is useful when controls are created dynamically and their events must be dynamically attached.

Figure 7.8 Browser output using the response.write method as the SaidHi event is raised.

```
Private Sub MyWebControl1_SaidHi(ByVal UserName As String) _
    Handles MyWebControl1.SaidHi
        Response.Write("* " & UserName & " Rendered *<BR>")
    End Sub
    Private Sub CustomWebControl_Load(ByVal sender As Object, _
    ByVal e As System.EventArgs) Handles MyBase.Load
        Dim m As MyWebControl
        Dim h As HiItem
        Dim f As Control = FindControl("Form1")
        Dim x As Integer
        m = New MyWebControl()
        AddHandler m.SaidHi, AddressOf MyWebControl1_SaidHi
        f.Controls.Add(m)
        For x = 1 To 5
            h = New HiItem()
            m.AddHiItem(h)
            If Not IsPostBack Then
                h.UserName = "User #" & x.ToString()
            End If
        Next
    End Sub
```

In this example, an instance of MyWebControl was dynamically created when the button was clicked. The SaidHi event was attached to the same method as in the previous example, using the AddHandler command. Five HiItem controls were added to the custom control.

Retrieving Postback Data

A custom server control has been created based on the information that has been covered so far. This custom control inherits from System.Web.UI.Control.

The control is a simple TextBox, except that the font is larger. The code for LargeText is as follows:

```
Public Class LargeText
     Inherits System.Web.UI.Control
     Public Property Text() As String
          Get
               If ViewState("Text") Is Nothing Then
                    Return String.Empty
               Else
                    Return CType(ViewState("Text"), String)
               End If
          End Get
          Set(ByVal Value As String)
               viewstate("Text") = Value
          End Set
     End Property
     Protected Overrides Sub render(ByVal w As HtmlTextWriter)
          w.AddAttribute("Name", Me.UniqueID)
          w.AddStyleAttribute("font-size", "18pt")
          w.AddAttribute("value", Text)
          w.RenderBeginTag("input")
          w.RenderEndTag()
     End Sub
End Class
```

The problem with this control is that the value in the TextBox is not maintained between calls to the server. When the Submit button is clicked, the page posts back to the server, but the response page will have an empty TextBox.

To make a control to handle postback information, the IPostBackDataHandler interface must be implemented, which contains two methods.

LoadPostData.   Allows access to the data that is posted back to the server. This method passes two arguments and returns a Boolean. The first argument is the post data key, which is a string value containing the ID of the current object. The second argument is the post collection, which contains a name value collection of all of the posted data. The return value that from this function is a Boolean, which is an indicator of whether the control has changed. This value will be held until all posted data has been loaded and then the value will be used to execute the RaisePostDataChangeEvent methods.

RaisePostDataChangedEvent.   Raises the changed event for a control. This method typically contains a line of code that raises an event to indicate that the control has changed.

This following code implements these methods. The LoadPostData method gets the posted value and compares it to the value that was in ViewState. If the values are the same, the function returns false, indicating that there is no change to the data. If the values are different, the posted value is assigned to the ViewState value and the function returns true.

```
Public Class LargeText
    Inherits System.Web.UI.Control
    Implements IPostBackDataHandler
    Public Event TextChanged(ByVal sender As Object, _
     ByVal e As EventArgs)
    Public Function LoadPostData(ByVal PostDataKey As String, _
     ByVal PostCollection As NameValueCollection) As Boolean _
     Implements IPostBackDataHandler.LoadPostData
        Dim PostedValue As String
        PostedValue = PostCollection(Me.UniqueID)
        If PostedValue = Text Then
            Return False
        End If
        Text = PostedValue
        Return True
    End Function
    Public Sub RaisePostDataChangedEvent() _
     Implements IPostBackDataHandler.RaisePostDataChangedEvent
        OnTextChanged(EventArgs.Empty)
    End Sub
    Protected Sub OnTextChanged(ByVal e As EventArgs)
        RaiseEvent TextChanged(Me, e)
    End Sub
    Public Property Text() As String
        Get
            If ViewState("Text") Is Nothing Then
                Return String.Empty
            Else
                Return CType(ViewState("Text"), String)
            End If
        End Get
        Set(ByVal Value As String)
            viewstate("Text") = Value
        End Set
    End Property
    Protected Overrides Sub render(ByVal w As HtmlTextWriter)
        w.AddAttribute("Name", Me.UniqueID)
        w.AddStyleAttribute("font-size", "18pt")
        w.AddAttribute("value", Text)
        w.RenderBeginTag("input")
        w.RenderEndTag()
    End Sub
End Class
```

The RaisePostedDataChangedEvent method contains a single call to the OnTextChangedMethod, which then raises the TextChanged event. This event is now available for use on the Web page. With the addition of the above code, the control responds to a postback and maintains state across calls to the server.

Composite Controls

Creating user controls was easier than creating custom Web controls, since existing controls were used to create the user control and the examples of creating custom Web controls have been geared around building a control from scratch. It is possible to create a custom Web control from existing controls as well. This is known as a composite control.

An example of a composite control might be a LoginControl that has a User-Name and Password TextBoxes, along with LiteralControls containing the formating, and a Submit button. The following code is an example of adding many controls to a custom Web control.

```
Public Class LoginControl
      Inherits Control
      Implements INamingContainer
      Protected Overrides Sub CreateChildControls()
            Dim pnl As New Panel()
            Dim txtUserName As New TextBox()
            Dim txtPassword As New TextBox()
            Dim btnSubmit As New Button()
            'start control buildup
            Controls.Add(pnl)
            'add user name row
            pnl.Controls.Add(New LiteralControl("<table><tr><td>"))
            pnl.Controls.Add(New LiteralControl("User Name:"))
            pnl.Controls.Add(New LiteralControl("</td><td>"))
            pnl.Controls.Add(txtUserName)
            pnl.Controls.Add(New LiteralControl("</td></tr>"))
            'add password row
            pnl.Controls.Add(New LiteralControl("<tr><td>"))
            pnl.Controls.Add(New LiteralControl("Password:"))
            pnl.Controls.Add(New LiteralControl("</td><td>"))
            pnl.Controls.Add(txtPassword)
            pnl.Controls.Add(New LiteralControl("</td></tr>"))
            'add submit button row
            pnl.Controls.Add(New LiteralControl( _
                  "<tr><td colspan=""2"" align=""center"" >"))
            pnl.Controls.Add(btnSubmit)
            pnl.Controls.Add(New LiteralControl("</td></tr></table>"))
            'set up control properties
            pnl.Style.Add("background-color", "silver")
            pnl.Style.Add("width", "275px")
```

```
                txtUserName.ID = "UserName"
                txtUserName.Style.Add("width", "170px")
                txtPassword.ID = "Password"
                txtPassword.TextMode = TextBoxMode.Password
                txtPassword.Style.Add("width", "170px")
                btnSubmit.Text = "Submit"
        End Sub
    End Class
```

The previous code creates a control hierarchy by adding a Panel control to the custom Web control and then adding a series of LiteralControls, TextBoxes, and Button controls in the Panel (Figure 7.9). Placing the controls inside a Panel control gives the custom Web control an outer HTML div tag on which to set styles.

Notice that the custom control implements INamingContainer. The INamingContainer is a marking interface, like an indicator, that signifies the start of a new namespace for controls. This allows the addition of multiple custom controls to the Web page even though every control may have a UserName TextBox.

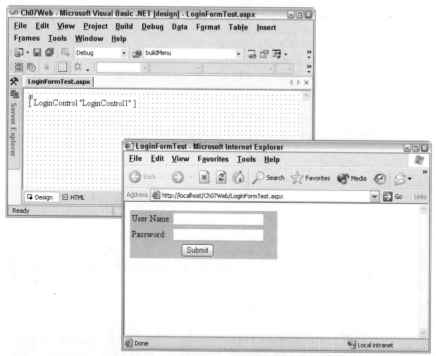

Figure 7.9 The control in Visual Studio .NET designer (left) and rendered in the browser (right).

Testing this control reveals that the TextBoxes implement their own View-State and the Button does post back to the server. The problem is that there doesn't seem to be an easy way to get to the Text properties of the TextBoxes, so an event handler method needs to be added for the Button. To get the data to and from the TextBoxes, the UserName and Password properties are added to the control. The code is as follows:

```
Public Sub New()
        Me.EnsureChildControls()
End Sub
Public Property UserName() As String
    Get
        Dim txt As TextBox
        txt = CType(Me.FindControl("UserName"), TextBox)
        Return txt.Text
    End Get
    Set(ByVal Value As String)
        Dim txt As TextBox
        txt = CType(Me.FindControl("UserName"), TextBox)
        txt.Text = Value
    End Set
End Property
Public Property Password() As String
    Get
        Dim txt As TextBox
        txt = CType(Me.FindControl("Password"), TextBox)
        Return txt.Text
    End Get
    Set(ByVal Value As String)
        Dim txt As TextBox
        txt = CType(Me.FindControl("Password"), TextBox)
        txt.Text = Value
    End Set
End Property
```

The constructor is added and includes a call to the EnsureChildControls method. This method starts by checking the ChildControlsCreated property to see if the child controls have been created yet. If not, a call is made to the CreateChildControls method. Next, the appropriate TextBox is searched for and then the Text value either is returned or assigned.

Although it may seem desirable to place the code for the Submit button inside the custom server control, in many cases the authentication method will not be known. A better solution is to raise an event to the page, passing the name and password as arguments. An event has been added to the class called Login. A new class called LoginEventArgs is created, which includes the User-Name and Password. The Login event has two arguments, the current object (Me) and the LoginEventArgs.

The Submit button's click has been attached to the SubmitClicked procedure, which calls the OnLogin method, which raises the event. The finished code looks like the following:

```
Public Class LoginEventArgs
      Inherits EventArgs
      Public UserName, Password As String
End Class
Public Class LoginControl
      Inherits Control
      Implements INamingContainer
      Public Event Login(ByVal sender As Object, _
          ByVal e As LoginEventArgs)
      Protected Sub OnLogin(ByVal e As LoginEventArgs)
          RaiseEvent Login(Me, e)
      End Sub
      Protected Sub SubmitClicked(ByVal sender As Object, _
              ByVal e As EventArgs)
          Dim args As New LoginEventArgs()
          args.UserName = UserName
          args.Password = Password
          OnLogin(args)
      End Sub
      Public Sub New()
          Me.EnsureChildControls()
      End Sub
      Public Property UserName() As String
          Get
              Dim txt As TextBox
              txt = CType(Me.FindControl("UserName"), TextBox)
              Return txt.Text
          End Get
          Set(ByVal Value As String)
              Dim txt As TextBox
              txt = CType(Me.FindControl("UserName"), TextBox)
              txt.Text = Value
          End Set
      End Property
      Public Property Password() As String
          Get
              Dim txt As TextBox
              txt = CType(Me.FindControl("Password"), TextBox)
              Return txt.Text
          End Get
          Set(ByVal Value As String)
              Dim txt As TextBox
              txt = CType(Me.FindControl("Password"), TextBox)
              txt.Text = Value
```

```
            End Set
        End Property
        Protected Overrides Sub CreateChildControls()
            Dim pnl As New Panel()
            Dim txtUserName As New TextBox()
            Dim txtPassword As New TextBox()
            Dim btnSubmit As New Button()
            'start control buildup
            Controls.Add(pnl)
            'add user name row
            pnl.Controls.Add(New LiteralControl("<table><tr><td>"))
            pnl.Controls.Add(New LiteralControl("User Name:"))
            pnl.Controls.Add(New LiteralControl("</td><td>"))
            pnl.Controls.Add(txtUserName)
            pnl.Controls.Add(New LiteralControl("</td></tr>"))
            'add password row
            pnl.Controls.Add(New LiteralControl("<tr><td>"))
            pnl.Controls.Add(New LiteralControl("Password:"))
            pnl.Controls.Add(New LiteralControl("</td><td>"))
            pnl.Controls.Add(txtPassword)
            pnl.Controls.Add(New LiteralControl("</td></tr>"))
            'add submit button row
            pnl.Controls.Add(New LiteralControl( _
                "<tr><td colspan=""2"" align=""center"" >"))
            pnl.Controls.Add(btnSubmit)
            pnl.Controls.Add(New LiteralControl("</td></tr></table>"))
            'set up control properties
            pnl.Style.Add("background-color", "silver")
            pnl.Style.Add("width", "275px")
            txtUserName.ID = "UserName"
            txtUserName.Style.Add("width", "170px")
            txtPassword.ID = "Password"
            txtPassword.TextMode = TextBoxMode.Password
            txtPassword.Style.Add("width", "170px")
            btnSubmit.Text = "Submit"
            AddHandler btnSubmit.Click, AddressOf Me.SubmitClicked
        End Sub
    End Class
```

Accessing the custom server control is rather easy. In fact, Figure 7.10 shows that a rendered version of the control is showing now that the constructor has added the call to EnsureChildControls. The following code shows the code-behind page programming of the Login event method.

```
Public Class LoginFormTest
    Inherits System.Web.UI.Page
        Protected WithEvents LoginControl1 As Ch07Web.LoginControl
        ' Web Form Designer Generated Code
```

```
Private Sub LoginControl1_Login(ByVal sender As Object, _
     ByVal e As Ch07Web.LoginEventArgs) Handles LoginControl1.Login
     If e.UserName = "Glenn" And e.Password = "1234" Then
          Response.Write("Success")
     Else
          Response.Write("Denied")
     End If
End Sub
End Class
```

Inheriting from Existing Controls

Rather than reinventing the wheel every time a new custom server control is required, it is often much preferable to inherit from an existing control. Inheriting from an exiting control allows the new control to receive the benefits of the base control while being able to add new features.

The following code takes the Login control one more step. Instead of inheriting from Control, the Login control is now inheriting from WebControl. The WebControl class is a base class to most of the Web server controls. By using this class, the new Login control can be dynamically positioned on the screen and can take advantage of many of the properties that the WebControl exposes.

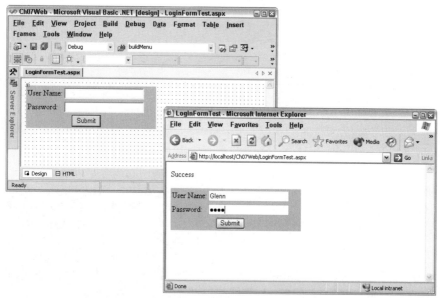

Figure 7.10 The rendered control in the Visual Studio .NET designer (left) and the successful handling of the Login event (right).

```vb
Public Class LoginPanel
    Inherits WebControl
    Implements INamingContainer
    Public Event Login(ByVal sender As Object, _
        ByVal e As LoginEventArgs)
    Protected Sub OnLogin(ByVal e As LoginEventArgs)
        RaiseEvent Login(Me, e)
    End Sub
    Protected Sub SubmitClicked(ByVal sender As Object, _
            ByVal e As EventArgs)
        Dim args As New LoginEventArgs()
        args.UserName = UserName
        args.Password = Password
        OnLogin(args)
    End Sub
    Public Sub New()
        Me.EnsureChildControls()
    End Sub
    Public Property UserName() As String
        Get
            Dim txt As TextBox
            txt = CType(Me.FindControl("UserName"), TextBox)
            Return txt.Text
        End Get
        Set(ByVal Value As String)
            Dim txt As TextBox
            txt = CType(Me.FindControl("UserName"), TextBox)
            txt.Text = Value
        End Set
    End Property
    Public Property Password() As String
        Get
            Dim txt As TextBox
            txt = CType(Me.FindControl("Password"), TextBox)
            Return txt.Text
        End Get
        Set(ByVal Value As String)
            Dim txt As TextBox
            txt = CType(Me.FindControl("Password"), TextBox)
            txt.Text = Value
        End Set
    End Property
    Protected Overrides Sub CreateChildControls()
        Dim pnl As WebControl = Me
        Dim txtUserName As New TextBox()
        Dim txtPassword As New TextBox()
        Dim btnSubmit As New Button()
        'start control buildup
        'add username row
```

```
            pnl.Controls.Add(New LiteralControl("<table><tr><td>"))
            pnl.Controls.Add(New LiteralControl("User Name:"))
            pnl.Controls.Add(New LiteralControl("</td><td>"))
            pnl.Controls.Add(txtUserName)
            pnl.Controls.Add(New LiteralControl("</td></tr>"))
            'add password row
            pnl.Controls.Add(New LiteralControl("<tr><td>"))
            pnl.Controls.Add(New LiteralControl("Password:"))
            pnl.Controls.Add(New LiteralControl("</td><td>"))
            pnl.Controls.Add(txtPassword)
            pnl.Controls.Add(New LiteralControl("</td></tr>"))
            'add submit button row
            pnl.Controls.Add(New LiteralControl( _
                "<tr><td colspan=""2"" align=""center"" >"))
            pnl.Controls.Add(btnSubmit)
            pnl.Controls.Add(New LiteralControl("</td></tr></table>"))
            'set up control properties
            txtUserName.ID = "UserName"
            txtUserName.Style.Add("width", "170px")
            txtPassword.ID = "Password"
            txtPassword.TextMode = TextBoxMode.Password
            txtPassword.Style.Add("width", "170px")
            btnSubmit.Text = "Submit"
            AddHandler btnSubmit.Click, AddressOf Me.SubmitClicked
        End Sub
    End Class
```

Besides inheriting from WebControl, the CreateChildControls method was reworked. The variable called pnl now points to Me and is no longer being added to the controls collection in the *Start control buildup* section. Also, in the *set up control properties* section, no style attributes are assigned to pnl, since they are settable from the Visual Studio .NET designer (Figure 7.11).

Another example of inheriting from an existing control occurs when it is preferable to set up a control like the DataGrid with many default setting. The following code shows an example of a new custom control called Default-DataGrid, which inherits from DataGrid. It has many default settings in the constructor.

```
    Public Class DefaultDataGrid
        Inherits DataGrid
        Public Sub New()
            'general settings
            BorderStyle = BorderStyle.Ridge
            BorderColor = Color.White
            CellSpacing = 1
            BorderWidth = New Unit(4, UnitType.Pixel)
            BackColor = Color.Black
            CellPadding = 3
            GridLines = GridLines.None
            Width = New Unit(425, UnitType.Pixel)
```

```
        AllowPaging = True
        Height = New Unit(300, UnitType.Pixel)
        'selected items
        SelectedItemStyle.BackColor = Color.FromArgb(&H94, &H71, &HDE)
        SelectedItemStyle.Font.Bold = True
        SelectedItemStyle.ForeColor = Color.White
        'alternating items
        AlternatingItemStyle.BackColor = Color.Silver
        'items
        ItemStyle.ForeColor = Color.Black
        ItemStyle.BackColor = Color.FromArgb(&HE0, &HE0, &HE0)
        'header
        HeaderStyle.Font.Bold = True
        HeaderStyle.ForeColor = Color.FromArgb(&HE7, &HE7, &HFF)
        HeaderStyle.BackColor = Color.FromArgb(&H4A, &H3C, &H8C)
        'footer
        FooterStyle.ForeColor = Color.Black
        FooterStyle.BackColor = Color.FromArgb(&HC6, &HC3, &HC6)
        'pager
        PagerStyle.HorizontalAlign = HorizontalAlign.Right
        PagerStyle.ForeColor = Color.Black
        PagerStyle.BackColor = Color.FromArgb(&HC6, &HC3, &HC6)
        PagerStyle.Mode = PagerMode.NumericPages
    End Sub
End Class
```

The DefaultDataGrid is initialized with the settings in the constructor. Figure 7.12 shows the DefaultDataGrid when it is placed on the Web page in the Visual Studio .NET Designer.

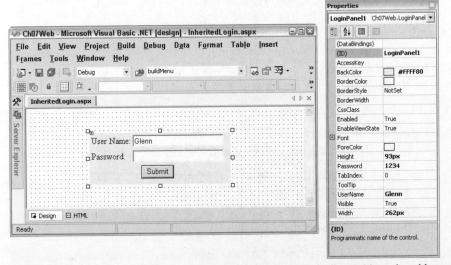

Figure 7.11 The Login custom control (left) can be dynamically positioned and has many more properties (right).

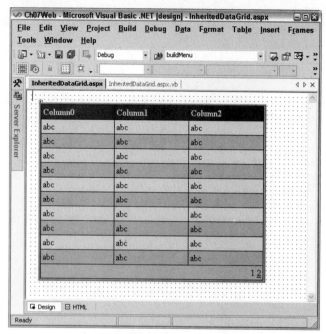

Figure 7.12 The DefaultDataGrid placed in the Web page.

Lab 7.1: User Control

In this lab, you will create a user control that can be used as a page banner for your Web pages. After that, you will convert a Web Form to a user control.

Creating a User Control

In this section, you will create a banner user control. This control will contain a Label with your company name. This user control will be dropped onto every page that requires a banner.

1. Open the OrderEntrySolution from Lab 6.1.

2. Right-click the OrderEntrySolution in the Solution Explorer, and click Check Out. This will check out the complete solution.

3. Right-click the Inventory project in the Solution Explorer, and click Set As StartUp Project.

4. Right-click the Inventory project and click Add, Add Web User Control. Name the control Banner.ascx.

5. Type *Welcome to My Home Page* directly on the user control. Note that the layout is set to FlowLayout by default, which allows text to be typed onto the control.

6. Use your mouse to select all the banner text, and then click Format, Justify, Center.

7. While the text is still selected, change the font to Arial and the font size to 6.

8. Close the user control.

9. Save your work.

Test the user control by placing it on a Web page and viewing the page. In this section of the lab, you will add the user control to the ProductList.asp page and view the result.

1. Open the ProductList.aspx page from the Inventory project.

2. Right-click the page, click Properties, and change the Page Layout to FlowLayout.

3. Move the DataGrid a bit with the mouse. When the mouse button is released, the DataGrid will snap into FlowLayout mode.

4. From the Solution Explorer, drag the Banner.ascx and drop it onto the ProductList.aspx page. The result should appear as shown in Figure 7.13.

5. Save your work.

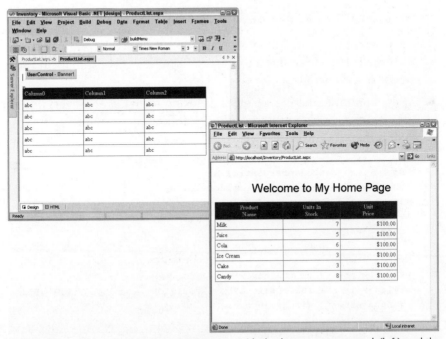

Figure 7.13 The Visual Studio .NET Designer with the banner user control (left) and the output when rendered in the browser (right).

Creating a User Control from a Web Form

In this section, you will create a copy of the NewCustomer.aspx page, and convert the copy to a user control.

1. Right-click the NewCustomer.aspx page in the Customer project and click Copy.

2. Right-click the customer project and click Paste. This creates a copy of the NewCustomer.aspx page to a page called Copy Of NewCustomer.aspx.

3. Right-click the copy and click Rename. Rename the page to NewCustomerControl.ascx. Click Yes to accept the warning message.

4. Double-click the NewCustomerControl.ascx file to open it in the Visual Studio .NET designer.

5. Click the HTML tab to reveal the HTML of the page. There are several changes that need to be done to convert this Web Form into a user control.

6. Change the first line from a Page directive to a Control directive. Change the code-behind page to NewCustomerControl.ascx .vb. Change the inherits class need to Customer.NewCustomer Control.

```
<%@ Control Language="vb" AutoEventWireup="false"
Codebehind="NewCustomerControl.ascx.vb"
Inherits="Customer.NewCustomerControl"%>
```

7. The user control is not allowed to have a form server control. Delete all of the HTML from line 2 to the the form server control, including the form server control.

8. At the bottom of the file, delete the closing form tag and everything after it. Your code should look like the following (though you may have different state codes).

```
<%@ Control Language="vb" AutoEventWireup="false"
Codebehind="NewCustomerControl.ascx.vb"
Inherits="Customer.NewCustomerControl"%>
<asp:label id="lblCustomer"
style="Z-INDEX: 103; LEFT: 50px; POSITION: absolute; TOP: 45px"
 runat="server">
    Customer Name
</asp:label>
<asp:textbox id="txtCustomerName"
style="Z-INDEX: 101; LEFT: 170px; POSITION: absolute; TOP: 45px"
 runat="server" Width="300px">
</asp:textbox>
<asp:label id="lblAddress"
style="Z-INDEX: 104; LEFT: 50px; POSITION: absolute; TOP: 75px"
```

```
 runat="server">
      Address
</asp:label>
<asp:textbox id="txtAddress1"
style="Z-INDEX: 102; LEFT: 170px; POSITION: absolute; TOP: 75px"
 runat="server" Width="300px">
</asp:textbox>
<asp:textbox id="txtAddress2"
style="Z-INDEX: 111; LEFT: 170px; POSITION: absolute; TOP: 105px"
 runat="server" Width="300px">
</asp:textbox>
<asp:label id="lblCity"
style="Z-INDEX: 106; LEFT: 20px; POSITION: absolute; TOP: 135px"
 runat="server">
      City
</asp:label>
<asp:textbox id="txtCity"
style="Z-INDEX: 105; LEFT: 55px; POSITION: absolute; TOP: 135px"
 runat="server" Width="150px">
</asp:textbox>
<asp:label id="lblState"
style="Z-INDEX: 107; LEFT: 266px; POSITION: absolute; TOP: 135px"
 runat="server">
      State
</asp:label>
<asp:dropdownlist id="drpState"
style="Z-INDEX: 110; LEFT: 314px; POSITION: absolute; TOP: 135px"
 runat="server" Width="75px">
      <asp:ListItem></asp:ListItem>
      <asp:ListItem Value="AK">AK</asp:ListItem>
      <asp:ListItem Value="AL">AL</asp:ListItem>
      <asp:ListItem Value="AR">AR</asp:ListItem>
      <asp:ListItem Value="AZ">AZ</asp:ListItem>
</asp:dropdownlist>
<asp:label id="lblZipCode"
style="Z-INDEX: 108; LEFT: 455px; POSITION: absolute; TOP: 136px"
 runat="server">
      Zip
</asp:label>
<asp:textbox id="txtZipCode"
style="Z-INDEX: 109; LEFT: 487px; POSITION: absolute; TOP: 134px"
 runat="server" Width="100px">
</asp:textbox>
<asp:Button id="btnAddCustomer"
style="Z-INDEX: 112; LEFT: 183px; POSITION: absolute; TOP: 177px"
 runat="server" Text="Add Customer">
</asp:Button>
<asp:Label id="lblConfirmation"
style="Z-INDEX: 113; LEFT: 52px; POSITION: absolute; TOP: 215px"
```

```
        runat="server" Width="520px" Height="75px">
        </asp:Label>
        <asp:RequiredFieldValidator id=valReqCustomerName
        style="Z-INDEX: 114; LEFT: 480px; POSITION: absolute; TOP: 48px"
         runat="server" ErrorMessage="Customer Name is Required"
        ToolTip="Customer Name is Required"
        controltovalidate="txtCustomerName">Error</asp:RequiredFieldValid
        ator>
        <asp:RequiredFieldValidator id=valReqAddress1
        style="Z-INDEX: 115; LEFT: 483px; POSITION: absolute; TOP: 80px"
         runat="server" ErrorMessage="Address Line 1 is Required"
        ToolTip="Address Line 1 is Required"
        controltovalidate="txtAddress1">Error</asp:RequiredFieldValidator
        >
        <asp:RequiredFieldValidator id=valReqCity
        style="Z-INDEX: 116; LEFT: 213px; POSITION: absolute; TOP: 136px"
         runat="server" ErrorMessage="City is Required"
        ToolTip="City is Required" controltovalidate="txtCity">
         Error</asp:RequiredFieldValidator>
        <asp:RequiredFieldValidator id=valReqState
        style="Z-INDEX: 117; LEFT: 398px; POSITION: absolute; TOP: 138px"
         runat="server" ErrorMessage="State is Required"
        ToolTip="State is Required"
        controltovalidate="drpState">Error</asp:RequiredFieldValidator>
        <asp:RequiredFieldValidator id=valReqZipCode
        style="Z-INDEX: 118; LEFT: 597px; POSITION: absolute; TOP: 136px"
         runat="server" ErrorMessage="Zip Code is Required"
        ToolTip="Zip Code is Required" controltovalidate="txtZipCode"
        enableclientscript="False">Error</asp:RequiredFieldValidator>
        <asp:RegularExpressionValidator id=valExpZipCode
        style="Z-INDEX: 119; LEFT: 597px; POSITION: absolute; TOP: 136px"
         runat="server" ErrorMessage="Zip Code Must be 99999 or
        99999-9999"
         tooltip="Zip Code Must be 99999 or 99999-9999"
        validationexpression="\d{5}(-\d{4})?"
        controltovalidate="txtZipCode"
        enableclientscript="False">Error</asp:RegularExpressionValidator>
        <asp:Button id=btnCancel
        style="Z-INDEX: 120; LEFT: 345px; POSITION: absolute; TOP: 177px"
         runat="server" Width="121px" Text="Cancel"
        CausesValidation="False"></asp:Button>
        <asp:ValidationSummary id=valSummary
        style="Z-INDEX: 121; LEFT: 245px; POSITION: absolute; TOP: 307px"
         runat="server" Width="164px" Height="21px"
        ShowMessageBox="True"
        ShowSummary="False"></asp:ValidationSummary>
```

9. Close and save the file.

10. Open the code-behind page by double-clicking the NewCustomer-Contol.ascx.vb file.

11. Change the name of the class on the first line to NewCustomControl and change this class to inherit from UserControl, as follows:

```
Public Class NewCustomerControl
        Inherits System.Web.UI.UserControl
```

12. Close and save the code-behind page.

Test the user control by placing it on a Web page and viewing the page. Here's how you can add the user control to a new page called AddCustomer.aspx and view the result:

1. Right-click the Customer project in the Solution Explorer, and click Set As StartUp Project.

2. Right-click the the Customer project, click Add, New Web Form, and name the new page AddCustomer.aspx.

3. Add a Label control to the top of the page. Change its Text property to Enter New Customer Information.

4. Add a Panel control under the Label control. The Panel will hold a NewCustomerControl. Make the size of the Panel large enough for the rendered size of the NewCustomerControl.

5. From the Solution Explorer, drag the NewCustomerControl, and drop it onto the Panel. The result should appear as shown in Figure 7.14.

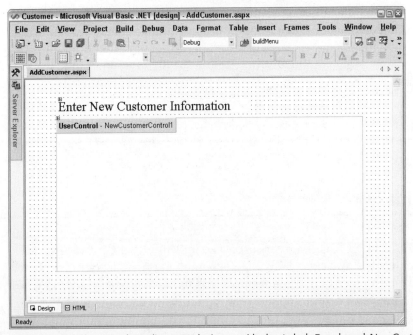

Figure 7.14 The Visual Studio .NET designer with the Label, Panel, and NewCustomer Control added.

6. Right-click the AddCustomer.aspx page in the Solution Explorer, and click Set as Start Page.

7. Save your work.

8. Start the Web application. Test the NewCustomerControl by creating errors to verify that the Validator controls are functioning properly. Figure 7.15 shows the completed page with the validators functioning properly.

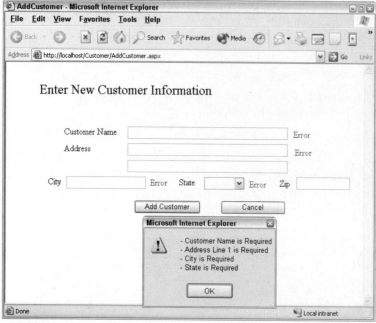

Figure 7.15 The completed AddCustomer.aspx page.

9. Check your work back into Visual SourceSafe.

Summary

- This chapter covered many aspects of creating user controls. A user control is similar to a Web page, where it is container for other controls. The difference between a user control and a Web page is that the user control must be placed on a Web page.

- User control data can be accessed by creating public properties on the user control.

- A user control can be positioned on a Web page that is configured for GridLayout by adding a Panel, positioning the Panel, and then adding the user control into the Panel.

- The Page's LoadControl method may be used to dynamically load a user control.

- Custom Web server controls may be created by having them inherit from System.Web.UI.Control, which allows you to create a control from scratch.

- Custom Web server controls may be created by combining existing controls.

- Custom Web server controls may be created by having them inherit from System.Web.UI.WebControls.WebControl, which gives the control much more built-in functionality. This allows the control to be dynamically positioned on a Web page that is set for GridLayout.

Review Questions

1. What is the file extension for a user control? Why is this important?
2. What is the command to dynamically load a user control?
3. How can a user control be positioned on a page with FlowLayout?
4. How can a user control be positioned on a page with GridLayout?

Answers to Review Questions

1. .ascx. ASP.NET does not allow an .ascx file to be retrieved by itself. The .ascx file must be part of a Web Form.

2. Page.LoadControl.

3. Any of the traditional methods of positioning can be used, such as placing the user control inside a table cell.

4. The user control can be placed inside a Panel control.

Data Access with ADO.NET

Previous chapters covered many of the basic elements of Visual Studio .NET, the .NET Framework, ASP.NET Web Forms, and controls. These chapters were intended to provide enough of a .NET foundation to get to the core of most applications: data access.

Data access is an important factor in most ASP.NET applications. The .NET Framework includes ADO.NET, which provides access to data in many locations. ADO.NET is not just another version of ADO; it represents a complete paradigm shift in data retrieval and manipulation.

ADO.NET is a set of classes to work with data. ADO.NET supports unstructured, structured, hierarchical, and relational data storage, which allows access to data wherever it is. It has a consistent object model, so learning how to retrieve and manipulate data in one data source is similar to working with most other data sources.

Many companies have already embraced XML in some form. Being able to integrate XML data was a primary design constraint of ADO.NET. Integration between ADO.NET and XML is done at with many levels, with ADO.NET being able to use many of the XML classes that are built into the .NET Framework. This allows for seamless use of ADO.NET to read and write XML data.

This chapter starts by comparing connected and disconnected data, and then covers the primary ADO.NET objects, looking at many details and examples. After covering the objects, this chapter covers different methods of performing data manipulation, sorting, and filtering using the DataGrid control.

Classroom Q & A

Q: Is it possible to load and save data as XML using ADO.NET?

A: Absolutely. ADO.NET represents a major change to ADO; ADO.NET is much more XML-centric than past versions of ADO.

Q: I heard that ADO.NET is focused on disconnected data. Is there a way to get connected data?

A: Yes. ADO.NET is indeed focused around disconnected data, but ADO.NET has limited support for connected data via a read-only, forward-only result set. This will be covered in more detail in this chapter.

Q: Can the DataGrid be used to add, delete, and edit the data?

A: Yes. This chapter will take a close look the DataGrid in detail, and you will see how the DataGrid can give you everything you're looking for.

Connected versus Disconnected Data

Previous versions of ADO were connection-centric, meaning that most of the data functionality was exposed via a maintained connection to the database. ADO supported disconnected recordsets and Remote Data Objects (RDO), but this certainly was not the focus of ADO.

One problem that is associated with connected data is that any data that is accessed will potentially create locks on rows in the database. Depending on the type of lock, user access to a given row may be paused while waiting for a lock to free up. Row locking at the database can be the cause of many performance and scalability problems.

ADO.NET is a disconnected-data-centric. Disconnected data retrieves the data from the data store and then closes the connection. One advantage of this model is that the data can be downloaded to the client, the connection can be closed, and the user can work with the data while offline. Updates can be sent back to the server when appropriate.

One of the problems with working with disconnected data is that changes can be made to the data from multiple locations at the same time, and when it comes time to update the data at the data store, concurrency errors may take place. ADO.NET provides the ability to deal with concurrency issues in a clean fashion.

ADO.NET Data Providers

A data provider supplies a bridge from the application to the data source. Think of the data provider as a set of drivers that are specific to a data store. Different providers include those discussed in the following subsections.

SQL Data Provider

The SQL Server .NET data provider contains classes that provide functionality that is similar to the generic OleDb data provider, but these classes are tuned for SQL Server data access. Although the OleDb data provider can be used to access SQL Server, the SQL data provider is the recommended data provider for SQL Server 7.0+ data access. The prefix for SQL provider objects is Sql, so a connection is a SqlConnection class.

OleDb Data Provider

The OleDb data provider contains classes for general-purpose access to many data sources, such as SQL Server 6.5 and earlier, Oracle, SyBase, DB2/400, and Microsoft Access. The prefix for OleDb provider objects is OleDb, so a connection is an OleDbConnection class.

Odbc Data Provider

The Odbc data provider contains classes for access to SQL Server, Oracle, and Access. The ODBC provider is available via free download from the Microsoft Solution Developer Network (MSDN) Web site at http://msdn.microsoft.com/downloads/sample.asp?url=/msdn-files/027/001/668/msdncompositedoc.xml.

To use ODBC, download and install the ODBC provider, and then add a reference to the Microsoft.Data.ODBC.dll file. The prefix for ODBC provider objects is Odbc, so a connection is an OdbcConnection class.

Oracle Data Provider

The Oracle data provider contains classes for access to Oracle 8i+ database servers. The Oracle provider is available for free download from the

MSDN Web site at http://msdn.microsoft.com/downloads/sample.asp?url=/
MSDN-FILES/ 027/001/940/msdncompositedoc.xml.

To use the Oracle data provider, download and install the provider and add
a reference to the System.Data.OracleClient.dll file. The prefix for Oracle
provider is Oracle, so a conection is an OracleConnection.

ADO.NET Data Namespaces

The .NET Framework is divided into logical namespaces. ADO.NET has its
own logical namespaces and extends some of the existing .NET Framework
namespaces. Table 8.1 lists most of the available ADO.NET namespaces.

When working with these namespaces, a reference must be set to the Sys-
tem.Data.dll file and any data provider .dll files. In addition, using the Imports
statement as follows can save typing.

```
Imports System.Data
Imports System.Data.SqlClient
```

Table 8.1   ADO.NET Namespaces

NAMESPACE	DESCRIPTION
System.Data	Provides the main namespace for ADO.NET, which contains many of the primary data classes.
System.Data.Common	Contains many utility and helper classes that are primarily used by data provider developers.
System.Data.SqlClient	Contains the SQL Server specific classes for the SQL Server .NET data provider.
System.Data.OleDb	Contains the OleDb specific classes for the OleDb .NET data provider, which provides access to OleDb specific data sources.
System.Data.SqlTypes	Provides SQL Server classes that are native to SQL Server. Explicitly creating instances of these classes when accessing SQL results in faster and cleaner code.
System.Xml	Provides standards-based support for accessing and modifying XML data.
Microsoft.Data.ODBC	Provides the classes for ODBC specific data access, which allows ODBC access to SQL Server, Oracle, and Access.
System.Data.OracleClient	Provides the classes for Oracle specific data access.

Primary Data Objects

Several primary data objects are covered in this section. Some of the primary objects are provider specific, while others are not provider specific. The provider-specific data objects, regardless of the provider, provide a core set of functionality, which will be covered in this section.

Provider-Specific Data Objects

The following data objects are provider specific: the Connection, DataAdapter, Command, Parameter, CommandBuilder, and the DataReader. This means that these objects will have a provider prefix. For example, the SQL Server objects have a SQL prefix, while the OleDb objects have an OleDb prefix. Provider-specific objects are tweaked for that provider, although the objects essentially provide the same functionality.

 Most of the examples in this section are done with SQL Server using the SQL Server data provider, but the examples can be converted to a different provider by simply changing the provider prefix of the data objects and the connection string.

Connection

The connection is required to access data in a data store. The connection requires a connection string, which is a list of settings for the connection. Connection strings typically identify the name of the computer that has the data store, the user name and password to connect to the data store, and the name of the data store. Additional settings that may be available depending on the type of data store are connection pooling, integrated security, packed size, and protocol.

Connection Security

Connecting to a data store usually requires security information of some sort, depending on the data store that is being accessed. When SQL Server is installed, it can be set up to use either Windows Authentication or Mixed Mode security. The default setting on SQL Server 2000+ is Windows Authentication.

With Windows Authentication, the SQL Server verifies that the user is authenticated based on the user's Windows login name as well as the Windows groups that the user is a member of. There is no separate login to get into SQL Server. Windows Authentication is more secure than Mixed Mode. Window Authentication is also referred to as Trusted Security and Integrated Security.

Mixed Mode, which is the default for SQL Server 7 and earlier, is available for situations where SQL Server will be accessed by users who do not have Windows networking accounts. The users who may not have a Windows networking account includes users who are accessing a non-Microsoft network, such as Novell NetWare. This also includes users who are running SQL Server in a workgroup environment. In situations like this, SQL Server maintains its own list of login names and passwords.

In Mixed Mode, SQL Server still allows users to connect using Windows Authentications. Windows Authentication cannot be turned off manually, but it will be off in situations where SQL Server is installed on a Windows 98 or Window ME operating system, which has no support for Windows Authentication.

ConnectionString

Coming up with a ConnectionString can be the hardest task to accomplish when accessing a data store. The ConnectionString contains the settings for the connection that will be opened to the data store. Every data store supports different settings but Table 8.2 names the more common settings.

Table 8.2 Typical Connection String Settings

SETTING	DESCRIPTION
Provider	(OleDb provider only) Contains the name of the provider that will be used. Think of the provider as the driver for the data store.
Connection Timeout or Connect Timeout	Number of seconds to wait for a connection to the data store before terminating the attempt for a connection and throwing an exception.
Initial Catalog	The name of the database.
Data Source	The name of the computer to be used when accessing data, or the Microsoft Access database full filename.
User ID	The user name for authentication.
Password	The password for authentication.
Integrated Security or Trusted Connection	Indicates that the connection will use Windows Authentication instead of Mide Mode security. Possible values are true, false, and SSPI (SSPI is true).
Persist Security Info	When set to false, the password and other security information will not be returned as part of the connection if the connection is open or has ever been in an open state. Default is false.

Although there are many ConnectionString options, a connection may be created by using just a couple of these settings. ConnectionStrings are created by concatenating the name and value settings together, separated by a semicolon. ConnectionsStrings typically are not case sensitive. Although spaces are supposed to be ignored, it is usually preferable to eliminate all spaces except the space that may be included in some setting names, such as User ID and Workstation ID. Some valid Connection strings follow:

```
'Microsoft Access connection
Dim cnstr as string = "Provider=Microsoft.Jet.OLEDB.4.0;"
cnstr &= "Data Source=C:\Samples\northwind.mdb"
```

This connects to the Microsoft Access database that is located at C:\Samples\ northwind.mdb if security has not been enabled on this database.

```
'Microsoft Access connection
Dim cnstr as string = "Provider=Microsoft.Jet.OLEDB.4.0;"
cnstr &= "Data Source=C:\mypath\nowind.mdb;"
cnstr &= "user id=admin;password=hello"
```

This connects to the Microsoft Access database that is located at c:\mypath\ nowind.mdb with the user name of admin and a password of hello.

```
'Excel spreadsheet
Dim cnstr as string = "Provider=Microsoft.Jet.OLEDB.4.0;"
cnstr &= "Data Source=C:\MyExcel.xls;Extended Properties=Excel 8.0;"
cnstr &= "HDR=yes"
```

This connects to an Excel spreadsheet using OleDb. The HDR=yes indicates that the first row contains column names of the data.

In addition to the connection settings listed in Table 8.2, the SQL Server provider offers the additional settings shown in Table 8.3.

As mentioned earlier in this chapter, it is usually preferable to eliminate all spaces except the space that may be included in some setting names, such as User ID and Workstation ID. Some valid SQL Connection strings are as follows:

```
'Sql Server
Dim cnstr as string = "integrated security=true;database=northwind"
```

This connects to the default instance of SQL Server on the local computer using Windows Authentication connecting to the northwind database.

```
'Sql Server
Dim cnstr as string = "server=remoteComputer;"
cnstr &= "integrated security=true;database=pubs"
```

Table 8.3   SQL Server Provider ConnectionString Settings

SQL SERVER SETTING	DEFAULT	DESCRIPTION
Application Name or App	.Net SqlClient Data Provider	The name of the current application. This is primarily used for logging. If the value is assigned, SQL Server uses this as the name of the process when querying SQL server for active connections (sp_who2 or "Select * from master.dbo.sysprocesses").
Connect Timeout, Connection Timeout or Timeout	15	Number of seconds to wait for a connection to the data store before terminating the attempt for a connection and throwing an exception.
Connection Lifetime	0	Used to determine whether a connection should be destroyed. When a connection is returned to the pool, its creation time is compared with the current time and the connection is destroyed if that time span (in seconds) exceeds the value specified by connection lifetime. This option can be useful in clustered configurations to force load balancing between a running server and a server just brought online.
Connection Reset	true	Determines whether the database connection is reset when being removed from the pool. Setting this to false avoids the making of an additional server round trip when obtaining a connection, but the programmer must be aware that the connection state is not being reset.
Current Language		The SQL Server Language record name.

Table 8.3 *(continued)*

SQL SERVER SETTING	DEFAULT	DESCRIPTION
Data Source, Server, Address, Addr, or Network Address		The name or network address of the instance of SQL Server to which to connect. This setting may also contain the instance name when attempting to connect to a nondefault instance of SQL Server. When empty, this will connect to the default instance of the local SQL Server. Can also be set to "." (period), "(local)," or "localhost" to select the local machine.
Enlist	true	When true, the pooler automatically enlists the connection in the creation thread's current transaction context.
Encrypt	false	Set the communications method to encrypted.
Initial FileName, Extended Properties, or AttachDBFileName		The full pathname of the primary file of an attachable database. If this setting is specified, the Database or Initial Catalog setting must also be specified.
OLE DB Services		Set this to -4 to disable the automatic pooling of connections.
Initial Catalog or Database		The name of the database.
Integrated Security or Trusted_Connection	false	Whether the connection is a secure connection.
Max Pool Size	100	The maximum number of connections allowed in the pool.
Min Pool Size	0	The minimum number of connections allowed in the pool.
Network Library or Net	'dbmssocn'	The network library used to establish a connection to an instance of SQL Server. The default value, dbnssocn, specifies TCP/IP. Other values include dbnmpntw (Named Pipes), dbmsrpcn (Multiprotocol), dbmsadsn (Apple Talk), dbmsgnet (VIA), dbmsipcn (Shared Memory), and dbmsspxn (IPX/SPX). The corresponding network DLL must be installed on the system to which you connect.

(continued)

Table 8.3   *(continued)*

SQL SERVER SETTING	DEFAULT	DESCRIPTION
Packet Size	8192	Size in bytes of the network packets used to communicate with an instance of SQL Server.
Persist Security Info or PersistSecurityInfo	false	When set to false, security-sensitive information, such as the password, is not returned as part of the connection if the connection is open or has ever been in an open state. Resetting the connection string resets all connection string values, including the password.
Pooling	true	When true, the SQLConnection object is drawn from the appropriate pool, or if necessary is created and added to the appropriate pool.
Password or Pwd		User's password.
User ID or Uid		The SQL Server Mixed Mode login account to use.
Workstation ID or Wsid	Local computer name	The name of the workstation connecting to SQL Server.

This connects to the default instance of SQL Server on a computer called remoteComputer using Windows Authentication and connecting to the pubs database.

```
'Sql Server
Dim cnstr as string = "server=remoteComputer;"
cnstr &= "user id=glenn;password=hello;database=pubs"
```

This connects to the default instance of SQL Server on a computer called remoteComputer using a SQL Server account called glenn with a password of hello and connecting to the pubs database.

```
'Sql Server
Dim cnstr as string = "server=.;"
Cnstr &= "timeout=30;"
cnstr &= "uid=glenn;pwd=hello;database=pubs"
```

This connects to the default instance of SQL Server on the local computer using a SQL Server account called glenn with a password of hello and connecting to the pubs database with a connection timeout of 30 seconds.

```
'Sql Server
Dim cnstr as string = "server=GJ\PortalSite;"
cnstr &= "integrated security=true;database=portal"
```

This connects to the PortalSite instance of SQL Server on a computer called GJ using a SQL Server Windows Authentication and connecting to the portal database.

Creating, Opening, Closing, and Destroying a Connection

In the previous section, many ConnectionString samples were presented. Now it's time to create and open a connection. A connection can be created as follows:

```
Dim cnstr as string = "integrated security=true;database=northwind"
Dim cn as new SqlConnection(cnstr)
cn.Open( )
'Do lots of data access here.
cn.Close( )
'can be reopened and closed here
cn.Dispose( )
cn=nothing
```

The first lines of code create a SqlConnection object using the specified ConnectionString and then open the connection. The ConnectionString could have been assign by using the ConnectionString property of cn as well.

After the connection has been opened, many commands may be executed over the connection. When finished, the connection can be closed, disposed, and assigned to nothing. See the accompanying *Close versus Dispose* sidebar for related details.

Exception Handling

When working with connection objects, it is usually advisable to place their code into an exception handling routine, since breaks in communication can cause application crashes. The previous code has been modified to reflect changes to handle any error that may occur, as follows:

```
Dim cn As New SqlConnection()
Dim cnstr as string = _
"server=asd;integrated security=yes;database=northwind"
Try
     cn.ConnectionString = cnstr
     cn.Open() 'Try to connect to nonexistent server.
     'lots of data access stuff here
Catch ex As SqlException
     Dim myErrors As SqlErrorCollection = ex.Errors
     Dim eItem As SqlError
     For Each eItem In myErrors
```

```
            Response.Write( _
            String.Format("Class: {0}<br>", eItem.Class))
            Response.Write( _
            String.Format( _
            "Error #{0}: {1} on line {2}.<br>", _
            eItem.Number, eItem.Message, eItem.LineNumber))
            Response.Write( _
            String.Format("{0} reported Error connecting to {1}<br>", _
                eItem.Source, eItem.Server))
          Response.Write( _
          String.Format("Nothing was written to database.<br>"))
    Next
Catch
      'Throw the previous exception to the caller.
      Throw
Finally
      cn.Dispose()
      cn = Nothing
End Try
```

 This book will not use the try/catch block in each example to keep focused on the subject at hand. Using a try/catch block is the recommended method of opening a connection and performing data access in a production environment.

In the previous code, the cn had to be declared outside the try block because variables that are declared inside the try block only live within the try block. Since the Finally block needs to access cn, cn's declaration was outside of the try block.

When a SqlException takes place, the exception will be caught. There is only one .NET exception for any SQL Server exception, but looping through the Errors collection of the SqlException will reveal more details about the type of SqlErrors that took place. If the exception was not a SqlException, the Exception is simply thrown to the caller.

The Finally block of code will execute regardless of whether or not an exception occurred. This is especially important in situations where the exception is being thrown to the caller, because the Finally block will even execute in this case, just prior to throwing the exception to the caller.

Command

The Command object is used to issue a command to the data store. The Command can be a command to retrieve data or a command to insert, update, or delete data. To issue a command to a data store, a connection object is required. The connection may be passed into the Command constructor or may be attached to the Command's Connection property after the Command is created. The following code examples show how a Command may be created and initialized.

```
Dim cnstr as string = _
    "server=asd;integrated security=yes;database=northwind"
Dim cn as new SqlConnection()
Dim cmd as new SqlCommand("Select * from customers", cn)
```

This is probably the simplest method of creating a Command object. The first constructor argument is the SQL command to execute. The second constructor argument is the connection. The connection must be opened before the command may be executed.

♦ Close versus Dispose

By convention, all .NET Framework classes that access unmanaged resources should implement the IDisposable interface, which contains the Dispose method. The Dispose method is responsible for cleaning up unmanaged resources and can be called to proactively clean up the unmanaged resources when they are no longer needed.

Objects that implement the IDisposable interface typically program the finalizer (conceptually similar to a class destructor) to call the Dispose method automatically if the programmer didn't. The problem is that the object may be retained in memory for a much longer time if the developer let the runtime handle the automatic call to Dispose.

If a class has a Dispose method, it should always be called as quickly as possible to free up unmanaged resources and allow the object to be garbage collected sooner.

So where does the Close method come into play? The Close method exists for two purposes. First, the Close method is a carryover from older technologies that have the notion of opening something and then closing it. Second, the Close method does not imply that all unmanaged resources will be freed up. The Close method actually implies that there may be a chance of the connection being reopened, where the Dispose implies that all unmanaged resources are freed up and there will not be a reopening of the connection.

Many books suggest that the Close method be executed just before the Dispose method. This is rather redundant, since the Dispose method calls the Close method before it finishes cleaning up the rest of the unmanaged resources. The right way to finish using a connection is as follows:

```
Dim cnstr as string = "integrated security=true;database=northwind"
Dim cn as new SqlConnection(cnstr)
cn.Open( )
'Do lots of data access here.
cn.Dispose( ) 'no longer needed, Dispose will call the Close method
cn=nothing
```

If a class has a Dispose method, always call the Dispose method and then assign the variable to nothing to expedite garbage collection.

```
Dim cnstr as string = _
    "server=asd;integrated security=yes;database=northwind"
Dim cn as new SqlConnection()
Dim cmd As New SqlCommand()
cmd.CommandText = "Select * from customers"
cmd.Connection = cn
```

This is just another way of creating and initializing the command. It assigns the appropriate properties after the Command has been created.

```
Dim cnstr as string = _
    "server=asd;integrated security=yes;database=northwind"
Dim cn as new SqlConnection()
Dim cmd As New SqlCommand()
cmd.CommandText = "uspGetCustomers"
cmd.CommandType = CommandType.StoredProcedure
cmd.Connection = cn
```

This is an example of a Command that executes a stored procedure. Notice that the CommandText property contains the name of the stored procedure, while the CommandType indicates that this will be a call to a stored procedure.

Command Parameters

Stored procedures often require values to be passed to them to execute. For example, a user-defined stored procedure called *uspGetCustomer* may require a customer ID to be passed into the store procedure to retrieve a particular customer. Parameters can be created by using the Parameters.Add method of the Command object as follows:

```
'Connection
Dim cn As New SqlConnection()
Dim cnstr as string = "integrated security=yes;database=northwind"
cn.ConnectionString = cnstr
'Command
Dim cmd As New SqlCommand()
cmd.CommandText = "CustOrdersOrders"
cmd.CommandType = CommandType.StoredProcedure
cmd.Connection = cn
'Parameters
cmd.Parameters.Add("@CustomerID", "AROUT")
```

This code creates a Connection object and configures the Command object to execute a stored procedure called *CustOrdersOrders*, which requires a single parameter called *@CustomerID*, which will contain the value *AROUT*.

The OleDb provider requires the parameters to be defined in the same order that they are defined in the stored procedure. This means that the names that are assigned to parameters do not need to match the names that are defined in the stored procedure.

The SQL Server provider requires parameter names to match the names of the parameters as defined in SQL Server, but the parameters may be created in any order.

In either case, the name that is assigned to a parameter object is the name that can be used to access the parameter in the code. For example, to retrieve the value that is currently in the SqlParameter called @CustCount, use the following code:

```
Dim x as integer = cmd.Parameters("@CustCount")
```

ExecuteNonQuery Method

The execution of the Command is done differently depending on the data being retrieved or modified. The ExecuteNonQuery method is used when a command is not expected to return any rows, such as an update, insert, or delete query. This method returns an integer that represents the quantity of rows that were affected by the operation. The following example executes a store procedure to archive data and returns the quantity of rows that were archived. Notice that the delimiter for the DateTime data types is the pound sign (#).

```
'Connection
Dim cn As New SqlConnection()
Dim cnstr as string = "integrated security=yes;database=northwind"
cn.ConnectionString = cnstr
'Command
Dim cmd As New SqlCommand()
cmd.CommandText = "ArchiveOrders"
cmd.CommandType = CommandType.StoredProcedure
cmd.Connection = cn
'Parameters
cmd.Parameters.Add("@ArchiveYear", #1/1/1997#)
'Execute
cn.Open()
Dim x As Integer = cmd.ExecuteNonQuery()
'Do something with x.
'x contains the quantity of rows that were affected.
'Cleanup
cn.Dispose()
cn = Nothing
```

ExecuteScalar Method

Many times a query is executed that is expected to return a single row with a single column. In these situations, the results can be treated as a single return value. For example, the following SQL stored procedure returns a single row with a single column.

```
CREATE PROCEDURE dbo.OrderCount
    (
            @CustomerID nvarchar(5)
    )
AS
    Select count(*) from orders where customerID = @CustomerID
RETURN
```

Using the ExecuteScalar method, the count can be retrieved into a variable as follows:

```
'Connection
Dim cn As New SqlConnection()
Dim cnstr as string = "integrated security=yes;database=northwind"
cn.ConnectionString = cnstr
'Command
Dim cmd As New SqlCommand()
cmd.CommandText = "ArchiveOrders"
cmd.CommandType = CommandType.StoredProcedure
cmd.Connection = cn
'Parameters
cmd.Parameters.Add("@CustomerID", "AROUT")
'Execute
cn.Open()
Dim x As Integer = cmd.ExecuteScalar()
'do something with x
'x contains the count of orders for
'Cleanup
cn.Dispose()
cn = Nothing
```

ExecuteReader Method

The ExecuteReader method returns a DataReader instance. The following code is an example of the ExecuteReader method. See the *DataReader* section later in this chapter for more information.

```
'Connection
Dim cn As New SqlConnection()
Dim cnstr as string = "integrated security=yes;database=northwind"
cn.ConnectionString = cnstr
'Command
Dim cmd As New SqlCommand()
cmd.CommandText = "CustOrderHist"
cmd.CommandType = CommandType.StoredProcedure
cmd.Connection = cn
'Parameters
cmd.Parameters.Add("@CustomerID", "AROUT")
'Execute
```

```
cn.Open()
Dim dr As SqlDataReader = cmd.ExecuteReader()
While (dr.Read())
     Response.Write(dr("ProductName") & " - " _
       & dr("Total").ToString() & "<br>")
End While
'Cleanup
dr.Close()
cn.Dispose()
cn = Nothing
```

ExecuteXmlReader Method

The ExecuteXmlReader returns a XmlReader instance. The following code is an example of the ExecuteXmlReader method. See the *XmlReader* section in Chapter 9, "Working with XML Data" for more information.

```
'Connection
Dim cn As New SqlConnection()
Dim cnstr as string = "integrated security=yes;database=northwind"
cn.ConnectionString = cnstr
'Command
Dim cmd As New SqlCommand()
cmd.CommandText = "Select * from customers for xml auto"
cmd.Connection = cn
'Execute
cn.Open()
Dim dr As XmlReader = cmd.ExecuteXmlReader()
While (dr.Read())
     Response.Write(dr("CustomerID") & " - " _
       & dr("CompanyName") & "<br>")
End While
'Cleanup
dr.Close()
cn.Dispose()
cn = Nothing
```

DataReader

The DataReader is used to retrieve connected data from the server. The DataReader requires a command and connection (see Figure 8.1). The Data-Reader returns a forward-only, read-only data stream from a data source. This stream represents the fastest way to retrieve data, but has the least functionality.

The DataReader object cannot be created using the *New* key word. To create a DataReader, use the ExecuteReader method of the Command object. The following code is an example of the DataReader.

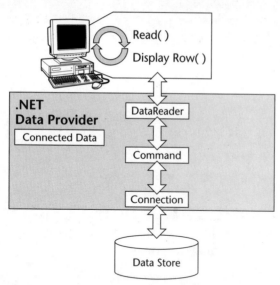

Figure 8.1 The DataAdapter requires Command and Connection objects. Use the Read method to retrieve one row at a time.

```
'Connection
Dim cn As New SqlConnection()
Dim cnstr as string = "integrated security=yes;database=northwind"
cn.ConnectionString = cnstr
'Command
Dim cmd As New SqlCommand()
cmd.CommandText = "CustOrderHist"
cmd.CommandType = CommandType.StoredProcedure
cmd.Connection = cn
'Parameters
cmd.Parameters.Add("@CustomerID", "AROUT")
'Execute
cn.Open()
Dim dr As SqlDataReader = cmd.ExecuteReader()
While (dr.Read())
    Response.Write(dr("ProductName") & " - " -
    & dr("Total").ToString() & "<br>")
End While
'Cleanup
dr.Close()
cn.Dispose()
cn = Nothing
```

In this example, the ExecuteReader method was used to create a DataReader object. The information is displayed by executing a loop, which executes the Read method, returning true each time a valid row is read.

The DataReader can be used for populating read-only controls like List-Boxes. The following code populates a ListBox with the CompanyName and the CustomerID.

```
'Connection
Dim cn As New SqlConnection()
Dim cnstr as string = "integrated security=yes;database=northwind"
cn.ConnectionString = cnstr
'Command
Dim cmd As New SqlCommand()
cmd.CommandText = "Select * from customers"
cmd.Connection = cn
'Execute
cn.Open()
Dim dr As SqlDataReader = cmd.ExecuteReader()
ListBox1.DataSource = dr
ListBox1.DataTextField = "CompanyName"
ListBox1.DataValueField = "CustomerID"
DataBind()
'Cleanup
dr.Close()
cn.Dispose()
cn = Nothing
```

Notice that a call is made to the dr.Close method. The DataReader's Close method should be called when cleaning up resources.

The DataReader provides the IsClosed and RecordsAffected properties that are available after the DataReader is closed. The DataReader also contains several helper methods that can be used to retrieve typed data without requiring the use of CType to cast to a particular data type. Table 8.4 lists these methods.

Table 8.4 DataReader's Typed Methods

GetBoolean	GetByte	GetBytes
GetChar	GetChars	GetDataTypeName
GetDateTime	GetDecimal	GetDouble
GetFieldType	GetFloat	GetGuid
GetInt16	GetInt32	GetInt64
GetName	GetOrdinal	GetString
GetValue	GetValues	IsDBNull
NextResult	GetSchemaTable	

In addition to these helper methods, each data provider has additional helper methods to aid in data retrieval. For example, the Sql provider contains many helper methods that are tuned to work with SQL Server, such as GetSqlBinary and GetSqlMoney. Use the Object Browser (Ctrl+Alt+J) to view available methods.

DataAdapter

The DataAdapter is responsible for moving data between the data store and a DataTable or DataSet. The DataAdapter can have four commands assigned to it: select, insert, update, and delete. Each command requires a connection, but can share the same connection object. The select command is required at a minimum. The select command may be created explicitly and assigned to the DataAdapter. Or, the select command may be created implicitly by providing the command text (see Figure 8.2).

The DataAdapter's primary method is the fill method. The fill method is responsible for filling one or more disconnected tables or a DataSet. The DataAdapter does not require the connection to be opened explicitly before the fill command is executed. If the connected is closed, the DataAdapter opens the connection automatically. After the DataAdapter is finished, the connection will be placed into its original state.

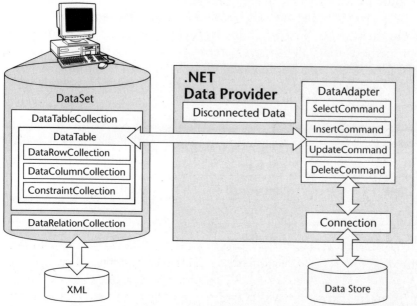

Figure 8.2 The DataAdapter's role in filling a DataSet.

Internally, the DataAdapter uses a DataReader to retrieve and update data, which is completely transparent to the developer. The following code is an example of using a DataAdapter to fill a DataTable and bind it to a DataGrid.

```
'Create objects
Dim cnstr As String = "integrated security=yes;database=northwind"
Dim da As New SqlDataAdapter("Select * from customers", cnstr)
Dim dt As New DataTable("MyTable")
'Execute
da.Fill(dt)
DataGrid1.DataSource = dt
DataBind()
'Cleanup
dt.Dispose()
da.Dispose()
```

This code sample represents an attempt to populate the DataGrid by creating the fewest objects. When the DataAdapter is created, strings are passed into the constructor to implicitly create Command and Connection objects. The connection does not need to be explicitly opened because it will be automatically opened and closed as needed. A DataTable was created and filled with rows from the customers table in SQL Server. The DataTable's constructor optionally allows assigning a table name to this memory-based table. Normally this table name should be assigned the same name as the table in SQL Server, but notice that this is not a requirement. If a table name is not supplied, its name will be *Table*. Notice that the DataAdapter and the DataTable contain a Dispose method that should always be called as part of the cleanup code.

Using a Single DataAdapter

When filling DataTables, how many DataAdapters are required? Certainly, a single DataAdapter could be provided, which could be reused to fill each table, as shown in Figure 8.3. If data in the DataTable will be inserted, updated, or deleted, consider using a DataAdapter for each DataTable. If the DataTables will contain read-only data, it may make more sense to use a single DataAdapter and change the CommandText prior to filling each DataTable.

Using Multiple DataAdapters

In situations where each DataTable will be updated, it usually makes sense to create a DataAdapter for each DataTable. This allows the select, insert, update, and delete commands to be assigned to the DataAdapter, and the DataAdapter will execute the appropriate command as needed when the DataAdaptor's Update method is called. Figure 8.4 shows an example of using multiple DataAdapters. Updating data sources is covered later in this chapter.

```
'fill DataTable1
Sql="Select * from customers"
Dim da as new SqlDataAdapter( Sql, cn)
Dim dt1 as new DataTable("DataTable1")
da.fill(dt1)


'fill DataTable2
Sql="Select * from orders"
da.SelectCommand.CommandText=Sql
Dim dt2 as new DataTable("DataTable2")
da.fill(dt2)
```

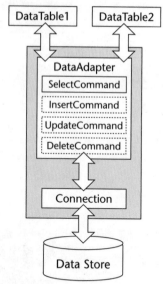

Figure 8.3 DataAdapter being reused to fill multiple DataTables.

Non-Provider-Specific Data Classes

The System.Data namespace provides classes that are not specific to any provider. This means that these classes can be used without having connectivity to a data provider. This section explores these classes.

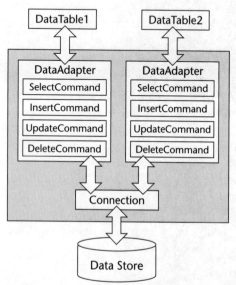

Figure 8.4 Multiple DataAdapters to fill multiple DataTables.

DataSet

The DataSet is a major component in ADO.NET as an in-memory, relational database. The DataSet contains a collection of DataTable objects and a collection of DataRelation objects (see Figure 8.5). Each DataTable can contain unique and foreign key constraints to enforce data integrity. The DataRelation can be used to navigate the table hierarchy. This essentially creates a path from DataTable to DataTable, which can be traversed by code.

The DataSet can read and write XML and XML Schema data. The XML information may be transferred across a network via many protocols, including HTTP. The DataSet also provides methods for copying, merging, and retrieving changes.

The following code shows an example of the creation of a DataSet.

```
'Create objects
Dim cnstr As String = "integrated security=yes;database=northwind"
Dim cn As New SqlConnection(cnstr)
Dim daCustomers As New SqlDataAdapter("Select * from customers", cn)
Dim daOrders As New SqlDataAdapter("Select * from orders", cn)
Dim ds As New DataSet("NW")
'Execute
daCustomers.Fill(ds, "Customers")
daOrders.Fill(ds, "Orders")
'Create the relation and constraints.
ds.Relations.Add("CustomersOrders", _
    ds.Tables("Customers").Columns("CustomerID"), _
    ds.Tables("Orders").Columns("CustomerID"), _
    True)
DataGrid1.DataSource = ds.Tables("Customers")
DataGrid2.DataSource = ds.Tables("Orders")
DataBind()
'Cleanup
ds.Dispose()
daCustomers.Dispose()
daOrders.Dispose()
```

This code creates a DataAdapter for the Customers table and another DataAdapter for the Orders table. After the DataTables are filled, a DataRelation is created. The creation of a DataRelation must include the parent and child columns. Optionally, the DataRelation may create the constraints when the DataRelation is created. When the constraints are created, an attempt to add a row into a child table that doesn't reference a row in the parent table will throw an exception. For example, if an order is entered into the Orders table but doesn't belong to a valid customer (the parent table), an exception will be thrown. By default, constraints are created, but it is possible to create a DataRelation without creating the constraints.

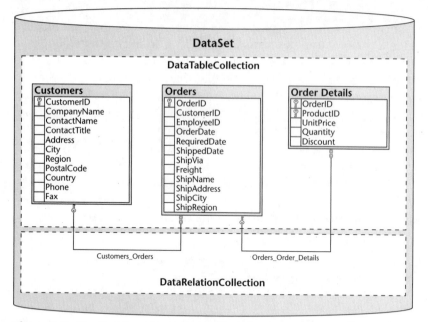

Figure 8.5 The DataSet with its DataTableCollection and DataRelationCollection.

When the DataSet is created, an optional DataSet name may be assigned by passing the name to its constructor. When writing the data as XML, the name, which is the DataSetName property, is important because the DataSetName will be the root-level element in the XML document.

When writing XML data, the parent table is written, followed by the child data. The DataRelation contains a nested property that will cause the child table data to be nested in each row of parent data. For example, the following code can be added to nest the Orders in the Customers table:

```
ds.Relations("CustomersOrders").Nested=True
```

DataTable

The DataTable is an in-memory table with rows, columns, and constraints. The DataTable is the central object for disconnected data access. The DataTable contains DataRows, DataColumns, Constraints, and references to ParentRelations and ChildRelations, as shown in Figure 8.6. A DataTable can be implicit or explicit. Implicit DataTable creation can be done by creating a DataAdapter and using its fill method to create the DataTable with the appropriate schema, as shown in the following code sample.

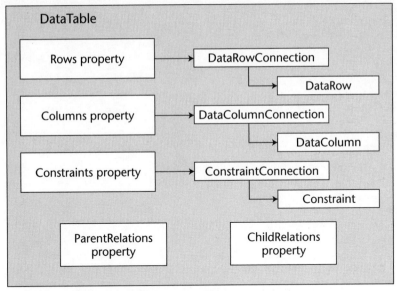

Figure 8.6 The main DataTable properties.

```
'Create objects
Dim cnstr As String = "integrated security=yes;database=northwind"
Dim cn As New SqlConnection(cnstr)
Dim sql As String = "Select * from customers"
Dim daCustomers As New SqlDataAdapter(sql, cn)
Dim dt As New DataTable("Customers")
'Execute
daCustomers.Fill(dt)
'Create the relation and constraints
DataGrid1.DataSource = dt
DataBind()
'Cleanup
dt.Dispose()
daCustomers.Dispose()
```

The DataTable is created and named Customers. Next, the DataTable is populated with the fill method. This will create the columns as necessary and populate all of the rows.

Creating DataColumn Objects

Explicit DataTable creation involves manually creating each column and constraint, and then populating the rows. This is useful in situations where data is not from a persistent date store. The following code builds a table, one column at a time.

```
Dim dt As New DataTable("Customers")
'Customer ID Column
Dim col As New DataColumn("CustomerID")
col.DataType = Type.GetType("System.String")
col.MaxLength = 5
col.Unique = true
col.AllowDBNull = false
col.Caption = "Customer ID"
dt.Columns.Add(col)
'Company Name Column
col = New DataColumn("CompanyName")
col.DataType = Type.GetType("System.String")
col.MaxLength = 40
col.Unique = false
col.AllowDBNull = false
col.Caption = "Company Name"
dt.Columns.Add(col)
```

This code creates a DataTable and then adds a column for the CustomerID and another column for the CompanyName. The DataTable may still be populated using a DataAdapter or may be populated manually via other code.

The DataColumn can also be a calculated column by assigning an expression to the column. This can be especially beneficial when data is available but not in the correct format. An example might be a DataTable that contains a Quantity and Price column, but a Total column is required. A new column can be created with an expression of "Quantity * Price." The following same code creates a column with concatenation of the CustomerID and the Company-Name.

```
'Both Columns
col = New DataColumn("Both")
col.DataType = Type.GetType("System.String")
col.MaxLength = 60
col.Unique = False
col.AllowDBNull = True
col.Caption = "Both of them"
col.Expression = "CustomerID + ' - ' + CompanyName"
dt.Columns.Add(col)
```

Enumerating the DataTable

It's often desirable to move through each row and each column of a DataTable. The following code shows how the rows and columns of a DataTable can be enumerated.

```
'Create objects
Dim cnstr As String = "integrated security=yes;database=northwind"
Dim cn As New SqlConnection(cnstr)
```

```
Dim sql As String = "Select * from customers"
Dim daCustomers As New SqlDataAdapter(sql, cn)
Dim dt As New DataTable("Customers")
'Execute
daCustomers.Fill(dt)
'Build HTML Table
Response.Write("<table border='1'>")
'Build the Column Headings
Dim dcol As DataColumn
Response.Write("<tr>")
For Each dcol In dt.Columns
    Response.Write("<th>")
    'This could also be the ColumnName property
    'but the Caption is changeable to a user-
    'friendly appearance.
    Response.Write(dcol.Caption.ToString())
    Response.Write("</th>")
Next
Response.Write("</tr>")
'Build Data Rows.
Dim drow As DataRow
For Each drow In dt.Rows
    Response.Write("<tr>")
    'Build Data Columns.
    Dim ditem As Object
    For Each ditem In drow.ItemArray
        Response.Write("<td>")
        Response.Write(ditem.ToString())
        Response.Write("</td>")
    Next
    Response.Write("</tr>")
Next
Response.Write("</table>")
'Cleanup
dt.Dispose()
daCustomers.Dispose()
cn.Dispose()
```

This code fills a DataTable, then builds an HTML table by writing the table tag; then, the column headers are written by retrieving the caption of each column. Finally, the DataRows are enumerated, and for each column in a DataRow, the object data in the column is written to the browser.

DataView

A DataView is a window into a DataTable. A DataTable can have many DataViews assigned to it, which allows the data to be viewed in many different ways without requiring the data to be read again from the database.

The following code sample shows the use of the RowFilter to view customers whose CustomerID begins with the letter *A*.

```
'Create objects
Dim cnstr As String = "integrated security=yes;database=northwind"
Dim cn As New SqlConnection(cnstr)
Dim sql As String = "Select CustomerID, CompanyName from customers"
Dim daCustomers As New SqlDataAdapter(sql, cn)
Dim dt As New DataTable("Customers")
'Execute
daCustomers.Fill(dt)
Dim dv As New DataView( )
dv.Table = dt
dv.RowFilter = "CustomerID like 'A%'"
DataGrid1.DataSource = dv
DataBind( )
```

Notice that the DataView is assigned to a DataTable. The RowFilter represents a SQL *where* clause. The DataGrid's DataSource is assigned directly to the DataView.

The next code sample shows the use of the Sort property to sort the customers on the Region in ascending order, followed by the CompanyName in descending order.

```
'Create objects
Dim cnstr As String = "integrated security=yes;database=northwind"
Dim cn As New SqlConnection(cnstr)
Dim sql As String = "Select CustomerID, CompanyName from customers"
Dim daCustomers As New SqlDataAdapter(sql, cn)
Dim dt As New DataTable("Customers")
'Execute
daCustomers.Fill(dt)
Dim dv As New DataView()
dv.Table = dt
dv.Sort = "Region ASC, CompanyName DESC"
DataGrid1.DataSource = dv
DataBind()
```

The sort expression is the SQL *order by* clause. Notice that the sort columns are comma separated, and ASC or DESC can be supplied to indicate ascending or descending order, respectively.

The following example shows the use of the RowStateFilter to view rows that are marked for deletion.

```
'Create objects
Dim cnstr As String = "integrated security=yes;database=northwind"
Dim cn As New SqlConnection(cnstr)
Dim sql As String = "Select * from customers"
```

```
Dim daCustomers As New SqlDataAdapter(sql, cn)
Dim dt As New DataTable("Customers")
'Execute
daCustomers.Fill(dt)
Dim x As Integer
For x = 5 To 10
    dt.Rows(x).Delete()
Next
Dim dv As New DataView()
dv.Table = dt
dv.RowStateFilter = DataViewRowState.Deleted
DataGrid1.DataSource = dv
DataBind()
```

This code deletes rows 5 through 10 and then creates a DataView with the RowStateFilter set to see only deleted rows.

The DataView can also combine the Sort, RowFilter, and RowStateFilter methods as needed. A single table can have many DataView objects assigned to it.

Enumerating the DataView

Many times it is desirable to walk through the rows and columns of a DataView. Although the procedure is similar to enumerating a DataTable, the objects are different. The following code enumerates the rows and columns of a DataView.

```
'Create objects
Dim cnstr As String = "integrated security=yes;database=northwind"
Dim cn As New SqlConnection(cnstr)
Dim sql As String = "Select * from customers"
Dim daCustomers As New SqlDataAdapter(sql, cn)
Dim dt As New DataTable("Customers")
'Execute
daCustomers.Fill(dt)
'Create DataView
Dim dv As New DataView(dt)
dv.RowFilter = "Region like 'S%'"
'Build HTML Table
Response.Write("<table border='1'>")

'Build the Column Headings.
Dim dcol As DataColumn
Response.Write("<tr>")
For Each dcol In dv.Table.Columns
    Response.Write("<th>")
    'This could also be the ColumnName property
    'but the Caption is changeable to a user-
    'friendly appearance.
```

```
        Response.Write(dcol.Caption.ToString())
        Response.Write("</th>")
Next
Response.Write("</tr>")
'Build Data Rows.
Dim drow As DataRowView
For Each drow In dv
        Response.Write("<tr>")
        'Build Data Columns,
        Dim ditem As Object
        For Each ditem In drow.Row.ItemArray
            Response.Write("<td>")
            Response.Write(ditem.ToString())
            Response.Write("</td>")
        Next
        Response.Write("</tr>")
Next
Response.Write("</table>")
'Cleanup
dt.Dispose()
daCustomers.Dispose()
cn.Dispose()
```

This code fills a DataTable and creates a DataView based on the Region beginning with the letter S. Next, the code builds an HTML table by writing the table tag. Then, the column headers are written by retrieving the caption of each column. When it's time to enumerate the DataView, each row is returned as a DataViewRow. The DataRowView contains a Row property, which allows access to the DataRow that the DataRowView is pointing to. The Row is enumerated; and for each column in the DataRow, the object data in the column is written to the browser.

Modifying Table Data

One of the main features of ADO.NET is its ability to work with disconnected data. This data is represented as one or more DataTable objects that optionally may be located inside a DataSet object. The goal is to be able to perform additions, updates, and deletes on the data, and at some point, send all of the changes to the data store. This section covers the modification of data in a DataTable or DataSet, and the next section covers the updating of data at the data store.

Setting the Primary Key

Before changes can be made to the DataTable, the DataTable's PrimaryKey property should be assigned. The PrimaryKey property expects an array of columns to be assigned, which allows DataTables with composite primary keys to be used with ADO.NET. The following code is an example of setting the PrimaryKey property. It creates a new DataColumn array and initializes it to the Datatable's CustomerID column. If the PrimaryKey property is not assigned, an exception will be thrown when updates are attempted.

```
dt.PrimaryKey = New DataColumn() {dt.Columns("CustomerID")}
```

Adding DataRow Objects

After the DataTable is created and its DataColumn objects have been defined, the DataTable can be populated with DataRow objects.

To add a DataRow to the DataTable, first create the DataRow. A DataRow will have different columns, based upon the DataTable that the row will be placed into, so the proper method of creating a DataRow is to execute the NewRow method on the DataTable instance. The following is an example of adding a new DataRow.

```
'Create objects
Dim cnstr As String = "integrated security=yes;database=northwind"
Dim cn As New SqlConnection(cnstr)
Dim sql As String = "Select CustomerID, CompanyName from customers"
Dim daCustomers As New SqlDataAdapter(sql, cn)
Dim dt As New DataTable("Customers")
'Execute
daCustomers.Fill(dt)
'Add New DataRow
Dim dr As DataRow = dt.NewRow()
dr("CustomerID") = "AAAAA"
dr("CompanyName") = "My Company"
dt.Rows.Add(dr)
'Create the relation and constraints.
DataGrid1.DataSource = dt
DataBind()
'Cleanup
dt.Dispose()
daCustomers.Dispose()
```

This code added a new DataRow to the DataTable. Remember that the SQL Database does not have the changed row. Sending updates is covered later in this chapter.

The DataRow goes through a series of states that can be viewed and filtered at any time, as shown in Table 8.5. The RowState can be viewed at any time to determine the current state of a DataRow. Figure 8.7 shows how the RowState changes at different stages of the DataRow's life.

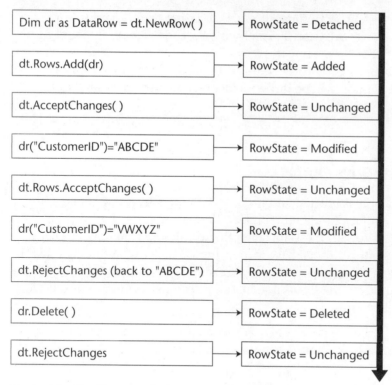

Figure 8.7   The life cycle of a DataRow and its RowState.

A DataRow can also contain different versions of the data, which can be filtered and viewed using the RowVersion property. This can be handy when it's desirable to look at the deleted or changed rows of a DataTable. Table 8.6 shows the list of available RowVersions. This will be covered in more detail in the following sections of this chapter.

Table 8.5   A DataRow's RowState

ROWSTATE	DESCRIPTION
Detached	The DataRow has been created but not attached to a DataTable.
Added	The DataRow has been created and Added to the DataTable.
Unchanged	The DataRow has not changed since the AcceptChanges method has been called. When the AcceptChanges method is called, the Row immediately changes to this state.
Modified	The DataRow has been changed since the last time that the AcceptChanges method has been called.
Deleted	The DataRow has been deleted using the Delete method of the DataRow.

Table 8.6 The DataRow's RowVersion

ROWVERSION	DESCRIPTION
Current	The row contains current values.
Default	The default row version according to the current DataRowState.
Original	The row contains its original values.
Proposed	The row contains a proposed value.

Deleting Rows

DataRows can be deleted by executing the Delete method of the DataRow. This marks the row as deleted, but the row will still exist in the DataTable. Later, when changes are sent to the data store, rows that were marked for deletion will be deleted.

The following code deletes a customer whose CustomerID is *AAAAB*. When the DataRow is deleted, it will only be viewable using a DataView that has its RowStateFilter set to Deleted rows.

```
'Create objects
Dim cnstr As String = "integrated security=yes;database=northwind"
Dim cn As New SqlConnection(cnstr)
Dim sql As String = "Select CustomerID, CompanyName from customers"
Dim daCustomers As New SqlDataAdapter(sql, cn)
Dim dt As New DataTable("Customers")
'Execute
daCustomers.Fill(dt)
dt.PrimaryKey = New DataColumn() {dt.Columns(0)}
Dim dr As DataRow = dt.Rows.Find("AAAAB")
dr.Delete()
DataGrid1.DataSource = dt
Dim dv As New DataView(dt)
dv.RowStateFilter = DataViewRowState.Deleted
DataGrid2.DataSource = dv
DataBind()
'Cleanup
dt.Dispose()
daCustomers.Dispose()
```

This code uses the Find method of the Rows collection to locate customer AAAAB and marks the row for deletion. The DataTable is bound to DataGrid1 and then a view is created with the RowStateFilter set to display only deleted rows. The DataView is then bound to DataGrid2. Figure 8.8 shows the output.

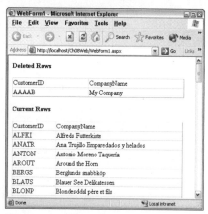

Figure 8.8 The DataGrid controls, which display the deleted rows (top) and the undeleted rows (bottom).

tip   **Be sure to use the Delete method of the DataRow if changes are going to be sent back to the data store using the DataAdapter. If the Remove method of the DataTable.Rows collection is used, the DataRow will be completely removed from the DataTable, but there will be no deletion of the row at the data store.**

Editing Rows

In its simplest form, a DataRow can be edited by assigning new contents to DataRow. Using this method, however, triggers validation with each change. It is better to use the BeginEdit method of the DataRow, which will postpone validation until the EndEdit method is executed. When you use the BeginEdit method, the changes may be rolled back by executing the CancelEdit method. The following code is an example of editing a DataRow.

```
'Create objects
Dim cnstr As String = "integrated security=yes;database=northwind"
Dim cn As New SqlConnection(cnstr)
Dim sql As String = "Select CustomerID, CompanyName from customers"
Dim daCustomers As New SqlDataAdapter(sql, cn)
Dim dt As New DataTable("Customers")
'Execute
daCustomers.Fill(dt)
'Assign the primary key.
dt.PrimaryKey = New DataColumn() {dt.Columns("CustomerID")}
Dim dr As DataRow = dt.Rows.Find("AAAAB")
dr.BeginEdit()
     dr("CustomerID") = "AAAAE"
```

```
         dr("CompanyName") = "A New Company Name"
    dr.EndEdit() 'can call dr.CancelEdit to abort
    DataGrid1.DataSource = dt
    DataBind()
    'Cleanup
    dt.Dispose()
    daCustomers.Dispose()
```

This code uses the Find method to find customer AAAB and then changes the CustomerID and the CompanyName. Notice that primary key changes are allowed.

Using the DataGrid to Modify Data

The DataGrid was previously introduced in this book, but it's now time to put it to work. The balance of this chapter focuses on using the DataGrid to view and modify data. To prepare for this, the following code obtains data from the data store, and the data will be stored in a Session variable. This code also contains the column layouts.

```
Private Sub Page_Load( _
 ByVal sender As System.Object, _
 ByVal e As System.EventArgs) Handles MyBase.Load
     If Not IsPostBack Then
          BindTable()
     End If
End Sub
Public Sub BindTable()
     'Create objects.
     Dim dt As DataTable
     If Session("Employee") Is Nothing Then
          Dim cnstr As String = "integrated security=yes;database=pubs"
          Dim cn As New SqlConnection(cnstr)
          Dim sql As String = "Select * from employee"
          Dim daEmployee As New SqlDataAdapter(sql, cn)
          dt = New DataTable("Employee")
          'Execute
          daEmployee.Fill(dt)
          'Assign the Primary Key
          dt.PrimaryKey = New DataColumn() {dt.Columns("emp_id")}
          'Store for the Session
          Session("Employee") = dt
          'Cleanup
          daEmployee.Dispose()
     Else
          dt = CType(Session("Employee"), DataTable)
End If
     dgEmployee.DataSource = dt
```

```
        DataBind()
    End Sub
    Private Sub dgEmployee_Init( _
     ByVal sender As Object, _
     ByVal e As System.EventArgs) Handles dgEmployee.Init
        dgEmployee.AutoGenerateColumns = False
        Dim colWidth As Integer = 110
        dgEmployee.DataKeyField="emp_id"
        Dim colEdit As New EditCommandColumn()
        colEdit.ButtonType = ButtonColumnType.PushButton
        colEdit.EditText = "Edit"
        colEdit.CancelText = "Cancel"
        colEdit.UpdateText = "Update"
        colEdit.ItemStyle.Width = New Unit(colWidth, UnitType.Pixel)
        dgEmployee.Columns.Add(colEdit)
        Dim col As New BoundColumn()
        col.HeaderText = "Employee<BR>ID"
        col.DataField = "emp_id"
        col.ItemStyle.HorizontalAlign = HorizontalAlign.Left
        col.HeaderStyle.HorizontalAlign = HorizontalAlign.Center
        col.ItemStyle.Width = New Unit(colWidth, UnitType.Pixel)
        dgEmployee.Columns.Add(col)
        'Store this info for later use.
        dgEmployee.Attributes(col.DataField) = _
            dgEmployee.Columns.Count - 1
        col = New BoundColumn()
        col.HeaderText = "Last<BR>Name"
        col.DataField = "LName"
        col.HeaderStyle.HorizontalAlign = HorizontalAlign.Center
        col.ItemStyle.Width = New Unit(colWidth, UnitType.Pixel)
        dgEmployee.Columns.Add(col)
        dgEmployee.Attributes(col.DataField) = _
            dgEmployee.Columns.Count - 1
        col = New BoundColumn()
        col.HeaderText = "First<BR>Name"
        col.DataField = "FName"
        col.HeaderStyle.HorizontalAlign = HorizontalAlign.Center
        col.ItemStyle.Width = New Unit(colWidth, UnitType.Pixel)
        dgEmployee.Columns.Add(col)
        dgEmployee.Attributes(col.DataField) = _
            dgEmployee.Columns.Count - 1
        col = New BoundColumn()
        col.HeaderText = "Middle<BR>Init"
        col.DataField = "minit"
        col.ItemStyle.HorizontalAlign = HorizontalAlign.Center
        col.HeaderStyle.HorizontalAlign = HorizontalAlign.Center
        col.ItemStyle.Width = New Unit(colWidth, UnitType.Pixel)
        dgEmployee.Columns.Add(col)
        dgEmployee.Attributes(col.DataField) = _
            dgEmployee.Columns.Count - 1
        col = New BoundColumn()
        col.HeaderText = "Hire<BR>Date"
```

```
        col.DataField = "hire_date"
        col.DataFormatString = "{0:d}"
        col.ItemStyle.HorizontalAlign = HorizontalAlign.Right
        col.HeaderStyle.HorizontalAlign = HorizontalAlign.Center
        col.ItemStyle.Width = New Unit(colWidth, UnitType.Pixel)
        dgEmployee.Columns.Add(col)
        dgEmployee.Attributes(col.DataField) = _
            dgEmployee.Columns.Count - 1
        col = New BoundColumn()
        col.HeaderText = "Job<BR>ID"
        col.DataField = "job_id"
        col.ItemStyle.HorizontalAlign = HorizontalAlign.Right
        col.HeaderStyle.HorizontalAlign = HorizontalAlign.Center
        col.ItemStyle.Width = New Unit(colWidth, UnitType.Pixel)
        dgEmployee.Columns.Add(col)
        dgEmployee.Attributes(col.DataField) = _
            dgEmployee.Columns.Count - 1
        col = New BoundColumn()
        col.HeaderText = "Job<BR>Level"
        col.DataField = "job_lvl"
        col.ItemStyle.HorizontalAlign = HorizontalAlign.Right
        col.HeaderStyle.HorizontalAlign = HorizontalAlign.Center
        col.ItemStyle.Width = New Unit(colWidth, UnitType.Pixel)
        dgEmployee.Columns.Add(col)
        dgEmployee.Attributes(col.DataField) = _
            dgEmployee.Columns.Count - 1
    End Sub
```

Editing a DataRow with the DataGrid

The DataGrid can be used to edit a DataRow by setting the EditItemIndex property of the DataGrid to the item number to be edited (see Figure 8.9). In addition, canceling the edit must set the EditItemIndex to -1. The following code shows the implementation.

```
    Private Sub dgEmployee_EditCommand( _
        ByVal source As Object, _
        ByVal e As System.Web.UI.WebControls.DataGridCommandEventArgs) _
        Handles dgEmployee.EditCommand
        dgEmployee.EditItemIndex = e.Item.ItemIndex
        BindTable()
    End Sub

    Private Sub dgEmployee_CancelCommand( _
        ByVal source As Object, _
        ByVal e As System.Web.UI.WebControls.DataGridCommandEventArgs) _
        Handles dgEmployee.CancelCommand
        dgEmployee.EditItemIndex = -1
        BindTable()
    End Sub
```

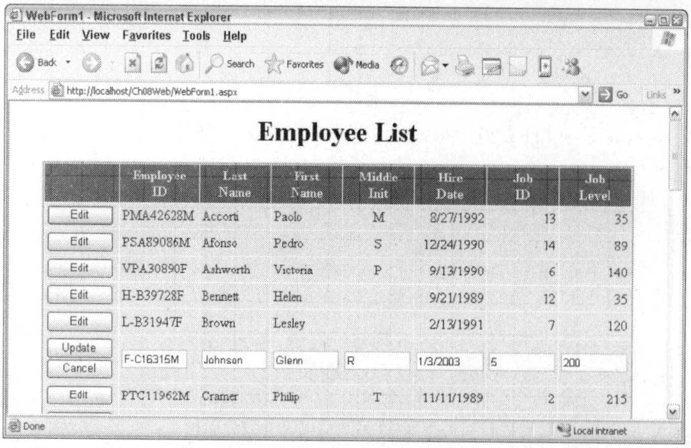

Figure 8.9 The DataGrid in edit mode.

This code allows dgEmployee to be displayed with edit buttons, and clicking edit causes the row to go into edit mode. Clicking cancel cancels edit mode. Note that the BindTable method must be executed after the EditItemIndex is changed. Otherwise, the button needs to be clicked twice to get into edit mode and twice to cancel it.

The last piece of code that needs to be added is the code to update the Data-Table. This code is placed into the dgEmployee_UpdateCommand as follows:

```
Private Sub dgEmployee_UpdateCommand( _
    ByVal source As Object, _
    ByVal e As System.Web.UI.WebControls.DataGridCommandEventArgs) _
    Handles dgEmployee.UpdateCommand
    'Get the DataTable from the Session.
    Dim dt As DataTable = CType(Session("Employee"), DataTable)
    'get the DataRow to be updated
    Dim PrimaryKey As String = dgEmployee.DataKeys(e.Item.DataSetIndex)
    Dim dr As DataRow = dt.Rows.Find(PrimaryKey)
    'Start editing this row.
    dr.BeginEdit()
    'Loop through all the columns.
    Dim col As DataGridColumn
    For Each col In dgEmployee.Columns
        'Check to see if this is a data column.
        If TypeOf col Is BoundColumn Then
            'Cast this col to a bound column.
            Dim colItem As BoundColumn = CType(col, BoundColumn)
            'Check to see if there is data worth getting.
            If colItem.Visible And _
            (colItem.DataField.ToString().Length > 0) Then
                'Get the field name.
                Dim colName As String = colItem.DataField
                'Find the cell number from the saved number.
```

```
            Dim cellNumber As Integer = _
             Integer.Parse(dgEmployee.Attributes(colName))
            'The cell has a text box with data.
            Dim curText As TextBox
            curText = _
                CType(e.Item.Cells(cellNumber).Controls(0), _
                TextBox)
            'Assign the data.
            dr(colName) = curText.Text
          End If
        End If
    Next
    'finished!
    dr.EndEdit()
    dt.DefaultView.RowFilter = ""
    dgEmployee.EditItemIndex = -1
    BindTable()
End Sub
```

This code starts by retrieving the DataTable from Session state. When items are retrieved from Session state, they are returned as objects and must be cast to the proper type using the CType function. The DataRow is then retrieved from the DataTable, based on the DataSetIndex that was automatically saved in the DataGrid. Then, the updating of the DataRow begins.

A loop enumerates all of the DataGrid columns. Each column is checked to see if it is a BoundColumn. If the column is a BoundColumn, then the column is cast to a BoundColumn and placed into the colItem variable. Invisible columns and columns that have no DataField are ignored in the loop.

The colName variable is assigned the name of the DataField. The colName retrieves the cellNumber from the dgEmployee attributes. The cell number was explicitly stored when the columns were created in the dgEmployee init method. Without this number, each cell would be accessed by a hard-coded cell number. Each of the edited cells contains a TextBox control, which is the first control in the cell. This TextBox is referenced with the curText variable, then the text is retrieved and stored in the DataRow's field. Finally, the editing is completed, the EditItemIndex is set to -1, and the DataGrid is bound.

Adding a DataRow with the DataGrid

Adding a DataRow to the DataGrid is probably the most difficult task to accomplish in terms of modifying data with a DataGrid. To add a DataRow to the DataGrid, the best approach is to add a new DataRow to the DataTable. A button needs to be added to the DataGrid to add a new DataRow. The button can be added anywhere on the Web page, but this button will be added to the header of the Edit button column. The following example shows the Add button code:

```
Dim colEdit As New EditCommandColumn()
colEdit.ButtonType = ButtonColumnType.PushButton
colEdit.HeaderText = _
        "<input type='submit' runat='server' name='" & _
        " dgEmployee:Add' value='Add' />"
colEdit.EditText = "Edit"
colEdit.CancelText = "Cancel"
colEdit.UpdateText = "Update"
colEdit.ItemStyle.Width = New Unit(colWidth, UnitType.Pixel)
dgEmployee.Columns.Add(colEdit)
```

Next, this new Add button will post back to the Web server; a method needs to be added to detect when this has been clicked. This is done by changing the Load method as follows:

```
Private Sub Page_Load( _
  ByVal sender As System.Object, _
  ByVal e As System.EventArgs) Handles MyBase.Load
      If Not IsPostBack Then
            BindTable()
      ElseIf Request("dgEmployee:Add") = "Add" Then
            AddEmployee()
      End If
End Sub
```

This code checks to see if the Add button was clicked. If so, a call is made to the AddEmployee method. The AddEmployee method checks to see if a new row already exists. If it does, this row will be used. If not, a new row is appended to the DataTable. Unfortunately, the primary key field is a string, and it is required. An arbitrary string is assigned to the primary key field. This would be much better in an environment with an autonumber primary key field, because the autonumber.field would automatically assign the next available number. The AddEmployee method follows:

```
Private Sub AddEmployee()
      Const newId As String = "*NEW ID*"
      dgEmployee.EditItemIndex = 0
      'Get the DataTable from the Session.
      Dim dt As DataTable = CType(Session("Employee"), DataTable)
      'Get the DataRow to be updated.
      Dim dr As DataRow = dt.Rows.Find(newId)
      If dr Is Nothing Then
            dr = dt.NewRow()
            'Start editing this row.
            dr.BeginEdit()
            'This is better with an autonumber key.
            dr("emp_id") = newId
            dt.Rows.Add(dr)
      Else
```

```
            dr.CancelEdit()
            dr.BeginEdit()
      End If
      dt.DefaultView.RowFilter = "emp_id='" & newId & "'"
      BindTable()
  End Sub
```

This code sets a RowFilter to the added row. This ensures that the correct row will be in edit mode and no other rows are available to distract the user. Finally, the Cancel method is modified to delete the new row if the Cancel button has been clicked. This code follows:

```
Private Sub dgEmployee_CancelCommand( _
 ByVal source As Object, _
 ByVal e As System.Web.UI.WebControls.DataGridCommandEventArgs) _
 Handles dgEmployee.CancelCommand
      dgEmployee.EditItemIndex = -1
      'Get the DataTable from the Session.
      Dim dt As DataTable = CType(Session("Employee"), DataTable)
      'Get the DataRow to be canceled.
      Dim PrimaryKey As String = dgEmployee.DataKeys(e.Item.DataSetIndex)
      'would be better if this was an autonumber
      If PrimaryKey = "*NEW ID*" Then
            Dim dr As DataRow = dt.Rows.Find(PrimaryKey)
            dt.Rows.Remove(dr)
      End If
      dt.DefaultView.RowFilter = ""
      BindTable()
  End Sub
```

Figure 8.10 shows the Add method in action. Notice that when the Add button is clicked, the DataGrid automatically resizes to a single row, which is the row that is being added. The only thing left is to allow the deletion of DataRows.

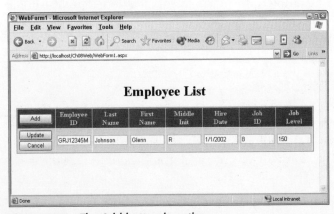

Figure 8.10 The Add button in action.

Deleting a DataRow with the DataGrid

Deleting a DataRow with the DataGrid is a relatively easy task. A Delete button column and a little bit of code are needed to handle the button. The new Delete button code follows:

```
Dim colDel As New ButtonColumn()
colDel.CommandName = "Delete"
colDel.Text = "Delete"
colDel.ButtonType = ButtonColumnType.PushButton
colDel.ItemStyle.Width = New Unit(colWidth, UnitType.Pixel)
dgEmployee.Columns.Add(colDel)
```

This code adds a ButtonColumn and sets the button type to a PushButton. The next code snippet shows the code for the Delete button.

```
Private Sub dgEmployee_DeleteCommand( _
      ByVal source As Object, _
      ByVal e As System.Web.UI.WebControls.DataGridCommandEventArgs) _
      Handles dgEmployee.DeleteCommand
      'Get the DataTable from the Session.
      Dim dt As DataTable = CType(Session("Employee"), DataTable)
      'Get the DataRow to be updated.
      Dim PrimaryKey As String = dgEmployee.DataKeys(e.Item.DataSetIndex)
      Dim dr As DataRow = dt.Rows.Find(PrimaryKey)
      dr.CancelEdit()
      'Delete the row.
      dr.Delete()
      dt.DefaultView.RowFilter = ""
      dgEmployee.EditItemIndex = -1
      dgEmployee.SelectedIndex = -1
      BindTable()
End Sub
```

This code locates the DataRow and marks it for deletion. The last items ensure that the RowFilter is clear and no Item is being edited. The completed DataGrid with the Delete button is shown in Figure 8.11.

Updating the Data Store

Until now, all data modification has been done in a local DataTable or DataSet. This section examines several methods of updating the data store. The Data-Grid from the previous section will be used as a graphical interface for these operations.

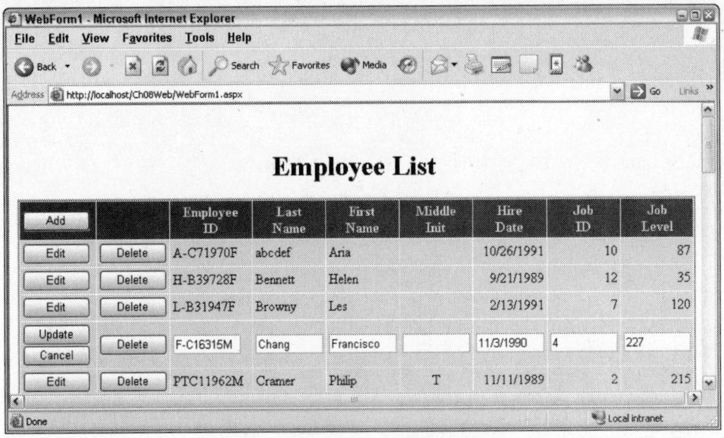

Figure 8.11 The completed DataGrid contains the Add, Edit, and Delete buttons.

The DataAdapter can be used to update the data store. The DataAdapter requires select, insert, update, and delete commands to successfully send changes back to the data store. Rather that create each of these commands, ADO.NET offers a class called the CommandBuilder, which can create the insert, update, and delete commands as long as the select command has been supplied. The command builder can only be used when the data store that is being updated represents a single table.

In this example, a command button is placed in the header of the delete column. When the command button is clicked, the UpdateDB method is executed. The following code shows the UpdateDB button.

```
Dim colDel As New ButtonColumn()
colDel.HeaderText = _
"<input type='submit' runat='server' " & _
    " name='dgEmployee:UpdateAll' value='Update DB' />"
colDel.CommandName = "Delete"
colDel.Text = "Delete"
colDel.ButtonType = ButtonColumnType.PushButton
colDel.ItemStyle.Width = New Unit(colWidth, UnitType.Pixel)
dgEmployee.Columns.Add(colDel)
```

The Page Load method has been modified to called the UpdateDB method, as shown in the following code:

```
Private Sub Page_Load( _
 ByVal sender As System.Object, _
 ByVal e As System.EventArgs) Handles MyBase.Load
     If Not IsPostBack Then
         BindTable()
     ElseIf Request("dgEmployee:Add") = "Add" Then
         AddEmployee()
```

```
        ElseIf Request("dgEmployee:UpdateAll") = "Update DB" Then
                UpdateDB()
        End If
End Sub
```

Finally, the UpdateDB method contains the code to modify the data store. This code follows:

```
Public Sub UpdateDB()
    Dim dt As DataTable
    If Not Session("Employee") Is Nothing Then
        Dim cnstr As String = "integrated security=yes;database=pubs"
        Dim cn As New SqlConnection(cnstr)
        Dim sql As String = "Select * from employee"
        Dim daEmployee As New SqlDataAdapter(sql, cn)
        Dim cmdBld As New SqlCommandBuilder(daEmployee)
        dt = CType(Session("Employee"), DataTable)
        daEmployee.Update(dt)
    End If
    BindTable()
End Sub
```

This code starts by connecting to the Session variable that contains the DataTable. Next, the connection and DataAdapter are created. Finally, a CommandBuilder is created, which will create the insert, update, and delete commands automatically when required. The finished Web page is shown in Figure 8.12.

 tip Although the CommandBuilder object was used in the example, separate command objects may be assigned to each of the DataAdapter's commands. The commands may contain calls to stored procedures as well.

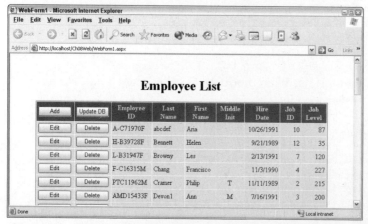

Figure 8.12　The completed DataGrid with Add, Delete, Edit, and Update DB buttons added.

Paging the DataGrid

A DataGrid can be set up to allow paging of data. This is especially useful when displaying a significant amout of data. Paging can be enabled by adding the following settings into the init code of the DataGrid.

```
Private Sub dgEmployee_Init( _
 ByVal sender As Object, _
 ByVal e As System.EventArgs) Handles dgEmployee.Init
     dgEmployee.AllowPaging = True
     dgEmployee.PageSize = 10
     dgEmployee.PagerStyle.Mode = PagerMode.NumericPages
     dgEmployee.PagerStyle.PageButtonCount = 5
     dgEmployee.PagerStyle.HorizontalAlign = HorizontalAlign.Right
        'Other code to initialize columns here
End Sub
```

This code turns on paging and sets the PageSize and the style of paging. Meanwhile, the following code must be added for the paging to operate.

```
Private Sub dgEmployee_PageIndexChanged( _
        ByVal source As Object, _
        ByVal e As _
        System.Web.UI.WebControls.DataGridPageChangedEventArgs) _
     Handles dgEmployee.PageIndexChanged
        dgEmployee.CurrentPageIndex = e.NewPageIndex
        dgEmployee.EditItemIndex = -1
        BindTable()
End Sub
```

This code simply changes the CurrentPageIndex to the NewPageIndex and then assures that no item is being edited. Figure 8.13 shows the DataGrid with paging enabled.

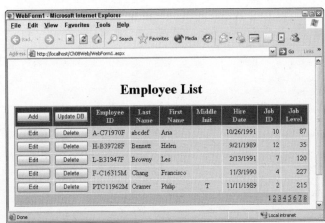

Figure 8.13 The DataGrid with paging enabled.

Sorting Data with the DataGrid

A DataGrid also can allow the user to select which column to edit. Sorting is enabled by setting the AllowSorting property of the DataGrid to true in the Init method, as follows:

```
dgEmployee.AllowSorting = True
```

Next, the SortExpression must be set for each column for which sorting is enabled. This can be done by adding the following line of code to the DataGrid Init method for each of these columns. Be sure to add this line of code after the assignment of the DataField.

```
col.SortExpression = col.DataField
```

Finally, code needs to be added to the DataGrid's sort command. This code will read the Sort Expression from the column and compare it with the value that was stored.

```
Private Sub dgEmployee_SortCommand( _
ByVal source As Object, _
ByVal e As System.Web.UI.WebControls.DataGridSortCommandEventArgs) _
Handles dgEmployee.SortCommand
    'Get the DataTable from the Session.
    Dim dt As DataTable = CType(Session("Employee"), DataTable)
    Dim PrevSortExpression As String = ""
    Dim PrevSortOrder As String = ""
    If Not dgEmployee.Attributes("SortExpression") Is Nothing Then
      PrevSortExpression = _
        dgEmployee.Attributes("SortExpression").ToString()
    End If
    If Not dgEmployee.Attributes("SortOrder") Is Nothing Then
        PrevSortOrder = dgEmployee.Attributes("SortOrder").ToString()
    End If
    Dim NewSortOrder As String = ""
    If PrevSortExpression = e.SortExpression Then
        If PrevSortOrder = "DESC" Then
            NewSortOrder = "ASC"
        Else
            NewSortOrder = "DESC"
        End If
    Else
        NewSortOrder = "ASC"
    End If
    dgEmployee.Attributes("SortExpression") = e.SortExpression
    dgEmployee.Attributes("SortOrder") = NewSortOrder
    dt.DefaultView.Sort = e.SortExpression & " " & NewSortOrder
    BindTable()
End Sub
```

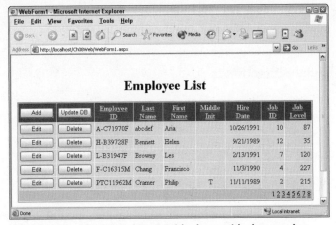

Figure 8.14 The sorted DataGrid, along with data paging.

The completed DataGrid with sort capabilities is shown in Figure 8.14.

Lab 8.1 Data Access

In this lab, you will add a new page to browse the customer table in the Northwind database. First, you will create a customer list page. After the page is created and the controls are placed on the page, you will add code to fill the DataGrid. Finally, you will test your work.

Creating the Customer List Page

In this section, you will create a Web page to display the customer table in the Northwind database.

1. Open the OrderEntrySolution from Lab 7.1.

2. Right-click the OrderEntrySolution in the Solution Explorer, and click Check Out to check out the complete solution.

3. Right-click the Customer project in the Solution Explorer, and then click Set As StartUp Project.

4. Right-click the Inventory project, and click Add, Add Web Form. Name the page CustomerList.aspx.

5. Change the layout to FlowLayout, which allows text to be simply typed onto the control and will push other controls downward when upper controls are too large.

6. Type Customer List at the top of the page.

7. Drag a DataGrid on to the Web Page. Change the name of the DataGrid to *dgCustomers*.

8. User your mouse to select everything on the page, and then click Format, Justify, Center.

9. Select the text, and change the font to Arial and the font size to 6.

10. Save your work. Figure 8.15 shows the page.

Filling the DataGrid

In this section, you will create a connection to the Northwind database.

1. Open the CustomerList.aspx.vb code-behind page.

2. Add an Imports state to the top of the code for System.Data and for System.Data.SqlClient. Locate the Page_Load event method and add a test to check for the postback. (If this is the first time that the page is being called, make a call to the BindTable method.) Your code should look like the following:

```
Imports System.Data
Imports System.Data.SqlClient
'....other code
Private Sub Page_Load( _
        ByVal sender As System.Object, _
        ByVal e As System.EventArgs) Handles MyBase.Load
            If Not IsPostBack Then
                    BindTable()
                End If
    End Sub
```

3. Add the BindTable method, which will contain code as described in the following steps.

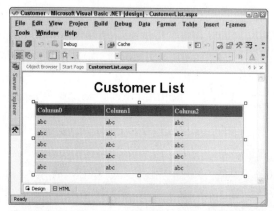

Figure 8.15   CustomerList Web page with DataGrid.

    a. Add code to create a SqlConnection, along with the connection string.

    b. Add a variable called sql, which will contain the command to retrieve the CustomerID, CompanyName, ContactName fields, and all rows from the Customers table.

    c. Add code to create a SqlDataAdapter, using the SqlConnection and the sql variable.

    d. Add code to create a variable called dt, which is a DataTable called Customers.

    e. Fill the DataTable using the SqlDataAdapter.

    f. Add a DataBind command. The completed BindTable code should like the following:

```
Public Sub Bindtable()
    Dim cnstr As String
    cnstr = "server=.;integrated security=yes;" _
        & "database=northwind"
    Dim cn As New SqlConnection(cnstr)
    Dim sql As String
    Sql = "Select CustomerID, CompanyName, ContactName" _
        & "from customers"
    Dim daCustomers As New SqlDataAdapter(sql, cn)
    Dim dt As New DataTable("Customers")
    'Execute
    daCustomers.Fill(dt)
    dgCustomers.DataSource = dt
    DataBind()
End Sub
```

4. Save your work.

Testing the DataGrid

You can test the DataGrid by setting the CustomerList.aspx as the start page and running the application.

1. Set the Customer project to be the startup project. This can be done by right-clicking the Customer project in the Solution Explorer and clicking Set As StartUp Project.

2. Set the CustomerList page as the startup page. This can be done by right-clicking the CustomerList.aspx page and clicking Set As Start Page.

3. Run the application. The result should look like Figure 8.16.

4. Check your work back into Visual SourceSafe.

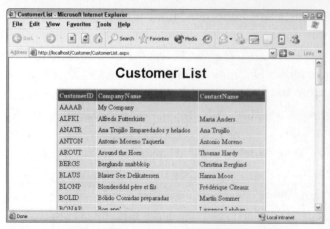

Figure 8.16 The CustomerList page filled with Customers.

Summary

- ADO.NET is a disconnected-data-centric environment. Disconnected data retrieves the data from the data store and then closes the connection. An advantage of this model is that the data can be downloaded to the client, the connection can be closed, and the user can work with the data while offline. Updates can be sent back to the server when appropriate.

- A data provider supplies a bridge from the application to the data source. Think of the data provider as a set of drivers that are specific to a data store.

- The following data objects are provider specific: the Connection, DataAdapter, Command, Parameter, CommandBuilder, and DataReader.

- The Command object is used to issue a command to the data store. The command can be a command to retrieve data or a command to insert, update, or delete data.

- The DataSet is a complete in-memory database.

- The DataTable contains DataRows, DataColumns, Constraints, and references to ParentRelations and ChildRelations.

- The DataView is a window into a DataTable that provides filtering and sorting.

- The DataAdapter is responsible for moving data between a data store and a DataTable or DataSet.

- Before changes can be made to the DataTable, the DataTable's Primary-Key property should be assigned.

- The DataGrid has abilities for adding, deleting, and in-place editing, sorting, and paging.

- A DataRow can be edited by assigning new contents to the DataRow. Using this method, however, triggers validation with each change. It is better to use the BeginEdit method of the DataRow, which will postpone validation until the EndEdit method is executed.

Review Questions

1. What is the proper method for creating a DataRow?

2. How is a DataReader created?

3. What is the purpose of BeginEdit and EndEdit?

4. Name two of the objects that are contained in a DataSet.

5. Name four data providers.

6. What method of which object is used to send all of the modified data in a DataSet back to the data store?

7. What is the most efficient method of the Command object that can retrieve the result of the following SQL statement: "Select count(*) from Employees"?

Answers to Review Questions

1. Use the DataTable's NewRow method.
2. Use the Command's ExecuteReader method.
3. BeginEdit postpones validation checking until the EndEdit method is executed.
4. DataTable and DataRelation objects.
5. Sql, OleDb, Odbc, and Oracle.
6. The Update method of the DataAdapter.
7. Use the ExecuteScaler method.

CHAPTER 9

Working with XML Data

Companies have always had a need to communicate with each other in an automated fashion. Communication between companies has been problematic, primarily due to the type of data that was being exchanged. Data has been exchanged using delimited files, fixed-width files, structured files, and everything in between. Each type of data had limitations. Delimited and fixed-width files could not easily reflect a relational structure, and structured data files were typically custom implementations that were not reusable. A method of communicating data that could be used by everyone was required. This new communications method needed features such as the support for structured data, validation, and extensibility, and the capability to pass through firewalls.

The World Wide Web Consortium (W3C) was created in October 1994 to help further the Web's potential by developing common protocols to ensure interoperability. In February 1998, the W3C published "The XML 1.0 Recommendation." Extensible Markup Language (XML) provides a foundation for text-based data communications that support validation, structured data, and extensibility, and the capability to pass through firewalls.

The world has big plans for XML and its supporting technologies. Many companies have already embraced XML, and many companies are planning implementations of XML technologies in new applications. The W3C envisions the future Web as being completely based on XML technologies.

This chapter looks at Microsoft's approach to XML in the .NET Framework. The chapter starts by examining the XML classes. After the classes have been examined, the chapter presents various ways of implementing these classes.

Classroom Q & A

Q: Is it possible to apply XML transformations with the .NET Framework?

A: It sure is. The XslTransform class can be used. Also, ASP.NET provides an XML Web control, which can perform transformations and produce output to the browser.

Q: When working with our vendors, we need to verify that each vendor is providing XML files to us in the correct format. Ideally, we don't want to attempt to process a document if it is not valid. Is there a way to check an XML file to see if it has extra nodes or if it is missing mandatory nodes?

A: Yes. The XmlValidatingReader class can be used with the other classes. This class throws an exception if the file is not validated against a data type definition (DTD) or an XML Data Reduced (XDR) or an XML Schema (XSD) file.

Q: Is there a way to use XPath queries on a DataSet?

A: Yes. The XmlDataDocument class was created to provide the ability to connect to a DataSet and allow XPath queries.

XML in the .NET Framework

The .NET Framework provides vast support for XML. The implementation of XML is focused on performance, reliability, and scalability. Many of the XML classes are stream based and require only small portions of the document to be in memory when it's being read.

The integration of XML with ADO.NET offers the ability to use XML documents as a data source. DataSets offer many XML methods, such as the ability to read and write XML documents. When a DataSet is transferred from one location to another, it is sent in an XML format.

The XML Document Object Model

The W3C has provided standards that define the structure and provide a standard programming interface that can be used in a wide variety of environments and applications for XML documents. This is called the Document Object Model (DOM). Classes that support the DOM are typically capable of random access navigation and modification of the XML document.

XML Namespace

The XML classes can be accessed by setting a reference to the System.XML.dll file, and adding the Imports System.XML directive to the code.

The System.Data.dll file also extends the System.XML namespace. This is the location of the XmlDataDocument class. If this class is required, a reference must be set to the System.Data.dll file.

XML Objects

This section covers the primary XML classes in the .NET Framework. Each of these classes offers varying degrees of functionality. It's important to look at each of the classes in detail, in order to make the correct decision on which classes should be used. Figure 9.1 shows a high-level view of the objects that are covered.

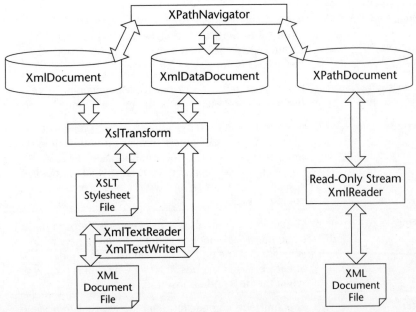

Figure 9.1 Some of the objects that are covered in this chapter and how they relate to each other.

XmlDocument and XmlDataDocument

These are in-memory representations of XML using the Document Object Model (DOM) Level 1 and Level 2. These classes can be used to navigate and edit the XML nodes.

The XmlDataDocument is inherited from XmlDocument and also represents relational data. The XmlDataDocument can expose its data as a DataSet to provide relational and nonrelational views of the data. The XmlDataDocument is located in the System.Data.dll assembly.

These classes provide many methods in order to implement the Level 2 specification, and also contain methods to facilitate common operations. The methods are summarized in Table 9.1. The XmlDocument contains all of the methods for creating XmlElements and XmlAttributes.

Table 9.1   XmlDocument and XmlDataDocument Methods

METHOD	DESCRIPTION
CreateNodeType	Creates an XML node in the document. There are Create methods for each node type.
CloneNode	Creates a duplicate of an XML node. This method takes a Boolean argument called deep. If deep is false, only the node is copied. If deep is true, all child nodes are recursively copied as well.
GetElementById	Locates and returns a single node based on its ID attribute. Note that this requires a DTD that identifies an attribute as being an ID type. An attribute whose name is ID is not an ID type by default.
GetElementsByTagName	Locates and returns an XmlNodeList containing all of the descendent elements based on the element name.
ImportNode	Imports a node from a different XmlDocument into this document. The source node remains unmodified in the original XmlDocument. This method takes a Boolean argument called deep. If deep is false, only the node is copied. If deep is true, all child nodes are recursively copied as well.
InsertBefore	The XmlNode immediately before the referenced node. If the referenced node is nothing, then the new node is inserted at the end of the child list. If the node already exists in the tree, the original node is removed when the new node is inserted.
InsertAfter	The XmlNode immediately after the referenced node. If the referenced node is nothing, then the new node is inserted at the beginning of the child list. If the node already exists in the tree, the original node is removed when the new node is inserted.

Table 9.1 *(continued)*

METHOD	DESCRIPTION
Load	Loads an XML document from a disk file, URL, or Stream.
LoadXml	Loads an XML document from a string.
Normalize	Normalize assures that there are no adjacent text nodes in the document. This is like saving the document and reloading it. This method may be desirable when text nodes are being programmatically added to an XmlDocument, and the text nodes could be side-by-side. Normalizing combines the adjacent text nodes to produce a single text node.
PrependChild	This method inserts a node at the beginning of the child node list. If the new node is already in the tree, it is removed before it is inserted. If the node is an XmlDocumentFragment, the complete fragment is added.
ReadNode	Loads a node from an XML document using an XmlTextReader or XmlNodeReader object. The reader must be on a valid node before executing this method. The reader reads the opening tag, all child nodes, and the closing tag of the current element. This repositions the reader to the next node.
RemoveAll	This removes all children and attributes from the current node.
RemoveChild	This removes the referenced child.
ReplaceChild	This replaces the referenced child with a new node. If the new node is already in the tree, it is removed first.
Save	Saves the XML document to a disk file, URL, or stream.
SelectNodes	Selects a list of nodes that match the XPath expression.
SelectSingleNode	Selects the first node that matches the XPath expression.
WriteTo	Writes a node to another XML document using an XmlTextWriter.
WriteContentsTo	Writes a node and all of its descendents to another XML document using an XmlTextWriter.

XPathDocument

The XPathDocument provides a cached read-only XmlDocument that can be used for performing quick XPath queries. This constructor for this class requires a stream object in order to create an instance of this object. The only useful method that this class exposes is the CreateNavigator method.

XmlConvert

The XmlConvert class has many static methods for converting between XSD data types and the common language runtime data types. This class is especially important when working with data sources that allow names that are not valid XML names. For example, if a column in a database table is called *List Price*, trying to create an element or attribute with a space character throws an exception. Using XmlConvert to encode the name converts the space to _0x0020_, so the XML element name becomes List_x0020_Price. Later, this name can be decoded using the XmlConvert.DecodeName method.

XmlConvert also provides many static methods for converting strings to numeric values.

XPathNavigator

The DocumentNavigator provides efficient navigation of an XmlDocument by providing XPath support for navigation. The XPathNavigator uses a cursor model and XPath queries to provide read-only, random access to the data. The XPathNavigator supports XSLT and can be used as the input to a transform.

XmlNodeReader

The XmlNodeReader provides forward-only access to data in an XmlDocument or XmlDataDocument. It provides the ability to start at a given node in the XmlDocument, and sequentially read each node.

XmlTextReader

The XmlTextWrite provides noncached, forward-only access to XML data. It parses XML tokens, but makes no attempt to represent the XML document as a DOM. The XmlTextReader does not perform document validation, but it checks the XML data to ensure that it is well formed.

XmlTextWriter

The XmlTextWriter provides noncached, forward-only writing of XML data to a stream or file, ensuring that the data conforms to the W3C XML 1.0 standard.

The XmlTextWriter contains logic for working with namespaces and resolving namespace conflicts.

XmlValidatingReader

The XmlValidatingReader provides an object for validating against DTD, XML Schema Reduced (XDR), or XML Schema Definition (XSD). The constructor expects a Reader or a string as the source of the XML that is validated.

XslTransform

The XslTransform can transform an XML document using an XSL stylesheet. The XslTransform supports XSLT 1.0 syntax and provides two methods: Load and Transform.

The Load method is used to load an XSLT stylesheet from a file or a stream. The Transform method is used to perform the transformation. The Transform method has several overloads, but essentially expects a XmlDocument or XmlNode as the first argument, an XsltArgumentList, and an output stream.

Working with XML Documents

There are certainly many ways of working with XML data in the .NET Framework. This section covers some of the methods, such as creating a new XML file from scratch, reading and writing XML files, searching XML data, and transforming XML data.

Creating a New XmlDocument from Scratch

The following code shows how an XmlDocument can be created from scratch, and saved to a file:

```
'Declare and create new XmlDocument.
Dim xmlDoc As New XmlDocument()
Dim el As XmlElement
Dim childCounter As Integer
Dim grandChildCounter As Integer
'Create the XML declaration first.
xmlDoc.AppendChild( _
 xmlDoc.CreateXmlDeclaration("1.0", "utf-8", Nothing))
'Create the root node and append into doc
el = xmlDoc.CreateElement("myRoot")
xmlDoc.AppendChild(el)
'Child loop
```

```
For childCounter = 1 To 4
     Dim childelmt As XmlElement
     Dim childattr As XmlAttribute
     'Create child with ID attribute
     childelmt = xmlDoc.CreateElement("myChild")
     childattr = xmlDoc.CreateAttribute("ID")
     childattr.Value = childCounter.ToString()
     childelmt.Attributes.Append(childattr)
     'Append element into the root element
     el.AppendChild(childelmt)
     For grandChildCounter = 1 To 3
          'Create grandchildren.
          childelmt.AppendChild(xmlDoc.CreateElement("GrandChild"))
     Next
Next
'Save to file
xmlDoc.Save("C:\xmltest.XML")
```

This code starts by creating an instance of an XmlDocument. Next, the XML declaration is created and placed inside the child collection. Figure 9.2 shows the XML file. An exception is thrown if this is not the first child of the Xml-Document. If the root element already exists, the declaration may be inserted as follows:

```
xmlDoc.PrependChild( _
     xmlDoc.CreateXmlDeclaration("1.0", "utf-8", Nothing))
```

This code creates the XML declaration and inserts it before all other child nodes.

Figure 9.2   The XML file created from scratch.

The previous code also works with the XmlDataDocument, but the Xml-DataDocument has more features for working with relational data. These features are explored later in this chapter.

Parsing XmlDocument Using the DOM

An XmlDocument can be parsed by using a recursive routine to loop through all elements. The following code has an example of parsing an XmlDocument:

```
Private Sub Button2_Click( _
 ByVal sender As System.Object, _
 ByVal e As System.EventArgs) _
 Handles Button2.Click
      Dim xmlDoc As New XmlDocument()
      xmlDoc.Load("C:\xmltest.XML")
      RecurseNodes(xmlDoc.DocumentElement)
End Sub
Public Sub RecurseNodes(ByVal node As XmlNode)
      'Start recursive loop with Level 0.
      RecurseNodes(node, 0)
End Sub
Public Sub RecurseNodes(ByVal node As XmlNode, ByVal level As Integer)
      Dim s As String
      Dim n As XmlNode
      Dim attr As XmlAttribute
      s = s.Format("{0} <b>Type:</b>{1} <b>Name:</b>{2} <b>Attr:</b> ", _
          New String("-", level), node.NodeType, node.Name)
      For Each attr In node.Attributes
          s &= s.Format("{0}={1} ", attr.Name, attr.Value)
      Next
      Response.Write(s & "<br>")
      For Each n In node.ChildNodes
          RecurseNodes(n, level + 1)
      Next
End Sub
```

The output of this code is shown in Figure 9.3. This code starts by loading an XML file and then calling a procedure called RecurseNodes. The Recurse-Nodes procedure is overloaded. The first call simply passes the xmlDoc's root node. The recursive calls pass the recursion level. Each time the RecurseNodes procedure executes, the node information is printed, and for each child that the node has, a recursive call is made.

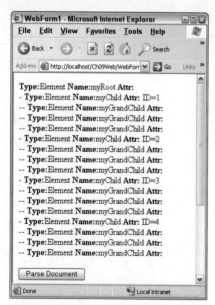

Figure 9.3 Parsing the XmlDocument.

Parsing XmlDocument Using the XPathNavigator

The XPathNavigator provides an alternate method of walking the XML document recursively. This object does not use the methods that are defined in the DOM. Instead, it uses XPath queries to navigate the data. It offers many methods and properties that can be used as shown in the following code example:

```
Private Sub Button3_Click( _
  ByVal sender As System.Object, _
  ByVal e As System.EventArgs) _
  Handles Button3.Click
    Dim xmlDoc As New XmlDocument()
    xmlDoc.Load("C:\xmltest.XML")
    Dim xpathNav As XPathNavigator = xmlDoc.CreateNavigator()
    xpathNav.MoveToRoot()
    RecurseNavNodes(xpathNav)
End Sub
Public Sub RecurseNavNodes(ByVal node As XPathNavigator)
    'Start recursive loop with Level 0.
    RecurseNavNodes(node, 0)
End Sub
```

```
Public Sub RecurseNavNodes(ByVal node As XPathNavigator, _
        ByVal level As Integer)
    Dim s As String
    s = s.Format("{0} <b>Type:</b>{1} <b>Name:</b>{2} <b>Attr:</b> ", _
        New String("-", level), node.NodeType, node.Name)
    If node.HasAttributes Then
        node.MoveToFirstAttribute()
        Do
            s &= s.Format("{0}={1} ", node.Name, node.Value)
        Loop While node.MoveToNextAttribute()
        node.MoveToParent()
    End If
    Response.Write(s & "<br>")
    If node.HasChildren Then
        node.MoveToFirstChild()
        Do
            RecurseNavNodes(node, level + 1)
        Loop While node.MoveToNext()
        node.MoveToParent()
    End If
End Sub
```

This is recursive code that works in a similar fashion to the DOM example that was previously covered. The difference is the methods that are used to get access to each node.

To get access to the attributes, there is a HasAttributes property that is true if the current node has attributes. The MoveToFirstAttribute and MoveToNext-Attribute method are used to navigate the attributes. After the attribute list has been navigated, the MoveToParent method moves back to the element.

The HasChildren property returns true if the current node has child nodes. The MoveToFirstChild and MoveToNext are used to navigate the child nodes. After the children have been navigated, the MoveToParent method moves back to the parent element.

Depending on the task at hand, it may be more preferable to use the XPath-Navigator instead of the DOM. In this example, other than syntax, there is little difference between the two methods.

Searching the XmlDocument Using the DOM

The DOM provides the GetElementById and the GetElementsByTagName methods for searching an XmlDocument. The GetElementById method locates an element based on its ID. The ID refers to an ID type that has been defined in a DTD document. In order to demonstrate this, the XML document in Listing 9.1 is used.

```
<?XML version="1.0" encoding="utf-8"?>
<!DOCTYPE myRoot [
     <!ELEMENT myRoot ANY>
     <!ELEMENT myChild ANY>
     <!ELEMENT myGrandChild EMPTY>
     <!ATTLIST myChild
     ChildID ID #REQUIRED
>
]>
<myRoot>
     <myChild ChildID="ref-1">
          <myGrandChild/>
          <myGrandChild/>
          <myGrandChild/>
     </myChild>
     <myChild ChildID="ref-2">
          <myGrandChild/>
          <myGrandChild/>
          <myGrandChild/>
     </myChild>
     <myChild ChildID="ref-3">
          <myGrandChild/>
          <myGrandChild/>
          <myGrandChild/>
     </myChild>
     <myChild ChildID="ref-4">
          <myGrandChild/>
          <myGrandChild/>
          <myGrandChild/>
     </myChild>
</myRoot>
```

Listing 9.1   Sample XML document with an embedded data type definition (DTD). This file is used in many of the chapter's examples.

The ChildID has been defined as an ID data type, and the IDs are required to begin with a character, underscore, or colon. The following code performs a lookup of the element with an ID of ref-3:

```
Private Sub Button5_Click( _
 ByVal sender As System.Object, _
 ByVal e As System.EventArgs) _
 Handles Button5.Click
     Dim s As String
     'Declare and create new XmlDocument
     Dim xmlDoc As New XmlDocument()
```

```
xmlDoc.Load("C:\xmltest.XML")
Dim node As XmlNode
node = xmlDoc.GetElementById("ref-3")
s = s.Format("<b>Type:</b>{0} <b>Name:</b>{1} <b>Attr:</b>", _
 node.NodeType, node.Name)
Dim a As XmlAttribute
For Each a In node.Attributes
     s &= s.Format("{0}={1} ", a.Name, a.Value)
Next
Response.Write(s & "<br>")
End Sub
```

The browser output is shown in Figure 9.4. When an ID data type is defined, the ID must be unique. This code locates ref-3 and displays the node and attributes information.

The SelectSingleNode method can also be used to locate an element. The SelectSingleNode method requires an XPath query to be passed into the method. The call to GetElementById, shown in the previous code sample, can be changed to SelectSingleNode to achieve the same result, as shown next.

```
node = xmlDoc.SelectSingleNode("//myChild[@ChildID='ref-3']")
```

Note that this method does not require a DTD to be provided, and it can perform an XPath lookup on any element or attribute where the SelectSingleNode required an ID data type.

The GetElementsByTagName method returns an XmlNodeList containing all matched elements. This following code returns a list of nodes whose tag name is myGrandChild:

```
Private Sub Button4_Click( _
 ByVal sender As System.Object, _
 ByVal e As System.EventArgs) _
 Handles Button4.Click
    Dim s As String
    'Declare and create new XmlDocument
    Dim xmlDoc As New XmlDocument()
    xmlDoc.Load("C:\xmltest.XML")
    Dim elmts As XmlNodeList
    elmts = xmlDoc.GetElementsByTagName("myGrandChild")
    Dim node As XmlNode
    For Each node In elmts
         s = s.Format("<b>Type:</b>{0} <b>Name:</b>{1}", _
           node.NodeType, node.Name)
         Response.Write(s & "<br>")
    Next
End Sub
```

Figure 9.4 The brower output when using the GetElementById method to locate an XML node.

This code retrieves the list of elements whose tag name is myGrandChild. The browser output is shown in Figure 9.5. This method does not require a DTD to be included, which makes this method preferable even for a single node lookup.

The SelectNodes method can also be used to locate an XmlNodeList. The SelectNodes method requires an XPath query to be passed into the method. In the previous code sample, the call to GetElementsByTagName can be changed to SelectNodes to achieve the same result as follows:

```
elmts = xmlDoc.SelectNodes("//myGrandChild")
```

Note that this method can perform an XPath lookup on any element or attribute, with much more querying flexibility where the SelectElementsBy-TagName was limited to a tag name.

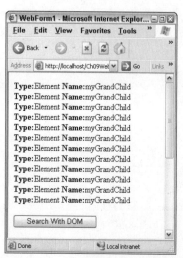

Figure 9.5 The browser output when executing the GetElementsByTagName method.

Searching XPathDocument Using the XPathNavigator

The XPathNavigator offers much more flexibility for performing searches than what is available through the DOM. The XPathNavigator has many methods that are focused around XPath queries, using a cursor model. The XPathNavigator works with the XmlDocument, but the XPathDocument object is tuned for the XPathNavigator and uses fewer resources than the XmlDocument. If the DOM is not required, use the XPathDocument instead of the XmlDocument. The following code example performs a search for the myChild element where the ChildID attribute equals ref-3:

```
Private Sub Button8_Click( _
  ByVal sender As System.Object, _
  ByVal e As System.EventArgs) _
  Handles Button8.Click
      Dim s As String
      Dim xmlDoc As New XPathDocument("C:\xmltest.XML")
      Dim nav As XPathNavigator = xmlDoc.CreateNavigator()
      Dim expr As String = "//myChild[@ChildID='ref-3']"
      'Display the selection.
      Dim iterator As XPathNodeIterator = nav.Select(expr)
      Dim navResult As XPathNavigator = iterator.Current
      While (iterator.MoveNext())
            s = s.Format("<b>Type:</b>{0} <b>Name:</b>{1} ", _
              navResult.NodeType, navResult.Name)
          If navResult.HasAttributes Then
                navResult.MoveToFirstAttribute()
                s &= "<b>Attr:</b> "
                Do
                    s &= s.Format("{0}={1} ", _
                      navResult.Name, navResult.Value)
                Loop While navResult.MoveToNextAttribute()
            End If
            Response.Write(s & "<br>")
      End While
  End Sub
```

Figure 9.6 shows the browser output. This code uses an XPath query to locate the myChild element. The Select method is called with the query string. The Select method returns an XPathNodeIterator object, which allows navigation over the node or nodes that are returned. The XPathNodeIterator has a property called Current, which represents the current node and is, in itself, an XPathNavigator data type. Rather than use iterator.Current throughout the code, a variable called navResult is created, and assigned a reference to iterator.Current. Note that the call to MoveToParent is not required when finishing the loop through the attributes. This is because the iterator.MoveNext doesn't care where the current location is, because it is simply going to the next node in its list.

Figure 9.6　Searching for a node with the XPathNavigator.

Some of the real power of the XPathNavigator starts to show when the requirement is to retrieve a list of nodes, and sort the output. Sorting involves compiling an XPath query string to an XPathExpression object, and then adding a sort to the compiled expressions. The following is an example of compiling and sorting:

```
Private Sub Button9_Click( _
 ByVal sender As System.Object, _
 ByVal e As System.EventArgs) _
 Handles Button9.Click
    Dim s As String
    Dim xmlDoc As New XPathDocument("C:\xmltest.XML")
    Dim nav As XPathNavigator = xmlDoc.CreateNavigator()
    'Select all myChild elements.
    Dim expr As XPathExpression
    expr = nav.Compile("//myChild")
    'Sort the selected books by title.
    expr.AddSort("@ChildID", _
     XmlSortOrder.Descending, _
     XmlCaseOrder.None, "", _
     XmlDataType.Text)
    'Display the selection.
    Dim iterator As XPathNodeIterator = nav.Select(expr)
    Dim navResult As XPathNavigator = iterator.Current
    While (iterator.MoveNext())
        s = s.Format("<b>Type:</b>{0} <b>Name:</b>{1} ", _
         navResult.NodeType, navResult.Name)
        If navResult.HasAttributes Then
            navResult.MoveToFirstAttribute()
            s &= "<b>Attr:</b> "
            Do
                s &= s.Format("{0}={1} ", _
                 navResult.Name, navResult.Value)
            Loop While navResult.MoveToNextAttribute()
        End If
        Response.Write(s & "<br>")
    End While
End Sub
```

Figure 9.7 The browser output when compiling and sorting an XPath query.

Figure 9.7 shows the browser output. This code is similar to the previous example, with the exception of the creation of the expr variable. The expr variable is created by compiling the query string to an XPathExpression. After that, the AddSort method is used to sort the output in descending order, based on the ChildID attribute.

When working with XML, it may seem easier to use the DOM methods to access data, but there are limits to the search capabilities that could require walking the tree to get the desired output. On the surface, the XPathNavigator may appear to be more difficult to use, but having the ability to perform XPath queries and sorting make this the object of choice for more complex XML problem solving.

Writing a File Using the XmlTextWriter

The XmlTextWriter can be used to create an XML file from scratch. This class has many properties that aid in the creation of XML nodes. The following sample creates an XML file called EmployeeList.XML, and writes two employees to the file:

```
Private Sub Button10_Click( _
  ByVal sender As System.Object, _
  ByVal e As System.EventArgs) _
  Handles Button10.Click
    Dim xmlWriter As New _
      XmlTextWriter("C:\EmployeeList.XML", _
      System.Text.Encoding.UTF8)
    With xmlWriter
        .Formatting = Formatting.Indented
        .Indentation = 5
        .WriteStartDocument()
        .WriteComment("XmlTextWriter Test Date: " & _
         DateTime.Now.ToShortDateString())
        .WriteStartElement("EmployeeList")
        'New employee
        .WriteStartElement("Employee")
```

```
            .WriteAttributeString("EmpID", "1")
            .WriteAttributeString("LastName", "GaryLast")
            .WriteAttributeString("FirstName", "Gary")
            .WriteAttributeString("Salary", XmlConvert.ToString(50000))
            .WriteElementString("HireDate", _
                XmlConvert.ToString(#1/1/2003#))
            .WriteStartElement("Address")
            .WriteElementString("Street1", "123 MyStreet")
            .WriteElementString("Street2", "")
            .WriteElementString("City", "MyCity")
            .WriteElementString("State", "My")
            .WriteElementString("ZipCode", "12345")
            'Address
            .WriteEndElement()
            'Employee
            .WriteEndElement()
            'New employee
            .WriteStartElement("Employee")
            .WriteAttributeString("EmpID", "2")
            .WriteAttributeString("LastName", "RandyLast")
            .WriteAttributeString("FirstName", "Randy")
            .WriteAttributeString("Salary", XmlConvert.ToString(40000))
            .WriteElementString("HireDate", _
                XmlConvert.ToString(#1/2/2003#))
            .WriteStartElement("Address")
            .WriteElementString("Street1", "234 MyStreet")
            .WriteElementString("Street2", "")
            .WriteElementString("City", "MyCity")
            .WriteElementString("State", "My")
            .WriteElementString("ZipCode", "23456")
            'Address
            .WriteEndElement()
            'Employee
            .WriteEndElement()
            'EmployeeList
            .WriteEndElement()
            .Close()
        End With
        Dim xmlDoc As New XmlDocument()
        xmlDoc.PreserveWhitespace = True
        xmlDoc.Load("C:\EmployeeList.XML")
        Response.Write("<pre>")
        Response.Write(Server.HtmlEncode(xmlDoc.OuterXml))
        Response.Write("</pre>")
    End Sub
```

Figure 9.8 shows the browser output. This code starts by opening the file as part of the constructor for the XmlTextWriter. The constructor also expects an encoding type. Since an argument is required, passing *Nothing* causes the encoding type to be UTF-8, which is that same as the value that is explicitly being passed.

There are many statements that are doing nothing more that writing to the textWriter using xmlWriter. Typing time is saved by the use of *With xmlWriter* statement, which allows a simple dot to be typed to represent the xmlWriter object.

The XmlTextWriter handles the formatting of the document by setting the Formatting and Indentation properties.

The WriteStartDocument method writes the XML declaration to the file. The WriteComment writes a comment to the file.

When writing elements, either the WriteStartElement method can be used, or the WriteElementString method can be used. The WriteStartElement only writes the starting element, but keeps track of the nesting level, and adds new elements inside this element. The element is completed when a call is made to the WriteEndElement method. The WriteElementString simply writes a closed element to the file.

The WriteAttribute method take a name and value pair, and writes the attribute into the current open element.

When writing is complete, a call to the Close method must be called to avoid losing data. The file is now saved.

The last part of this procedure is used to display the file on the browser, as shown in Figure 9.8. This procedure reads the document back into an XmlDocument, turns on the WhiteSpacePreserve property, and sends the outerXML of the XmlDocument to the browser by encoding it in HTML, between the HTML pre tags.

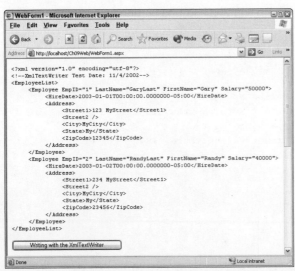

Figure 9.8 The browser output when an XML file is created. The file is then read into an XmlDocument and displayed.

Reading a File Using the XmlTextReader

The XmlTextReader is used to read an XML file, node by node. The reader provides forward-only, noncaching, access to an XML data stream. The reader is ideal for use when there is a possibility that the information that is desired is near the top of the XML file, and the file is large. If random access is required, use the XPathNavigator or the XmlDocument. The following code reads the XML file that was created in the previous example and displays information about each node:

```
Private Sub Button11_Click( _
  ByVal sender As System.Object, _
  ByVal e As System.EventArgs) _
  Handles Button11.Click
      Dim xmlReader As New _
        XmlTextReader("C:\EmployeeList.XML")
      Do While xmlReader.Read()
          Select Case xmlReader.NodeType
              Case XmlNodeType.XmlDeclaration, _
                XmlNodeType.Element, _
                XmlNodeType.Comment
                  Dim s As String
                  s = s.Format("{0}: {1} = {2}<br>", _
                      xmlReader.NodeType, _
                      xmlReader.Name, _
                      xmlReader.Value)
                  Response.Write(s)
              Case XmlNodeType.Text
                  Dim s As String
                  s = s.Format(" - Value: {0}<br>", _
                    xmlReader.Value)
                  Response.Write(s)
          End Select
          If xmlReader.HasAttributes Then
              Do While xmlReader.MoveToNextAttribute()
                  Dim s As String
                  s = s.Format(" - Attribute: {0} = {1}<br>", _
                    xmlReader.Name, xmlReader.Value)
                  Response.Write(s)
              Loop
          End If
      Loop
      xmlReader.Close()
  End Sub
```

Figure 9.9 shows the browser output. This code opens the EmployeeList file and then performs a simple loop, reading one element at a time until finished. For each node that is read, a check is made on the NodeType, and the node information is printed.

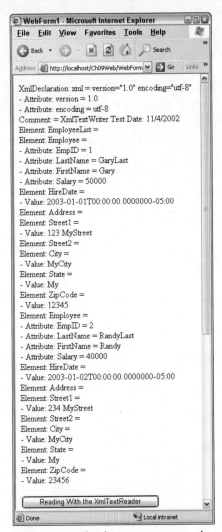

Figure 9.9 The browser output when reading an XML file and displaying information about each node.

When a node is read, its corresponding attributes are read as well. A check is made to see if the node has attributes, and, if so, they are displayed.

XslTransform

The XslTransform class provides a simple method of transforming an XML file, using an xsl stylesheet. The XslTransform supports XSLT 1.0 syntax. The XSLT stylesheet must reference the following namespace:

```
http://www.w3.org/1999/XSL/Transform
```

This class has two methods: Load and Transform. The Load method is used to load an xsl stylesheet. The Transform method has several overloads, but basically expects an XML source, a destination, and, optionally, an XsltArgumentList object.

The XSL stylesheet supports script as well as .NET languages. The example that follows embeds a Visual Basic .NET function to format the hire date of the employee before placing the date into the HTML table.

The following example uses the EmployeeList.XML file that was created in the previous XmlTextWriter example (see Figure 9.8). This example takes an XSL stylesheet, and transforms the EmployeeList into formatted HTML. The HTML is sent to a file, and then the HTML is sent to right out to the Response stream to the browser. The following is the EmployeeList.xsl file:

```
<xsl:stylesheet version="1.0"
        xmlns:xsl="http://www.w3.org/1999/XSL/Transform"
        xmlns:msxsl="urn:schemas-microsoft-com:xslt"
        xmlns:labs="http://labs.com/mynamespace">
    <msxsl:script implements-prefix='labs' language='VB'>
      <![CDATA[
      'Add code here.
        function FormatDate( _
                d as System.XML.XPath.XPathNodeIterator ) as string
            dim ret as string=""
            dim nav as XPathNavigator = d.Current
            nav.MoveToFirstChild()
            ret = XmlConvert.ToDateTime( _
                nav.Value).ToShortDateString()
            return ret
        end function
      ]]>
    </msxsl:script>
    <xsl:template match="/">
        <html>
            <head>
                <title>Employee List</title>
            </head>
            <body>
                <center>
                <h1>Employee List</h1>
                <xsl:call-template name="CreateHeading"/>
                </center>
            </body>
        </html>
    </xsl:template>
    <xsl:template name="CreateHeading">
        <table border="1" width="100%" cellpadding="4">
            <tr >
                <th><font size="4">
                        <b>Employee ID</b>
                </font></th>
```

```
                    <th><font size="4">
                            <b>Last Name</b>
                    </font></th>
                    <th><font size="4">
                            <b>First Name</b>
                    </font></th>
                    <th><font size="4">
                            <b>Hire Date</b>
                    </font></th>
                    <th><font size="4">
                            <b>Salary</b>
                    </font></th>
                </tr>
                <xsl:call-template name="CreateTable"/>
                <xsl:call-template name="GetTotal"/>
            </table>
    </xsl:template>
    <xsl:template name="CreateTable">
        <xsl:for-each select="/EmployeeList/Employee">
            <tr>
                <td align="center">
                    <xsl:value-of select="@EmpID"/>
                </td>
                <td>
                    <xsl:value-of select="@LastName"/>
                </td>
                <td>
                    <xsl:value-of select="@FirstName"/>
                </td>
                <td>
                    <xsl:value-of select=
                        "labs:FormatDate(HireDate)"/>
                </td>
                <td align="right">
                    <xsl:value-of select=
                        "format-number(@Salary,'$#,##0.00')"/>
                </td>
            </tr>
        </xsl:for-each>
    </xsl:template>
    <xsl:template name="GetTotal">
            <tr>
                <td align="right" colspan="4">
                    <font size="4">
                        <b>Total Salaries:</b>
                    </font>
                </td>
                <td align="right"><font size="4">
                    <b><xsl:value-of select=
                    "format-number(sum(
                        /EmployeeList/Employee/@Salary),
                    '$#,##0.00')"/></b>
```

```
                        </font></td>
                    </tr>
            </xsl:template>
        </xsl:stylesheet>
```

The first part of the stylesheet defines a function called FormatDate, which is written in Visual Basic .NET. This function receives an XPathNodeIterator, which is pointing to the current node. The XmlConvert class is then used to format the output and return the short date representation of the hire date.

The next part of the XSL stylesheet contains the main template, which is a search for a matching root node, and is essentially the entry point into the XSL stylesheet. This section creates the HTML formatted output, and makes a call to the CreateHeading template.

The CreateHeading template sets up the HTML table, along with the table header. It then makes a call to the CreateTable template, which has a for-each loop to enumerate the Employee nodes. This prints the Employee information, making calls to the FormatDate function as required.

Finally, the CreateHeading template also calls the GetTotal template, which outputs a total of all salaries as the last row of the table.

There is a good amount of stylesheet code, but there is very little code to execute the transformation. The following code executes the transformation:

```
Private Sub Button12_Click( _
 ByVal sender As System.Object, _
 ByVal e As System.EventArgs) _
 Handles Button12.Click
     'Added to top of code
     'Imports System.XML.Xsl
     Dim xfrm As New XslTransform()
     xfrm.Load("c:\EmployeeList.xsl")
     'Transform to output file
     xfrm.Transform("c:\EmployeeList.XML", _
       "c:\EmployeeList.htm")
     'Transform to response stream
     Dim xpDoc As New XPathDocument("c:\EmployeeList.XML")
     Dim xpNav As XPathNavigator = xpDoc.CreateNavigator()
     xfrm.Transform(xpNav, Nothing, Response.OutputStream)
 End Sub
```

This code sample loads the XSL stylesheet and executes the Transform method. The first time that the Transform is executed, the output is sent to the EmployeeList.htm file.

The second transform took a few more lines of code, but the output is not sent to a file. Instead, the output is sent directly to the output stream, which goes directly to the browser. Figure 9.10 show the browser output.

Figure 9.10 The browser output when performing XSL transformation on the EmployeeList file.

The ASP.NET XML Web Control

The ASP.NET XML Web server control can perform XSL transformations. This control can be dragged and dropped onto a Web form, as shown in Figure 9.11. The properties allow a XSL transformation to be assigned and an XML document to be assigned. The output is automatically sent to the browser.

DataSets and XML

In the last chapter, the DataSet was covered in detail, and in this chapter, many aspects of XML have been covered in detail. This section takes a closer look at the DataSet and how it can use XML.

The DataSet can load XML directly from a file. The DataSet can also use the XmlDataDocument to populate a DataSet. This section takes a look at both methods of working with XML data.

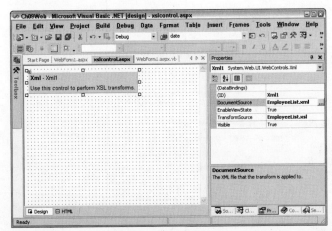

Figure 9.11 The ASP.NET XML Web server control along with its properties window.

Reading an XML Document into the DataSet

Reading XML data into a DataSet can be done by simply using the ReadXml method of the DataSet. This method has several overloads, but one of the overloads allows a filename to be passed into the method. The filename must be a physical path, which means that when the XML document is on the Web server, the Server.MapPath method can be used with a relative virtual address to obtain the physical path. The following code shows an example of reading an XML file into the DataSet and then displaying the data in a DataGrid:

```
Private Sub Button13_Click( _
  ByVal sender As System.Object, _
  ByVal e As System.EventArgs) _
  Handles Button13.Click
      Dim ds As New DataSet("MyCompany")
      ds.ReadXml("C:\EmployeeList.XML")
      DataGrid1.DataSource = ds.Tables("Employee")
      DataBind()
End Sub
```

The browser output is shown in Figure 9.12. This code reads the EmployeeList.XML file into the DataSet. The DataSet parses the repeating rows into tables. The end result is that two tables are created: the Employee table and the Address table.

The DataSet does well at identifying the XML data, but all of the data types are strings and many of the data types, such as dates and numbers, produce the desired results. This can be corrected by supplying an XML schema. An XSL schema can be supplied as a separate file, or it can be embedded into the XML file. For the EmployeeList.XML file, an XML schema might look like the following:

```
<?XML version="1.0" standalone="yes"?>
<xs:schema id="EmployeeList" xmlns=""
    xmlns:xs="http://www.w3.org/2001/XMLSchema"
    xmlns:msdata="urn:schemas-microsoft-com:XML-msdata">
    <xs:element name="EmployeeList" msdata:IsDataSet="true">
      <xs:complexType>
        <xs:choice maxOccurs="unbounded">
          <xs:element name="Employee" id="EmpID">
            <xs:complexType>
              <xs:sequence>
                <xs:element name="HireDate"
                      type="xs:dateTime"
                      minOccurs="0"
                      msdata:Ordinal="0" />
                <xs:element name="Address"
                      minOccurs="0"
                      maxOccurs="unbounded">
```

```
                    <xs:complexType>
                        <xs:sequence>
                            <xs:element name="Street1"
            type="xs:string"
                                minOccurs="0" />
                            <xs:element name="Street2"
                                type="xs:string"
                                minOccurs="0" />
                            <xs:element name="City"
                                type="xs:string"
                                minOccurs="0" />
                            <xs:element name="State"
            type="xs:string"
                                minOccurs="0" />
                            <xs:element name="ZipCode"
            type="xs:string"
                                minOccurs="0" />
                        </xs:sequence>
                    </xs:complexType>
                </xs:element>
            </xs:sequence>
            <xs:attribute name="EmpID"
                type="xs:integer" use="required" />
        <xs:attribute name="LastName" type="xs:string" />
        <xs:attribute name="FirstName" type="xs:string" />
                <xs:attribute name="Salary" type="xs:decimal" />
            </xs:complexType>
        </xs:element>
    </xs:choice>
    </xs:complexType>
  </xs:element>
</xs:schema>
```

Using this schema, the DataSet knows that the HireDate is indeed a date field, the EmpID is an integer, and the Salary is a decimal.

The DataSet has a WriteXmlSchema method that can save the derived schema to a file. This produces a baseline schema that can modified and loaded back into the DataSet using the ReadXmlSchema.

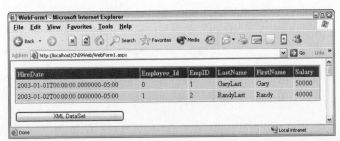

Figure 9.12   The EmployeeList is read into memory and bound to the DataGrid.

Writing an XML Document from the DataSet

A DataSet can be saved to an XML file using the WriteXml method, regardless of its original source. One option that is available is the ability to change the output type of each column when writing the data. For example, the HireDate can be an element or an attribute. The following code changes all columns of all tables to attributes and then writes the XML with an embedded schema to a file called EList.XML:

```
Private Sub Button14_Click( _
      ByVal sender As System.Object, _
      ByVal e As System.EventArgs) _
      Handles Button14.Click
    Dim ds As New DataSet("MyCompany")
    ds.ReadXmlSchema("c:\el.xsd")
    ds.ReadXml("C:\EmployeeList.XML")
    Dim t As DataTable
    For Each t In ds.Tables
        Dim c As DataColumn
        For Each c In t.Columns
            c.ColumnMapping = MappingType.Attribute
        Next
    Next
    ds.WriteXml("c:\EList.XML", XmlWriteMode.WriteSchema)
End Sub
```

The code changes all columns by changing the ColumnMapping properties of all Columns of all Tables to MappingType.Attribute. The options for the MappingType are Attribute, Element, Hidden, or SimpleContent.

Another change that can be made to the XML output is nesting of parent and child tables. The relation has a Nested property that can be set to control the nesting. The following code sets the Nested property to false for all relationships in the DataSet:

```
Dim r As DataRelation
For Each r In ds.Relations
    r.Nested = False
Next
```

When the columns are all changed to attributes and the nesting is set to false, the XML output looks like the following:

```
<?XML version="1.0" standalone="yes"?>
<EmployeeList>
  <Employee HireDate="2003-01-01T00:00:00.0000000-05:00" EmpID="1"
     LastName="GaryLast" FirstName="Gary" Salary="50000"
     Employee_Id="0" />
  <Employee HireDate="2003-01-02T00:00:00.0000000-05:00" EmpID="2"
     LastName="RandyLast" FirstName="Randy" Salary="40000"
     Employee_Id="1" />
  <Address Street1="123 MyStreet" Street2="" City="MyCity"
     State="My" ZipCode="12345" Employee_Id="0" />
  <Address Street1="234 MyStreet" Street2="" City="MyCity"
     State="My" ZipCode="23456" Employee_Id="1" />
</EmployeeList>
```

The Employee_ID is a column that was dynamically added in order to maintain the relationship between the Employee table and the Address table.

Last, the name that is passed into the DataSet's constructor is the name of the DataSet, and also the name of the root element for the XML output.

Using the XmlDataDocument with a DataSet

There may be times when is it more desirable to work with data in an XML fashion instead of table rows and columns. This can be done by creating an XmlDataDocument and passing a DataSet into the class constructor. In the following example, the Suppliers table is read from the Northwind database, and then an XmlDataDocument is created from the DataSet. Finally, a resultant table is created, containing the SupplierID, CompanyName, and Contact-Name, as shown in Figure 9.13.

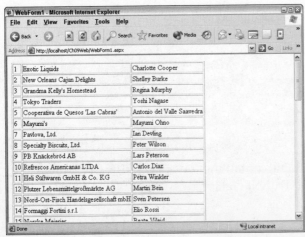

Figure 9.13 Creating an HTML table by navigating the XmlDataDocument.

```
Private Sub Button15_Click( _
    ByVal sender As System.Object, _
    ByVal e As System.EventArgs) _
    Handles Button15.Click
        'Connection
        Dim cn As New SqlConnection()
        Dim cnstr As String
        cnstr = "server=.;integrated security=yes;database=northwind"
        cn.ConnectionString = cnstr
        'Command
        Dim cmd As New SqlCommand()
        cmd.CommandText = _
        "Select SupplierID, CompanyName, ContactName from Suppliers"
        cmd.Connection = cn
        Dim da As New SqlDataAdapter(cmd)
        Dim ds As New DataSet("NW")
        da.Fill(ds, "Suppliers")
        Dim x As New XmlDataDocument(ds)
        Dim nav As XPathNavigator = x.CreateNavigator()
        Dim node As XPathNodeIterator
        node = nav.Select("//Suppliers")
        Response.Write("<table border='1'>")
        Do While node.MoveNext()
            Response.Write("<tr>")
            Dim nav2 As XPathNavigator
            nav2 = node.Current
            Response.Write("<td>")
            nav2.MoveToFirstChild()                'ID
            Response.Write(nav2.Value & "    ")
            Response.Write("</td>")
            Response.Write("<td>")
            nav2.MoveToNext()
            Response.Write(nav2.Value & "    ")
            Response.Write("</td>")
            Response.Write("<td>")
            nav2.MoveToNext()
            Response.Write(nav2.Value & "<br>")
            Response.Write("</td>")
            Response.Write("</tr>")
        Loop
        Response.Write("</table>")
    End Sub
```

This code builds a simple table containing the SupplierID, CompanyName,
and ContactName, using an XPathNavigator.

Validating XML Documents

Having the ability to define the structure of an XML document and then validate the XML document against its defined structure is an important element of being able to exchange documents between disparate systems. The .NET Framework offers the ability to perform validation against a document type definition (DTD) or schema. This section explores XML document validation using the XmlValidatingReader class.

XmlValidatingReader

The XmlValidatingReader class performs forward-only validation of a stream of XML. The XmlValidatingReader constructor can be passed to an XmlReader, a string, or a stream. This class has a ValidationType property that can be set to Auto, DTD, None, Schema, or XDR. If the setting is set to None, this class becomes an XmlTextReader.

In the next example, the file in Listing 9.1 is validated using the following code:

```
Private Sub Button16_Click( _
      ByVal sender As System.Object, _
      ByVal e As System.EventArgs) _
      Handles Button16.Click
          Dim vr As New XmlValidatingReader( _
           New XmlTextReader("C:\xmltest.XML"))
          vr.ValidationType = ValidationType.DTD
          Dim xd As New XmlDocument()
          xd.Load(vr)
          Response.Write("Valid Document!<br>")
          vr.Close()
End Sub
```

This code simply opens the XML file with an XmlTextReader, and the reader is used as the input to the XmlValidatingReader. Since this code has an embedded DTD, the document is validated.

In the next test, the input file has been modified.

```
<?XML version="1.0" encoding="utf-8"?>
<!DOCTYPE myRoot [
    <!ELEMENT myRoot ANY>
    <!ELEMENT myChild ANY>
    <!ELEMENT myGrandChild EMPTY>
    <!ATTLIST myChild
    ChildID ID #REQUIRED
  >
```

```
]>
<myRoot>
    <myChild ChildID="ref-1">
        <myGrandChild/>
        <myGrandChild>Hi</myGrandChild>
        <myGrandChild/>
    </myChild>
    <myChild ChildID="ref-2">
        <myGrandChild/>
        <myGrandChild/>
        <myGrandChild/>
    </myChild>
    <myChild ChildID="ref-3">
        <myGrandChild/>
        <myGrandChild/>
        <myGrandChild/>
    </myChild>
    <myChild ChildID="ref-4">
        <myGrandChild/>
        <myGrandChild/>
        <myGrandChild/>
    </myChild>
</myRoot>
```

The DTD states that the myGrandChild element must be empty, but one of
the myGrandChild elements of myChild ref-1 has a myGrandChild element
containing the word Hi. This causes an error, as shown in Figure 9.14.
Attempts to read from the XmlValidatingRead should always occur within a
Try/Catch block to catch possible validation exceptions.

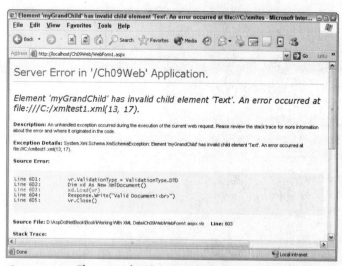

Figure 9.14   The error that is generated when an invalid document is validated using the
XmlValidatingReader.

Lab 9.1: Working with XML Data

You have a requirement to be able to save a customer's orders, along with the order details, to an XML file. The XML file must have only three levels of elements. The first level is the root element, which is called Customers, and has attributes for the CustomerID, CompanyName, and Contact-Name. The second level is the Orders element, which contains an Orders element for each order that the customer has. The third level contains Order_Details elements, which contain an element for each item in the order. The XML document essentially contains an element for each row of each table, and all column data must be presented as XML attributes.

In this lab, you modify the DataGrid from the previous lab, to add a Save Orders button to the DataGrid; this button writes the current customer's orders to an XML file.

Retrieving the Data

In this section, you modify the Bindtable method to retrieve the customers, orders and order details for all customers, and store the results in a Session variable. DataRelations also is created to join these tables together, and the ColumnMapping must be set to be an attribute for every column in the DataSet.

1. Start this lab by opening the OrderEntrySolution from Lab 8.1.

2. Right-click the OrderEntrySolution in the Solution Explorer, and click Check Out. This checks out the complete solution.

3. Open the CustomerList.aspx.vb code-behind page.

4. In the Bindtable method, modify the code to check for the existence of a Session variable named Customers. If it exists, assign the Session variable to a DataSet.

5. If the Session variable does not exist, populate a new DataSet with Customers, Orders, and Order Details from the Northwind SQL database. Add relations between the Customers and Orders tables, and between the Orders and Order Details tables.

6. Add a loop, which enumerates all tables and all columns of the DataSet, setting the ColumnMapping to Attribute.

7. Store the DataSet in the Customers Session variable. Your code should look like the following:

```
Public Sub Bindtable()
    Dim ds As DataSet
    If Session("Customers") Is Nothing Then
        Dim cnstr As String
```

```vb
cnstr = "server=.;integrated security=yes;" _
    & "database=northwind"
Dim cn As New SqlConnection(cnstr)
Dim sql As String = _
sql = "Select CustomerID, CompanyName, ContactName " _
    & " from customers"
Dim da As New SqlDataAdapter(sql, cn)
ds = New DataSet("NW")
'Fill Customers
da.Fill(ds, "Customers")
ds.Tables("Customers").PrimaryKey = _
 New DataColumn() _
 {ds.Tables("Customers").Columns("CustomerID")}
'Fill Orders
sql = "Select * from Orders"
da.SelectCommand.CommandText = sql
da.Fill(ds, "Orders")
ds.Tables("Orders").PrimaryKey = _
 New DataColumn() _
 {ds.Tables("Orders").Columns("OrderID")}
'Fill Order Details
sql = "Select * from [Order Details]"
da.SelectCommand.CommandText = sql
da.Fill(ds, "Order_Details")
ds.Tables("Order_Details").PrimaryKey = _
 New DataColumn() _
 {ds.Tables("Order_Details").Columns("OrderID"), _
 ds.Tables("Order_Details").Columns("ProductID")}
'Create Customers to Orders Relation
ds.Relations.Add( _
 "CustomersOrders", _
 ds.Tables("Customers").Columns("CustomerID"), _
 ds.Tables("Orders").Columns("CustomerID"), _
 True)
ds.Relations("CustomersOrders").Nested = True
'Create Orders to Order Details Relation
ds.Relations.Add( _
 "OrdersOrderDetails", _
 ds.Tables("Orders").Columns("OrderID"), _
 ds.Tables("Order_Details").Columns("OrderID"), _
 True)
ds.Relations("OrdersOrderDetails").Nested = True
'Change all columns to attributes
Dim t As DataTable
For Each t In ds.Tables
    Dim c As DataColumn
    For Each c In t.Columns
        c.ColumnMapping = MappingType.Attribute
    Next
Next
Session("Customers") = ds
Else
```

```
        ds = CType(Session("Customers"), DataSet)
    End If
    dgCustomers.DataSource = ds.Tables("Customers")
    dgCustomers.DataKeyField = "CustomerID"
    DataBind()
End Sub
```

Preparing the Data Grid

The DataGrid needs to be updated to have a Save button beside each customer. The Save button is used to initiate the storing of customer data in an XML file.

1. In the Init event method of the DataGrid, add code to create a button column.

2. Set the properties of the button. Be sure that the CommandName is called *Save*. This is used in the ItemCommand method, in order to find out which button was pressed.

3. Your code should look like the following:

```
Private Sub dgCustomers_Init( _
ByVal sender As Object, _
ByVal e As System.EventArgs) _
Handles dgCustomers.Init
    Dim colButton As New ButtonColumn()
    With colButton
        .ButtonType = ButtonColumnType.PushButton
        .CommandName = "Save"
        .ItemStyle.Width = New Unit(100, UnitType.Pixel)
        .ItemStyle.HorizontalAlign = HorizontalAlign.Center
        .HeaderStyle.HorizontalAlign = HorizontalAlign.Center
        .HeaderText = "Save Orders<br>as XML"
        .Text = "Save"
    End With
    dgCustomers.Columns.Add(colButton)
End Sub
```

Save Customer's Orders to XML File

In this section, you add code to the ItemCommand method of the Data-Grid. This code retrieves the customer primary key of the selected customer. The code then uses an XmlDataDocument to get data from the DataSet and write the data to the XML file.

1. Add an if statement to the ItemCommand, which checks to see if the Command is Save. All additional code is placed inside the if statement.

2. Add code to retrieve the DataSet from the Session variable.

3. Declare a variable called XML as a XmlDataDocument. Check to see if a Session variable called CustomersXml exists. If so, assign the

Session variable to the XML variable. If not, create a new XmlData-Document, based on the DataSet, and assign it to the XML variable.

4. The XML file is stored in the current Web site folder. Add code to get the current path.

5. Add a variable called CustomerKey. Retrieve the CustomerKey from the DataKeys collection of the DataGrid.

6. Declare a variable called xmlWriter, and assign a new instance of the XmlTextWriter to it. The filename is the CustomerKey name, with a .XML extension. This file is stored in the current folder.

7. Write an XML declaration to the file.

8. Write code to locate the customer within the XmlDataDocument, and write the customer details to the file.

9. Add code to close the XmlTextWriter.

10. Save your work. Your code should look the following:

```
    Private Sub dgCustomers_ItemCommand( _
ByVal source As Object, _
ByVal e As System.Web.UI.WebControls.DataGridCommandEventArgs) _
Handles dgCustomers.ItemCommand
    If e.CommandName = "Save" Then
        Dim ds As DataSet = _
            CType(Session("Customers"), DataSet)
        Dim XML As XmlDataDocument
        If Session("CustomersXml") Is Nothing Then
            XML = New XmlDataDocument(Session("Customers"))
            Session("CustomersXml") = XML
        Else
            XML = CType( _
                Session("CustomersXml"), XmlDataDocument)
        End If
        Dim path As String = Server.MapPath(".") & "\"
        'Get Customer Key
        Dim CustomerKey As String
        CustomerKey = dgCustomers.DataKeys(e.Item.ItemIndex)
        path &= CustomerKey & ".XML"
        'Open the XmlWriter.
        Dim xmlWriter As New XmlTextWriter(path, _
         System.Text.Encoding.UTF8)
        xmlWriter.WriteStartDocument()
        Dim CustomerXml As XmlNode
        Dim xPathQuery As String
        xPathQuery = String.Format( _
         "//Customers[@CustomerID='{0}']", CustomerKey)
        CustomerXml = XML.SelectSingleNode(xPathQuery)
        CustomerXml.WriteTo(xmlWriter)
        xmlWriter.Close()
    End If
End Sub
```

Test the DataGrid

The DataGrid can be tested by setting the CustomerList.aspx as the start page and running the application.

1. Right-click the Customer project in the Solution Explorer. Click Set As StartUp Project.

2. Right-click the CustomerList.aspx page. Click Set As Start Page.

3. Run the application. The result should look like that shown in Figure 9.15.

Figure 9.15   The CustomerList page filled with Customers.

4. Click the Save button for CustomerID ANTON. The browser output is shown in Figure 9.16. Notice that there is only one root element, which represents ANTON, followed by the orders and order items.

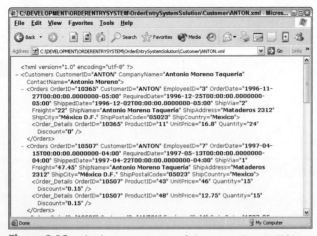

Figure 9.16   The browser output of CustomerID = ANTON.

5. Check you work back into Visual SourceSafe.

Summary

- XML documents can be accessed using the Document Object Model (DOM) Level 1 and Level 2.

- The XPathNavigator uses a cursor model and XPath queries to provide read-only, random access to the data.

- The XmlValidatingReader provides an object for validation against DTD, XML Schema Reduced (XDR), or XML Schema Definition (XSD).

- The XslTransform class provides a simple method of transforming an XML file, using an XSL stylesheet.

- The DataSet provides methods for easily reading and writing XML files.

Review Questions

1. What class can be used to create an XML document from scratch?

2. What class can be used to perform data type conversion between .NET data types and XML types?

3. What class can be used to perform XSL transformations?

4. What is the simplest method of storing a DataSet in an XML file?

5. How are large XML files quickly searched without loading the complete file into memory?

Answers to Review Questions

1. The XmlDocument class.
2. The XmlConvert class.
3. The XslTransform class or the ASP.NET XML Web control.
4. Using the WriteXml method of the DataSet.
5. Using the XPathDocument class with the XpathNavigator.

Streams, File Access, and Serialization

When data must be transferred from one location to another, a method of moving data across the media is required. This method typically involves the sending of bytes in a sequential fashion and the ability to read and process these bytes in chunks, while the information is still being received. Streams are the answer to this problem.

The previous chapters have looked at data access using ADO.NET and XML technologies. Although those technologies should be the primary technologies for storing and retrieving data, there are many instances where the need for file and folder access is necessary.

It's also a common requirement to persist, or store, objects with their state, and to retrieve these persisted objects. This is sometimes referred to as object dehydration and rehydration, but is more commonly called serialization.

Many of the types covered in this chapter are located in the System.IO namespace. This chapter starts by exploring streams in detail. After that, file and folder classes are covered. Finally, this chapter covers serialization.

Classroom Q & A

Q: Is it possible to access the file system to display a list of files that are in a folder and allow a user to select a file to download?
A: Yes. Using the file and directory objects, you can create a view of files and folders from which users can select a file for downloading.

Q: Is it possible to allow users to upload files to the Web server?
A: Yes. The HTML file field control can be used for this. We will look at this control in this chapter.

Q: Can serialization be used to make copies of objects?
A: Absolutely. Serialization can be used to perform a deep copy of an object by serializing to a memory stream then deserializing to a new object.

Stream Classes

In the .NET Framework, many classes require the ability to move data. This data movement may be to and from a file, a TCP socket, memory, or something else. If a class were written to simply write to a file, there could be a problem later when the requirement for writing to a file changed to writing content to a browser window. This is where streams can help.

The stream provides a method for moving data to and from somewhere, depending on the stream class that is implemented. Instead of writing to a file, a class should write to a stream. This allows the programmer to decide what the destination of the stream will be.

In the .NET Framework, some .NET streams have endpoints, or data sinks, such as a file stream. The .NET Framework also provides intermediate streams that provide processing and are spliced into other streams, such as the buffered stream and the Crypto stream.

All streams typically have the same pattern for reading and writing data, as shown here. This section examines each of these streams in detail.

```
'Writing data
Open the stream
While more data exists
     Write the data
Close the stream
'Reading data
```

```
Open the stream
While more data exists
     Read the data
     Process the data
Close the stream
```

The .NET Framework provides stream classes, which are classes that derive from System.IO.Stream, and helper classes, which are wrapper classes that use a stream and provide additional methods to simplify stream access. The helper classes are typically called reader and writer classes. Figure 10.1 shows the relationship between the stream and reader/writer classes.

Stream

The Stream class is an abstract base class for all stream classes. The constructor for this class is protected, which means that it is not possible to create a new instance of this class. The Stream class members are shown in Table 10.1.

The Stream class has a Close method, which releases all resourses, such as file handles and windows sockets. The opening of the stream is accomplished in the constructor of the Stream class.

Using one of the available streams helps to isolate the programmer from the low-level operating system and device details.

All stream classes handle the movement of binary data using bytes or byte arrays. The System.Text.Encoding class provides routines for converting bytes and byte arrays to and from Unicode text.

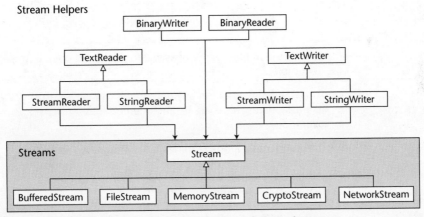

Figure 10.1 Stream class children and stream helper classes.

Table 10.1 Stream Properties and Methods

STREAM MEMBER	DESCRIPTION
Null	A static property that can be used to send data to the bit bucket. Use this when a stream is required, but there is no desire to actually move data.
CanRead	Returns a Boolean, indicating whether the stream can be read. This is an abstract method that must be overridden.
CanSeek	Returns a Boolean, indicating whether this stream supports seeking. This is an abstract method that must be overridden.
CanWrite	Returns a Boolean, indicating whether this stream can be written to. This is an abstract method that must be overridden.
Length	Returns a Long, indicating the length of the stream. This is an abstract method that must be overridden.
Position	This changeable property can be used to get or set the position within the stream. The stream must support seeking to use this property. This is an abstract method that must be overridden.
BeginRead	Starts an asynchronous read from the stream.
BeginWrite	Starts an asynchronous write from the stream.
Close	Closes the stream. This method will also flush all data that is buffered. All resources, including file and socket handles will be released.
EndRead	Called to wait for a pending asynchronous read operation to complete.
EndWrite	Called to wait for a pending asynchronous write operation to complete.
Flush	Forces the movement of any data that is in memory to its destination. This is an abstract method that must be overridden.
Read	If the stream supports reading, this method is used to retrieve a sequence of bytes from the stream and update the position within the stream. This is an abstract method that must be overridden.
ReadByte	If the stream supports reading, this method is used to read a single byte from a stream and update the position within the stream.

Table 10.1 *(continued)*

STREAM MEMBER	DESCRIPTION
Seek	This method is used to set the position within the stream. The stream must support seeking to execute this method. This method requires an offset and a relative origin. The relative origin can be Begin, Current, or End. This is an abstract method that must be overridden.
SetLength	If the stream supports writing and seeking, this method can be used to expand or truncate the current stream. This is an abstract method that must be overridden.
Write	If the stream supports writing, this writes a sequence of bytes to the current stream and advances the position. This is an abstract method that must be overridden.
WriteByte	If the stream supports writing, this method writes a byte to the current stream and advances the position.

FileStream

The FileStream class provides the ability to move data to and from a disk file. This class inherits all the methods in the Stream class and has additional file-centric properties and methods.

FileStream Constructor

The following parameters may be passed to the constructor when opening a file.

FilePath

This is the location of the file that is to be opened. The path can be absolute or relative, and the path can be a UNC path. The path can also be a system device.

FileMode

The FileMode indicates how the file will be opened. This parameter is always required to open a file. The following FileModes are available.

Append. Using the Append mode opens the file and sets the position to the end of the file. If the file does not exist, a new file is created. This option can only be used with the FileAccess property set to Write. An attempt to read from the file will throw an ArgumentException.

Create. Using the Create mode opens a new file if the file does not exist. If the file does exist, the file will be truncated.

CreateNew. The CreateNew mode creates a new file if the file does not exist. If the file exists, an IOException will be thrown.

Open. The Open mode opens an existing file. If the file does not exist, a FileNotFound exception will be thrown.

OpenOrCreate. The OpenOrCreate mode opens the file if it exists. If the file does not exist, a new file is created. This mode differs from the CreateNew mode in that this mode does not truncate an existing file.

Truncate. The Truncate mode opens and truncates an existing file for writing. If the file does not exist, a FileNotFoundException is thrown. If an attempt is made to read from the file, an exception will be thrown.

FileAccess

The FileAccess parameter specifies whether the file is being opened for read or write access. This is a bit enumeration method, which means that settings can be combined with the *Or* operator. The following settings are available.

Read. Read access is used to specify that the file will be opened for read-only use.

Write. Write access is used to specify that the file will be opened for write-only use.

ReadWrite. ReadWrite access is used to specify that the file will be opened for read or write access.

FileShare

The FileShare parameter is used to specify how other streams can access this file. Available options are listed here. Generally, the best setting is None (the default), unless all users need read-only access to the file, in which the setting could be set to Read.

Inheritable. The Inheritable share specifies that the file handle is inheritable by child processes. This option is not available with Win32.

None. The None share does not allow any sharing of this file until the file is closed. This is the default when the FileShare parameter is not specified. An additional attempt to open the file will result in an IOException being thrown.

Read. The Read share allows other processes to also open the same file for read access. The file cannot be opened for write access until the file has been closed.

ReadWrite. The ReadWrite share allows other processes to open this file for reading and writing.

Write. The Write share allows other processes to open this file for writing. This file cannot be opened for read access until the file has been closed.

BufferSize

The BufferSize specifies the size of the buffer to be used when accessing this file. If the number is between zero and eight, the buffer size will be set to eight. Generally, performance gains can be realized by increasing this number.

UseAsync

The UseAsync setting can be used to allow asynchronous access to the file. When set to true, file access is done by using the BeginRead and BeginWrite methods.

FileStream Examples

The section examines several ways of creating a FileStream object. These examples explore several options that are available when opening and working with the FileStream.

Opening and Writing to a File

The following code examples show how a file can be opened, written to, and closed:

```
Private Sub Button1_Click( _
    ByVal sender As System.Object, _
    ByVal e As System.EventArgs) _
    Handles Button1.Click
        Dim s1 As New FileStream( _
          "c:\test.txt", FileMode.Create)
        Dim s1options As String
        s1options = String.Format( _
        "s1 - CanRead:{0} CanSeek:{1} CanWrite:{2}<br>", _
         s1.CanRead, _
         s1.CanSeek, _
         s1.CanWrite)
        Response.Write(s1options)
        Dim b As Byte()
        b = System.Text.Encoding.Unicode.GetBytes("Hello World")
        s1.Write(b, 0, b.Length)
        s1.Close()
    End Sub
```

The browser displays the following information about the stream:

```
s1 - CanRead:True CanSeek:True CanWrite:True
```

Figure 10.2 shows the file contents when viewed in the Visual Studio .NET binary editor. Viewing the output in the binary editor reveals that the message was saved using two bytes per character (Unicode). Writing to the stream required either a byte or an array of bytes. Therefore, this code converts the Unicode string to an array of bytes and writes the byte array, starting at offset zero of the byte array, and writing all bytes by setting the count to the length of the byte array.

Writing and Reading from the FileStream

Since the CanRead and CanSeek properties were set to true, the code can be modified to reset the position to the beginning of the file and read its contents. The following code shows the writing and reading of the file:

```
Private Sub Button1_Click( _
  ByVal sender As System.Object, _
  ByVal e As System.EventArgs) _
  Handles Button1.Click
      Dim s1 As New FileStream( _
        "c:\test.txt", FileMode.Create)
      Dim s1options As String
      s1options = String.Format( _
      "s1 - CanRead:{0} CanSeek:{1} CanWrite:{2}<br>", _
        s1.CanRead, _
        s1.CanSeek, _
        s1.CanWrite)
      Response.Write(s1options)
      Dim b As Byte()
      b = System.Text.Encoding.Unicode.GetBytes("Hello World")
      s1.Write(b, 0, b.Length)
      Dim strOutput As String = ""
      Dim bInput(9) As Byte
      Dim count As Integer = bInput.Length
      Do While (count > 0)
          count = s1.Read(bInput, 0, bInput.Length)
          strOutput &= _
            System.Text.Encoding.UTF8.GetString(bInput, 0, count)
      Loop
      s1.Close()
      Response.Write(strOutput & "<br>")
  End Sub
```

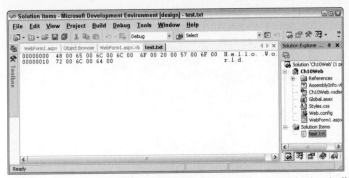

Figure 10.2   Displaying the file in the binary editor reveals that hello world was stored using two bytes per character (Unicode).

To read the file, a byte array must be supplied to act as a buffer. The size of the buffer could be set much higher to achieve better performance. Each time the loop is executed, count will hold the quantity of bytes read from the stream. This loop will run until the Read method returns zero, then the file is closed and the string is output to the browser. The browser output is shown in Figure 10.3.

 The stream is not obliged to fill the buffer each time the Read method is executed. The stream is only obliged to return one or more bytes. If no bytes have been received, the call will block until a single byte has been received. This operation works especially well in situations where a slow stream is involved. The loop can process bytes while the slow stream is sending data.

Opening the Same File with Multiple Streams

In this example, two streams can be opened. Both streams are opening the same file, and each stream has its own position.

Figure 10.3   Browser output when writing and reading a file.

```
Private Sub Button2_Click( _
        ByVal sender As System.Object, _
        ByVal e As System.EventArgs) _
        Handles Button2.Click
    Dim s1 As New FileStream( _
        "c:\test.txt", _
        FileMode.OpenOrCreate, _
        FileAccess.Read, FileShare.Read)
    Dim s1options As String
    s1options = String.Format( _
        "s1 - CanRead:{0} CanSeek:{1} CanWrite:{2}<br>", _
        s1.CanRead, _
        s1.CanSeek, _
        s1.CanWrite)
    Dim s2 As New FileStream( _
        "c:\test.txt", _
        FileMode.OpenOrCreate, _
        FileAccess.Read, FileShare.Read)
    Dim s2options As String
    s2options = String.Format( _
        "s2 - CanRead:{0} CanSeek:{1} CanWrite:{2}<br>", _
        s2.CanRead, _
        s2.CanSeek, _
        s2.CanWrite)
    Response.Write(s1options)
    Response.Write(s2options)
    s1.Seek(0, SeekOrigin.Begin)
    s2.Seek(0, SeekOrigin.Begin)
    Dim strOutput As String = ""
    Dim bInput(10) As Byte
    Dim count As Integer
    count = s1.Read(bInput, 0, bInput.Length)
    Do While (count > 0)
        strOutput &= _
            System.Text.Encoding.UTF8.GetString(bInput, 0, count)
        count = s1.Read(bInput, 0, bInput.Length)
        strOutput &= "<br>"
    Loop
    count = s2.Read(bInput, 0, bInput.Length)
    Do While (count > 0)
        strOutput &= _
            System.Text.Encoding.UTF8.GetString(bInput, 0, count)
        count = s2.Read(bInput, 0, bInput.Length)
        strOutput &= "<br>"
    Loop
    s1.Close()
    s2.Close()
    Response.Write(strOutput & "<br>")
End Sub
```

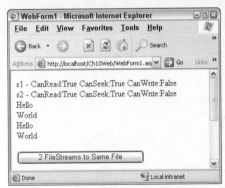

Figure 10.4 Browser output with two streams open for reading.

This code would normally throw an IOException, but does not because the FileAccess is set to Read on both streams. Also, an HTML line break has been added to the output each time through the loops. This gives an indication of the number of times that the loop has run. Figure 10.4 shows the browser output.

Null Stream

The Null Stream is a bit bucket, meaning that it is a dummy stream. This can be useful in situations where a stream is required to execute a process, but there is no desired endpoint.

The following code example shows how a Null stream can be written to and read from. Note that a new Stream instance is not, and cannot be, created. The Stream class is abstract, which means that it must be inherited. Instead, the assignment is made to System.Null.

```
Private Sub Button4_Click( _
        ByVal sender As System.Object, _
        ByVal e As System.EventArgs) _
        Handles Button4.Click
    Dim s1 As Stream = Stream.Null
    Dim s1options As String
    s1options = String.Format( _
        "s1 - CanRead:{0} CanSeek:{1} CanWrite:{2}<br>", _
        s1.CanRead, _
        s1.CanSeek, _
        s1.CanWrite)
    Response.Write(s1options)
    Dim b As Byte()
    b = System.Text.Encoding.Unicode.GetBytes("Hello World")
    s1.Write(b, 0, b.Length)
    s1.Seek(0, SeekOrigin.Begin)
    Dim strOutput As String = ""
```

```
        Dim bInput(10) As Byte
        Dim count As Integer = bInput.Length
        count = s1.Read(bInput, 0, bInput.Length)
        Do While (count > 0)
            strOutput &= _
            System.Text.Encoding.UTF8.GetString(bInput, 0, count)
            count = s1.Read(bInput, 0, bInput.Length)
        Loop
        s1.Close()
        Response.Write(strOutput & "<br>")
    End Sub
```

This code is the same as the code in the FileStream example for opening and writing to a file, except that the FileStream was replaced with the Stream class and initialized to Stream.Null. The browser output is shown in Figure 10.5.

When writing to the Null stream, calling the Write method results in it simply returning without writing anything, and executing the Read method returns zero, indicating that the end of the stream has been reached. CanRead returns true, CanWrite returns true, and CanSeek returns true.

MemoryStream

The MemoryStream class provides the ability to move data to and from a memory buffer. This class inherits all methods in the Stream class and has additional memory-centric properties and methods. MemoryStreams are useful in helping to eliminate the need for temporary files when processing data. The memory buffer that is created by the memory stream is directly accessible as well.

MemoryStream Constructor

The following parameters may be passed to the constructor when opening the stream.

Buffer.   An optional byte array that may be passed to the MemoryStream constructor. If this parameter is used, the buffer size cannot be increased, but it can be truncated. Use of this parameter will isolate the internal buffer, which means that executing the GetBuffer method will throw an exception.

Capacity.   An optional integer that sets the initial size of the internal buffer. Writing past the end of the buffer will cause the buffer to increase its size. Using the SetLength method will also update the length of the buffer.

Figure 10.5   Browser output when using the Null stream.

Writeable.   An optional setting that can be used with the Buffer parameter to indicate whether the buffer can be written to.

Index.   An optional parameter that can be used with the Buffer parameter; it indicates the starting location in the buffer that will be used.

Count.   An optional parameter that can be used with the Buffer parameter; it indicates the quantity of bytes that may be used in the buffer.

Publicly Visible.   An optional parameter that enables the GetBuffer method. The GetBuffer method returns the buffer as an unsigned byte array.

MemoryStream Examples

The section examines several ways of working with the MemoryStream object. These examples explore several of the options that are available when opening and working with the MemoryStream.

Opening and Writing to a MemoryStream

The following code example shows how a Memory stream can be written to and read from.

```
Private Sub Button3_Click( _
        ByVal sender As System.Object, _
        ByVal e As System.EventArgs) _
        Handles Button3.Click
    Dim s1 As New MemoryStream()
    Dim s1options As String
    s1options = String.Format( _
        "s1 - CanRead:{0} CanSeek:{1} CanWrite:{2}<br>", _
        s1.CanRead, _
        s1.CanSeek, _
        s1.CanWrite)
    Response.Write(s1options)
    Dim b As Byte()
```

```
    b = System.Text.Encoding.Unicode.GetBytes("Hello World")
    s1.Write(b, 0, b.Length)
    s1.Seek(0, SeekOrigin.Begin)
    Dim strOutput As String = ""
    Dim bInput(10) As Byte
    Dim count As Integer
    count = s1.Read(bInput, 0, bInput.Length)
    Do While (count > 0)
        strOutput &= _
        System.Text.Encoding.UTF8.GetString(bInput, 0, count)
            count = s1.Read(bInput, 0, bInput.Length)
    Loop
    s1.Close()
    Response.Write(strOutput & "<br>")
End Sub
```

This code is the same as the code in the FileStream example for opening and writing to a file, except that the FileStream was replaced with the Memory-Stream class and initialized with the empty constructor. The browser output is shown in Figure 10.6. CanRead returns true, CanWrite returns true, and CanSeek returns true.

Accessing the MemoryStream's Buffer

The following code example shows how a Memory stream's internal buffer can be accessed directly. This simplifies retrieving the data, and doesn't require changing the stream's position.

```
Private Sub Button5_Click( _
        ByVal sender As System.Object, _
        ByVal e As System.EventArgs) _
        Handles Button5.Click
    Dim s1 As New MemoryStream()
    Dim s1options As String
    s1options = String.Format( _
    "s1 - CanRead:{0} CanSeek:{1} CanWrite:{2}<br>", _
     s1.CanRead, _
     s1.CanSeek, _
     s1.CanWrite)
    Response.Write(s1options)
    Dim b As Byte()
    b = System.Text.Encoding.Unicode.GetBytes("Hello World")
    s1.Write(b, 0, b.Length)
    Dim strOutput As String = ""
    Dim bInput() As Byte = s1.GetBuffer()
    strOutput &= _
     System.Text.Encoding.UTF8.GetString(bInput, 0, bInput.Length)
    s1.Close()
    Response.Write(strOutput & "<br>")
End Sub
```

Figure 10.6 Browser output when using the MemoryStream.

NetworkStream

The NetworkStream class provides the ability to move data to and from a network endpoint. This class inherits all the methods in the Stream class and has additional network-centric properties and methods. NetworkStreams can be used to access a Web site, as well as to communicate between local computers.

It takes a little bit more code to set up the NetworkStream. Figure 10.7 shows a high-level view of the program flow when using the NetworkStream to retrieve the default Web page from a Web server.

The following helper objects are required in order to communicate using the NetworkStream class:

IPAddress. The IPAddress class is used to encapsulate an IP address that represents the URL of the final endpoint. This uses the static Resolve method of the Dns class to perform a Domain Name Service (DNS) search of the Internet for the IP address that corresponds to the domain name that is supplied by the user. Since the endpoint may be part of a Web farm, an array of addresses may be returned, of which the first address is customarily used, unless there is a communication failure.

IPEndPoint. The IPEndPoint class consists of the IPAddress and the Port number of the endpoint. The IPEndPoint is required to create a Socket.

Encoder.ASCII. The Encoder.ASCII class is used to create an encoder that will be used to convert ASCII strings to byte arrays and back.

NetworkStream Constructor

The following parameters may be passed to the constructor when opening the stream.

Socket

The Socket class provides the .NET managed transport service. The Socket requires an IPEndPoint, an AddressFamily, and a ProtocolType. Examples of the AddressFamily are AppleTalk, Ipx, DecNet, and InternetNetwork (IP). Examples of the ProtocolType are SPX, TCP, and UDP.

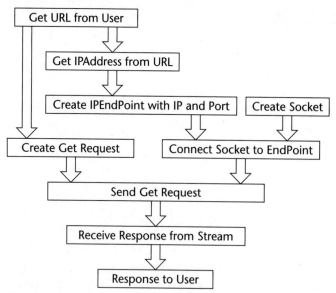

Figure 10.7 A high-level view of the progam flow when working with the NetworkStream to retrieve the default Web page from a Web server.

OwnsSocket

Setting this to true causes the Close method of the NetworkStream to also call the Close method of the Socket. The default is false, so this should always be set to true unless the Socket is being used for other purposes.

NetworkStream Example

The section examines the creation and use of a NetworkStream object. This example looks up the IP address of www.wiley.com, then creates an IPAddress object based on the URL. Next, the IPEndPoint will be created, and finally the Socket is created and connected. The code is as follows:

```
Private Sub Button6_Click( _
        ByVal sender As System.Object, _
        ByVal e As System.EventArgs) _
        Handles Button6.Click
    Dim strServer As String = "www.wiley.com"
    Dim getCmd As String
    Dim getBytes As Byte()
    Dim recvBytes(1024) As Byte
    Dim strRespose As String = ""
    Dim enc As Encoding = Encoding.ASCII
```

```
'Resolve the DNS name to an IP Address.
'by taking the first address in the resolved list
Dim host As IPAddress = Dns.Resolve(strServer).AddressList(0)
Dim EPhost As New IPEndPoint(host, 80)
'Creates the Socket for sending data over TCP
Dim sokt As New Socket(
 AddressFamily.InterNetwork, _
 SocketType.Stream, _
 ProtocolType.Tcp)
getCmd = String.Format( _
    "GET / HTTP/1.1{0}Host: {1}{0}Connection: Close{0}{0}", _
    ControlChars.CrLf, strServer)
getBytes = enc.GetBytes(getCmd)
' Connects to the host using IPEndPoint.
sokt.Connect(EPhost)
If Not sokt.Connected Then
        strRespose = "Cannot connect to host: " & strServer
        Response.Write(strRespose)
End If
Dim s1 As New NetworkStream(sokt, True)
Dim s1options As String
s1options = String.Format( _
        "s1 - CanRead:{0} CanSeek:{1} CanWrite:{2}<br>", _
        s1.CanRead, _
        s1.CanSeek, _
        s1.CanWrite)
Response.Write(s1options)
s1.Write(getBytes, 0, getBytes.Length)
Dim strOutput As String = ""
Dim bInput(10) As Byte
Dim count As Integer
count = s1.Read(bInput, 0, bInput.Length)
Do While (count > 0)
        strOutput &= _
         System.Text.Encoding.UTF8.GetString(bInput, 0, count)
        count = s1.Read(bInput, 0, bInput.Length)
Loop
s1.Close()
Response.Write(strOutput)
End Sub
```

The browser output, shown in Figure 10.8, demonstrates that the stream's CanRead and CanWrite properties are true, while the CanSeek property is set to false. An attempt to seek will cause an exception to be thrown.

This stream operates much like the previous streams that have been examined, except that more setup is required in order to communicate over the network.

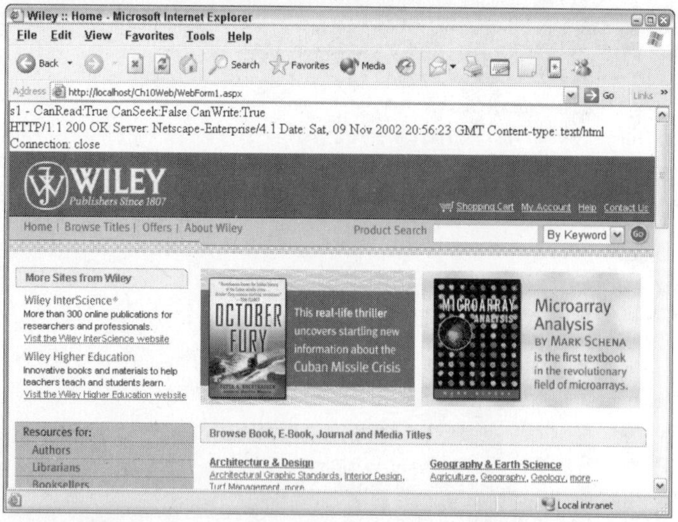

Figure 10.8 An example of using the NetworkStream to read a Web page.

CryptoStream

The CryptoStream class provides the ability to move and process data from one stream to another. This stream does not have an endpoint. This class inherits all the methods in the Stream class and has additional cryptographic-centric properties and methods. CryptoStream can be used to encrypt any data.

The CryptoStream provides the ability to perform symmetrical encryption with little extra work. Symmetrical encryption is done by sharing a secret. In this case, the secret will be the initialization vector (IV) and the key. Depending on the usage, it may be desirable to regenerate the IV and key each time that a session has started, or it may be desirable to store the IV and key for repeated use.

CryptoStream Constructor

The following parameters may be passed to the constructor when opening a CryptoStream for encryption or decrytpion.

Stream

The stream that is passed to the constructor is the input (decryption) or output (encryption) stream.

SymmetricAlgorithm

The SymmetricAlgorithm class can be used to create a CryptoServiceProvider. This is an abstract class and, although this can be used to create the

TripleDESCryptoServiceProvider, it may be better to use one of the explicit CryptoServiceProvider classes. The following CryptoServiceProvider classes are available:

- RijndaelManaged
- DESCryptoServiceProvider
- RC2CryptoServiceProvider
- TripleDESCryptoServiceProvider

ICryptoTransform

The CryptoServiceProvider class contains a Create and CreateDecryptor method. Each of these methods returns an object that implements the ICrypto-Transform interface, which is used to perform encryption and decryption.

CryptoStream Encryption Example

The following example shows how encryption may be done by encrypting the words *Encrypted Hello World* and placing them in a file called c:\test.txt.

```
Private Sub Button7_Click( _
        ByVal sender As System.Object, _
        ByVal e As System.EventArgs) _
        Handles Button7.Click
    Dim s1 As New FileStream( _
        "c:\test.txt", FileMode.Create)
    Dim s1options As String
    s1options = String.Format( _
        "s1 - CanRead:{0} CanSeek:{1} CanWrite:{2}<br>", _
        s1.CanRead, _
        s1.CanSeek, _
        s1.CanWrite)
    Response.Write(s1options)
    Dim cryptoProvider As TripleDESCryptoServiceProvider
    cryptoProvider = TripleDESCryptoServiceProvider.Create()
    If Session("iv") Is Nothing Then
        Session("iv") = cryptoProvider.IV
        Session("key") = cryptoProvider.Key
        txtIV.Text = Convert.ToBase64String(cryptoProvider.IV)
        txtKey.Text = Convert.ToBase64String(cryptoProvider.Key)
    End If
    Dim xfrm As ICryptoTransform
    xfrm = cryptoProvider.CreateEncryptor( _
        Session("key"), Session("iv"))
    Dim c1 As New CryptoStream(s1, xfrm, CryptoStreamMode.Write)
    Dim c1options As String
    s1options = String.Format( _
        "c1 - CanRead:{0} CanSeek:{1} CanWrite:{2}<br>", _
```

```
        c1.CanRead, _
        c1.CanSeek, _
        c1.CanWrite)
    Response.Write(c1options)
    Dim b As Byte()
    b = System.Text.Encoding.Unicode.GetBytes( _
      "Encrypted Hello World")
    c1.Write(b, 0, b.Length)
    c1.Close()
    s1.Close()
  End Sub
```

This code creates a FileStream, then creates the TripleDESCryptoService-Provider. The TripleDESCryptoServiceProvider will generate an IV and key, which must be recorded to decrypt the message. They are saved into Session variables. Next, the CreateEncryptor method is executed to produce an ICrypto-Transform, and finally the CryptoStream is opened with the appropriate parameters. The browser output, shown in Figure 10.9, demonstrates that although the FileStream supports reading, writing, and seeking, the CryptoStream only supports writing.

CryptoStream Decryption Example

The following example shows how decryption may be done by decrypting the words *Encrypted Hello World* from the file called c:\test.txt and sending them to the browser.

```
Private Sub Button8_Click( _
        ByVal sender As System.Object, _
        ByVal e As System.EventArgs) _
        Handles Button8.Click
    Dim s1 As New FileStream( _
      "c:\test.txt", FileMode.Open)
    Dim s1options As String
    s1options = String.Format( _
        "s1 - CanRead:{0} CanSeek:{1} CanWrite:{2}<br>", _
        s1.CanRead, _
        s1.CanSeek, _
        s1.CanWrite)
    Response.Write(s1options)
    Dim cryptoProvider As TripleDESCryptoServiceProvider
    cryptoProvider = TripleDESCryptoServiceProvider.Create()
    Dim xfrm As ICryptoTransform
    xfrm = cryptoProvider.CreateDecryptor(Session("key"),
        Session("iv"))
```

```
Dim c1 As New CryptoStream(s1, xfrm, CryptoStreamMode.Read)
Dim c1options As String
c1options = String.Format( _
    "c1 - CanRead:{0} CanSeek:{1} CanWrite:{2}<br>", _
    c1.CanRead, _
    c1.CanSeek, _
    c1.CanWrite)
Response.Write(c1options)
Dim strOutput As String = ""
Dim bInput(10) As Byte
Dim count As Integer
count = c1.Read(bInput, 0, bInput.Length)
Do While (count > 0)
    strOutput &= _
     System.Text.Encoding.UTF8.GetString(bInput, 0, count)
    count = c1.Read(bInput, 0, bInput.Length)
Loop
Response.Write(strOutput & "<br>")
c1.Close()
s1.Close()
End Sub
```

The browser output, Figure 10.10, shows the decrypted file contents. The FileStream supports reading, writing, and seeking, but the CryptoStream only supports reading. Also note that the IV and key were initialized from the storedSession variables.

BufferedStream

The BufferedStream class provides the ability to take an existing stream and give it buffering capabilities. This stream does not have an endpoint. This class inherits all the methods in the Stream class and has additional buffer-centric properties and methods.

Figure 10.9 Encryption IV and key. This also reveals that the CryptoStream only supports writing.

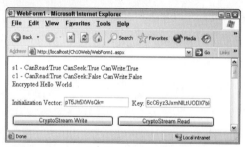

Figure 10.10   The file is decrypted and displayed in the browser.

BufferedStream Constructor

The following parameters may be passed to the constructor when opening a BufferedStream.

Stream.   The stream passed to the constructor is the stream that will benefit from being buffered.

BufferSize.   If a buffer size is provided, a shared buffer is created. If the size of the buffer needs to increase beyond the size of BufferSize, an internal buffer will be used.

BufferedStream Example

The following example shows how a BufferedStream can be used with the existing FileStream:

```
Private Sub Button9_Click( _
        ByVal sender As System.Object, _
        ByVal e As System.EventArgs) _
        Handles Button9.Click
    Dim s1 As New FileStream( _
        "c:\test.txt", FileMode.Create)
    Dim s1options As String
    s1options = String.Format( _
        "s1 - CanRead:{0} CanSeek:{1} CanWrite:{2}<br>", _
        s1.CanRead, _
        s1.CanSeek, _
        s1.CanWrite)
    Response.Write(s1options)
    Dim b1 As New BufferedStream(s1)
    Dim b1options As String
    b1options = String.Format( _
```

```
            "b1 - CanRead:{0} CanSeek:{1} CanWrite:{2}<br>", _
            b1.CanRead, _
            b1.CanSeek, _
            b1.CanWrite)
    Response.Write(b1options)
    Dim b As Byte()
    b = System.Text.Encoding.Unicode.GetBytes("Hello World")
    b1.Write(b, 0, b.Length)
    b1.Seek(0, SeekOrigin.Begin)
    Dim strOutput As String = ""
    Dim bInput(10) As Byte
    Dim count As Integer
    count = b1.Read(bInput, 0, bInput.Length)
    Do While (count > 0)
        strOutput &= _
            System.Text.Encoding.UTF8.GetString(bInput, 0, count)
        count = b1.Read(bInput, 0, bInput.Length)
    Loop
    b1.Close()
    s1.Close()
    Response.Write(strOutput & "<br>")
End Sub
```

The browser output is shown in Figure 10.11. Notice that the buffered stream supports reading, writing, and seeking.

Response.OutputStream

The Response.OutputStream is an instance of the Stream object. The Output-Stream can be used when outputting binary information to the browser. The following example (see Figure 10.12) opens a FileStream containing a picture. The FileStream is read and then written to the OutputStream.

Figure 10.11 In this browser output, notice that the BufferedStream supports reading, writing, and seeking.

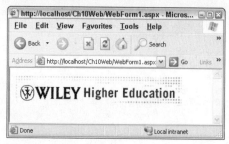

Figure 10.12 An image file is read with a FileStream object and written to the Response object's output stream.

```
Private Sub Button10_Click( _
        ByVal sender As System.Object, _
        ByVal e As System.EventArgs) _
        Handles Button10.Click
    Response.Clear()
    Response.ContentType = "image/gif"
    Dim s1 As New FileStream( _
        "c:\whe_logo.gif", FileMode.Open)
    Dim s2 As Stream = Response.OutputStream()
    Dim b(512) As Byte
    Dim count As Integer
    count = s1.Read(b, 0, b.Length)
    Do While (count > 0)
        s2.Write(b, 0, count)
        count = s1.Read(b, 0, b.Length)
    Loop
    Response.End()
End Sub
```

To ensure that the image is output properly without being corrupted, the response buffer is cleared first. Next, the content type is set to image/gif, which tells the browser what kind of file is being sent. Finally, a loop is created, which reads a block of bytes from the FileStream, and outputs the block to the OutputStream.

This same concept can be applied to delivering other document types, such as Word documents and Excel spreadsheets.

Stream Helper Classes

Many stream helper classes can be used to simplify the coding of the streams that have been covered in this chapter. This section explores some of these classes and provide examples where appropriate.

BinaryWriter

The BinaryReader class provides many Write overloads to simplify writing to a file. The following example shows how this can be used:

```
Private Sub Button14_Click( _
        ByVal sender As System.Object, _
        ByVal e As System.EventArgs) _
        Handles Button14.Click
            Dim s1 As New FileStream( _
                "c:\test.txt", FileMode.Create)
            Dim b1 As New BinaryWriter(s1, Encoding.Unicode)
            b1.Write("Hello BinaryWriter World")
            b1.Close()
        s1.Close()
End Sub
```

This code can reduce the complexity of working with the stream directly, but the BinaryWriter requires a stream to be passed to its constructor.

BinaryReader

The BinaryWriter class provides many Read overloads to simplify the reading of data from files. The following is an example of its use:

```
Private Sub Button15_Click( _
        ByVal sender As System.Object, _
        ByVal e As System.EventArgs) _
        Handles Button15.Click
    Dim s1 As New FileStream( _
        "c:\test.txt", FileMode.Open)
    Dim b1 As New BinaryReader(s1, Encoding.Unicode)
    Response.Write(b1.ReadString())
    b1.Close()
    s1.Close()
End Sub
```

This code simplifies the retrieval of data, but requires that two streams be opened.

TextWriter and TextReader

These classes are abstract and provide many methods that simplify reading and writing textual information.

StreamWriter

The StreamWriter class inherits from TextWriter and can be used to easily write text to a file. The following code shows an example of StreamWriter class:

```
Private Sub Button12_Click( _
        ByVal sender As System.Object, _
        ByVal e As System.EventArgs) _
        Handles Button12.Click
    Dim s1 As New StreamWriter("C:\test.txt", False, Encoding.Unicode)
    s1.Write("Hello StreamWriter World")
    s1.Close()
End Sub
```

This is substantially less code than writing directly to the FileStream. The second parameter is a Boolean that specifies whether the file should be appended. Notice that the encoding is set up in the constructor as well.

StreamReader

The StreamReader inherits from TextWriter and can be used to read text easily from a file. The following code shows how this can be used:

```
Private Sub Button13_Click( _
        ByVal sender As System.Object, _
        ByVal e As System.EventArgs) _
        Handles Button13.Click
    Dim s1 As New StreamReader("C:\test.txt", Encoding.Unicode)
    Response.Write(s1.ReadToEnd())
    s1.Close()
End Sub
```

This code is also much simpler than accessing the FileStream to read its contents. The constructor optionally accepts an encoding type. Notice that the ReadToEnd method is provided to read the entire contents of the file and return a string. The returned string is passed to the Write method of the Response object.

HttpWebRequest

HttpWebRequest can be used to simplify the use of the NetworkStream. This class has the ability to use proxy settings and can also operate with SSL. The constructor of this class is not used. Instead, the Create method returns a valid instance of this class. The following code shows the use of HttpWebRequest:

```
Private Sub Button16_Click( _
        ByVal sender As System.Object, _
        ByVal e As System.EventArgs) _
```

```
        Handles Button16.Click
    Dim h As HttpWebRequest
    h = CType(HttpWebRequest.Create("http://www.wiley.com"), _
        HttpWebRequest)
    Dim r As WebResponse = h.GetResponse()
    Dim s1 As Stream = r.GetResponseStream()
    Dim count As Integer
    Dim b(128) As Byte
    count = s1.Read(b, 0, b.Length)
    Do While count > 0
        Response.OutputStream.Write(b, 0, count)
        count = s1.Read(b, 0, b.Length)
    Loop
    s1.Close()
End Sub
```

This greatly simplifies the use of the NetworkStream. Notice that there is no need to create IPAddresses, EndPoints, and Sockets. HttpWebRequest also provides all the functionality to communicate through proxy servers, communicate via SSL, and log in using credentials.

File Classes

The .NET Framework provides file classes that are used when manipulating files on the disk. The file classes covered in this section are File, FileInfo, and File Upload control. Each of these classes provides different functionality, although the File and FileInfo classes have a fair amount of overlap.

File Class

The File class provides many static classes that perform file manipulation. The File class is typically used when performing a single file operation that requires a string for the file path. Table 10.2 show a list of the static methods that are provided by the File class.

Table 10.2 File Class Static Methods to Manipulate a File

FILE METHOD	DESCRIPTION
AppendText	Creates and returns a StreamWriter that can be used to append to the current file.
Copy	Copies an existing source file to the destination location. Throws an IOException if the destination file already exists.

(continued)

Table 10.2   *(continued)*

FILE METHOD	DESCRIPTION
Create	Creates a file and returns a FileStream using a fully qualified path.
CreateText	Creates a file and returns a StreamWriter using the fully qualified path.
Delete	Deletes the file that is specified by its fully qualified path. This does not throw an exception if the file does not exist.
Exists	Returns a Boolean, indicating the existence of the specified file.
GetAttributes SetAttributes	Retrieves and sets the attributes of the specified file as a FileAttributes bitwise enumeration. Note that each attribute is exposed as a property of the enumeration.
GetCreationTime SetCreationTime	Retrieves and sets the time that the file was created.
GetLastAccessTime SetLastAccessTime	Retrieves and sets the last access time on the file.
GetLastWriteTime SetLastWriteTime	Retrieves and sets the last time of the last write to the file.
Move	Moves the file to a new location. This will throw an exception if the destination file already exists, or if the source file does not exist.
Open	Opens the file and returns a FileStream that can be used to access the file.
OpenRead	Opens the file for read-only access and returns a FileStream object.
OpenText	Opens the file and returns a StreamReader object for read only access.
OpenWrite	Opens the file for write access and returns a FileStream object.

The File class provides many methods; this section shows some examples of File class use. The following code provides a simple example of copying a file from one location to another:

```
Private Sub Button17_Click( _
        ByVal sender As System.Object, _
        ByVal e As System.EventArgs) _
        Handles Button17.Click
```

```
        'Copies from the source, to the destination
        File.Copy("C:\test.txt", "C:\testbackup.txt")
    End Sub
```

This is a simple example of moving a file from one location to another:

```
Private Sub Button17_Click( _
        ByVal sender As System.Object, _
        ByVal e As System.EventArgs) _
        Handles Button17.Click
    'Moves from the source, to the destination
    File.Move("C:\test.txt", "C:\testbackup.txt")
End Sub
```

This example retrieves the last write time and displays it in the browser as a formatted string:

```
Private Sub Button21_Click( _
        ByVal sender As System.Object, _
        ByVal e As System.EventArgs) _
        Handles Button21.Click
    Dim lastWrite As String
    lastWrite = File.GetLastWriteTime("C:\test.txt").ToUniversalTime()
    Response.Write(lastWrite & "<br>")
End Sub
```

This example sets the last write time on the file to Jan 1, 2005 at midnight:

```
Private Sub Button22_Click( _
        ByVal sender As System.Object, _
        ByVal e As System.EventArgs) _
        Handles Button22.Click
    Dim d As DateTime
    d = DateTime.Parse("Jan 1, 2005")
    File.SetLastWriteTime("C:\test.txt", d)
End Sub
```

This code reads the attributes of a file. First, the attributes are enumerated and displayed, then a test is made to see if a certain attribute is set.

```
Private Sub Button19_Click( _
        ByVal sender As System.Object, _
        ByVal e As System.EventArgs) _
        Handles Button19.Click
    Dim a As FileAttributes
    a = File.GetAttributes("C:\test.txt")
    'Display all attributes
    Dim attrArray As Integer()
    attrArray = System.Enum.GetValues(a.GetType())
```

```
        Dim attr As Integer
        For Each attr In attrArray
            If attr And a Then
                    Response.Write(System.Enum.GetName(a.GetType, attr))
                    Response.Write("<br>")
            End If
        Next
        'Check a single attribute.
        If a.ReadOnly And a Then
            Response.Write("This is a Read Only File"
            Response.Write("<br>")
        End If
    End Sub
```

The following code example initially demonstrates the setting of a single attribute that clears other attributes. The next line retrieves the existing attributes and adds the ReadOnly attribute.

```
Private Sub Button23_Click( _
        ByVal sender As System.Object, _
        ByVal e As System.EventArgs) _
        Handles Button23.Click
    'Explicitly set Hidden attribute
    File.SetAttributes("C:\test.txt", FileAttributes.Hidden)
    'Retrieve existing settings and add ReadOnly
    File.SetAttributes( _
        "C:\test.txt", File.GetAttributes("c:\test.txt") _
        Or FileAttributes.ReadOnly)
End Sub
```

FileInfo Class

The FileInfo class provides many of the same methods as the File class, except that FileInfo requires an instance to be created. When the FileInfo instance is created, the name and path to the file must be specified in the constructor. After that, the object can be reused to perform subsequent operations on the same file. This can translate to increased performance over the File class when the same file is being manipulated many times. Table 10.3 lists the methods that are available in the FileInfo class.

The following example shows how the FileInfo class can be used to copy files. A CopyTo method is used to copy a file. The CopyTo method returns a FileInfo object that points to the destination file. The returned FileInfo object is assigned to a variable, and the information is sent to the browser, as shown in Figure 10.13.

Table 10.3   FileInfo Methods

FILEINFO METHOD	DESCRIPTION
AppendText	Creates and returns a StreamWriter that can be used to append text to the file.
CopyTo	Copies an existing file to a new file. This method has an overload that allows the passing of a Boolean overwrite indicator. If the overwrite is true, the destination file will be overwritten without error. If the overwrite is false, an exception will be thrown if an attempt is made to overwrite a file that already exists.
Create	Creates a new file and returns a FileStream object that can be used to access the file.
CreateText	Creates a file and returns a StreamWriter that can be used to access the file.
Delete	Deletes the file. If the file does not exist, no exception will be thrown.
MoveTo	Moves a file to the destination.
Open	Opens the file and returns a FileStream object that may be used to manipulate the file.
OpenRead	Opens the file and returns a read-only FileStream object.
OpenText	Opens the file and returns a StreamReader object that can be used to write text.
OpenWrite	Opens the file and returns a write only FileStream.
Refresh	Refreshes the state of the file.

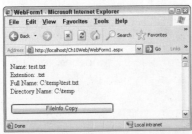

Figure 10.13 The returned FileInfo object has been assigned to a variable, and the information has been sent to a browser.

```
Private Sub Button24_Click( _
        ByVal sender As System.Object, _
        ByVal e As System.EventArgs) _
        Handles Button24.Click
    Dim f As New FileInfo("C:\test.txt")
    Dim d As FileInfo = f.CopyTo("C:\temp\test.txt", True)
    Response.Write("Name: " & d.Name & "<br>")
    Response.Write("Extention: " & d.Extension & "<br>")
    Response.Write("Full Name: " & d.FullName & "<br>")
    Response.Write("Directory Name: " & d.DirectoryName & "<br>")
End Sub
```

Notice that the CopyTo method has a Boolean parameter. This parameter is used to specify whether an existing file should be overwritten by the copy operation. If this option is false, or not specified, an attempt to copy over an existing file will throw an exception.

File Uploading with the File Field Control

The File Field upload control is used to allow users to upload documents to a directory on the Web server, without the need to use Visual Studio .NET. This is an HTML server control.

To use the File Field control, drag a File Field to the Web page. The File Field is located in the HTML tab of the Toolbox. Right-click the control, and click Run As Server Control. Next, add a button that will post the file when clicked. Figure 10.14 shows the designer screen with the File Field control and the Upload button.

In the HTML of the page, the form tag must be modified to specify that it will be posting a file. This is done by making the following change to the form tag:

```
<form id="Form1"
    method="post"
    enctype="multipart/form-data"
    runat="server">
```

The accept property of the File Field control can also be modified to allow only certain types of files to be uploaded. This is done by adding the following attribute to the File Field:

```
accept="image/*"
```

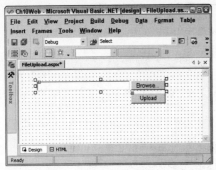

Figure 10.14   The HTML file field and the Upload button.

In the code-behind page, the button click event method must have the following code to process the uploaded file:

```
Private Sub Button1_Click( _
        ByVal sender As System.Object, _
        ByVal e As System.EventArgs) _
        Handles Button1.Click
    Dim fileTarget As String = "C:\MyUploadDocs\"
    If UpLoadControl.PostedFile Is Nothing Then
        Response.Write("No file uploaded.<br>")
        Return
    End If
    fileTarget &= _
        Path.GetFileName(UpLoadControl.PostedFile.FileName.ToString())
    If File.Exists(fileTarget) Then
        Response.Write("File already exists.<br>")
        Return
    End If
    Response.Write("File Uploaded to: " + fileTarget + "<BR>")
    Response.Write( _
        UpLoadControl.PostedFile.ContentType.ToString() + "<BR>")
    Response.Write( _
        UpLoadControl.PostedFile.ContentLength.ToString() + "<BR>")
    UpLoadControl.PostedFile.SaveAs(fileTarget)
End Sub
```

The upload control can be used to upload very large files. Care should be taken to ensure that the destination of the uploaded files does not allow execution of an uploaded file.

Directory Classes

Two Directory classes assist in browsing and manipulation of the operating system directories: Directory and DirectoryInfo. These classes contain a fair amount of overlapping methods. If directory information or manipulation needs to take place only once on a directory, then use the Directory class. If there will be repeated calls to access the directory information, then use the DirectoryInfo class.

Directory Class

The Directory class contains many static methods for accessing and manipulating a directory; thus, there is no need to create an instance of the Directory class. When specifying a path, the path may be absolute or relative, and it may be a UNC path. These methods are listed in Table 10.4.

Table 10.4 Directory Class Methods

DIRECTORY METHOD	DESCRIPTION
CreateDirectory	Creates a new directory and any required subdirectories.
Delete	Deletes the specified directory.
Exists	Returns a Boolean true if the specified directory exists.
GetCreationTime SetCreationTime	Gets and sets the creation time of the specified folder.
GetCurrentDirectory SetCurrentDirectory	Gets and sets the current default directory.
GetDirectories	Returns a string array containing a list of all directories that are under the specified directory.
GetDirectoryRoot	Gets the name of the root directory or volume information of the specified directory. For example, if c:\test\abc\def is specified as the directory, this method returns C:\ as the directory root.
GetFiles	Returns a string array containing a list of files that are in the specified directory.
GetFileSystemEntries	Returns a string array containing the list of all files and folders in the specified directory.
GetLastAccessTime SetLastAccessTIme	Gets and sets the last access time of the specified directory.
GetLastWriteTime SetLastWriteTime	Gets and sets the last write time of the specified directory.

Table 10.4 *(continued)*

DIRECTORY METHOD	DESCRIPTION
GetLogicalDrives	Retrieves a list of logical drives on the current machine. This method does not return mapped drives.
GetParent	Returns the parent directory of the specified directory.
Move	Moves the specified directory to a new location.

The following examples show how the Directory class can be used. Notice that an instance of the Directory class does not need to be created, since the methods are static.

Get All File and Folder Entries

The following code is an example of reading the files and folders in a directory and using the list to populate a ListBox.

```
Private Sub Button25_Click( _
        ByVal sender As System.Object, _
        ByVal e As System.EventArgs) _
        Handles Button25.Click
    Dim f As String
    Dim d As String
    d = "C:\DEVELOPMENT\ORDERENTRYSYSTEM\OrderEntrySystemSolution"
    For Each f In Directory.GetFileSystemEntries(d)
        ListBox1.Items.Add(f)
    Next
End Sub
```

Figure 10.15 shows the browser output. Notice that the full path is retrieved for each entry, even though they are in the same directory.

Get Computer Drive List

The following code shows how to obtain a list of logical drives that are on the current machine. This list will not include mapped drives, however.

```
Private Sub Button27_Click( _
        ByVal sender As System.Object, _
        ByVal e As System.EventArgs) _
        Handles Button27.Click
    Dim d As String
    For Each d In Directory.GetLogicalDrives()
        ListBox1.Items.Add(d)
    Next
End Sub
```

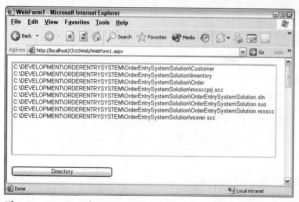

Figure 10.15 The Directory class can be used to retrieve a list of files and folders and populate a ListBox.

Figure 10.16 shows the browser output. Notice that the drives have the colon and backslash already appended to each letter.

DirectoryInfo Class

The DirectoryInfo class provides many of the same methods that the Directory class provides, except that DirectoryInfo requires an instance to be created. When the DirectoryInfo instance is created, the path must be specified in the constructor. After that, the object can be reused to perform subsequent operations on the same directory. This can translate to increased performance over the Directory class when the same directory is being manipulated many times. Table 10.5 lists some of the methods that are available in the DirectoryInfo class.

Figure 10.16   The Directory class can be used to retrieve a list of logical drives on the current machine.

Table 10.5 DirectoryInfo Methods

DIRECTORYINFO METHOD	DESCRIPTION
Create	Creates a new directory under the current directory. No exception is thrown if the current directory already exists.
CreateSubdirectory	Creates a new directory under the current directory; this directory can be several directories under the current directory and any required subdirectories will be created.
Delete	Deletes the current directory and its contents.
GetDirectories	Gets the directories that are in the current directory and returns them as an array of DirectoryInfo objects.
GetFiles	Gets the files that are in the current directory and returns them as an array of FileInfo objects.
GetFileSystemInfos	Gets the files and directories that are in the current directory and returns them as an array of FileSystemInfo objects. The FileSystemInfo class is the base class for both the FileInfo and DirectoryInfo classes.
MoveTo	Moves the current directory to a new location.
Refresh	Refreshes the state of the directory.

The following example shows how the DirectoryInfo class can be used to create a new directory along with any required directories. In this situation, a folder called temp exists, but it is empty. The new directory is C:\temp\abc\ def\ghi\jkl\mno\pqr\stu\vwx\yz.

```
Private Sub Button26_Click( _
        ByVal sender As System.Object, _
        ByVal e As System.EventArgs) _
        Handles Button26.Click
    Dim d As String
    d = "C:\temp"
    Dim di As New DirectoryInfo(d)
    di.CreateSubdirectory("abc\def\ghi\jkl\mno\pqr\stu\vwx\yz")
End Sub
```

The created folder structure is shown in Figure 10.17. Notice that each directory was created as needed in order to create the final yz directory. Also, the new folder is listed relative to the current folder.

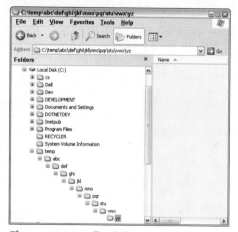

Figure 10.17 All subdirectories were automatically created in order to create the final yz folder.

Isolated Storage

One problem that developers have been challenged with is the ability to store data on the local user's machine. Part of the problem is that there may be security permissions required that the current user does not have, as is the case when the program attempts to store data in the same folder in which a Windows application normally resides (under the Program Files folder). Another problem is that an unauthorized program may attempt to read this information.

Isolated storage provides a method of storing information on a user's fixed disk without requiring any additional security and without exposing the information to other programs. The developer need only be concerned with the data that is to be stored, not the location of the data.

The data store may include files and folders arranged hierarchically. This is up to the developer's discretion. The data store is assigned a *scope,* and if code is not included within the assigned scope, the code will not be able to access the data store. Scopes may be assigned based on application domain, assembly, or user. An administrator may also set a quota on the size of the data store.

Each data store is physically isolated from other data stores. Therefore, an assembly that resides on the local drive will have a data store different from that of the same assembly loaded from the Internet. To use Isolated Storage be sure to import the System.IO.IsolatedStorage namespace.

The following example creates a file within Isolated Storage and writes Hello World.

```
Private Sub Button1_Click( _
        ByVal sender As System.Object, _
        ByVal e As System.EventArgs) _
        Handles Button1.Click
    Dim s1 As New IsolatedStorageFileStream("\test.txt", _
        FileMode.Create)
    Dim s1options As String
    s1options = String.Format( _
    "s1 - CanRead:{0} CanSeek:{1} CanWrite:{2}<br>", _
     s1.CanRead, _
     s1.CanSeek, _
     s1.CanWrite)
    Response.Write(s1options)
    Dim b As Byte()
    b = System.Text.Encoding.Unicode.GetBytes("Hello World")
    s1.Write(b, 0, b.Length)
    s1.Seek(0, SeekOrigin.Begin)
    Dim strOutput As String = ""
    Dim bInput(10) As Byte
    Dim count As Integer
    count = s1.Read(bInput, 0, bInput.Length)
    Do While (count > 0)
        strOutput &= _
          System.Text.Encoding.UTF8.GetString(bInput, 0, count)
        count = s1.Read(bInput, 0, bInput.Length)
    Loop
    s1.Close()
    Response.Write(strOutput & "<br>")
End Sub
```

◆ Where Did the Isolated Storage File Go?

Although the intent is that the developer does not need to be concerned with the location of the Isolated Storage file, the first thing that most people ask is whether the file is being backed up.

A search on the hard drive, using the Windows search, does not expose the file. A search from the command prompt using the following command does find the file:

```
Dir \test.txt /s
```

This search starts at the root directory and searches each subdirectory, looking for all instances of test.txt. The file turned up in the following location:

```
C:\Documents and Settings\LocalService\Local Settings\
Application Data\IsolatedStorage\ljytwfxx.wrt\rpgje1zq.e4o\
Url.f44my4kvl2hzhmacq1gws4w0cswi1zr0\
Url.z0hlqcdjxqmjeuh3hglpmfpz3cbo1c5w\Files
```

This location will probably be different on each machine, and it will be different based on the scope of the data store. The good news is that the file can be found, and this means that the ability to verify that the file is being backed up does exist.

Notice that this code is identical to the code example for the FileStream, except that the IsolatedStorageFileStream is created. The accompanying sidebar explains the location of isolated storage files.

Serialization

Serialization is the process of converting an object into a stream of data, which allows the object to be transported. For example, an instance of a Car class might contain the Car's vehicle identification number (VIN), color, make, model, and year. If several instances of the Car class are in memory, it might be desirable to transport these to disk storage, and later transport the instances back to memory to deserialize the Car instances without losing the data.

The .NET Framework has support for binary, SOAP, and XML serialization. The different reasons for choosing one type of serialization over another will be covered in this section.

It is usually better to serialize a single item to a stream, although this item could be a collection, such as an ArrayList. This is especially important with SOAP serialization, in which serializing more that one object creates an XML document with multiple root elements.

To serialize an object, the class must implement the <Serializable( )> attribute. If there are any members of the class that should not be serialized, those members may contain the <NonSerialized( )> attribute.

In Visual Basic .NET, Attributes are placed only on the same line as the class or member definition. Thus, the LineItem class would appear as follows:

```
<Serializable()>Public class LineItems
```

Most other .NET languages place the attribute on the line above the definition, which may look and feel better. This can be done in Visual Basic .NET by using the line continuation character, which looks like this:

```
<Serializable()> _
Public class LineItems
```

In this section, an ArrayList is serialized. The ArrayList is called ShoppingCart and contains instances of the LineItem class, which are items that a potential customer wishes to purchase. Listing 10.1 shows the code for the LineItem class and the manual population of the ShoppingCart collection.

```
Imports System.Runtime.Serialization.Formatters.Binary
Imports System.Collections
Imports System.IO
```

Listing 10.1 ShoppingCart code that will be used and modified with the serialization examples.

```
Public Class SerializationTest
    Inherits System.Web.UI.Page
    Protected WithEvents btnRestoreCart As _
        System.Web.UI.WebControls.Button
    Protected WithEvents btnPopulateCart As _
        System.Web.UI.WebControls.Button
    Private Sub Page_Load( _
            ByVal sender As System.Object, _
            ByVal e As System.EventArgs) _
            Handles MyBase.Load
        'Put user code to initialize the page here.
    End Sub
    Private Sub btnPopulateCart_Click( _
            ByVal sender As System.Object, _
            ByVal e As System.EventArgs) _
            Handles btnPopulateCart.Click
        Dim ShoppingCart As New ArrayList()
        ShoppingCart.Add(New LineItem("Apple-123", 1))
        ShoppingCart.Add(New LineItem("Orange-234", 2))
        ShoppingCart.Add(New LineItem("Pear-567", 3))
        ShoppingCart.Add(New LineItem("Plum-890", 4))
        ShoppingCart.Add(New LineItem("Grape-999", 5))
    End Sub
    Private Sub btnRestoreCart_Click( _
            ByVal sender As System.Object, _
            ByVal e As System.EventArgs) _
            Handles btnRestoreCart.Click
    End Sub
End Class
<Serializable()> _
Public Class LineItem
    Private _productID As String
    Private _Quantity As Integer
    Public Sub New(ByVal ProductID As String, _
            ByVal Quantity As Integer)
        _productID = ProductID
        _Quantity = Quantity
    End Sub
    Public ReadOnly Property ProductID() As String
        Get
            Return _productID
        End Get
    End Property
    Public Property Quantity() As Integer
        Get
            Return _Quantity
        End Get
        Set(ByVal Value As Integer)
```

Listing 10.1   *(continued)*

```
                 If Quantity > 1000 Then
                     Throw New ArgumentOutOfRangeException( _
                     "Quantity must be less than 1000")
                 End If
                 _Quantity = Value
             End Set
         End Property
     End Class
```

Listing 10.1 *(continued)*

Binary Serialization

Binary serialization is the fastest and most compact serialization type. Binary serialization is included in the base class library, mscorlib.dll, so no references need be made to external .dll files.

Binary serialization classes are located in the System.Runtime.Serialization .Formatters.Binary namespace. To serialize and store the ShoppingCart to a disk file, the btnPopulateCart_click method can be modified as follows:

```
Private Sub btnPopulateCart_Click( _
        ByVal sender As System.Object, _
        ByVal e As System.EventArgs) _
        Handles btnPopulateCart.Click
    Dim ShoppingCart As New ArrayList()
    ShoppingCart.Add(New LineItem("Apple-123", 1))
    ShoppingCart.Add(New LineItem("Orange-234", 2))
    ShoppingCart.Add(New LineItem("Pear-567", 3))
    ShoppingCart.Add(New LineItem("Plum-890", 4))
    ShoppingCart.Add(New LineItem("Grape-999", 5))
    Dim filename As String = "c:\cart.bin"
    Dim s As New FileStream(filename, FileMode.Create)
    Dim f As New BinaryFormatter()
    f.Serialize(s, ShoppingCart)
    s.Close()
End Sub
```

Figure 10.18 shows the cart.bin file contents, using the Visual Studio .NET binary editor. Although some of the information is not readable, a good amount of the data is readable.

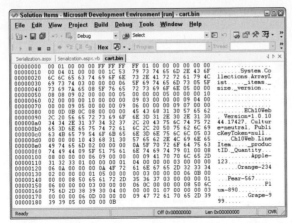

Figure 10.18 The cart.bin file contents, using the Visual Studio .NET binary editor.

Deserializing the shopping cart is a relatively simple task. The following code deserializes the ShoppingCart and displays the LineItems in a DataGrid:

```
Private Sub btnRestoreCart_Click( _
        ByVal sender As System.Object, _
        ByVal e As System.EventArgs) _
        Handles btnRestoreCart.Click
    Dim ShoppingCart As ArrayList
    Dim filename As String = "c:\cart.bin"
    Dim s As New FileStream(filename, FileMode.Open)
    Dim f As New BinaryFormatter()
    ShoppingCart = CType(f.Deserialize(s), ArrayList)
    s.Close()
    DataGrid1.DataSource = ShoppingCart
    DataBind()
End Sub
```

This code declares an ArrayList, but does not create the instance of the ArrayList. The stream is created, thus essentially opening the file. The ShoppingCart is deserialized, but the BinaryFormatter always returns an object data type, so the CType command is used to cast the object to the desired ArrayList.

Finally, the ShoppingCart is assigned to the DataGrid, and the DataBind command is executed. The browser output is shown in Figure 10.19.

SOAP Serialization

SOAP serialization is the most cross-platform-compatible method of serialization, but it is also the most verbose serialization type. SOAP serialization is not included in the base class library, so a reference must be added to the System .Runtime.Serialization.Formatters.Soap.dll file.

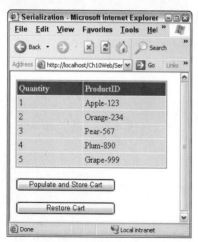

Figure 10.19   Shows the deserialized ShoppingCart in the DataGrid.

The SOAP serialization classes are located in the System.Runtime.Serialization .Formatters.Soap namespace, so the following imports statement is added to the top of the code-behind page:

```
Imports System.Runtime.Serialization.Formatters.Soap
```

To serialize and store the ShoppingCart to a disk file, the btnPopulateCart_click method can be modified as follows:

```
Private Sub btnPopulateCart_Click( _
        ByVal sender As System.Object, _
        ByVal e As System.EventArgs) _
        Handles btnPopulateCart.Click
    Dim ShoppingCart As New ArrayList()
    ShoppingCart.Add(New LineItem("Apple-123", 1))
    ShoppingCart.Add(New LineItem("Orange-234", 2))
    ShoppingCart.Add(New LineItem("Pear-567", 3))
    ShoppingCart.Add(New LineItem("Plum-890", 4))
    ShoppingCart.Add(New LineItem("Grape-999", 5))
    Dim filename As String = "c:\cart.xml"
    Dim s As New FileStream(filename, FileMode.Create)
    Dim f As New SoapFormatter()
    f.Serialize(s, ShoppingCart)
    s.Close()
End Sub
```

Deserializing the shopping cart is the same as using the binary formatter, except that the filename and formatter are different. The following code deserializes the ShoppingCart and displays the LineItems in a DataGrid:

```
Private Sub btnRestoreCart_Click( _
        ByVal sender As System.Object, _
        ByVal e As System.EventArgs) _
        Handles btnRestoreCart.Click
    Dim ShoppingCart As ArrayList
    Dim filename As String = "c:\cart.xml"
    Dim s As New FileStream(filename, FileMode.Open)
    Dim f As New SoapFormatter()
    ShoppingCart = CType(f.Deserialize(s), ArrayList)
    s.Close()
    DataGrid1.DataSource = ShoppingCart
    DataBind()
End Sub
```

The only change is the filename and the use of the SoapFormatter instead of the BinaryFormatter. This code produces the XML file shown in Figure 10.20. Note that the data is very readable, but is very verbose, which may influence whether a programmer chooses to use SOAP serialization.

Before looking at XML serialization, some changes can be made to the code to reduce the verbosity of this file. First, much of the verbosity is from namespaces. This can be reduced by declaring a very short namespace for the List-Item class. If the namespace is eliminated, the class cannot be deserialized, so a dot (.) is used as the namespace, as shown in the following attribute:

```
<System.Runtime.Remoting.Metadata.SoapType(XmlNamespace:="."), _
Serializable()> _
Public Class LineItem
End Class
```

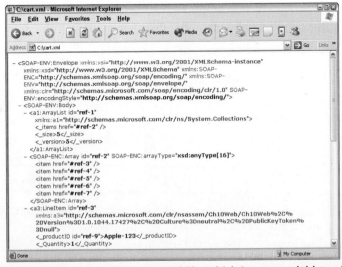

Figure 10.20 Part of the cart.xml file, which is very readable and very verbose.

Next, because fully qualified namespaces are not being used, the assembly's data types need to be preloaded into SoapServices in order for the data types to be found when deserializing. This requires importing more namespaces at the top of the code-behind page as follows:

```
Imports System.Reflection
Imports System.Runtime.Remoting
```

The deserialization code now looks like this:

```
Private Sub btnRestoreCart_Click( _
        ByVal sender As System.Object, _
        ByVal e As System.EventArgs) _
        Handles btnRestoreCart.Click
    Dim ShoppingCart As ArrayList
    Dim filename As String = "c:\cart.xml"
    Dim s As New FileStream(filename, FileMode.Open)
    Dim f As New SoapFormatter()
    Dim a As [Assembly] = [Assembly].GetExecutingAssembly()
    SoapServices.PreLoad(a)
    ShoppingCart = CType(f.Deserialize(s), ArrayList)
    s.Close()
    DataGrid1.DataSource = ShoppingCart
    DataBind()
End Sub
```

The cart.xml file is shown in Figure 10.21. Note that the use of the shortened namespace dramatically reduces the file size. This may be a desired option, but remember that namespaces exist to prevent name collision, so the namespace should be set to something that makes logical sense.

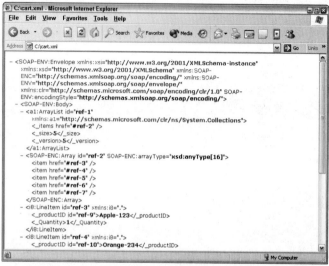

Figure 10.21   The cart.xml file with the shortened namespace.

XML Serialization

XML serialization is sometimes considered as a compromise between using binary serialization and SOAP serialization. Although this produces a very readable output, the lack of a standard implementation means that it should not be used for exchanging data across platforms.

Another problem with XML serialization is that it requires the implementation of the empty constructor for all serialized classes. Thus, the LineItem class needs to be modified by adding the empty constructor.

Yet another problem with XML serialization is that read-only properties are not serialized. Therefore, the ProductID property must be modified to a changeable property.

The new LineItem class follows:

```vb
<Serializable()> _
Public Class LineItem
    Private _productID As String
    Private _Quantity As Integer
    Public Sub New()
    End Sub
    Public Sub New(ByVal ProductID As String, _
            ByVal Quantity As Integer)
        _productID = ProductID
        _Quantity = Quantity
    End Sub
    Public Property ProductID() As String
        Get
            Return _productID
        End Get
        Set(ByVal value As String)
            _productID = value
        End Set
    End Property
    Public Property Quantity() As Integer
        Get
            Return _Quantity
        End Get
        Set(ByVal Value As Integer)
            If Quantity > 1000 Then
                Throw New ArgumentOutOfRangeException( _
                "Quantity must be less than 1000")
            End If
            _Quantity = Value
        End Set
    End Property
End Class
```

XML serialization is not included in the base class library. Therefore, a reference to the System.XML.dll file must be added. Because the XML serialization classes are located in the System.XML.Serialization namespace, the following statements need to be added to the top of the code-behind page:

```
Imports System.XML
Imports System.XML.Serialization
```

To serialize and store the ShoppingCart to a disk file, the btnPopulate-Cart_click method can be modified as follows:

```
Private Sub btnPopulateCart_Click( _
        ByVal sender As System.Object, _
        ByVal e As System.EventArgs) _
        Handles btnPopulateCart.Click
    Dim ShoppingCart As New ArrayList()
    ShoppingCart.Add(New LineItem("Apple-123", 1))
    ShoppingCart.Add(New LineItem("Orange-234", 2))
    ShoppingCart.Add(New LineItem("Pear-567", 3))
    ShoppingCart.Add(New LineItem("Plum-890", 4))
    ShoppingCart.Add(New LineItem("Grape-999", 5))
    Dim filename As String = "c:\cart.xml"
    Dim s As New FileStream(filename, FileMode.Create)
    Dim extraTypes() As Type = {Type.GetType("Ch10Web.LineItem")}
    Dim f As New XmlSerializer( _
     Type.GetType("System.Collections.ArrayList"), _
     extraTypes)
    f.Serialize(s, ShoppingCart)
    s.Close()
End Sub
```

Notice that the serialization required a list of types to be preloaded into the XmlSerializer. The cart.xml file is shown in Figure 10.22. Notice that this file is not too verbose, but some of the limitations that have already been identitified may make this a bad choice.

The deserialization code looks like this:

```
Private Sub btnRestoreCart_Click( _
        ByVal sender As System.Object, _
        ByVal e As System.EventArgs) _
        Handles btnRestoreCart.Click
    Dim ShoppingCart As ArrayList
    Dim filename As String = "c:\cart.xml"
    Dim s As New FileStream(filename, FileMode.Open)
    Dim extraTypes() As Type = {Type.GetType("Ch10Web.LineItem")}
    Dim f As New XmlSerializer( _
     Type.GetType("System.Collections.ArrayList"), _
     extraTypes)
    ShoppingCart = CType(f.Deserialize(s), ArrayList)
    s.Close()
    DataGrid1.DataSource = ShoppingCart
    DataBind()
End Sub
```

```
C:\cart.xml - Microsoft Internet Explorer
File   Edit   View   Favorites   Tools   Help
Back          x  2         Search    Favorites   Media
Address     C:\cart.xml                              Go    Links

    <?xml version="1.0" ?>
  - <ArrayOfAnyType
      xmlns:xsd="http://www.w3.org/2001/XMLSchema"
      xmlns:xsi="http://www.w3.org/2001/XMLSchema-instance">
    - <anyType xsi:type="LineItem">
        <ProductID>Apple-123</ProductID>
        <Quantity>1</Quantity>
      </anyType>
    - <anyType xsi:type="LineItem">
        <ProductID>Orange-234</ProductID>
        <Quantity>2</Quantity>
      </anyType>
    - <anyType xsi:type="LineItem">
        <ProductID>Pear-567</ProductID>
        <Quantity>3</Quantity>
      </anyType>
    - <anyType xsi:type="LineItem">
        <ProductID>Plum-890</ProductID>
        <Quantity>4</Quantity>
      </anyType>
    - <anyType xsi:type="LineItem">
        <ProductID>Grape-999</ProductID>
        <Quantity>5</Quantity>
      </anyType>
    </ArrayOfAnyType>

Done                                      My Computer
```

Figure 10.22   The serialized cart.xml file, using the XmlSerializer.

This code is similar to the serialization code in that the data types were required to be preloaded before they could be deserialized.

Final Notes on Serialization

Serialization is used extensively throughout the .NET Framework. Anytime data needs to be transported from one location to another, serialization is used. As a general rule, binary serialization or SOAP serialization should be used, because of the limitations of XML serialization.

Lab 10.1: Working with File and Directory Objects

You are required to allow users to upload files to the Web server, and the files need to be immediately available for download by other users.

In this lab, you will create an upload page and a download page. The upload page will contain a File Field control for uploading. The download page will contain a ListBox that will cause the file to be sent to the ResponseStream.

Uploading the File
In this section, you will add a new page with the File Field control.

1. Start this lab by opening the OrderEntrySolution from Lab 9.1.

2. Right-click the OrderEntrySolution in the Solution Explorer and clickCheck Out. This will check out the complete solution.

3. Add a new Web Form page called DocumentUpload.aspx to the Customer project.

4. Add a new folder to the Customer project called Uploaded-Documents. This will hold all documents that have been uploaded.

5. From the HTML tab in the Toolbox, add a File Field control. Right-click the contol, and click Run As Server Control. Change the ID and name of the control to *UploadControl*.

6. Change to the Web Forms tab in the Toolbox. Add a button from this menu to the page. Set the Text of the control to *Upload*. Change the ID of the button to *btnUpload*.

7. Click the HTML tab on the page. Change the form tag to look like this:

```
<form id="Form1"
      method="post"
      enctype="multipart/form-data"
      runat="server">
```

8. Double-click the button to go to the button's click event in the code-behind page.

9. Add Imports System.IO to the top of the code-behind page.

10. Add code to store the uploaded document in the Uploaded-Documents folder. Your code should look like the following:

```
Private Sub btnUpload_Click( _
           ByVal sender As System.Object, _
           ByVal e As System.EventArgs) _
           Handles btnUpload.Click
   If UploadControl.PostedFile Is Nothing Then
       Response.Write("No file uploaded.<br>")
       Return
   End If
   Dim fileTarget As String = Server.MapPath( _
       "UploadedDocuments\")
   fileTarget &= Path.GetFileName( _
       UploadControl.PostedFile.FileName.ToString())
   If File.Exists(fileTarget) Then
       Response.Write("File already exists.<br>")
       Return
   End If
   Response.Write("File Uploaded to: " & fileTarget _
       & "<BR>")
```

```
Response.Write( _
    UploadControl.PostedFile.ContentType.ToString() _
        & "<BR>")
Response.Write( _
    UploadControl.PostedFile.ContentLength.ToString() _
        & "<BR>")
UploadControl.PostedFile.SaveAs(fileTarget)
End sub
```

Test File Uploading

The File Field control can be tested by setting the DocumentUpload.aspx as the start page and running the application.

1. Right-click the Customer project in the Solution Explorer. Click Set As StartUp Project.

2. Right-click the DocumentUpload.aspx page. Click Set As Start Page.

3. Run the application. Upload some text and picture files.

4. After stopping the program, check the folder to verify that the files are being saved properly.

Create the Download Page

In this section, a download page will be created. This page will use the DirectoryInfo class to populate a ListBox with the file list.

1. Add a new Web Form page called DocumentDownload.aspx to the Customer project.

2. Add a ListBox to the page.

3. Set the AutoPostBack property of the ListBox to true.

4. Double-click the ListBox to go to the code-behind page.

5. Add Imports System.IO to the top of the code-behind page.

6. Add code to the Page_Load to populate the ListBox if the page is not being posted back. The code should look like the following:

```
Private Sub Page_Load( _
ByVal sender As System.Object, _
ByVal e As System.EventArgs) _
Handles MyBase.Load
    'Put the user code to initialize the page here.
    If Not IsPostBack Then
        Dim d As DirectoryInfo
        d = New DirectoryInfo(Server.MapPath( _
            "UploadedDocuments/"))
        Dim fi() As FileInfo
        fi = d.GetFiles()
        Dim f As FileInfo
```

```
                For Each f In fi
                      ListBox1.Items.Add( _
                            New ListItem(f.Name, f.FullName))
                Next
            End If
        End Sub
```

7. Add code to the ListBox's SelectedIndexChanged method to deliver the file to the user. Your code should look like the following:

```
Private Sub ListBox1_SelectedIndexChanged( _
ByVal sender As System.Object, _
ByVal e As System.EventArgs) _
Handles ListBox1.SelectedIndexChanged
        Dim f As String
        f = ListBox1.SelectedItem.Value
        If File.Exists(f) Then
              Response.Clear()
              'Default to force the save messagebox
              Response.ContentType = "application/octet-stream"
              If String.Compare( _
                        Path.GetExtension(f), ".gif", True) Then
                    Response.ContentType = "image/gif"
              End If
              Response.WriteFile(f)
              Response.End()
        Else
              Response.Write("File not found<br>")
        End If
    End Sub
```

8. Check your work back into Visual SourceSafe.

Test File Downloading

The download can be tested by setting the DownLoadDocument.aspx as the start page and running the application.

1. Right-click the Customer project in the Solution Explorer. Click Set As StartUp Project.

2. Right-click the DownLoadDocument.aspx page. Click Set As Start Page.

3. Run the application. Click some of the files that are in the ListBox.

Summary

- Using one of the available streams helps to isolate the programmer from the low-level operating system and device details.
- The File class provides many static classes that perform file manipulation.
- The FileInfo class requires an instance to be created.
- The Directory class contains many static methods for accessing and manipulating a directory.
- The DirectoryInfo class requires an instance to be created.
- Isolated storage provides a method of storing information on a user's fixed disk without requiring any additional security and without exposing the information to other programs.
- Serialization is the process of converting an object into a stream of data, which allows the object to be transported.

Review Questions

1. What are three of the Stream classes?

2. What are three of the Stream helper classes?

3. What is the difference between the File and FileInfo class?

4. What control can be used to upload files to the Web server?

5. How can you save data to the file system without needing to worry about the location and file system type for the data?

6. What type of serialization should be used for optimal performance?

Answers to Review Questions

1. The FileStream, NetworkStream, Null Stream, MemoryStream, CryptoStream, BufferedStream.

2. The BinaryWriter, BinaryReader, TextWriter, TextReader, StreamWriter, StreamReader, HttpWebRequest.

3. The File class uses static methods, whereas the FileInfo class uses instance methods.

4. The File Field HTML control.

5. Use Isolated Storage.

6. Binary Serialization.

Working with GDI+ and Images

Until now, the focus of this book has been on the use of textual data in a Web application. There is often a requirement to work with images, either by storing and retrieving images on the Web server, or by creating images on the fly.

This chapter starts by looking at the image and bitmap classes. These classes can be used to work with images, by using most of the techniques that have been defined in previous chapters.

The latter part of the chapter looks closely at GDI+ and the ability to create images on the fly. Many of the types that are covered in this chapter are located in the System.Drawing and System.Drawing.Imaging namespaces.

Classroom Q & A

Q: Is it possible to upload images to a database?
A: Yes. This chapter covers uploading images to a database and retrieving images from the database.

Q: How difficult is it to rotate or flip an image?
A: Actually, it's very easy to rotate or flip an image after it's loaded into memory. The Image class contains a RotateFlip method that simplifies this process.

Q: I have a graphical menu on my site, and I would like to generate on-the-fly text graphics for the menu selections. Is this possible in ASP.NET?

A: It sure is. This chapter covers the creation of on-the-fly graphics.

Understanding How the Browser Retrieves Images

When a user requests a Web page, the Web page typically contains HTML content, which may also include <img src="image1.gif"> tags. When the browser receives this image tag, the browser then needs go to the source and request the image. In effect, when the browser sees an image tag, the browser knows that the content isn't included in the Web page, it is in a different file, which must be retrieved to display the image. Figure 11.1 shows an example of the requests and responses between the browser and the Web server.

The source of the image tag is typically a file, such as Image1.gif, but it doesn't need to be a file. Instead, the source attribute could be set to a handler that will locate the image and respond with it. The handler may be a simple .aspx page that has no HTML content, but the code-behind page may be retrieving the image from a database, and sending the image to the browser. Think of this handler as being the *image engine* for the site. The query string could contain the ID of the image to be retrieved and the image engine will locate and respond with the correct image, as shown in Figure 11.2.

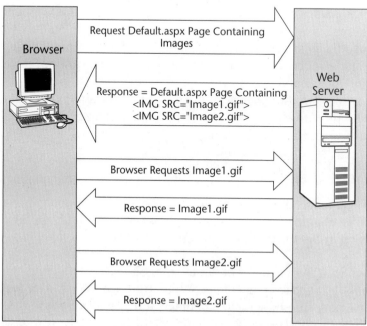

Figure 11.1　The typical series of requests and responses between the browser and the Web server when images appear on the Web page.

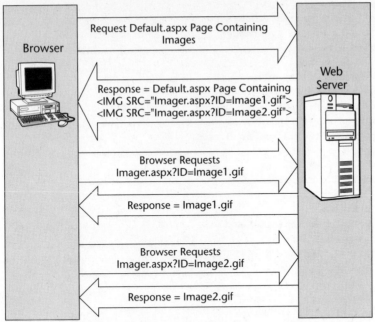

Figure 11.2 The image tags contain a URL to the image. The URL is always the same, but the QueryString is different for each image.

Creating the image engine has many advantages. These advantages become more apparent as more graphics are added to the site. Some advantages are as follows:

Logging.   All requests for images can be logged.

Sizing.   All images can be sized to the same size that the browser will be using to display the image. This lowers the bandwidth requirements by downloading only thumbnails instead large graphics.

Storage.   The images don't need to be stored on the file system. Instead the images may be located in a database.

Building the Image Engine

The first step in building an image engine is to add a Web page to the project. In this example, it will be called Imager.aspx. When you click the HTML tab, all HTML is removed from the page except for the first line, which contains the page directive.

In the code-behind page, the Imports System.IO directive is added to the top of the page to provide access to the File and Path classes. The following code is added to locate an image in the images folder and write the file to the response stream:

```
Private Sub Page_Load( _
        ByVal sender As System.Object, _
        ByVal e As System.EventArgs) _
        Handles MyBase.Load
    Dim ImageID As String
    ImageID = Request("ID").ToString()
    Dim fileLocation As String
    fileLocation = Server.MapPath("images/" + ImageID)
    If Not File.Exists(fileLocation) Then
        Response.Write("Image not found")
        Return
    End If
    'Get extension to use with
    'the MIME content type
    Dim ext As String
    ext = Path.GetExtension(fileLocation)
    ext = ext.Replace(".", "")
    'Ensure that nothing has already been
    'sent to the browser.
    Response.Clear()
    Response.ContentType = "image/" & ext
    Response.WriteFile(fileLocation)
    Response.End()
End Sub
```

This code retrieves the ID from the Request object. The Request("ID")
retrieves the ID, regardless of whether the ID is in the query string or in posted
form data. Next, the code verifies the existence of the file. If the file exists, the
extension is extracted from the file and used to build the MIME ContentType
that is sent to the browser. Finally, the image is written to the browser stream.
It's important to make sure that no other information is sent to the browser.
You do this by executing the Response.Clear and Response.End methods.

You test this code by adding some pictures to the images folder and then
adding image tags to a Web page as follows:

```
<body>
  <form id="Form1" method="post" runat="server"> 
   <img src="imager.aspx?ID=flower3.jpg" >
   <img src="imager.aspx?ID=cat1.jpg" >
  </form>
</body>
```

The images that are being requested are 1,152 pixels by 864 pixels. This presents a problem, because the user's screen may only be 800 pixels by 600 pixels. A simple solution to this problem is to add a width attribute to the image
tags, as shown in the following code:

```
<body >
  <form id="Form1" method="post" runat="server"> 
   <img src="imager.aspx?ID=flower3.jpg" width="300px">
```

```
    <img src="imager.aspx?ID=cat1.jpg" width="300px">
  </form>
</body>
```

Adding these attributes solves the problem of being able to see the images in an 800 x 600 window, as shown in Figure 11.3. The problem with simply setting the width attribute to 300 px is that the large image still downloads to the browser and is scaled at the browser, which uses bandwidth. Displaying the properties of each image reveals that flower3.jpg is 518,484 bytes, and cat1.jpg is 551,831 bytes.

The ideal solution is to have the Web server scale the image appropriately and deliver a smaller file to the browser. This is where the image and bitmap classes can help. The next section covers these classes in detail and presents a solution to this problem.

Image

The Image class is an abstract class that provides the base functionality for the Bitmap and the Imaging.Metafile class. The Image class is located in the System .Drawing.dll file and in the System.Drawing namespace. Don't confuse this with the image that is in the System.Web.UI.WebControls namespace. Confusion can be avoided by adding the following imports statement to the top of the code-behind page:

```
Imports System.Drawing
Imports Image = System.Drawing.Image
```

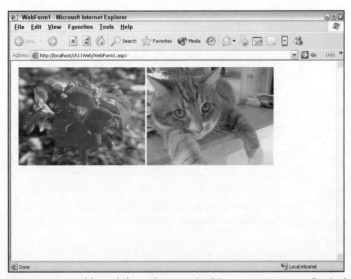

Figure 11.3   Although large images, in this case 800 x 600, fit nicely in the browser window, the complete 1,152 x 864 images are downloaded to the browser.

The second imports statement sets the image to explicitly resolve to the System.Drawing.Image. The properties are shown in Table 11.1.

The methods are shown in Table 11.2.

Although the Bitmap class has many properties and methods, the real power is in the Bitmap class, which is the focus of this section.

 The Image and Bitmap classes that are part of the System.Drawing namespace represent in-memory objects. By themselves, these objects have no visual component. These objects are visible when assigned to a control that will render the object.

Table 11.1 Properties

IMAGE PROPERTIES	DESCRIPTION
Flags	Gets the flags for the current image. The flag will be a member of the System.Drawing.Imaging.ImageFlags enumeration.
FrameDimensionList	This property gets an array of globally unique IDs (GUIDs) that represent the dimensions of frames within the current image. This property is used with images object that contain multiple images in one package, such as animated .gif files, which contain a sequence of images, or images that contain the same image, but at different resolutions.
Height	This property retrieves the height of the image.
HorizontalResolution	This property retrieves the horizontal pixels per inch of the current image.
Palette	This property gets or sets the color palette for the current image.
PhysicalDimension	This property returns a SizeF structure representing the height and width of the current image.
PixelFormat	This property returns a member of the PixelFormat enumeration. There are many formats, but they include indexed color and 32-bit color.
RawFormat	This property returns the ImageFormat of the current image. Some of the Image formats are .bmp, .gif, .icon, .jpeg, .tiff.
Size	This property returns a Size data type, indicating the height and width of the image.
VerticalResolution	This property represents the vertical resolution in pixels per inch.
Width	This property retrieves the width of the current image.

Table 11.2   Methods

IMAGE METHODS	DESCRIPTION
Clone	Creates a deep copy of the image.
FromFile	Static; creates a new images by loading the image from a file.
FromHbitmap	Static; creates a new bitmap by loading the image from a Window handle.
FromStream	Static; creates a new image by loading the image from a stream.
GetBounds	This method returns the bounding rectangle as a RectangleF data type with the specified units.
GetEncoderParameterList	This method returns information about the parameters that are supported by the specified image encoder.
GetFrameCount	This method returns the quantity of frames that are a specified dimension in this image.
GetPixelFormatSize	Static; this method returns the color depth of a specified pixel format.
GetPropertyItem	This method retrieves the specified property item from the image object.
GetThumbnailImage	This property returns an image that represents the thumbnail of the current image, by first looking inside the image to see whether it contains an embedded thumbnail, and then generating a thumbnail image if an embedded one does not exist.
IsAlphaPixelFormat	Static; this method returns true if the image contains alpha information.
IsCanonicalPixelFormat	Static; this method returns true if the pixel's format is known (canonical).
IsExtendedPixelFormat	Static; this method returns true if the pixel's format is extended.
RemovePropertyItem	This method removes a property from the image.
RotateFlip	This method rotates or flips the current image.
Save	This method saves the current image to a file or stream.
SaveAdd	This method can be used to add information from the specified image to the current image and then save it. The EncoderParameters determine how the information is incorporated into the image.

Bitmap

The Bitmap class is derived from the Image class. The Bitmap class has all of the properties and methods that the Image class has, plus a few more methods. Table 11.3 lists the additional methods that the Bitmap class has. In addition, the Bitmap class has several constructors that simplify the creation of a bitmap.

Using the Bitmap Class to Resize an Image

The image engine needs the ability to resize the image that is being retrieved from the disk file. This resizing is done by using the Bitmap's constructor, which allows the bitmap to be resized as the object is being created.

The image engine needs to be flexible enough to be able to respond to requests for different sized images, so the source of the image tags will be changed to include a width as follows:

```
<body >
  <form id="Form1" method="post" runat="server"> 
   <img src="imager.aspx?ID=flower1.jpg&Width=300" width="300px" >
   <img src="imager.aspx?ID=cat1.jpg&Width=300" width="300px">
  </form>
</body>
```

Table 11.3 Bitmap Methods

BITMAP METHOD	DESCRIPTION
FromHIcon	Static; this method creates a bitmap from a Windows handle to an icon.
FromResource	Static; this method creates a bitmap from the specified Windows resource.
GetHBitmap	This method creates an HBITMAP from the image. The Windows.DeleteObject(handle) must be called to deallocate the bitmap.
GetHIcon	This method returns the handle to an icon.
GetPixel	This method gets the color of the specified pixel in the current bitmap.
LockBits	This method locks the bitmap into the system memory.
MakeTransparent	This method passes a color to be marked as the transparent color for the bitmap.
SetPixel	This method sets the color of the specified pixel in the current bitmap.

Table 11.3   *(continued)*

BITMAP METHOD	DESCRIPTION
SetResolution	This method sets the resolution for the current bitmap.
UnlockBits	This method unlocks the bitmap from the system memory.

In the Imager code-behind page, the Page_Load method is modified to resize the bitmap, based on the width or height that is supplied. The following code loads an image from the file, determines whether the width or height are specified, and then calculates any unassigned values based on maintaining the image proportions.

```
Private Sub Page_Load( _
        ByVal sender As System.Object, _
        ByVal e As System.EventArgs) _
        Handles MyBase.Load
    Dim ImageID As String
    If Request("ID") is nothing then
        Return
    else
        ImageID = Request("ID").ToString()
    End if
    Dim fileLocation As String
    fileLocation = Server.MapPath("images/" + ImageID)
    If Not File.Exists(fileLocation) Then
        Response.Write("Image not found")
        Return
    End If
    Dim i As Image = Image.FromFile(fileLocation)
    Dim newWidth As Integer = 0
    Dim newHeight As Integer = 0
    If Not Request("Width") Is Nothing Then
        newWidth = CType(Request("Width"), Integer)
    End If
    If Not Request("Height") Is Nothing Then
        newHeight = CType(Request("Height"), Integer)
    End If
    If (newWidth = 0) And (newHeight = 0) Then
        newWidth = i.Width
        newHeight = i.Height
    End If
    If newWidth = 0 Then
        newWidth = (i.Width * newHeight) / i.Height
    End If
    If newHeight = 0 Then
        newHeight = (i.Height * newWidth) / i.Width
    End If
```

```
        Dim b As New Bitmap(i, newWidth, newHeight)
        'Ensure that nothing has already been
        'sent to the browser.
        Response.Clear()
        Response.ContentType = "image/jpg"
        b.Save(Response.OutputStream, Imaging.ImageFormat.Jpeg)
        Response.End()
    End Sub
```

After the new dimensions are calculated, the bitmap is created, based on the existing image and the new sizes. You can save the Save method of the bitmap to a stream, which allows the bitmap to transfer the data straight to the response's OutputStream without requiring the bitmap to be saved to a file first. The preceding code also calls the Save method, which requires an image format parameter. Regardless of the type of file that was loaded, the bitmap may be saved as a .jpeg to the stream.

The browser output looks the same as the output shown in Figure 11.3, but the size of the files has changed. The flower3.jpg properties reveal that the image size is 12,991 bytes, and cat1.jpg is 13,305 bytes. This represents a significant change in size and bandwidth usage.

 This example uses the constructor of the Bitmap class to generate a resized image. Careful examination of the Image class will reveal that there is a GetThumbnail method. If the GetThumbnail method is used, an attempt is made to go to the original stream or file to see whether the image contains any embedded thumbnails of the requested size. If no thumbnail exists, one is created. The problem is that the stream must be left open for this method to operate properly. If the stream is closed, the program crashes. It may be better to always use the Bitmap's constructor to build the thumbnail on the fly.

Uploading Images to a Database

The previous chapter covered file uploading with the File Field control. In the data access chapter, saving data to the database was covered. In this section, many of the previous topics are combined to enable users to upload images to a database.

In this example a new page is added, called ImageView.aspx. This page has an HTML File Field, called UploadImage, as a server control. The encoding attribute must be set on the form to allow file uploads. Finally, an Upload button is placed on the form, which causes the file to be uploaded to the Web server, and a title is placed on the form. The HTML looks like the following. (See Figure 11.4.)

Figure 11.4 The Web page in the browser.

```
<form id="Form1" method="post"
        enctype="multipart/form-data"  runat="server">
    <P align=center>
        <FONT face="Comic Sans MS" size="7">
        <STRONG>My Photo Gallery</STRONG>
        </FONT></P>
    <P align=center>
        <INPUT type="file"
            id=UploadImage name=UploadImage
            runat="server"> 
        <asp:Button id=" btnUpload"
            runat="server" Text="Upload"
            Width="75px" Height="23px">
        </asp:Button></P>
    <P align=center> </P>
    <P> </P>
</form>
```

To store images in the database, a table must be created to hold the data. In this example, the table is created in the Northwind database. It is called Image-Gallery and contains the fields shown in Table 11.4.

Table 11.4 Fileds in ImageGallery

FIELD NAME	DATA TYPE
ImageID	Int; identity (auto number)
ImageName	varChar(255)
ImageType	VarChar(255)
ImageData	Image

The SQL script to create the table and primary key looks like the following:

```
CREATE TABLE [dbo].[ImageGallery] (
    [ImageID] [int] IDENTITY (1, 1) NOT NULL ,
    [ImageName] [varchar] (255) NOT NULL ,
    [ImageType] [varchar] (255) NOT NULL ,
    [ImageData] [image] NOT NULL
) ON [PRIMARY] TEXTIMAGE_ON [PRIMARY]
```

The btnUpload's click method contains code to add the image to the database. The code checks to see whether a file has been posted. The code then retrieves the uploaded file data, such as the filename, content type, content length, and a reference to the InputStream.

A memory stream is created to retrieve the uploaded file. A loop is created to continue reading the InputStream into the MemoryStream until the file has finished uploading.

After the file is uploaded, a SQL Server connection is created to connect to the local Northwind database. A new SQL command, which inserts the data into the ImageGallery table, is created. SQL parameters are created, and the command is executed using the ExecuteNonQuery method. The code is as follows:

```
Private Sub btnUpload_Click( _
        ByVal sender As System.Object, _
        ByVal e As System.EventArgs) _
        Handles btnUpload.Click
    If UploadImage.PostedFile Is Nothing Then
        Response.Write("No file uploaded.<br>")
        Return
    End If
    Dim imageStream As Stream = UploadImage.PostedFile.InputStream
    Dim imageLength As Integer = UploadImage.PostedFile.ContentLength
    Dim imageType As String = UploadImage.PostedFile.ContentType
    Dim imageName As String
    imageName = Path.GetFileName(UploadImage.PostedFile.FileName)
    Dim mStream As New MemoryStream()
    Dim imageData(1024) As Byte
    Dim count As Integer = imageData.Length
    count = imageStream.Read(imageData, 0, imageData.Length)
    Do While count > 0
        mStream.Write(imageData, 0, count)
        count = imageStream.Read(imageData, 0, imageData.Length)
    Loop
    Dim sqlConnect As String
    sqlConnect = "server=.;database=northwind;Trusted_Connection=true"
    Dim cn As New SqlConnection(sqlConnect)
    Dim sqlCmd As String
```

```
      sqlCmd = "insert into ImageGallery(imageName,imageType,imageData)"
      sqlCmd &= " values ( @imageName, @imageType, @imageData )"
      Dim cmd As New SqlCommand(sqlCmd, cn)
      cmd.Parameters.Add("@imageName", imageName)
      cmd.Parameters.Add("@imageType", imageType)
      cmd.Parameters.Add("@imageData", mStream.GetBuffer())
      cn.Open()
      cmd.ExecuteNonQuery()
      cn.Close()
  End Sub
```

Figure 11.5 shows the SQL server view of the ImageGallery table after uploading several images to the server.

Retrieving Images from the Database

Just as images can be saved to the database server, they can also be retrieved from the database. This section uses most of the topics that were covered in previous chapters to display images in the browser.

The images will be displayed as thumbnail image in a DataList control on the ImageGallery.aspx page. If an image is clicked, a new browser window will open with the full-sized image.

The Imager.aspx image engine needs to be modified to retrieve data from the database instead of the file system. You make this modification by adding another item, called Source, to the query string. Source is set to DB to specify that it is retrieving data from the database. If the Source is DB, a SQL Server connection is created, and a command is executed to retrieve the imageType and imageData for the imageID that was requested. Then, the image that was originally populated from a file is populated from a MemoryStream that represents the imageData field. The file access should still operate. The following code shows the changes to the Imager code-behind page:

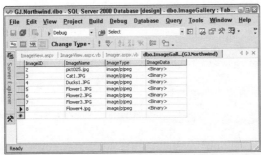

Figure 11.5   The ImageGallery table reveals that several images were successfully uploaded.

```vb
Sub Page_Load( _
        ByVal sender As System.Object, _
        ByVal e As System.EventArgs) _
        Handles MyBase.Load
    'Ensure that nothing as already been
    'sent to the browser.
    Response.Clear()
    Dim ImageID As String
    If Request("ID") Is Nothing Then
        Return
    Else
        ImageID = Request("ID").ToString()
    End If
    Dim i As Image
    Dim fileLocation As String
    If Not Request("Source") Is Nothing Then
        If (String.Compare( _
        Request("Source").ToString(), _
        "DB", True) = 0) Then
            'Retrive from DB
            Dim sqlConnect As String
            sqlConnect = _
        "server=.;database=northwind;Trusted_Connection=true"
            Dim cn As New SqlConnection(sqlConnect)
            Dim sqlCmd As String
            sqlCmd = _
            "Select imageType, imageData from ImageGallery where "
            sqlCmd &= " imageID = @imageID"
            Dim cmd As New SqlCommand(sqlCmd, cn)
            cmd.Parameters.Add("@imageID", ImageID)
            cn.Open()
            Dim dr As SqlDataReader = cmd.ExecuteReader()
            If Not dr.Read() Then
                Response.Write("Image not found")
                Return
            End If
            Response.ContentType = dr("imageType").ToString()
            Dim mStream As MemoryStream
            Dim byteData() As Byte
            byteData = dr("imageData")
            mStream = New MemoryStream(byteData)
            cn.Close()
            i = Image.FromStream(mStream)
        Else
            Response.Write("Unknown source")
            Return
        End If
    Else
        'Retrieve from file
        fileLocation = Server.MapPath("images/" + ImageID)
        If Not File.Exists(fileLocation) Then
            Response.Write("Image not found")
```

```
                Return
            End If
            i = Image.FromFile(fileLocation)
            Response.ContentType = "image/jpg"
        End If
        'Common items
        Dim newWidth As Integer = 0
        Dim newHeight As Integer = 0
        If Not Request("Width") Is Nothing Then
            newWidth = CType(Request("Width"), Integer)
        End If
        If Not Request("Height") Is Nothing Then
            newHeight = CType(Request("Height"), Integer)
        End If
        Dim b As Bitmap
        If (newWidth = 0) And (newHeight = 0) Then
            b = New Bitmap(i)
        Else
            If newWidth = 0 Then
                newWidth = (i.Width * newHeight) / i.Height
            End If
            If newHeight = 0 Then
                newHeight = (i.Height * newWidth) / i.Width
            End If
            b = New Bitmap(i, newWidth, newHeight)
        End If
        b.Save(Response.OutputStream, Imaging.ImageFormat.Jpeg)
        Response.End()
End Sub
```

The HTML of the ImageView.aspx page needs to be changed to provide a DataList containing thumbnail images from the database, along with the image-Name. The images will be 150 pixels wide, but may be different heights to maintain the proportion of the original image. To accommodate the different heights and place the image name neatly under the image, an HTML table containing a row for the image and a row for the imageName is placed inside the ItemTemplate of the DataList. The height of the image row is fixed at 125 pixels, and the height of the image name row is fixed at 25 pixels.

The image and the image name are inside hyperlink (<a>) tags, which have the target set to _blank_. Setting the target to _blank causes a new browser window to open, containing the image. Notice that no size is set for the image that is to be displayed in the new window. This allows the image to be delivered to the browser at full size.

The image is displayed using an IMG tag. The source of the image tag is set to the Imager.aspx page, passing the ID of the image, a Source of DB, and a Width of 150 pixels. The following code shows the ImageView.aspx page:

```
<form id="Form1" method="post"
    enctype="multipart/form-data"  runat="server">
```

```
      <P align=center>
            <FONT face="Comic Sans MS" size="7">
            <STRONG>My Photo Gallery</STRONG>
            </FONT></P>
      <P align=center>
            <INPUT type="file"
                  id=UploadImage name=UploadImage
                  runat="server"> 
            <asp:Button id="btnUpload"
                  runat="server" Text="Upload"
                  Width="75px" Height="23px">
            </asp:Button></P>
      <P align=center> </P>
      <P align=center>
<asp:DataList id="DataList1" runat="server"
      RepeatDirection="Horizontal" RepeatColumns="4">
<ItemTemplate>
      <table><tr><td height="125px">
      <A href='Imager.aspx?ID=<%#
            container.dataitem("ImageID") %>&amp;Source=DB'
            target="_blank">
      <IMG src='Imager.aspx?ID=<%#
            container.dataitem("ImageID") %>&amp;Source=DB&amp;Width=125'
            border="0"></a></td></tr>
      <tr><td height="25px">
      <A href='Imager.aspx?ID=<%#
            container.dataitem("ImageID") %>&amp;Source=DB'
            target="_blank">
      <%# container.dataitem("ImageName") %></a></td></tr>
      </table>
</asp:DataList></P>
</form>
```

The ImageView code-behind page needs to be modified to retrieve the image data from the ImageGallery table. This code is a simple database query for the imageID and imageName fields. Note that the imageData is not required here, because the Web browser calls the Imager.aspx page to get the imageData. The following code contains the changes to the code-behind page. Figure 11.6 shows the final Web page.

```
Private Sub Page_Load( _
            ByVal sender As System.Object, _
            ByVal e As System.EventArgs) _
            Handles MyBase.Load
      If Not Page.IsPostBack Then
            BindData()
      End If
End Sub
Public Sub BindData()
      Dim sqlConnect As String
      sqlConnect = "server=.;database=northwind;Trusted_Connection=true"
```

```
            Dim cn As New SqlConnection(sqlConnect)
            Dim sqlCmd As String
            sqlCmd = "Select ImageID,ImageName from ImageGallery"
            Dim cmd As New SqlCommand(sqlCmd, cn)
            Dim da As New SqlDataAdapter(cmd)
            Dim dt As New DataTable("ImageGallery")
            da.Fill(dt)
            DataList1.DataSource = dt
            DataBind()
    End Sub
    Private Sub btnUpload_Click( _
            ByVal sender As System.Object, _
            ByVal e As System.EventArgs) _
            Handles btnUpload.Click
        'Existing code from previous example
        DataBind()
    End Sub
```

The final Web page displays the populated DataList control, and still allows new images to be uploaded. Click the image or the image name to view the full-sized photo in a new browser window, as shown in Figure 11.7.

This really is just the beginning of working with Images in a database. Some things that should be added include the ability to delete images, allow flipping and rotating, a check to see whether the filename already exists, and caching of the images. Chapter 14 covers caching in detail, and this application is used to perform baseline testing. The sidebar titled, *Retrieving Existing Images from the Northwind Database,* also describes the method for retrieving the images that contain OLE header information, such as the images that are stored in the Employees table of the Northwind database.

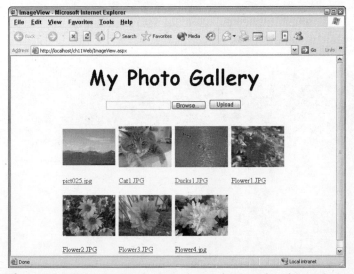

Figure 11.6   The final Web page shows the populated DataList control.

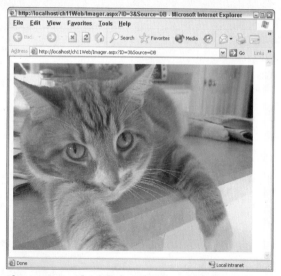

Figure 11.7 The full-sized photo, which was opened in a new window when the thumbnail was clicked. The URL is for the Imager.aspx page, and the proper ID and Source are included.

♦ Retrieving Existing Images from the Northwind Database

The code to upload and retrieve images works fine in new scenarios. This code doesn't seem to work with the existing images in the Northwind database.

The existing images were saved from within Microsoft Access and contain OLE header information. To disregard the header information, the first 78 bytes (0–77) of data must be skipped.

Besides changing the query to retrieve the pictures from the appropriate table, the code needs to change to ignore the first 78 bytes, as shown in the following example:

```
Dim mStream As MemoryStream
Dim byteData() As Byte
byteData = dr("imageData")
mStream = New MemoryStream(byteData)
mStream = New MemoryStream( byteData, 78, byteData.Length - 78)
```

The MemoryStream in this example contains only the picture, which is a .bmp file. The MemoryStream can be assigned directly to the Image object. Because these embedded files were originally .bmp files, the bitmap's Save method must include the .gif or .jpeg format to be viewable in most browsers.

GDI+

The first part of this chapter dealt with the storage and retrieval of existing images. There was very little manipulation of the image, except to create the thumbnail image.

This section explores the creation of an image on the fly, covering several of the help types, then pen and brushes, and finally fonts.

GDI+ Helper Data Types

GDI+ contains several helper types that you will use extensively. In most cases, there are two versions of the helper type. One version has a letter F suffix, which indicates that this version uses floating-point numbers. The floating-point types are desirable in situations where precision is important. This book attempts to list the floating-point types, but uses only the standard versions of these classes.

Point/PointF

The Point is a structure used to identify an x and y location in a two-dimensional plane. The Point has X and Y properties, and methods for converting PointF objects to Point objects. The operators are overloaded to provide the ability to add Point and Size instances, and check Point instances for equality. There are several ways to create a new Point, but the most common method is as follows:

```
Dim myLocation As New Point(10, 20)
```

In this case, 10 is the x coordinate and 20 is the y coordinate.

Rectangle/RectangleF

The Rectangle is a structure that is used to define a rectangular region. The Rectangle consists of an origin point and a size, which is the width and height of the rectangle.

You can create a Rectangle object by specifying the origin and size, or by specifying the X, Z, width, and height as four integers when creating the Rectangle.

The Rectangle provides many functions, such as the ability to inflate union, intersect, and check for equality. Also some methods for converting RectangleF to Rectangle are included.

Size/SizeF

The Size is a structure that is used to define a width and height of a rectangular region. The Size provides methods to test for equality, and to convert from SizeF to Size. Methods are also provided to add and subtract Size instances.

Color

The Color is a structure that represents a color in terms of its Alpha, Red, Green, and Blue byte values (ARGB). The Alpha component refers to the opacity of the color, where 255 is the most opaque, and 0 is transparent.

The Color has static properties that represent many of the colors that are available by name. You create a Color by using the following code:

```
Dim myColor As Color = Color.Red
```

The Color also has methods for creating a color from different color types.

Pen

All drawing requires a Pen object, a Brush object, or both. The Pen is used to draw lines and curves. The Pen class is not inheritable or serializable.

Brush

The Brush is an abstract class. A brush is used to fill regions. To create a brush, you must use one of the classes that inherits from the Brush class, such as SolidBrush, TextureBrush, or LinearGradientBrush. The Brush class is not serializable.

Graphics

The Graphics class is the class that provides all the methods necessary for drawing on a device. The device may be a visible or invisible window. The Graphics object is related to the handle to a device context (HDC) that GDI used in the past, except that the GDI+ Graphics object encapsulates this low-level functionality.

When a Graphics object is created, it is associated with a Window (WinForms) or an object that will be rendered, such as a bitmap. No drawing can occur until a valid Graphics instance has been obtained.

The Graphics class provides many properties, as shown in Table 11.5.

Table 11.5   The Graphics Class Properties

GRAPHICS PROPERTY	DESCRIPTION
Clip	This changeable Region object can be used to limit the drawing region of this Graphics object.
ClipBounds	This read only RectangleF structure defines the bounds of the clipping region of this Graphics object.
CompositingMode	This read-only value specifies how composite images are drawn to this Graphics object.
CompositingQuality	This changeable value represents the rendering quality of composite images drawn to this Graphics object.
DpiX	This read-only value represents the horizontal resolution of this Graphics object.
DpiY	This read-only value represents the vertical resolution of this Graphics object.
InterpolationMode	This changeable value represents the interpolation mode associated with this Graphics object.
IsClipEmpty	This read-only value represents a value indicating whether the clipping region of this Graphics object is empty.
IsVisibleClipEmpty	This read-only value represents a value indicating whether the visible clipping region of this Graphics object is empty.
PageScale	This changeable value represents the scaling between world units and page units for this Graphics object.
PageUnit	This changeable value represents the unit of measure used for page coordinates in this Graphics object.
PixelOffsetMode	This changeable value represents a value specifying how pixels are offset during rendering of this Graphics object.
RenderingOrigin	This changeable value represents the rendering origin of this Graphics object for dithering and for hatch brushes.
SmoothingMode	This changeable value represents the rendering quality for this Graphics object.

(continued)

Table 11.5 *(continued)*

GRAPHICS PROPERTY	DESCRIPTION
TextContrast	This changeable value represents the gamma correction value for rendering text.
TextRenderingHint	This changeable value represents the rendering mode for text associated with this Graphics object.
Transform	This changeable value represents the world transformation for this Graphics object.
VisibleClipBounds	This changeable value represents the bounding rectangle of the visible clipping region of this Graphics object.

The Graphics class also provides the methods shown in Table 11.6.

Table 11.6 The Graphics Class Methods

GRAPHICS METHOD	DESCRIPTION
AddMetafileComment	Adds a comment to the current Metafile object.
BeginContainer	Saves a graphics container with the current state of this Graphics object and opens and uses a new graphics container.
Clear	Clears the entire drawing surface and fills it with the specified background color.
Dispose	Releases all resources used by this Graphics object.
DrawArc	Draws an arc representing a portion of an ellipse specified by a pair of coordinates, a width, and a height.
DrawBezier	Draws a Bézier spline defined by four point structures.
DrawBeziers	Draws a series of Bézier splines from an array of point structures.
DrawClosedCurve	Draws a closed cardinal spline defined by an array of point structures.
DrawCurve	Draws a cardinal spline through a specified array of point structures.
DrawEllipse	Draws an ellipse defined by a bounding rectangle specified by a pair of coordinates, a height, and a width.

Table 11.6 *(continued)*

GRAPHICS METHOD	DESCRIPTION
DrawIcon	Draws the image represented by the specified Icon object at the specified coordinates.
DrawIconUnstretched	Draws the image represented by the specified Icon object without scaling the image.
DrawImage	Draws the specified Image object at the specified location and with the original size.
DrawImageUnscaled	Draws the specified Image object with its original size at the location specified by a coordinate pair.
DrawLine	Draws a line connecting the two points specified by coordinate pairs.
DrawLines	Draws a series of line segments that connect an array of point structures.
DrawPath	Draws a GraphicsPath object.
DrawPie	Draws a pie shape defined by an ellipse specified by a coordinate pair, a width, a height, and two radial lines.
DrawPolygon	Draws a polygon defined by an array of point structures.
DrawRectangle	Draws a rectangle specified by a coordinate pair, a width, and a height.
DrawRectangles	Draws a series of rectangles specified by rectangle structures.
DrawString	Draws the specified text string at the specified location with the specified Brush and Font objects.
EndContainer	Closes the current graphic container and restores the state of this Graphic object to the state saved by a call to the BeginContainer method.
EnumerateMetafile	Sends the records in the specified Metafile object, one at a time, to a callback method for display at a specified point.
ExcludeClip	Updates the clip region of this Graphics object to exclude the area specified by a rectangle structure.
FillClosedCurve	Fills the interior with a closed cardinal spline curve defined by an array of point structures.

(continued)

Table 11.6 *(continued)*

GRAPHICS METHOD	DESCRIPTION
FillEllipse	Fills the interior of an ellipse defined by a bounding rectangle specified by a pair of coordinates, a width, and a height.
FillPath	Fills the interior of a GraphicsPath object.
FillPie	Fills the interior of a pie section defined by an ellipse specified by a pair of coordinates, a width, and a height and two radial lines.
FillPolygon	Fills the interior of a polygon defined by an array of points specified by point structures.
FillRectangle	Fills the interior of a rectangle specified by a pair of coordinates, a width, and a height.
FillRectangles	Fills the interiors of a series of rectangles specified by rectangle structures.
Flush	Forces execution of all pending graphics operations and returns immediately without waiting for the operations to finish.
FromHdc	Creates a new Graphics object from the specified handle to a device context.
FromHwnd	Creates a new Graphics object from the specified handle to a window.
FromImage	Creates a new Graphics object from the specified Image object.
GetHalftonePalette	Gets a handle to the current Windows halftone palette.
GetHdc	Gets the handle to the device context associated with this Graphics object.
GetNearestColor	Gets the nearest color to the specified Color structure.
IntersectClip	Updates the clip region of this Graphics object to the intersection of the current clip region and the specified rectangle structure.
IsVisible	Indicates whether the point specified by a pair of coordinates is contained within the visible clip region of this Graphics object.
MeasureCharacterRanges	Gets an array of Region objects, each of which bounds a range of character positions within the specified string.

Table 11.6 *(continued)*

GRAPHICS METHOD	DESCRIPTION
MeasureString	Measures the specified string when it is drawn with the specified Font object.
MultiplyTransform	Multiplies the world transformation of this Graphics object and specified the Matrix object.
ReleaseHdc	Releases a device context handle obtained by a previous call to the GetHdc method of this Graphics object.
ResetClip	Resets the clip region of this Graphics object to an infinite region.
ResetTransform	Resets the world transformation matrix of this Graphics object to the identity matrix.
Restore	Restores the state of this Graphics object to the state represented by a GraphicsState object.
RotateTransform	Applies the specified rotation to the transformation matrix of this Graphics object.
Save	Saves the current state of this Graphics object and identifies the saved state with a GraphicsState object.
ScaleTransform	Applies the specified scaling operation to the transformation matrix of this Graphics object by prepending it to the object's transformation matrix.
SetClip	Sets the clipping region of this Graphics object to the Clip property of the specified Graphics object.
TransformPoints	Transforms an array of points from one coordinate space to another, using the current world and page transformations of this Graphics object.
TranslateClip	Translates the clipping region of this Graphics object by specified amounts in the horizontal and vertical directions.
TranslateTransform	Prepends the specified translation to the transformation matrix of this Graphics object.

Drawing an Image on the Fly

This example shows how to create an image on the fly and send it to the browser. In previous image examples, a second page was used to render and deliver the image to the browser. In this example, one page is used to create an image on the fly, as shown in Figure 11.8.

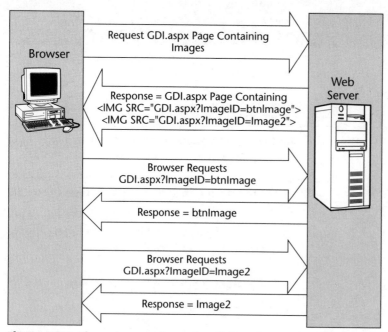

Figure 11.8 The same page is used to deliver the HTML content and the images. Notice that there are three calls to the page: one call for the HTML and a call for each of the images.

Code in the Page_Load method allows the browser to make a call to the same page to retrieve any images that the page has created. The following code handles a request for an image that was built and saved as a Session variable. This code should be ahead of any other code in the Page_Load method:

```
Priv ate Sub Page_Load( _
        ByVal sender As System.Object, _
        ByVal e As System.EventArgs) _
        Handles MyBase.Load
    If Not Request("ImageID") Is Nothing Then
        If Not Session(Request("ImageID")) Is Nothing Then
            Dim b As Bitmap
            b = CType(Session(Request("ImageID")), Bitmap)
            Response.Clear()
            Response.ContentType = "image/jpeg"
            b.Save(Response.OutputStream, ImageFormat.Jpeg)
            Response.End()
            Return
        End If
    End If
    'More code goes here...
End Sub
```

This code checks to see whether the Request object has an ImageID. If so, the image is retrieved from a session variable, and the image is saved to the response stream, then the response is ended. Remember that this portion of code should operate only when the browser tries to render an image, and the image's URL is the name of this page, plus "?ImageID=Image1". A normal request for this page doesn't have the ImageID information.

With the delivery code in place, it's time to create an image. This example starts by creating a blank image and placing the image into an ImageButton control called btnImage.

After the image is created, code is added to draw lines from each point on the image that the user clicks. The following code creates a blank image in the Page's PreRender method:

```
Private Sub Page_PreRender( _
        ByVal sender As Object, _
        ByVal e As System.EventArgs) _
        Handles MyBase.PreRender
    Dim bmp As New Bitmap(700, 350)
    Dim bmpGraphics As Graphics
    bmpGraphics = Graphics.FromImage(bmp)
    bmpGraphics.Clear(Color.Yellow)
    Session("btnImage") = bmp
    btnImage.ImageUrl = Request.ServerVariables("SCRIPT_NAME") _
     & "?ImageID=btnImage"
End Sub
```

This code creates an instance of the Bitmap class that represents a bitmap that will be 700 pixels high by 350 pixels wide. After the bitmap is created, a Graphics object that handles drawing in the bitmap must be obtained. The Graphics object is used to clear the bitmap with the color yellow.

The bitmap must be saved to a Session variable, which allows the browser to make a request to this page for the stored image. Finally, the ImageButton control is assigned a URL for the image, which is the URL to this page, but the URL includes the "?ImageID=btnImage" request.

Adding Drawing Code

In this section, code is added to the btnImage's click event method. Instead of drawing the image in this routine, the location of the click is simply added into a points array called DrawPoints. DrawPoints is then saved to a SessionVariable called Session("DrawPoints"). Notice the use of UBound, which retrieves the upper boundary of the array. The array uses this number to redimension the array, adding an extra element. This variable is retrieved during the PreRender method, and is used to build the bitmap. The code is as follows:

```
Private Sub btnImage_Click( _
        ByVal sender As System.Object, _
        ByVal e As System.Web.UI.ImageClickEventArgs) _
        Handles btnImage.Click
    Dim DrawPoints() As Point
    If Session("DrawPoints") Is Nothing Then
        DrawPoints = New Point() {New Point(e.X, e.Y)}
    Else
        DrawPoints = CType(Session("DrawPoints"), Point())
        ReDim Preserve DrawPoints(UBound(DrawPoints) + 1)
        DrawPoints(UBound(DrawPoints)) = New Point(e.X, e.Y)
    End If
    Session("DrawPoints") = DrawPoints
End Sub
```

The PreRender code needs to be modified to include drawing lines to connect the points that were clicked. The first time that the user clicks, there is not enough information to be able to draw a line, so a dot is placed where the first click took place. Additional clicks cause lines to be added, drawing from point to point. The modified PreRender code is as follows:

```
Private Sub Page_PreRender( _
        ByVal sender As Object, _
        ByVal e As System.EventArgs) _
        Handles MyBase.PreRender
    Dim bmp As New Bitmap(700, 350)
    Dim bmpGraphics As Graphics
    bmpGraphics = Graphics.FromImage(bmp)
    bmpGraphics.Clear(Color.Yellow)
    Dim DrawPoints() As Point
    If Not Session("DrawPoints") Is Nothing Then
        DrawPoints = CType(Session("DrawPoints"), Point())
        If DrawPoints.Length = 1 Then
            bmpGraphics.DrawEllipse(New Pen(Color.Blue, 3), _
            DrawPoints(0).X, DrawPoints(0).Y, 3, 3)
        Else
            bmpGraphics.DrawLines(New Pen(Color.Blue), DrawPoints)
        End If
    End If
    Session("btnImage") = bmp
    btnImage.ImageUrl = Request.ServerVariables("SCRIPT_NAME") _
        & "?ImageID=btnImage"
End Sub
```

Figure 11.9 shows the browser output after clicking various places on the btnImage control. Notice the use of the DrawEllipse method to draw a dot on the screen. The Graphics' draw methods typically require a pen or brush. The

DrawEllipse requires a pen, so a new blue pen is created. To make sure that the dot is visible, the pen's width is set to 3. The height and width of the ellipse are also set to 3. If the array contains at least two points, the DrawLines method is executed. This method draws a line from point to point, using the specified pen.

Some items that could be added are a DropDownList for the line color, a pen width setting, and a button to clear the array and start over.

Fonts

The .NET Framework provides support for working with fonts. This support carries over to ASP.NET. This section explores some of the font classes, and contains sample code for creating bitmaps containing text created on the fly.

FontFamilies

FontFamilies define a group of typefaces that have a distinct design, but may have variations, such as size, and FontStyles, such as bold and italic. A typical FontFamily is Arial, and another one is Courier. The FontFamilies class has a GetFamilies method, which returns an array of the FontFamily objects supported by a given Graphics context.

Figure 11.9   The browser output when creating lines by clicking the btnImage control.

Font Metrics

When working with fonts, the font measurements are relative to the baseline, which is an imaginary line that all characters sit on. Characters such as *g, q, j,* and *y* drop below the baseline. The distance to the bottom of these characters is called the *descent*. Characters such as *a, e, o,* and *u* rise above the baseline to an imaginary line called the *ascent*. Uppercase characters, such as the *M, N, S,* and *O* rise higher to another imaginary line. The distance from the ascent to the top of the uppercase characters is called the *leading* distance. Figure 11.10 shows these font metrics.

Fonts

Before you can draw any text to a bitmap, you must create an instance of the Font class. The font is created from one of the FontFamilies and has a size and style.

Creating a Text Bitmap on the Fly

This example shows how to create a text bitmap on the fly and send it to the browser. This process is useful when a complex graphical menu has been created, and you need to write text on an existing bitmap, or supply a new bitmap with text.

Another common use for this feature occurs when a Web site allows a new account to be created, and the Web administrator wants to ensure that an account can't be programmatically created. Imagine the problems that a hacker could cause by creating a program that adds millions of new users to someone's Web application. A unique ID can be generated and placed on a bitmap image, and the user would be prompted to read the ID and type it into a form for verification that the account is being created by a person. The bitmap could even have random lines through the image, just to make it more difficult for the would-be hacker.

This page in this example contains several DropDownList boxes that will be populated by enumerating colors and FontFamilies. Figure 11.11 shows the Web page containing the controls. The DropDownList boxes and the TextBox have AutoPostBack turned on, which causes the bitmap to regenerate each time a change is made.

Figure 11.10   The font metrics.

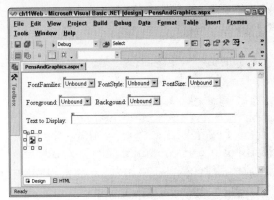

Figure 11.11   The Web page in Design mode.

The Page's Load event method is similar to the previous example, except that it also includes code to populate the DropDownList boxes.

```
Private Sub Page_Load( _
        ByVal sender As System.Object, _
        ByVal e As System.EventArgs) _
        Handles MyBase.Load
    If Not Request("ImageID") Is Nothing Then
        If Not Session(Request("ImageID")) Is Nothing Then
            Dim b As Bitmap
            b = CType(Session(Request("ImageID")), Bitmap)
            Response.Clear()
            Response.ContentType = "image/jpeg"
            b.Save(Response.OutputStream, ImageFormat.Jpeg)
            Response.End()
            Return
        End If
    End If
    If Not Page.IsPostBack Then
        LoadColors(drpForeground)
        LoadColors(drpBackground)
        LoadFamily(drpFontFamily)
        LoadFontStyles(drpFontStyle)
        LoadFontSizes(drpFontSize)
        'Set defaults.
        TextBox1.Text = "Type some text into the text box."
        Dim i As ListItem
        i = drpForeground.Items.FindByText("Red")
        drpForeground.SelectedIndex = drpForeground.Items.IndexOf(i)
        i = drpBackground.Items.FindByText("Silver")
        drpBackground.SelectedIndex = drpBackground.Items.IndexOf(i)
        i = drpFontFamily.Items.FindByText("Arial")
        drpFontFamily.SelectedIndex = drpFontFamily.Items.IndexOf(i)
        i = drpFontStyle.Items.FindByText("Bold")
```

```
        drpFontStyle.SelectedIndex = drpFontStyle.Items.IndexOf(i)
        i = drpFontSize.Items.FindByText("24")
        drpFontSize.SelectedIndex = drpFontSize.Items.IndexOf(i)
    End If
End Sub
```

The first part of this code delivers the bitmap to the browser. The second part of the code populates the DropDownList boxes and then sets a default value for each of them. Setting the default value is done by executing the Find-ByText method, which returns a ListItem object containing the default item. After that, the IndexOf method executes to retrieve the index of the ListItem and assigns it to the SelectedIndex of the DropDownList.

Enumerating the Colors

To enumerate the list of colors, you can use the System.Enum class to execute the GetNames method. This procedure returns an array of strings, which you can use to populate the DropDownList:

```
Public Sub LoadColors(ByVal ddl As DropDownList)
    Dim n As String
    For Each n In System.Enum.GetNames(GetType(KnownColor))
        ddl.Items.Add(n)
    Next
End Sub
```

Enumerating the FontFamilies

To enumerate the list of FontFamilies, you can create a temporary bitmap with the Graphics class. The FontFamily has a static method called GetFamilies, which requires a valid Graphics object. This method returns an array of the FontFamilies available when you are working with Bitmap objects. You enumerate the array and add the FontFamilies to the DropDownList as follows:

```
Public Sub LoadFamily(ByVal ddl As DropDownList)
    Dim fFamily As FontFamily
    Dim b As New Bitmap(1, 1)
    Dim g As Graphics = Graphics.FromImage(b)
    Dim arFamily() As FontFamily = FontFamily.GetFamilies(g)
    For Each fFamily In arFamily
        ddl.Items.Add(fFamily.Name)
    Next
End Sub
```

Enumerating the FontStyles

Enumerating the FontStyles is similar to enumerating the colors as previously described. The System.Enum class can be used to get the names of the items in an enumeration.

```
Public Sub LoadFontStyles(ByVal ddl As DropDownList)
    Dim n As String
    For Each n In System.Enum.GetNames(GetType(FontStyle))
        ddl.Items.Add(n)
    Next
End Sub
```

Loading the Font Sizes

You populate the font size DropDownList by adding the numbers 6–100 to the DropDownList, as follows:

```
Public Sub LoadFontSizes(ByVal ddl As DropDownList)
    Dim X As Integer
    For X = 6 To 100
        ddl.Items.Add(X.ToString())
    Next
End Sub
```

Rendering the Text

Rendering the text involves parsing the data in the DropDownList boxes and then using a temporary bitmap to measure the size of the text, creating the final bitmap, based on the size of the text, and finally drawing the text on the bitmap.

```
Private Sub Page_PreRender( _
        ByVal sender As Object, _
        ByVal e As System.EventArgs) _
        Handles MyBase.PreRender
    'Initialize
    Dim imgBitmap As New Bitmap(1, 1)
    Dim fStyle As FontStyle
    fStyle = System.Enum.Parse(GetType(FontStyle), _
            drpFontStyle.SelectedItem.Text)
    Dim fSize As Single
    fSize = Single.Parse(drpFontSize.SelectedItem.Text)
    Dim strFont As Font
```

```
strFont = New Font(drpFontFamily.SelectedItem.Text, fSize, fStyle)
Dim str As String = TextBox1.Text
Dim cBackground As Color
cBackground = Color.FromName(drpBackground.SelectedItem.Text)
Dim cForeground As Color
cForeground = Color.FromName(drpForeground.SelectedItem.Text)
'Get the size of the text string.
If str = "" Then str = "No text defined."
Dim g As Graphics = Graphics.FromImage(imgBitmap)
Dim strSize As Size
strSize = g.MeasureString(str, strFont).ToSize()
'Create the bitmap.
imgBitmap = New Bitmap(strSize.Width, strSize.Height)
g = Graphics.FromImage(imgBitmap)
g.Clear(cBackground)
g.DrawString(str, strFont, New SolidBrush(cForeground), 0, 0)
Session("imgBitmap") = imgBitmap
img.ImageUrl = Request.ServerVariables("SCRIPT_NAME") & _
        "?ImageID=imgBitmap"
End Sub
```

This code places the drawn bitmap into the imgBitmap Session variable, which is available when the browser attempts to request the bitmap from this page. Figure 11.12 shows the browser output with settings changed.

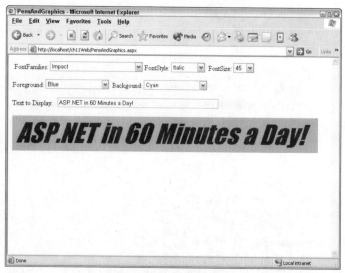

Figure 11.12   The browser output with setting changes.

Lab 11.1: Working with File and Directory Objects

In the last chapter's lab, you created a Web page that allowed users to upload files to the server. You are concerned that someone will try to programmatically upload thousands of files to the server. To solve this problem, you have decided to implement a validation image scheme, where a GUID is generated and placed into a bitmap, and the user must type the GUID into a TextBox. Upon validation, the Upload controls will be displayed. After a file has been uploaded, the GUID is cleared to force a user to type the GUID to upload a new file.

Hiding Existing Controls and Adding New Controls

In this section, you add a new page with the File Field control.

1. Start this lab by opening the OrderEntrySolution from Lab 10.1.

2. Right-click the OrderEntrySolution in the Solution Explorer, and click Check Out. This checks out the complete solution.

3. Open the Web Form page called DocumentUpload.aspx that exists in the Customer project.

4. To simplify the enabling and disabling of many controls, the Web page has been changed to FlowLayout, and two HTML Grid panels must be added to the Web page. One will be called pnlValidate, and the other will be called pnlUpload. Be sure to right-click each of these controls, and then click Run As A Server Control.

5. Add a Button called btnValidate, a TextBox called txtValidate, and an Image called Img to the pnlValidate panel. Also add a Label control with instructions. Figure 11.13 Shows the Visual Studio .NET designer screen.

6. Add Imports System.Drawing.Imaging to the top of the code-behind page.

7. In the code-behind page, add code to the Page_Load event method that will deliver a bitmap, if the Request object contains an ImageID field. Also, add code to check for Not IsPostBack, txtValidate having an empty string, or Session("Validate") being Nothing. If any of these is true, a call is made to a new method called SetupValidate. The added code should look like the following:

```
If Not Request("ImageID") Is Nothing Then
    If Not Session(Request("ImageID")) Is Nothing Then
        Dim b As Bitmap
        b = CType(Session(Request("ImageID")), Bitmap)
```

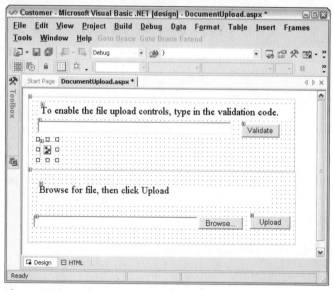

Figure 11.13 The Visual Studio .NET Designer screen with the image upload page, and the controls that are required.

```
            Response.Clear()
            Response.ContentType = "image/jpeg"
            b.Save(Response.OutputStream, ImageFormat.Jpeg)
            Response.End()
            Return
        End If
    End If


    If (Not IsPostBack) _
            Or (txtValidate.Text = "") _
            Or (Session("Validate") Is Nothing) Then
        SetupValidate()
    End If
```

8. Add a new method called ServerValidate. The method hides the pnlUpload and shows the pnlValidate. The method contains code to create a globally unique ID (GUID), convert it to a string, and assign the first eight characters to a string variable called guidValidate. Add code to clear the txtValidate TextBox control.

9. In the ServerValidate code, add code to create a temporary bitmap called imgBitmap, and use this bitmap to measure the size of guidValidate, using the Impact, 24-point font.

10. After the size has been calculated, create the bitmap and store it in a Session variable called imgBitmap. Set the imageURL of the Img control to request imageID=imgBitmap. Your code for the Setup-Validate should look like the following:

```
Public Sub SetupValidate()
    pnlUpload.Visible = False
    pnlValidate.Visible = True
    Dim guidValidate As String
    guidValidate = Guid.NewGuid().ToString.Substring(0, 8)
    Session("Validate") = guidValidate
    txtValidate.Text = ""
    'Initialize
    Dim imgBitmap As New Bitmap(1, 1)
    Dim strFont As Font
    strFont = New Font("Impact", 24, FontStyle.Regular)
    'Get the size of the text string.
    Dim g As Graphics = Graphics.FromImage(imgBitmap)
    Dim strSize As Size
    strSize = g.MeasureString(guidValidate, strFont).ToSize()
    'Create the bitmap.
    imgBitmap = New Bitmap(strSize.Width, strSize.Height)
    g = Graphics.FromImage(imgBitmap)
    g.Clear(Color.Silver)
    g.DrawString(guidValidate, strFont, _
        New SolidBrush(Color.Blue), _
        0, 0)
    Session("imgBitmap") = imgBitmap
    Img.ImageUrl = Request.ServerVariables("SCRIPT_NAME") & _
     "?ImageID=imgBitmap"
End Sub
```

11. Add code to the btnValidate's click event method. This code verifies that the GUID that was entered is the same as the GUID that was saved to the Session variable. If they are equal, pnlUpload is displayed and pnlValidate is hidden. Your code should look like the following:

```
Private Sub btnValidate_Click( _
 ByVal sender As System.Object, _
 ByVal e As System.EventArgs) _
 Handles btnValidate.Click
    Dim guidValidate As String
    guidValidate = Session("Validate")
    If (String.Compare(txtValidate.Text, _
            guidValidate, True) = 0) Then
        pnlUpload.Visible = True
        pnlValidate.Visible = False
    Else
        SetupValidate()
    End If
End Sub
```

12. At the end of the btnUpload click event method, add a call to the SetupValidate method to force the user to type in a new validation code for each file that is uploaded.

Test File Uploading

The File Field control can be tested by setting DocumentUpload.aspx as the start page and running the application.

1. Right-click the Customer project in the Solution Explorer. Click Set As StartUp Project.

2. Right-click the DocumentUpload.aspx page. Click Set As Start Page.

3. Run the application. The browser should prompt you to enter the validation code, as shown in Figure 11.14.

4. Upload some text and picture files.

5. After stopping the program, check the folder to verify that the files were saved properly.

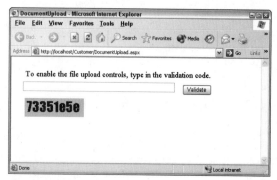

Figure 11.14 The validation screen. After entering the validation code, the upload panel will be displayed.

Summary

- When the browser sees an image tag, the browser knows that the content isn't included in the Web page. The browser must get the image that is at the URL of the image source.

- The pen is an object that is used to draw lines and curves.

- A brush is used to fill regions.

- The Graphics class is the class that provides all the methods for drawing on a display device. The Graphics object is related to the handle of a device context (HDC) that GDI used in the past, except the GDI+ Graphics object encapsulate this low-level functionality.

- GDI+ allows images to be drawn on the fly.

Review Questions

1. What are two ways of displaying a thumbnail image?

2. If a bitmap is stored in a database as a Windows Paintbrush (.bmp) file, how can it be retrieved and sent to a browser that only supports .gif and .jpg files?

3. What's the difference between the Point and the PointF classes?

4. What do the letters ARGB mean?

5. What is the Graphics class used for?

6. How can a bitmap be created that is the same size as a string of text that is to be written using Arial Black, 36-point font?

Answers to Review Questions

1. Use the GetThumbNail method, or use the constructor of the Bitmap class.

2. Use the Save method of the Bitmap class to save to the Response.OutputStream as a Imaging.ImageFormat.Jpeg image type.

3. The Point class uses integers, whereas the PointF class uses floats.

4. Alpha, Red, Green, Blue.

5. The Graphics class contains a handle to the device context and provides methods for drawing.

6. Use the MeasureString method of the Graphics class.

ASP.NET Applications

One of the challenges involved with Web development is the sharing of data amongst many Web pages to make a collection of Web pages into a seamless Web application. Sharing data means sharing *state*. For example, on the customer page, an order is selected, which causes a new page to be displayed. The new page still knows who the customer is, and also knows which order is to be displayed. This is the sharing of state.

Being able to treat a group of Web pages like an application also involves being able to access application- and session-level events. There may be objects that need to be initialized when the application starts, or when a session starts.

Even from a security perspective, it makes sense to log on to an application, rather than logging on to every page. Security is covered in detail in the next chapter, but the need for security and defining the scope of a login are primary factors in justifying the need to treat a collection of Web pages as a Web application.

It seems as though it should not be a big deal to share state. The Windows application on a user's desktop can share state seamlessly as many Windows forms are opened with an application. The problem is that there is a finite amount of resources that are available on a computer. Where the single-user machine needs to be concerned with only the currently logged on person, the

Web server may have thousands of users logged on. If the server is holding state data for thousands of users, this severely affects the performance and scalability of the server. From the Web server's perspective, if the Web server could deliver a page to the user and simply close the connection and release all resources, the Web server would use only a small amount of resources. From the developer's perspective, if the Web server could simply remember all of the global variables on every page, it would take the developer less time to create a Web application.

This chapter explores several aspects of ASP.NET application programming. The first section covers the global.asax file and the HttpApplication class. Next, the chapter explores HTTP handlers and modules. After that, state management within an ASP.NET application is explored in detail. This chapter also covers several other items that come in handy when connecting pages together.

Classroom Q & A

Q: On my last project, we built a shopping cart application and used session variables to share data between Web pages, because session variables are so easy to use. We deployed the application on a Web farm, and found that the application did not work because the Web servers didn't know about each other's sessions. This turned into a major rewrite of the application. Does ASP.NET do anything to solve this problem?

A: Yes. Lots of developers had the same problem, especially since session variables are so easy to use. ASP.NET corrects the problem that you experienced, by providing a session server or SQL Server to manage session state. We explore this is more detail in this chapter.

Q: Is there a way to store data during a request? Our company likes to use Server.Transfer, but there doesn't seem to be a way of retrieving the data that was posted to the original page.

A: There sure is. You can expose data from the original page by using public fields or properties. Also, ASP.NET provides a collection called Context.Items, which is scoped to the page request.

Q: Is there a way to cache data that is normally retrieved from the database and very rarely updated?

A: Absolutely. You can retrieve the data from the database and store a DataTable or DataSet in the Cache. This improves performance significantly.

ASP.NET Applications

An ASP.NET application is a collection of pages that are grouped together under a common virtual directory structure. This means that all of the Web pages that reside in a single virtual directory are part of the same Web application. Global variables are shared among these pages.

Chapter 2, "Solutions, Projects, and the Visual Studio .NET IDE," explained how to create a virtual directory. When a new Visual Studio .NET Web application is begun, a virtual directory is created for the group of pages in the Visual Studio .NET Web application.

The Web application does not begin immediately when the Web server starts. Instead, it begins when the first person requests a code page from the site. After the application starts, a session begins for that person. The Application continues to run until the application is directly shut down via IIS or until the server is shut down.

A virtual directory that contains ASP and ASP.NET pages does not share the same application scope, because ASP and ASP.NET run in a different context. This can be a problem when migrating from ASP to ASP.NET.

The Global.asax File

The Global.asax file is an optional file into which the developer may place application- and session-level event handler code. The Global.asax file is sometimes called the application file.

The Global.asax file must be located in the root of the Web Application. The Global.asax file can coexist with a Global.asa file, since ASP and ASP.NET are very much isolated.

The Global.asax file is cached in memory, but is dependent on the timestamp of the file. If a change is made to the Gobal.asax file, the Web application shuts down, and the next person that requests a Web page causes the Web application to restart.

In Visual Studio .NET, the Global.asax file also contains a code-behind page. The code-behind page contains several methods that can be used in an ASP.NET application. Traditional ASP programmers recognize the Application_Start and Application_End methods, as well as the Session_Start and Session_End methods. The following sections explain how these methods operate.

Application_Start

The Application_Start method is invoked only once, when the first request is made for a page that contains server-side code. This could be used to initialize variables or load global information from a data store.

Application_End

The Application_End method executes once, when the Web is being shut down. This can be used to log the fact that the application is ending and to clean up any shared resources.

Session_Start

The Session_Start method executes when a user starts a new session at the Web site. A session is started when the user requests a page that contains server-side code. With Internet Explorer, if the user clicks File, New, Window, a new browser window opens, but this window is in the same ASP.NET session. Any new browser windows that are spawned from a window automatically join the existing window's session.

Session_End

The Session_End method executes when the user's session is terminated. This typically happens when the session times out. The default timeout is 20 minutes, and this is set in Internet Information Server. The timeout can also be overridden from within code by setting the Session.Timeout to the number of minutes that is desired.

The HttpApplication Class

The Global.asax.vb code-behind page contains a class called Global, which inherits from the HttpApplication class. During the lifetime of a Web application, there could be many HttpApplication instances, because ASP.NET allocates a pool of these instances when the Web application starts. ASP.NET assigns an HttpApplication instance to each Web page request that is received. An HttpApplication instance can only handle one request and is responsible for managing the request from start to finish.

The HttpApplication class contains an Init method and a Disposed method. The Init and Dispose methods execute for each instance of the HttpApplication, so they are very different from the Application_Start and Application_End event methods that are available in the Global.asax.vb code-behind page. These methods can be overridden in the Global.asax.vb code-behind file by providing the following code:

```
Public Overrides Sub Init()
     'Cool code here...
End Sub
Public Overrides Sub Disposed()
     'Cool code here...
End Sub
```

During the lifetime of a request, the HttpApplication raises the following events. These events are presented in the order that they are raised.

BeginRequest.   This event is raised as the first event when an ASP.NET request arrives at the server.

AuthenticateRequest.   This event is raised when the security module has established that the identity of the current user is valid. The user's credentials have been validated just prior to this event. More details are covered in Chapter 13, "Site Security."

AuthorizeRequest.   This event is raised when the security module has verified that a user is authorized to access the resources. More details are covered in Chapter 13, "Site Security."

ResolveRequestCache.   This event is raised when ASP.NET has completed the authorization. This informs the caching modules to serve the request from the cache, thus bypassing the execution of the handler. This improves the performance of the Web site, and this event can be used to judge if the contents are used from the cache or not.

AcquireRequestState.   This event is raised when ASP.NET acquires the current state, such as the session state, that is associated with the current request.

PreRequestHandlerExecute.   This event is raised just before ASP.NET begins executing a handler such as a page or a Web service. The session state is available in this event method.

PreSendRequestHeaders.   This event is raised just before ASP.NET sends HTTP Headers to the client.

PreSendRequestContent.   This event is raised just before ASP.NET sends content to the client.

Page Processing – Possible Error.   Page processing isn't an event. This is where the normal page processing by the ASP.NET handler takes place. If an error occurs, an Error event is raised.

PostRequestHandlerExecute.   This event is raised when the ASP.NET handler finishes execution.

ReleaseRequestState.   This event is raised after ASP.NET finishes executing all request handlers. This event causes state modules to save the current state data.

UpdateRequestCache.   This event is raised when ASP.NET finishes executing a handler in order to let caching modules store responses that are used to serve subsequent requests from the cache.

EndRequest.   This event is raised as the last event when ASP.NET responds to a request.

The HttpContext Class

The HttpContext class is a wrapper class that provides a simple object model of the actual request and response. The HttpContext class contains most of the properties that a developer would typically need to access the request and response as follows:

ApplicationInstance.   The HttpApplication instance that is processing the current request.

Handler.   The Handler that is processing the request.

Request.   The HTTP request message from the browser.

Response.   The HTTP response message to the browser.

Cache.   Application scoped cache state.

Application.   Application scoped, cross-request state data.

Session.   Session scoped, cross-request state data.

Items.   Request scoped state data.

Server.   Contains many utility functions.

User.   The current user, based on authentication.

HttpContext is available on the processing thread by using the static property called HttpContext.Current.

Pipeline Processing of the Request

When a user requests a page from a Web server, Internet Information Server (IIS) receives the request, and ASPNET_ISAPI.DLL receives the request from the IIS ISAPI Extension Manager. ASPNET_ISAPI.DLL passes the request, through a named pipe, to the ASP.NET Worker Process, which is called ASPNET_WP.EXE. This process is diagrammed in Figure 12.1.

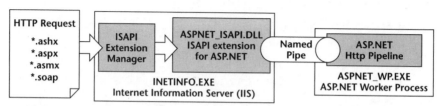

Figure 12.1   ASPNET_ISAPI.DLL is responsible for forwarding a request to ASPNET_WP.EXE, which provides the HttpRuntime Pipeline.

The ASP.NET Worker Process processes the request by using HttpRuntime, which is the entry point to the HttpPipeline. HttpRuntime uses HttpWorker-Request, which is the low-level request, to create an HttpContext object, as shown in Figure 12.2.

HttpRuntime retrieves an HttpApplication instance from HttpApplication-Factory. HttpApplicationFactory is responsible for maintaining the pool of HttpApplication instances for the current virtual directory.

HttpApplication processes the request and response by using zero-to-many modules and a single handler.

The modules are used to hook into the request in a prehandler and posthandler fashion. The module can intercept and modify the request and response.

HttpRuntime retrieves an instance of the handler from HttpHandlerFactory. HttpHandlerFactory is responsible for maintaining a pool of handlers. The handler performs the actual processing of the request and generates the response code.

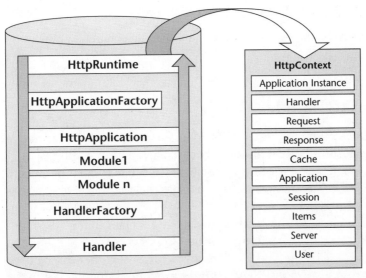

Figure 12.2 The HttpPipeline showing the HttpRuntime entry point, which creates the HttpContext. The HttpContext is available through the entire pipeline.

The HTTP Handler

The HTTP handler is responsible for processing the request and generating the response. Although most developers can create many Web sites without ever creating a handler, the key benefit of developing a handler is its reusability. The handler can be snapped into other Web sites rather easily.

Built-in HTTP Handlers

Many Web sites are set up to allow actions against some files, but not other files. For example, it's usually not desirable to allow someone to download the Web.config file, which contains the settings for the Web site, possibly including database connection information and so on.

ASP.NET includes the following handlers that can be used to eliminate the ability to download certain files, based on their extension.

- HttpForbiddenHandler
- HttpMethodNotAllowedHandler
- HttpNotFoundHandler
- HttpNotImplementedHandler

Creating an HTTP Handler

Handlers can be created very easily. In this section, a new handler is created to respond to any request for a file with the .abc extension.

To create a handler, a new class library project (.dll project) must be created in Visual Studio .NET. The new project must have a reference to the System.Web.dll file.

An HTTP handler class can be created by creating a class that implements the IHttpHandler interface. The IHttpHandler interface exposes a method called ProcessRequest. This method receives an HttpContext that can be used to access the request and response. The method must be implemented in the handler class.

The IHttpHandler interface also exposes a read-only property called IsReusable. This property must be implemented to return true if the class is poolable, or false if not.

The following code shows a simple implementation of the IHttpHandler interface:

```
Imports System.Web
Public Class HandlerTestClass
    Implements IHttpHandler
    Public Overridable Sub ProcessRequest( _
```

```
      ByVal context As HttpContext) _
      Implements IHttpHandler.ProcessRequest
          With context
              .Response.Write("<h1>This is a handler test.</h1><br>")
              .Response.Write("<h2>Requested file: ")
              .Response.Write(.Request.ServerVariables("PATH_INFO"))
              .Response.Write("</h2><br>")
          End With
      End Sub
      Public Overridable ReadOnly Property IsReusable() _
       As Boolean _
       Implements IHttpHandler.IsReusable
          Get
                Return True
          End Get
      End Property
  End Class
```

The class definition includes the Implement IhttpHandler, and the method and property to implement the appropriate IHttpHandler members. Since ProcessRequest receives a valid HttpContext, the request and response are available. This example is being used to display the path and filename that were requested. An interesting note is that the file does not need to exist, because this handler is doing all the work.

The IsReusable property simply returns true, since this class is not using or holding any resources that would require it to return false.

This project can be compiled, and the .dll can be used in a Web application.

Installing the HTTP Handler

Installing the HTTP Handler involves setting a reference to the Handler's .dll, adding an *httpHandlers* configuration in the Web.config file, and adding an Application Mapping to IIS.

Adding the reference to the Handler's .dll file can be done by right-clicking the References folder in the project, then clicking Add Reference. Browse to the folder containing the .dll file, and select it.

To add the httpHandlers configuration to the Web.config file, the Web.config file is opened, and the httpHandlers section is added into the <system.web> XML element as follows:

```
<configuration>
   <system.web>
      <httpHandlers>
          <add verb="*" path="*.abc"
          type="HandlerTest.HandlerTestClass, HandlerTest" />
      </httpHandlers>
   </system.web>
</configuration>
```

Figure 12.3   The Internet Information Server Web application settings screen.

This handler is being set up to handle any file with an .abc extension. The verb can be changed to handle GET, POST, HEAD, TRACE, or any combination of verbs. The path can have an explicit filename, or it can use wildcard characters. The type attribute of the add element must be the fully qualified path to the handler class. The first item in the type is the namespace.name of the class. The second item is the friendly name of the assembly, which is the name of the assembly without the extension.

To add the Application Mapping to IIS, the Internet Service Manager must be opened, and then the properties of the Web application need to be selected (see Figure 12.3).

The execute permissions of the Web application should be set to Scripts. In the Configuration section, the Mappings tab (see Figure 12.4) shows all of the existing mappings of file extensions to executables.

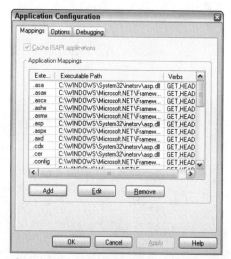

Figure 12.4   The existing application mappings are shown. An additional mapping needs to be added for the .abc extension.

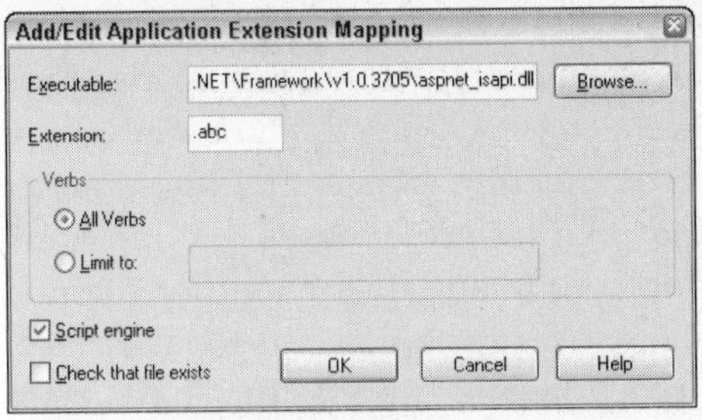

Add/Edit Application Extension Mapping

Executable: .NET\Framework\v1.0.3705\aspnet_isapi.dll   Browse...

Extension: .abc

Verbs
- All Verbs
- Limit to:

☑ Script engine
☐ Check that file exists   OK   Cancel   Help

Figure 12.5   The application mapping is added to IIS.

Clicking the Add button allows a new application mapping to be added (see Figure 12.5). The executable is set to the following:

```
C:\WINDOWS\Microsoft.NET\Framework\v1.0.3705\aspnet_isapi.dll
```

The extension is set to .abc so that any request for a file with an .abc extension is forwarded to the aspnet_isapi.dll filter. aspnet_isapi.net locates the handler definition in the Web.config file and executes the ProcessRequest method.

 In IIS 5.1 on Windows XP, a bug exists whereby the OK button on the Add/Edit Application Extension Mapping dialog stays disabled even after the executable and extension for the mapping have been selected. The workaround for this bug is to click on the executable text box after using the Bowse button. This fully expands the path and enables the OK button so the mapping can be saved.

The HTTP Module

HTTP modules extend the middle of the HTTP pipeline, and allow the request and response messages to be examined and modified as they pass between the browser and the HTTP handler. This HTTP module is another entity that most developers never need to create, but a key benefit of developing a module is its reusability. The module, like the handler, can be snapped into other Web sites rather easily.

HTTP modules are notified of the request and response messages' progress through events.

Creating an HTTP Module

In this section, a new module is created to respond to all requests within the Web site.

To create a module, a new class library project (.dll project) must be created in Visual Studio .NET. The new project must have a reference to the System.Web.dll file.

An HTTP module class can be created by creating a class that implements the IHttpModule interface. The IHttpModule interface exposes two methods called Init and Dispose. This Init method is used to add event handlers, which can be thought of as telling the module to listen for certain events to take place. The events that are available are the HttpApplication events that have been identified earlier in this chapter.

```
Imports System.Web
Public Class ModuleTestClass
    Implements IHttpModule
    Public Sub Init(ByVal httpApp As HttpApplication) _
            Implements IHttpModule.Init
        AddHandler httpApp.BeginRequest, AddressOf Me.OnBeginRequest
        AddHandler httpApp.EndRequest, AddressOf Me.OnEndRequest
    End Sub
    Public Sub Dispose() Implements IHttpModule.Dispose
    End Sub
    Public Sub OnBeginRequest(ByVal o As Object, ByVal e As EventArgs)
        Dim httpApp As HttpApplication = CType(o, HttpApplication)
        Dim ctx As HttpContext = HttpContext.Current
        With ctx
        .Response.Write("<h1>ModuleTest Begin Request</h1><br>")
        End With
    End Sub
    Public Sub OnEndRequest(ByVal o As Object, ByVal e As EventArgs)
        Dim httpApp As HttpApplication = CType(o, HttpApplication)
        Dim ctx As HttpContext = HttpContext.Current
        With ctx
        .Response.Write("<h1>ModuleTest End Request</h1><br>")
        End With
    End Sub
End Class
```

The code for this module is set up to listen for the BeginRequest and EndRequest events, and output a small message. The httpApp is retrieved from the object parameter, primarily to show how this can be done. The HttpContext is available from the HttpContext.Current property, and is used in order to write data back to the browser.

Installing the HTTP Module

Installing the HTTP Module involves setting a reference to the Module's .dll and adding an *httpModules* configuration in the Web.config file.

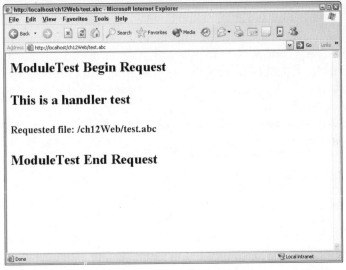

Figure 12.6 The browser output when requesting an .abc page.

Adding the reference to the Handler's .dll file can be done by right-clicking the References folder in the project, then clicking Add Reference. Browse to the folder containing the .dll file, and select it.

The Web.config file is opened, and the httpModules section is added into the <system.web> XML element as follows:

```
<configuration>
  <system.web>
    <httpModules>
        <add name="ModuleTestClass"
             type="HandlerTest.ModuleTestClass, HandlerTest" />
    </httpModules >
  </system.web>
</configuration>
```

In this example, the HTTP module was created in the same project (HandlerTest) as the HTTP handler that was previously described. Figure 12.6 shows the output when testing the HTTP module by requesting an .abc page.

Note that this module works with every request to the Web site, not just the request for the Web page that is shown.

Maintaining State

There are several ways of maintaining state in a Web application. Which method to use depends on the data that is being shared and the scope of the sharing. This section explores some of the methods.

Application State Data

Application variables were available with traditional ASP and are still available using ASP.NET. The HttpContext exposes the Application property, which is an instance of the HttpApplicationState class. The HttpApplication-State exposes a dictionary of key-value pairs. Only one instance of the HttpApplication State is created for a Web application.

Probably the most common method of accessing the HttpApplicationState is through the Application property of the Page. This allows the user to simply type the following:

```
Application("Test")="This is a test."
```

This syntax is the same as that used in previous versions of ASP. The impact of using global variables such as these should be considered before using Application variables. These variables have an application scope, which means that these variables can be accessed from any thread, handler, module, or page by any user. This can be a problem if users are reading and changing data simultaneously.

Application variables are not destroyed until the application ends or until the code replaces or deletes the variable. It's not a good idea to assign large, seldom-used datasets to Application variables. Caching this data may be a better solution.

When accessing Application variables, the HttpApplicationState class provides the Lock and Unlock methods to ensure synchronized access to the data. Although locks can be used to protect the integrity of global resources, locks have a negative impact on the performance and scalability of an application. In general, if an Application variable is to be used, it should be locked for the least amount of time that is possible. If Unlock is not explicitly called, ASP.NET automatically removes the lock when a request is completed, when the request times out, or if an unhandled error occurs that causes the request processing to fail.

Application state is not shared across servers in a Web farm, where a Web application is hosted by many Web servers. Application state is also not shared across a Web garden, where a Web application is hosted by many processors on a multiple-processor machine. An example of using an Application variable is as follows:

```
Application.Lock( )
Application("ActiveSessions") = _
    CType(Application("ActiveSessions "), Integer) + 1
Application.UnLock( )
```

Notice that when the value is retrieved from an Application variable, the value needs to be cast to the proper data type using the CType function.

Session State Data

Session variables were also available with traditional ASP and are still available using ASP.NET. Session variables store data that needs to be shared across requests to the server. This data might be a user's shopping cart, the ID of the current user, or even the user's preferences. The HttpContext exposes the Session property, which is an instance of the HttpSessionState class. The HttpSessionState exposes a dictionary of key-value pairs. There is an instance of the HttpSessionState for each user who has an active session within the Web application.

A common method of accessing the HttpSessionState is through the Session property of the Page. This allows the user to simply type the following:

```
Session("Test")="This is a test."
```

This syntax is the same as was used in previous versions of ASP. Retrieving the session variable is a bit different though. The session variable always returns a data type of object, so the following code can be used to retrieve the data that was stored in the previous example.

```
Dim str as string
str = Ctype(Session("Test"),String)
```

A session has a 120-bit SessionID assigned, which contains characters that can be placed into a URL, if necessary. The SessionID also has uniqueness to ensure that two sessions do not collide. To prevent malicious attacks, the SessionID is generated with a degree of randomness. This keeps a would-be hacker from retrieving a SessionID and simply adding or subtracting one to get someone else's SessionID.

The SessionID is typically placed on the user's machine in the form of a cookie. It is also possible to configure an ASP.NET Web application to place the SessionID in the URL, which works with browsers that don't support cookies.

Session variables have always been a compelling choice because of their ease of use. The problem is that the previous version of ASP did not support sessions across a Web farm or Web garden. As a result, many developers have suffered the consequences of choosing to use session variables when a single-server Web application required additional servers to accommodate the user load.

With ASP.NET, the session infrastructure has been changed significantly. The developer can start with maintaining session data in memory, and can simply change the configuration as needed to accommodate the demands of the Web site.

The configuration for session management is stored in the Web.config file within the Web application. The following section is the default configuration for session management.

```
<sessionState
    mode="InProc"
    stateConnectionString="tcpip=127.0.0.1:42424"
    sqlConnectionString="data source=127.0.0.1;user id=sa;password="
    cookieless="false"
    timeout="20"
/>
```

The mode attribute can be set to either InProc, StateServer, SQLServer, or none. The InProc setting is the same as traditional session state management, where the session data is stored in the same process as the Web application and does not support Web farms and gardens. With this mode, if the Web service needs to be reset (iisreset), all session data is destroyed. The number one reason to use this option is performance.

The StateServer option provides compatibility with Web farms and gardens by using a common server to manage session information for all servers that host the Web application. This can be done by starting the ASP.NET State Service on a machine and pointing all machines to this machine. To start the service, use either of the following commands from the command prompt:

```
net start aspnet_state
net start "asp.net state service"
```

The State Service was installed as part of the .NET Framework SDK. If this service is used, the service should also be configured to start up automatically when the server is started. This can be done through Control Panel, Services.

The Web.config file needs to be changed for the StateServer option to operate. The mode needs to be changed to StateServer, the stateConnectionString needs to be configured to be the same for all machines that share session state as follows:

```
<sessionState
    mode="StateServer"
    stateConnectionString="tcpip=MainServer:42424"
    sqlConnectionString="data source=127.0.0.1;user id=sa;password="
    cookieless="false"
    timeout="20"
/>
```

The StateServer option is compatible with Web farms and gardens, but is also a good choice for single server installations, where it may be necessary to reset IIS and it's important not to lose session state data. Be aware that the session data is still being stored in memory, but not in the Web application's process.

The SQLServer option is very similar to the StateServer option, except the session data is sent to a SQL Server. This option is compatible with Web farms and gardens, but is not as fast as the other options. The mode is set to SQLServer, and the sqlConnectionString must be set to a machine that has SQL Server installed. The following is a sample of the Web.config settings:

```
<sessionState
    mode="SQLServer"
    stateConnectionString="tcpip=127.0.0.1:42424"
    sqlConnectionString="data source=MainServer;user id=sa;password="
    cookieless="false"
    timeout="20"
/>
```

In order to use the SQLServer option, the SQL Server must be set up by running a SQL script called InstallSqlState.sql, which is in the following location:

```
%SystemRoot%\Microsoft.NET\Framework\v1.0.3705
```

The SQL script can be run from the SQL Server Query Analyzer or from the osql.exe command line tool. This script creates a new database with several stored procedures, and a couple tables in tempdb, which is a high-performance database that is not persistant.

Another option that is available is the cookieless option. By setting cookieless to true, the SessionID is automatically embedded into the URL as follows:

```
http://localhost/ch12Web/(41udo145kjgvrlugwgjnkf55)/WebForm1.aspx
```

The use of this option requires that relative links be used throughout. Care must be used to avoid losing session data due to using explicit paths.

Session variables are not destroyed until the session ends or until the code replaces or deletes the variable, or until the Session.Abandon method has been executed in the code. Because each user has an isolated session, each user may have a copy of a session variable that contains a different value. For example, each user may have a session variable called UserName, which contains the current user's name. It's also not a good idea to assign large, seldom-used datasets to session variables, because there could be thousands of copies of this data on the server, depending on the quantity of active sessions that the server currently has. Caching is still the better solution.

Request State Data

Request variables store data that needs to be shared between pages and classes during a single request to the server. This data might be a user's selected item to be added to the shopping cart, or the ID of the current user. HttpContext exposes the Items property, which is a Dictionary Object, containing key-value pairs that are available during a request. There is an instance of the Items property for each request to the server. As the request is being processed through the HTTP runtime pipeline, Context.Items is available and shareable.

A common method of accessing the Items property is through the Context property of the Page. This allows the user to simply type the following:

```
Context.Items("Test")="This is a test."
```

The Items property always returns a data type of object, so the following code can be used to retrieve the data that was stored in the previous example.

```
Dim str as string
str = Ctype(Context.Items("Test"),String)
```

Cache

There are many cases where it's desirable to share data globally, but if the data changes, there needs to be a method of updating the global data. In addition, if the system needs more memory, it may be desirable to allow the system to reclaim the resources that are being used by seldom-used global data. Caching is the answer to these problems.

The cache has an application scope, like application variables. Although concurrency is still an issue, the cache has built-in locking. Items that are cached can be expired, which means that a check always needs to be done to verify that the item is still cached, prior to using the item.

Cache Dependency

An item in the Cache can be expired by setting a dependency on the timestamp of a file. For example, an XML file on a Web site may contain the settings for the Web site's menu system, as shown in Figure 12.7. The contents of this file are shared among all site users. Instead of loading the file everytime someone hits the site, the file can be cached, with a dependency set to the XML file.

The XML file is called WebMenu.xml and contains the following data:

```
<?xml version="1.0" encoding="utf-8" ?>
<mainmenu>
    <menuitem displayname="Home" url="default.aspx" />
    <menuitem displayname="About" url="about.aspx" />
</mainmenu>
```

In this example, the HTML contains a DataList to display menu items with links to the selected page.

```
<form id="Form1" method="post" runat="server">
    <asp:DataList id="DataList1"
        runat="server"
        RepeatDirection="Horizontal">
    <ItemTemplate>
```

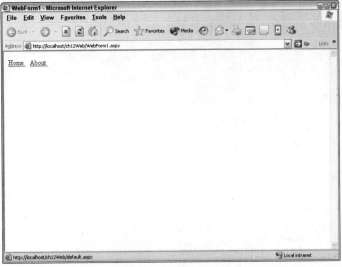

Figure 12.7 The DataList is populated from an XML file containing the settings.

```
        <a href='<%#Container.DataItem("url")%>'>
            <%#Container.DataItem("displayname")%>
        </a>  
    </ItemTemplate>
    </asp:DataList>
</form>
```

The code to display the menu is in the Page_Load method, but the real work is done in the MenuSettings property as follows:

```
Private Sub Page_Load( _
    ByVal sender As System.Object, _
    ByVal e As System.EventArgs) _
    Handles MyBase.Load
    DataList1.DataSource = MenuSettings
    DataList1.DataMember = "menuitem"
    DataBind()
End Sub
Public ReadOnly Property MenuSettings() As DataSet
    Get
        Dim ds As DataSet
        If Cache("MenuSettings") Is Nothing Then
            'Load the DataSet.
            ds = New DataSet()
            ds.ReadXml(Server.MapPath("WebMenu.xml"))
            'Set up file dependency
            Dim cDepend As Caching.CacheDependency
            cDepend = New Caching.CacheDependency( _
              Server.MapPath("WebMenu.xml"))
            'Insert to cache
```

```
                     Cache.Insert("MenuSettings", ds, cDepend)
             Else
                     ds = CType(Cache("MenuSettings"), DataSet)
             End If
             Return ds
      End Get
  End Property
```

The MenuSettings are exposed as a property, but it is dependent on the Web-Menu.xml file. Any change to the file causes the cache to be invalidated, which causes the file to be reread the next time the property is read. Figure 12.8 shows the browser after a menu item has been added to the file.

Cache dependencies can also be set up based on other cache keys. For example, if a Cache object called NextMenu is dependent on the MenuSettings Cache object, a dependency can be set up as follows:

```
'Insert to cache (from previous example)
Cache.Insert("MenuSettings", ds, cDepend)
'Add dependent menu (added dependency)
Dim obj As New Object()
Dim oDepend As Caching.CacheDependency
oDepend = New Caching.CacheDependency( _
      Nothing, New String() {"MenuSettings"})
Cache.Insert("NextMenu", obj, oDepend)
```

Notice that the CacheDependency class can be based on a file, an array of files, or an array of cache keys, or any combination of these. In this example, a file dependency was not desirable, because it is more desirable to simply allow the MenuSettings to control its own dependencies independently.

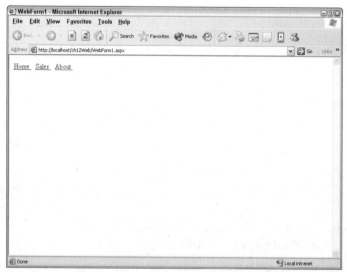

Figure 12.8   The browser output after a menu item has been added to the file.

Cache Timeout

An item in the cache can be expired by setting an absolute expiration date, a sliding date, or a priority. The absolute expiration date allows the expiration to take place at a specified date and time. The sliding expiration allows a time span to be specified from the last time that the object was accessed.

```
Cache.Insert("MenuSettings", ds, cDepend, _
    DateTime.MaxValue, _
    New TimeSpan(0, 2, 0))
```

In this example, a dependency still exists on the file, but a sliding window of 2 minutes has also been added to have the cache automatically expire after 2 minutes of not accessing the menu from the cache. If the absolute expiration is not required, DateTime.MaxValue is supplied.

Static Variables

In addition to Application variables and caching, static variables can be created which essentially have an application scope. A static variable is created within a class, and has the following syntax:

```
Public Shared ds As DataSet
```

The use of the *Shared* keyword identifies ds as being a static variable. Static variables can be accessed without creating an instance of the class that the variable was defined in. If ds was in a class called Settings, ds could be accessed as follows:

```
Settings.ds = new DataSet( )
```

Another method of creating static variables is to add a module file to the project. A module automatically exposes all variables as shared, without requiring the Shared keyword. In addition, access to the variable doesn't require the module name unless there is a potential name conflict.

Web Configuration File

The Web configuration file, called Web.config, contains many of the Web site settings that can be changed without requiring a recompiling of the Web application. This file is read and cached when the Web application starts. The cached file has a dependency on the File timestamp, which force the file to be reread after the file has been changed.

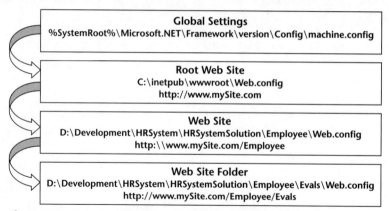

Figure 12.9 The Web configuration file hierarchy.

The Web configuration settings are organized in a hierarchical fashion, as shown in Figure 12.9. The most global setting file is the machine.config file. The settings in the most local folder typically override the parent and global settings, but this can be different, based on the actual configuration setting that is being accessed. Some settings are only allowed in specific locations. For example, a subdirectory of the Web site might contain security information, but it cannot contain handler and module configuration settings.

This chapter explores some of the Web.config file settings. Other Web configuration settings are covered in other areas of this book.

Error Handling

The global.asax.vb code-behind page contains an Application_Error event method, which is called when any unhandled Exception occurs. This is can be used to log any errors that have occurred and possibly transfer a common error page as follows:

```
Sub Application_Error(ByVal sender As Object, ByVal e As EventArgs)
    Dim evlog As New EventLog("Application")
    evlog.Source = "Chapter12"
    Dim message As String
    message = String.Format( _
    "Exception:{1}{0}Message:{0}{2}{0}{0}Stack Trace:{0}{3}", _
        vbCrLf, Server.GetLastError().GetType(), _
        Server.GetLastError().Message, _
        Server.GetLastError().StackTrace)
    evlog.WriteEntry(message, EventLogEntryType.Error)
    evlog.Close()
End Sub
```

Error handling can also be done at the page level using the following routine in the page itself:

```
Private Sub Page_Error( _
        ByVal sender As Object, _
        ByVal e As System.EventArgs) _
        Handles MyBase.Error
            'Page error handling here
End Sub
```

The Web.config file contains settings for configuring the custom error handling using the customErrors XML tag. This contains options for setting a default redirect page, the ability to turn the handling on or off or make the error redirect only operate from remote machines, and the ability to set up a different error page for each HTTP error. The default error configuration is as follows:

```
<?xml version="1.0" encoding="utf-8" ?>
<configuration>
    <system.web>
        <!--  CUSTOM ERROR MESSAGES
        Set customErrors mode="On" or "RemoteOnly" to
        enable custom error messages, "Off" to disable.
        Add <error> tags for each of the errors you want to handle.
        -->
        <customErrors mode="RemoteOnly" />
    </system.web>
</configuration>
```

The default configuration is configured to redirect to custom error pages, but only if the user is accessing the Web site from a remote computer. No custom errors are configured, so any error that takes place causes the default ASP.NET error page to be displayed, as shown in Figure 12.10.

The mode attribute can be set to On, Off, or Remote Only. This means that it is very easy to turn off the custom error pages while debugging the code, and turn them back on when in production. Better yet, leaving the setting at RemoteOnly means that the developer can work on the local Web server without seeing the custom errors, but the remote users see the custom errors.

The customErrors tag also has a defaultRedirect attribute. This attribute can be set to a URL to assign a default error page to the Web application. The following XML snippet shows how to redirect all errors to a default error page:

```
<?xml version="1.0" encoding="utf-8" ?>
<configuration>
    <system.web>
        <!--  CUSTOM ERROR MESSAGES
        Set customErrors mode="On" or "RemoteOnly" to
        enable custom error messages, "Off" to disable.
        Add <error> tags for each of the errors you want to handle.
        -->
        <customErrors defaultRedirect="error.aspx"
```

```
            mode="RemoteOnly" />
      </system.web>
  </configuration>
```

There may be a need to cause some errors to display specific pages as well as having a default redirect location. This can be done by embedding custom error information into the customErrors XML tag, as shown in the following code sample:

```
<?xml version="1.0" encoding="utf-8" ?>
<configuration>
    <system.web>
        <!--  CUSTOM ERROR MESSAGES
        Set customErrors mode="On" or "RemoteOnly" to
        enable custom error messages, "Off" to disable.
        Add <error> tags for each of the errors you want to handle.
        -->
        <customErrors defaultRedirect="error.aspx" mode="On" >
            <error statusCode="404"
                redirect="NotFound.aspx"/>
            <error statusCode="500"
                redirect="InternalError.aspx"/>
        </customErrors>
    </system.web>
</configuration>
```

In this example, a File Not Found (404) or an Internal Server Error (500) displays custom error pages, as shown in Figure 12.11, and any other error displays the error.aspx page.

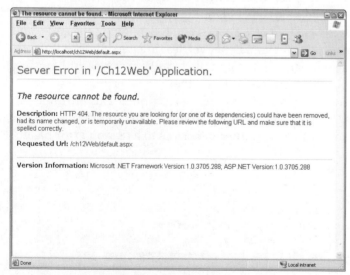

Figure 12.10   The default error ASP.NET error page.

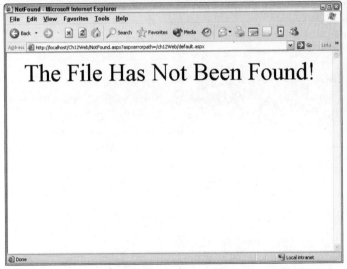

Figure 12.11 The custom Web page for a File Not Found (404) error.

Page Navigation

ASP.NET requires a page to post back to itself. How can control be transferred to a different page? This section offers several solutions, along with the benefits and drawbacks of each.

In the following examples, the user is presented with a list of orders. The user selects an order and clicks the GetDetails button. A control called ctlOrderID, is assumed to hold the OrderID of the order in which the user wishes to view details.

HyperLink and HyperLink Control

The HyperLink control allows page navigations through the HyperLink's NavigateURL property. The NavigateURL property can be set from within the code-behind page, and it may contain a constructed URL. The following code sample shows how to program the Page_Load method of the code-behind page. This sample assumes that the Web form page contains a HyperLink control called HyperLink1.

```
Private Sub Page_Load(ByVal sender As System.Object, _
        ByVal e As System.EventArgs) Handles MyBase.Load
    'Put user code to initialize the page here
    Dim OrderID as Integer
```

```
                'Assign OrderID to a value obtained from the database
                HyperLink1.NavigateUrl = _
                    "OrderDetails.aspx?OrderID=" & OrderID
                HyperLink1.Target = "_blank"
            End Sub
```

This code builds and sets the NavigateURL, typically based on a database query result. The Hyperlink also has a Target property, which is the type HTML target attribute. When set to "_blank," a new browser is opened to contain the OrderDetails page.

The advantages of the Hyperlink control include the following:

- This method can be used to call ASP pages as well as ASPX pages.
- This method allows a new browser child window to be opened to hold the results.

The disadvantages to it include the following:

- This method does not post any data. This means that all data entered on the Order page can be lost.
- The URL is limited in size. The URL should be limited to 1,024 bytes in order to accommodate all browsers.
- Although this method can open a new browser window, the child window is not easily accessible from the parent window, so it is difficult to close the child window when the parent window is closed.

Window.Open

Window.Open is a client-side script command. This can be used when it is desirable to open the OrderDetails in a second window. Using this approach requires the use of a standard HTML tag to execute the client-side script. The following is a sample implementation:

```
<%@ Page Language="vb" Codebehind="Order.aspx.vb"
        Inherits="ch3.Orders"%>
<HTML>
    <HEAD>
        <script language="javascript">
            <!--
            var w=null;
            function btnClick()
            {
                var URL;
                URL = "OrderDetails.aspx?OrderID=" +
                    document.all["OrderID"].value;
```

```
                        w=window.open(URL);
                }
                function closewindows()
                {      //was the window opened?
                    if(w != null)
                    {      //if so, was it closed?
                        if(!w.closed)
                        {      //close it
                            w.close();
                        }
                    }
                }
                //-->
            </script>
        </HEAD>
        <body  onunload="return closewindows();">
            <form id="Form1" method="post" runat="server">
                <asp:textbox id="OrderID"
                    runat="server">
                </asp:textbox>
                <input type="button" id="GetOrder"
                    value="GetOrder"
                    onclick="return btnClick();" />
            </form>
        </body>
    </HTML>
```

If the OrderID is 123, the btnClick method constructs a URL of OrderDe-
tails.aspx?OrderID=123, and then the window.open function is used to open a
new browser window, using the URL that was created.

The sample also shows how window.open returns a reference to the window that was opened. In the body tag, onunload is programmed to execute
closewindows, which uses the reference to the OrderDetails to close the window when this window is closed.

The OrderDetails.aspx.vb code-behind page can extract the OrderID from
the QueryString with the following code:

```
Private Sub Page_Load(ByVal sender As System.Object, ByVal _
        e As System.EventArgs) Handles MyBase.Load
    Dim OrderID As String = Request.QueryString("OrderID")
    'Look up order details based on this order
End Sub
```

The advantages to using the window.open function are as follows:

- This method can be used to call ASP pages as well as ASPX pages.

- This method allows a new browser child window to be opened to hold
  the results, and the child can be autoclosed if the parent window is
  closed.

The disadvantages include the following:

- This method, as shown, does not post any data, but some creative client-side programming could accomplish this. This means that all data entered on the Order page can be lost.

- The URL is limited in size. The URL should be limited to 1,024 bytes in order to accommodate all browsers.

Response.Redirect

In the server-side event-handling code, a Response.Redirect statement can be issued to get to the new page. Clicking on the GetDetails button causes the page to post back to the server. The GetDetails_Click event handler contains code to redirect to the OrderDetails page as shown.

```
Private Sub GetDetails_Click(ByVal sender As System.Object, _
        ByVal e As System.EventArgs) Handles Button1.Click
    Response.Redirect("OrderDetails.aspx?OrderID=" & _
        HttpUtility.UrlEncode(ctlOrderID.Text))
End Sub
```

If the OrderID is 123, then the GetDetails_Click event constructs a URL of OrderDetails.aspx?OrderID=123 and issues a redirect back to the browser with the newly constructed URL. The browser then requests the new URL. HttpUtility.UrlEncode is a helper method that converts characters, such as @ % . / ? : \ and so on, to a form that can be placed within the URL.

The OrderDetails.aspx.vb code-behind page can extract the OrderID from the QueryString with the following code:

```
Private Sub Page_Load(ByVal sender As System.Object, ByVal _
        e As System.EventArgs) Handles MyBase.Load
    Dim OrderID As String = Request.QueryString("OrderID")
    'Look up order details based on this order.
End Sub
```

The advantages to using a Response.Redirect statement include the following:

- This method can be used to call ASP pages as well as ASPX pages.

- The redirect can be to a different Web server.

The disadvantages are as follows:

- Response.Redirect sends a command back to the browser, essentially saying "go here instead." The browser then places a request for the new URL. This results in an extra round trip between the server and browser.

- Response.Redirect does not include the posted data. This means that all data entered on the Order page can be lost.

- The URL is limited in size. The URL should be limited to 1,024 bytes in order to accommodate all browsers.

Server.Transfer

Instead of using Response.Redirect, Server.Transfer can be used. The GetDetails_Click event handler contains code to transfer control to the OrderDetails page as shown.

```
Private Sub GetDetails_Click(ByVal sender As System.Object, _
        ByVal e As System.EventArgs) Handles Button1.Click
    Server.Transfer("OrderDetails.aspx?OrderID=" & _
        HttpUtility.UrlEncode(ctlOrderID.Text))
End Sub
```

If the OrderID is 123, the GetDetails_Click event constructs a URL of OrderDetails.aspx?OrderID=123 and issues a transfer to the Web server.

The OrderDetails.aspx.vb code-behind page can extract the OrderID from the QueryString with the following code:

```
Private Sub Page_Load(ByVal sender As System.Object, ByVal _
        e As System.EventArgs) Handles MyBase.Load
    Dim OrderID As String = Request.QueryString("OrderID")
    'Look up order details based on this order
End Sub
```

One of the advantages of this method is that it can be used to call ASP pages as well as ASPX pages. The disadvantages include the following:

- The transfer must be to a page on the same Web server.
- Although Server.Transfer can be used to transfer from one ASP page to another ASP page, or one ASPX page to another ASPX page, it cannot transfer from an ASPX page to an ASP page. This is because the ASP page attempts to load into the ASP.NET application, which is not allowable.
- Server.Transfer does not include the posted data. This means that all data entered on the Order page can be lost.
- The URL is limited in size. The URL should be limited to 1,024 bytes in order to accommodate all browsers.

Object-Oriented Approach

All of the previous examples used the QueryString as a method of passing a value to a different page. The size limitation of the QueryString poses a big problem, especially if many values need to be passed to the new page.

With the object-oriented approach, Server.Transfer is used to navigate to the new page, but there is no need to pass data using the QueryString because the new page can get access to the original page via the HttpContext. The following Web Form page contains a Button called btnGetOrder and a TextBox called OrderID. Here is the code-behind page:

```
Public Class Order
    Inherits System.Web.UI.Page
    Public WithEvents OrderID As System.Web.UI.WebControls.TextBox
    Protected WithEvents btnGetOrder As System.Web.UI.WebControls.Button
    Private Sub Page_Load(ByVal sender As System.Object, _
            ByVal e As System.EventArgs) Handles MyBase.Load
        'Put user code to initialize the page here.
    End Sub
    Private Sub btnGetOrder_Click(ByVal sender As System.Object, _
            ByVal e As System.EventArgs) Handles btnGetOrder.Click
        Server.Transfer("OrderDetails.aspx")
    End Sub
End Class
```

The code-behind page is performing a simple Server.Transfer. Notice that the OrderID TextBox has been changed to Public. This allows access to the OrderID from the OrderDetails page. The OrderDetails Web Form page contains a label control called Label1. The following is the OrderDetails code-behind page:

```
Public Class OrderDetails
    Inherits System.Web.UI.Page
    Protected WithEvents Label1 As System.Web.UI.WebControls.Label
    Private Sub Page_Load(ByVal sender As System.Object, _
            ByVal e As System.EventArgs) Handles MyBase.Load
        'Put user code to initialize the page here.
        Dim o As Order
        o = CType(HttpContext.Current.Handler, Order)
        Label1.Text = o.OrderID.Text
    End Sub
End Class
```

The Page_Load method can get access to the original page through the HttpContext.Current.Handler. The Handler is the page that was originally called, and can be assigned to a variable, but must be *cast* to the Order class. (Casting is covered in the next chapter.) Since the OrderID TextBox is public, it is available, and the Text property is assigned to Label1's Text property.

This method of page navigation should always be considered first, due to its ability to get access to all of data from the original page. One of the advantages to using an object-oriented approach is that it allows all data from the original

Order page to be available to the OrderDetails page. This means that all posted data is available. The disadvantages include the following:

- The transfer must be to a page on the same Web server.
- This method can only transfer to an ASPX page.
- This method would require some client-side code in order to open a new child browser window.

Panels

This method does not perform page navigation; instead, it provides an illusion of page navigation. Panel navigation can be used when many settings need to be entered in a wizardlike fashion. A single page can be arranged with a sequence of panel controls. The panel control is a container for other controls. If the visible property is false, the panel and its contained controls are not displayed at the browser. In fact, if the user looks at the source code, there is no apparent sign of the panel and its controls!

Using panels effectively involves setting the page's pageLayout property to FlowLayout. When FlowLayout is selected, hidden panels do not take up space on the form. This allows the visible panel to essentially float to the top of the form.

Figure 12.12 shows an example of sequenced panels on a WebForm. This pageLayout property is set to FlowLayout, and the panels are HTML Grid-LayoutPanels. After the GridLayoutPanels are placed on the WebForm, right-click on the panel, and click Run As Server Control.

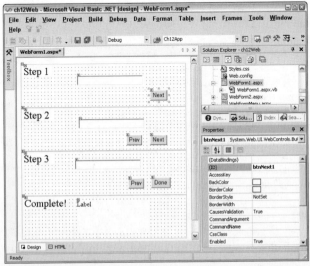

Figure 12.12   The sequenced panel layout is created on a single Web page.

The following is the HTML code for the page shown in Figure 12.12.

```
<%@ Page Language="vb" AutoEventWireup="false"
        Codebehind="WebForm1.aspx.vb" Inherits="ch12Web.WebForm1" %>
<!DOCTYPE HTML PUBLIC "-//W3C//DTD HTML 4.0 Transitional//EN">
<HTML>
  <HEAD>
            <title>WebForm1</title>
            <meta name="GENERATOR" content=
                "Microsoft Visual Studio.NET 7.0">
            <meta name="CODE_LANGUAGE" content="Visual Basic 7.0">
            <meta name="vs_defaultClientScript" content="JavaScript">
            <meta name="vs_targetSchema"
                content="http://schemas.microsoft.com/intellisense/ie5">
  </HEAD>
    <body>
            <form id="Form1" method="post" runat="server">
            <DIV id="DIV1" style=
                "WIDTH: 389px; POSITION: relative; HEIGHT: 100px"
                 runat="server" ms_positioning="GridLayout">
            <asp:TextBox id="txtStep1" style=
              "Z-INDEX: 101; LEFT: 133px; POSITION: absolute; TOP: 27px"
              runat="server"></asp:TextBox>
            <asp:Label id="lblStep1" style=
              "Z-INDEX: 102; LEFT: 7px; POSITION: absolute; TOP: 4px"
              runat="server" Width="71px" Height="25px"
              Font-Size="Large">Step 1</asp:Label>
            <asp:Button id="btnNext1" style=
              "Z-INDEX: 104; LEFT: 305px; POSITION: absolute; TOP: 62px"
              runat="server" Text="Next"></asp:Button>
            </DIV>
            <DIV id="DIV2" style=
              "WIDTH: 389px; POSITION: relative; HEIGHT: 100px"
              runat="server" ms_positioning="GridLayout">
            <asp:Label id="lblStep2" style=
              "Z-INDEX: 102; LEFT: 7px; POSITION: absolute; TOP: 4px"
              runat="server" Width="71px" Height="25px"
              Font-Size="Large">Step 2</asp:Label>
            <asp:Button id="btnNext2" style=
              "Z-INDEX: 103; LEFT: 304px; POSITION: absolute; TOP: 64px"
              runat="server" Text="Next" Width="40px"></asp:Button>
            <asp:Button id="btnPrev1" style=
              "Z-INDEX: 104; LEFT: 248px; POSITION: absolute; TOP: 64px"
              runat="server" Text="Prev"></asp:Button>
            <asp:TextBox id="txtStep2" style=
              "Z-INDEX: 105; LEFT: 136px; POSITION: absolute; TOP: 26px"
              runat="server"></asp:TextBox>
            </DIV>
            <DIV id="Div3" style=
              "WIDTH: 389px; POSITION: relative; HEIGHT: 102px"
              runat="server" ms_positioning="GridLayout">
```

```
<asp:Label id="lblStep3" style=
  "Z-INDEX: 102; LEFT: 6px; POSITION: absolute; TOP: 4px"
  runat="server" Width="71px" Height="25px"
  Font-Size="Large">Step 3</asp:Label>
<asp:Button id="btnDone" style=
  "Z-INDEX: 103; LEFT: 306px; POSITION: absolute; TOP: 62px"
  runat="server" Text="Done"></asp:Button>
<asp:Button id="btnPrev2" style=
  "Z-INDEX: 104; LEFT: 252px; POSITION: absolute; TOP: 63px"
  runat="server" Text="Prev"></asp:Button>
<asp:TextBox id="txtStep3" style=
  "Z-INDEX: 105; LEFT: 127px; POSITION: absolute; TOP: 20px"
  runat="server"></asp:TextBox>
  </DIV>
<DIV id="Div4" style=
  "WIDTH: 389px; POSITION: relative; HEIGHT: 100px"
  runat="server" ms_positioning="GridLayout">
<asp:Label id="lblDone" style=
  "Z-INDEX: 101; LEFT: 130px; POSITION: absolute; TOP: 10px"
  runat="server" Width="168px" Height="75px">Label</asp:Label>
<asp:Label id="lblComplete" style=
  "Z-INDEX: 102; LEFT: 6px; POSITION: absolute; TOP: 4px"
  runat="server" Width="71px" Height="25px"
  Font-Size="Large">Complete!</asp:Label>
  </DIV>
  </form>
</body>
</HTML>
```

Each of the sections is composed of an HTML Panel control, which is simply a DIV tag with a runat attribute set to server, and an attribute called ms_positioning, which is set to GridLayout. The code-behind page for this sample is as follows:

```
Public Class WebForm1
    Inherits System.Web.UI.Page
    Protected WithEvents Div1 As _
        System.Web.UI.HtmlControls.HtmlGenericControl
    Protected WithEvents Div2 As _
        System.Web.UI.HtmlControls.HtmlGenericControl
    Protected WithEvents Div3 As _
        System.Web.UI.HtmlControls.HtmlGenericControl
    Protected WithEvents Div4 As _
        System.Web.UI.HtmlControls.HtmlGenericControl
    Protected WithEvents lblStep1 As _
        System.Web.UI.WebControls.Label
    Protected WithEvents lblStep2 As _
        System.Web.UI.WebControls.Label
    Protected WithEvents lblStep3 As _
        System.Web.UI.WebControls.Label
```

```vbnet
        Protected WithEvents lblDone As _
             System.Web.UI.WebControls.Label
        Protected WithEvents lblComplete As _
             System.Web.UI.WebControls.Label
        Protected WithEvents btnNext1 As _
             System.Web.UI.WebControls.Button
        Protected WithEvents btnNext2 As _
             System.Web.UI.WebControls.Button
        Protected WithEvents btnPrev1 As _
             System.Web.UI.WebControls.Button
        Protected WithEvents btnPrev2 As _
             System.Web.UI.WebControls.Button
        Protected WithEvents btnDone As _
             System.Web.UI.WebControls.Button
        Protected WithEvents txtStep1 As _
             System.Web.UI.WebControls.TextBox
        Protected WithEvents txtStep2 As _
             System.Web.UI.WebControls.TextBox
        Protected WithEvents txtStep3 As _
             System.Web.UI.WebControls.TextBox
    #Region " Web Form Designer Generated Code "
        'This call is required by the Web Form Designer.
        <System.Diagnostics.DebuggerStepThrough()> _
         Private Sub InitializeComponent()
         End Sub
         Private Sub Page_Init(ByVal sender As System.Object, _
             ByVal e As System.EventArgs) Handles MyBase.Init
            'CODEGEN: This method call is required by the Web Form Designer
            'Do not modify it using the code editor.
             InitializeComponent()
        End Sub
    #End Region
        Private Sub Page_Load(ByVal sender As System.Object, _
             ByVal e As System.EventArgs) Handles MyBase.Load
            If Not Page.IsPostBack Then
                GoPage(1)
            End If
        End Sub
        Private Sub GoPage(ByVal page As Integer)
            Div1.Visible = IIf(page = 1, True, False)
            Div2.Visible = IIf(page = 2, True, False)
            Div3.Visible = IIf(page = 3, True, False)
            Div4.Visible = IIf(page = 4, True, False)
        End Sub
        Private Sub btnNext1_Click(ByVal sender As System.Object, _
             ByVal e As System.EventArgs) Handles btnNext1.Click
            GoPage(2)
        End Sub
        Private Sub btnPrev1_Click(ByVal sender As System.Object, _
             ByVal e As System.EventArgs) Handles btnPrev1.Click
```

```
            GoPage(1)
        End Sub
        Private Sub btnNext2_Click(ByVal sender As System.Object, _
            ByVal e As System.EventArgs) Handles btnNext2.Click
            GoPage(3)
        End Sub
        Private Sub btnPrev2_Click(ByVal sender As System.Object, _
            ByVal e As System.EventArgs) Handles btnPrev2.Click
            GoPage(2)
        End Sub
        Private Sub btnDone_Click(ByVal sender As System.Object, _
            ByVal e As System.EventArgs) Handles btnDone.Click
            GoPage(4)
            Dim lf As String = "<br>"
            lblDone.Text = txtStep1.Text & lf & _
                txtStep2.Text & lf & _
                txtStep3.Text & lf
        End Sub
    End Class
```

The browser output for this page is shown in Figure 12.13. Notice how the only visible panel is displayed at the top of the page. This is because invisible panels don't generate any HTML. The settings for the controls that are with the panel are contained in ViewState so that the data is available, even when the panel is invisible.

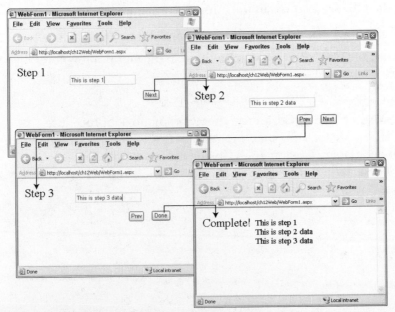

Figure 12.13 Using panels to present the illusion of switching between pages.

The advantages of using Panel navigation include the following:

- Because all of the panels are on the same page, the form data remains available.

- Although this example was done with server-side code, this method could be done with client-side code as well.

The one disadvantage is that grouping many panels on a page can become somewhat unmanageable.

Lab 12.1: Maintaining State

In this lab, you explore several methods of maintaining state in an ASP.NET application while changing from one Web page to another. You work with the CustomerList.aspx page, which currently displays a list of customers in a DataGrid and contains a button to save a customer's orders to an XML file. The program is modified by adding a summary information page. After saving, the page transfers the user to the summary information page. This page retrieves data from the CustomerList.aspx page and displays it.

Modify the Customer List Page

In this section, you modify the CustomerList.aspx code-behind page to expose the data that is required in the InformationSummary page.

1. To start this lab, open the OrderEntrySystemSolution from Lab 11.1.

2. Right-click the OrderEntrySystemSolution in the Solution Explorer, and click Check Out.

3. Open the CustomerList.aspx code behind page.

4. At the bottom of the dgCustomers_ItemCommand subprocedure, add code to store the customer information from the DataGrid in the following variables: CustomerID, CustomerName, and Contact-Name. These variables are scoped to be available anywhere within the request.

5. Add code to transfer to the InformationSummary.aspx page. The following code shows the finished subroutine:

```
Private Sub dgCustomers_ItemCommand( _
 ByVal source As Object, _
 ByVal e As System.Web.UI.WebControls.DataGridCommandEventArgs) _
 Handles dgCustomers.ItemCommand
     If e.CommandName = "Save" Then
          Dim ds As DataSet = CType(Session("Customers"),
DataSet)
          Dim xml As XmlDataDocument
          If Session("CustomersXml") Is Nothing Then
               xml = New XmlDataDocument(
                    Session("Customers"))
               Session("CustomersXml") = xml
          Else
               xml = CType( _
                    Session("CustomersXml"), XmlDataDocument)
          End If
          Dim path As String = Server.MapPath(".") & "\"
          'Get Customer Key
          Dim CustomerKey As String
          CustomerKey = dgCustomers.DataKeys(e.Item.ItemIndex)
          path &= CustomerKey & ".xml"
          'Open the XmlWriter.
          Dim xmlWriter As New XmlTextWriter(path, _
           System.Text.Encoding.UTF8)
          xmlWriter.WriteStartDocument()
          Dim CustomerXml As XmlNode
          Dim xPathQuery As String
          xPathQuery = String.Format( _
           "//Customers[@CustomerID='{0}']", CustomerKey)
          CustomerXml = xml.SelectSingleNode(xPathQuery)
          CustomerXml.WriteTo(xmlWriter)
          xmlWriter.Close()
          Context.Items("CustomerKey") = CustomerKey
          Context.Items("CompanyName") = e.Item.Cells(2).Text
          Context.Items("ContactName") = e.Item.Cells(3).Text
          Server.Transfer("InformationSummary.aspx")
     End If
End Sub
```

Create the Summary Information Form

In this section, you create a Web Form that displays summary information.

1. Right-click the Customer project. Click Add, click Add Web Form, and name the new page InformationSummary.aspx.

2. Change the PageLayout properties to FlowLayout.

3. Add a title to the page. The title should be *Information Summary*.

4. Add a label control under the title.

5. In the code-behind page, add code to retrieve the CustomerID, CustomerName, and ContactName from the CustomerList.aspx page, and display this data in the Label control. The following code shows the finished Page_Load method:

```
Private Sub Page_Load( _
  ByVal sender As System.Object, _
  ByVal e As System.EventArgs) _
  Handles MyBase.Load
      Label1.Text = "Customer ID: " & _
          Context.Items("CustomerKey") & "<br>"
      Label1.Text &= "Customer:     " & _
          Context.Items("CompanyName") & "<br>"
      Label1.Text &= "Contact:      " & _
          Context.Items("ContactName") & "<br>"
  End Sub
```

Test the Information Summary Page

To test the ability to store data while transferring the user to another page, the CustomerList page must be set as the startup page, and the project can be started. After that, a customer is selected, and the data should be displayed on the InformationSummary page.

1. Right-click the CustomerList.aspx page in the Solution Explorer, and click Set As Start Page.

2. Run the application. The results should appear as shown in Figure 12.14.

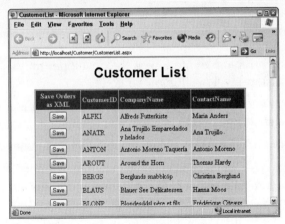

Figure 12.14 The CustomerList.aspx page.

3. Click the Save button of one customer. This saves the customer's orders as XML, and performs a transfer to the InformationSummary.aspx page, as shown in Figure 12.15.

4. Save the Solution, and check it back into Visual SourceSafe.

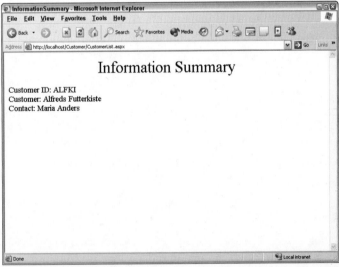

Figure 12.15 The browser output when passing data between pages by using the Context.Items collection.

Summary

- The Global.asax file is an optional file into which the developer may place application- and session-level event handler code.

- The HttpContext class is a wrapper class that provides a simple object model of the actual request and response.

- The HTTP handler is responsible for processing the request and generating the response.

- HTTP modules extend the middle of the HTTP pipeline and allow a request and a response message to be examined and modified as they pass between the browser and the HTTP handler.

- State management can be provided by the use of Application, Session, Context.Items, Cache, or Shared (static) variables.

- Page navigation can be done by hyperlinks, Window.Open, Response.Redirect, Server.Transfer, the OO Approach, or Panels.

Review Questions

1. What are three methods of saving session state?

2. What is the scope of variables that are stored in the Context.Items collection?

3. What is a disadvantage to using the Response.Redirect method to navigate to a new Web page?

4. What are three methods of storing data with an Application-wide scope?

5. How can page navigation occur at the server and still allow access to the original page data?

Answers to Review Questions

1. InProc, SQLServer, and StateServer.

2. These items are scoped to the request. This means that the Items are available when using Server.Transfer.

3. The Response.Redirect method causes extra network traffic, because this method sends a message back to the browser to tell the browser to request a different page.

4. Application variables, shared (static) variables, and cached variables.

5. The object-oriented approach uses Server.Transfer to navigate to another page, and data can be exposed on the original page by creating public properties or public data members.

CHAPTER 13

Site Security

There is a rewarding feeling when a Web site is created and put into production on the Web. The site can be viewed from anywhere that has Internet access. The fruit of everyone's labor is finally realized and everyone is proud of the work that is globally visible.

For hackers, a new target is born. A globally visible Web site is exposed to the world of hackers. Some hackers want to penetrate site security just to see if they can. Others are interested in stealing data and products. Still others are interested in defacing or destroying a site.

There is never a good time to be hacked, but it always seems to happen when there are a million other things going on. A hacker who destroys a site can force a Web site administrator to scramble for the latest backup, which hopefully was recent.

For a long time, many people figured their site would never be hacked because there are many bigger targets on the Internet. And, for a long time this was true. But hackers are now writing programs that start at IP address 0.0.0.0 and increment through 255.255.255.255, and look for opportunities to hack any site that has a security hole. Hackers can enlist millions of computers into their hacker army in order to perform attacks on larger targets.

Staying current with the latest security patches, running antivirus software, and providing firewalls with logging software is a requirement for public Web sites. There are also many things that can be done to control access to resources on a Web site. Some parts of a Web site may be public, but other parts of a Web site may require authorization to access private data. This section covers many of these aspects in order to ensure that only authorized people have access to private data.

Classroom Q & A

Q: Is there a way to display a custom login page instead of the ugly gray box that is displayed when I set up security in Internet Information Server?

A: Yes. ASP.NET provides Forms authentication which allows you to provide your own customized Web page for logging into the Web site.

Q: I want to use SSL on my Web site to encrypt credit card information, but the SSL port is grayed out in Internet Information Server. How can I get this to operate?

A: The SSL port is probably grayed out because you have not installed a digital certificate for your site. SSL is an important part of Web e-commerce, and this chapter covers SSL in great detail.

Q: Is there a way to confine code to being able to have access to a certain folder, regardless of who is logged in?

A: Yes. The .NET Framework provides Code Access Security, which allows you to assign permissions to the code, as opposed to assigning permissions to the user.

Understanding Security Basics

Before diving too deeply into security, it is important to understand some fundamentals about security and the types of security that are available to protect a Web site. Figure 13.1 shows the different areas where security is available. When the browser communicates to the server, the communications can be encrypted using Secure Sockets Layer (SSL).

When Internet Information Server (IIS) receives a request, IIS may require the user to be authenticated first, by means of Standard, Windows, or Digest authentication. If the user is requesting a file that is not handled by ASP.NET, then IIS retrieves the file directly from the file system, but the user must be authorized to receive the file by the file system. If the file is handled by ASP.NET, then ASP.NET has the ability to provide its own authentication by using Windows, Forms, or Passport authentication. After being authenticated, any code that is run must be authorized by Code Access Security, and any files that are requested must be authorized by the file system. This chapter covers these aspects of security.

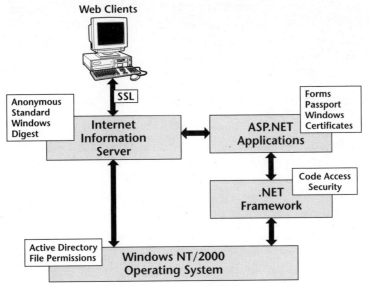

Figure 13.1 Areas where security is available.

Authentication

Authentication is the process of obtaining identification credentials, such as name and password, from a user and validating those credentials against an authority, as shown in Figure 13.2. The credentials typically contain an identifier and proof, which could be a username and password, an email address and password, an email address and digital certificate, and so on.

Authenticating a user does not imply the granting of any permission to access resources. This is done though authorization.

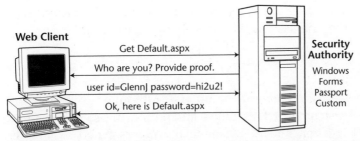

Figure 13.2 Authentication involves providing an identifier and proof.

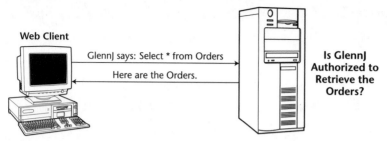

Figure 13.3 Authorization requires determining if a user should have a specific type of access to a resource.

Authorization

Authorization is the process of determining whether a user should be granted a specific type of access to a resource. The resource may be a file, a printer, a database, the Registry, or any other controlled resource. The type of access may be read, write, add, or delete, or it may be resource specific, such as print (see Figure 13.3).

Authorization may be performed on a user basis, a role basis, or a combination of the two. Using roles can simplify the management of permissions. If a role is created for managers, it is easy to assign write permissions to the manager's role, instead of assigning permissions separately to each manager.

Impersonation

Impersonation is the process of allowing applications to execute with the identity of the client on whose behalf they are operating. If ASP.NET is impersonating a user when executing code, any authorization that is required is based on permissions that have been granted to the user. This method can be used to allow IIS to impersonate a user in order to retrieve a file, where NTFS file permissions dictate whether the user is authorized to retrieve the file.

Delegation

Delegation is impersonation across computers. Although impersonation works fine within a machine, it fails when attempting to access resources across machines. Delegation allows a user to be impersonated to another machine to access remote resources.

Windows Security

Microsoft Windows provides a directory of users and user roles for all users who are allowed to access a computer, domain, or enterprise.

Workgroup Environment

In a workgroup environment, each computer has its own directory of users who need to access the computer (see Figure 13.4). If four users exist, and each user needs access to all machines, then matching accounts must be created in all machines. Roles or groups also can be created in each machine to simplify the assignment of users to resources. For example, a group could be created called Managers. The Managers group can be assigned to all resources to which managers have access. When a manager is hired, the manager can be simply placed into the Managers group. This is much quicker that authorizing a user for each individual resource.

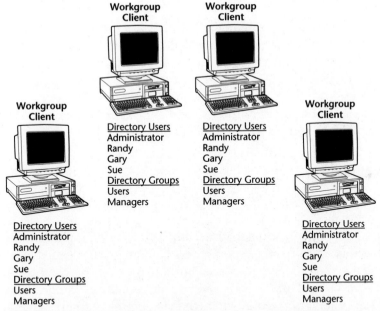

Figure 13.4 The workgroup environment. If any user maintenance is required it must be done on all four machines.

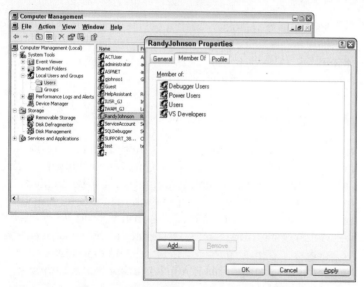

Figure 13.5   The Local Users and Groups snap-in. The user called RandyJohnson has been selected, and the groups that he is a member of are displayed.

Depending on the operating system that is installed, adding users and groups can be done by clicking Start, Control Panel, Administrative Tools, Computer Management, Local Users and Groups, or by clicking Start, Control Panel, User Accounts. Figure 13.5 shows the Local Users and Groups. The Local Users and Groups program provides the ability to create new users, and add users to groups. In the workgroup environment, account maintenance, such as changing the password, is repeated on all machines.

Domain Environment

In a domain or enterprise environment, servers that act as domain controllers contain a directory, called Active Directory, which contains the list of users who have access to the domain or enterprise. Although workstation machines still contain a directory, this directory should only contain groups, called local groups, which are assigned to resources (see Figure 13.6).

Accounts that are created in Active Directory automatically replicate to other Active Directory servers. Account maintenance, such as changing a password or deleting a user, only needs to be done at one location.

Adding users to Active Directory is done by using the Active Directory Users and Computers tool. This tool allows new users to be added and even allows objects, such as computers, to be partitioned into separate administrative units, called organizational units. Any changes that are performed while in Active Directory are propagated to other domain controllers automatically.

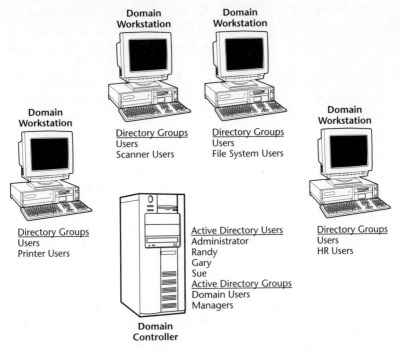

Figure 13.6 The domain environment containing Active Directory.

Active Directory is very extensible, and can store other information, such as certificates, user preferences, printer location information, and email information. Active Directory is intended to holds thousands of users.

NTFS File System

Windows provides NTFS, FAT, and FAT32 file systems. The FAT and FAT32 file systems do not offer any security, and should not be used in a Web environment. FAT (File Allocation Table) and FAT32 are intended to be used when it is necessary to upgrade or coexist with a Windows 95, 98, or Me operating system.

NTFS (NT File System) is much more stable than FAT and FAT32, because it provides the following:

- A transacted file system that can perform an autorecovery if power is abruptly lost.
- Disk quota management, which allows an administrator to limit the amount of disk space that can be used by any user.
- Events that are triggered when a file is added, deleted, or modified on the file system. This is great when it is necessary, and processes any new files that are placed into the folder.

Most importantly, however, NTFS provides security. Permissions may be assigned at the folder or file level. Each file and folder has a Discretionary Access Control List (DACL) that contains an Access Control Entry (ACE) for each user or group who is assigned permissions.

When permissions are assigned to a resource, the user receives the combined permissions of all groups that the user is a member of, except when a Deny ACE exists. Figure 13.7 shows an example of a file called SalesData.xml with its corresponding DACL. Sue's effective permission is Full Control, since she receives the union of the permissions of all groups that she is a member of, and her specific permissions. Glenn's effective permission is Read and Execute. Although Glenn is a member of Managers, which should give Glenn Write permission, Glenn has a Deny Write ACE. Regardless of granted permissions, the Deny Write always takes precedence.

In summary, any Web site that is exposed to the public should always be hosted on an NTFS partitioned drive. This is the safest and most secure storage method that the Windows operating system provides.

 NTFS file security makes the final determination of whether a user can access a file or not, based on the file's DACL, regardless of settings in IIS and ASP.NET.

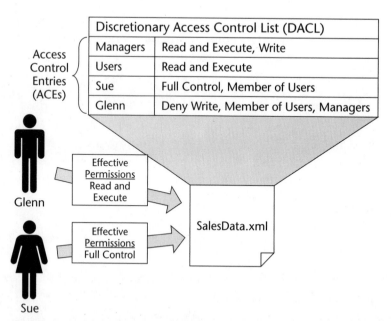

Figure 13.7 The effective permission is the union of all granted permissions minus any denied permissions.

Internet Information Server Security

Internet Information Server provides several security mechanisms that can be implemented based on the needs of the Web site. Security can be applied at the file, folder, Web site, or computer level. Security settings are typically applied at the computer level, and all Web sites, folders, and files inherit the settings. Settings can then be overridden as necessary at the Web site, folder, or file level.

This section explores authentication methods, IP address and domain name restrictions, and secure communications resources that are available in IIS, as shown in Figure 13.8.

Authentication Methods

IIS authentication can be used to require users to provide a valid Windows username and password in order to access the Web site, folder, or file. This section covers the authentication options that are available.

Anonymous

Anonymous access is typically used when allowing users to access public areas of a Web site without requiring users to enter a username and password. This method of access uses an account called the IUSR_*machinename* (commonly referred to as the I-User account) to access resources such as files.

The IUSR account is created on the Web server when IIS is installed. This account has limited permissions. The only Windows group that this account is a member of is the Guests group.

Figure 13.8 The security options that are available in IIS.

When attempting to access a resource, such as a file, IIS impersonates the IUSR account and attempts to access the resource. If the access is successful, the resource is available to the anonymous Web site user. If the access is not successful, IIS attempts to use another access method, if other methods are available.

 When using ASP.NET, the IUSR account is not used. A new account is created when ASP.NET is installed, called ASPNET. This is the default account for ASP.NET anonymous access.

Basic

Basic authentication is the most common method of collecting a username and password in order to authenticate them against a Windows user account. With Basic authentication selected, the username and password are base64 encoded and sent across the network. Base64 encoding provides a method of sending special characters without interfering with the regular HTTP communications.

Base64 encoding is not encryption. Base64 encoders and decoders are readily available in many languages. The .NET Framework's Convert class contains a FromBase64String method and a ToBase64String method that can easily be used to read usernames and passwords that have been Base64 encoded. Secure Sockets Layer (SSL) encrypted communications can be used with Basic authentication in order to ensure that the username and password cannot be intercepted.

 Basic authentication with SSL is the most common method of authentication on the Internet, because it operates on most of today's browsers and can pass through most of today's firewalls.

Digest

Digest authentication provides authentication by sending an MD5 hash of the user's credentials across the network. This is a one-way hash, which is not decipherable. When the hash is received, the hash is compared against the hash of the credentials that the server has. If the hash codes are the same, the user is authenticated.

Like Basic authentication, Digest authentication can pass through firewalls, but the use of Digest authentication requires a browser that supports HTTP 1.1 protocol as defined in the RFC 2617 specification at www.w3c.org. This requirement limits the use of Digest authentication to a small number of browsers.

Digest authentication requires IIS to be installed in a Windows Active Directory Domain, and the user must also have a valid account in the domain.

In order to use Digest authentication, the user credentials must be stored as clear text in Active Directory. There is another version of Digest authentication called Advanced Digest, which is the same as Digest authentication, except that the user credentials are stored in Active Directory as a hash, instead of being stored as clear text.

Digest authentication is not a good choice for Internet sites, where there is no control of the browser. This authentication method may be a good choice for server-to-server communications in an intranet or extranet environment, where the servers are in the same domain, and it is not necessary to pass through firewalls.

Integrated Windows

Integrated Windows authentication, formerly known as NTLM and NT Challenge/Response, is a secure method of authentication. The user's credentials are hashed, and the hash is passed across the network.

Integrated Windows authentication is currently supported by Internet Explorer. This authentication is not capable of passing through most of today's firewalls.

Integrated Windows authentication provides the ability to be transparently authenticated, meaning that the currently logged-on user's credentials are used without requiring the user to reenter a username and password.

The use of Integrated Windows authentication is a bad choice for public sites, but a great choice for an intranet site.

Certificate

Internet Information Server provides the ability to use server certificates and client certificates. A server certificate is used for Server authentication, which means that the server certificate proves that the server is the server it claims it is. A server certificate must be installed on the server in order to enable Secure Sockets Layer (SSL) encrypted communications. Secure Sockets Layer encrypted communications should be used when private data is being transferred across the Internet.

Certificates can also be used to perform User authentication. This requires each user to have a certificate. The user certificate is presented to the server in order to prove that the user is who the user claims to be. The certificate is then mapped to a Windows user account, which is used to access protected resources. Internet Information Server also allows groups of client certificates to be mapped to a single Windows user account. In this scenario, the certificate provides the identity, while the Windows user account provides the authorized access to resources.

Certificates can pass through a firewall. Certificates must be obtained from a mutually trusted certificate authority (CA), such as Entrust.net or Verisign.com. A server certificate is required for any public Web site that retrieves private data from a user. User certificates are optional for secure communications.

IP Address and Domain Name Restrictions

One method of restricting access to a Web site is through the IP Address and Domain Name Restrictions option. This option can be set to grant or deny access to everyone, and then you can enter the exceptions. IP Address and Domain Name Restrictions are best used in an intranet environment to deny access to everyone except the people who are trying to access the site from any IP address that is within the corporate intranet. This option is available only on Windows Server products.

Secure Communications

Secure Sockets Layer (SSL) communications provide encrypted communications when private data is being sent across the network. A server certificate must be obtained and installed in order to use Secure Sockets Layer communications. The server certificate contains information about the Web server and company that is providing the Web site. The certificate also contains a public key, which can be used by the client when encrypting messages to the server.

Server certificates must be issued by a mutually trusted Certificate Authority (CA) in order to be successfully used for encrypted communications. The Certificate Authority is responsible for verifying the server certificate.

Obtaining the server certificate from the certificate authority typically requires providing information about the company. The amount of information that is required depends on the certificate authority and the level of security that is desired. The Certificate Authority reviews items, such as your organization's Dun & Bradstreet number and Articles of Incorporation. The Certificate Authority may also complete a thorough background check to ensure that the organization is what it claims to be and is not claiming a false identity

The success of certificate authentication requires that the party receiving a certificate trust the Certificate Authority who issued the certificate, and that the Certificate Authority properly verified the owner of the certificate.

Providing a digital certificate helps to eliminate Web site spoofing. It is rather easy to set up an illegitimate Web site that looks like someone else's and then capture unsuspecting customer's credit information.

How SSL Works

When a user navigates to a URL that starts with *https*, negotiation for a session key begins. The negotiation is done via the SSL handshake protocol. The client starts by sending a hello message to the server. The server must respond with a hello message.

The server's hello message also contains its certificate. This certificate contains its public key, which has been digitally signed by its Certificate Authority's private key (see Figure 13.9).

If the browser has the trusted Certificate Authority's certificate installed, the browser can use the Certificate Authority's public key to validate the digital signature that is on the server's public key.

If the server's public key is valid, the browser generates a session key, encrypts the session key with the server's public key, and transfers the encrypted session key to the server.

The server can decrypt the session key with its private key and start an encrypted communication session with the browser.

 The default operation of some browsers, such as Internet Explorer, does not check with the Certificate Authority to see if the certificate has been revoked prior to the certificate's normal expiration. On Internet Explorer, this option can be enabled by clicking Tools, Internet Options, Advanced, Check For Server Revocation.

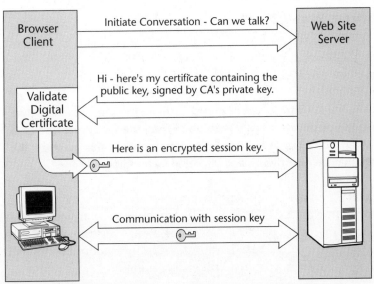

Figure 13.9 When the browser navigates to a URL that starts with https, negotiation for a session key starts.

Client Certificates

Internet Information Server also provides the ability to require client certificates in order to prove that the client is who the client claims to be. Client certificates are typically used in an environment where a high degree of security is required, and a method to distribute client certificates has been established. The use of client certificates is not a requirement for providing e-commerce on a public Web site.

Secure Sockets Layer (SSL) Setup

There are several steps involved in setting up Secure Sockets Layer communication. It's easy to make mistakes anywhere during the process. Most Certificate Authorities assist with changes that are required for a short time, and then charge for changes that need to be made. This section goes through the steps that are required to set up SSL, back up the certificate, and restore the certificate.

Using SSL on Computers that Host Multiple Web Sites

Windows supports the ability to host many Web sites. Each Web site must have its own unique IP address, port, or host header. With the lack of available IP addresses, most hosting companies use host headers to provide hosting services for multiple domain names.

SSL does not work with host headers. In order to use SSL on a machine that hosts multiple domain names, a unique IP address must be provided for each Web site that uses SSL.

Create the Certificate Request

The Web Server Certificate wizard can be used to generate a certificate request file. After starting the wizard, click Create a New Certificate. Next, click Prepare The Request Now, But Send It Later.

 The Web Server Certificate wizard must be run on the same machine that processes the certificate when it is received from the Certificate Authority. After the certificate has been received and processed in this machine, the certificate may be exported to and imported by another machine.

The next screen is a prompt for a friendly name for the certificate and a bit length. The friendly name is visible on the certificate, but can be any name that is desired. The default bit length of 1,024 results in 128-bit encryption, which is the recommended setting for U.S.-based Web sites. For international sites, 512 bit should be selected, which results in 40-bit encryption.

The Organization Information screen prompts for the organization name and the organization unit. The organization unit is typically the name of a branch office or department within the company.

The Site's Common Name screen prompts for the common name. This is one of the most important screens in the request process. The name that is entered in this text box is the name that is required when an https request is made (see Figure 13.10). For example, if www.ByRef.com is entered in this text box, then https://www.ByRef.com *must* be the beginning part of the URL when encrypted communication is required.

If the request is made to https://localhost/ch13Web/WebForm1.aspx, a message box is displayed, indicating that the name on the certificate (www.ByRef.com) does not match the name of the site (localhost). The common name is not case sensitive on Internet Information Server.

 Many Web sites generate certificate error messaages because the developer has used a common name such as www.ByRef.com, but a link on the site points to a URL such as https://secure.ByRef.com. Since www.ByRef.com does not match secure.ByRef.com, the error message box is displayed.

The geographical information screen requests country/region, state/province, and city/locality information. The country must be the two-character country code. The state and city must not be abbreviated.

The certificate request filename screen prompts for a location for the certificate request. The file is an encrypted text file and contains the organization's public key, the name, locality, and the common name. The local certificate store holds the complete certificate request, including the private key.

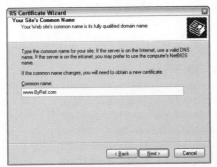

Figure 13.10 The common name must match the URL that is used when encrypted communication is required.

Submit the Certificate Request

The certificate request is also known as the Certificate Signing Request (CSR). This certificate request is submitted to the Certificate Authority with the intention of receiving a digitally signed certificate, which was signed with the Certificate Authority's private key. Depending on the level of security that is required, this could take one week to several weeks. The delay is due to the Certificate Authority's performing a check to ensure that the certificate is being issued to the correct entity.

Care should be taken to choose a Certificate Authority that has a trusted certificate installed by most browsers. Some Certificate Authorities are:

- www.entrust.net
- www.thawte.com
- www.baltimore.com
- www.verisign.com

The Certificate Authority prompts for the Certificate Signing Request. The text file that was created from Internet Information Server can be opened, and the contents are copied and pasted into the text box that is provided.

The Certificate Authority prompts for other information as well. After this information is complete, there is a delay of several days before the signed certificate is received, usually via email.

Processing the Certificate

The certificate typically arrives from the Certificate Authority by email. If the certificate is an attachment, it can simply be saved to disk. If the certificate is embedded as encrypted text, it can be copied and pasted into a file with Notepad. The file should have a .cer extension and should contain data that looks like the following. Notice that the header and footer are included in the file.

```
-----BEGIN CERTIFICATE-----
MQswCQYDVQQGEwJVUzEgMB4GA1UEChMXU1NBIERhdGEgU2VjdXJpdHksIEluYy4x
LjAsBgNVBAsTJVN1Y3VyZSBTZXJ2ZXIgQ2VydGlmaWNhdGlvbiBBdXRob3JpdHkw
HhcNMDEwMzE2MDAwMDAwWhcNMDExMTE3MjM1OTU5WjCBuzELMAkGA1UEBhMCVVMx
DTALBgNVBAgTBE9oaW8xEjAQBgNVBAcUCUF2b24gTGFrZTEpMCcGA1UEChQgR0xF
Tk4gSk9IT1NPTiBURUNITk1DQUwgVFJBSU5JTkcxEjAQBgNVBAsUCUNPU1BPUkFU
Z24sIEluYy4wAwIBARo9VmVyaVNpZ24ncyBDUFMgaW5jb3JwLiBieSByZWZlcmVu
Y2UgbGlhYi4gbHRkLiAoYyk5NyBWZXJpU2lnbjAdBgNVHSUEFjAUBggrBgEFBQcD
AQYIKwYBBQUHAwIwGQYKYIZIAYb4RQEGDwQLFgkxMDMzMTQ3OTAwDQYJKoZIhvcN
AQEFBQADfgCMjTCDYjvLb75QjSp3AsHoI0RF5X59SgW3+WKsmNnTC4LJr8yg4kIN
vTvdesOKoxfU2egMYauwScazA6kgsR1Y8XdUq+EQYoDgbJAn1Q==
-----END CERTIFICATE-----
```

The Web Server Certificate wizard must be run to process the certificate. The first screen is a prompt to process the certificate request, or delete it.

The next screen prompts for the location of the .cer file. Simply browse to the file, and click Next.

The next screen displays the certificate summary information. This information should match the information that was originally submitted. When the wizard has finished, the certificate is installed in the local computer's certificate store and is attached to the Web site for which the certificate was requested.

Backing Up and Exporting a Certificate

Backing up the certificate is extremely important in order to ensure recovery in the event of a disaster. Also, if the certificate needs to be copied to additional servers, this process is used to retrieve the certificate so it can be installed in other Web farm computers.

The Certificate snap-in must be executed. This is a component of the Microsoft Management Console (MMC). To execute, click Start, Run, MMC.exe to start the Management Console. Next, click File, Add, Remove Snap-In, Add, Certificates. The snap-in prompts for the desired certificate store to manage. Click Computer Account. Next, click Local Computer.

After the snap-in is installed, open Certificates (Local Computer), Personal, Certificates to reveal the certificate that was installed. Right-click the certificate, click All Tasks, Export, as shown in Figure 13.11.

The Certificate Export Wizard is started. Be sure to select the option to export the private key. This option is required to be able to restore the key later.

The next screen prompts for the export file format. The default PKCS @12 is acceptable, which creates a .pfx file that can be imported into any machine.

The next screen prompts for a password. A password should always be provided. When you import a password a prompt is displayed, and the text box for the password on this screen cannot be left blank.

The next screen prompts for the filename. The file should have a .pfx extension. After the file is saved, the export is complete.

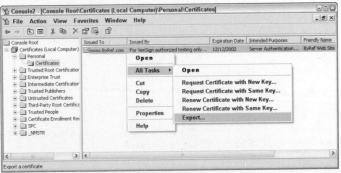

Figure 13.11 Export the certificate using the Certificate Snap-in in the Microsoft Management Console.

Restoring and Importing a Certificate

The Certificate Snap-In can be used to import or restore a certificate. For information on executing the Certificate Snap-In, see the previous topic: *Backing Up and Exporting a Certificate*. Open the snap-in and click Certificates (Local Computer), Personal, Certificates. Right-click Certificates, and click All Tasks, Import as shown in Figure 13.12.

The Certificate Import wizard starts and prompts for the location of the .pfx file to be imported.

Next, the wizard prompts for the password that was assigned to the file. Note that this screen contains a check box to indicate that the private key can be exported. Ideally, the .pfx file should be placed in a secure location, and should be the only way to get access to the private key. If this check box is selected, the certificate with its private key can be exported from this machine.

The next screen prompts for the destination certificate store. The personal certificate store should be selected. When the wizard has finished, the certificate is available to be attached to a Web site.

Attaching an Imported Certificate to a Web Site

When a certificate has been imported using the Certificate Import wizard, it is placed into the local computer's personal certificate store. The certificate can then be bound to a Web site on the local computer.

When the Web Server Certificate wizard is started, the server certificate screen provides the ability to assign an existing certificate. The certificate must exist in the local computer's personal certificate store. The wizard displays a list of all certificates that are in the local computer's personal certificate store. A certificate must be selected, and it is bound to the current Web site.

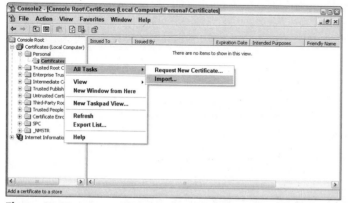

Figure 13.12   The Certificate Snap-In is used to import certificates.

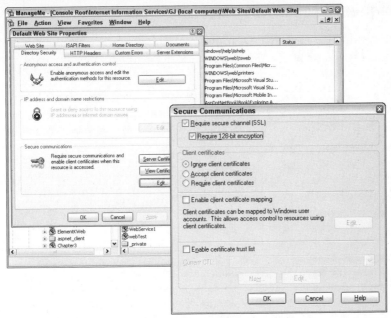

Figure 13.13   The Secure Communications window is used to require SSL communication.

Configuring IIS to Require SSL

After obtaining and processing a certificate, SSL communications may be used on any page on the site by using https instead of http in the URL. The problem is that http can also be used.

To require SSL to be used, edit the properties of the desired folders and files. Select the security tab, and then click Edit in the secure communications section of the security window. The Secure Communications window is displayed, as shown in Figure 13.13. This screen contains the settings to require SSL, and also require client certificates, if necessary. If a file is configured to require SSL and a user attempts to retrieve the file using http instead of https, an HTTP 403.4 error is displayed, which states that access is forbidden and SSL is required.

ASP.NET Security

ASP.NET provides an extensible framework for implementing security. Out of the box, ASP.NET provides the ability to authenticate against Windows, Forms, and Passport authorities. The developer can provide custom authentication as well. Before ASP.NET authentication is covered, it is important to understand the overall security process that is involved.

ASP.NET Request Processing Account

Figure 13.14 shows the process, from a high-level perspective, of delivering a requested resource to the browser. When a request for a resource is received by Internet Information Server, the normal checks are done to ensure that the request came from an IP address and domain that are acceptable. Internet Information Server also authenticates the user in accordance with its authentication settings. If the authentication is successful, the request is passed to ASP.NET for processing.

ASP.NET uses the user's account if impersonation is active or the IUSR account if anonymous access is active. Identity impersonation is settable in the machine.config file or in the Web.config file by using the identity XML tag. Some samples of the proper use of the identity XML tag are as follows:

```
<!--
    identity Attributes:
    impersonate="[true|false]" - Impersonate Windows User
    userName="Windows user account to impersonate" | empty string
        implies impersonate the LOGON user specified by IIS
    password="password of above specified account" | empty string
-->
    <identity impersonate="false" />
    <identity impersonate="true" userName="joe" password="joepass" />
    <identity impersonate="true" userName="" password="" />
    <identity impersonate="true" />
```

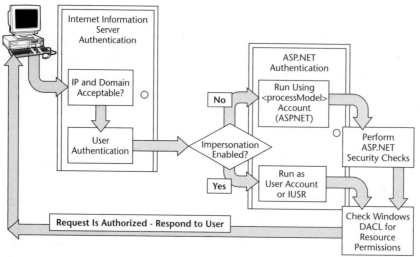

Figure 13.14 The process of delivering a requested resource to the browser.

The first example disables impersonation. The other examples enable impersonation. When impersonation is enabled, it is possible to specify a user name and password that is used by all users. If the name and password are not specified as shown in the last two examples, the username of the current user is used. This account is used to access the desired resource, and if authorized, the resource is delivered to the browser.

ASP.NET uses the user's account if impersonation is not active, and it uses the account that has been configured in the <processModel> tag of the machine.config file if anonymous access is enabled. The process model account can be one of the following:

Machine. Run as a low-privilege user account named *ASPNET*.

System. Run as the LocalSystem account, which is a high-privilege admin account on the local machine. Use of this account is not recommended since a hacker might be able to get access to the operating system using the process account. Using an account with low permissions limits the exposure if a hacker is able to penetrate security.

Windows. Specify a regular Windows account to be used.

The password for Machine and System should be set to AutoGenerate. For regular Windows accounts, the actual password is required.

If the account is authorized to access the resource, the resource is delivered to the browser.

In many cases, the Internet Information Server settings don't need to be changed when using ASP.NET security, but these settings can be used in conjunction with ASP.NET to further tighten the security of the Web site.

 If ASP.NET is installed on a Windows machine that is configured as a domain controller, it may be necessary to change the process model account to System. Since this is typically not recommended, installing ASP.NET on a domain controller is not recommended.

ASP.NET Authentication

In addition to the authentication that is available in Internet Information Server, ASP.NET offers other methods of authenticating a Web site user. The ASP.NET authentication methods offer more flexibility and can be tailored to suit the needs of most customers.

Default (IIS)

The Default authentication that is built into Internet Information Server is still available, but access to resources is strictly limited to the username that is being used to access the resource, and to the DACL that is associated with the resource. The following settings can be included in the Web.config file to set up the default authentication:

```
<configuration>
    <system.web>
        <authentication mode="None" />
        <identity impersonate="true" />
    </system.web>
</configuration>
```

Windows

With Windows authentication, Internet Information Server provides the initial authentication via the authentication methods that are configured in Internet Information Server. Resources then can be accessed using the authenticated account. ASP.NET can use this account to verify authorized access to resources. The following settings can be included in the Web.config file to set up Windows authentication:

```
<configuration>
    <system.web>
        <authentication mode="Windows" />
        <identity impersonate="true" />
    </system.web>
</configuration>
```

Windows authentication can be a compelling choice for intranet applications, especially when the user accounts already exist in the domain and a transparent login can be obtained for users who are already logged into the domain.

Passport

Microsoft Passport authentication uses centralized authentication that is provided by Microsoft. Passport offers the ability to provide Single Sign On (SSO) to multiple sites, and it plays an important role in Microsoft's Web services ventures. The following settings can be included in the Web.config file to set up Passport authentication:

```
<configuration>
    <system.web>
        <authentication mode="Passport" >
            <passport redirectUrl="internal|url" />
        </authentication>
        <identity impersonate="false" />
    </system.web>
</configuration>
```

Using Passport authentication requires paying a subscription fee to Microsoft, and buying and installing special software from Microsoft. More information can be retrieved from the www.microsoft.com/netservices/passport Web site.

Forms

With Forms authentication, any unauthenticated requests are automatically redirected to a Web Form page using a client-side redirect (Response.Redirect) method. The user must provide the required credentials and submit the page back for authentication.

If the site authenticates the user, a cookie is issued to the user, which indicates the identity of the user and the authority that authenticated the user. When the user requests any page on the site, the cookie is passed with the request. The following settings can be included in the Web.config file to set up Forms authentication:

```
<configuration>
    <system.web>
        <authentication mode="Forms" >
            <forms name="cookie-name"
                   path="cookie-path"
                   loginUrl="url"
                   protection="protection-mode"
                   timeout="number-of-minutes" >
                <credentials passwordFormat="format" >
                    <user name="name" password="pwd" />
                </credentials>
            </forms>
        </authentication>
        <identity impersonate="false" />
    </system.web>
</configuration>
```

Forms authentication is probably the most compelling solution for most public Web sites. Figure 13.15 shows the communication that takes place in order to authenticate a user. When a user requests a protected resource from the Web server, the Web server checks to see if an authentication cookie has been received with the request. If no authentication cookie has been received, the Web server redirects the user to the login page that was defined using the loginUrl attribute of the forms attribute. The redirect includes the return URL in the response querystring, which is the page that was originally requested. The browser transparently requests the login page, which is displayed on the browser. After the user enters the appropriate credentials and submits the login form, the user is authenticated. If the user is authenticated, the user is redirected to the original page that was requested and an authentication cookie is sent to the browser. The browser requests the original page and passes the authentication cookie. The Web server validates the authentication cookie and responds with the page that was originally selected.

The following is a sample of the settings that are placed in the Web.config file to set up Forms authentication:

```
<configuration>
    <system.web>
        <authentication mode="Forms" >
            <forms name="AuthTicket"
                    path="/"
                    loginUrl="login.aspx"
                    protection="All"
                    timeout="20" >
                <credentials passwordFormat="Clear" >
                    <user name="Joe" password="pwd1" />
                    <user name="Mary" password="pwd2" />
                </credentials>
            </forms>
        </authentication>
        <identity impersonate="false" />
    </system.web>
</configuration>
```

In this example, the name attribute is called AuthTicket, which is the name of the authentication cookie. The path defines the scope of the cookie, which typically is set to "/". The loginUrl attribute is set to login.aspx, which is the name of the login page that the user is redirected to for authentication.

In this example, the authentication cookie is both validated and encrypted. The protection attribute may be set to one of the following settings:

All. The authentication cookie is encrypted and validated.

None. No protection.

Encryption. The authentication cookie is encrypted.

Validation. The authentication cookie is validated to ensure that it has not been tampered with.

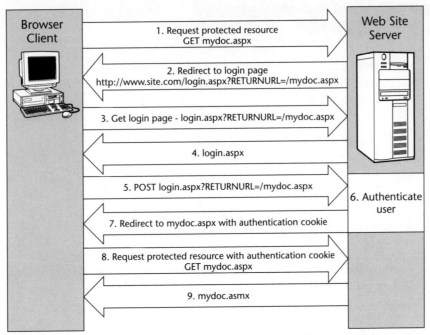

Figure 13.15 The communication that takes place in order to authenticate a user when the user requests a protected resource from the Web server.

The timeout for inactivity is set to 20 minutes. Attempting to retrieve a resource after 20 minutes of inactivity causes a redirect back to the login page.

The credentials section is optional. This section may be used to define users who may be authenticated. Currently, this section contains two users. The password format can be set Clear, SHA1, or MD5.

The credentials section can be useful in a development environment or on a site that has few users. For larger sites, this section would be abandoned in favor of a database for storing users.

Forms authentication requires the creation of a login page to collect the user's credentials and authenticate the user. This is usually preferred over displaying the gray Windows login pop-up menu. A simple login form can be created as shown in Figure 13.16. This form contains a text box for the user's name and password, a check box to prompt for persisting the credentials, a login button, and a label to display messages. The password text box has its TextMode property set to password to hide the password as it's being entered.

By default, this form sends the user name and password by clear text. Secure Sockets Layer encrypted communications should be used to send the login credentials to the Web server.

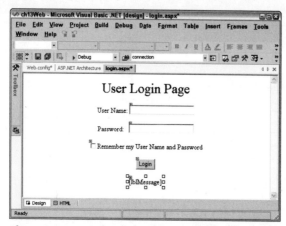

Figure 13.16 A simple login form for Forms authentication.

To authenticate the user, the following code can be placed into the login button's click event method:

```
Imports System.Web.Security
Public Class login
    Inherits System.Web.UI.Page
    Protected WithEvents txtUserName As _
        System.Web.UI.WebControls.TextBox
    Protected WithEvents txtPassword As _
        System.Web.UI.WebControls.TextBox
    Protected WithEvents chkRemember As _
            System.Web.UI.WebControls.CheckBox
    Protected WithEvents btnLogin As System.Web.UI.WebControls.Button
    Protected WithEvents lblMessage As System.Web.UI.WebControls.Label
    Private Sub btnLogin_Click( _
            ByVal sender As System.Object, _
            ByVal e As System.EventArgs) _
            Handles btnLogin.Click
        If FormsAuthentication.Authenticate( _
                txtUserName.Text, txtPassword.Text) Then
            FormsAuthentication.RedirectFromLoginPage( _
            txtUserName.Text, chkRemember.Checked)
        Else
            lblMessage.Text = "<b>Authentication Failure.</b>"
        End If
    End Sub
End Class
```

The FormsAuthentication.Authenticate method looks in the Web.config file for the name and password of the user that is attempting to login. This method returns true if the user is authenticated or false if not.

The FormsAuthentication.RedirectFromLoginPage method creates an encrypted cookie, adds it to the response headers, and redirects the user to the page that was originally requested. The login normally generates a memory-based session cookie that is valid for the time that is set in the Web.config file, or until the browser is closed, whichever comes first. If chkRemember is true, the cookie is persistant at the browser and the user is not required to log back into the application. The FormsAuthentication class also provides separate methods to individually perform the steps that the RedirectFromLoginPage performs when more granular control is required.

Forms Authorization

The only way that a user is directed to the login page is when the user attempts to access a resource that the user is not authorized to access. In many cases, this is because the user is logged in anonymously, and the resource may only allow access to authenticated users.

The default authorization for resources is that everyone has access. This is set in the machine.config file, and if not overridden, this setting prevails. The setting is as follows:

```
<configuration>
    <system.web>
        <authorization>
            <!--
                allow/deny Attributes:
                users="[*|?|name]"
                  * - All users
                  ? - Anonymous users
                [name] - Named user
                roles="[name]"
            -->
            <allow users="*" />
        </authorization>
    </system.web>
</configuration>
```

This authorization tag is used to allow or deny access. This is accomplished by nesting a combination of allow and deny tags into the authorization tag. These tags may contain a comma-separated list of names. In addition, the use of the asterisk denotes *all users*, and the use of the question mark denotes *anonymous users*.

In addition to allowing and denying user access, the authorization tag also allows roles to be allowed or denied. The Web.config file does not have provisions for adding users to roles, but when using a database to store security information, roles can be added as well. The following example shows how user and role access can be used:

```
<configuration>
    <system.web>
        <authorization>
            <allow users="Joe,Mary" roles="Admins,Managers" />
            <deny users="*" />
        </authorization>
    </system.web>
</configuration>
```

In this example, Joe and Mary have access to the files in the folder that this Web.config is in. In addition, members of the Admins and Managers role also have access to the files. All other users are denied access.

The authorization tag may be placed in the machine.config, the Web site root, each subweb, and each subdirectory. When authorization is required for a resource, ASP.NET starts looking for a username match in the Web.config file at the current directory, and continues to search up through the folder structure until a match is found, or until ASP.NET reaches the machine.config file. As soon as a match is found with the username, the user receives the matched permission, which either is allowed or denied. There is no further checking for additional matches. Figure 13.17 shows the search path for a username match.

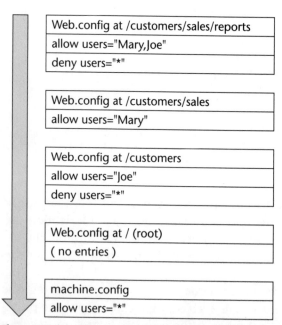

Figure 13.17 The search path for a username match. As soon as a match is found, the search ends, and the user receives the permissions of the match.

In the figure, Mary and Joe have permission for the files in /customers/ sales. Mary's permission is quite apparent, since she is explicitly given permission in that directory. When Joe tries to access a resource in the /customers/ sales folder, ASP.NET looks in the /customers/sales folder for a match. There is no match for Joe, so ASP.NET looks at the /customers folder and finds a match for Joe. As soon as this match is found, the search stops and Joe has access.

If another user, named Peter, were trying to access a resource in the /customers/sales folder, he would not have permission, because ASP.NET would search until it found the first match to Peter, which is in the Web.config file in the /customers folder. The match is on the deny *users="*" line*. Because Peter is a match to all users, Peter receives the matched permission, which is to deny access. No further searching is done. When it is desirable to stop the searching through the parent folders, one of two entries should be placed in the Web.config file: *allow users="*"* or *deny users="*"*.

Authorization is processed from the top to the bottom of each authorization tag. The following examples are different. Here is the code for the first example:

```
<configuration>
    <system.web>
        <authorization>
            <allow users="Joe" />
            <deny users="*" />
        </authorization>
    </system.web>
</configuration>
```

Here is the code for the second example.

```
<configuration>
    <system.web>
        <authorization>
            <deny users="*" />
            <allow users="Joe" />
        </authorization>
    </system.web>
</configuration>
```

In the first example, Joe has access to the files in this folder. In the second example, Joe does not have access to the files in the folder. This is because every user matches on the deny *users="*"* tag.

Sometimes it is desirable to set permissions at the file level, instead of at the folder level. This can be done by using the following syntax inside the Web.config file:

```
<configuration>
    <location path="File1.aspx">
        <system.web>
            <authorization>
```

```
                <deny users="?"/>
            </authorization>
        </system.web>
    </location>
     <location path="File2.aspx">
        <system.web>
            <authorization>
                <deny users="?"/>
            </authorization>
        </system.web>
    </location>
</configuration>
```

In many situations, it is desirable to simply deny access to anonymous users. This is done by using the question mark as follows:

```
<deny users="?" />
```

Using this entry in the authorization tag immediately redirects all anonymous users to the login page.

Windows Authorization

Windows Authorization is very similar to Forms authorization. The only difference is the format of the user names and the ability to use Windows roles. The following example allows the members of the Administrators role, the Administrator, and User1 access to resources in the folder that contains this Web.config file:

```
<configuration>
    <system.web>
        <authorization>
            <allow roles="BUILTIN\Administrators"
                users="MYDomain\Administrator, MyDomain\User1"/>
            <deny users="*" />
        </authorization>
    </system.web>
</configuration>
```

Notice that the built-in Windows groups have a different prefix from the user-defined and domain groups. Also notice that the user must be identified with the computer name or domain name prefix.

Identity and Principal

The .NET Framework defines a common model for working with user information. This is through the use of the Identity and Principal classes. In the simplest terms, the Identity class represents a user, while the Principal class represents the user and the user's roles. This section explores the use of these classes from the ASP.NET perspective.

Identity

An Identity object represents an authenticated user, containing at minimum, the name of the user and the authority that authenticated the user. The .NET Framework contains the WindowsIdentity, FormsIdentity, GenericIdentity, and the PassportIdentity classes. An Identity class must implement the IIdentity interface, which contains the read-only properties for AuthenticationType, Name, and IsAuthenticated (see Figure 13.18). It is possible to create custom Identity classes by simply implementing the IIdentity interface in the custom class.

The following code example demonstrates how the Identity class can be used in a Web page. It displays the Identity information for the currently logged-in user.

```
Private Sub Page_Load( _
        ByVal sender As System.Object, _
        ByVal e As System.EventArgs) _
        Handles MyBase.Load
    Dim Message As String
    Message = String.Format("Hello {0},  Authenticated:{1}  By:{2}", _
    User.Identity.Name, _
    User.Identity.IsAuthenticated, _
    User.Identity.AuthenticationType)
    Response.Write(Message)
End Sub
```

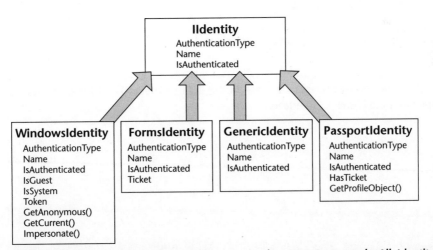

Figure 13.18 The Identity classes that are in the .NET Framework. All Identity classes implement the IIdentity interface.

The following message is displayed when using Forms authentication:

```
Hello Joe, Authenticated:True By:Forms
```

When using Windows authentication on Windows XP Professional, the message appears as follows:

```
Hello GJ\GlennJohnson, Authenticated:True By:Negotiate
```

This computer is not a member of a Windows domain, so the computer name (GJ) is placed in front of the username instead of the domain name.

Principal

A Principal object represents the security context that the code is running under. This is done by encapsulating the user's identity and the roles to which the user belongs. Applications that use role-based security grant access to resources based on the roles that are contained within a Principal object.

The .NET Framework contains the WindowsPrincipal and GenericPrincipal classes. A Principal class must implement the IPrincipal interface, which contains a property for the current user Identity, and an IsInRole method, which can be used to determine whether the current user is in a particular role (see Figure 13.19). It is possible to create custom Principal classes simply by implementing the IPrincipal interface.

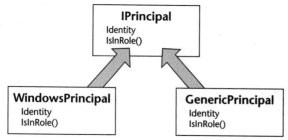

Figure 13.19 The Principal classes that are in the .NET Framework. All Principal classes must implement the IPrincipal interface.

In an ASP.NET application, an instance of the Principal object, called User, is available. User is a property of the HttpContext and the Page class (the Web Form). The following code example demonstrates the use of the Principal object:

```
Dim PMessage As String
PMessage = String.Format("Administrator? {0} Developer? {1}<br>", _
    User.IsInRole("BUILTIN\Administrators"), _
    User.IsInRole("GJ\VS Developers"))
Response.Write(PMessage)
```

The output of this code is as follows:

```
Administrator? True Developer? True
```

Another way to test for membership in one of the built-in roles is to use the WindowsBuiltInRole enumeration. There are enumeration values for each of the built-in Windows roles. The following code example produces the same output as the previous example:

```
Dim PMessage As String
PMessage = String.Format("Administrator? {0} Developer? {1}<br>", _
    User.IsInRole(WindowsBuiltInRole.Administrator), _
    User.IsInRole("GJ\VS Developers"))
Response.Write(PMessage)
```

Forms Authentication Example Using Database Access

This section explores the use of SQL Server to perform Forms authentication, and includes the use of roles. This example focuses primarily on using SQL Server data to authenticate the user and construct a Principal object containing roles from SQL Server.

Database Setup

The SQL Server database is set up with three tables, Users, Roles, and Users-Roles. The UsersRoles table is a junction table that creates a many-to-many relationship between the Users and the Roles table. Figure 13.20 shows the database schema. Each table contains a surrogate primary key, which is an Identity (autonumber) field.

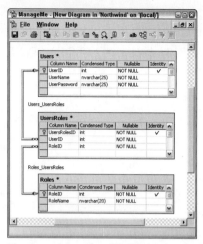

Figure 13.20 The database schema for the Forms authentication example.

The database has been populated with sample data. Figure 13.21 shows the data that has been added to the tables.

Although stored procedures should be created for all calls to SQL Server, this sample passes SQL statements to SQL Server in the interest of brevity.

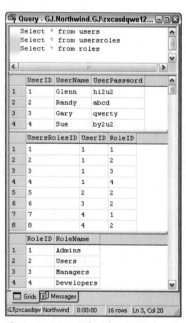

Figure 13.21 The database has been populated with sample data.

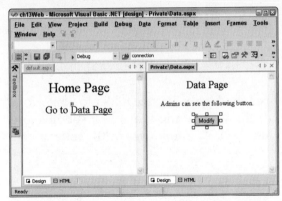

Figure 13.22   The default.aspx home page and the protected Data.aspx page.

The Project File and Folder Structure

The Web project is set up to allow access to any file that is in the root of the Web site. A folder, Private, is created and is accessible only to authenticated users. A single page, called Data.aspx, is placed into the Private folder, and it contains a button called btnModify, which is available only to users in the Admins role.

The root of the Web site contains a modified version of the login page that is shown in Figure 13.16. The code-behind page is modified to access the database. This folder also contains a home page called default.aspx which has a hyperlink control with a link to the Data.aspx page, as shown in Figure 13.22.

Web.config Settings

The Web.config file in the Web site root must contain the directive to use Forms authentication. The user credentials are not included since the users are in the database. The Web.config file also contains authorization to allow access by all users. The following XML code shows the settings that have been updated in the Web.config file:

```
<authentication mode="Forms">
    <forms name="AuthTicket"
        path="/"
        loginUrl="login.aspx"
        protection="All"
        timeout="20" >
    </forms>
```

```
</authentication>
<identity impersonate="false" />
<authorization>
    <allow users="*" />
</authorization>
```

An additional Web.config file is required in the Private folder to limit access to resources in this directory. Since this Web.config file is in a subdirectory, only the permissions should be included. The following XML code is contained in the Web.config file:

```
<?xml version="1.0" encoding="utf-8" ?>
<configuration>
    <system.web>
        <authorization>
            deny users="?" />
        </authorization>
    </system.web>
</configuration>
```

Login Page Authentication

The btnLogin must be changed to perform a lookup in the database. This can be done by creating a function called SqlValidateUser, which executes a command to get the count of rows that have the name and password that have been typed into the login page. If the count is one, then the user is authenticated. The following code contains the updated Login.aspx page. It queries the database to authenticate the user and, if successful, queries the database for the list of roles.

```
Imports System.Security.Principal
Imports System.Web.Security
Imports System.Data.SqlClient
Public Class login
    Inherits System.Web.UI.Page
    Protected WithEvents txtUserName As _
        System.Web.UI.WebControls.TextBox
    Protected WithEvents txtPassword As _
        System.Web.UI.WebControls.TextBox
    Protected WithEvents chkRemember As _
            System.Web.UI.WebControls.CheckBox
    Protected WithEvents btnLogin As System.Web.UI.WebControls.Button
    Protected WithEvents lblMessage As System.Web.UI.WebControls.Label
    Public Function SqlValidateUser( _
            ByVal UserName As String, _
            ByVal Password As String) As Boolean
        Dim cn As New SqlConnection( _
        "server=.;database=northwind;trusted_connection=true")
```

```
        Dim Sql As String
        Sql = "Select count(*) from Users "
        Sql &= " where UserName='{0}' and UserPassword='{1}' "
        Sql = String.Format(Sql, UserName, Password)
        Dim cmd As New SqlCommand(Sql, cn)
        Dim valid As Integer = 0
        cn.Open()
        valid = CType(cmd.ExecuteScalar(), Integer)
        cn.Close()
        Return (1 = valid)
    End Function
    Public Function GetRoles() As String
        Dim cn As New SqlConnection( _
        "server=.;database=northwind;trusted_connection=true")
        Dim Sql As String
        Sql = "SELECT RoleName FROM Roles r "
        Sql &= " INNER JOIN UsersRoles ur "
        Sql &= " ON r.RoleID = ur.RoleID "
        Sql &= " INNER JOIN Users u "
        Sql &= " ON u.UserID = ur.UserID "
        Sql &= " WHERE u.UserName='{0}' "
        Sql = String.Format(Sql, txtUserName.Text)
        Dim cmd As New SqlCommand(Sql, cn)
        Dim arRoles As New ArrayList()
        cn.Open()
        Dim dr As SqlDataReader = cmd.ExecuteReader()
        While (dr.Read())
            arRoles.Add(dr("RoleName").ToString())
        End While
        cn.Close()
        Dim roles(arRoles.Count - 1) As String
        arRoles.CopyTo(roles)
        Return String.Join(";", roles)
    End Function
    Private Sub btnLogin_Click( _
     ByVal sender As System.Object, _
     ByVal e As System.EventArgs) _
     Handles btnLogin.Click
        If SqlValidateUser(txtUserName.Text, txtPassword.Text) Then
            Dim tkt As FormsAuthenticationTicket
            Dim cookieStr As String
            Dim ck As HttpCookie
            Dim roles as string = GetRoles()
            tkt = New FormsAuthenticationTicket(1, _
                    txtUserName.Text, DateTime.Now(), _
                DateTime.Now.AddMinutes(30), _
                        chkRemember.Checked, roles)
            cookieStr = FormsAuthentication.Encrypt(tkt)
            ck = New HttpCookie( _
                    FormsAuthentication.FormsCookieName(), _
                    cookieStr)
```

```
        If (chkRemember.Checked) Then
            ck.Expires = tkt.Expiration
        End If
        Response.Cookies.Add(ck)
        Dim strRedirect As String
        strRedirect = Request("ReturnURL")
        If strRedirect <> "" Then
            Response.Redirect(strRedirect, True)
        Else
            strRedirect = "default.aspx"
            Response.Redirect(strRedirect, True)
        End If
    Else
        lblMessage.Text = "<b>Authentication Failure.</b>"
    End If
  End Sub
End Class
```

Notice that the SqlValidateUser call replaces the Forms Authentication .Authenticate method, which was used to search the Web.config file for a valid user. The SqlValidateUser method performs a lookup in SQL Server, returning the count of records that have the same name and password. If the count is one, the user is validated and the SqlValidateUser returns true.

If the user is valid, the code could simply perform a redirect to the original page as done in previous examples. The problem is that the user's roles need to be retrieved and stored, so future SQL Server lookups are not required during the login session. A session variable seems like a compelling choice, but the roles need to be available in the Application_AuthenticateRequest event method in the Global.asax.vb page. As it turns out, session variable are not yet available when this method is called. The next best choice is to place the roles into a cookie, but the roles must be encrypted to ensure that they can't be read and modified by the user. This requires the authentication ticket cookie to be constructed manually, so the roles can be inserted into the encrypted cookie.

Before the authentication ticket cookie is created, the roles are retrieved by calling the GetRoles method. This method queries SQL Server for the list of roles for the current user. The roles are returned in the SqlDataReader. The roles are moved to an ArrayList, then copied to a String array, and then the array is joined into a string with the semicolon delimiter and returned.

The FormsAuthenticationTicket class can be used to create the encrypted authentication cookie. The first argument of the constructor is the version number. This is reserved for future use, and one is placed into that parameter. The next argument is the username. The username is simply the name of the user who is logging in. This also could be the primary key of the Users table, or it could be some other value that uniquely identifies the user. Then next parameter is the date and time that the cookie was issued, and the next parameter is the expiration date and time of the cookie. These parameters simply use Date-Time.Now and DateTime.Now.AddMinutes(30) for values. The next parameter specifies whether the cookie should be persistant, and is set to the value in the check box. The last parameter allows user data to be added to the cookie. This parameter is set to the roles.

After the FormsAuthenticationTicket has been created, it is encrypted, and a new cookie is created based on the cookie name that is in the Web.config file. The cookie is then placed into the Response's cookies collection.

The last thing to do is check to see if there is a redirect page. If so, redirect to the originally requested page. If not, always redirect to the default.aspx page.

Attaching the Roles to the Principal

The user's roles need to be attached to the Principal object everytime a request is made to the server. This has to be done as early as possible, in order to ensure that the user has the permissions that are assigned to the roles.

The roles need to be read from the authentication ticket and then attached to the Principal object in the Application_AuthenticateRequest method. The following code shows how this is accomplished:

```
Sub Application_AuthenticateRequest( _
  ByVal sender As Object, ByVal e As EventArgs)
     If (Not HttpContext.Current.User Is Nothing) Then
          If (HttpContext.Current.User.Identity.IsAuthenticated) Then
               If (TypeOf HttpContext.Current.User.Identity Is _
                        FormsIdentity) Then
                    Dim id As FormsIdentity = _
                    CType( HttpContext.Current.User.Identity, _
                             FormsIdentity)
                    Dim ticket As FormsAuthenticationTicket = _
                             id.Ticket
                    'Get the stored user-data,
                         ' in this case, our roles.
                    Dim userData As String = ticket.UserData
                    Dim roles As String() = userData.Split(";")
                    HttpContext.Current.User = _
                             New GenericPrincipal(id, roles)
               End If
          End If
     End If
  End Sub
```

When the userData is retrieved from the authentication ticket, it is a semicolon-delimited string. This string is then split into an array of strings. A new GenericPrincipal is created, using the ID from the original Principal object and the roles that have been extracted form the userData.

Declarative Security Authorization

Another method of authorizing users is declarative security. Declarative security can be implemented by the use of attributes on methods and classes. From a code management perspective, this might be a better choice than embedding the User.IsInRole method in the code.

The PrincipalPermissionAttribute can be used to specify the permissions that are required in order to execute the code. The following example requires a user named Glenn, and Glenn must be in the Admins role.

```
<PrincipalPermissionAttribute(SecurityAction.Demand, _
        Name:="Glenn", Role:="Admins")> _
Private Sub btnModify_Click( _
        ByVal sender As System.Object, _
        ByVal e As System.EventArgs) _
        Handles btnModify.Click
    Response.Write("Made it!")
End Sub
```

The next example requires the user to be a member of the Admins role only.

```
<PrincipalPermission(SecurityAction.Demand, Role:="Admins")> _
Private Sub btnModify_Click( _
        ByVal sender As System.Object, _
        ByVal e As System.EventArgs) _
        Handles btnModify.Click
    Response.Write("Made it!")
End Sub
```

Attributes that end with Attribute can be abbreviated as shown in the previous example. Also, attributes are supposed to be defined directly in front of the method in Visual Basic .NET, but in other .NET languages the attribute is defined on the line before the method. Using the line continuation characters (space, then underscore), allows placement on the line before while satisfying the Visual Basic .NET syntactical requirements.

The next example requires the user be authenticated to execute the method.

```
<PrincipalPermission(SecurityAction.Demand, Authenticated := True)> _
Private Sub btnModify_Click( _
        ByVal sender As System.Object, _
        ByVal e As System.EventArgs) _
        Handles btnModify.Click
    Response.Write("Made it!")
End Sub
```

In the above examples, if the user does not have the required permissions, an SecurityException is thrown. Any code that calls a method with a PrincipalPermissionAttribute should wrap the call in a try/catch block.

Imperative Security

Imperative Security can be used to force a security check in a code block. This can be done with the PrincipalPermission class. The PrincipalPermission class can be created with a username and role. If the user is Joe, and the role is Managers, only Joe in the Managers role has access to the code that follows. This means that the user and role are ANDed together, not ORed. For other users, a SecurityException is thrown.

The user or role may be omitted by passing Nothing as the parameter. This forces a match on the valid parameter only. The following sample demonstrates the use of the PrincipalPermission class to allow only Joe in the Managers role access to the code.

```
Public Sub test()
     Dim id1 As String = "Joe"
     Dim role1 As String = "Managers"
     Dim Perm1 As New PrincipalPermission(id1, role1)
     Perm1.Demand()
     Response.Write("Made it!")
End Sub
```

Instances of PrinciplePermission objects may be ANDed and ORed together. This allows many users and roles to be defined, even at different scopes, and they can be combined as needed to achieve the desired access level. The following example shows how two PrincipalPermission instances can be ORed together using the Union method. It allows users in the Developers and Managers role to access the following code:

```
Public Sub test()
     Dim id1 As String = Nothing
     Dim role1 As String = "Developers"
     Dim Perm1 As New PrincipalPermission(id1, role1)
     Dim id2 As String = Nothing
     Dim role2 As String = "Managers"
     Dim Perm2 As New PrincipalPermission(id2, role2)
     Dim Perm3 as PrincipalPermission
     Perm3 = Perm1.Union(Perm2)
     Perm3.Demand()
     Response.Write("Made it!")
End Sub
```

The next example shows how two PrincipalPermission instances can be ANDed together by the Intersect method. The first part of the code creates Perm3, which contains the Developers and Managers roles. The second part of the code creates Perm6, which contains Admins and Managers. If Perm3 is ANDed with Perm6, the result is Managers, since Managers is common to Perm3 and Perm6. Only Managers may execute the code that follows:

```
Public Sub test()
    Dim id1 As String = Nothing
    Dim role1 As String = "Developers"
    Dim Perm1 As New PrincipalPermission(id1, role1)
    Dim id2 As String = Nothing
    Dim role2 As String = "Managers"
    Dim Perm2 As New PrincipalPermission(id2, role2)
    Dim Perm3 as PrincipalPermission
    'Developers and Managers
    Perm3 = Perm1.Union(Perm2)
    Dim id4 As String = Nothing
    Dim role4 As String = "Admins"
    Dim Perm4 As New PrincipalPermission(id1, role1)
    Dim id5 As String = Nothing
    Dim role5 As String = "Managers"
    Dim Perm5 As New PrincipalPermission(id2, role2)
    'Admins and Managers
    Perm6 = Perm4.Union(Perm5)
    Dim Perm7 as PrincipalPermission
    'Just Managers
    Perm7 = Perm3.Intersect(Perm6)
    Perm7.Demand()
    Response.Write("Made it!")
End Sub
```

Imperative Security versus Declarative Security

One of the primary differences between Imperative Security and Declarative Security is that Declarative Security places its data into the metadata of the assembly, while Imperative Security places its data into the IL code. Other benefits of Declarative Security actions are as follows:

- Actions can be easily viewed without looking through the code.

- Actions are expressed on methods and take place at the beginning of the method. This can help to ensure that code was not executed before the security check had taken place.

- Declarative Security actions can also be placed at the class level. This causes the security action to take place on every method, constructor, and property.

Listed below are some benefits of Imperative Security.

- Security logic can be much more complex in code. Conditional bodies of code can have different security actions.

- Imperative Security actions can be created dynamically. This allows security action settings to be dynamically loaded from a database or XML file.

Code Access Security Basics

One of the problems that has been associated with security in the past is that security has always been based entirely on the user's permissions. For example, a person who is logged on as an administrator has full permission to execute virtually any code on the machine, while a person who is logged on as a simple user has very limited permissions.

This really doesn't sound like a problem, but it is. The problem becomes apparent when a hacker finds a way to get the administrator to execute unsafe code. The unsafe code runs with administrator permissions, doing damage to everything in its path as it was programmed to do.

Code Access Security can help minimize the problem of users unintentionally executing unsafe code. Code Access Security can be used to limit the resources that code has access to. This means that a hacker who finds a way to get into the code can still be halted from doing damage because the code itself only has limited access to resources. This is done by using permissions and permission sets, by providing evidence of the code's origin, and by applying security policies. Evidence about an assembly is used to grant permissions, based upon a security policy. When code needs to access a resource, a demand is made for the appropriate permissions, and the .NET Framework security system determines if the code is able to perform the desired operation.

Evidence

Evidence is the collection of information about an assembly and its origin. Evidence includes the following:

Strong name.   This consists of the assembly's public key, friendly name, and version.

Publisher.   This is the Microsoft Authenticode signature.

Zone.   This is the origination of the assembly, such as the local computer, intranet, or Internet zone.

Location.   This is the actual location of the assembly, which can be expressed as a URL, Universal Naming Convention (UNC) path, or local computer folder.

Cryptographic hash.   This is the cryptographic hash of the assembly.

Some evidence is considered to be stronger that other types of evidence. Security policies can be based on the strength of the evidence. For example, strong names and Authenticode signatures are much stronger than the location and zone information.

Code Access Permissions

Code Access Permissions are the rights to access certain resources. There are many types of Code Access Permission in the .NET Framework. Many of these permissions are implemented within the .NET Framework to secure the system resources. Table 13.1 contains a list of the Code Access Permissions that are included in the .NET Framework.

Table 13.1 The Code Access Permissions Included in the .NET Framework

PERMISSION	DESCRIPTION
DnsPermission	Controls the ability to access DNS servers
EnvironmentPermission	Controls access to the system and user environment variables
EventLogPermission	Controls access to the event logs
FileDialogPermission	Controls access to file dialog boxes in the user interface
FileIOPermission	Controls access to files and folders on the file system
IsolatedStorgeFilePermission	Controls access to isolated storage
MessageQueuePermission	Controls access to message queues
OleDbPermission	Controls database access by the OLEDB data access provider
PerformanceCounterPermission	Controls access to performance counters
PrintingPermission	Controls access to printers
ReflectionPermission	Controls access to type metadata by reflection
RegistryPermission	Controls access to the Registry
SecurityPermission	Controls ability to execute code, assert permissions, and call unmanaged code
ServiceControllerPermission	Controls the ability to start or stop services
SocketPermission	Controls the ability to connect to other computers by means of sockets
SqlClientPermission	Controls database access by the Microsoft SQL Server data access provider
UIPermission	Controls access to windows and other user interface elements
WebPermission	Controls the ability to connect to other computers by means of HTTP

Working with Code Access Security

The .NET Framework grants a set of permissions to every assembly that is loaded. These permissions are used to access resources and are *permission sets*. The security policy looks at the assembly's evidence and decides what permissions should be assigned to the assembly.

Code Groups

Code groups are used to define the permissions that an assembly should receive. An assembly can be a member of many code groups. When a code group is created, it is assigned a membership condition and a set of permissions that its members should receive. For example, there is a code group called Internet_Zone. Its membership condition is that the assembly be located on the Internet. It has no permissions. There is another code group called My_Computer_Zone. Its membership condition is that the assembly be located on the current user's machine. This code group has several permissions assigned to it. The assembly receives the union of the permissions that are assigned to every code group of which it is a member.

Security Policy Levels

Security policy levels are levels of security that may be applied for the Enterprise, the Local Computer, the User, and the Application Domain. Each of these policy levels contains its own hierarchy of code groups. The Enterprise policies can be set by the network administrator, and affect all managed code in the domain. The Local Computer policies can be set by the local computer administrator. The User policies can be set by the local user or local administrator. The Application Domain policies are optional and provide isolation, unloading, and security boundaries that are used for managed code execution.

An assembly's effective permissions are calculated by looping through each policy level. Within each policy level, the assembly's evidence is collected and code group membership is evaluated. Permissions are assigned based on code group membership. The assembly receives the *union* of the permissions, based on code group membership. The resultant permissions are then *intersected* with the permissions of the next policy, and so on (see Figure 13.23).

The effective security permissions that an assembly has can be different on every machine. This means that the developer must be intimately involved with the runtime security system, using Declarative and Imperative security calls. The runtime already contains security calls for the system resources, to ensure that the required permissions are assigned to the assembly.

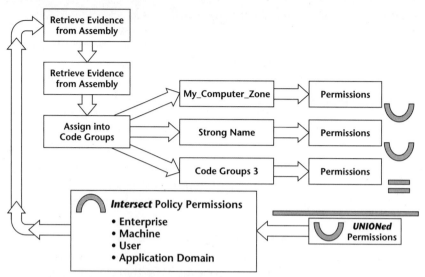

Figure 13.23 The calculation of an assembly's effective permissions.

Requested Permissions

The developer needs to document all permissions that are required throughout the assembly, request the desired permissions through Declarative and Imperative security calls, and perform testing with the minimum security policy.

Declarative permissions may also be assigned at the assembly level, by placing the Declarative permission request inside the AssemblyInfo.vb file and using the Assembly prefix in the attribute, before the desired permission request. An example of an assembly permission request is as follows:

```
'Imports statements required for the following permission
Imports System.Security
Imports System.Security.Permissions
Imports System.Diagnostics
'The actual permission request.
<Assembly: EventLogPermission(SystemSecurityAction.RequestMinimum)>
```

This attribute requests EventLogPermission from the .NET security system. If the permissions are not granted, the assembly does not load.

In addition to requesting individual permissions, the .NET Framework provides permission sets that can be used to request many permissions in one attribute. Table 13.2 contains a list of the permission sets that are available in the .NET Framework.

The assembly permission request types are RequestMinimum, RequestOptional, and RequestRefuse. These types are evaluated when the assembly is loaded.

Table 13.2 The Permission Sets Available in the .NET Framework

PERMISSION SET	DESCRIPTION
Nothing	This set provides no permissions. Code cannot run with this permission.
Execution	This provides permission for code to run.
Internet	This permission set allows code to execute and create top-level windows and file dialog boxes. This code can also make Internet connections to the same site that the assembly came from, and use Isolated Storage with a quota. All code from Trusted zone receives this permission set.
LocalIntranet	This permission set allows code to execute and unrestricted creation of user interface elements. This allows unrestricted use of isolated storage with no quota. This also allows DNS usage, and the reading of the USERNAME, the TEMP, and TMP environment variables. This code can also make Internet connections to the same site that the assembly came from. This permission set also allows files to be read that are in the same folder. All code from the LocalIntranet zone receives this permission set.
Everything	This permission set contains all standard permissions except the permission to skip validation.
FullTrust	This permission set provides full access to all resources. All code from the LocalComputer zone receives this permission set.

The *RequestMinimum* request is used to define the minimum permissions that are required in order for the assembly to operate effectively. If these permissions are not granted, the .NET runtime throws a policy exception and the assembly is not loaded. If a request is not made for minimum permissions, the permissions that are granted are the equivalent to a RequestMinimum of Nothing.

The *RequestOptional* request is used to define the permissions that the code could use to run more efficiently, but the code still operates even if the permissions are not granted. The assembly still is allowed to load and run, even when these permissions are not granted. If a request is not made for optional permissions, the permissions that are granted are equivalent to a RequestOptional of FullTrust. This is an important point, because your code ends up requesting, and possibly receiving full permissions. It's better to add code for a RequestOptional of Nothing, which won't give the assembly any extra permission. This forces the assembly to run with the least permissions.

The *RequestRefuse* permission is used to identify permissions that the assembly is never to be granted, even if the security policy allows the permission to be granted. If a request is not made for the RequestRefuse permission, the permissions that are granted are equivalent to a RequestRefuse of Nothing.

The permissions that are finally granted (FG) to the assembly are based on the security policy permissions (SP) intersected with the permissions that were requested by the assembly. The permissions that were requested are the union of the RequestMinimum (M) and RequestOptional (O), minus the RequestRefuse (R), as shown below.

```
FG = SP ∩ ((M ∪ O) - R)
```

Some other examples of assembly permission requests are as follows:

```
<Assembly: UIPermissionAttribute( _
    SecurityAction.RequestMinimum, _
    Window:=UIPermissionWindow.AllWindows, _
    ClipBoard:=UIPermissionClipboard.NoClipboard)>
```

This example requests a minimum UIPermission for AllWindows and NoClipboard.

```
<Assembly:PermissionSet( _
    SecurityAction.RequestOptional, _
    Unrestricted:=false)>
```

This code optionally requests no access. This means that this assembly does not receive any permissions other that the permissions that were minimally requested.

Exception Handling

Using security requires exception handling to be added to code in order to gracefully handle any potential security exception that may be thrown. Exception handling can be done with try/catch blocks, as shown in the following code:

```
Imports System.Security
Imports System.IO
Dim fs As FileStream
Try
    fs = New FileStream("C:\myFile.txt",FileMode.Create)
Catch xcp As SecurityException
    ' Display error message.
    Response.Write("Security Exception: " & xcp.Message )
End Try
```

Security Policy Administration

The Microsoft .NET Framework Configuration (Mscorcfg.msc) tool can be used to review and change the security policies. This tool is located under Administrative Tools. Figure 13.24 shows the Microsoft .NET Framework Configuration tool. This tool has a node called the Runtime Security Policy, which contains a node for Enterprise, Machine, and User policy settings. Each of these nodes has Code Groups, Permission Sets, and Policy Assemblies nodes.

Figure 13.24 shows the Machine node, and its subnodes, fully opened. The Code Groups node has one top level code group, called All_Code. A glance at the properties of this node reveals that the Membership Condition to this code group is *All Code*. This means that all assemblies are a member of this group. The permission set for this node is Nothing, which means that no permissions are assigned at this level. Since there is a match at this level, the security system searches for membership in subnodes as well.

Under the All Code node is a node for each of the zones, which represents the location of the assembly that is to be evaluated. If the assembly is located on the computer, the assembly is a member of the My_Computer_Zone. The Permission Set for this node is Full Trust, which means that an assembly that is located on the local computer has full trust.

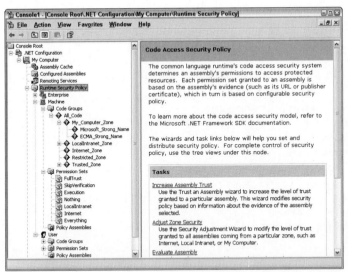

Figure 13.24   The Microsoft .NET Framework Configuration tool.

Under the My_Computer_Zone are two more nodes, Microsoft_Strong_Name and ECMA_Strong_Name. Membership to these nodes is based on the assembly having a specific public key. The permission set for these nodes is Full Trust. These permissions are UNIONed with the permissions that the assembly has already acquired. As it turns out, the My_Computer_Zone is already assigned Full Trust, but if these permissions were reduced at this node, Microsoft and ECMA strong-named assemblies would still receive Full Trust.

The permissions that are granted finally are not based simply on the Machine node. These permissions must be INTERSECTed with the Enterprise and User policy settings. As it turns out, the default settings for these groups are *Full Trust*. This means that by default, the Machine node settings are the permissions that are finally granted.

Testing Code Access Security

To test Code Access Security, a new code group, called Ch13Test, has been created under the Machine's All_Code/My_Computer_Zone node. This membership condition for this group is set to URL, and the URL is set to the following location:

```
file://D:/AspDotNetBook/Book/ASPdotNet Security/Ch13Web/bin/TestAccess.dll
```

This is the location of a .dll file to which the Web site has a reference. On the next screen, a new permission set is created, called ch13permission. The permission set has Security added, with Enable Assembly Execution and Assert any permission that has been granted selected. This permission set also has FileIO added, with c:\xml read permissions added.

The TestAccess class has the following code:

```
Imports System.Data.SqlClient
Imports System.Security.Permissions
Imports System.Security
Public Class TestClass
    Public Function GetData() As DataSet
        Dim ds As New DataSet()
        ds.ReadXml("C:\xml\myfruit.xml")
        Return ds
    End Function
End Class
```

A page on the Web site contains a Button and a DataGrid. The Button's click event method contains the following code to get the myfruit.xml file and display it in the grid.

```
Imports System.Data.SqlClient
Imports System.Security.Permissions
Public Class WebForm2
    Inherits System.Web.UI.Page
    Protected WithEvents btnGetData As _
        System.Web.UI.WebControls.Button
    Protected WithEvents DataGrid1 As _
        System.Web.UI.WebControls.DataGrid
    Public Sub GetData()
        Dim c As New TestAccess.TestClass()
        DataGrid1.DataSource = c.GetData()
        DataBind()
    End Sub
    Private Sub btnGetData_Click( _
     ByVal sender As System.Object, _
     ByVal e As System.EventArgs) _
     Handles btnGetData.Click
        GetData()
    End Sub
End Class
```

This code should be able to make a call to populate the grid, as shown in Figure 13.25. The myfruit.xml file was read into a DataSet, and the DataSet was returned to the Web page, and bound to the grid.

If the myfruit.xml file is moved to c:\myfruit.xml, the code should not be able to run, as shown in Figure 13.26. This throws a security exception, stating that there is a FileIOPermission problem.

Figure 13.25   The TestAccess.dll file has access to the c:\xml folder.

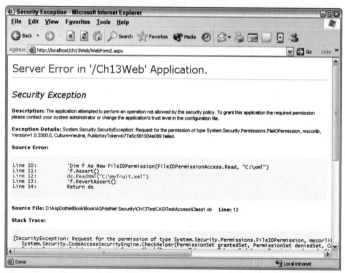

Figure 13.26   Trying to access a file in a location that permissions have not been assigned for throws a security exception.

Lab 13.1: Adding Forms Authentication

In this lab, you add Forms authentication to the Customers Web site. You create a simple list of users, which are placed in the Web.config file. After Forms authentication is added, you test the application by trying to view the CustomerList.aspx page, which is only available to users who are logged into the Web site.

Adding the Login Page

In this section, you add a new Web page called login.aspx.

1. To start this lab, open the OrderEntrySystemSolution from Lab 12.1.

2. Right-click the OrderEntrySystemSolution in the Solution Explorer, and click Check Out.

3. Add a new Web Form, called login.aspx, to the Customers site.

4. Add a TextBox for the username and another TextBox for the password.

5. Add a CheckBox that the user can select to have the application remember the login credentials.

6. Add a logon Button and a Label for any message that is to be displayed.

7. Your login page should look like the one that is shown in Figure 13.16.

8. Add the following code to authenticate the user and redirect the user to the page that was originally requested.

```
Imports System.Web.Security
Public Class login
    Inherits System.Web.UI.Page
    Protected WithEvents txtUserName As
        System.Web.UI.WebControls.TextBox
    Protected WithEvents txtPassword As _
        System.Web.UI.WebControls.TextBox
    Protected WithEvents chkRemember As _
        System.Web.UI.WebControls.CheckBox
    Protected WithEvents btnLogin As _
        System.Web.UI.WebControls.Button
    Protected WithEvents lblMessage As _
        System.Web.UI.WebControls.Label
    Private Sub btnLogin_Click( _
            ByVal sender As System.Object, _
            ByVal e As System.EventArgs) _
            Handles btnLogin.Click
        If FormsAuthentication.Authenticate( _
         txtUserName.Text, txtPassword.Text) Then
            FormsAuthentication.RedirectFromLoginPage( _
            txtUserName.Text, chkRemember.Checked)
        Else
            lblMessage.Text = "<b>Authentication Failure.</b>"
        End If
    End Sub
End Class
```

Modify the Web.config File

In this section, you make changes to the Web.config file to enable Forms authentication and protect the CustomerList.aspx page from being viewed by anonymous users.

1. Open the Web.config file.

2. Locate the *<authentication mode="Windows">* tag. Replace this tag with a tag to enable Forms authentication. Within the forms tag, add credentials for three users. Your code should look like the following:

```
<authentication mode="Forms">
<forms name="AuthTicket" protection="All"
loginUrl="login.aspx" path="/" timeout="20">
<credentials passwordFormat="Clear" >
            <user name="John" password="hi2u" />
            <user name="Mary" password="hi2uAll" />
            <user name="Glenn" password="hi2u2" />
        </credentials>
    </forms>
</authentication>
```

3. Add code to authorize nonanonymous users to view the CustomerList.aspx page. Your code should look like the following. This code should be located between the </system.web> and the </configuration> tags that are at the bottom of the Web.config file.

```
<location path="CustomerList.aspx">
    <system.web>
        <authorization>
            <deny users="?"/>
        </authorization>
    </system.web>
</location>
```

Test the Login Page

To test the application's ability to force a login if someone tries to access the CustomerList.aspx page, the CustomerList page must be set as the startup page, and the project can be started. The login.aspx page should be displayed, instead of the CustomerList.aspx page. After logging in, the CustomerList.aspx page should be displayed.

1. Right-click the CustomerList.aspx page in the Solution Explorer, and click Set As Start Page.

2. Run the application. The login.aspx page should be displayed.

3. Log in with one of the accounts that you created. You should be redirected to the CustomerList.aspx page.

4. Save the Solution and check it back into Visual SourceSafe.

Summary

- Authentication is the process of obtaining identification credentials, such as name and password, from a user and validating those credentials against an authority.

- Authorization is the process of determining whether a user should be granted a specific type of access to a resource.

- Impersonation is the process of allowing applications to execute with the identity of the client on whose behalf they are operating.

- Delegation is impersonation across computers. Although impersonation works fine within a machine, it fails when attempting to access resources across machines.

- Secure Sockets Layer (SSL) communication provides encrypted communications when private data is being sent across the network.

- An Identity object represents an authenticated user containing, at minimum, the name of the user and the authority that authenticated the user.

- A Principal object represents the security context that the code is running under. This is done by encapsulating the user's identity and the roles to which the user belongs.

- Code Access Security can help minimize the problem of users unintentionally executing unsafe code. Code Access Security can be used to limit the resources to which code has access.

Review Questions

1. What are the three types of authentication that ASP.NET supports?

2. What is required in order to enable SSL communications?

3. When is the IUSR account used, and when is the ASPNET account used?

4. What does the *<deny users="?"/>* tag mean?

5. What are the four security policy levels?

Answers to Review Questions

1. Forms, Windows, and Passport.

2. A digital certificate.

3. The IUSR account is the anonymous account that is used when identity impersonation is set to true. The ASPNET account is the anonymous account that is used when impersonation is false.

4. Deny anonymous users.

5. Enterprise, Machine, User, and Optionally AppDomain.

Performance Tuning and Application Instrumentation

One of the most common questions that a customer will ask is "How many users will this Web site be able to handle?" and the most common answer is, "It depends." It depends on the equipment that is being used, the bandwidth available to the Web site, the processor speed, the quantity of processors, memory, disk access speed, the software, and many other factors.

Load testing can help you identify how many users the Web site can handle. Load testing typically encompasses the areas of performance, scalability, and stability. It's important to address these areas in all phases of development to ensure that there are no surprises when the system is being deployed. Even if the system has undergone serious load testing prior to deployment, there is always a chance that new bugs will surface, or that the hardware won't perform as well as was expected.

In many cases, a small change to the code can have an enormous impact on the performance of a Web site, so knowing the tools to use can help you identify potential problems much earlier. This chapter covers several performance tools covered in detail. In addition, several tips and tricks will be explored in detail.

The topics that are covered in this chapter are not meant to replace formal load testing. Instead, the topics in this chapter are intended to help you think about performance before formal load testing starts. To be more explicit, this chapter focuses on developer's ability to optimize the software, although the developer's ability to identify potential hardware bottlenecks can play a key role in determining the hardware that should be provided in the production system.

Classroom Q & A

Q: Is there a way to see the debug messages when running my Web application without using Visual Studio .NET?

A: Yes. The Window Platform SDK provides a program called DbMon.exe that can be run on the Web server. This is a console application that will display debug and trace messages. Debug and trace are covered in detail in this chapter.

Q: Is there a way to load test a Web server that is running on Windows XP Professional to see how many connections the server can handle?

A: Well, that's a loaded question. The answer is yes, but you don't need to perform a load test to find out. As it turns out, Windows 2000 Professional and Windows XP Professional have a 10-connection limit. After the connection limit has been reached, the Web server will refuse to process additional requests.

Q: Is there a way to create a Performance Monitor counter for my Web application?

A: There sure is. The .NET Framework provides classes that simplify the creation of Performance Monitor counters. This is covered in detail in this chapter.

Load Testing

Load testing involves the creation of a testing environment that closely matches the environment of the production system. Ideally, this environment should match the production environment. The problem is that it is difficult to extrapolate calculations from different equipment to predict the performance of the production equipment. If new equipment is being supplied for the Web site, the new equipment could be used in the load-testing phase to help predict the quantity of users that the Web site can handle.

Formal load testing should be implemented to identify the quantity of users that the Web site can handle, as well as to identify scalability issues.

Performance Tuning in a Development Environment

Performance tuning is the process of running specific tests on isolated parts of the software, making changes to the software, and rerunning the tests in an effort to identify bottlenecks and increase the performance of the software.

Many types of performance tuning can be done in the development environment, because many of the tests are relative tests. This means that each test is meant to identify whether the performance increased or decreased with each test. It would be difficult to perform Web farm performance tuning in a development environment, because most development environments don't have Web farms. On the other hand, it's easy to test the relative performance of a Web page on the developer's machine. The developer can test changes to the Web page code to obtain the fastest relative performance of the Web page.

Performance tuning in a development environment is not meant to identify the quantity of users that the Web site can handle, but successful performance tuning in the development environment increases the quantity of users that the Web site can handle.

Identifying Bottlenecks

Identifying bottlenecks is the process of interpreting load test data and investigating system performance in an effort to locate the slowest parts of the system. Eliminating a bottleneck can result in substantial gains in performance to the overall system.

Locating bottlenecks in a development environment can be difficult at best. The problem is that a bottleneck in the development environment may not be a bottleneck in the production environment. For example, a bottleneck may exist when communicating to the SQL Server database. This may be due to the type of hardware that the developers are using, the bandwidth that is available, or the quantity of users. Most of these bottlenecks will not exist in the production environment. There may be different bottlenecks in the product environment.

In every case, when a bottleneck is identified, it should be documented and the software should be optimized to get the best possible performance. In cases where tuning requires hardware modification or trade-offs, it's better to document and retest within the proper environment.

 Proper load and performance testing requires the establishment of a baseline, and revisiting the baseline after changes have been made. This is the only way to identify whether a change to the system has had an impact on performance.

Performance and Instrumentation Tools

This section identifies some of the tools that are available within Visual Studio .NET. The first part of this section covers some of the classes that are in the System.Diagnostics namespace, such as Debug and Trace. These tools are useful when logging data that can be evaluated to identify potential bottlenecks.

Debug

The System.dll file contains the Debug class, which can be used to obtain information when running an application that has been compiled using the debug switch. The use of the Debug class requires the application to be compiled with the /d:DEBUG=True switch. In Visual Studio .NET, this can be done by clicking the project in the Solution Explorer, and then clicking Build, Configuration Manager, Debug. When the application is compiled for release, the debug code is not included in the compiled application. By default, the debug information is written to the Visual Studio .NET output window. This can be changed to send the information to a stream with the use of trace listeners, as shown in Figure 14.1.

Assert

Assert is used to test a condition, and if the condition evaluates to false, the assertion message will be output. The following code is an example of using debug.assert to check a counter and display a message in the Visual Studio .NET output window.

```
Debug.Assert(Count <> 0, "Count=0 Error", _
    "Count must not be 0 because the Count will be used for division.")
```

The output of this code shows up in the Visual Studio .NET output window, and looks like the following:

```
---- DEBUG ASSERTION FAILED ----
---- Assert Short Message ----
Count=0 Error
---- Assert Long Message ----
Count must not be 0 because Count is the denominator in next function.
    at WebForm1.Button1_Click(Object sender, EventArgs e)
        D:\AspDotNetBook\Book\ASP.NET Performance
        Tuning\Ch14Web\WebForm1.aspx.vb(31)
    at Button.OnClick(EventArgs e)
    at Button.System.Web.UI.IPostBackEventHandler.RaisePostBackEvent
        (String eventArgument)
    at Page.RaisePostBackEvent(IPostBackEventHandler sourceControl,
```

```
            String eventArgument)
    at Page.RaisePostBackEvent(NameValueCollection postData)
    at Page.ProcessRequestMain()
    at Page.ProcessRequest()
    at Page.ProcessRequest(HttpContext context)
    at CallHandlerExecutionStep.Execute()
    at HttpApplication.ExecuteStep(IExecutionStep step,
            Boolean& completedSynchronously)
    at HttpApplication.ResumeSteps(Exception error)
    at HttpApplication.System.Web.IHttpAsyncHandler.BeginProcessRequest(
            HttpContext context, AsyncCallback cb, Object extraData)
    at HttpRuntime.ProcessRequestInternal(HttpWorkerRequest wr)
    at HttpRuntime.ProcessRequest(HttpWorkerRequest wr)
    at ISAPIRuntime.ProcessRequest(IntPtr ecb, Int32 iWRType)
```

This code performs the test expression when the value of Count is 0. The assertion message is displayed with the call stack to help you understand how the software got to this point in the code.

Write, WriteLine

These methods output debug information. The Write method does not append a new line to the end of the information, whereas the WriteLine method does append a new line to the end of the information. The following is an example of the WriteLine method:

```
Debug.WriteLine("End of button click event")
```

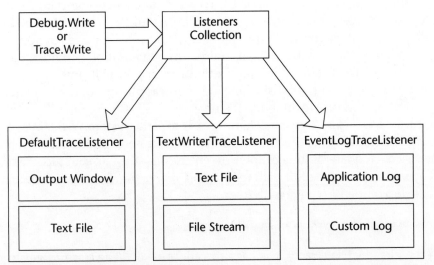

Figure 14.1 The Debug and Trace output may be directed to many locations by using any combination of TraceListener classes.

WriteIf, WriteLineIf

These methods conditionally output debug information. These methods have a Boolean expression parameter and a message parameter. The following is an example of the WriteLineIf method:

```
Debug.WriteLineIf(x=0,"x is set to zero")
```

Fail

This Fail method outputs debug information and is typically used inside exception catch blocks. The Fail event is essentially an Assert method that always evaluates to false. Like Assert, this method has a message parameter and a detail message parameter. The following is an example of the Fail method:

```
Debug.Fail("Count=0 Error", _
    "Count must not be 0 because the Count will be used for division.")
```

Trace

The System.dll file contains the Trace class, which can be used to obtain information while the system is running. At times, such as when working with a multitier or multithreaded application, using the debugger to retrieve data doesn't work. This is where tracing can provide troubleshooting data. You enable tracing by adding the /d:TRACE=True switch when compiling the code. By default, the trace switch is enabled in Visual Studio .NET, which means that trace code is compiled into the debug and release builds of applications, which produces instrumented builds. Instrumentation provides the ability to monitor the health of an application running in real time. Tracing helps isolate problems without disturbing a running application. All the methods of the Debug class are included in the trace.

Two Trace classes exist: System.Diagnostics.Trace and System.Web.UI.Page .Trace. The System.Diagnostics.Trace class is covered here, and System.Web .UI.Trace is covered later in this chapter. To ensure that the correct Trace class is used, you can specify the full path to System.Diagnostics.Trace, or create an alias at the top of the Web page as follows:

```
Imports DiagTrace = System.Diagnostics.Trace
```

With the alias of DiagTrace, it is easy to call Trace or DiagTrace to get to either of the Trace classes. The alias is used in the examples that follow.

Switches

Switches can be used in an application to control the Debug and Trace output from the application's configuration file. Two concrete switch classes inherit from the abstract (MustInherit) Switch class: BooleanSwitch and TraceSwitch.

BooleanSwitch

You can set the BooleanSwitch to 1 or 0 in the Web.config file, as shown in the following example:

```
<configuration>
    <system.diagnostics>
        <switches>
            <add name="myBoolSwitch" value="0" />
            <add name="myOtherBoolSwitch" value="1" />
        </switches>
    </system.diagnostics>
</configuration>
```

To use these switches in the program, you can create instances of the BooleanSwitch and use them in any conditional statement, such as Debug.WriteIf, Trace.WriteLineIf, or a simple If statement. The following sample shows how the BooleanSwitch class can be used:

```
Imports DiagTrace = System.Diagnostics.Trace
Public Class WebForm1
    Inherits System.Web.UI.Page
    Shared myBool As New BooleanSwitch( _
        "myBoolSwitch", "This is a boolean switch")
    Shared myOtherBool As New BooleanSwitch( _
            "myOtherBoolSwitch", "This is a Boolean switch")
    Private Sub Button1_Click( _
            ByVal sender As System.Object, _
            ByVal e As System.EventArgs) Handles Button1.Click
        Debug.WriteLineIf( _
        myBool.Enabled, "myBoolSwitch is on")
        Debug.WriteLineIf( _
            myOtherBool.Enabled, "myOtherBoolSwitch is on")
        DiagTrace.WriteLineIf( _
            Not myBool.Enabled, "myBoolSwitch is off")
        DiagTrace.WriteLineIf( _
            Not myOtherBool.Enabled, "myOtherBoolSwitch is off")
    End Sub
End Class
```

The output is as follows:

```
myOtherBoolSwitch is on
myBoolSwitch is off
```

When the first switch is checked, the Switch class reads all switch settings from the Web.config file. The settings are stored in a private HashTable inside the Switch class. When any other switch is checked, the value is retrieved from the Switch class's internal HashTable.

 For optimum performance, Switch instances should be configured as static (shared) variables. The switches in previous code example, myBoolSwitch and myOtherBoolSwitch, are examples of the proper configuration.

TraceSwitch

The TraceSwitch is similar to the BooleanSwitch, except TraceSwitch is multi-valued. The values that the TraceSwitch can handle are included in the TraceLevel enumeration as shown in Table 14.1.

You set the TraceSwitch in the Web.config file as follows:

```
<configuration>
    <system.diagnostics>
        <switches>
            <add name="myTraceSwitch" value="4" />
        </switches>
    </system.diagnostics>
</configuration>
```

Table 14.1 TraceLevel Values

TRACELEVEL	VALUE
Off	0
Error	1
Warning	2
Info	3
Verbose	4

When the TraceSwitch is set to 4, all the levels will be output. If the switch is set to 3, levels 1 through 3 will output, and so on. The following code example uses the TraceSwitch:

```
Imports DiagTrace = System.Diagnostics.Trace
Public Class WebForm1
    Inherits System.Web.UI.Page
    Shared myTrace As New TraceSwitch( _
            "myTraceSwitch", "This is a Trace switch")
    Private Sub Button1_Click( _
            ByVal sender As System.Object, _
            ByVal e As System.EventArgs) Handles Button1.Click
        Debug.WriteLineIf( _
            myTrace.TraceVerbose, "This is the Verbose Trace = 4")
        Debug.WriteLineIf( _
            myTrace.TraceInfo, "This is the Info Trace = 3")
        DiagTrace.WriteLineIf( _
            myTrace.TraceWarning, "This is the Warning Trace = 2")
        DiagTrace.WriteLineIf( _
            myTrace.TraceError, "This is the Error Trace = 1")
    End Sub
End Class
```

The output of the code when the trace setting is set to 4 is as follows:

```
This is the Verbose Trace = 4
This is the Info Trace = 3
This is the Warning Trace = 2
This is the Error Trace = 1
```

If the value of the trace setting is changed in the Web.config file, the Switch class rereads the Web.config file and uses the new settings.

Debug Monitor Utility

The Debug Monitor Utility (DbMon.exe) is a tool that displays the messages that have been written to the OutputDebugString function in the Kernel32 API. This tool can display Trace and Debug messages that have been written using the DefaultTraceListener. The Debug Monitor Utility is provided with the Windows Platform SDK. Figure 14.2 shows the Trace output when running the previous Trace example code. The benefit of this tool is that a program that contains many trace messages can be run outside of Visual Studio .NET and the Debug Monitor Utility will listen for the trace messages and display them. This does not require a recompilation of the program, and the program works normally as the messages are displayed.

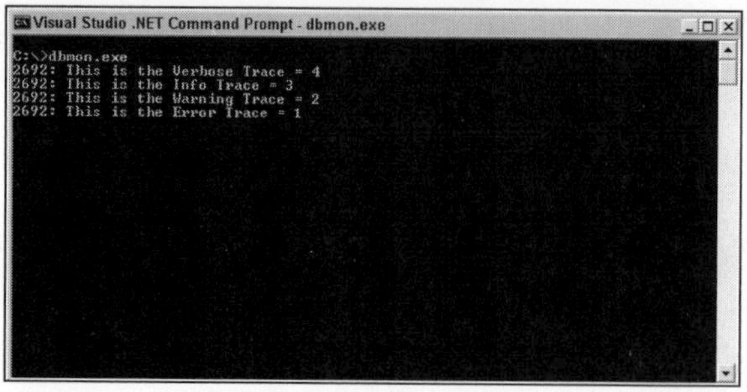

Figure 14.2 The Debug Monitor Utility displays Trace and Debug output.

> **tip** **This tool works when the Web application is run outside the Visual Studio .NET debugger. The Visual Studio .NET debugger contains its own output window that displays the DefaultTraceListener output.**

TraceListener

You can use TraceListener to direct Debug or Trace output to an alternate location, such as a stream, file, or an event log. Debug and Trace have a Listeners collection, which enables you to add many Listeners. The TraceListener class is a base class for the DefaultTraceListener, TextWriterTraceListener, and the EventLogTraceListener. Debug and Trace automatically receive an instance of the DefaultTraceListener.

DefaultTraceListener

The DefaultTraceListener sends its output to the output window, but also has a LogFileName property that you can use to direct the output to a file.

The following code directs the Debug output to a file. Note that the output still goes to the output window, and both outputs contain stack trace information.

```
Dim defListener As DefaultTraceListener
defListener = CType(Debug.Listeners(0), DefaultTraceListener)
defListener.LogFileName = "c:\defautListener.txt"
Debug.Assert(Count <> 0, "Count=0 Error", _
    "Count must not be 0 because the Count will be the denominator" & _
    " in the next function.")
```

TextWriterTraceListener

It may not be desirable to see the stack trace information, which is generated by the DefaultTraceListener. The following code creates a TextWriterTraceListener, which is used to output Debug information to a text file and does not generate stack trace information to the file.

```
Sub Application_Start(ByVal sender As Object, ByVal e As EventArgs)
    ' Fires when the application is started
    Dim fname As String = "C:\debug.txt"
    Dim fs As New FileStream(fname, FileMode.OpenOrCreate, _
            FileAccess.Write)
    Dim tr As New TextWriterTraceListener(fs, "file")
    Debug.Listeners.Add(tr)
    Debug.AutoFlush=true
End Sub
Sub Application_End(ByVal sender As Object, ByVal e As EventArgs)
    ' Fires when the application ends
    Dim tr As TraceListener
    tr = Debug.Listeners("file")
    tr.Close()
    Debug.Listeners.Remove("file")
End Sub
```

This code opens a file when the Web application starts and closes the file when the Web application ends. Notice that AutoFlush is set to true to ensure that data is not held in the buffer for a long period.

EventLogTraceListener

Use the EventLogTraceListener to output Debug and Trace information to an event log. The following example creates an instance of the EventLog class and then an instance of the EventLogTraceListener with the EventLog instance.

```
Sub Application_Start(ByVal sender As Object, ByVal e As EventArgs)
    ' Fires when the application is started
    Dim elog As New EventLog("Application")
    elog.Source = "Ch14Web"
    Dim el As New EventLogTraceListener(elog)
    el.Name = "eventLog"
    Debug.Listeners.Add(el)
End Sub
Sub Application_End(ByVal sender As Object, ByVal e As EventArgs)
    ' Fires when the application ends
```

```
        Dim el As TraceListener
        el = Debug.Listeners("eventLog")
        el.Close()
        Debug.Listeners.Remove(el)
    End Sub
```

The Application_Start event method creates the EventLogTraceListener and adds it to the Debug.Listeners collection. The Application_End event method removes the EventLogTraceListener. Figure 14.3 shows the event in the Application event log.

 When a new source is being defined, the EventLogTraceListener code shown in this section attempts to create the event log source on the fly. This requires the write permissions in the Registry that the default ASPNET account does not have. If the event log source already exists, no additional permissions are required for the ASPNET account. To correct the problem, temporarily turn on impersonation in the Web.config file by adding the following tag after the authentication tag:

```
<identity impersonate="true" userName="admin" password="pwd"/>
```

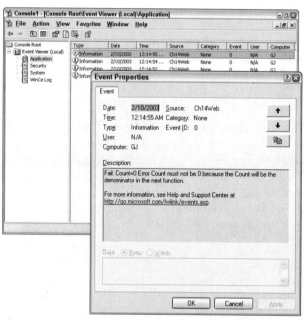

Figure 14.3 The Application event log showing events that have been written to the log using the EventLogTraceListener.

Web Trace

The previous sections covered the System.Diagnostics.Trace class, but the System.Web.UI.Page class has a Trace property, which is an instance of the TraceContext class. This class provides a simple solution to Web page instrumentation by building an HTML representation of the Trace output information.

With ASP, the developer used Response.Write statements to display various bits of information to help with debugging a Web page. With Trace, the debugging information can be easily turned on or off. The Trace output displays the Trace messages that have been added to the code and displays information about the Web page, such as the QueryString, the form data, header information, and the time that was required to build the page.

Trace provides you with the ability to perform page- or application-level tracing. Page-level tracing is configured at the Web page; whereas application-level tracing is configured in the Web.config file.

Trace information is written by using the Trace.Write and Trace.Warn methods. Trace.Warn displays its message using red font.

Page-Level Trace

You turn on page-level tracing at the Web page by placing the following code at the top of the HTML page:

```
<%@ Page Trace="true" TraceMode="SortByCategory" %>
```

After tracing is turned on at the page, the trace output is appended to the Web page output. If the PageLayout is set to FlowLayout, the trace output appears at the bottom of the Web page. If the PageLayout is set to GridLayout, the trace output is displayed as a background to the page. The following sample code produces the output shown in Figure 14.4:

```
Public Class WebForm2
    Inherits System.Web.UI.Page
    Protected WithEvents Button1 As System.Web.UI.WebControls.Button
    Private Sub btnLogin_Click( _
            ByVal sender As System.Object, _
            ByVal e As System.EventArgs) Handles btnLogin.Click
        Trace.Write("Button1", "This is the start of Button1_Click")
        Trace.Warn("Button1", "In the middle of Button1_Click")
        Trace.Write("Button1", "This is the end of Button1_Click")
    End Sub
End Class
```

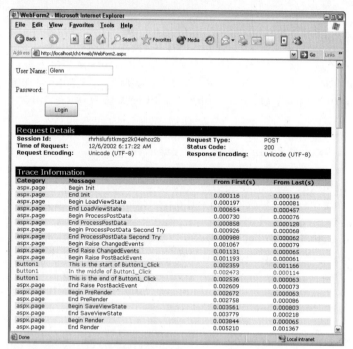

Figure 14.4 The Trace output when using the Trace.Write and Trace.Warn methods.

In addition to turning on tracing at the top of the Web page, you can also turn it on with the IsEnabled property. This turns on the Trace, starting at the current code location. The following code enables tracing:

```
Trace.IsEnabled = True
```

You can also use the IsEnabled property to verify that tracing is turned on.

Application-Level Trace

Tracing at the Web application level allows one setting to be changed to enable or disable tracing across the complete Web site. Tracing is controlled at the Web application level by changing the settings in the Web.config file. This Web.config file contains a setting for a trace that looks like the following:

```
<trace enabled="false"
       requestLimit="10"
       pageOutput="false"
       traceMode="SortByTime"
       localOnly="true" />
```

If the enabled attribute is changed to true, all Web pages on the site will have tracing enabled; but notice that the pageOutput attribute is set to false.

Although tracing is enabled, the results are held in memory instead of being appended to the bottom of each page. This is a nice feature, because the trace results can be cleanly viewed and printed. To view the result after navigating around the Web site, request the trace.axd page. There is no file called trace.axd; but there is an HttpHandler that listens for a request for trace.axd, and the handler generates the Web page on the fly, as shown in Figure 14.5.

The requestLimit attribute defaults to 10, but you can change it as required. When the request limit is reached, the server stops recoding trace messages. If the *clear current trace* link is clicked (see Figure 14.5), all trace data is erased and the server starts recording trace data again. Also, if any change is made to the Web.config file, the Web application restarts, and the trace information is erased.

Set the localOnly attribute to true to be at the Web server to view the trace data. This helps to ensure that users or customers don't see the trace information.

The traceMode attribute can be set to SortByTime or SortByCategory, which is the default.

Using Trace in Components

When working with components, Web tracing can still be used to output data to the Web trace page. This feature allows all trace information to be displayed on a single page. Web tracing can be extended into .dll libraries by adding a reference to the System.Web.dll assembly, and adding Imports System.Web to the top of the code page. The following is an example of a simple component containing a class with a buildString method:

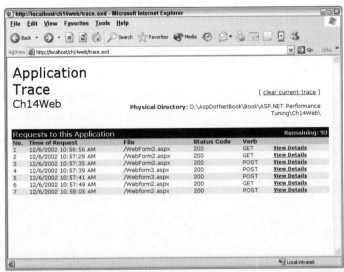

Figure 14.5 The main menu screen is displayed when a request is made for trace.axd.

```
'Be sure to set a reference to System.Web.dll.
Imports System.Web
Public Class AbcClass
    Public Function BuildString()
        Dim x As Integer = 0
        Dim s As String = ""
        Dim webTrace As TraceContext
        webTrace = HttpContext.Current.Trace
        webTrace.Warn("AbcClass", "Starting contruction of string")
        For x = 1 To 5000
            s = s & "The current value of x=" & x.ToString() & ","
        Next
        webTrace.Warn("AbcClass", "Ended contruction of string")
        Return s
    End Function
End Class
```

The buildString method gets access to the trace of the current HttpContext, which is assigned to a variable called webTrace. Use the Write and Warn methods of the webTrace variable to output trace data.

In the following example, a Web page, which has a single button, is created. When the button is clicked, an instance of the AbcClass is created and the BuildString method is executed.

```
Imports Ch14Component
Public Class WebForm3
    Inherits System.Web.UI.Page
    Protected WithEvents Button1 As System.Web.UI.WebControls.Button
    Private Sub Button1_Click( _
     ByVal sender As System.Object, _
     ByVal e As System.EventArgs) Handles Button1.Click
        Dim a As New AbcClass()
        Response.Write(a.BuildString())
    End Sub
End Class
```

The trace results are shown in Figure 14.6. The most important metric to focus on is the warning that was output when the construction of the string ended. Figure 14.6 shows the warning, which states that it took 25.360157 seconds to execute this method.

Performance Monitor

You can use Windows Performance Monitor to look at many aspects of Windows and the .NET Framework. Performance Monitor can be used to monitor system resources, such as memory usage, processor utilization, disk access, and network bandwidth. In addition, the .NET Framework provides many counters, and many applications, such as SQL Server and Internet Information Server, provide counters.

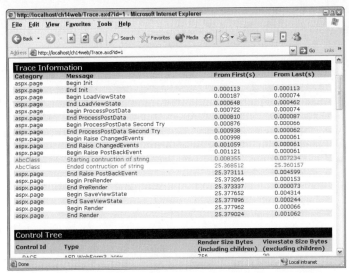

Figure 14.6 The trace results reveal the warning that was generated when the string construction ended. The warning states that it took 25.360157 seconds to build the string.

Performance Monitor is available under the Administrative Tools. Performance Monitor is an ActiveX control called the System Monitor Utility that can be added to the Microsoft Management Console. Performance Monitor supports graphical logging to the screen, as well as logging to a file. It is also possible to create Performance Monitor alerts, which you can use to execute a program when a counter reaches a user-settable level. You can also monitor performance counters on remote machines, which makes this a compelling resource to use when attempting to instrument a multitier Web farm.

Performance Monitor displays symptoms, such as abnormally high processor usage, or excessive disk IO, but it takes a keen person to identify the root cause of these symptoms. To see a more complete picture of the system, monitoring should always include processor, memory, disk, and network counters. For example, at times when monitoring processor utilization, and disk IO, these counters may have excessively high metrics. You might deduce that a faster hard drive is required, but if you monitor memory, you might see that the system is low on RAM, which is causing excessive page swapping. The better solution in this case is to add more RAM.

A Web page containing a Button control, Label control, and the following code has been added to a Web project and was run with the Performance Monitor watching % Processor Time, Available Megabytes of RAM, % Disk Time, and Network Byte Total per Second:

```
Public Class WebForm5
    Inherits System.Web.UI.Page
    Protected WithEvents Button1 As System.Web.UI.WebControls.Button
    Protected WithEvents Label1 As System.Web.UI.WebControls.Label
```

```
Private Sub Button1_Click( _
        ByVal sender As System.Object, _
        ByVal e As System.EventArgs) Handles Button1.Click
    Label1.Text = BuildString()
End Sub
Public Function BuildString()
    Dim x As Integer = 0
    Dim s As String = ""
    For x = 1 To 5000
        s = s & "abcdefghijklmnopqrstuvwxyz"
        s = s & " The value of x=" & x.ToString()
        s = s & "<br>"
    Next
    Return s
End Function
End Class
```

The button was clicked and there was a lengthy delay before the page finished its processing. The Performance Monitor output is shown in Figure 14.7. The highlight (Ctrl+H) feature is being used to identify the % Processor Usage. As soon as the button was clicked, the % Processor Usage went to 100%, and stayed there until the page was done being processed. The other counters hardly moved, except for the % Disk Time, which jumped for a brief moment toward the end of processing. So where is the bottleneck? Based on the counters that are being monitored, increasing the processor speed or finding a way to reduce the processor requirements would probably deliver the most gain in overall performance. For now, the focus is on the tools, but solving this problem is covered later in the performance-tuning part of this chapter.

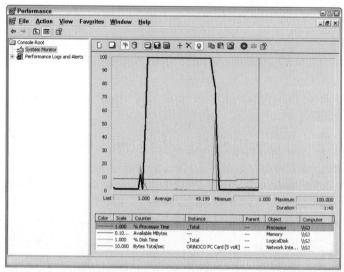

Figure 14.7 The performance counters show that processor usage spikes when the button on the Web page is clicked.

Performance Counters

You add counters in the Performance Monitor window by clicking the icon that looks like a plus sign. The Add Counters window opens, enabling you to select the computer, performance object, performance counter, and instance of the counter.

In addition to adding counters, you can create new counters in Visual Studio .NET, which allows the presentation of more specific information to Performance Monitor. To create new counters for monitoring the StringLength and the LoopCount, add the following code to the Global.asax.vb class:

```vb
Imports System.Web
Imports System.Web.SessionState
Imports System.Diagnostics
Imports System.IO
Public Class Global
    Inherits System.Web.HttpApplication
    Sub Application_Start(ByVal sender As Object, ByVal e As EventArgs)
        ' Fires when the application is started
        Dim catName As String = "MyPerformanceObject"
        If (Not PerformanceCounterCategory.Exists(catName)) Then
            Dim myCounterData As New _
                CounterCreationDataCollection()
            Dim ccd As New CounterCreationData()
            ccd.CounterName = "StringLength"
            ccd.CounterType = _
                PerformanceCounterType.NumberOfItems64
            ccd.CounterHelp = _
                "Displays character count in the string"
            myCounterData.Add(ccd)
            ccd = New CounterCreationData()
            ccd.CounterName = "LoopValue"
            ccd.CounterType = _
                PerformanceCounterType.NumberOfItems64
            ccd.CounterHelp = _
                "Displays the value of the loop counter"
            myCounterData.Add(ccd)
            PerformanceCounterCategory.Create(catName, _
                "This Is the Category Help.", myCounterData)
        End If
    End Sub
    Sub Session_Start(ByVal sender As Object, ByVal e As EventArgs)
        ' Fires when the session is started
        Dim pcStringLength As New PerformanceCounter( _
            "MyPerformanceObject", _
            "StringLength", _
            Session.SessionID.ToString(), False)
        Session("pcStringLength") = pcStringLength
        Dim pcLoopVaue As New PerformanceCounter( _
            "MyPerformanceObject", _
```

```
                "LoopValue", _
                Session.SessionID.ToString(), False)
            Session("pcLoopVaue") = pcLoopVaue
      End Sub
      Sub Application_BeginRequest( _
                ByVal sender As Object, ByVal e As EventArgs)
            ' Fires at the beginning of each request
      End Sub
      Sub Application_AuthenticateRequest( _
                ByVal sender As Object, ByVal e As EventArgs)
            ' Fires upon attempting to authenticate the use
      End Sub
      Sub Application_Error( _
        ByVal sender As Object, ByVal e As EventArgs)
            ' Fires when an error occurs
      End Sub
      Sub Session_End(ByVal sender As Object, ByVal e As EventArgs)
            ' Fires when the session ends
      End Sub
      Sub Application_End(ByVal sender As Object, ByVal e As EventArgs)
            ' Fires when the application ends
      End Sub
  End Class
```

A performance counter requires a category and a counter name. The following code checks to see whether the category exists, and if it doesn't, the category and counters are created.

 When a new Performance Monitor category and counters are not defined, the code in this section attempts to create the category and counters on the fly. This requires permissions that the default ASPNET account does not have. If the category and counters already exist, no additional permissions are required for the ASPNET account. To correct the problem, temporarily turn on impersonation in the Web.config file by adding the following tag after the authentication tag:

```
<identity impersonate="true" userName="admin" password="pwd"/>.
```

Session_Start creates a new instance of both counters and stores the instances in Session variables. The instance names are assigned to the current SessionID, which you can view in the browser by navigating to the Web page to start a session, and then typing the following into the Internet Explorer address bar:

```
javascript:alert(document.cookie);
```

This line displays a message box containing all the current cookies for the current site, which includes the SessionID.

The BuildString function has also been updated to include the new counters as shown in the following code:

```
Public Function BuildString()
      Dim x As Integer = 0
      Dim s As String = ""
      Dim pcStringLength As PerformanceCounter
      Dim pcLoopValue As PerformanceCounter
      pcStringLength = CType(Session("pcStringLength"), _
          PerformanceCounter)
      pcLoopValue = CType(Session("pcLoopVaue"), _
          PerformanceCounter)
      For x = 1 To 3000
          s = s & "abcdefghijklmnopqrstuvwxyz"
          s = s & " The value of x=" & x.ToString()
          s = s & "<br>"
          'Update the counters.
          pcStringLength.RawValue = s.Length
          pcLoopValue.RawValue = x
      Next
      'Clear the counters.
      pcStringLength.RawValue = 0
      pcLoopValue.RawValue = 0
      Return s
End Function
```

This BuildString function assigns the Session variables to local variables. Each time the loop is run, the counters are updated. When the loop is done, the counters are reset to zero.

The Web application needs to be run at least once to create the new category and counter. To add a counter, press Ctrl+I or click the plus button. Figure 14.8 shows the addition of the new counters to the Performance Monitor window. The local computer is selected, and then the Performance object is set to the new category called MyPerformanceObject, which reveals the new counters and the session instances that are available.

Figure 14.9 shows Performance Monitor with the counters added. Each counter has scale, color, line width, and line style properties you can set. The LoopValue has a dotted line style with a scale of .01, whereas the StringLength has a thicker line style with a scale of .0001. When the button is clicked to execute the BuildString method, the processor usage immediately rises to 100 percent. The custom counters initially rise quickly, and then rate of rise slows down. This suggests that as the loop counter increases, it takes more time to process the loop.

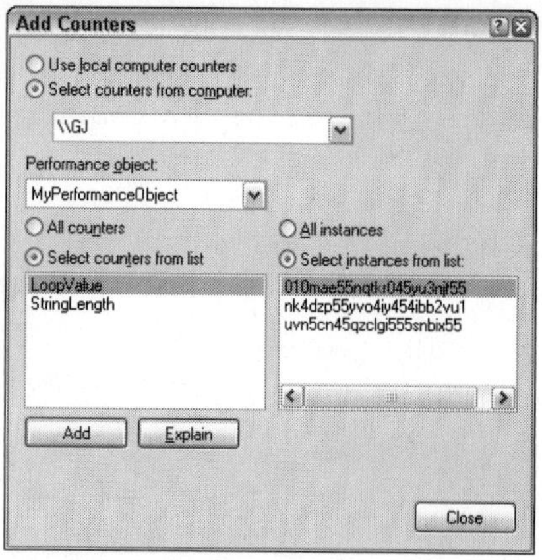

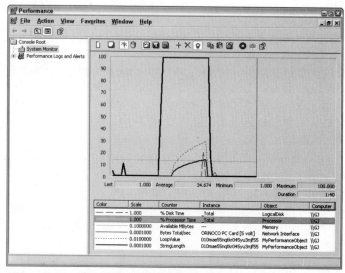

Figure 14.8 The addition of the new custom counters requires the selection of a SessionID.

Application Center Test

Application Center Test (ACT) is a software tool included with Visual Studio .NET that can help you gather data and make capacity decisions about a Web application. With the ACT, you can create tests that simulate many users hitting the Web site simultaneously. The results of the tests are recorded so you can review them to identify a site's stability, speed, scalability, and responsiveness issues.

Figure 14.9 The Performance Monitor displays the new custom counters, overlayed with the existing system counters.

An ACT project can be created that identifies many tests. Each test can be created by letting ACT record the browser navigation. Alternatively, an empty test can be created, and the test code can be manually written. Writing the test code provides full control of the test. A single test can be run many times, and the results are recorded each time.

Getting started with Application Center Test is as easy as creating a new test from the Action menu, clicking New Test, the scripting language, and the Start Recoding button. Internet Explorer starts, and Application Center Test will record all Web navigation within the browser window. An appropriate test would be navigating to the desired site and clicking through the links on the site in the same fashion as a typical user. When finished, the browser window can be closed, and the Stop Recording button can be clicked to stop and record the test. Finally, the wizard prompts you for a test name, and saves the test.

Before a test is run, you need to set the test properties by right-clicking the test and clicking Properties, as shown in Figure 14.10. The test properties window allows you to set the quantity of simultaneous browser connections and the run duration. The Users tab allows the selection of users, which can be handy when authentication is required for the site. The Counters tab allows Performance Monitor counters to be queried while the test is progressing. The counter information is stored with the recorded test data.

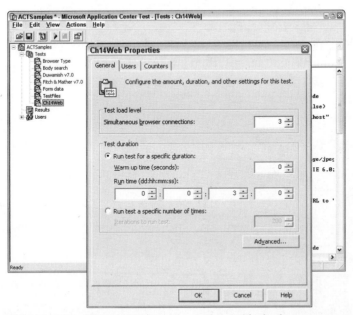

Figure 14.10 The test properties window with the browser connections set to 3 and the duration set to 3 minutes.

The test being run in Figure 14.10 is against the same Web page, with its button and Label controls, that was just created in the Performance Monitor section of this chapter. When the button is clicked, a call is made to a superslow function called BuildString. When the test was recoded, the Web page was navigated to and then the Button was clicked. ACT repeats this test for the duration that is specified. The test properties have been set to three browser connections, and a 3-minute run duration. The results of the test are shown in Figure 14.11.

The test results show that there were only 12 total requests to the Web page in 3 minutes with three browser connections. The low number is due to the time that is required to execute the BuildString function.

The BuildString function is performing a rather simple loop that exists in many Web pages. Based on the tracing and performance counters that have been covered in this chapter, it's obvious that the BuildString function is the bottleneck. The next section, *Performance Tips*, examines this bottleneck in detail and provides alternatives to dramatically increase the performance of this Web page.

The test can be copied, so changes can be made to the properties or the test code and the test can be rerun. The previous test was copied, and the browser connections set to 6, and then copied again with the browser connections set to 9, and then copied again with the browser connections set to 12. The test was run again for each of the new tests.

After the desired tests are run, click the Results node to reveal all the recoded test data. The reports can be displayed with overlapping data from each test by clicking the Results node, and then clicking the check box of each report that is to be displayed. See Figure 14.12.

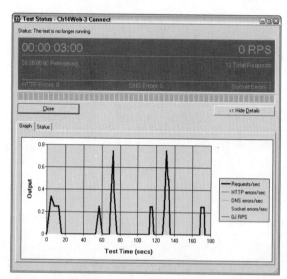

Figure 14.11   The test results with three browser connection for 3 minutes.

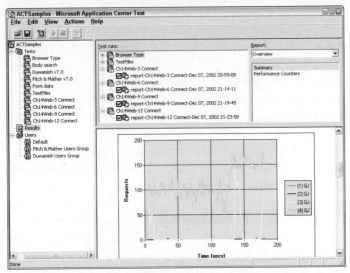

Figure 14.12 The results of the four test runs, where the browser connection settings were the only change (3, 6, 9, and 12 connections).

At first glance, it may look like the Web server responds well to more connections. The graph shows the quantity of requests per second, and the 12-connection test has many more requests than the other test. Unfortunately, this is not the complete story. You must take errors into account. As more connections were used, the error count increased dramatically. The bottom of the report shows the real result. See Figure 14.13.

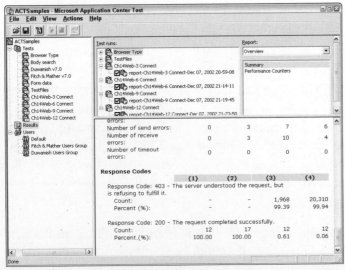

Figure 14.13 The bottom of the report shows the quantity of errors and successful requests.

Notice that only two response code types were received. The first one was response code 403, which is "The server understood the request, but is refusing to fulfill it." The second one is response code 200, which is "The request completed successfully."

The quantity of successful responses is almost the same across all tests. Although the six-browser connection test had the highest quantity of successful responses, it still had three socket errors, which means that the only test without errors was the three-connection test.

There are two primary reasons why there were so many errors. First the processor was so busy handling each request that it failed to respond to new requests. The other problem relates to the operating system that is being run for these tests. On Window 2000 and Windows XP Professional, only 10 connections are allowed into the Web server. After that, additional requests are rejected. The problem is compounded by the fact that Internet Information Server implements keep-alives, which are usually desirable for better performance, but with connection limits, they hurt performance. Keep-alives are connections that stay open after the browser requests a Web page, because there is a good chance that the browser will request another page from the Web site. If a connection is left open, it takes away from the 10-connection limit on Windows Professional. The net result is that ACT makes requests that are immediately rejected by Internet Information Server, thereby generating a quick HTTP error, so ACT keeps trying until a connection finally opens.

 When using Windows 2000 Professional or Windows XP Professional for load testing with ACT, turn off HTTP keep-alives in Internet Information Server, and keep the simultaneous browser connections under five to ensure the most accurate results without receiving errors.

Performance Tips

Now that several performance and instrumentation tools have been covered, it's time to look at performance tips and tricks. This section is certainly not all-encompassing, but the tips and techniques defined here could help identify other potential bottlenecks.

String Concatenation

In the .NET Framework, the string data type is immutable. This means that when a value is assigned to a string, it cannot be changed. This seems like a rather bazaar statement, since developers always use code such as the following:

```
Dim s as string
s = "This is a test. "
s = s & "More data here"
```

This may look like s is being changed, but it is not. The last line of code is creating a new string that contains the concatenation of s, and "More data here" and the new string is being assigned to s. The old string is being abandoned in memory, and garbage collection will reclaim this memory (see Figure 14.14).

One way to increase performance is to avoid concatenation. The following code is faster, because movement of data in memory is reduced. The Build-String function that has been used in the previous ACT and Performance Monitor tests uses concatenation three times within the loop. The use of Web Trace can identify the time that it takes to run this loop. The revised BuildString method is as follows:

```
Public Function BuildString()
     Dim x As Integer = 0
     Dim s As String = ""
     Dim pcStringLength As PerformanceCounter
     Dim pcLoopValue As PerformanceCounter
     pcStringLength = CType(Session("pcStringLength"), _
       PerformanceCounter)
     pcLoopValue = CType(Session("pcLoopVaue"), _
       PerformanceCounter)
     Trace.Warn("BuildString", "Start of loop")
     For x = 1 To 3000
          s = s & "abcdefghijklmnopqrstuvwxyz"
          s = s & " The value of x=" & x.ToString()
          s = s & "<br>"
          'Update the counters.
          pcStringLength.RawValue = s.Length
          pcLoopValue.RawValue = x
     Next
     Trace.Warn("BuildString", "End of loop")
     'Clear the counters.
     pcStringLength.RawValue = 0
     pcLoopValue.RawValue = 0
     Return s
End Function
```

When the test was run three times, the loop run times were 23.907289, 30.436777, and 30.360770. In the following code, the BuildString is modified to concatenate only once within the loop:

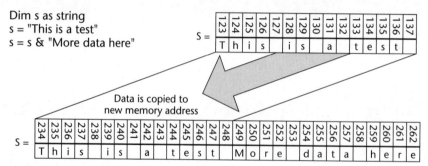

```
Dim s as string
s = "This is a test"
s = s & "More data here"
```

Figure 14.14 Because strings are immutable, string concatenation involves the creation of a new string containing the old string plus the new string. This means that string data must be copied to the new memory address.

```
Public Function BuildString()
    Dim x As Integer = 0
    Dim s As String = ""
    Dim pcStringLength As PerformanceCounter
    Dim pcLoopValue As PerformanceCounter
    pcStringLength = CType(Session("pcStringLength"), _
        PerformanceCounter)
    pcLoopValue = CType(Session("pcLoopVaue"), _
        PerformanceCounter)
    Trace.Warn("BuildString", "Start of loop")
    For x = 1 To 3000
s &= "abcdefghijklmnopqrstuvwxyz The value of x=" & x.ToString()& "<br>"
        'Update the counters.
        pcStringLength.RawValue = s.Length
        pcLoopValue.RawValue = x
    Next
    Trace.Warn("BuildString", "End of loop")
    'Clear the counters.
    pcStringLength.RawValue = 0
    pcLoopValue.RawValue = 0
    Return s
End Function
```

When the test was run three times, the loop run times were 8.758217, 10.050231, and 10.023658. By performing one third of the concatenations, the time to run the loop was reduced to approximately one third of the original time.

StringBuilder

The previous example demonstrated how performance can be increased by reducing the concatenations of strings. The problem is that the code is still performing concatenation 3,000 times while the loop is running.

The StringBuilder class addresses the issue of string concatenation. The StringBuilder is a memory buffer that can dynamically grow, without requiring the data to be moved. When working with large strings, this can increase performance dramatically. Concatenation is accomplished by using the Append method of the StringBuilder. When modifications are complete, the StringBuilder can be converted to a string by using the ToString method as shown in the following example:

```
Public Function BuildString()
    Dim x As Integer = 0
    Dim s As New System.Text.StringBuilder()
    Dim pcStringLength As PerformanceCounter
    Dim pcLoopValue As PerformanceCounter
    pcStringLength = CType(Session("pcStringLength"), _
        PerformanceCounter)
    pcLoopValue = CType(Session("pcLoopVaue"), _
        PerformanceCounter)
    Trace.Warn("BuildString", "Start of loop")
    For x = 1 To 3000
        s.Append("abcdefghijklmnopqrstuvwxyz The value of x=")
        s.Append( x.ToString())
        s.Append( "<br>")
        'Update the counters.
        pcStringLength.RawValue = s.Length
        pcLoopValue.RawValue = x
    Next
    Trace.Warn("BuildString", "End of loop")
    'Clear the counters
    pcStringLength.RawValue = 0
    pcLoopValue.RawValue = 0
    Return s.ToString()
End Function
```

The StringBuilder class is in the System.Text namespace. Inside the loop, the Append method can be run many times, because it is simply adding data to the end of the existing data. When this code was run three times, the resulting times to execute the loop were 0.014790, 0.046475, and 0.021009, which represents a major improvement in performance. Comparing the fastest execution before the change was made (8.758217) to the slowest speed with the change (0.046475), the speed has increased by over 180 times.

After this change, it's time to run ACT to see what kind of performance can be obtained on the tests that were defined. The original test was run with three browser connections, because that was the only test that did not generate errors. The result of the new test also had no errors. Figure 14.15 shows the difference between the two tests.

Comparing the graph of the original test against the new test shows a substantial difference in performance. Neither of these tests generated errors. What was once an extremely slow site now responds significantly better. The original test delivered a mere 12 responses, whereas the latest test delivered 2,204 responses. This is over 180 times the original test.

Caching

Caching data can result in substantial performance gains. In situations where many users would normally make calls to the database for data that rarely changes, caching the data on the Web server can completely bypass the call to the database server.

The cache has a global scope and includes the necessary locking mechanism to allow items to be added and read from the cache by many users. Caching specifics are covered in more detail in Chapter 12, "ASP.NET Applications." This section explores some of the performance gains derived from caching.

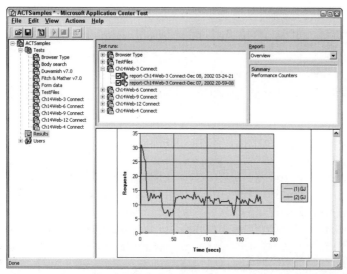

Figure 14.15 The original three-browser connection test overlaid with a new three-browser connection test.

Page Caching

Page caching is probably the easiest caching method to implement. This is a compelling choice for many Web applications. To enable Web page caching, the following information must be added to the HTML at the top of the Web page:

```
<%@ OutputCache Duration="60" VaryByParam="customerId;pageNumber" %>
```

This setting caches the page output for 60 seconds, after which, the cache is invalidated, and the next request for the page results in execution of the code that is on the page.

The VaryByParam setting can be set to none, *, valid querystring, or form parameter names, separated by a semicolon. If VaryByParam is set to none, only one copy of the page is cached. If VaryByParam is set to *, there will be a cached copy of the page for each combination of parameters that changes when the page is retrieved. If the parameter is set to customerId;pageNumber, there will be a cached copy of the page for each customerId and pageNumber combination.

Figure 14.16 shows the ACT output after running the same test that was used with the StringBuilder, but the page was cached using the following statement in the Web page HTML:

```
<%@ OutputCache Duration="60" VaryByParam="*" %>
```

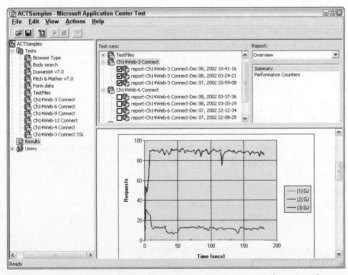

Figure 14.16   The Application Center Test report when implementing caching.

Caching improved performance significantly over the last test where the StringBuilder was implemented. This required only a single line of code and resulted in a substantial gain.

The test was done using three browser connections, and no errors were reported when running the test. Notice that the request count went from 12 to 2,204 to 15,837. This represents an increase of over seven times the previous test. It's worth noting that if the code were not changed to use the String-Builder, the change would have been from 12 requests to 15,837 requests. This would represent an increase of over 1,300 times.

Object Caching

In the previous example, caching was implemented with a single line of code. In some cases, this type of caching is wasteful. For example, if a large amount of data is being sent to the browser and that same data is being sent to the browser from a different page, multiple copies of the same data could be held by the Web server. Often, part of the Web page needs to be dynamic, whereas another part of the page is cached.

Object caching involves writing the code to cache objects rather than the entire page. The Cache object is used to add items into the cache. The following code shows how the BuildString method's result can be cached:

```
Public Function BuildString()
    Dim retString As String
    If Cache("BuildString") Is Nothing Then
        Dim x As Integer = 0
        Dim s As New System.Text.StringBuilder()
        Dim pcStringLength As PerformanceCounter
        Dim pcLoopValue As PerformanceCounter
        pcStringLength = CType(Session("pcStringLength"), _
          PerformanceCounter)
        pcLoopValue = CType(Session("pcLoopVaue"), _
          PerformanceCounter)
        Trace.Warn("BuildString", "Start of loop")
        For x = 1 To 3000
            s.Append("abcdefghijklmnopqrstuvwxyz The value of x=")
            s.Append(x.ToString())
            s.Append("<br>")
            'Update the counters.
            pcStringLength.RawValue = s.Length
            pcLoopValue.RawValue = x
        Next
        Trace.Warn("BuildString", "End of loop")
        'Clear the counters.
        pcStringLength.RawValue = 0
        pcLoopValue.RawValue = 0
```

```
          retString = s.ToString()
          Cache("BuildString") = retString
     Else
          retString = CType(Cache("BuildString"), String)
     End If
     Return retString
End Function
```

The OutputCache directive was removed from the HTML and the test was run again. Figure 14.17 shows the output of the test, overlaid with the previous test.

Test number 4 represents the object-caching test, which did not perform as well as the page cache test (test 3). The benefit is that other parts of the page are still dynamic. Figure 14.18 shows the metrics of the test. The page cache test (test 3) was over seven times faster than the StringBuilder test (test 2), but this test (test 4) is only about five times faster than the StringBuilder test.

Graphics Caching

When working with images, be sure to deliver the image to the browser using the same size that the browser uses to display the image. If a page is displaying thumbnail images that are 75 x 75 pixels, don't send the image to the browser at 1,200 x 1,200 pixels, because doing so uses all available network bandwidth. Images should be cached where possible, especially when the image is being loaded from a database.

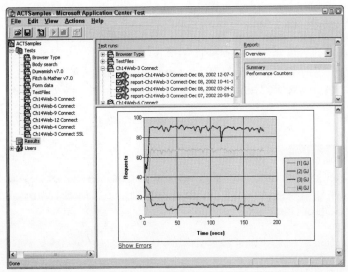

Figure 14.17   The output of the object-caching test, overlaid with previous tests.

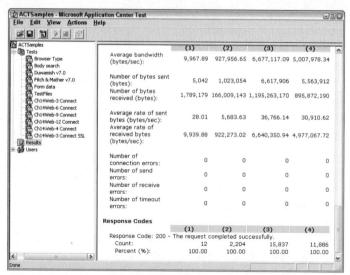

Figure 14.18 The metrics of the object-caching test show a decrease in performance over page caching, but parts of the page can still be dynamic.

ViewState

ViewState should be monitored, and a test should be run to determine whether it is better to store information in the ViewState or in the Session, Application, or Cache state. If a control is read-only, ViewState may not be necessary for the control.

ViewState is turned on at the page level by default, but you can turn it off when it's not required. Also, ViewState should be reviewed on a per control basis to determine the control's impact on performance.

Use a combination of Web Trace and ACT to determine what the impact of ViewState is for the current Web application. Performance will vary between Web pages.

Database Performance

In many situations, database performance can become the bottleneck of a Web application. SQL Server is a fast product, but you still need to be aware of items that can impact SQL Server performance.

Stored Procedures

Whenever possible, use stored procedures for making calls to the database. When a stored procedure is created, it is checked for syntax errors, compiled, and saved to disk. When SQL commands are sent to SQL Server from a Web application, SQL Server must check the SQL statement for syntax errors and compile the SQL before the SQL command can be executed.

When a call is made to the stored procedure, the first time it runs, it may be slower than sending a SQL statement directly to SQL Server, because the stored procedure must load into memory from the disk. After the stored procedure is in memory, the stored procedure will outperform ad hoc SQL statements.

Indexes

When creating SQL Server tables and relationships, be sure to designate a primary key for each table. Although the primary key can be an existing field or fields that identify uniqueness for a row, a surrogate primary key should be considered. A surrogate primary key exists solely to be a row identifier, which is a field that is added to the table and is usually an autonumber (also known as an identity) field. It's faster for SQL Server to maintain an index on a single numeric column than to maintain composite indexes. When a primary key is identified, a unique index is created for the key.

When a relationship is created between two tables, the relationship is usually between the primary key of one table and a foreign key of another table. Although the creation of a primary key automatically creates an index for the primary key, the creation of a foreign key does not create an index automatically. Big performance gains can be realized by adding indexes for all foreign key fields.

Calculated Fields

If a stored procedure or view is constantly performing mathematical operations on certain fields, a calculated field can be created that performs the math operation once prior to executing the stored procedure. This addition can lead to large gains when complex formulas are involved, such as trigonometry functions performed on the columns.

Lab 14.1: Using Application Center Test

In this lab, you explore the performance increase that can be obtained by using page caching. An Application Center Test will be used as the primary tool to record performance changes as caching is implemented.

Establishing Baseline Performance Data

In this section, you add a new Web page called login.aspx:

1. To start this lab, open the OrderEntrySystemSolution from Lab 13.1.

2. Right-click the OrderEntrySystemSolution in the Solution Explorer, and click Check Out.

3. Set Customer as the startup project.

4. Set the CustomerList.aspx page as the startup page.

5. Right-click the CustomerList.aspx page, and click View In Browser to ensure that the Web application has been started. Notice that you are redirected to the login page. Enter a name and password, and click the Login button to redirect the page to the CustomerList.aspx page. Close the browser.

6. Open Application Center Test by clicking Start, All Programs, Microsoft Visual Studio .NET, Visual Studio .NET Enterprise Features, Microsoft Application Center Test.

7. Click File, New Project to create a new project. When prompted for the project name, type Customer. Your screen should look like Figure 14.19.

8. Create a new test by clicking Actions, New Test to start the New Test Wizard. Click Record a New Test. Select VBScript as the language. Click Start Recording to start recording a test.

9. When the browser window is displayed, enter the following URL:

   ```
   http://localhost/Customer/CustomerList.aspx
   ```

10. This code redirects the page to the login.aspx page. Type a valid name and password, and click the Login button to redirect the page to the CustomerList.aspx page.

11. Click the browser's Refresh button to retrieve another copy of the CustomerList.aspx page.

12. Close the browser, and click the Stop Recording button.

13. On the next screen, type CustomerListTest for the test name.

14. After recoding the test, open the Tests node in Application Center Test. The CustomerListTest should be available; click CustomerListTest.

The upper-right window contains a message stating that notes can be entered. Enter the following note:

```
Baseline CustomerList Test with 3 Browser Connections for 3
Minutes.
```

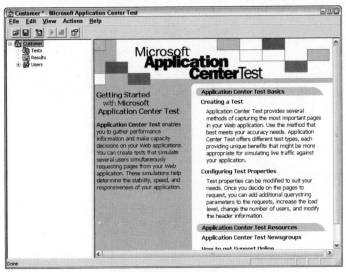

Figure 14.19 The Application Center Test screen after creating a new project called Customer.

15. Right-click the CustomerListTest, and click Properties. Set the Browser Connections to 3 and the Duration to 3 minutes.

16. Right-click the CustomerListTest, and click Start Test.

17. After the test is completed, add the following line to the HTML of the CustomerList.aspx page:

```
<%@ OutputCache Duration="600" VaryByParam="*" %>
```

18. Right-click the CustomerListTest, and click Copy. Rename the copy CustomerListCacheTest. In the upper-right pane, add the following note:

```
CustomerList Cache Test with 3 Browser Connections for 3 Minutes.
```

19. Right-click the CustomerListCacheTest, and click Start Test. Figure 14.20 shows the baseline test overlaid with the cache test. Actual numbers will vary, but there should be a significant difference in performance between the two tests.

20. Scroll to the bottom of report. Figure 14.21 shows the metrics of the test. There were no errors in either test. Your metrics will vary, but there should be a substantial difference between the two tests. Notice that there were two different response codes: The 200 is a success, and the

302 represents the redirect to the login page as well as the redirect back to the CustomerList.aspx page upon successful login. There were a total of 1,581 requests by the baseline test and a total of 20,222 requests by the cache test, which represents speed increase of over 12 times.

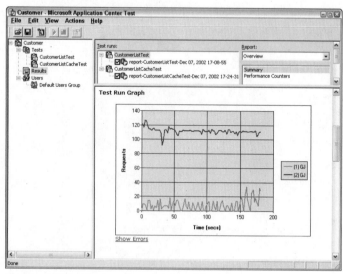

Figure 14.20   The baseline and the cached CustomerList.aspx page results.

21. Save your changes, and check the final solution back into Visual SourceSafe.

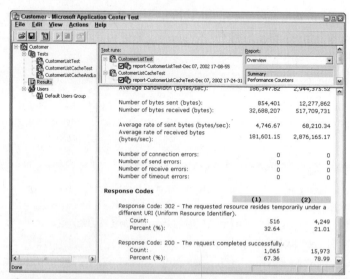

Figure 14.21   The metrics of the baseline and cached CustomerList.aspx page.

Summary

- Performance tuning is the process of running specific tests on isolated parts of the software, making changes to the software, and rerunning the tests to identify bottlenecks and increase the software's performance.

- Identifying bottlenecks is the process of interpreting load test data and investigating system performance to locate the slowest parts of the system. Eliminating a bottleneck can result in substantial gains in performance for the overall system.

- The System.dll file contains the Debug class, which can be used to obtain information when running an application that was compiled using the debug switch.

- The System.dll file contains the Trace class, which can be used to obtain information while the system is running, especially in a multitier or multithreaded application.

- Trace provides the ability to perform page- or application-level tracing. Page-level tracing is configured at the Web page, whereas application-level tracing is configured in the Web.config file.

- Performance Monitor can be used to monitor system resources, such as memory usage, processor utilization, disk access, and network bandwidth. In addition, the .NET Framework provides many counters, and many applications, such as SQL Server and Internet Information Server, provide counters.

- Strings are immutable in the .NET Framework. Concatenation of large strings should be avoided due to the resources that are required to move this data.

- The StringBuilder class can be used when string concatenation is required, because the StringBuilder class contains an Append method, which does not require excessive resources.

- Caching can increase Web performance substantially. For pages that are relatively static, page caching can be used. For pages that can't be cached, object caching can be implemented.

Review Questions

1. What must be established prior to load testing and performance tuning?

2. To receive verbose trace messages, what value should a TraceSwitch be set to?

3. What utility can be run outside of the Visual Studio .NET environment to display Debug and Trace messages that are written to the default listener?

4. When using Web application tracing with pageOutput set to false, what must be requested in order to view the trace information?

5. What is the best method of creating a string when the string is being constructed of a series of loops?

6. What Visual Studio .NET tool can be used to simulate many users hitting a Web site simultaneously?

7. When working with Windows XP Professional, what is the maximum quantity of connections that are allowed on the Web server?

Answers to Review Questions

1. A baseline for comparison as changes are made.

2. Set the value to 4 for verbose messages.

3. The Debug Monitor (DbMon.exe) utility can be run. This utility is included in the Windows Platform SDK.

4. A request for trace.axd must be made.

5. Use the StringBuilder class.

6. Application Center Test (ACT).

7. Windows XP Professional has a 10 connection limit.

Building and Versioning .NET Components

Building reusable components is something developers have done in the past and found beneficial in several ways. First, reusable components have reduced the amount of code developers have had to write, particularly when building large applications. Second, reusable components have encapsulated functionality that developers could reuse in other applications. Third, being compiled code, reusable components have had a performance edge over interpreted scripts.

Today, it's not necessary to build components to get a performance edge; scripted languages are equally fast. The other reasons for building reusable components are still valid, however, and there are some new benefits, such as cross-language inheritance.

One of the problems that have plagued components is versioning. With COM, versioning was done by providing new interfaces, and each interface was considered to be an immutable contract. The problem was that enforcement of the versioning was done by the developer. With .NET components, the runtime enforces versioning. Providing a different version of a component automatically breaks the code until the code is recompiled with the new assembly, or until the application code is redirected to the new component.

This chapter covers the methods of creating components, or reusable assemblies, by first creating a component and using it. After that, this chapter discusses versioning of assemblies, and the differences between private and shared assemblies. Much time is spent also on exploring strong names and binding policies. This chapter finishes by looking at cross-language inheritance.

Classroom Q & A

Q: Where are the Registry entries for .NET components? I am afraid of registering a new component and overwriting this setting by registering an older version of the .NET component.

A: There are no Registry entries for .NET components. This eliminates the problem that was affectionately known as DLL Hell in the past.

Q: If I have many copies of a .NET component on my machine, is there a way to find out which copy is actually being used?

A: Yes. There is a tool called the Fusion Log Viewer that can tell you which component is being used by a program.

Q: Is there a way to set a lookup path to my components so I don't have to keep placing them into the Global Assembly Cache when I am working on them?

A: Yes. You can use the DEVPATH environment variable. We look at this in detail in this chapter.

Building Reusable Components

Chapter 4, "The .NET Framework and Visual Basic .NET Object Programming," covered many of the aspects of object-oriented programming, including inheritance. Creating components allows much of the coding logic to be encapsulated, which can simplify the task of creating many user interfaces, from cell phone to Windows. In this section, a component example is presented that is used throughout the chapter.

Creating the Class Library Project

To build a reusable component, a Visual Studio .NET Class Library project must be created. This project compiles to a .dll file. To use the .dll file, a reference must be made to the .dll file from the Web application.

When the Class Library project is created, it includes an empty class file. The code in Listing 15.1 is included in the class file to provide easy access to the back end SQL Server.

```
Imports System.Data.SqlClient
Public Class Db
    Public Shared Function ExecuteScaler( _
     ByVal cn As SqlConnection, _
     ByVal cmdText As String) As Long
        Return ExecuteScaler( _
         cn, CommandType.Text, cmdText, Nothing)
    End Function
    Public Shared Function ExecuteScaler( _
     ByVal cn As SqlConnection, _
     ByVal cmdType As CommandType, _
     ByVal cmdText As String) As Long
        Return ExecuteScaler( _
         cn, cmdType, cmdText, Nothing)
    End Function
    Public Shared Function ExecuteScaler( _
     ByVal cn As SqlConnection, _
     ByVal cmdType As CommandType, _
     ByVal cmdText As String, _
     ByVal ParamArray prm() As SqlParameter) As Long
        Dim cmd As New SqlCommand(cmdText, cn)
        cmd.CommandType = cmdType
        AddParameters(cmd, prm)
        cn.Open()
        Dim retVal As Long
        retVal = CType(cmd.ExecuteScalar(), Long)
        cn.Close()
        Return retVal
    End Function
    Public Shared Function ExecuteDataSet( _
     ByVal cn As SqlConnection, _
     ByVal cmdText As String) As DataSet
        Return ExecuteDataSet( _
         cn, CommandType.Text, cmdText, Nothing)
    End Function
    Public Shared Function ExecuteDataSet( _
     ByVal cn As SqlConnection, _
     ByVal cmdType As CommandType, _
     ByVal cmdText As String) As DataSet
        Return ExecuteDataSet( _
         cn, cmdType, cmdText, Nothing)
    End Function
    Public Shared Function ExecuteDataSet( _
     ByVal cn As SqlConnection, _
     ByVal cmdType As CommandType, _
     ByVal cmdText As String, _
     ByVal ParamArray prm() As SqlParameter) As DataSet
        Dim cmd As New SqlCommand(cmdText, cn)
```

Listing 15.1 Data component code. This code contains common methods that encapsulate access to the database. This code is used throughout this chapter. *(continued)*

```
        cmd.CommandType = cmdType
        AddParameters(cmd, prm)
        Dim ds As New DataSet()
        Dim da As New SqlDataAdapter(cmd)
        da.Fill(ds)
        Return ds
    End Function
    Private Shared Sub AddParameters( _
     ByVal cmd As SqlCommand, _
     ByVal prm() As SqlParameter)
        If prm Is Nothing Then
            Return
        End If
        Dim p As SqlParameter
        For Each p In prm
            cmd.Parameters.Add(p)
        Next
    End Sub
End Class
```

Listing 15.1 *(continued)*

The methods that have been defined in Listing 15.1 are shared (static), which means that it is not necessary to create an instance of the Db class first. The method can be called by using simply the name of the class as follows:

```
x = Db.ExecuteScaler(cn, "Select count(*) from customers")
```

The Db class contains a method called ExecuteScaler that is overloaded so it can be called with a connection and SQL, or with additional arguments. The ExecuteScaler method returns the first column of the first row from the result set of the query. This method is typically used to retrieve a numeric value, so the return type is cast to a Long, using the CType function.

The ExecuteDataSet method contains the same overloads as the ExecuteScaler method. This method returns a DataSet that could contain many tables if the SQL command contained many select statements.

The AddParameters method is a private helper method that is used to enumerate a parameter array and add each parameter to the command's parameters collection.

After this code is added to the project, the project must be built. Building the project creates a .dll file, which is an assembly. The assembly can be revealed by clicking Show All Files in the Solution Explorer.

Using the Component

Using and reusing a component can save lots of development time. In this section, a new Web project is created that uses the DataComponent assembly. For the purposes of these examples, a second copy of Visual Studio .NET is opened, and a new Web site is created.

Setting a Reference to the Component

Using the component requires telling Visual Studio .NET that the external assembly is to be used with a project. This is done by setting a reference. The reference is added to the Web project by right-clicking the References node in the Solution Explorer and clicking Add Reference.

The Add Reference dialog box has three tabs; .NET, COM, and Projects. If the component was written with Visual Studio .NET, the .NET tab could be used to Browse to the desired folder. Selecting the .dll file using this method does not cause the assembly to be rebuilt when the current project is built.

The COM tab is used to set references to COM components. If a reference is set to a COM component, Visual Studio .NET creates a COM Callable Wrapper class, that can be used to access the COM component.

The Project tab is used to set a reference to a project instead of an assembly. Setting a reference to a project tells Visual Studio .NET that the project must be built prior to building the current project. This essentially sets up the build order for the solution. The only projects that are visible in this tab are the projects that are in the current solution. This means that the DataComponent project must be loaded in the current solution to be able to select it. Setting a reference to the project is generally considered to the best selection, because building the solution builds all of the projects in the correct order.

In this example, a reference is set to the DataComponent.dll assembly instead of the project. This allows the projects to be out of sync for the testing purposes.

Calling the Component

In the new Web project, the following code has been added to the Web page to test the ExecuteScaler functionality.

```
Imports DataComponent
Imports System.Data.SqlClient
Public Class WebForm1
    Inherits System.Web.UI.Page
    Private Sub Page_Load( _
```

```
            ByVal sender As System.Object, _
            ByVal e As System.EventArgs) Handles MyBase.Load
                Dim cn As New SqlConnection( _
                    "server=.;database=northwind;trusted_connection=true")
                Dim x As Long
                x = Db.ExecuteScaler( _
                 cn, "Select count(*) from customers")
                Response.Write("Count of Customers=" & x.ToString())
        End Sub
    End Class
```

When the application is run, a Web page is displayed that contains the count of the customers in the customers table.

To test the ExecuteDataSet functionality, a Datagrid is added to the Web page, and it displays the contents of the DataSet that is returned from the Exe-cuteDataSet method. The page now contains the following code:

```
Imports DataComponent
Imports System.Data.SqlClient
Public Class WebForm1
    Inherits System.Web.UI.Page
    Protected WithEvents DataGrid1 As
        System.Web.UI.WebControls.DataGrid
    Private Sub Page_Load( _
                ByVal sender As System.Object, _
                ByVal e As System.EventArgs) _
                Handles MyBase.Load
          Dim cn As New SqlConnection( _
              "server=.;database=northwind;trusted_connection=true")
          Dim x As Long
          x = Db.ExecuteScaler( _
           cn, "Select count(*) from customers")
          Response.Write("Count of Customers=" & x.ToString())
          Dim SQL As String
          SQL = "Select " _
          & " CustomerID, CompanyName, ContactName, ContactTitle " _
          & " from customers " _
          & " where CompanyName like 'A%'"
          DataGrid1.DataSource = Db.ExecuteDataSet(cn, SQL)
          DataBind()
      End Sub
  End Class
```

The browser output is shown in Figure 15.1. The advantage of using the DataComponent is that the developer did not need to be concerned about the specifics of accessing the database, and this saved several lines of code in the Web project. This component, which is compiled into an assembly, is available for use in many applications.

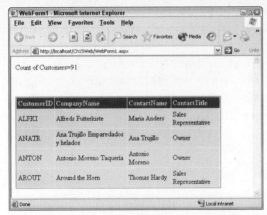

Figure 15.1   The DataComponent simplifies access to the data store.

Locating the Component at Run Time

Some questions that may come to mind are, How is the reference to the project or assembly stored in the Web application? Does the .dll file need to be in the same folder as it currently is in when the Web application is deployed? What Registry entries are required on the production Web server in order to get the Web application to locate the DataComponent?

The .NET common language runtime needs to locate and bind to the assembly at run time. The process or set of steps and logic involved in locating the assembly is called probing. Probing is discussed in more detail a little later in this chapter.

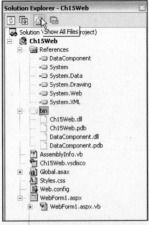

Figure 15.2   Setting a reference to an external assembly automatically creates a copy of the assembly to the bin folder of the Web application.

Currently, the common language runtime is located in the DataComponent by searching in the same directory as the Web application's assembly, which is the bin folder of the Web application. There's no mistake in that statement; when the reference was set to the DataComponent project, a copy of the assembly was made to the Web application's bin folder, as shown in Figure 15.2. The copy was only made if the DataComponent was built prior to setting the reference to the project. If the assembly doesn't exist, it is copied when the solution is built.

Assembly Versioning

When an assembly is built, its current version is stored in the manifest metadata of the assembly. The version can be set by using an assembly attribute called AssemblyVersion. By default, this attribute is located in the Assembly-Info.vb file of each project. The default value for this attribute is as follows:

```
<Assembly: AssemblyVersion("1.0.*")>
```

The assembly version is made up of four numbers, as shown in Figure 15.3. The first two numbers indicate the major and minor version of the assembly. A change to the major or minor version number usually indicates that the assembly contains new functionality, either by adding or changing properties, method, or events. By default, assemblies that have different major and minor version numbers are not considered to be compatible.

The third number of the version represents the revision of the assembly. The revision number is usually updated when applying service packs. No assumption of compatibility can be made between different revision numbers.

<Assembly: AssemblyVersion("1.0.*")>

- Assembly version is automatically updated
  Revision = days since 1/1/2000
  Build = seconds since midnight divided by 2
- To fix the version, manually type it:
  <Assembly: AssemblyVersion("3.0.24.1109")>

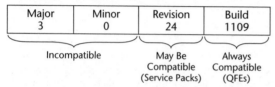

Major 3	Minor 0	Revision 24	Build 1109
Incompatible		May Be Compatible (Service Packs)	Always Compatible (QFEs)

Figure 15.3   The versioning of an assembly.

The fourth number of the version represents the build of the assembly. Assemblies that have the same major, minor, and revision numbers, but have a different build number are considered to be compatible. An assembly with a different build number is usually deployed to correct software bugs through Quick Fix Engineering (QFE) builds.

When using the asterisk to provide autonumbering of the assembly, the third number contains the number of days since January 1, 2000, and the fourth number contains the number of seconds since midnight, divided by two. Depending on the current daylight savings setting, this number may start at midnight or 1:00 A.M.

The System.Version class can be used to obtain the version of an assembly. The following code has been added to the DataComponent to allow retrieval of the version of the assembly:

```
'Add Imports System.Reflection to top of this code file.
Public Shared ReadOnly Property Version() As Version
    Get
        Dim a As [Assembly] = [Assembly].GetExecutingAssembly()
        Dim aName As AssemblyName = a.GetName()
        Return aName.Version
    End Get
End Property
```

This code requires the Imports System.Reflection directive at the top of the code file because the System.Reflection namespace contains the Assembly class and the AssemblyName class. The Assembly class is enclosed within brackets because Assembly is also a keyword. The Assembly class has several shared methods for obtaining a reference to an assembly. In this case, GetExecutingAssembly method returns a reference to the DataComponent assembly.

The Version class contains properties called Major, Minor, Revision, and Build. The ToString method provides the version as a string. Also, the operators =, <>, <, >, >=, <= are overloaded to allow comparison of version instances. Visual Basic .NET does not support operator overloading, but methods exist that Visual Basic .NET can use to perform comparisons as shown in Figure 15.4. These methods are static methods, and can be called as follows:

```
If Version.op_equality(myVersion,yourVersion) then
    Response.Write("The versions are equal")
End If
```

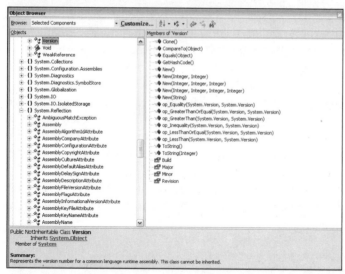

Figure 15.4   The Object Browser, displaying the Version class and its methods. Notice the Assembly and AssemblyName classes in the System.Reflection namespace.

The Web page has been updated to display this version of the assembly. This comes in handy in some of the later examples. The following line of code has been added to the Page_Load event method:

```
Response.Write(Db.Version.ToString() & "<br>")
```

Private Assemblies

Private assemblies are assemblies that are used solely by the Web application with which it has been deployed. Private assemblies are required to be located in the main folder as the Web application (bin), or a subdirectory of the Web application. In the example of the Web site that is using the DataComponent, setting the reference to the DataComponent copied the DataComponent assembly to the bin folder of the Web site.

Deployment of Web applications that use private assemblies is simply a matter of copying the files to the new location, and creating a Web share, as was done in Chapter 2, "Solutions, Projects, and the Visual Studio .NET IDE." The common language runtime probes for the DataComponent in the bin folder of the Web application.

By default, there is no runtime version control on private assemblies. This means that different versions of the assembly simply can be copied into the bin folder of the Web site. Assuming that the assemblies are compatible, the ASP.NET starts using the new assembly.

Private assemblies are considered to be the deployment model of choice by some people. Be careful, because although it is simple to deploy assemblies by simply copying the files to the destination, this could become unmanageable as an assembly is used with many applications. Shared Assemblies are covered in this chapter, which is a more manageable choice.

When working with private assemblies, the common language runtime looks for the assembly in the same folder as the Web application, which is the bin folder. The common language runtime starts by looking for the assembly by its friendly name plus the .dll extension. If the file is not found, the common language runtime attempts to locate the assembly by using its friendly name plus the .exe extension.

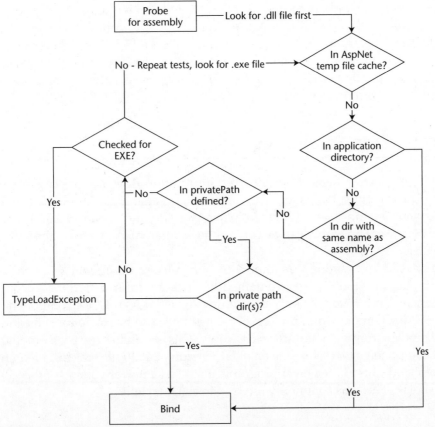

Figure 15.5 The probing sequence that the common language runtime uses when locating a private assembly that has no strong name.

If the assembly is not found in the bin folder, the common language runtime checks for the existence of a folder that has the same name as the assembly's friendly name. If the folder exists, the common language runtime attempts to locate the assembly in that folder.

It may be desirable to place all of the referenced assemblies in a common subdirectory. This can be done by placing a probing privatePath directive into the Web.config file as follows:

```
<configuration>
    <runtime>
        <assemblyBinding xmlns="urn:schemas-microsoft-com:asm.v1">
            <probing privatePath="bin\salesDll;bin\customerDll" />
        </assemblyBinding>
    </runtime>
</configuration>
```

This code sets a lookup path to the bin\salesDll and bin\customerDll folders. If the assembly is not found in the bin folder, the common language runtime looks in the privatePaths that are defined. Figure 15.5 shows the probing sequence that the common language runtime uses when attempting to locate a private assembly that has no strong name. Probing for assemblies is covered in more detail later in this chapter.

Side-by-Side Versioning

Copying over the assembly in one Web application does not affect private assemblies for other Web sites. This means that version 2.0.0.0 of the Data-Component assembly can be running in one Web site, and version 3.0.0.0 of the DataComponent assembly can be running in a different Web site on the same computer.

Side-by-side versioning was impossible when using traditional COM components, because the Registry contained the location information for a COM component, and there was only one setting for any given COM component. With the .NET Framework, no Registry entries need to be made for the common language runtime to locate an assembly. This eliminates the problem that COM components had, whereby an older version of a .dll file was installed on a system and caused the newer programs that used a newer version of the .dll file to break. This was commonly referred to as DLL Hell.

Strong-Named Assemblies

Being able to copy over an assembly that is being referenced may be a benefit, but can also be problem. The reason that this is allowable is because the assembly is private, and private assemblies do not need to have a strong name.

A strong name is a unique name that is assigned to an assembly, which would force the version to be the version that was compiled with the application, unless the version is explicitly overridden.

A strong name consists of the assembly's friendly name, which is the name of the assembly without the file extension (.dll), version number, culture information, plus a public key and a digital signature. Visual Studio .NET can assign strong names to an assembly when the assembly is compiled. Two assemblies with the same strong name are considered to be identical.

Strong names guarantee name uniqueness by using a public and private key pair. Only the entity that holds the private key can create an assembly with the same strong name. This means that the private and public keys provide a method of identifying the entity that created the assembly.

Strong names are used to maintain the version lineage of an assembly. A strong name ensures that nobody can produce a different version of an assembly if they don't have the private key. Users can be certain that a version of a strong-named assembly comes from the original publisher.

Strong names provide an integrity check that guarantees that the contents of the assembly have not been tampered with since the assembly was compiled.

Be careful, a strong name does not guarantee that a publisher is who it says it is. The strong name only states that the publisher is the same as in the previous versions. To be sure that the publisher is who it says it is, the assembly should contain a digital signature and digital certificate.

When you reference a strong-named assembly, versioning enforcement is provided as well as naming protection. Also, strong-named assemblies can reference only other strong-named assemblies.

Creating a Strong-Named Assembly

Creating a strong-named assembly requires a public and private key pair. The key pair can be generated by using the strong-name utility (sn.exe). The strong-name utility is a console application that can be run by starting the Visual Studio .NET command prompt and executing the following command:

```
Sn.exe -k c:\myKey.snk
```

This creates a key pair, stored in the myKey.snk file. This file contains both the private and public key, and should be stored and protected. This program should only be run once to create the key pair. Every strong-named assembly should use the same key pair. Keep in mind that the key pair is used to identify the publisher, and the key is required to maintain the version lineage on the assemblies.

After the key pair is obtained, there are two things that need to be done in the component project: assign a fixed version number and assign the key file to the assembly. The AssemblyInfo.vb file contains the AssemblyVersion attribute, which simply can be edited. By default, the AssemblyKeyFile attribute is not included in the AssemblyInfo.vb file, but this can be added. The following changes have been made to the DataComponent project's AssemblyInfo.vb file:

```
Imports System.Reflection
Imports System.Runtime.InteropServices
' General information about an assembly is controlled
' through the following set of attributes. Change these
' attribute values to modify the information
' associated with an assembly.
' Review the values of the assembly attributes.
<Assembly: AssemblyTitle("Data Component")>
<Assembly: AssemblyDescription("Provides easy access to SQL Server")>
<Assembly: AssemblyCompany("MyCompany")>
<Assembly: AssemblyProduct("DataComponent")>
<Assembly: AssemblyCopyright("Copyright (c) 2001-2010")>
<Assembly: AssemblyTrademark("Trademark Here")>
<Assembly: CLSCompliant(True)>
' The following GUID is for the ID of the typelib if this
' project is exposed to COM.
<Assembly: Guid("921E7039-7D26-40A2-9A51-FA105B6D717F")>
' Version information for an assembly consists of the
' following four values:
'       Major Version
'       Minor Version
'       Build Number
'       Revision
' You can specify all the values or you can default the
' Build and Revision Numbers
' by using the '*' as shown below:
<Assembly: AssemblyVersion("2.0.0.0")>
<Assembly: AssemblyKeyFile("c:\myKey.snk")>
```

The significant changes are the last two lines. These changes automatically create this assembly as a strong-named assembly. The strong name, or full name, of the compiled assembly is as follows:

```
DataComponent, Version=2.0.0.0, _
        Culture=neutral, PublicKeyToken=4fa8f612df7c8110
```

The strong name consists of the friendly name, the version, the culture (which should always be set to neutral for the main assembly file), and the public-key token. The public-key token represents an abbreviated version of the public key.

In Chapter 13, "Site Security," code access security was covered. One of the important considerations when using code access security is the strength of the evidence. Different permissions may be provided based on a public-key token. For example, Microsoft has granted itself full permissions, based on their public key. There may be situations in which it is important to grant a certain company's code more permissions than those that are normally granted. This can be easily done at the company level if the company only has a single public key. Figure 15.6 shows how a code group can be added for MyCompany, based on a public key. All code that is published by MyCompany has the permissions that are assigned to the code group.

When the DataComponent assembly is compiled, the assembly's manifest can be viewed with ILDASM.exe and contains the public key, as shown in Figure 15.7. Also notice that the version has been updated to reflect the fixed setting of version 2.0.0.0.

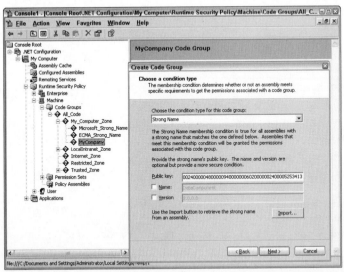

Figure 15.6   The code group is added for MyCompany based on the public-key evidence.

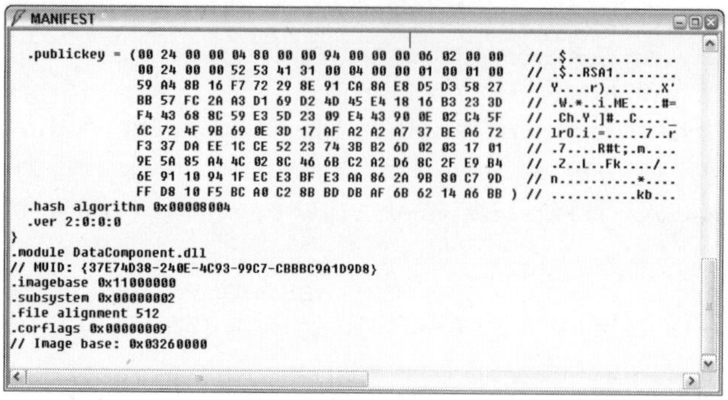

Figure 15.7 The public key is included in the manifest of a strong-named assembly.

Using Strong-Named Assemblies

When an assembly is referenced in an application, a record of the referenced assembly is included in the application assembly's manifest. If the assembly does not contain a string name, the manifest records the friendly name and version of the referenced assembly. The following is an example of the manifest data for the DataComponent when the DataComponent does not have a strong name.

```
.assembly extern DataComponent
{
    ver 1:0:1073:39385
}
```

Although the version is recorded, the version is not used to enforce versioning because this is not a strong-named assembly.

When a strong-named assembly is referenced in an application, the record of the assembly contains the friendly name, the public-key token, and the version. The presence of the public-key token indicates that this is a strong-named assembly, and the version number is enforced.

```
.assembly extern DataComponent
{
    .publickeytoken = (4F A8 F6 12 DF 7C 81 10 )    // O....|..
    .ver 2:0:0:0
}
```

The Web application has been compiled with version 2.0.0.0 of the Data-Component. If the DataComponent has been updated to version 2.0.0.1 and the new version is copied to the bin folder of the Web application (copying over private assembly version 2.0.0.0 of DataComponent), an error message is displayed in the browser, as shown in Figure 15.8.

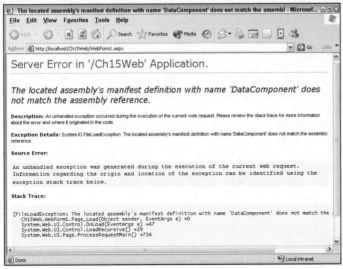

Figure 15.8 Copying a new version of a private strong-named assembly over the old version generates an error, because the Web application is enforcing versioning.

Fusion Log Viewer (FusLogVw.exe)

Although Figure 15.8 displays a message stating that the DataComponent assembly has a problem, it's not too clear as to the actual problem. To see more information, the .NET Framework SDK contains a tool called the Fusion Log Viewer (FusLogVw.exe). This tool can be used to get more detailed information about the error.

To use FusLogVw.exe with ASP.NET, the processModel account must be set to System. The processModel account setting is located in the machine.config file. After changing this setting, either reboot the machine, or execute iisreset from the command prompt.

The Fusion Log Viewer utility also can be tweaked to display all bindings instead of the failures. This can be a handy learning tool, and also can be used when an assembly is actually loading, but it's not the assembly that should have loaded. To view all assembly bindings, add the following key into the Registry:

```
HKEY_LOCAL_MACHINE\SOFTWARE\Microsoft\Fusion\ForceLog=dword:1
```

The Fusion Log Viewer displays an entry in its window indicating the application, the assembly, and the date. Double-click the application to display the following information when version 2.0.0.0 is overwritten with version 2.0.0.1 of the DataComponent:

```
*** Assembly Binder Log Entry  (12/9/2002 @ 11:59:38 PM) ***

The operation failed.
Bind result: hr = 0x80131040. No description available.

Assembly manager loaded from:
C:\WINDOWS\Microsoft.NET\Framework\v1.0.3705\fusion.dll
Running under executable
C:\WINDOWS\Microsoft.NET\Framework\v1.0.3705\aspnet_wp.exe
--- A detailed error log follows.

=== Pre-bind state information ===
LOG: DisplayName = DataComponent, Version=2.0.0.0, Culture=neutral,
 PublicKeyToken=4fa8f612df7c8110
 (Fully-specified)
LOG: Appbase = file:///D:/AspDotNetBook/Book/Building and Versioning
 .NET Components/Ch15Web
LOG: DEVPATH = C:\DevAssemblie
LOG: Initial PrivatePath = bin
LOG: Dynamic Base =
C:\WINDOWS\Microsoft.NET\Framework\v1.0.3705\Temporary ASP.NET
 Files\ch15web\0baf2047
LOG: Cache Base = C:\WINDOWS\Microsoft.NET\Framework\v1.0.3705\Temporary
 ASP.NET Files\ch15web\0baf2047
LOG: AppName = 5feb88b4
Calling assembly : Ch15Web, Version=1.0.1073.42703, Culture=neutral,
 PublicKeyToken=null.
===

LOG: Processing DEVPATH.
LOG: Unable to find assembly in DEVPATH location:
 C:\DevAssemblie\DataComponent.DLL.
LOG: Unable to find assembly in DEVPATH location:
 C:\DevAssemblie\DataComponent.EXE.
LOG: Unable to find assembly in DEVPATH.
LOG: Publisher policy file is not found.
LOG: No redirect found in host configuration file
(C:\WINDOWS\Microsoft.NET\Framework\v1.0.3705\aspnet.config).
LOG: Using machine configuration file from
 C:\WINDOWS\Microsoft.NET\Framework\v1.0.3705\config\machine.config.
LOG: Post-policy reference: DataComponent, Version=2.0.0.0,
Culture=neutral, PublicKeyToken=4fa8f612df7c8110
LOG: Cache Lookup was unsuccessful.
LOG: Attempting download of new URL
 file:///C:/WINDOWS/Microsoft.NET/Framework/v1.0.3705/Temporary ASP.NET
 Files/ch15web/0baf2047/5feb88b4/DataComponent.DLL.
LOG: Attempting download of new URL
 file:///C:/WINDOWS/Microsoft.NET/Framework/v1.0.3705/Temporary ASP.NET
 Files/ch15web/0baf2047/5feb88b4/DataComponent/DataComponent.DLL.
```

```
LOG: Attempting download of new URL
  file:///D:/AspDotNetBook/Book/Building and Versioning .NET
Components/Ch15Web/bin/DataComponent.DLL.
LOG: Assembly download was successful. Attempting setup of file:
  D:\AspDotNetBook\Book\Building and Versioning .NET
Components\Ch15Web\bin\DataComponent.DLL
LOG: Entering download cache setup phase.
WRN: Comparing the assembly name resulted in the mismatch:
Revision Number
ERR: The assembly reference did not match the assembly definition found.
ERR: Setup failed with hr = 0x80131040.
ERR: Failed to complete setup of assembly (hr = 0x80131040).

Probing terminated.
```

The pre-bind state information displays the assembly that the Web application requires. The last lines of this log entry shows that DataComponent.dll was found, but the Revision Number did not match.

The Fusion Log Viewer should be used to assist with any errors when an application is failing to locate a referenced assembly.

Shared Assemblies

Shared assemblies are assemblies that are located in a common repository, called the Global Assembly Cache (GAC). Shared assemblies can be used by any application on the computer. Installing assemblies into the Global Assembly Cache provides the ability to keep a single copy of each version of an assembly on the machine, in a common location. This simplifies assembly management and minimizes the quantity of assembly copies that are located on the machine.

By default, the Global Assembly Cache is located in the %SystemRoot%\ Assembly folder. For example, on most Windows 2000 computers, this is the C:\Winnt\Assembly folder, while on Windows XP computers this is the C:\Windows\Assembly folder.

Installing an assembly into the Global Assembly Cache requires the assembly to have a strong name. The assembly can be dragged and dropped into the Global Assembly Cache folder. Figure 15.9 shows the Global Assembly Cache after dragging and dropping version 2.0.0.0 and version 2.0.0.1 of the DataComponent into it.

The accompanying sidebar, *How Does the Assembly Folder Hold Multiple Copies of Files That Have the Same Filename?* explains how the Global Assembly Cache can maintain multiple copies of files that have the same name.

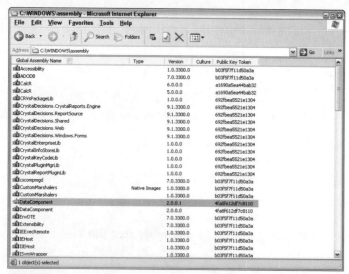

Figure 15.9 The Global Assembly Cache after dragging and dropping version 2.0.0.0 and version 2.0.0.1 of the DataComponent into it.

The .NET Framework also includes a program called the GacUtil.exe, which could be used to install and uninstall assemblies with a batch file. The GacUtil program can be run from the Visual Studio .NET Command Prompt, and this utility has options for adding, deleting, and list assemblies that are in the Global Assembly Cache.

When working with shared assemblies in a development environment, it may be more desirable to set a lookup path to the location of the component project's output, rather than continuously moving the component into the Global Assembly Cache. This can be done by assigning a lookup path to the DEVPATH system environment variable. For example, if the component project is in the c:\ myComponent folder, the DEVPATH could be set to C:\myComponent\Bin\ to indicate the location of the myComponent.dll assembly.

After the DEVPATH environment variable is set, the following entry needs to be added to the machine.config file:

```
<configuration>
    <runtime>
        <developmentMode developerInstallation="true">
    </runtime>
</configuration>
```

tip **Note that this setting must be in the machine.config file. This setting does not work in the Web.config. Also, be sure to add the backslash to the end of the path.**

♦ How Does the Assembly Folder Hold Multiple Copies of Files That Have the Same Filename?

When a file such as DataComponent.dll exists in a folder and a new version of this file is copied into the folder, the new copy overwrites the old copy. So how can this folder behave differently?

Although the Global Assembly Cache appears as a single folder, it is really a folder structure. A COM component called shfusion.dll is responsible for presenting the pretty output that is shown in Figure 15.9. To reveal the folder structure that is hidden by shfusion.dll, simply unregister the shfusion.dll component. This can be done by starting the Visual Studio .NET Command Prompt, which is located in the Visual Studio .NET Tools menu. At the prompt, the following information can be typed:

```
Regsvr32 -u shfusion.dll
```

After the shfusion.dll file is unregistered, opening the Assembly folder reveals two temporary folders and a folder called GAC and another folder called NativeImage1_version.

The NativeImages folder contains .NET components that have been precompiled using the ngen.exe utility. If a .NET assembly has been precompiled with ngen.exe, it is not JIT compiled when it is run.

The GAC folder contains the .NET components that are shared on the machine. Components that are in the GAC folder must have strong names. Navigating further into the folder structure of the GAC, there is actually a folder for each assembly name. Inside the Data-Component folder, there is a folder called 2.0.0.0__4fa8f612df7c8110 and another folder called 2.0.0.1__4fa8f612df7c8110 (see Figure 15.10). These folders contain the actual versions of the DataComponent that were dragged and dropped into the assembly folder.

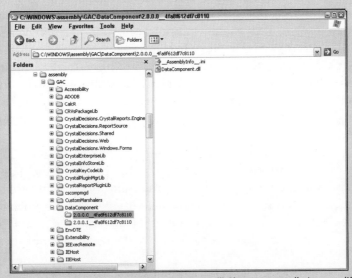

Figure 15.10 The two DataComponent.dll files are actually in two different folders.

continued

> ### ◆ How Does the Assembly Folder Hold Multiple Copies of Files That Have the Same Filename?
> *(continued)*
>
> In reality, the shfusion.dll file displays a flattened version of this folder hierarchy, which is how files with the same filename can be dropped into the GAC without the files overwriting each other.
>
> After viewing the folder structure, the shfusion.dll must be registered as follows:
>
> ```
> regsvr32  shfusion.dll
> ```
>
> Use this command to reregister the shfusion.dll component any time that the folder layout is visible in the assembly folder.

The DEVPATH environment variable only works with strong-named assemblies. This setting is ignored for assemblies without strong names.

Assembly-Binding Policies

Although strong-named assemblies provide enforcement of versioning between the Web application and the referenced assembly, there are many cases where it is desirable to copy a new version of an assembly to the Web server, without being forced to recompile the Web application.

Performing a version redirect is a function of assembly policies. The four primary types of assembly polices are application, publisher, ASPNET, and administrator.

Changes that are made to the application policy are unique to the Web application. Changes that are made to the publisher policy are global to the machine. Changes that are made to ASPNET policy apply to all Web sites on the machine. Changes to the administrator policy override all other policies and are global to the machine.

Each policy is applied in a specific order as shown in Figure 15.11. The Application policy is stored in the Web.config file. This policy is evaluated first. If the application required version 2.0.0.0 of the DataComponent assembly, the application binding could be redirected to a different version, such as version 2.0.0.1 of the assembly. The application policy also has the ability to skip over evaluation of the publisher policy by using the optional publisherPolicy attribute.

The following XML code performs a redirect from version 2.0.0.0 to version 2.0.0.1 and directs the runtime to skip the publisher policy:

```
<configuration>
    <runtime>
        <assemblyBinding xmlns="urn:schemas-microsoft-com:asm.v1">
            <dependentAssembly>
                <assemblyIdentity name="DataComponent"
                    publicKeyToken="4FA8F612DF7C8110" culture=""/>
                <bindingRedirect oldVersion="2.0.0.0"
                    newVersion="2.0.0.1"/>
                <publisherPolicy apply="no" />
            </dependentAssembly>
        </assemblyBinding>
    </runtime>
</configuration>
```

The oldVersion also supports ranges. For example, the oldVersion could have been specified as "1.0.0.0-2.0.0.0". Each number of the version can be between 0 and 65535, so "1.0.0.0-1.65535.65535.65535" is a valid method of specifying any major version 1 of the component.

The assembly-binding redirect does not have to go from a lower to higher version number. It is possible to redirect from any version to any version.

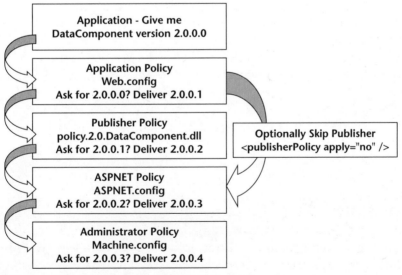

Figure 15.11   The assembly-binding policy order.

Notice that the strong name is composed of the friendly name of the assembly, the public-key token, the culture, and the version. What happens if two vendors supply an assembly with the same name, a different version, and the same culture? If the public-key token is different, the two assemblies, even though they have the same filename, have different version lineages. One does not interfere with the other.

What happens if a company loses their key pair and simply creates a new key pair for the next release of their program? When this program is installed, the program appears to have been written by a different company. There is no way to create a binding policy to redirect from one version with key A to a different version with key B because this is like trying to perform a redirect from company A to company B. This means that every effort should be taken to protect the key pair from being lost or stolen.

Microsoft .NET Framework Configuration Tool

The Microsoft .NET Framework Configuration Tool is an administration tool that can be used to configure the application (Web.config) and administrator (machine.config) policies. This tool can be executed from the Administrative Tools menu.

The application policy for a Web application can be edited by right-clicking Applications, clicking Add, and then navigating to the Web.config file, as shown in Figure 15.12.

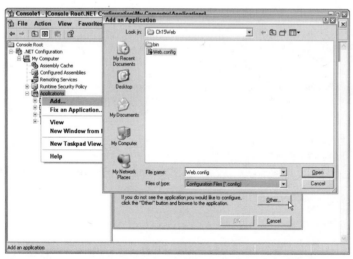

Figure 15.12   Add the Web.config file to the list of applications.

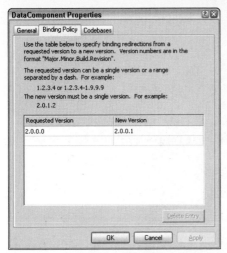

Figure 15.13   The Binding Policy tab is used to redirect the binding to a different version.

After the Web application is added, a configured assembly can be added to set the binding policy for the assembly. The assembly can be selected from the Global Assembly Cache, and the settings can be entered as shown in Figure 15.13. The General tab also allows the Publisher Policy to be overridden, while the Codebases tab allows the entry of a download location. The changes are saved to the Web.config file.

The Microsoft .NET Framework Configuration Tool also allows global changes on the machine by configuring an assembly at the computer level. The changes that are made at this level are saved to the machine.config file.

Publisher Policies

Creating publisher policies requires more work than the other policies. The vendor or publisher can specify that a new version of an assembly should be used. Publisher policies are compiled to .dll files and placed into the Global Assembly Cache. By default, the publisher policy overrides the application policy but this can be also overridden.

Creating a publisher policy requires an XML file with the binding redirect information. An example of the XML file is as follows:

```
<configuration>
    <runtime>
        <assemblyBinding xmlns="urn:schemas-microsoft-com:asm.v1">
            <dependentAssembly>
                <assemblyIdentity name="DataComponent"
                    publicKeyToken="4FA8F612DF7C8110" culture=""/>
                <bindingRedirect oldVersion="2.0.0.1"
                    newVersion="2.0.0.2"/>
```

```
                </dependentAssembly>
            </assemblyBinding>
        </runtime>
    </configuration>
```

This file can be saved with any name, but for this example, the file is saved as PubDataComponent.config.

Next, the Assembly Linker (AL.exe) must be used to package this file into a .dll file. The command to package the PubDataComponent is as follows:

```
AL.exe /link:PubDataConponent.config
       /out:policy.2.0.DataComponent.dll
       /keyfile:c:\myKey.snk
       /version:1.0.0.0
```

In this example, the *link* switch is the name of the binding policy file source XML file. The *out* switch is the name of the output file, which has a special syntax. The filename must start with the word policy, followed by the major and minor version of the source assembly that is redirected. The *keyfile* switch is the name of the key file that should be used for all assemblies, including this one. The *version* is the version of this assembly.

> **tip** **The version switch is the version of the publisher policy. If multiple versions of the publisher file exist, the highest version number is automatically used.**

After the policy.2.0.DataComponent.dll file is created, it must be installed into the Global Assembly Cache. This can be done by dragging and dropping the file into the Global Assembly Cache, or by using the gacutil.exe tool.

Probing for Assemblies

When an assembly needs to be located, there is a series of checks to locate the assembly. The process of locating an assembly is called probing.

The first thing that the class loader checks is that the DEVPATH environment variable exists, and that the assembly exists at the location that is pointed to in the DEVPATH, as shown in Figure 15.14.

Next, the assembly is checked to see if it has a strong name. If the assembly does not have a strong name, the class loader searches for a .dll file that has the same name as the assembly's friendly name plus the .dll extension. First, the ASP.NET's temporary file cache is checked. Next, the application's bin folder is searched for the .dll file.

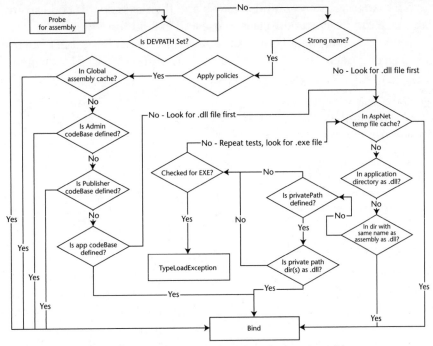

Figure 15.14 The runtime probes many locations for an assembly.

Probing continues to check for the .dll in the bin\myComponent folder. If it is not found, probing checks the Web.config to see if a privatePath has been configured. If so, each of the paths that are configured in the privatePath variable is searched.

If the .dll file has not been found, probing starts over, but this time the search is for an .exe file. If the .exe file is not found, a TypeLoadException occurs.

If the assembly has a strong name, the assembly policies are applied. After the policies are applied, the class loader looks for the assembly in the Global Assembly Cache.

If the assembly is not is the Global Assembly Cache, the class loader checks to see if a publisher codebase or application codebase exists. If neither exists, probing continues in the application directory, and follows the same path as it would for an assembly without a strong name.

Cross-Language Inheritance

A new benefit of .NET components is that they support cross-language inheritance. For example, a component that has been written in C# can be used as a base class for a new Visual Basic .NET component. This allows a developer to use any .NET language to accomplish a task and then expose this code so any .NET language can derive a new class to use and extend the code.

The following C# component is an example of how Visual Basic .NET can use and extend a component that has been written in a different .NET language:

```csharp
using System;
using System.Web;
using System.Web.Mail;
namespace csMessaging
{
    public class csEmail
    {
        private string server;
        public string Server
        {
            get
            {
                return SmtpMail.SmtpServer;
            }
            set
            {
                server = value;
            }
        }
        public virtual void Send(
            string from,
            string to,
            string subject,
            string messageText)
        {
            SmtpMail.SmtpServer=server;
            SmtpMail.Send(from,to,subject,messageText);
        }
    }
}
```

This component has a single method called Send, which is called with its calling parameters, and a property called Sever. This component is compiled to an assembly called csMessaging.dll, which can be used by any .NET language.

A new Visual Basic .NET Class Library project called vbMessaging has been created. Although the C# component could be instantiated and used in the Visual Basic .NET application, there is a requirement to add functionality, where the From, To, Subject, and Message could be entered as properties, and the Send method could be executed. This functionality also required the ability to be able to execute the Send method again, but with a different message, and the message would use the stored properties to get the From, To, and Subject.

In the vbMessaging project, a reference is set to the csMessaging project. A new class, called vbEmail, is added into the vbMessaging component, and it inherits from csEmail.

```vb
Public Class vbEmail
    Inherits csMessaging.csEmail
    Private _sendFrom As String
    Private _subject As String
    Private _message As String
    Private _sendTo As String
    Public Property SendFrom() As String
        Get
            Return _sendFrom
        End Get
        Set(ByVal Value As String)
            _sendFrom = Value
        End Set
    End Property
    Public Property SendTo() As String
        Get
            Return _sendTo
        End Get
        Set(ByVal Value As String)
            _sendTo = Value
        End Set
    End Property
    Public Property Subject() As String
        Get
            Return _subject
        End Get
        Set(ByVal Value As String)
            _subject = Value
        End Set
    End Property
    Public Property Message() As String
        Get
            Return _message
        End Get
        Set(ByVal Value As String)
            _message = Value
        End Set
    End Property
    Public Overloads Sub Send()
        Send(_sendFrom, _sendTo, _subject, _message)
    End Sub
    Public Overloads Sub Send(ByVal message As String)
        _message = message
        Send(_sendFrom, _sendTo, _subject, _message)
    End Sub
    Public Overloads Sub Send( _
            ByVal subject As String, _
            ByVal message As String)
        _subject = subject
        _message = message
        Send(_sendFrom, _sendTo, _subject, _message)
```

```
    End Sub
    Public Overloads Sub Send( _
            ByVal sendTo As String, _
            ByVal subject As String, _
            ByVal message As String)
        _sendTo = sendTo
        _subject = subject
        _message = message
        Send(_sendFrom, _sendTo, _subject, _message)
    End Sub
    Public Overloads Overrides Sub Send( _
            ByVal sendTo As String, _
            ByVal sendFrom As String, _
            ByVal subject As String, _
            ByVal message As String)
        _sendTo = sendTo
        _sendFrom = sendFrom
        _subject = subject
        _message = message
        MyBase.Send(_sendFrom, _sendTo, _subject, _message)
    End Sub
    Public Sub SendMessageTo(ByVal sendTo As String)
        _sendTo = sendTo
        Send(_sendFrom, _sendTo, _subject, _message)
    End Sub
End Class
```

The SendMessageTo method also was added to allow the same message to be sent to a different recipient.

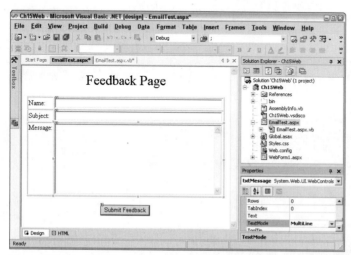

Figure 15.17 The Feedback page that uses the vbMessaging component to send email to the Webmaster.

Both projects were given a version number of 1.0.0.0 and a strong name, and installed into the Global Assembly Cache. It's important to note that any assembly that has a strong name must reference assemblies that have a strong name.

The accompanying sidebar, *Getting Assemblies to Show in the .NET Tab*, explains how to add entries to the Registry, which exposes the assemblies on the .NET tab when adding assembly references to a project.

A new Web project is created that displays a feedback form to the user. When the user submits the feedback form, the message is sent to two recipients. The feedback page contains TextBoxes for the Name, Subject, and Message, as shown in Figure 15.17.

♦ Getting Assemblies to Show in the .NET Tab

Although it's easy to browse for the .dll file when adding a reference to an assembly, assemblies that are frequently used could be placed in the .NET tab of Visual Studio .NET's Add Reference dialog box. This is done by adding a Registry entry, which tells Visual Studio .NET to display the assemblies that are in a given folder.

To make the vbMessaging and the csMessaging components visible in the .NET tab, the following Registry entries are added:

```
Windows Registry Editor Version 5.00
[HKEY_LOCAL_MACHINE\SOFTWARE\Microsoft\.NETFramework\
AssemblyFolders\csMessaging]
@="D:\\AspDotNetBook\\Book\\
Building and Versioning .NET Components\\csMessaging\\bin\\Debug"
[HKEY_LOCAL_MACHINE\SOFTWARE\Microsoft\.NETFramework\
AssemblyFolders\vbMessaging]
@="D:\\AspDotNetBook\\Book\\
Building and Versioning .NET Components\\vbMessaging\\bin"
```

If these lines are typed into Notepad and saved with a .reg extension, the .reg file can be executed to add the proper keys. Figure 15.15 shows the added Registry keys.

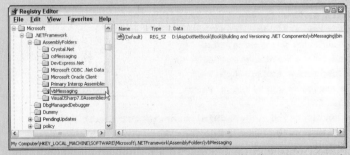

Figure 15.15 The Registry keys to add to display the components in the .NET tab of the Add Reference dialog box.

continued

◆ **Getting Assemblies to Show in the .NET Tab** *(continued)*

Adding these Registry keys is not required to use the components. In the Add Reference dialog box, the developer could simply browse to the components. This procedure is used only if it is desirable to display the components in the .NET tab, as shown in Figure 15.16.

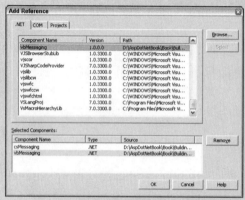

Figure 15.16 The Add Reference dialog box contains the new components.

Visual Studio .NET must be restarted in order to see the components.

The code in the button's click event method simply creates an instance of the vbEmail, and send the feedback to the Webmaster. After that, the message is also sent to the Web administrator. The code is as follows:

```
Private Sub Button1_Click( _
      ByVal sender As System.Object, _
      ByVal e As System.EventArgs) Handles Button1.Click
         Dim email As New vbMessaging.vbEmail()
         email.Server = "localhost"
         email.SendFrom = txtName.Text
         email.SendTo = "WebMaster@GJTT.com"
         email.Subject = txtSubject.Text
         email.Message = txtMessage.Text
         email.Send()
         email.SendMessageTo("WebAdministrator@GJTT.com")
         Response.Write("Message Sent <br>")
End Sub
```

To use this code, SMTP mail must be installed. Also, this may generate a message stating the following:

```
The server rejected one or more recipient addresses.
The server response was: 550 5.7.1 Unable to relay for ...
```

This can be corrected by editing the relay properties of the SMTP server, which is accessible from the Internet Information Server tool. The relay property should be set to allow address 127.0.0.1 (localhost) to relay. Do not grant this access to everyone, because many hackers exploit this.

Lab 15.1: Creating a Visual Basic .NET Data Component

In this lab, you create a Visual Basic .NET component that can be reused in many applications. This component is installed into the Global Assembly Cache, and configured to be available from the .NET tab of the Add Reference dialog box.

Adding the DataComponent Project

In this section, you add a new Visual Basic .NET Class Library project to the existing solution. This project compiles to a .dll file.

1. To start this lab, open the OrderEntrySystemSolution from Lab 14.1. Right-click the OrderEntrySystemSolution in the Solution Explorer, and click Check Out.

2. Right-click on the OrderEntrySystemSolution, and click Add, New Project. For the project name, type DataComponent. Be sure to verify that the project is located under the OrderEntrySystemSolution folder.

3. Rename Class1.vb to Db.vb, and open the class file. Rename Class1 to Db.

4. Add the Imports System.Data.SqlClient statement to the top of the code.

5. In the Db class, add a method called ExecuteDataSet. This method requires parameters for the connection, command type, and command text, and an array of command parameters. The return type is a DataSet.

6. In the body of the ExecuteDataSet function, add code to create a new SqlCommand. Assign the connection, command type, and the command text to the command.

7. Execute a call to a method that hasn't been defined yet, called AddParameters. This method requires the command and the parameter array as arguments.

8. In the ExecuteDataSet method, create a new DataSet and Sql-DataAdapter. Fill the dataset and return the dataset. The completed code should look like the following:

```
Public Shared Function ExecuteDataSet( _
        ByVal cn As SqlConnection, _
        ByVal cmdType As CommandType, _
        ByVal cmdText As String, _
        ByVal ParamArray prm() As SqlParameter) As DataSet
    Dim cmd As New SqlCommand(cmdText, cn)
    cmd.CommandType = cmdType
    AddParameters(cmd, prm)
    Dim ds As New DataSet()
    Dim da As New SqlDataAdapter(cmd)
    da.Fill(ds)
    Return ds
End Function
```

9. Add a new method called AddParameter, that requires parameters for the command and array of parameters. This method does not return a value.

10. In the AddParameter method, add code to test the parameter array to see if it is Nothing, and return if so. Add a loop that adds each parameter in the array to the command object's collection of parameters. The code should look like the following:

```
Private Shared Sub AddParameters( _
            ByVal cmd As SqlCommand, _
            ByVal prm() As SqlParameter)
    If prm Is Nothing Then
        Return
    End If
    Dim p As SqlParameter
    For Each p In prm
        cmd.Parameters.Add(p)
    Next
End Sub
```

11. Add overload to the ExecuteDataSet method that requires only a connection and the command text. Rather than rewrite the code, this method should call the method that has already been written. The code should like the following:

```
Public Shared Function ExecuteDataSet( _
            ByVal cn As SqlConnection, _
            ByVal cmdText As String) As DataSet
    Return ExecuteDataSet( _
        cn, CommandType.Text, cmdText, Nothing)
End Function
```

12. Build the project and save your work.

Testing the DataComponent

Before adding DataComponent to the Global Assembly Cache, the assembly is tested by rewriting the ProductList.aspx page. After the Data-Component is working, you add it to the Global Assembly Cache, and add the Registry entry to expose the DataComponent in the .NET tab of the add references.

1. Right-click the Inventory project in the Solution Explorer, and click Set As Startup Project.

2. Right-click the ProductList.aspx page, and click Set As Start Page.

3. Right-click the References node in the Inventory project, and click Add Reference. Add a reference to the DataComponent project.

4. Open the ProductList.aspx.vb code-behind page. Add the Imports System.Data.SqlData directive to the top of the page.

5. Notice that the BindProducts method has an if statement that checks to see whether the session variable called Products exists. If the session variable does not exist, an ArrayList is populated and assigned to the session variable.

6. Comment the code that is inside the if statement.

7. Inside the if statement, add code to create a DataSet called Products, and assign it to the session variable called Products. The data is retrieved from the Products table of the Northwind database. Be sure to use the new DataComponent. Your BindProducts method should look like the following:

```vb
Public Sub BindProducts()
    If Session("Products") Is Nothing Then
        'Dim Products As New ArrayList()
        'Products.Add(New Beverage(1, "Milk"))
        'Products.Add(New Beverage(2, "Juice"))
        'Products.Add(New Beverage(3, "Cola"))
        'Products.Add(New Confection(4, "Ice Cream"))
        'Products.Add(New Confection(5, "Cake"))
        'Products.Add(New Confection(6, "Candy"))

        'Dim b As BaseProduct
        'For Each b In Products
        '    b.UnitPrice = 100
        '    b.UnitsInStock = Rnd() * 10
        'Next

        Dim cn As New SqlConnection( _
            "server=.;database=northwind;" _
            & "trusted_connection=true")
        Dim sql As String
```

```
Dim Products As DataSet

sql =  _ "Select ProductName, UnitsInStock, UnitPrice " _
          & " from Products"

Products = DataComponent.Db.ExecuteDataSet(cn, sql)
Session("Products") = Products
End If
ProductGrid.DataSource = Session("Products")
DataBind()
End Sub
```

8. Run the Web application. The ProductList page should be displayed shown in Figure 15.18.

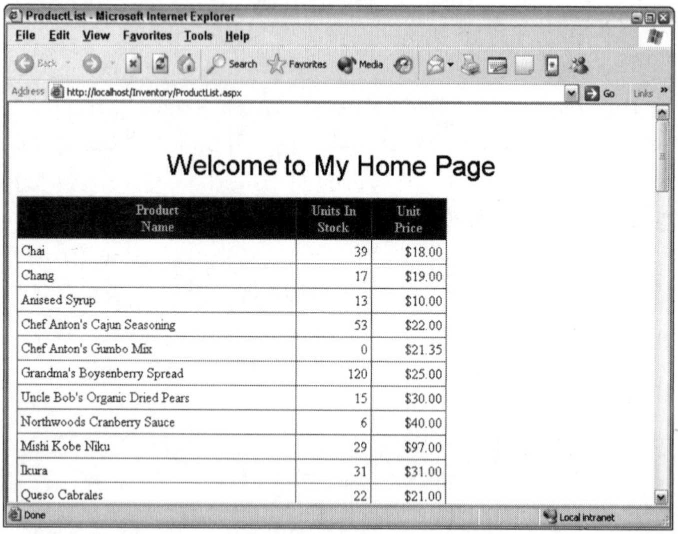

Figure 15.18 The revised ProductList.aspx page.

Adding the DataComponent to the Global Assembly Cache

In this section, you assign a strong name to the DataComponent and assign 1.0.0.0 to the version. After that, you install the assembly into the Global Assembly Cache.

1. Open the Visual Studio .NET Command Prompt.

2. Create a key pair file for use when strong-naming assemblies. The command should be as follows:

```
sn -k c:\Development\StrongName.snk
```

3. The key is checked into Visual SourceSafe, but since this key is used for all projects, it should be stored at the C:\Development folder, and then should be manually placed into Visual SourceSafe.

4. Open Visual SourceSafe. Click the Development folder. Click File, Add Files. This displays the Add File dialog box. Click the Strong-Name.snk file, and click Add (see Figure 15.19).

Figure 15.19   Add the StongName.snk file to the Visual SourceSafe.

 Adding the StrongName.snk to Visual SourceSafe may not be a good idea in an untrustworthy environment. It is possible to extract the public key to a file and check the public key into Visual SourceSafe while locking the private and public key pair file in a safe place. For more information on this topic, see Delay Signing an Assembly in the Visual Studio .NET Help.

5. Close Visual SourceSafe. Close the Visual Studio .NET Command Prompt.

6. Open the AssemblyInfo.vb file that is in the DataComponent project.

7. Change the AssemblyVersion to 1.0.0.0.

8. Add another line of code to assign the strong name to the assembly. The code should look like the following:

```
<Assembly: AssemblyVersion("1.0.0.0")>
<Assembly: AssemblyKeyFile("C:\Development\StrongName.snk")>
```

9. Save your changes and build the project.

10. Open Windows Explorer. Navigate to the folder that contains the DataComponent.dll file. It looks like the following:

```
C:\DEVELOPMENT\ORDERENTRYSYSTEM\OrderEntrySystemSolution\DataComp
onent\bin
```

11. Open another copy of Windows Explorer. Navigate to the assembly folder. On Windows 2000, this is C:\Winnt\Assembly, and on Windows XP or .NET, this is C:\Windows\Assembly.

12. Drag the DataComponent.dll file, and drop it into the assembly folder. The DataComponent should be displayed along with its version and public-key token.

Adding the Assembly to the .NET Tab of the Add Reference Dialog

In this section, you add a key to the Registry, which displays the Data-Component.dll in the .NET tab of the Add Reference dialog box.

1. Open the Registry editor program by clicking Start, Run, type Regedit.exe, and click Ok.

2. Open the following key:

```
HKEY_LOCAL_MACHINE\
      SOFTWARE\
            Microsoft\
                  .NETFramework\
                        AssemblyFolders\
```

3. Notice that there are already some keys at this location.

4. Right-click on AssemblyFolders and click New, Key. The new key name is insignificatant, so name the key DataComponent.

5. In the detail window, double-click the (Default) value. In the dialog box, set the value to the following:

```
C:\DEVELOPMENT
      \ORDERENTRYSYSTEM
            \OrderEntrySystemSolution
                  \DataComponent
                        \bin
```

6. Close the Registry Editor. Close Visual Studio .NET.

7. Reopen Visual Studio .NET. In the Inventory project, delete the existing reference to the DataComponent project.

8. Add a reference to the DataComponent. It should be available on the .NET tab, as shown in Figure 15.20.

9. Build the project and test.

10. Save your changes and check the final solution back into Visual SourceSafe.

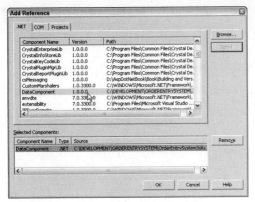

Figure 15.20   Setting a reference to the DataComponent. Notice that it is available in the .NET tab.

Summary

- To build a reusable component, a Visual Studio .NET Class Library project must be created.

- Using the component requires telling Visual Studio .NET that the external assembly is to be used with a project.

- The process of locating the assembly is called probing. Probing is the set of steps and logic involved in locating the assembly.

- A strong name is a unique name that is assigned to an assembly, which dictates that the version is the version that was compiled with the application, unless the version is explicitly overridden.

- A strong name consists of the assembly's friendly name, which is the name of the assembly without the file extension (.dll), version number, and culture information, plus a public key and a digital signature.

- Performing a version redirect is a function of assembly policies. The four primary types of assembly polices are application, publisher, ASP-NET, and administrator policies.

- A new benefit of .NET components is that they support cross-language inheritance.

Review Questions

1. What are the four binding policy types that are available in ASP.NET?

2. Assemblies that do not have a strong name are still version checked. True or false?

3. What tool can be used to see the attempted assembly bindings when the runtime cannot find an assembly?

4. What can be done to allow an assembly to be downloaded from the Internet on demand?

Answers to Review Questions

1. Application, publisher, ASPNET, and administrator policies.
2. False.
3. The Fusion Log Viewer (FusLogVw.exe).
4. Set the codeBase property to the URL of the assembly.

Creating Web Services

Visual Studio .NET components were covered in the last chapter, as were the benefits of building and using reusable components. Reusable components really shine when you use Web services. Web services are components that are accessible across a network. This opens a new world of reusability and can be used to distribute application logic across many machines, thus delivering better performance on large systems.

A Web service (also known as an XML Web service) is a programmable entity that provides a particular element of functionality, such as application logic, and is accessible to any number of potentially disparate systems using Internet standards such as XML and HTTP. Web services require XML and other Internet standards to create an infrastructure that supports interoperability among many applications.

Existing technologies, such as CORBA (Common Object Request Broker Architecture) and DCOM (Distributed Component Object Model) were attempts to reuse components across the network, but these technologies have problems, such as the inability to penetrate firewalls and the lack of cross-platform support. Because communication between companies is easier than ever using open industry standard protocols such as HTTP and SOAP, if it's not necessary for a technique to be platform independent and there is no need to penetrate a firewall, remoting (the replacement for DCOM) can be used.

Remoting provides better runtime performance, but does not offer cross-platform, open standards implementation.

Web services are loosely coupled. When a client makes a call to the Web service, the Web service processes the call, returns a result, and closes the connection. Web services may even extend their interface by adding new methods and properties. This won't affect existing clients as long as the existing methods and properties have not been changed.

One of the best features of Visual Studio .NET is its ability to work with Web services in a seamless way. This chapter explores Web services from the Visual Studio .NET perspective, by looking at some of the Web service basics and then consuming an existing Web service. The balance of the chapter focuses on creating a Web service.

Classroom Q & A

Q: My office uses a firewall that requires a name and password to surf the Web. Is there a way for my internal programs to use Web services through this type of firewall?

A: Yes. The Web service has a Proxy property that can be set to an instance of the Webproxy class. The WebProxy class has a property called Credentials that can have an instance of NetworkCredential assigned to it. Keep in mind that this allows the Web service to authenticate with the proxy, but you may still need to use the traditional methods of authentication at the destination Web server.

Q: Is there a way to charge for Web service use?

A: Sure. All the logging and tracing methods that have been covered to date can be used.

Q: Some of the Web services that I hit take a long time to execute. I know that they need to perform a substantial amount of work, but I am currently executing calls to three different long-running Web services. Is there a way to execute all three calls at the same time?

A: Absolutely. Web service methods can be executed asynchronously. The key to executing Web service methods is not the call to the method, but deciding when and how to end the method. This chapter covers asynchronous Web service access in detail.

The Role of Web Services

A Web server is to a user as a Web service is to a Web application. A user browses to a Web server, looking for information. The Web server content provides an interactive experience to the user, but ultimately provides data to the user. The Web service provides data to the Web application, but the Web application is interested in specific data, so there is no need to provide an interactive experience to the Web application. Although a Web browser could communicate to a Web service, usually the application communicates to the Web service.

This section examines some ways that Web services are implemented with today's applications.

Business Scenarios

It is important to understand the benefits that a Web service can provide. In its simplest form, a Web service can provide a single function to a client, such as the calculation of sales tax in an e-commerce application. Because dealing with issues such as changes to tax codes can be time-consuming and costly to a company, such tasks may be best left to a company that focuses on these issues and is responsive to changes. Ideally, companies that wish to get sales tax calculations could send an XML message across the Internet to a tax calculation Web service, and the Web service could respond with an XML message that contains the amount of sales tax to charge.

Web services can be used in a departmental fashion in the corporate intranet. Different departments may expose data via a Web service, and complete applications may be built by simply gluing the Web service pieces together.

A Web service can also act as a node in a workflow application. Products such as Microsoft BizTalk Server provide much of the glue that enables long-running transactions across many computers, and Web services can provide a seamless connection to BizTalk Server.

Show Me the Money

One way to ensure the success of Web services is to make sure that they can be used to make money. If a company can find a way to make money with a technology, then the technology can succeed.

Money can be made with Web services by charging subscriber fees or pay per use fees. It's easy to log the usage by customer and charge a periodic fee based on the usage of the Web service.

Web Service Basics

Web services provide a method for one application to communicate with another application, leveraging existing technologies and protocols. On the Windows platform, Internet Information Server (IIS) can be used to host a Web service, and the authentication, encryption (SSL), and load-balancing technologies that are built into Internet Information Server can be used with Web services.

A typical Web application might use Web services to acquire data from another source that can be consumed by the Web application, as shown in Figure 16.1. Note that Web services are not just for Web applications. Windows and Console applications can also consume Web services.

Several steps are involved in creating and consuming a Web service. The following steps help identify the big picture and are covered in detail in this chapter (see Figure 16.2).

1. Build the Web service by creating a Visual Studio .NET Web service project.

2. Advertise the Web service in a UDDI (Universal Description Discovery Integration) directory.

3. Locate a Web service by querying the UDDI directory.

4. Get the Web service description in the form of a Web service Description Language (WSDL, pronounced as *wiz-dill*) document.

5. Build a proxy at the client by using the WSDL document data.

6. Call the Web service using the SOAP protocol over HTTP.

7. Process the returned data from the Web service using SOAP over HTTP.

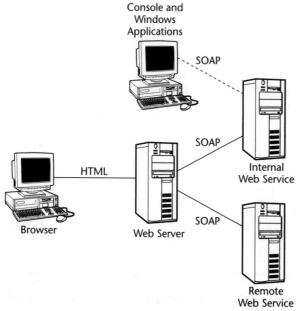

Figure 16.1 Web applications may call internal and external Web services. Windows and Console applications may also call Web services.

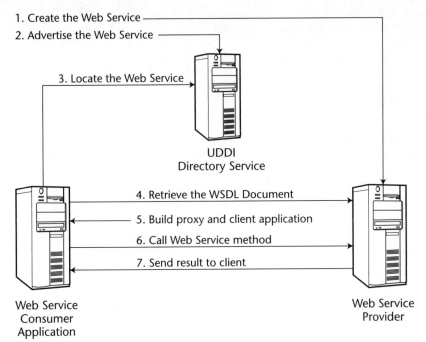

1. Create the Web Service
2. Advertise the Web Service

3. Locate the Web Service

UDDI
Directory Service

4. Retrieve the WSDL Document
5. Build proxy and client application
6. Call Web Service method
7. Send result to client

Web Service
Consumer
Application

Web Service
Provider

Figure 16.2 The primary steps involved in creating and consuming a Web service.

Simple Object Access Protocol (SOAP)

Simple Object Access Protocol (SOAP) is the protocol used to transfer data to and from the Web service. SOAP is XML based, and at the time of its inception, SOAP leveraged the XML specifications. SOAP is itself a W3C specification.

The SOAP protocol consists of three parts. First is the envelope, which defines what is in a message and how to process it. Second is a set of encoding rules for expressing instances of data types that are defined in an application. Third is the remote procedure call (RPC) representation and its RPC responses.

Although SOAP can be used in combination with a variety of other protocols, only HTTP is used in relation to SOAP and Web services.

SOAP Message

The following code shows an example of a SOAP message that is posted to a Web service to retrieve the latest trade price of a stock:

```
<soap:Envelope
       xmlns:soap="http://schemas.xmlsoap.org/soap/envelope/"
       soap:encodingStyle="http://schemas.xmlsoap.org/soap/encoding/"
    xmlns:m="Some-URI">
```

```
    <soap:Body>
        <m:GetLastTradePrice>
        <symbol>MSFT</symbol>
        </m:GetLastTradePrice>
    </soap:Body>
</soap:Envelope>
```

The SOAP envelope is the top-level element and includes attributes for the SOAP envelope namespace and the encoding style. Inside the envelope is the SOAP body, which carries the message payload. The namespace that is defined inside the body ("Some-URI") is the namespace of the Web service provider.

When the Web service receives the SOAP envelope, it executes the GetLast-TradePrice method, using MSFT as a parameter.

The following code is an example of the SOAP message response to the consumer:

```
<soap:Envelope
    xmlns:soap="http://schemas.xmlsoap.org/soap/envelope/"
    soap:encodingStyle="http://schemas.xmlsoap.org/soap/encoding/">
    <soap:Body>
        <m:GetLastTradePriceResponse xmlns:m="Some-URI">
            <Price>52.5</Price>
        </m:GetLastTradePriceResponse>
    </soap:Body>
</soap:Envelope>
```

The returned SOAP message resembles the message that was sent, but has the results in the message payload. It's important to note that there is nothing in either message that ties SOAP to HTTP, although when SOAP is used with Web services, HTTP is the protocol used.

SOAP Header

The SOAP header provides a mechanism for extending a message without prior knowledge between the communicating parties. SOAP headers are typically used for authentication and transaction management. The Header element must be the first immediate child element of the SOAP Envelope XML element. An example of a SOAP Header follows:

```
<soap:Envelope xmlns:soap="http://schemas.xmlsoap.org/soap/envelope/"
soap:encodingStyle="http://schemas.xmlsoap.org/soap/encoding/"
xmlns:m="SomeWebServiceURI">
    <soap:Header
xmlns:soap="http://schemas.xmlsoap.org/soap/envelope/">
        <m:MyHeader>
            <Username>MyUsername</Username>
```

```
            <Password>MyPassword</Password>
        </m:MyHeader>
    </soap:Header>
    <soap:Body>
        <m:GetLastTradePriceResponse>
            <Price>52.5</Price>
        </m:GetLastTradePriceResponse>
    </soap:Body>
</soap:Envelope>
```

SOAP Fault

The SOAP Fault element is used to transport error and status information within a SOAP message. If the SOAP Fault element is present, it must be a body entry and may not appear more than once within the Body element. The SOAP Fault element defines four child elements, as shown in Table 16.1.

The following code shows a SOAP fault message that might be generated when an attempt is made to get the stock price of an invalid symbol. (For more information on the SOAP protocol, access www.w3.org/TR/SOAP/.)

Table 16.1 Fault Child Elements Describing the Fault

FAULT ELEMENT	DESCRIPTION
faultcode	Used by the Web service consumer to identify the fault. This element must be present within the SOAP Fault element. SOAP defines a small set of SOAP fault codes that covers the basic SOAP faults.
faultstring	Provides a human-readable explanation of the fault. Faultstring must be present within the SOAP Fault element and must provide information explaining the nature of the fault.
faultactor	Provides information about what caused the fault within the message path. It indicates the source of the fault. The value of the faultactor element is a URI that identifies the source. Applications that are not the ultimate destination of the SOAP message must include the faultactor element in the SOAP Fault element.
detail	Holds application-specific error information related to the Body element. It is included if the contents of the Body element could not be successfully processed. The absence of the detail element within the Fault element indicates that the fault is not related to the processing of the Body element.

```
<soap:Envelope
    xmlns:soap="http://schemas.xmlsoap.org/soap/envelope/"
    soap:encodingStyle="http://schemas.xmlsoap.org/soap/encoding/"
    xmlns:m="Some-URI">
    <soap:Body>
        <soap:Fault>
            <faultcode>soap:Server</faultcode>
            <faultstring>Ticker Error</faultstring>
            <detail>
                <m:myfaultdetails>
                    <message>
                        The ticker was invalid.
                    </message>
                    <errorcode>
                        12345
                    </errorcode>
                </m:myfaultdetails>
            </detail>
        </soap:Fault>
    </soap:Body>
</soap:Envelope>
```

Web Service Description Language

Web Service Description Language (WSDL) is used to describe the Web service's interface. This is the metadata of the Web service component. In COM, IDL was used to perform the same task. WSDL is a W3C specification.

The WSDL document uses XML to describe network services as a collection of communication endpoints, or ports, which can exchange messages. The following example shows a WSDL document that has been generated by Visual Studio .NET for a Web service called HiWorld, which has a class called Hi and a method called SayHi.

```
<?xml version="1.0" encoding="utf-8"?>
<definitions
    xmlns:http="http://schemas.xmlsoap.org/wsdl/http/"
    xmlns:soap="http://schemas.xmlsoap.org/wsdl/soap/"
    xmlns:s="http://www.w3.org/2001/XMLSchema"
    xmlns:s0="http://gjtt.com/"
    xmlns:soapenc="http://schemas.xmlsoap.org/soap/encoding/"
    xmlns:tm="http://microsoft.com/wsdl/mime/textMatching/"
    xmlns:mime="http://schemas.xmlsoap.org/wsdl/mime/"
    targetNamespace="http://gjtt.com/"
    xmlns="http://schemas.xmlsoap.org/wsdl/">
    <types>
        <s:schema elementFormDefault="qualified"
            targetNamespace="http://gjtt.com/">
            <s:element name="SayHi">
```

```xml
                        <s:complexType/>
                </s:element>
                <s:element name="SayHiResponse">
                        <s:complexType>
                                <s:sequence>
                                        <s:element minOccurs="0"
                                                maxOccurs="1"
                                                name="SayHiResult"
                                                type="s:string"/>
                                </s:sequence>
                        </s:complexType>
                </s:element>
                <s:element name="string"
                                nillable="true"
                                type="s:string"/>
        </s:schema>
</types>
<message name="SayHiSoapIn">
        <part name="parameters" element="s0:SayHi"/>
</message>
<message name="SayHiSoapOut">
        <part name="parameters" element="s0:SayHiResponse"/>
</message>
<message name="SayHiHttpGetIn"/>
<message name="SayHiHttpGetOut">
        <part name="Body" element="s0:string"/>
</message>
<message name="SayHiHttpPostIn"/>
<message name="SayHiHttpPostOut">
        <part name="Body" element="s0:string"/>
</message>
<portType name="HiSoap">
        <operation name="SayHi">
                <input message="s0:SayHiSoapIn"/>
                <output message="s0:SayHiSoapOut"/>
        </operation>
</portType>
<portType name="HiHttpGet">
        <operation name="SayHi">
                <input message="s0:SayHiHttpGetIn"/>
                <output message="s0:SayHiHttpGetOut"/>
        </operation>
</portType>
<portType name="HiHttpPost">
        <operation name="SayHi">
                <input message="s0:SayHiHttpPostIn"/>
                <output message="s0:SayHiHttpPostOut"/>
        </operation>
</portType>
<binding name="HiSoap" type="s0:HiSoap">
        <soap:binding
```

```
                transport="http://schemas.xmlsoap.org/soap/http"
                 style="document"/>
        <operation name="SayHi">
            <soap:operation soapAction="http://gjtt.com/SayHi"
                        style="document"/>
            <input>
                <soap:body use="literal"/>
            </input>
            <output>
                <soap:body use="literal"/>
            </output>
        </operation>
    </binding>
    <binding name="HiHttpGet" type="s0:HiHttpGet">
        <http:binding verb="GET"/>
        <operation name="SayHi">
            <http:operation location="/SayHi"/>
            <input>
                <http:urlEncoded/>
            </input>
            <output>
                <mime:mimeXml part="Body"/>
            </output>
        </operation>
    </binding>
    <binding name="HiHttpPost" type="s0:HiHttpPost">
        <http:binding verb="POST"/>
        <operation name="SayHi">
            <http:operation location="/SayHi"/>
            <input>
                <mime:content
                type="application/x-www-form-urlencoded"/>
            </input>
            <output>
                <mime:mimeXml part="Body"/>
            </output>
        </operation>
    </binding>
    <service name="Hi">
        <port name="HiSoap" binding="s0:HiSoap">
            <soap:address
                location="http://localhost/HiWorld/Hi.asmx"/>
        </port>
        <port name="HiHttpGet" binding="s0:HiHttpGet">
            <http:address
                location="http://localhost/HiWorld/Hi.asmx"/>
        </port>
        <port name="HiHttpPost" binding="s0:HiHttpPost">
            <http:address
                location="http://localhost/HiWorld/Hi.asmx"/>
```

```
      </port>
    </service>
</definitions>
```

Notice that the WSDL document uses XML Schema (XSD) syntax. The defintions element is the root element. This element defines all namespaces that are used in this document. The WSDL document uses the following elements in the definition of network services:

Types.   A list of data type definitions that will be used by the Web service.

Message.   An abstract, typed definition of the data being communicated.

Operation.   An abstract description of an action supported by the service.

Port Type.   An abstract set of operations supported by one or more endpoints.

Binding.   A concrete protocol and data format specification for a port.

Port.   An endpoint defined as a combination of a binding and a network address.

Service.   A collection of related endpoints.

The WSDL document essentially describes all data types that will be used to communicate to the Web service, and also describes the method of communication. For more information on Web service Description Language, visit www.w3.org/TR/wsdl.

Universal Description Discovery Integration

The Universal Description, Discovery, and Integration (UDDI) project creates a platform-independent, open framework for describing services, discovering businesses, and integrating business services using the Internet. UDDI is not a W3C standard, but is a cross-industry effort driven by all major platform and software providers, marketplace operators, and e-business leaders. The central location for most UDDI development, specifications, and forums can be found at www.uddi.org.

The UDDI project builds on WorldWide Web Consortium (W3C) and Internet Engineering Task Force (IETF) standards such as XML, HTTP, and Domain Name System (DNS) protocols. Cross-platform programming features are addressed through the use of Simple Object Access Protocol (SOAP). The UDDI protocol enables businesses to find and transact with one another quickly, easily, and dynamically using their preferred applications.

A growing number of UDDI sites exist on the Internet. Some UDDI sites that may be of interest are:

IBM. http://uddi.ibm.com.

Microsoft. http://uddi.microsoft.com.

SAP. http://uddi.sap.com.

UDDI also can be implemented in an intranet environment, thus allowing various departments to share Web services.

Discovery with Disco

Disco is a mechanism that allows the discovery of Web services that are available a server. Disco is not a W3C standard, but is a Microsoft-driven initiative to enable the location of Web services on a computer. This differs from UDDI, which enables the location of Web services on the Internet.

The Web service provider can create and make discovery information available to Web service consumer developers. This discovery information can be statically or dynamically generated, and it will contain links to the WSDL document for all the Web services hosted by the provider.

Static Discovery

Static discovery is used by creating a .disco file and placing it in the directory that contains the Web service. Static discovery can be used when the URL of the .disco file is known. A sample of a .disco file follows:

```
<?xml version="1.0"?>
<discovery xmlns:xsi="http://www.w3.org/2000/10/!XMLSchema-instance"
    xmlns:xsd="http://www.w3.org/2000/10/XMLSchema/"
    xmlns="http://schemas.xmlsoap.org/disco/">
    <discoveryRef ref="/HiWorld/HiWorld.disco"/>
    <contractRef
        ref="/HiWorld/Hi.asmx?wsdl"
        docRef="/HiWorld/Hi.asmx"
        xmlns="http://schemas.xmlsoap.org/disco/scl/"/>
</discovery>
```

This sample has two key elements; discoveryRef and contractRef. DiscoveryRef contains a link to other .disco documents, which essentially creates a chain of .disco files. ContractRef specifies the location of the Web service contracts, which are the WSDL documents.

This .disco files is static. The server administrator must maintain these files manually; thus, when additional Web services are added to the server, these documents must be manually updated to expose the new Web service.

Dynamic Discovery

Dynamic discovery is used with Internet Information Server and ASP.NET to provide discovery information, when only the name of the endpoint computer is required. ASP.NET places a file called Default.vsdisco in the root Web site. The following is a sample of the Default.vsdisco file:

```
<?xml version="1.0" ?>
<dynamicDiscovery xmlns="urn:schemas-dynamicdiscovery:disco.2000-03-17">
    <exclude path="_vti_cnf" />
    <exclude path="_vti_pvt" />
    <exclude path="_vti_log" />
    <exclude path="_vti_script" />
    <exclude path="_vti_txt" />
</dynamicDiscovery>
```

ASP.NET answers discovery requests by enumerating the folder structure, including virtual directories, of the Web site looking for WSDL documents and .NET assemblies. The .vsdisco file contains the list of paths to exclude from the search for Web services.

When an assembly is found, reflection is used to search through the assembly's metadata, looking for methods that have a *WebMethod* attribute. Reflection is a .NET technology that can be used to query an assembly's metadata to locate and instantiate data types, as well as invoke methods dynamically. Reflection is used dynamically to build WSDL documents on the fly.

The use of static .disco files is supported with dynamic discovery by renaming the .disco file to a .vsdisco file. (See the following sidebar for information on enabling dynamic discovery.)

The Disco.exe Utility

The .NET Framework SDK provides a utility called Disco.exe that can be used to locate the available Web services on a computer by using either .disco or .vsdisco files. Figure 16.3 shows the output when executing a query to get the static Default.disco file.

The output of the query for the static Default.disco file shows the location of the Hi.asmx?Wsdl file, as well as the locations of all .disco files. This also retrieved the files and stored them to disk, using the dir command. An additional file is created, called the results.discomap, which can be fed into the WSDL.exe utility.

♦ Dynamic Discovery Does Not Work

For security reasons, dynamic discovery is turned off in Visual Studio .NET but may be enabled by editing the machine.config file and adding the following line in the httpHandlers section:

```
<add verb="*" path="*.vsdisco"
     type="System.Web.Services.Discovery.DiscoveryRequestHandler,
     System.Web.Services,
     Version=1.0.3300.0, Culture=neutral,
          PublicKeyToken=b03f5f7f11d50a3a"
          validate="false"/>
```

This line is included in the machine.config file, but it is commented out, as part of the default install of Visual Studio .NET.

The processModel account also must belong to the VS Developers group. Therefore, the ASPNET account should be added to the VS Developers group to allow the enumeration of the folders and virtual directories. After adding the account to VS Developers, execute iisreset (or reboot the computer) from the command prompt so that the change is recognized.

The Disco.exe utility can also be used to perform dynamic discovery on ASP.NET computers. Figure 16.4 shows the output when querying the localhost. Notice that this query does not require an actual filename.

The same information is extracted from the Web server, except that the dynamic query finds both the static and dynamic entries.

Figure 16.3   Disco.exe utility is used to query the static Default.disco file.

Figure 16.4 Disco.exe utility is used to perform a dynamic query.

Web Service Proxies

When communicating to the Web service, SOAP messages must be constructed and sent to the Web service. The resulting SOAP message then must be parsed before it can be consumed by the application. This can be a very time-consuming task. The job of a proxy class is to encapsulate this code into a class that exposes the Web service data types and methods, but performs the assembly and disassembly of the SOAP messages transparently.

Proxies are entities that act on behalf of other entities. With Web services, proxies expose the same logical interface to a Web service consumer as a Web service itself exposes. Thus, Visual Studio .NET developers are still able to use strongly typed classes, and IntelliSense operates as though the Web service were a local class.

Visual Studio .NET can create a Web service proxy by assigning a reference to the WSDL document of the desired Web service. A tool called WSDL.exe can be used to create the Web service proxy.

The WSDL.exe utility is used to generate a proxy class that can be included in a Visual Studio .NET project. When using Visual Studio .NET, this tool is rarely required, since adding a Web reference to a project automatically generates the proxy class. However, there are times when this tool must be used, such as when a name and password are required to access a firewall. In this situation, the Visual Studio .NET graphical tools break, but the WSDL tool has options for using a firewall (or proxy) username and password.

The WSDL.exe utility can be executed from the Visual Studio .NET command prompt. It is possible to retrieve the WSDL document from a Web service and create a proxy class using WSDL /L:VB http://localhost/hiworld/hi.asmx?WSDL.

The default language that WSDL uses is C#, but the language can be selected with the /L switch. Use the /? switch to get a list of available options.

 For each method exposed by the Web service, synchronous and asynchronous methods are created. The synchronous methods use the standard class name. To execute a method asynchronously, use the methods having *Begin* and *End* prefixes.

Consuming a Web Service

When a developer drops a button control onto a Web page, she is using a control that was created by another party. A productive developer may use only components that have been produced by third parties, and she may never actually create a component herself. The same holds true for Web services. A developer may never create a Web service, but still can be very productive by using Web services that have been developed by third parties.

Here, we examine the steps of locating a Web service that converts text to an image. The code to accomplish this is covered in Chapter 11, but this example uses a Web service to accomplish the same function.

Create the Project

A Web service can be consumed by any project type—Console application, Windows Application, Web Application, or another Web service. In this example, a Web application is the Web service consumer.

Set a Web Reference

A Web Reference can be added to a project by right-clicking the References node in the project and clicking Add Web Reference. This displays the Web Service Directory list. Currently, the only directories are Microsoft's UDDI directory and the Microsoft Test UDDI Directory. Click the Microsoft UDDI directory to display the search dialog box.

The search dialog box allows the developer to enter a service name, the provider name, or use the drill-down categories. This service searches for a text-to-image service, so we type Text into the service name field and click the search button. The result is shown in Figure 16.5.

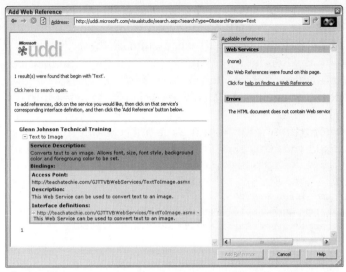

Figure 16.5   The search for text found a Web service that converts text to an image.

The interface definition is a hyperlink. Clicking it displays the Web service interface information, as shown in Figure 16.6. On the right pane, clicking View Contract reveals the WSDL document, which describes all the data types exposed by this Web service. Clicking View Contract simply calls the Web service page with "?wsdl." Visual Studio .NET creates the WSDL document on the fly.

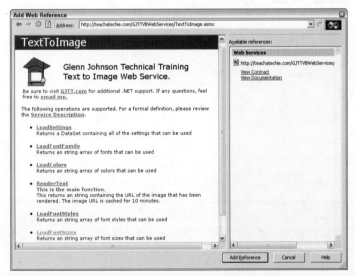

Figure 16.6   The Web service interface information shows the methods that are available for this service.

Each method may be tested without requiring the developer to create a test project. Clicking the link for each method displays information about the method. The Invoke button can be clicked to execute the method. Figure 16.7 shows the information for the RenderText method, which is the main method. This method accepts various parameters and returns a URL to the image that has been created. To see the image, the URL can be copied and pasted into the address bar in Internet Explorer.

After entering the information into the test page and clicking the Invoke button, a new page is displayed. This page will contain an XML response with the image URL as follows:

```
<?xml version="1.0" encoding="utf-8" ?>
<string xmlns="http://teachatechie.com/">
http://teachatechie.com/GJTTVBWebServices/ImageURL.aspx?ImageID=
8b54d349be7343dc9561d53a3a7536ce
</string>
```

The URL that has been created is the same, except that the ImageID will be different each time. If the image URL is copied and pasted into the Address bar of Internet Explorer, the image will be displayed as shown in Figure 16.8.

When the user is satisfied with the Web service, the Add Reference button may be clicked to add the Web reference to the current project.

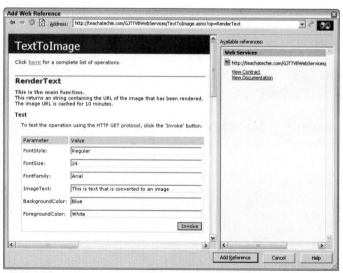

Figure 16.7 The RenderText method with various settings; this renders the test to an image and returns a URL to the image.

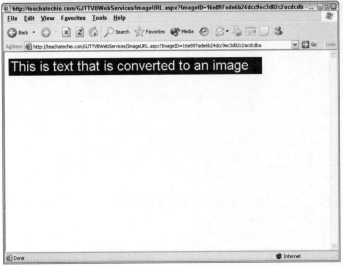

Figure 16.8 The image can be displayed by copying and pasting the image URL into Internet Explorer's Address.

When the Web reference is added, the reference will be displayed under Web References in the Solution Explorer. The domain name and host name will become the namespace of the Web service. In this case, the reference was to http://teachatechie.com, so the namespace for the Web service is com.teachatechie. If the reference were set to http://www.teachatechie.com, then the namespace would be com.teachatechie.www.

 After adding a Web reference, rename the Web reference to something that is more generic than the vendor name by right-clicking the reference and clicking Rename. If the reference is left as is, the vendor's name will show up in the code when you use the namespace. This allows the Web service to be replaced with a different Web service without requiring the code to be changed.

When the Web reference is added, Visual Studio .NET automatically loads the Reference.map, the .wsdl file, and the .disco file from the Web Server, and creates a proxy class that can be used to communicate to the Web service as though the Web service were on the client machine. Figure 16.9 shows the new files that have been automatically added to the project. In this case, the namespace was changed to TextImaging.

Figure 16.9 The Solution Explorer contains additional files after adding the Web reference. The namespace was renamed TextImaging.

Executing the Web Server Method

After the Web reference has been added and the namespace has been renamed, the Web service is ready to be used. This Web service contains a method called RenderText, which creates an image based on the parameters that are passed. Additional methods can be used to retrieve a list of valid values for each of the parameters. These are especially useful when populating DropDownList controls.

In this example, a Web page is opened and the page layout is set to FlowLayout. An Image has been added to the top of the page to display a custom heading, and the Image control is centered. The RenderText method can be easily used by assigning the ImageURL property to a call to RenderText in the Page_Load event method as follows:

```
Dim ti as TextImaging.TextToImage
Private Sub Page_Load( _
    ByVal sender As System.Object, _
    ByVal e As System.EventArgs) Handles MyBase.Load
    ti = New TextImaging.TextToImage()
    Image1.ImageUrl = ti.RenderText("Regular", _
        "36", "Impact", "My Home Page", "LightBlue", "Blue")
End Sub
```

The code to create an instance of the TextToImage class and execute the RenderText method is actually quite simple. The browser output is shown in Figure 16.10. The call to RenderText returned a URL to the image, which was assigned to the ImageURL property. Viewing the source HTML from the browser reveals the result of the RenderText call.

```
<!DOCTYPE HTML PUBLIC "-//W3C//DTD HTML 4.0 Transitional//EN">
<HTML>
    <HEAD>
        <title>WebForm1</title>
        <meta name="GENERATOR"
            content="Microsoft Visual Studio.NET 7.0">
        <meta name="CODE_LANGUAGE" content="Visual Basic 7.0">
        <meta name="vs_defaultClientScript" content="JavaScript">
        <meta name="vs_targetSchema"
        content="http://schemas.microsoft.com/intellisense/ie5">
    </HEAD>
    <body>
        <form name="Form1" method="post"
            action="WebForm1.aspx" id="Form1">
            <input type="hidden" name="__VIEWSTATE"
            value="dDw5OTg1NjA2Ozs+Hi6x4gaAuIZHihy9reVYgBFyY6E=" />
            <P align="center">
                <img id="Image1"
src="http://teachatechie.com/GJTTVBWebServices/ImageURL.aspx?ImageID=
9ef3e7522f0a48e7937e68b110953dc4" border="0" />
            </P>
            <P align="center">Welcome to my home page.</P>
            <P> </P>
        </form>
    </body>
</HTML>
```

Figure 16.10 The browser output, showing the custom heading created by calling the RenderText method.

Notice that the Image control became an HTML img tag, and src contains the URL to the image (View State was disabled on the Image control).

Adding More Web Service Functionality

In the next example, DropDownList controls are added to allow the user to select a value for each of the parameters required by the RenderText method. A call could be made to LoadColors, LoadFontStyles, LoadFontFamily, and LoadFontSizes, but another method, called LoadSettings, returns a DataSet that is populated with a table for each of the settings.

Figure 16.11 shows the modified page with DropDownList controls for each of the settings and a Render button and added Image control.

The following code has been added to retrieve the settings and display a new image into a second image control:

```
Public Class WebForm1
    Inherits System.Web.UI.Page
    Protected WithEvents drpFont As _
        System.Web.UI.WebControls.DropDownList
    Protected WithEvents drpSize As _
        System.Web.UI.WebControls.DropDownList
    Protected WithEvents drpStyle As _
        System.Web.UI.WebControls.DropDownList
    Protected WithEvents Image2 As System.Web.UI.WebControls.Image
    Protected WithEvents drpForeground As _
        System.Web.UI.WebControls.DropDownList
    Protected WithEvents drpBackground As _
        System.Web.UI.WebControls.DropDownList
    Protected WithEvents txtText As System.Web.UI.WebControls.TextBox
    Protected WithEvents btnRender As System.Web.UI.WebControls.Button
    Protected WithEvents Image1 As System.Web.UI.WebControls.Image
    Dim ti As TextImaging.TextToImage
    Private Sub Page_Load( _
        ByVal sender As System.Object, _
        ByVal e As System.EventArgs) Handles MyBase.Load
        ti = New TextImaging.TextToImage()
        Image1.ImageUrl = ti.RenderText("Regular", _
            "36", "Impact", "My Home Page", "LightBlue", "Blue")
        If Not Page.IsPostBack() Then
            Dim ds As DataSet
            If Cache("FontSettings") Is Nothing Then
                ds = ti.LoadSettings()
                Cache("FontSettings") = ds
            Else
                ds = CType(Cache("FontSettings"), DataSet)
            End If
            drpFont.DataSource = ds
            drpFont.DataMember = "FontFamily"
```

```
                drpFont.DataTextField = "FontName"
                drpStyle.DataSource = ds
                drpStyle.DataMember = "FontStyles"
                drpStyle.DataTextField = "StyleName"
                drpSize.DataSource = ds
                drpSize.DataMember = "FontSizes"
                drpSize.DataTextField = "Size"
                drpBackground.DataSource = ds
                drpBackground.DataMember = "Colors"
                drpBackground.DataTextField = "ColorName"
                drpForeground.DataSource = ds
                drpForeground.DataMember = "Colors"
                drpForeground.DataTextField = "ColorName"
                DataBind()
            End If
        End Sub
        Private Sub btnRender_Click( _
            ByVal sender As System.Object, _
            ByVal e As System.EventArgs) Handles btnRender.Click
            Image2.ImageUrl = ti.RenderText( _
                drpStyle.SelectedItem.Text, _
                drpSize.SelectedItem.Text, _
                drpFont.SelectedItem.Text, _
                txtText.Text, _
                drpBackground.SelectedItem.Text, _
                drpForeground.SelectedItem.Text)
        End Sub
    End Class
```

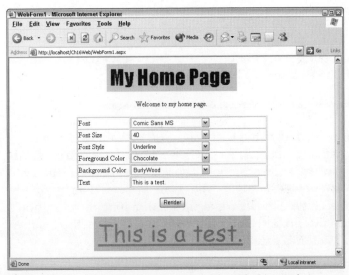

Figure 16.11   The revised Web page with added controls.

This code still displays the heading on the page, but also checks to see if the page has been posted back. If this is the first visit to the page, the DropDownList controls must be populated. A call is made to the LoadSettings method only if the DataSet is not in the cache. The balance of the Page_Load method is dedicated to assigning the DataSet to the DropDownList controls.

The btnRender method simply calls the RenderText method using the settings from the DropDownList controls. The returned URL is placed into the second Image control's ImageURL.

Additional Web Service Settings

The proxy class that has been created also contains settings that may need to be modified. This section addresses some of the most common settings.

Credentials

The proxy class has a Credentials property that can be used when the Web service requires authentication using Internet Information Server Basic or Windows authentication. A new instance of the System.Net.NetworkCredential class can be assigned to the Credentials property before the call is made to any method, as shown:

```
'Imports System.Net
ti = New TextImaging.TextToImage()
ti.Credentials = New NetworkCredential("Glenn", "password")
```

URL

The URL property contains the location of the Web service. This can be changed in the code if the Web service location changes.

```
ti.Url = "http://newServer.com/WebServices/TextToImage.asmx"
```

This is another reason to change the URL: Suppose that a power company creates a Web service with a method called GetPowerData. This Web service is installed on a computer at each power station. The Web client can use the same proxy class to query each power station for the current power data by simply creating a loop, where each time the loop executes, a different power station's URL is placed into the URL property, and the GetPowerData method is then executed to collect that station's data.

Proxy (Firewall)

The Proxy property allows proxy server information to be entered to get through the firewall. Some proxy servers also require a name and password. The following sample code shows how to connect through the proxy, and if credentials are required, they are set as well:

```
'Imports System.Net
ti.Proxy = New WebProxy("proxy.mycompany.com", 80)
ti.Proxy.Credentials = New NetworkCredential("glennProxy", "password")
```

Timeout

Slow Web services may cause frequent failures due to timeout conditions. The Timeout setting (in milliseconds) can be changed to tweak the maximum allotted time for a Web method to execute. The default setting is 100,000 milliseconds.

Executing an Asynchronous Method

When a Web proxy is created, each method that is exposed as a Web method has three associated methods in the Web proxy class. The three methods are a method with the same name as the Web service's method, the same method name but with a *Begin* prefix, and the same method with an *End* prefix. For example, the RenderText Web method has an associated RenderText, Begin-RenderText, and EndRenderText method in its proxy class.

Execution of RenderText method performs a synchronous call to the Web service's RenderText method. Code processing pauses until the Web service returns a result.

Execution of the BeginRenderText method performs an asynchronous call to the Web service's RenderText method. Code execution does not pause to wait for the result. This allows additional work to be performed while the Web service is performing its work. The EndRenderText method is called to retrieve the return value of the Web service's RenderText method.

The easiest part of asynchronous programming is executing the Begin method. The most difficult part is knowing when and how to end the asynchronous call. Two primary methods are used to end the asynchronous call: the use of synchronization objects or the use of callback functions.

Asynchronous Execution Using a Synchronization Object

The use of a synchronization object is required when the normal code execution must wait to ensure that a value has been returned before continuing. For example, in the case of the RenderText method, the URL to the image is required before the page can be rendered properly, so the code could be set up to wait for a returned value at the last possible moment, which would be in the PreRender method of the Web page. This allows the rest of the page processing to be accomplished while the BeginRenderText Web method is being executed.

When calling the Begin method, the return value will be a WebClientAsync-Result data type that implements the IAsyncResult interface. To get the original return value from the Web method, the End method can be used.

The IAsyncResult contains the following members:

AsyncState. The object that was provided in the last parameter to the Begin method call. This is useful for passing an object from the Begin to the End method. This object is not required.

AsyncWaitHandle. This WaitHandle type can be used to wait for an asynchronous operation to complete. The WaitAll, WaitAny, or WaitOne methods of the WaitHandle may be executed to block the current thread until this method has completed.

CompletedSynchronously. This value indicates whether the Begin call completed synchronously or not.

IsCompleted. This value indicates whether the asynchronous method has completed.

Abort. In addition to the members that IAsyncResult provides, the Web-ClientAsyncResult also contains the Abort method. The return value must cast as a WebClientAsyncResult using the CType command to execute this method. The Abort method cancels an asynchronous XML Web service request.

The following code is an example of asynchronously executing the Render-Text method:

```
Dim RenderResult As IAsyncResult
RenderResult = ti.BeginRenderText( _
"Regular", "36", "Impact", "My Home Page", "LightBlue", "Blue", _
Nothing, Nothing)
'Do some work
.RenderResult.AsyncWaitHandle.WaitOne()
Image1.ImageUrl = ti.EndRenderText(RenderResult)
```

In this example, the BeginRenderText method requires the same parameters as the RenderText method plus an additional parameter for a callback function and another parameter for the AsynchState object. These added parameters are not used with this approach, but are used in the following callback function approach.

After the BeginRenderText method has been executed, the code continues to execute without waiting for the return value. Additional work can be done, and when the additional work has been completed, the thread can be paused to wait for the asynchronous method to complete by executing the WaitOne method of the AsyncWaitHandle. Once the asynchronous method has completed, a call to the EndRenderText method retrieves the return value.

Asynchronous Execution Using a Callback Function

The use of the callback function is best suited for situations in which the executing code never needs to pause to wait for a result, but some processing may need to be executed upon return. For example, when printing a document, there is no need to wait for the document to print before continuing the code execution, but if the printing fails, a code in the callback can be used to notify the user of the failure.

When calling the Begin method, two addition parameters must be included; the callback and the AsyncState. In the previous example, these were set to nothing. In this example, a callback function will be supplied to handle the return value, and the AsyncState will be supplied to pass an object from the Begin method to the End method. The AsyncState object can be any object type, although it is usually the original object that called the Begin method.

The return value will be a WebClientAsyncResult data type that implements the IAsyncResult interface, which, optionally, may be used. To get the original return value from the Web method, the End method can be used. The End method should be executed within the callback function.

The following code can be used to execute a Web method asynchronously using a callback function to handle the returned value:

```
Dim ti As TextImaging.TextToImage
Public Sub RenderTextCallback(ByVal resAr As IAsyncResult)
    Dim i As System.Web.UI.WebControls.Image = _
    CType(resAr.AsyncState, System.Web.UI.WebControls.Image)
    i.ImageUrl = ti.EndRenderText(resAr)
End Sub
Private Sub Page_Load( _
    ByVal sender As System.Object, _
    ByVal e As System.EventArgs) Handles MyBase.Load
    ti = New TextImaging.TextToImage()
    Dim callback As New AsyncCallback(AddressOf RenderTextCallback)
    ti.BeginRenderText( _
        "Regular", "36", "Impact", _
        "My Home Page", "LightBlue", "Blue", _
        callback, Image1)
End Sub
```

In this example, a method called RenderTextCallback has been created to handle the assignment of the return value to the Image control's ImageURL property. The BeginRenderText method requires the same parameters as the

RenderText method plus an additional parameter for a callback function and another parameter for the AsynchState object. The callback parameter is assigned an instance of AsyncCallback, which is a reference to the Render-TextCallback method. The AsynchState parameter can contain a reference to any object and is used to pass an object from the Begin to the End method. In this case, the Image1 control was passed to the End method, which allows the End method to populate the ImageURL of Image1.

Building a Visual Studio .NET Web Service

The balance of this chapter is devoted to building a Web service and registering the Web service with the Microsoft UDDI provider.

Create the Project

A Web service can be created by starting Visual Studio .NET and creating an ASP.NET Web service Application, as shown in Figure 16.12. This example creates the Web service that was consumed in the previous session.

Create the TextToImage Class

A new class file, called TextToImage.asmx, has been added to the project. The TextToImage class contains the following code at the top of the file:

```
Imports System.Web.Services
Imports System.Drawing
<WebService(Namespace:="http://teachatechie.com/", _
 Description:="<table border='0'><tr><td>
<img src='http://teachatechie.com/GJTTVBWebServices/images/logo.gif'
```

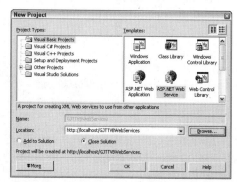

Figure 16.12   Create the Web service by selecting the ASP.NET Web service.

```
    border='0'></td><td><font size='4'>
Glenn Johnson Technical Training<br>
Text to Image Web Service.</font></td></tr><tr><td colspan='2'>
Be sure to visit <a href='http://gjtt.com'>GJTT.com</a>
for additional .NET support. If any questions, feel free to
<a href='mailto:glenn@GJTT.com?subject=Zip Code Web Service'>
email me.</a></td></tr></table>")> _
Public Class TextToImage
    Inherits System.Web.Services.WebService
```

In this code, the System.Drawing namespace is used. This also requires a reference to the System.Drawing.dll file.

The attribute that is called WebService has been placed before the TextToImage class. This attribute offers the ability to set the Web service namespace and assign a description to the Web service. The namespace assignment is a requirement for public Web services, but the Web service will still operate even if the WebService attribute does not exist.

The Description property of the attribute displays on the Web page that is automatically created when this .asmx page is displayed. Notice that the description may contain HTML tags.

The following methods are helper methods for the RenderText method, which performs the real work. Each method that contains a WebMethod attribute will automatically be exposed as a Web method. This is the required attribute to enable Web services:

```
<WebMethod(Description:="Returns a DataSet containing all " + _
        "of the settings that can be used")> _
Public Function LoadSettings() As DataSet
    Dim ds As New DataSet("TextSettings")
    'Create the Color table.
    ds.Tables.Add(MakeTable("Colors", "ColorName", LoadColors()))
    'Create the Font Family table.
    ds.Tables.Add(MakeTable("FontFamily", "FontName", _
            LoadFontFamily()))
    'Create the Font Styles table.
    ds.Tables.Add(MakeTable("FontStyles", "StyleName", _
            LoadFontStyles()))
    'Create the Font Sizes table.
    ds.Tables.Add(MakeTable("FontSizes", "Size", LoadFontSizes()))
    Return ds
End Function
Private Function MakeTable(ByVal TableName As String, _
        ByVal ColumnName As String, _
        ByVal StringArray As String()) As DataTable
    Dim dt As New DataTable(TableName)
    Dim dc As New DataColumn(ColumnName, GetType(String))
    dt.Columns.Add(dc)
    Dim stringValue As String
    For Each stringValue In StringArray
```

```
                    Dim dr As DataRow = dt.NewRow()
                    dr.Item(0) = stringValue
                    dt.Rows.Add(dr)
            Next
            Return dt
    End Function
    <WebMethod(Description:= _
            "Returns an string array of colors that can be used")> _
    Public Function LoadColors() As String()
            Return System.Enum.GetNames(GetType(KnownColor))
    End Function
    <WebMethod(Description:= _
            "Returns an string array of fonts that can be used")> _
    Public Function LoadFontFamily() As String()
            Dim b As New Bitmap(1, 1)
            Dim g As Graphics = Graphics.FromImage(b)
            Dim a As New ArrayList()
            Dim arFamily() As FontFamily = FontFamily.GetFamilies(g)
            Dim x As Integer
            Dim FontFamilyList(arFamily.Length - 1) As String
            For x = 0 To arFamily.Length - 1
                    FontFamilyList(x) = arFamily(x).Name
            Next
    Return FontFamilyList
    End Function
    <WebMethod(Description:= _
     "Returns an string array of font styles that can be used")> _
    Public Function LoadFontStyles() As String()
            Return System.Enum.GetNames(GetType(FontStyle))
    End Function
    <WebMethod(Description:= _
     "Returns an string array of font sizes that can be used")> _
    Public Function LoadFontSizes() As String()
            Dim startSize As Integer = 6
            Dim endSize As Integer = 100
            Dim FontSizeList(endSize - startSize) As String
            Dim X As Integer
            For X = 0 To endSize - startSize
                    FontSizeList(X) = (startSize + X).ToString()
            Next
            Return FontSizeList
    End Function
```

Each helper method is exposed as a Web method, which simplifies the task of populating drop-down boxes with valid data. Most of these methods return an array of strings, except the LoadSettings method. The LoadSettings method will execute each of the other load methods and populate a dataset with this information, which can be returned to the client as a single call. The MakeTable method is a helper method for the LoadSettings method and does not need to be exposed as a Web method.

The last Web method is the RenderText method. This method requires parameters for the font, background and foreground color, font size, font style, and the text to render. In the following code, this method creates a bitmap and returns a string containing the URL to the bitmap. This bitmap will be cached for 10 minutes.

```
<WebMethod(Description:="<font color='#FF0000'><b>" + _
        "This is the main function.</b></font><br>" + _
        "This returns an string containing the URL of the " + _
        "image that has been rendered. The image URL is " + _
        "cached for 10 minutes.")> _
    Public Function RenderText(ByVal FontStyle As String, _
            ByVal FontSize As String, _
            ByVal FontFamily As String, _
            ByVal ImageText As String, _
            ByVal BackgroundColor As String, _
            ByVal ForegroundColor As String) As String
        Dim imgBitmap As New Bitmap(1, 1)
        Dim fStyle As FontStyle
        fStyle = System.Enum.Parse(GetType(FontStyle), FontStyle)
        Dim fSize As Single
        fSize = Single.Parse(FontSize)
        Dim strFont As Font
        strFont = New Font(FontFamily, fSize, fStyle)
        Dim str As String = ImageText
        Dim cBackground As Color
        cBackground = Color.FromName(BackgroundColor)
        Dim cForeground As Color
        cForeground = Color.FromName(ForegroundColor)
        'Get the size of the text string.
        If str = "" Then str = "No text defined."
        Dim g As Graphics = Graphics.FromImage(imgBitmap)
        Dim strSize As Size
        strSize = g.MeasureString(str, strFont).ToSize()
        'Create the bitmap.
        imgBitmap = New Bitmap(strSize.Width, strSize.Height)
        g = Graphics.FromImage(imgBitmap)
        g.Clear(cBackground)
        g.DrawString(str, strFont, New SolidBrush(cForeground), 0, 0)
        Dim imgGuid As String
        imgGuid = GUID.NewGuid().ToString()
        imgGuid = imgGuid.Replace("-", "")
        Context.Cache.Insert(imgGuid, imgBitmap, Nothing, _
            DateTime.Now.AddMinutes(10), Nothing)
        Dim url As String
        If Context.Request.ServerVariables("https") = "off" Then
            url = "http://"
        Else
            url = "https://"
        End If
```

```
                url &= Context.Request.ServerVariables("HTTP_HOST")
                url &= Context.Request.ApplicationPath()
                url &= "/ImageURL.aspx"
                Return url & "?ImageID=" & imgGuid
        End Function
    End Class
```

The RenderText method creates the image based on the parameters that have been passed into the method. Chapter 11, "Working with GDI+ and Images," contains a more detailed explanation of the rendering process. Once the bitmap has been created, a Globally Unique ID (GUID) is created to represent this image. The dashes were removed from the GUID since they only add more length to the URL. The image is cached for 10 minutes. The last section of this method creates the URL to the cached bitmap.

Creating the ImageURL Page

The previous code was responsible for creating an image from the parameters supplied to the RenderText method. Because HTML image tags require a URL to the image, the RenderText creates the URL. The URL points to the ImageURL.aspx page, which expects to receive an ImageID GUID. This page will extract the image from the cache and deliver it to the client.

```
Imports System.Drawing
Imports System.Drawing.Imaging
Public Class ImageURL
    Inherits System.Web.UI.Page
    Private Sub Page_Load( _
        ByVal sender As System.Object, _
        ByVal e As System.EventArgs) _
        Handles MyBase.Load
        If Not Request("ImageID") Is Nothing Then
            If Not Cache(Request("ImageID")) Is Nothing Then
                Dim b As Bitmap
                b = CType(Cache(Request("ImageID")), Bitmap)
                Response.Clear()
                Response.ContentType = "image/jpeg"
                b.Save(Response.OutputStream, _
                    ImageFormat.Jpeg)
                Response.End()
                Return
            End If
        End If
    End Sub
End Class
```

If the image is not in the cache, a Not Found image could be created. Also, an image could be generated with any exception message as well. It's important to call Response.End after saving the image to the response stream, because this command will end the page's processing to ensure that none of the .aspx page is mistakenly sent to the client.

Registering the Web Service with a UDDI Registry

Registering a Web service with a UDDI business registry (UBR) requires a bit of work, but once the Web service is registered, users can locate and use the Web service. This section covers the registration process at Microsoft's UDDI site. Before starting the registration process, the Web service should be created and deployed on a server that is accessible from the Internet.

Visual Studio .NET makes it easy for developers to find Web services using UDDI, and then add the Web service into a project through the Add Web Reference feature. For a Web service to be visible via this feature, the Web service must be properly registered in the UDDI registry. The WSDL file must be registered as a tModel, and the Web service itself must be registered as a binding that refers to your tModel.

To follow the best practice and correctly register a Web service using the Microsoft Web interface at http://uddi.microsoft.com, a UDDI account must be obtained at the http://uddi.microsoft.com/register.aspx site. After an account has been registered, the following steps must be followed.

Create the Technology Model (tModel)

The term *tModel* is short for *technology model*. A tModel is typically used to provide technical information about a programmatic interface, such as a Web Service Description Language (WSDL) file, which describes the conventions that are supported by an interface.

Figure 16.13 shows the tModel screen, which contains several tabs. The Details tab contains the tModel name and description.

The Identifiers tab contains a list of Identifiers, which are optional descriptions intended to enhance the discovery of tModels and providers in Search. The Categories tab contains categorization schemes, which are predefined sets of categories that are represented in a hierarchical fashion. Searches for tModels may be performed by drilling the hierarchy. Add one or more categories by selecting from available schemes.

To ensure Web service visibility when using Visual Studio .NET to search for a Web service, be sure the following category is added to the tModel:

Categorization Scheme: uddi-org:types.

Key Name: Specification for a Web service described in WSDL.

Key Value: wsdlSpec.

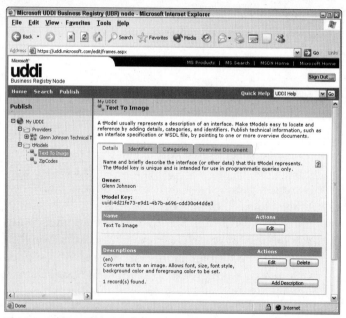

Figure 16.13 The tModel screen showing two tModels. The Details tab contains the tModel name and description.

The Document Overview tab is an HTTP-accessible resource, such as a WSDL file or specification document, that usually contains technical information for implementing or interacting with an interface. For Visual Studio .NET Web services, this should be the URL to the Web service. The following URL points to a Visual Studio .NET Web service:

```
http://teachatechie.com/GJTTVBWebservices/TextToImage.asmx
```

This URL will be displayed as a hyperlink that the prospective user will select to view the Web service information. This tab also includes the ability to add Descriptions of the Web service, each in a different language. The description will be displayed with the URL to the Web service.

Add the Service Information

After the tModel has been defined, the service must be defined and bound to the tModel. Figure 16.14 shows the services screen, which is available under the provider's node. Clicking the Add Service button displays the Details tab window, which allows the service name to be entered in any languages. Service descriptions may also be entered.

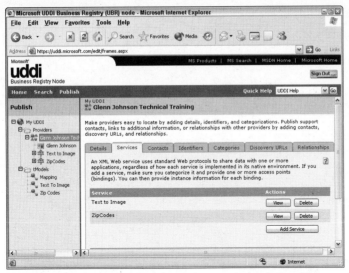

Figure 16.14 The Services tab. Services must be defined here and bound to the tModel.

The Bindings tab is used to bind, or connect, to a tModel. The Bindings section has three tabs: Details, Bindings, and Categories.

The Details tab holds the name and description of the service. The Bindings tab holds information that represents an access point for this service. A binding must be created to reference the tModel that has been created. The tModel is referenced in the Instance Info tab of the Binding. Figure 16.15 shows the link to the tModel. The Web service will not be found in a search from Visual Studio .NET until the reference to the tModel has been set.

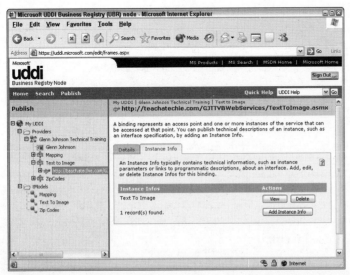

Figure 16.15 The reference from the service to the tModel must be set before the Web service will be located in a Visual Studio .NET search.

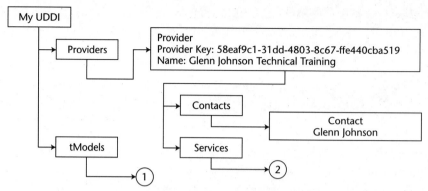

Figure 16.16 The registration properties must be set up first.

Understanding the UDDI Menu Hierarchy

The UDDI menu hierarchy can be confusing, especially when it shows more information than required. To help simplify this process, Figure 16.16, Figure 16.17, and Figure 16.18 show the menu hierarchy of the required elements.

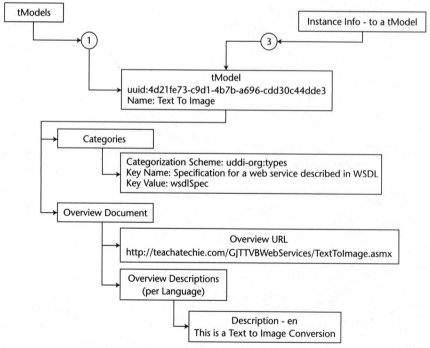

Figure 16.17 Second, the tModel properties must be set up.

The registration items are set up first, as shown in Figure 16.16. (Descriptions that contain the *en* label denote English.) This simply involves the creation of a provider and a contact.

A tModel must be set up next, as shown in Figure 16.17. This involves creating a tModel, assigning a name, a category, and an overview document. Be sure to assign the category called uddi-org:types as shown. This will expose the Web service to Visual Studio .NET users. The overview document must be set to the .asmx file of the Web service.

The Service properties must be set up last, as shown in Figure 16.18. The service requires a name to be assigned, a description for the service, and a binding to be created. The names and descriptions must exist in English, and optionally may exist in other languages. Notice that the binding will reference the tModel that was defined in Figure 16.16.

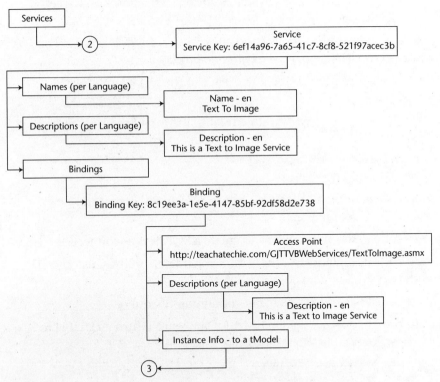

Figure 16.18 The Service properties must be set up last.

Lab 16.1: Creating a Web Service

In this lab, you will create a Visual Basic .NET Web service that can be used to return the orders that a customer has placed. This Web service will use the DataComponent from Lab 15.1 to access SQL Server.

Add the Web Service File to the Orders Project

Although a new Web service can be created by creating a Web service project, a Web service can be simply added to an existing Web application. In this section, you will add a new Web service file to the existing Order solution.

1. To start this lab, open the OrderEntrySystemSolution from Lab 15.1. Right-click the OrderEntrySystemSolution in the Solution Explorer, and click Check Out.

2. Right-click the Order project and click Add, Add Web service. For the Web service name, type CustomersOrders.asmx.

3. In the Order project, assign a reference to the DataComponent project.

4. Add the following Imports statement to the top of the Web service file:

```
Imports System.Data.SqlClient
Imports DataComponent
```

5. Add a Web method called GetOrders, which will accept the CustomerID as a parameter.

6. Add code to the Web method to create a SQL Server connection.

7. Add code to replace any single quote characters in the CustomerID with two single-quote characters.

8. Add code to create a SQL string containing the query.

9. Add code to execute the Db.ExecuteDataSet to return a DataSet to the user. Your code should look like this:

```
Imports System.Web.Services
Imports System.Data.SqlClient
Imports DataComponent
<WebService(Namespace := "http://tempuri.org/")> _
Public Class CustomersOrders
    Inherits System.Web.Services.WebService
    <WebMethod()> Public Function GetOrders( _
        ByVal CustomerID As String) As DataSet
```

```
        Dim cn As New SqlConnection( _
            "server=.;database=northwind;trusted_connection=true")
        CustomerID = CustomerID.Replace("'", "''")
        Dim Sql As String
        Sql = String.Format( _
            "Select * from Orders where CustomerID='{0}'",
    CustomerID)
        Return Db.ExecuteDataSet(cn, Sql)
    End Function
End Class
```

10. Build the project and save your work.

Testing the Web Service

In this section, you will test the Web service to verify that it operates as expected prior to implementing this service in your application.

1. Right-click the Order project in the Solution Explorer and click Set As StartUp project.

2. Right-click the CustomersOrders.asmx page and click Set As Start Page.

3. Run the Web Application. The Web service page should be displayed, as shown in Figure 16.19. Although the page appears to be functioning, a message is displayed that states that the namespace needs to be changed from tempura.org to a custom namespace.

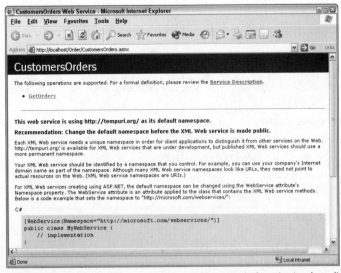

Figure 16.19 The Web service page. This page is functioning but displays a message to change the namespace from tempura.org to a custom namespace.

4. Click the GetOrders hyperlink. A test page will be displayed with a TextBox that allows a CustomerID to be entered. Enter a CustomerID, such as *ALFKI*, and click Invoke.

5. A new browser window will open. This window contains an XML document that represents a DataSet called *NewDataSet*, and contains a DataTable called *Table* (see Figure 16.20).

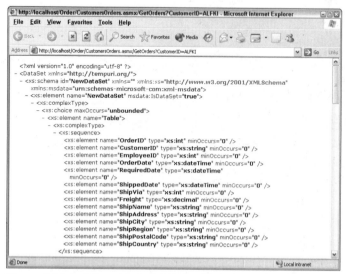

Figure 16.20   When GetOrders is invoked, the Web service returns a DataSet that is represented as XML.

6. Close the browser windows to end the Web service application.

Implementing the Web Service

In this section, you will implement the Web service in the Customers Web application. The CustomerList.aspx page will be modified by adding an Orders button for each customer. Clicking the Orders button will cause the page to change to a new page that will display the orders belonging to the customer. Note that this page already has code to retrieve the orders and order details tables, but that code will be ignored for the purpose of demonstrating the Web service implementation.

1. Right-click the Customer project, and click Set As StartUp Project.

2. Right-click the CustomerList.aspx page, and click Set As Start Page.

3. Open the CustomerList.aspx.vb code-behind page.

4. Add a public variable to the top of the CustomerList class that will expose the current customer ID. The code should look like this:

```
Public CurrentCustomerID As String
```

5. Locate the dgCustomers_Init method. This method is currently used to add the Save button. Add code after the first button's code to add another button to display the orders. Your code should look like this:

```
colButton = New ButtonColumn()
With colButton
    .ButtonType = ButtonColumnType.PushButton
    .CommandName = "ViewOrders"
    .ItemStyle.Width = New Unit(100, UnitType.Pixel)
    .ItemStyle.HorizontalAlign = HorizontalAlign.Center
    .HeaderStyle.HorizontalAlign = HorizontalAlign.Center
    .HeaderText = "View<br>Orders"
    .Text = "Orders"
End With
dgCustomers.Columns.Add(colButton)
```

6. When a DataGrid button is clicked, it executes the dgCustomers_ItemCommand method. Add code to transfer to the ShowOrders.aspx page after setting the CurrentCustomerID variable. Your code should look like this:

```
If e.CommandName = "ViewOrders" Then
    'Get Customer Key
    Dim CustomerKey As String
    CurrentCustomerID = dgCustomers.DataKeys(e.Item.ItemIndex)
    Server.Transfer("ShowOrders.aspx")
End If
```

7. Add a new Web Form to the Customer project, called ShowOrders.aspx. This page will display the orders in a DataGrid.

8. Add a DataGrid to the Web page.

9. Add a Web Reference to the Customer project. This is done by right-clicking the References node of the Customer project in the Solution Explorer and clicking Add Web Reference. In the Address box, type the following URL to the CustomersOrders.asmx page:

```
http://localhost/Order/CustomersOrders.asmx
```

10. When the Web service's test page is displayed, click the Add Reference button. A new node will be displayed, called Web References, and the Web service will be displayed as a localhost sub node. Rename the localhost to OrderInfo. This will display a Visual SourceSafe message stating that renaming a file will cause problems with the change history of the file. Click the Continue button.

11. Add code into the page's load event method to retrieve the current customer ID and call the Web method. Your code should look like the following:

```
Private Sub Page_Load( _
        ByVal sender As System.Object, _
        ByVal e As System.EventArgs) Handles MyBase.Load
        'Put user code to initialize the page here
        Dim ws As New OrderInfo.CustomersOrders()
        Dim custPage As CustomerList
        custPage = CType(Context.Current.Handler, CustomerList)
        Dim CurrentCustomerID As String
        CurrentCustomerID = custPage.CurrentCustomerID
        Dim ds As DataSet = ws.GetOrders(CurrentCustomerID)
        DataGrid1.DataSource = ds
        DataBind()
End Sub
```

12. Save your work.

13. Run the Web application. You may need to log into the Web site if you did not click the Remember check box previously. The CustomerList.aspx page should be displayed, which contains an Orders button for each customer.

14. Click the Orders button for one of the customers. This should cause the ShowOrders.aspx page to be displayed, as shown in Figure 16.21.

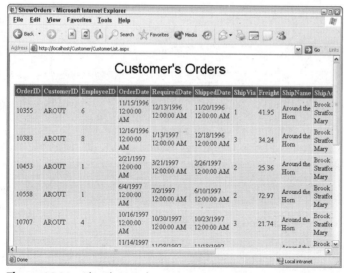

Figure 16.21 The ShowOrders.aspx page made the call to the Web service and returned a DataSet that only contained the orders for the current customer.

15. Save your changes and check the final solution back into Visual SourceSafe.

Summary

- Web services provide a method for one application to communicate with another application.

- Web services can be used in a departmental fashion in the corporate intranet. Different departments may expose data via a Web service, and complete applications may be built by simply gluing the Web service pieces together.

- Simple Object Access Protocol (SOAP) is the protocol used to transfer data to and from the Web service.

- Web Service Description Language (WSDL) is used to describe the Web service's interface.

- The Universal Description, Discovery, and Integration (UDDI) project creates a platform-independent, open framework for describing services, discovering businesses, and integrating business services using the Internet.

- Disco is a mechanism that allows the discovery of the Web services available to a server. Disco is not a W3C standard, but is a Microsoft-driven initiative to enable the location of Web services on a computer. This differs from UDDI, which enables the location of Web services on the Internet.

- The proxy class is responsible for encapsulating Web service code into a class that exposes the Web service data types and methods and transparently performs the assembly and disassembly of the SOAP messages.

- The term tModel is short for technology model. A tModel is typically used to provide technical information about a programmatic interface, such as a WSDL file that describes the conventions supported by an interface.

Review Questions

1. What are two methods that create a Web service proxy class?
2. Name three methods of calling a Visual Studio .NET Web service.
3. How is an asynchronous method identifiable?
4. What technology can be used to advertise your Web service on the Web?
5. What technology can be used to locate a Web service on a user's machine?

Answers to Review Questions

1. Use the WSDL.exe utility or simply add a Web reference from Visual Studio .NET.

2. POST, GET, and SOAP Message.

3. By the Begin and End prefixes.

4. UDDI.

5. Discovery with disco or vsdisco files.

Deployment and Migration

Complex software systems usually involve many applications communicating with each other and with databases. In the past, deploying large software systems required copying files to the destination location, because the COM components required Registry entries to operate.

It's not always possible to jump over to the .NET Framework, abandoning the hundreds of COM components that have been developed over the past several years. A phased approach can limit the risk involved.

Migrating to the .NET Framework usually means that a development team must decide which COM components will be migrated to .NET and which COM components will be used with COM interoperability. This comes with its own set of challenges.

The first part of this chapter explores some methods for migrating from ASP code to ASP.NET. Later, chapter examines early and late binding techniques for using COM components. Finally, the chapter covers some methods for deploying ASP.NET Web applications.

Classroom Q & A

Q: We currently have a Web application that was developed using Visual InterDev 6, and it contains several COM components. After making changes to a COM component and compiling it, we try to copy the COM component over the existing component that is on the production server, but we constantly get an Access Denied message. We usually have to either restart the WWW service or reboot the machine to be able to overwrite the file. Has anything been done to correct this problem with ASP.NET?

A: Yes. ASP.NET caches .NET components into memory when they are loaded. A new .NET component can be simply copied over the existing .NET component. ASP.NET will detect the new component and start using it without requiring a reboot or restart of Internet Information Server.

Q: Can Include files still be used with ASP.NET?

A: Yes. ASP.NET still allows Include files, but they are not recommended. You can achieve better performance, maintainability, and design by deriving your Web pages from a custom base class for your common routines.

Q: Can existing COM components be utilized with ASP.NET, and can they be early bound?

A: Absolutely. In this chapter we explore some methods for using COM components.

Migration

This section examines ASP to ASP.NET migration, Visual Basic to Visual Basic .NET language differences, COM to .NET migration, and COM interoperability.

ASP and ASP.NET Coexistence

Situations may exist where the size or complexity of the Web site dictates that an ASP.NET application run alongside the ASP application. Internet Information Server knows how to direct a request for an .asp or .aspx file to the correct processing engine, primarily because the ASP.NET file extensions are different from the ASP file extensions.

Being able to run ASP and ASP.NET pages in the same Web site does not mean that ASP and ASP.NET will share Application and Session variables.

These technologies reside in different processes and can coexist in a rather isolated fashion. Making ASP data available to the ASP.NET application is typically done by passing data in the QueryString or posting form data from an ASP page to an ASP.NET page.

In many cases, it may be desirable to make architectural changes to the application to take advantage of the ASP.NET or Visual Basic .NET features. This may require sections of an ASP Web application to be migrated to ASP.NET, rather than moving a page at a time.

ASP to ASP.NET Changes

One of the original design goals for ASP.NET was to be completely backward compatible. However, changes were needed to achieve the desired platform improvements and be compatible with the .NET Framework. This section examines these differences. The code block in Listing 17.1 will be used for several of the migration examples in this section.

```
<%@ Language=VBScript %>
<HTML>
<HEAD>
<META NAME="GENERATOR" Content="Microsoft Visual Studio 6.0">
</HEAD>
<BODY>
<%
if request("posted")="true" then
    Dim lineCount
    lineCount=1
    printList "mycar",lineCount
    printList "mytruck",lineCount
    Response.Write(lineCount & "<br>")
end if
sub printList(item,counter)
    Dim r
    set r = Response
    r.Write( "<u>First list for " & item & "</u><br>")
    counter=counter + 1
    r.Write( request(item) & "<br>")
    counter=counter + 1
    r.Write("<u>Next list for " & item & "</u><br>")
    counter=counter + 1
    Dim x
    for x=1 to request(item).Count
        r.Write(request(item)(x) & "<br>")
        counter=counter + 1
    next
end sub
```

Listing 17.1   Sample ASP code that needs to be migrated to ASP.NET. *(continued)*

```
%>
<form name="frm" action="" method="get">
Cars<br>
<INPUT type="text" id="text1" name="mycar" value="vw">
<INPUT type="text" id="text2" name="mycar" value="audi">
<INPUT type="text" id="text3" name="mycar" value="bmw">
<br>
Trucks<br>
<INPUT type="text" id="text4" name="mytruck" value="ford">
<br>
<INPUT type="submit" value="Submit" id=submit1 name=submit1>
<INPUT type="hidden" id="text5" name="posted" value="true">
</form>
<%for each i in Request("mycar")%>
Car: <%=i%><br>
<%Next%>
</BODY>
</HTML>
```

Listing 17.1 *(continued)*

The code in Listing 17.1 contains a form with several text boxes. Values were placed into the text boxes to eliminate the need to retype the values every time that page is run. One of the input tags is a hidden field. This field is used to indicate that the form has been submitted to the server. A server-side script block checks to see if the page has been submitted and if it has, processes the submitted data. A call is made to the printList subroutine for the cars and again for the trucks. After the calls are made, the total line count is output to the page. The printList subroutine first prints the Requested item and then enumerates the list to print it.

At the bottom of the ASP code, another set of server-side scripts is included to print a formatted list of all the cars. This routine uses a for-next loop to accomplish its work.

Figure 17.1 shows the browser output when this page is run in Visual Inter-Dev. To see this page, the Submit button must be clicked. The total line count is eleven.

This page can be included in a Visual Studio .NET by right-clicking the project, clicking Add, Add Existing Item, then clicking Files of Type *.* and navigate to the .asp page. After the page is added, rename it with an .aspx extension. When the page is renamed, a message box is displayed that states, "There is no class file in the project associated with the Web Form 'Inter-DevTest.aspx'. Create class file now?" The choice depends primarily on the amount of changes that are going to be made to the page when it is migrated to ASP.NET. In this case, the minimum amount of changes will be made, and the only goal in these samples will be to get the code to work with ASP.NET.

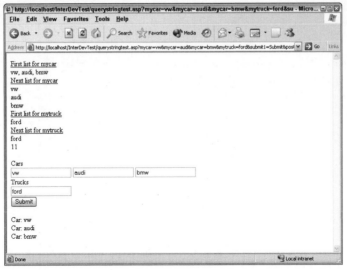

Figure 17.1   The browser output when the code in Listing 17.1 is run.

Subprocedures Require Parentheses

The first error that is exposed when running this page in ASP.NET states "Compiler Error Message: BC30800: Method arguments must be enclosed in parentheses." Visual Basic script does not require parentheses when making a call to a subprocedure (see Figure 17.2); however, in Visual Studio .NET, the parentheses are required. Correct this problem by using the Call keyword and then using parentheses.

The revised and corrected code follows. This code can be used on the original ASP page as well.

```
Call printList ("mycar",lineCount)
Call printList ("mytruck",lineCount)
```

Server-Side Script Blocks

The next error that is displayed when running this page states "Compiler Error Message: BC30289: Statement cannot appear within a method body. End of method assumed." (See Figure 17.3.) The best way to identify the cause of this error is by clicking the Show Complete Compilation Source link.

This link displays the source code generated to compile the aspx page. The key problem is as follows:

```
Line 78: Private Sub __Render__control1( _
            ByVal __output As System.Web.UI.HtmlTextWriter, _
            ByVal parameterContainer As System.Web.UI.Control)
Line 79: __output.Write(""&Microsoft.VisualBasic.ChrW(13)& _
            Microsoft.VisualBasic.ChrW(10)& _
```

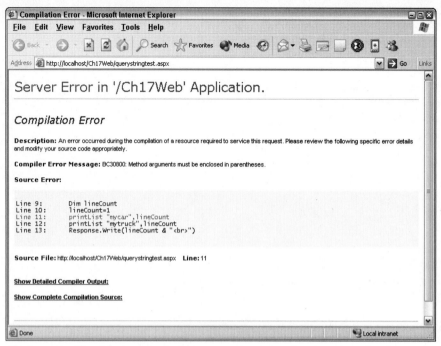

Figure 17.2 The first error to surface occurs because Visual Basic script does not require parentheses when making calls to a subprocedure.

```
          "<HTML>"&Microsoft.VisualBasic.ChrW(13)& _
          Microsoft.VisualBasic.ChrW(10)& _
          "<HEAD>"&Microsoft.VisualBasic.ChrW(13)& _
          Microsoft.VisualBasic.ChrW(10)& _
          "<META NAME="""GENERATOR"" "& _
          "Content=""""Microsoft Visual Studio 6.0"""">"& _
        Microsoft.VisualBasic.ChrW(13)&Microsoft.VisualBasic.ChrW(10)& _
Line 80:   "</HEAD>"&Microsoft.VisualBasic.ChrW(13)& _
          Microsoft.VisualBasic.ChrW(10)& _
          "<BODY>"&Microsoft.VisualBasic.ChrW(13)& _
          Microsoft.VisualBasic.ChrW(10))
Line 81:
Line 82:   #ExternalSource( _
              "http://localhost/Ch17Web/querystringtest.aspx",7)
Line 83:
Line 84:   if request("posted")="true" then
Line 85:       Dim lineCount
Line 86:       lineCount=1
Line 87:       Call printList ("mycar",lineCount)
Line 88:       Call printList ("mytruck",lineCount)
Line 89:       Response.Write(lineCount & "<br>")
Line 90:   end if
Line 91:
Line 92:    sub printList(item,counter)
Line 93:       Dim r
       'And so on
```

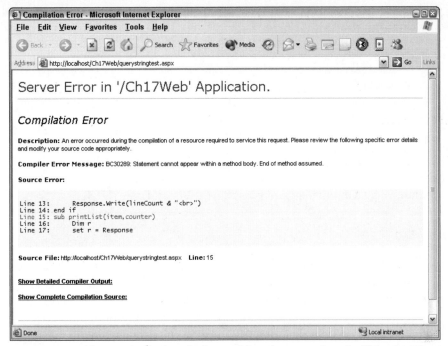

Figure 17.3 This error is displayed when subfunctions are placed within <% %> tags.

In this code, the contents of the server-side script block are included inside the Sub called __Render__control (line 78). Because the <% %> tags are now called *render blocks* and are only intended to be used for inline rendering, the compiler tried to embed the sub called printList (line 92) into the sub called __Render__control. To correct this error, only use <% %> for the inline script and place <script runat="server" language="VBScript"> </script> tags around the subprocedure as follows:

```
<%
if request("posted")="true" then
     Dim lineCount
     lineCount=1
     call printList ("mycar",lineCount)
     call printList ("mytruck",lineCount)
     Response.Write(lineCount & "<br>")
end if
%>
<script runat="server" language="VBScript">
sub printList(item,counter)
     Dim r
     set r = Response
     r.Write( "<u>First list for " & item & "</u><br>")
     counter=counter + 1
     r.Write( request(item) & "<br>")
     counter=counter + 1
```

```
        r.Write("<u>Next list for " & item & "</u><br>")
        counter=counter + 1
        Dim x
        for x=1 to request(item).Count
            r.Write(request(item)(x) & "<br>")
            counter=counter + 1
        next
    end sub
    </script>
```

Once again, this code change can be made in the original ASP page without any problem. The Visual Basic .NET compiler will automatically treat the VBScript language directive as a request to use Visual Basic .NET.

Set and Let

The next error that is displayed states "Compiler Error Message: BC30807: 'Let' and 'Set' assignment statements are no longer supported." This error relates to the use of the word *Set* to assign an object to a variable (see Figure 17.4). VBScript required the use of the word Set to identify whether an object is to be assigned to a variable or a default value was being assigned to a object currently referenced by the variable.

The solution to this error is to remove the word Set. Unfortunately, the word Set is required in the ASP page, so this change can't be proactively avoided.

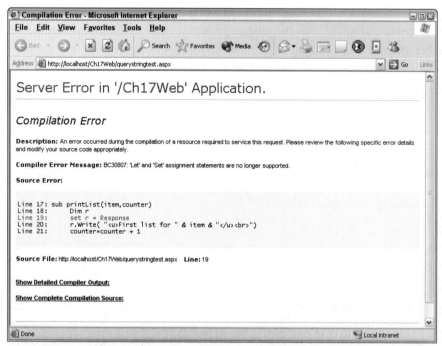

Figure 17.4 This error is displayed when the word Set or Let is used in an .aspx page.

Request Object

The next error that is displayed states "Compiler Error Message: BC30456: 'Count' is not a member of 'String'" (see Figure 17.5). This error relates to the many changes that have been made to the Request object.

Before this error is fixed, it's important to get a better grasp of the new Response object. This object is a property of the System.Web.UI.Page class as well as the HttpContext class, which means that it is available throughout the request. The name of this property is Request, but its data type is System.Web.HttpRequest.

When executing Request("mycar"), the code that is actually executed is Request.Item("mycar") because the HttpRequest has a DefaultMemberAttribute that sets the default member to Item property. A look at the IL code reveals that when using the Request("mycar") syntax, the code for Item property (get_Item) checks the QueryString to see if a value called "mycar" exists. If not, the code checks the Form to see if a form value called "mycar" was posted. If the value hasn't been found, the code checks cookies to see if there is one called "mycar." Finally, if the value has not been found, the code checks the ServerVariables to see if a ServerVariable named "mycar" exists. If the value is not found, a null value is returned. If the value is found, a string is returned (see Figure 17.6).

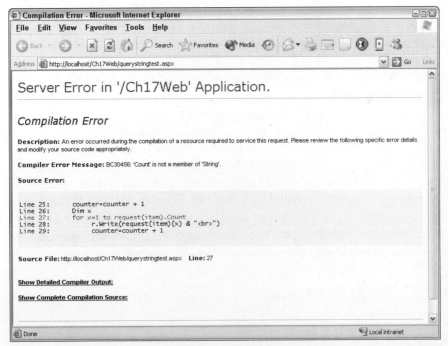

Figure 17.5 An error is displayed because Request(item) returns a string instead of an array.

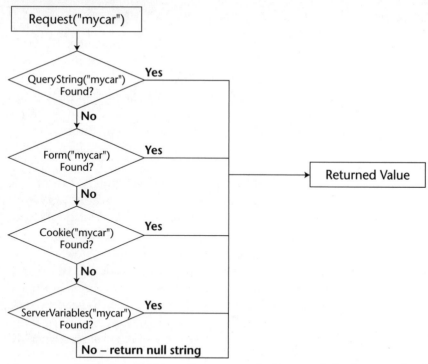

Figure 17.6   Using Request("mycar") syntax results in a search for the named variable.

   The search for a named variable is especially useful when the data may be posted or placed in the QueryString. Note that this syntax always returns a string; thus, in the case of the three cars, a comma was placed between each car. This can become a problem if the data is allowed to contain a comma.

   Although using the Request("mycar") is great for locating a named variable that is not an array, the better solution to working with a named array would be to work directly with the QueryString, Form or Cookie objects.

   The Request.QueryString and Request.Form object return a NameValueCollection that is in the System.Collections.Specialized namespace. The NameValueCollection class has a GetValues method that can be used to retrieve an array of strings. The .NET Array has a Length property instead of the Count property, and the array is zero-based (instead of the one-based collection that was used in ASP with VBScript). The following code shows the changes that must be made to work with the submitted "mycar" array:

```
<%
if request("posted")="true" then
    Dim lineCount
    lineCount=1
    Call printList ("mycar",lineCount)
```

```
      Call printList ("mytruck",lineCount)
      Response.Write(lineCount & "<br>")
  end if
%>
<script runat="server" language="VBScript">
sub printList(item,counter)
      Dim r
      r = Response
      r.Write( "<u>First list for " & item & "</u><br>")
      counter=counter + 1
      r.Write( request(item) & "<br>")
      counter=counter + 1
      r.Write("<u>Next list for " & item & "</u><br>")
      counter=counter + 1
      Dim x
      for x=0 to request.QueryString.GetValues(item).Length-1
          r.Write(request.QueryString.GetValues(item)(x) & "<br>")
          counter=counter + 1
      next
  end sub
</script>
```

After making these changes and executing this page, another exception is thrown. It states "Exception Details: System.NullReferenceException: Object reference not set to an instance of an object" (see Figure 17.7).

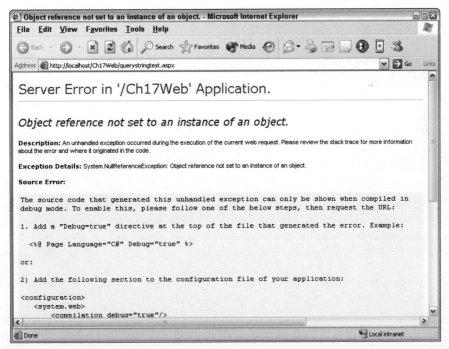

Figure 17.7   This exception is thrown because GetValues("mycar") returned a null value.

This exception is caused because the for-each loop returns an entry array under ASP, but now returns a null if there are no values. The revised code follows:

```
<%
dim i
if not Request.QueryString.GetValues("mycar") is nothing then
    for each i in Request.QueryString.GetValues("mycar")
%>
Car: <%=i%> <br>
<%
    Next
end if
%>
```

This code checks to see if the GetValues("mycar") returns anything prior to attempting to loop through the list. The code finally executes but does not quite operate the same as in the original ASP page.

Method Arguments

In the previous examples, the code from List 17.1 was modified as each exception was thrown. The code finally runs in ASP.NET, but because arguments are passed by reference by default in ASP, the lineCount appears as 1 instead of 11 To correct this error, the printList method must be modified by adding the ByRef keyword before the counter:

```
sub printList(item,ByRef counter)
```

The ASP.NET page now has the same output as the ASP version. Listing 17.2 shows the completed ASP.NET code.

```
<%@ Page Language="VBScript"%>
<HTML>
<HEAD>
<META NAME="GENERATOR" Content="Microsoft Visual Studio 6.0">
</HEAD>
<BODY>
<%
if request("posted")="true" then
    Dim lineCount
    lineCount=1
    Call printList ("mycar",lineCount)
    Call printList ("mytruck",lineCount)
    Response.Write(lineCount & "<br>")
end if
```

Listing 17.2 The revised code that works with ASP.NET

```
%>
<script runat="server" language="VBScript">
sub printList(item,ByRef counter)
    Dim r
    r = Response
    r.Write( "<u>First list for " & item & "</u><br>")
    counter=counter + 1
    r.Write( request(item) & "<br>")
    counter=counter + 1
    r.Write("<u>Next list for " & item & "</u><br>")
    counter=counter + 1
    Dim x
    for x=0 to request.QueryString.GetValues(item).Length-1
        r.Write(request.QueryString.GetValues(item)(x) & "<br>")
        counter=counter + 1
    next
end sub
</script>
<form name="frm" action="" method="get">
Cars<br>
<INPUT type="text" id="text1" name="mycar" value="vw">
<INPUT type="text" id="text2" name="mycar" value="audi">
<INPUT type="text" id="text3" name="mycar" value="bmw">
<br>
Trucks<br>
<INPUT type="text" id="text4" name="mytruck" value="ford">
<br>
<INPUT type="submit" value="Submit" id=submit1 name=submit1>
<INPUT type="hidden" id="text5" name="posted" value="true">
</form>
<%
dim i
if not Request.QueryString.GetValues("mycar") is nothing then
    for each i in Request.QueryString.GetValues("mycar")%>
Car: <%=i%> <br>
<%Next
end if%>
</BODY>
</HTML>
```

Listing 17.2 *(continued)*

Single Language per Page

In ASP.NET, only one server-side language can be used on a page, whereas ASP allows multiple languages to be mixed on a page. The language directive should be placed in a Page directive at the top of the ASP.NET page as follows:

```
<%@ Page Language="VBScript"%>
```

Visual Studio .NET tightens this constraint further by setting the limit to one language per project.

Option Explicit

In ASP, the developer needed to add the Option Explicit directive to generate an error if a variable is used before it is declared. Option Explicit is the default setting for ASP.NET.

Variables and Strong Typing

Variants are no longer available in the .NET Framework. In situations where a variable is defined without using a data type, the data type will be object. It's best to declare all variables with their actual data type; this keeps Visual Basic .NET from providing implicit casts where needed.

Include Files

The use of Include files in ASP is popular and is one of the easiest ways to get common code into many pages. Include files can still be used in ASP.NET, but they must be converted to use the same server-side language as the .aspx page. Many better ways exist to handle repetitive code in ASP.NET than using Include files. Depending on the content of the Include file, one method may be more appropriate than another.

One solution is to create new HttpModules that contain the same code as the Include file. Another solution is to create a new HttpHandler that contains the code from the Include files. Finally, one of the easiest solutions is to create a base page, from which all Web pages inherit, and include the code in the base page.

In this example, every page must contain a special footer that contains a copyright message. The ASP page uses the following line just before the end of the body of each page:

```
<!--#INCLUDE FILE="footer.inc"-->
```

The footer.inc file contains code that changes the font size, writes the copyright message, and displays the current time:

```
<p>
<font size="2">
<%
Response.Write "Copyright &copy; 2002-2004 MyCompany " & time()
%>
</font>
</p>
```

Two changes must be made to make this Include file work: the addition of parentheses for the Write method and the changing of time to DateTime.Now.ToShortTimeString( ):

```
<p>
<font size="2">
<%
Response.Write( "Copyright &copy; 2002-2004 MyCompany " & _
    DateTime.Now.ToShortTimeString())
%>
</font>
</p>
```

The code that executes inside the Include file must be the same language as the .aspx page. Visual Basic .NET doesn't know about the VBScript time method, but changing to the DateTime.Now.ToShortTimeString method fixes the problem.

A better solution might be to simply add a base class that all Web pages inherit from. Create a class that inherits from System.Web.UI.Page and then add the subprocedure to output the footer, as shown in the following code:

```
Public Class MyCommonBase
    Inherits System.Web.UI.Page
    Public Sub footer()
        Response.Write("<p><font size='2'>")
        Response.Write("Copyright &copy; 2002-2004 MyCompany " & _
          DateTime.Now.ToShortTimeString())
        Response.Write("</font></p>")
    End Sub
End Class
```

The revised ASP.NET page must inherit from the MyCommonBase page. The following code contains the AspComTest page with the footer:

```
<%@ Page Language="VBScript" AspCompat="true"
    Inherits="Ch17Web.MyCommonBase"%>
<HTML>
    <HEAD>
        <META NAME="GENERATOR" Content="Microsoft Visual Studio 6.0">
    </HEAD>
    <BODY>
        Saying hi:
        <%
        Dim h as new AspComTest.HiTest()
        h.SayHi()
        h=nothing
        %>
        <% footer() %>
    </BODY>
</HTML>
```

Two important changes to this code are the Inherits= "Ch17Web.MyCommon-Base," contained in the Page directive, and the <% footer() %> call at the bottom of the code.

If this page already contained a code-behind page, it would be modified to inherit from Ch17Web.MyCommonBase, instead of modifying the .aspx page.

Using this technique, common functions are compiled into the project .dll file when the project is compiled. This is a much better object-oriented approach; the developer has full use of IntelliSense, and the code is much easier to maintain.

Using COM Components

When migrating an ASP page that make calls to a COM component, the first decision that must be made is whether to upgrade the COM component to a .NET component or use the existing COM component. This section examines the use of the component as is, but then examines the use of the migration wizard to upgrade the COM component to a Visual Studio .NET component.

Figure 17.8 shows a sample COM component that was created in Visual Basic 6. This ActiveX.dll project has a reference set to the COM+ Services Type Library and the Microsoft Active Server Pages Object Library. This component contains a class called HiTest and a method called SayHi. The SayHi method gains access to the ASP Request object by using the following statement:

```
Set res = GetObjectContext.Item("Response")
```

In this code line, a reference is obtained to the Response object, which allows the COM component to write directly to the Response stream. This was a common method of bypassing the use of ASP scripting.

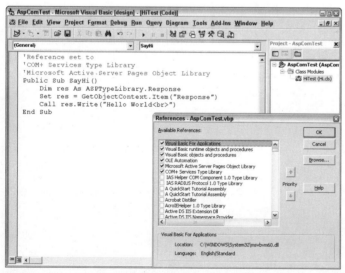

Figure 17.8 A sample COM component that writes directly to the response stream.

The following code is contained in an ASP page. This code creates an instance of the COM component and calls the SayHi method.

```
<%@ Language=VBScript %>
<HTML>
<HEAD>
<META NAME="GENERATOR" Content="Microsoft Visual Studio 6.0">
</HEAD>
<BODY>
Saying hi:
<%
    Dim h
    set h= server.CreateObject("AspComTest.HiTest")
    call h.SayHi()
    set h=nothing
%>
</BODY>
</HTML>
```

If this code is migrated to ASP.NET, the word Set must be removed from both locations.

AspCompat Switch

After the Set keyword is removed from the code, executing the page displays an exception that states "Exception Details: System.Web.HttpException: The component 'AspComTest.HiTest' cannot be created. Apartment threaded components can only be created on pages with an <%@ Page aspcompat=true %> page directive" (see Figure 17.9). This exception is thrown because ASP.NET uses Multi-Threaded Apartments (MTA), also known as free-threaded apartments. A call to a Visual Basic 6 component represents an attempt to make a call to a component that uses Single-Threaded Apartments (STA).

The AspCompat switch is used to direct the ASP.NET page to operate on a STA thread. The use of the AspCompat switch also allows COM 1.0+ components to access the underlying unmanaged ASP objects, such as Request and Response. The corrected code follows:

```
<%@ Page Language="VBScript" AspCompat="true"%>
<HTML>
<HEAD>
<META NAME="GENERATOR" Content="Microsoft Visual Studio 6.0">
</HEAD>
<BODY>
Saying hi:
<%
    Dim h
    h= Server.CreateObject("AspComTest.HiTest")
    call h.SayHi()
    h=nothing
```

```
%>
</BODY>
</HTML>
```

Performance is degraded when the AspCompat switch is set to true, so this switch should only be used where necessary.

Early Binding versus Late Binding

In the previous example, the ASP code was modified to work in ASP.NET. The previous code used late binding in the same fashion as it did when the code was in ASP.

Late binding uses the IDispatch interface to indirectly invoke a method at run time. In the example, the ASP page is used solely as a means of connecting the browser to the COM component via a single call. There won't be a big performance gain by changing to early binding because there is only one call to the COM component. In situations where there are many late bound calls, a substantial gain in performance can be achieved by switching to early binding.

The first step to early binding involves setting a reference to the COM component. This is done the same as a .NET component is referenced, except the COM component can be chosen from the COM tab in the Add References dialog box.

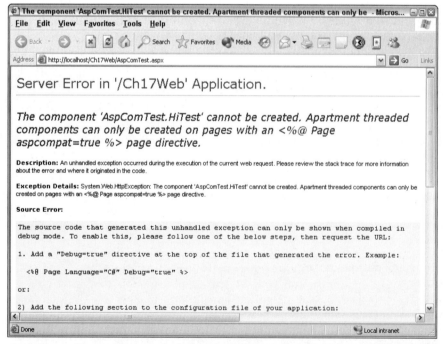

Figure 17.9 An error is caused when attempting to call a Single-Threaded Apartment (STA) component using ASP.NET.

When a reference is added to a COM component, Visual Studio .NET creates a proxy class called a Runtime Callable Wrapper (RCW), which is used to allow Visual Basic .NET code to communicate with the COM component. The Runtime Callable Wrapper is viewable in the Object Browser, and the .dll file can be seen by clicking the Show All Files button in the Server Explorer and then opening the bin folder, as shown in Figure 17.10.

After the reference is set and the proxy class created, the COM component can be created and used like a .NET component. The revised code follows:

```
<%@ Page Language="VBScript" AspCompat="true"%>
<HTML>
    <HEAD>
        <META NAME="GENERATOR" Content="Microsoft Visual Studio 6.0">
    </HEAD>
    <BODY>
        Saying hi:
<%
Dim h as new AspComTest.HiTest()
h.SayHi()
h=nothing
%>
    </BODY>
</HTML>
```

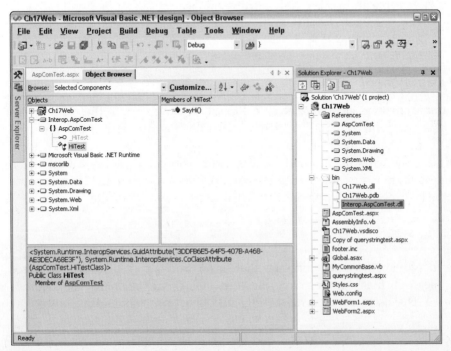

Figure 17.10 The object browser shows the Runtime Callable Wrapper, which is included in the bin folder.

   Although an extra layer of code sits on top of the COM component, this generally operates faster than its late bound counterpart.

Deployment

Deploying an ASP Web application has its share of problems, usually involving registering COM components and copying over COM components that were in use. When it comes time to deploy a Web site to a production environment, ASP.NET really shines. This section explores some methods for ASP.NET Web application deployment.

XCopy Deployment

One of the best features of the .NET Framework is the ability to deploy an application by copying the application's folder structure from one location to another. This is commonly called XCopy deployment because the XCopy command has command-line switches to copy files and folders. Thus, Windows Explorer can also be used to drag an application folder structure from one location and drop it onto another location.

   ASP.NET differs a bit from the XCopy deployment that Microsoft touts, but even deploying an ASP.NET Web application is substantially easier that traditional Web applications. The only additional task that must be done is to create a virtual directory for the Web site, so that XCopy deployment can be accomplished.

FTP Deployment

FTP deployment is closely related to XCopy deployment. In the past, it was extremely difficult to deploy a Web site to a hosting provider if the site used COM components that needed to be registered. With File Transfer Protocol (FTP) deployment, all files and folders can be simply copied via FTP to the hosting provider, and the ASP.NET components will operate. This requires that the hosting provider have ASP.NET installed on its Web site.

What to Copy

When deploying to a production site, there is no need to copy all files. The source code files (.vb files), the resource files (.resx files), and .webinfo files are not required. The .aspx, .ascx, .asmx, .config, .dll, .asax, and .css files are required.

Copy Project Button

The Visual Studio .NET Solution Explorer contains a Copy Project button that can be used to copy a project to a new location (see Figure 17.11). This button can be used to copy the current Visual Studio .NET project to a new location either by using Front Page Server Extensions or by using File Sharing. The Copy Project option also has options to select the files to be copied.

Before using this option, the virtual directory should be created in the desired location. If the virtual directory is not created, the files will be copied to a new folder under the c:\inetpub\wwwroot folder. The destination system also must have Internet Information Server installed.

Web Setup Project

Visual Studio .NET also provides the ability to create a Web setup project for deployment. The setup project has options for selecting the files to be deployed, adding Registry entries, selecting the deployment location, setting custom deployments actions, and more.

To create a Web setup project, click File, Add Project, New Project. Click Setup and Deployment Projects, Web Setup Project, and assign a name and location to the project, as shown in Figure 17.12. In this example, the project has been named WebDeploy. The project opens the File System Editor.

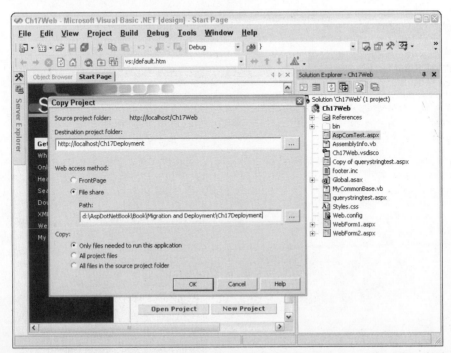

Figure 17.11 The Copy Project button in the Solution Explorer can be used to deploy the current project to a new location.

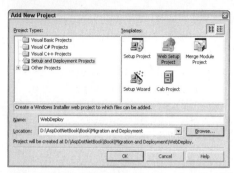

Figure 17.12 The Web setup project is added to the solution.

Next, the ProductName property of the project must be set to the default name of the installed project. In this example, the name will be set to Ch17Web. Notice that there are many project properties, such as the ability to remove existing installations of the Web application and to restart the WWW service after the installation has completed.

The Web setup project must be configured with a list of files to be included in the setup. This is done by clicking Web Application Folder in the File Editor window, and clicking Action, Add, Project Output. The Add Project Output Group dialog box is displayed, as shown in Figure 17.13. Click Primary Output and Content Files, and click OK to add the minimum required files.

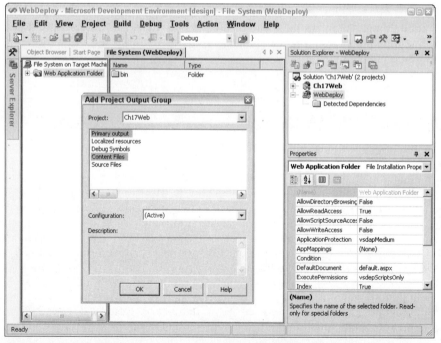

Figure 17.13 The Primary Output and Content Files must be clicked in the Add Project Output Group window.

The default virtual directory is set by clicking Web Application Folder and setting the VirtualDirectory property. In this example, the default virtual directory is set to Ch17WebVirtual.

The setup project is built by right-clicking the project and clicking Build. This collects all the required files and encapsulates them in the .msi installer file.

The installation is started by executing the setup.exe file, which launches the setup wizard's welcome screen with the product name. Clicking Next displays the virtual directory and port setup screen. After these are set, click Next to start the installation. When setup has completed, users will be able to browse to the new site.

ASP.NET Registration Utility (aspnet_regiis.exe)

Situations may exist in which the ASP.NET Registration Utility must be run to connect ASP.NET to an Internet Information Server Web site. In its simplest form, this utility is run by executing the following command from the .NET Command Prompt:

```
aspnet_regiis.exe -i
```

If Internet Information Server was installed on the machine after Visual Studio .NET was installed, this utility must be run. The typical symptom is that the .aspx files are rendered as text files. Depending on the content of the page, the page may be rendered in the browser as a blank page or as a page that displays the source content of the .aspx file. Use the /? option to see the additional options for installing ASP.NET on multiple Web sites.

Lab 17.1: Deploying the Customer Site

In this lab, you will add a Web setup project to the OrderEntrySystemSolution. This will be used to deploy the Customer Web site to a new site called Ch17Customer.

Add the Web Setup Project
The Web setup project will be added and configured to install in a default virtual directory called Ch17Customer.

1. To start this lab, open the OrderEntrySystemSolution from Lab 16.1. Right-click the OrderEntrySystemSolution in the Solution Explorer, and click Check Out.

2. Click File, Add Project, New Project. Click Setup and Deployment Projects, Web Setup Project to assign a project name of Customer-Setup and location as follows:

```
C:\DEVELOPMENT\ORDERENTRYSYSTEM\OrderEntrySystemSolution
```

3. The project will open with the File Editor window being displayed. Change the ProductName property to Customer Setup.

4. Add the minimum files to the Web Setup project. This is done by clicking Web Application Folder in the File Editor window, and then clicking Action, Add, Project Output. The Add Project Output Group dialog box will be displayed. Click Primary Output and Content Files. Click OK to add the minimum required files.

5. The default virtual directory must be set by clicking the Web Application Folder and setting the VirtualDirectory property. Set the default virtual directory to Ch17Customer.

6. Right-click the Web setup project, and click Build.

7. Save this Web project.

Testing the Web Setup Project

In this section, you will test the Web setup project by executing the setup.exe application and verifying that the site can be visited when complete.

1. Open Windows Explorer and navigate to the following folder:

   `C:\DEVELOPMENT\ORDERENTRYSYSTEM\OrderEntrySystemSolution\Customer Setup\Debug`

2. Execute the Setup.exe application. This starts the Web Setup wizard.

3. Click Next to go to the virtual directory and port number configuration screen. The screen should look like Figure 17.14. Accept the defaults; click Next, and Next again to start the installation.

4. When the setup is complete, click the Close button.

5. Using the Web browser, navigate to the following URL:

   `http://localhost/ch17Customer`

6. The login screen should be displayed. Type in the username and password, and click the Login button.

7. If the login was successful, the CustomerList.aspx page will be displayed.

8. Save your changes, and check the final solution back into Visual SourceSafe.

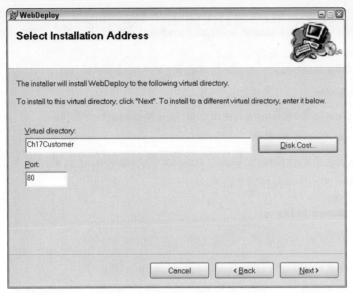

Figure 17.14 The Select Installation Address screen.

Summary

- ASP and ASP.NET do not share Application and Session variables. These technologies reside in different processes and can coexist in a rather isolated fashion.

- In Visual Basic .NET, parentheses are required for subprocedure parameters.

- In ASP.NET, the <% %> tags are now called render blocks and are only intended to be used for inline rendering.

- Use the <script runat= "server" language= "VBScript"> </script> tags when creating subprocedures.

- The use of Set and Let are no longer required and generate a compile error when used.

- When processing single items, the Request object code does not need to be changed. However, when multiple items are to be returned, the existing code must be changed.

- Method arguments are now passed by value instead of by reference.

- Use the AspCompat switch to call STA threaded COM components with ASP.NET.

- ASP.NET Web applications may be deployed by using XCopy, FTP, the Copy Project option, or a Web Setup Project.

Review Questions

1. What must be done to the following line of code for it to work in ASP.NET?

```
Set res = Response
```

2. What must be done to the following line of code for it to operate in ASP.NET?

```
Response.Write "Hello World"
```

3. What must be done to the following lines of code for them to operate in ASP.NET?

```
<%
    Sub Test(x)
        Response.Write(x)
    End Sub
%>
```

4. Before using XCopy to deploy a Web application, what must be done?

5. What deployment method may be used to automatically restart the WWW service after the deployment has been completed?

Answers to Review Questions

1. Remove the word *Set*.

2. Add parentheses around "Hello World."

3. The subprocedure must be enclosed in <script runat= "server"> tags.

4. The virtual directory must be created.

5. The Web setup project must be created.

APPENDIX

A

About the 60 Minutes Web Site

This appendix provides you with information on the contents of the Web site that accompanies this book. On this site, you will find information that will help you with each of the book's chapters.

This Web site contains:

- Streaming video presentations that introduce you to each chapter of the book. These presentations are intended to provide late-breaking information that can help you understand the content of the chapter.

- Sample code that is used throughout the book. The sample code is presented as files with a .txt extension, which will allow you to easily copy and paste the code into your Visual Studio .NET project.

- The lab starter and lab solution for each chapter. The lab starter and solution is presented as a folder structure that can be unzipped and used as necessary.

- Bonus chapter.

To access the site, visit www.wiley.com/compbooks/60minutesaday.

System Requirements

Make sure that your computer meets the minimum system requirements listed in this section. If your computer doesn't match up to most of these requirements, you may have a problem using the contents of the Knowledge Publisher Studio.

- PC with a Pentium processor running at 266 Mhz or faster with Windows NT4, Windows 2000, or Windows XP.
- At least 256 MB of total RAM installed on your computer; for best performance, we recommend at least 512 MB.
- A high-speed internet connection of at least 100K is recommended for viewing online video.
- Internet Explorer 6.0 or higher.
- Browser settings need to have Cookies enabled; Java must be enabled (including JRE 1.2.2 or higher installed) for chat functionality and live Webcast.
- Screen Resolution of 1024x768 pixels.

60 Minutes a Day Presentations

To enhance the learning experience and further replicate the classroom environment, *ASP.NET in 60 Minutes a Day* is complemented by a multimedia Web site which aggregates a streaming video and audio presentation. The multimedia Web site includes an online presentation and introduction to each chapter. The presentation, hosted by Glenn Johnson, includes a 10 to 15 minute video segment for each chapter that helps to deliver the training experience to your desktop and to convey advanced topics in a user-friendly manner.

Each video/audio segment introduces a chapter and details the important concepts and details of that chapter. After viewing the online presentation, you are prepped and prepared to read the chapter.

Upon reaching the companion site that contains the video content for this book you will be asked to register using a valid email address and self-generated password. This will allow you to bookmark video progress and manage notes, email, and collaborative content as you progress through the chapters. All video content is delivered "on demand," meaning that you can initiate the viewing of a video at any time of the day or night at your convenience.

Any video can be paused and replayed as many times as you wish. The necessary controls and widgets used to control the delivery of the videos use strict industry-standard symbols and behaviors, thus eliminating the necessity to learn new techniques. If you would like to participate in a complete five-minute online tutorial on how to use all features available inside the presentation panel, visit http://www.propoint.com/solutions/ and click on the DEMO NOW link located on the left hand side of the Web page.

This video delivery system may be customized somewhat to enhance and accommodate the subject matter within a particular book. In these cases, special effort has been made to ensure that all information is readily available and easy to understand. In the unlikely event that you should encounter a problem with the content on the site, please do not hesitate to contact us at Wiley Product Technical Support.

Code and Bonus Content

In addition to the presentations, you can download the sample code files and view additional resources. You'll also find the bonus chapter on Mobile Computing.

Troubleshooting

If you have trouble with the Web site, please call the Wiley Product Technical Support phone number: (800) 762-2974. Outside the United States, call 1 (317) 572-3994. You can also visit our Web site at www.wiley.com/techsupport. Wiley Publishing, Inc. will provide technical support only for installation and other general quality control items; for technical support on the applications themselves, consult the program's vendor or author.

Index